A MILITARY HISTORY OF THE WESTERN WORLD

VOLUME III
FROM THE AMERICAN CIVIL WAR TO THE END OF WORLD WAR II

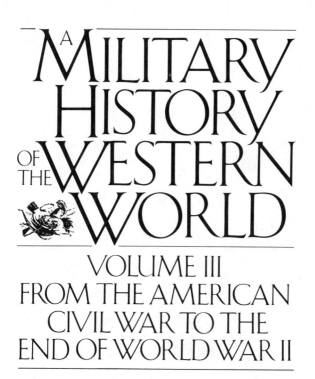

A MILITARY HISTORY OF THE WESTERN WORLD

VOLUME III
FROM THE AMERICAN CIVIL WAR TO THE END OF WORLD WAR II

J. F. C. FULLER

A DA CAPO PAPERBACK

Published by Da Capo Press, Inc.
A Subsidiary of Plenum Publishing Corporation
233 Spring Street, New York, N.Y. 10013

To

FRANCIS NEILSON

Acknowledgments

For their kindness in reading and commenting on part or whole of the text of volumes II and III of this book, I am especially indebted to Professor M. A. Lewis, M.A., Sir Charles Petrie, Bart., Mr. Bruce Catton, Mr. Frank Uhlig, Jnr., and Major W. G. F. Jackson, M.C., R.E. In addition I wish to tend my grateful thanks to my friend and publisher Mr. Douglas Jerrold for his unstinting assistance and advice, and to Mr. Anthony S. F. Rippon for preparing the typescript of both volumes for the press. Also I wish to thank my very dear friends Dr. Francis Neilson, Litt.D., and Miss Phyllis Evans for providing me with many books published in America on the First and Second World Wars, and for verifying quotations. While it would be difficult to exaggerate the value of the assistance I have received from the above, I am alone responsible for the text as it stands and for such errors as it may contain.

Contents

Maps and Diagrams

The industrial revolution and the rise of American imperialism

While the French Revolutionary and Napoleonic wars ploughed up the remnants of European feudalism, the greatest revolution the world had so far seen sowed the seeds of a new dispensation – a way of life based on coal, steam and machinery. After the outburst of nationalism awakened by the American and French Revolutions, in the century subsequent to Waterloo Cyclopean forces were unleashed which were to change the face of the world and to raise war from the cockpit of gladiatorial armies to the grand amphitheatre of contending continents. Even as early as 1825 – that is, only 10 years after Napoleon's final defeat – we find Stendhal in his *Racine et Shakespeare* writing: "What a change from 1785 to 1824! In the two thousand years of recorded world history, so sharp a revolution in customs, ideas and beliefs has perhaps never occurred before."

Before Stendhal's 1785, the Industrial Revolution, so far as it was fostered by steam power, had been nearly a century in gestation. It may be said to have been begotten by Thomas Savery's steam pumping engine of 1698, and Thomas Newcomen's atmospheric engine of 1705. But it was not until 1769 – the birth year of Napoleon and Wellington – that James Watt, a Glasgow instrument maker, matured the steam pumping engine, and in 1782 invented the double-acting engine. Also in 1769 Cugnot, in France, built and drove the first steam-propelled road carriage, and in 1785 came Edmund Cartwright's power-loom, and with this invention we reach Stendhal's initial date.

From 1785, because of the development of steam power and the introduction of the "puddling" process in the manufacture of bar iron, England strode ahead, and during the Napoleonic wars established a virtual monopoly of industrial manufactures. Admiral Lord Cochrane (later tenth Earl of Dundonald) on June 2, 1818, pointed out in the House of Commons that England would have been brought "to total ruin", but "for the timely intervention of the use of machinery."

As the discovery that gunpowder could be used as a propellant had led to an outburst of inventiveness which changed the technics of war, so did the use of steam power as a source of energy revolutionize armies; it made possible their movements and supply by steamship and railway. Further, it enabled vast improvements in armaments to be made, as well as their mass production.

The two outstanding military inventions of the first half of the nineteenth century were the percussion cap and the cylindro-conoidal bullet. The first was made possible by the discovery of fulminate of mercury in 1800. Seven years later the Rev. A. Forsyth patented a percussion powder for priming, and in 1816 Thomas Shaw, of Philadelphia, invented the copper percussion cap. The next improvement came in 1823, when Captain Norton, of the British 34th Regiment, designed a cylindro-conoidal bullet with a hollow base, so that when fired it would automatically expand and seal the bore. Though rejected by the British Government it was later taken up in France, and in 1849 M. Minié designed the Minié bullet which was adopted by the British Army, and rifles of the Minié pattern were issued to it in 1851. These two inventions revolutionized infantry tactics. The former made the musket serviceable in all weathers, and vastly reduced misfires; the latter made the rifle the most deadly weapon of the century.

The percussion cap made possible the expansive cartridge case, which in its turn rendered practicable the breech-loading system. This case revolutionized gunnery by preventing the escape of gases at the breech. First came the pin-fire cartridge in 1847; next the rim-fire, and lastly, in 1861, the central-fire cartridge. While other nations argued over the merits and demerits of flint and percussion lock muzzle-loaders, in 1841 Prussia took a bold step and issued to certain regiments the Dreyse breech-loading rifle, better known as the needle gun, a bolt-operated weapon firing a paper cartridge. Though, because of escape of gas at the breech, its effective range was considerably less than that of the Minié rifle, seven shots a minute could be fired with it instead of a maximum of two. But its main advantage was not its rapidity of loading; it was that a breech-operated rifle can easily be loaded in the prone position – that is, when the rifleman is lying down.

The development of artillery was slower, for although breech-loading and rifled cannon had long been known, it was not until 1845 that these two characteristics were combined in an effective breech-loading rifled cannon. But its cost was so great that no country would face its adoption until the outbreak of war in the Crimea, when some cast-iron muzzle-loading smooth-bore 68-pdrs. and 8-in. guns were converted into rifled pieces. Their greater range and accuracy made the bombardment of Sebastopol "a very hideous thing", and after the war all the Powers began to experiment with breech-loading rifled ordnance.

Another weapon which was developed at the opening of the nineteenth century was the war rocket, actually the oldest of all explosively propelled projectiles. For centuries it had been extensively used in Asia as an anti-cavalry weapon, and it was the rocket employed by Tipu Sultan at the siege of Seringapatam in 1799 that gave Colonel Sir William Congreve, an inventor of note, the idea of improving upon it. He informs us that he made rockets weighing from two ounces – "a species of self-moving musket-balls" – to three hundredweight. In 1806 his rocket was successfully tested in an attack on Boulogne, and he predicted: "The rocket is, in truth, an arm by which the whole system of military tactics is destined to be changed"; a prophecy which was to be fulfilled in the Second World War.

While these changes were under way, steam propulsion in the form of the marine engine and the locomotive laid the foundations of a totally new type of warship and opened to armies the possibility of adding vastly to their size. Although the paddle-wheel dated from Roman times and was the most obvious mechanical means for water propulsion, one of the earliest types of steamboat, constructed by James Rumsey, a Virginian, in 1775, was driven by water-jet propulsion: a steam pump sucked in water at her bow and ejected it at her stern. But he and other early steamboat designers were eclipsed by a young American, Robert Fulton, a man of extraordinary inventive genius. In 1797 he submitted to the Directory the plans of a "plunging boat" called the *Nautilus*, and tests with this early submarine[1] were carried out in Brest harbour in 1801, when she remained under water for about an hour. In 1803, Fulton experimented with a steamboat[2] on the Seine, the value of which was appreciated by Bonaparte. On July 21, 1804, he wrote that the project of moving ships by steam "is

[1] In 1776 David Bushnell invented a turtle-shaped submarine in which, during the American War of Independence, he dived beneath the British warship *Eagle* and tried to screw a "torpedo" into her bottom. Through an error of judgment he failed.
[2] The first practical steamboat was the *Charlotte Dundas*, tried out in the Forth in 1802. The first to cross the Atlantic was the American built *Savannah* in 1819.

one that may change the face of the world. . . . A great truth, a physical, palpable truth, is before my eyes."

Fulton returned to America in 1807 and built an improved steamship, the *Clermont*, which travelled the 150 miles from New York to Albany, in under 32 hours. Earlier he had invented a torpedo, which was tried by Lord Keith against the French flotilla outside Boulogne in September, 1804, and in 1813 he built the first steam-driven warship, the *Demologos* (later renamed the *Fulton*). She was of twin-hull construction with a central paddle-wheel between the hulls, and was protected by a belt of timber 58 in. thick. This monstrous vessel clearly showed that two things were required: a less vulnerable system of propulsion than the paddle-wheel and a less clumsy means of protection.

The first problem was solved by the introduction of the screw propeller, patented by Captain John Ericsson, of the Swedish army, in 1836, and the second by the substitution of iron for wooden armour, first proposed by Congreve in 1805. But it was not until the war in the Crimea that the Emperor Louis Napoleon ordered the construction of a flotilla of floating armoured batteries which could resist solid shot and explosive shell. Five were built, protected by 4 in. iron plate. They mounted 56-pdr. shell guns and were equipped with auxiliary steam machinery. Their success was complete. Not only was the need to armour ships proved beyond all doubt, but also that armour would necessitate the introduction of more powerful ordnance. This, by degrees, led to the general adoption of rifled ship cannon.

Soon after the Crimean war, France and Great Britain laid down the first two armoured steam warships, *La Gloire* and the *Warrior*. The latter was 380 ft. in length, of 8,830 tons displacement, her engines developed 6,000 initial h.p. and her speed was $14\frac{1}{2}$ knots. Her armament consisted of 28 7-in. guns, and her armour belt was $4\frac{1}{2}$ in. thick.

When we turn from sea to land, we find that the first practicable locomotive was designed by Richard Trevithick in England in 1801, and the first true railway was built by George Stephenson between Stockton and Darlington in 1825. Although the locomotive was wholly of British origin, it is no coincidence that the nation which produced Clausewitz was the first to grasp the supreme importance of the railway in war. Thus, in 1833, F. W. Harkort pointed out that a railway between Cologne and Minden and another between Mainz and Wesel would add enormously to the defence of the Rhineland, and C. E. Pönitz urged the general building of railways to protect Prussia against France, Austria, and Russia. Simultaneously, Friedrich List, an economist of unique genius, pointed out that from the position of a secondary military Power, whose weakness was that she was centrally placed between powerful potential enemies, Prussia could be raised by the railway into a formidable State. "She could be made into a defensive bastion in the very heart of Europe. Speed of mobilization, the rapidity with which troops could be moved from the centre of the country to its periphery, and the other obvious advantages of 'interior lines' of rail transport would be of greater relative advantage to Germany than to any other European country."

In 1833, before a single rail had been laid, this remarkable man projected a network of railways for Germany which is substantially that of to-day, and 13 years later, the year of his death, the first extensive troop movement by rail was made by a Prussian army corps 12,000 strong with horses and guns to Cracow. After this experiment the Prussian General Staff made a comprehensive survey of the military value of railways. Although during the revolutionary troubles of 1848–1850 Prussia gained further experience in rail movements, as also did Austria and Russia, it was not until the Franco-Italian War of 1859 that troop movements by rail may be said to have become fully established. Thus it came about that the genius of George Stephenson gave life to the Clausewitzian theory of the nation in arms, for without the railway the mass-armies of the second half of the nineteenth century could not have been supplied.

When Jomini[1] reviewed these changes, so far as they had advanced by 1836, he was of opinion that war would become "a bloody and most unreasonable struggle between great masses equipped with the weapons of unimaginable power. We might see again wars of peoples like those of the fourth century; we might be forced to live again through the centuries of the Huns, the Vandals and the Tartars." Further, he pointed out that unless governments combined to proscribe inventions of destruction, infantry would be obliged "to resume its armour of the Middle Ages, without which a battalion will be destroyed before engaging the enemy. We may then see again the famous men-at-arms all

[1] Baron Henri Jomini, Swiss military writer. Served under Napoleon as colonel and was aide to Marshal Ney. After 1813 was lieut.-gen. in Russian service and aide to the Tsar.

covered with armour, and horses also will require the same protection."

Yet out of the Industrial Revolution came changes deeper than Jomini could foresee. The ancient foundations of manual labour were fast uprooted; workers were torn from their homes and villages and regimented in factories, the power-houses of national wealth and the barracks of social revolution.

Widespread misery caused vast emigration; a veritable *Völkerwanderung* occurred between 1831 and 1852, when over three million people left Great Britain and Ireland for the United States, and many of those who were unable to do so turned towards Socialism, the new cult to which the Industrial Revolution had given birth.

The spiritual moulders of this age of power were the three Charles – Clausewitz, Marx, and Darwin. The first, in his *On War* (1832), expounded a return to Spartanism, which turned the State into a military machine; the second, in his *Communist Manifesto* (1848), based his social theorem on class antagonism; and the third, in his *Origin of Species* (1859), brought the whole apocalyptic vision to its summit in his hypothesis of the survival of the fittest through never ending conflict. All three were prophets of the mass-struggle – in war, in social life, and in biology.

Although, when the Machine Age was in its youth, the consensus was that it heralded an age of peace, sharp differences between one country and another caused discord and contributed to the intensification of nationalism, and as countries outside Europe became industrialized, the problem became world-wide. The road led from limited to total war and totalitarianism became the hidden philosophy of the age.

The first of the unlimited industrialized wars was the Civil War in America. It was the first great conflict of the steam age, and the aim of the Northern, or Federal, states was unconditional surrender – that is, total victory. Its character was, therefore, that of a crusade, and because of this, as well as because it put to the test the military developments of the Industrial Revolution, it opened a radically new chapter in the history of war.

While the French Revolutionary and Napoleonic wars were fought, a new empire began to take form in North America; for expansion – "Manifest Destiny" – was as much a product of the American Revolution as it was of the French. Indian territories were annexed and new states rapidly came into being. In 1803 the purchase of the vast region of Louisiana from France for $11,250,000 doubled the area of the United States, which was further increased by the purchase of Florida from Spain in 1819.

As the Louisiana Purchase abutted on Spanish America, friction with the Spaniards was constant. In 1821 Mexico broke away from Spain, and in 1822 was followed by Columbia, Chile, Peru, and Buenos Aires. Because President Monroe feared that some European Power might try to take possession of one or more of these newborn republics, on December 2, 1823, he announced in his Annual Message to Congress three principles, which became known as the Monroe Doctrine. In brief, they reserved the Americas for the Americans, and thereby removed the whole of the western hemisphere from future European colonization. It was, therefore, a total policy.

Thus a new form of expansion was created – expansion by reservation. The whole of the New World was excluded from European land hunger and placed in cold storage for the eventual economic exploitation of the United States.

In 1836, friction between the Americans and Mexicans over Texas led to the Texan War, and in 1846 to war with Mexico, by which the United States not only confirmed its annexation of Texas, but also gained the future states of New Mexico, Arizona, California, Nevada, Utah, and part of Colorado, an area as extensive as the Louisiana Purchase. At the same time the Oregon Country (states of Washington, Oregon, and Idaho) was obtained by treaty from Great Britain, and in 1853 the existing United States, less Alaska,[1] was created with the Gadsen Purchase from Mexico.

Thus, within the space of a lifetime (1783-1853) a vast yet largely empty empire was born, and as it expanded so did the problem not of how to secure it, but of how to prevent internal stresses and strains from disrupting it. For years the political outlooks of the Southern and Northern states had been shaped by the planting, slave-holding interest of the former, and the mercantile, shipping and financial interests of the latter; on one side stood agrarians and debtors, and on the other capitalists and creditors. After the Revolution, the former were represented by the Republicans (later Democrats) led by Thomas Jefferson, and the latter by the Federalists (later Republicans) under Alexander Hamilton, and as the frontier advanced, the schism between these two factions widened.

[1] Alaska was bought from Russia in 1867.

The primal factor in the dissensions which were to arise between these divergent interests was the political impotence of the Constitution under which the states were governed. It was an instrument devised to control a loose collection of extensive parishes, and was therefore totally inadequate to sustain the solidarity of a rapidly growing empire.

This Constitution originated from the breakdown of the Confederation, the Articles of which had been agreed in 1777. That Association of States was no more than "a firm league of friendship", each state followed its own path, and Congress had no power to levy taxes, to regulate trade with foreign countries or between the states, or to compel compliance with its ordinances. In 1787, a convention assembled at Philadelphia under the chairmanship of George Washington to consider the formulation of a Federal Constitution. Its master mind was Alexander Hamilton, who proposed a legislature of two Houses, a Senate and an Assembly – the one to have sole power to declare war, and the other to coin money, regulate trade, levy taxes, duties, imposts and excises, pay the debts of the United States, and provide for the common defence of the nation. These proposals were adopted in July, 1788.

This momentous change coincided with the outbreak of the French Revolution, which kept European nations fully occupied and for 20 years left the Americans free to consider their domestic affairs. During this interval of upheaval and war they were increasingly influenced by the economic revolutions which simultaneously took place in the Southern and Northern states. In the South, Eli Whitney's invention of the cotton gin revolutionized the cotton trade. The result was the political supremacy of the cotton planter in the South and an ever-increasing economic and therefore political divergence from the North. In the Southern states trade was vastly simplified; in the North it became more and more diversified because of the increasing commerce enjoyed during the 20 years of war in Europe which brought prosperity to New England and the commercial states, and because the long embargo of 1807–1812 and the 1812–1815 war with England forced industrialization upon them.

In the North, tariffs were essential to protect the young industries from being swamped by European competitors; in the South, which had to dispose of an ever-increasing cotton crop, they were a disadvantage. Thus differentiation rapidly led to a demand for separation and the crisis came to a head over what became known as the "Tariff of Abominations" of January, 1828, when the ships in Charleston harbour flew their flags at half-mast.

That same year, Georgia addressed a long memorial to the anti-tariff states, and in 1829 Mississippi advised resistance, and Virginia resolved that the tariff ought to be repealed. In 1832, Congress removed the duties on a long list of imports, but this only made the storm more violent. At once South Carolina called a State Convention, at which the Tariff Act of 1828 and the 1832 Amendment were declared null and void. At length in March the following year a compromise was agreed, and the first phase of the struggle for state rights terminated.

Once it had developed from an economic into a political question it was not long before the quarrel took upon itself a moral aspect and became deeply concerned with the rights and wrongs of slavery. Between 1781 and 1804 slavery had been abolished in the North, and by 1819, of the 22 states then existing 11 were slave-holding and 11 free. Trouble began when in that same year a Bill to admit Missouri as a state came before the House of Representatives. Was Missouri to be a free or a slave-holding state? In either case the balance between North and South would be broken. At length a compromise was agreed: Missouri was to be admitted as a slave-holding state, and the balance maintained by admitting Maine as a free state at the same time. It was a pure makeshift and no solution of the problem. John Quincy Adams saw it as such, for he recorded in his diary: "I take it for granted that the present question is a mere preamble – the title-page to a great, tragic volume."

As a moral issue, the dispute acquired a religious significance, state rights became wrapped in a politico-mysticism which defied definition and could be argued over forever without any hope of conclusion.

In 1829, a Negro, David Walker, published a pamphlet entitled *Walker's Appeal* in which he lauded the bravery of the blacks over the whites and urged the former to revolt. A rising of slaves in Virginia was attributed to this pamphlet as well as to the *Liberator*, a Boston newspaper edited by William Lloyd Garrison, whose followers were known as Abolitionists. In the South demands were made that they should be suppressed; yet, although anti-slave meetings were broken up and Negro schools sacked, anti-slave literature continued to pour into the Southern states. Thus the quarrel deepened, until for a time it was distracted by the insurrection in Texas, the Texan problem and the Mexican War, which, as we have seen, added hundreds of thousands of square miles to the United States. This accretion of land, as well as the discovery, in 1848, of gold in California, still further accentuated the differences between the North and South.

The finding of gold caused violent social disturbances throughout the recently acquired territory. Labourers left their fields, tradesmen their shops, seamen their ships and soldiers their barracks for the goldfields. Neither threats nor punishments could hold men to their legal engagements. Because Congress had not provided for a government in California, the people proceeded to establish one of their own. In September, 1849, a convention assembled at Monterey drew up a Free-State Constitution and made formal application for the admission of California into the Union. This was violently opposed by the South because it would upset the balance of power between the free and the slave states in the Senate. Nevertheless, after a series of debates, in 1850 a compromise was agreed. It settled nothing because in the new territories the problem of slavery remained in solution, and one day these territories would become states. So it came about that, while economically and demographically the South stood still, the North continued to expand, for the opening up of the West, like the opening of a sluice gate, gave freedom to the latter to flood into the undeveloped lands.

Meanwhile, changes beyond legal arguments pushed the contending parties farther and farther apart. Yearly, scores of thousands of immigrants poured into the United States. They cared little about politics and much about the gaining of wealth. Railways advanced daily, mile by mile; more than 6,000 miles were laid between 1840 and 1850, and the Morse telegraph was adopted in 1844. Yet the South did not grow, rather did her states shrink, for many of their citizens migrated to the North and the West.

It was not the actual existence of slavery that antagonized the North, but its possible extension to the new regions. Therefore, as long as this latter question remained unsettled the quarrel continued, to reach its climax during the Presidency of James Buchanan (1857–1861) which were years of trade depression. In 1858, a comparatively unknown man, Abraham Lincoln (1809–1865) appeared upon the scene. In his contest with Stephen A.

Douglas for the senatorial seat of Illinois he poured no little common sense on the burning question and won the ears of the whole country when he proclaimed: "A house divided against itself cannot stand. I believe this government cannot endure half slave and half free. I do not expect the house to fall, but I expect it will cease to be divided. It will become all one thing or all the other."

Next, in May, 1858, the Free State of Minnesota entered the Union, to be followed in 1859 by the Free State of Oregon, when the balance between free and slave-holding states was destroyed. Compromise was now at an end, and the inevitable clash was hastened when, on the night of October 16, John Brown, a fanatical Abolitionist, at the head of some 20 followers seized the arsenal at Harper's Ferry in Virginia in order to set on foot a servile insurrection. This blew the quarrel into white heat, for though he was speedily hanged his purpose was massacre; therefore, Union or no Union, anti-slavery had to be fought to the death.

Thus matters stood when on November 6, 1860, the Presidential elections were held. There were four candidates, Bell, Breckinridge, Douglas, and Lincoln. Lincoln was elected practically on the votes of the 18 free states of the Union and received no electoral votes in the South. This verdict announced to the South that its dream of an extension of slavery had ended, and that the North held the political balance of power.

Forthwith, on December 20, South Carolina passed an ordinance of secession; Georgia, Alabama, Mississippi, Florida, Louisiana, and Texas followed suit. Their militias were called out, and the federal forts, arsenals, and custom-houses in the Southern states were occupied. One thousand cannon and 115,000 stands of arms were seized. On January 5, 1861, a caucus of cotton-state senators in Washington drew up a revolutionary programme and called a convention to assemble at Montgomery, Alabama, to organize a confederacy of seceding states.

On February 4, the secession delegates met in Congress at Montgomery and formed a provisional government, known as the Confederate States of America, with Jefferson Davis (1808–1889), as its president. And a month later Lincoln, then aged 51, addressed an earnest appeal to the South which ended: "In your hands, my dissatisfied fellow-countrymen, and not in mine, is the momentous issue of civil war. You can have no conflict without being yourselves the aggressors."

CHAPTER I

The Seven Days Battle, 1862

What were the strategical considerations which faced the contenders? In themselves they were exceedingly simple: to re-establish the Union the North must conquer the South, and to maintain the Confederacy and all that it stood for the South must resist invasion. On the one side the attitude was offensive, on the other defensive. To conquer the North was out of the question; therefore the Southern attitude resolved itself into inducing Europe to intervene and exhausting the North so as to compel the Union to abandon the contest. Since it was uncertain what Europe would do, the latter consideration was the more important; consequently, of equal importance was the question of how long Southern resources could stand the strain, since the South depended on the industries of both the North and Europe.

On April 19, 1861, Lincoln proclaimed a blockade of the Southern ports. Simultaneously he called for the enrolment of 75,000 volunteers, in spite of the fact that the Federal Commander-in-Chief, Lieutenant-General Winfield Scott, considered that "300,000 men under an able general might carry the business through in two or three years."[1] Lincoln did not appreciate, as Scott did, the vital relationship between economic pressure and land attack, or how the former should be made the base of action of the latter. Consequently he failed to gauge the value of Scott's project, which was: (1) to capture New Orleans by a joint naval and military expedition, as well as to seal up all the Southern ports; and (2) to form two large armies, one to move down the Mississippi and cut the western Confederate states off from the eastern states, while the other threatened Richmond and so contained the main Confederate forces in Virginia.[2]

Of the ports and harbours between Cape Charles and the Mississippi there were only nine linked by railways with the

[1] *Leading American Soldiers*, R. M. Johnston (1907), p. 130.
[2] See *Papers of the Military Historical Society of Massachusetts*, vol. XIII, p. 396 (cited as *M.H.S.M.*), and *Campaigns of the Army of the Potomac*, William Swinton (1866), pp. 41–42.

interior – Newbern, Beaufort, Wilmington, Charleston, Savannah, Brunswick, Pensacola, Mobile, and New Orleans.

By the end of April, 1862, all except Mobile, Charleston, and Wilmington were closed, thanks largely to Scott's forethought in holding fast to Fort Monroe; for every expedition against the Southern coast was assembled under the protection of its guns. Although Scott was derided and ridiculed, the truth is that, had these three remaining ports been occupied in 1862, the war would most definitely have been shortened. For instance, on the outbreak of the war there were fewer than 200,000 muskets in the Confederate arsenals, which were equipped with no machinery "above the grade of a foot-lathe". One hundred thousand were required yearly for replacements alone, and more than 400,000 were imported during 1862–1863. Colonel William Lamb, who was in command at Fort Fisher from July, 1862, until its fall, says that there were at least 100 vessels engaged running in and out of Wilmington. "One ship ran to Nassau with almost the regularity of a mail packet."[1]

Because by force of policy and circumstances the defensive was thrust upon the South, Jefferson Davis should have recognized that the strategic and political frontiers of the Confederacy did not coincide. Whereas the latter ran from the Potomac to the Ohio, and thence to Columbus on the Mississippi and westward along the Missouri, the former ran from the Potomac along the Alleghany mountains to Chattanooga, thence along the Tennessee River to about Savannah, across to the Mississippi at Fulton, and thence to Little Rock on the Arkansas River. Had he recognized this, and had he realized that the states of Kentucky, Tennessee, and Missouri were no more than advanced positions, or tactical outworks, in the main strategic line of defence, his strategy would have taken concrete form. He would have seen that the key to it was the area Chattanooga–Atlanta, because the two main lateral railways in the Confederacy ran through these towns and linked the entire strategical area with the supply ports of Memphis, Vicksburg, New Orleans, Mobile, Pensacola, Savannah, Charleston,

[1] *M.H.S.M.*, vol. xiii, pp. 405–406. As late as April 23, 1862, we find General Lee suggesting to Brigadier-General French at Wilmington that "you might arm the regiment at Wilmington by placing pikes in the hands of the men at the heavy batteries and giving their muskets, as far as they will go, to the unarmed regiment, and make up deficiency by arming some of the center companies with pikes, the flanking companies having the rifles" (*The War of the Rebellion: A Compilation of the Official Records of the Union and Confederate Armies*, vol. ix, p. 463 – cited as *W.R.* See also *ibid.*, vol. ix, p. 719).

I. THE CONFEDERACY, 1861–1865

Wilmington, and Richmond. Should Chattanooga-Atlanta be lost, then, from a supply point of view, to all intents and purposes the Confederacy would be reduced to the Carolinas and Virginia.[1]

Had Davis understood this strategy he would also have seen that the Alleghany Mountains cut the main theatre of war, which lay between the Mississippi and the Atlantic, into two sub-theatres, political and strategical. In the political theatre the security of the two capital cities and their governments were the paramount factor; whereas the strategical theatre was largely determined by the great river lines of approach – namely, the Mississippi, Tennessee, Cumberland, and Ohio. He would then also have seen that, as the most certain means to win the war was to wear out the North – that is, to prolong the war indefinitely – the correct grand tactics were to base the main forces on Chattanooga and to carry out a defensive-offensive campaign in Tennessee, while a covering force operated in Virginia. Such a campaign, if pushed with vigour, would not only have protected the great supply states of Mississippi, Alabama, and Georgia, but would have kept open the vital crossings into Arkansas and Louisiana and stretched out a helping hand to Kentucky.

It may be said that, had these grand tactics been decided upon, the Federals would have occupied Virginia, from where they would have pushed south through the Carolinas. This is unlikely, even had Virginia been overrun, for not only would the Confederate operations in Tennessee have drawn the bulk of the Federal forces westward, but topographical conditions in the east would have proved as difficult to overcome as in 1775–1783. What did General Nathaniel Greene[2] do in North Carolina in 1781? He avoided pitched battles, and instead relied upon rapidity of manoeuvre to strike at weakness and the British lines of communication. Had the Federals penetrated into North Carolina they would have had to rely on the Danville railway, and every mile of advance would have laid that line open to more certain attack; therefore its protection would eventually have crippled their field army. Further, in order to protect this central line of supply, they would have been compelled to advance on an enormously

[1] According to the census of 1850, Texas possessed four times as many cattle and horses as all the other Southern states combined.
[2] Nathaniel Greene: American revolutionary general noted for campaigns in Carolina in 1781. Was Q.M.G. and during Washington's absence in September, 1780, was in supreme command of Continental Army.

extended front, and as the country they traversed was hostile their progress would have been excessively slow.

On the Federal side, the failure to adopt Scott's plan until late in the war and the failure on the part of Lincoln to find a general capable of grasping the strategical advantage of carrying the war into East Tennessee made strategy vague and confused. Not until Rosecrans's defeat at Chickamauga in September, 1863, was Lincoln's essentially sound idea accepted. This was mainly because from the opening of the struggle, and for more than two years following it, attention was riveted on the political theatre of the war, which included the enemy's capital.

Into the hands of Lincoln and Davis was thrust the destiny of a divided people. Lincoln was the product of the soil, Davis of the study. One had breathed the freedom of nature and could best express his inner feeling in parables; the other had breathed the air of the cloister, and his soul had grown stiff as the parchment it fed upon. Lincoln was very human, Davis artificial, autocratic and forever standing on the pedestal of his own conceit; a man of little humour who could dictate, but who could not argue or listen and who could not tolerate either help or opposition. Because he relied upon European intervention to scuttle the war, he had no foreign policy outside establishing cotton as king. Early in the war the Hon. James Mason, Confederate Commissioner in Europe, affirmed that all cotton in that continent would be exhausted by February, 1862, "and that . . . intervention would [then] be inevitable";[1] yet before the end of 1861 Europe was learning to do without cotton. Davis could not believe that he was wrong; he staked the fortunes of his government and his people on this commodity and lost. On the other hand, Lincoln pinned his faith on what he believed to be the common rights of humanity. In spite of division he saw one people, and in spite of climate and occupation, one nation. To him the Union was older than any state, for it was the Union which had created the States as states. He saw that whatever happened the nation could not permanently remain divided. His supreme difficulty was to maintain the unity of the North so that he might enforce unity upon the South; whereas Jefferson Davis's ship of state was wrecked on the fundamental principle of his policy that each individual state had the right to control its own destiny, a policy which was incapable of

[1] *An Aide-de-Camp of Lee, Papers of Colonel Charles Marshall*, edited by Major-General Sir Frederick Maurice (1927), pp. 10 and 19.

establishing united effort. At heart Lincoln was an imperialist, at bottom Davis was still a colonist.

Because the Confederacy was immense in size, badly supplied with roads, and pre-eminently agricultural, its soldiers naturally took to guerrilla warfare, as their forefathers had done during the War of Independence. In order to conquer such a people operations had to be methodical, for individual valour and initiative are best overcome by discipline and solidarity. Unfortunately for the Federals they sought to establish these conditions on the conventional European pattern. They copied instead of creating, and at the outbreak of the war, because they possessed the army headquarters and the bulk of the small regular establishment, they expanded it not only bodily but spiritually in the form in which they found it. In short the South, though less military, was more soldierlike and free from shibboleths; therefore the Confederate soldier could the better adapt himself to changing conditions, whereas the Federal soldier tried to overcome difficulties by textbook rules.

Except for his lack of discipline, the Southern soldier was probably the finest individual fighter of his day. The Confederate General D. H. Hill says:

"Self-reliant always, obedient when he chose to be, impatient of drill and discipline, he was unsurpassed as a scout or on the skirmish line. Of the shoulder-to-shoulder courage, bred of drill and discipline, he knew nothing and cared less. Hence, on the battlefield he was more of a free-lance than a machine. Whoever saw a Confederate line advancing that was not crooked as a ram's horn? Each ragged rebel yelling on his own hook and aligning on himself."[1]

This individualism was also largely stimulated by the change in firearms during the previous 20 years. In the Napoleonic wars the flintlock musket, which possessed an effective range of less than 100 yards, was considerably outranged by cannon firing grape or canister; therefore the gun was the superior weapon. But in 1861 the musket had given way to the muzzle-loading percussion-capped rifle,[2] a weapon with an effective range of 500 yards, which could outrange case and canister fired either by smooth-bore or rifled guns. The whole of fire tactics underwent a profound change. The

---

[1] *Papers of the Southern Historical Society*, vol. XIII, p. 261.
[2] The Minié rifle was largely used. Its weight was 10½ lb., length of barrel, 3 ft. 3 in., its barrel four-grooved, its bore .702 in., and it was sighted from 100 to 1,000 yards.

gun had to fall back behind the infantry and become a support weapon, and the infantry fire-fight opened at 400 yards' range instead of 50 to 100 yards. The result of this long range fire-fighting was that the bayonet assault died out; individual good shooting became more effective than volley firing, and for full effectiveness it demanded initiative and loose order. Therefore the percussion-cap rifle well fitted Confederate tactics and the character of the Southern soldier.

During the war we find that the Confederate soldier marched light, carried from 30 lb. to 40 lb. weight[1] – a rifle, a cartridge-box, an old blanket, and a "tooth brush stuck like a rose in his button-hole" – and the Federal carried about 60 lb.[2] A good description of the tactics of the Southern soldier is given by the Confederate Colonel Taylor, who writes:

"I was wonderfully impressed . . . by the Southern soldier and his independent action in battle as contrasted with the mechanical movement of the machine soldier. . . . First one man went forward, then another, then at intervals two or three; then there would be a wavering and falling back when the fire became hot; then there would be a repetition of this; one or two at a time encouraging the others, then small parties advanced; the officers waved their swords and called the men 'forward', and then with a yell the whole line rushed rapidly forward without precision or order, but irresistibly sweeping everything before them."[3]

In his turn, Watson, a Confederate private, says of the Federal soldiers:

"What told most against them was their strict adherence to military rigidity and form of discipline, by standing up close and maintaining their line in the open field, making themselves conspicuous marks for the fire of their opponents, who fought in open ranks and kneeled down, forming a less prominent mark. . . . They, knowing the superiority of their arms over ours, kept falling back to keep us at long shot, while we followed them up to keep them at close range. This was a considerable advantage to us. Our advancing upon them kept us enveloped in the dense smoke, while their falling back kept them in the clear atmosphere where they could be easily seen. Our men squatted down when loading, then advanced and squatted down again, and looking along

[1] *Life in the Confederate Army*, William Watson (1887), p. 184.
[2] *The Campaign of Chancellorsville*, Major John Biglow (1910), p. 175.
[3] *General Lee: His Campaigns in Virginia, 1861–1865*, Walter H. Taylor (1906), pp. 176–177.

under the smoke could take good aim, while the enemy firing at random into the smoke, much of their shot passed over our heads."[1]

In brief, the Federal soldier was semi-regular and the Confederate semi-guerrilla. The one strove after discipline, the other unleashed initiative. In battle the Confederate fought like a Berserker, but out of battle he ceased to be a soldier.[2] For instance, Robert Stiles, a Southerner, tells us that on his way to Gettysburg he rode up to a house, asked for a drink of water, rested there, chatted, wrote a letter, and after he had wasted an hour or two, rejoined his unit.[3] In the Confederate Army straggling was an inalienable right, a defect which jeopardized success time and again.

Such, in brief, was the background of the war, which opened at 4.30 a.m. on April 12, 1861, when the Confederates at Charleston bombarded Fort Sumter, which surrendered at noon on April 14.

When those guns opened fire, Colonel Robert E. Lee (1807–1870) was still in the United States Army. On April 20 he resigned his commission and three days later was entrusted with the defence of Virginia, which had seceded but had not yet joined the Confederacy. This was an event of the greatest importance for the South, for Lee's position as a soldier and as a citizen was outstanding. Son of General Henry Lee ("Light Horse Harry") he was born at Stratford, Virginia, on January 19, 1807, and, in 1831, when he married Mary Randolph Custis, great granddaughter of Martha Custis, the wife of George Washington, he became the representative of the family which more than any other had founded American liberty.

His first act was to send Colonel Thomas J. Jackson, soon to become famous as "Stonewall" Jackson, to seize Harper's Ferry. Later, on May 10, he was appointed commander-in-chief of the forces of the Confederacy, and held that appointment until June 8, when Jefferson Davis assumed direct control. Lee then became his nominal chief of staff, and his first task was to secure northern Virginia. He accomplished this by sending General Joseph E.

---

[1] William Watson, pp. 230 and 294.
[2] Lieutenant-General Richard Taylor writes: "They could always be relied on when a battle was imminent; but when no fighting was to be done they had best be at home attending to their families and interests" (*Destruction and Reconstruction*, 1879, p. 28).
[3] *Four Years under Marse Robert*, Robert Stiles (1903), p. 20.

Johnston and 11,000 men to Harper's Ferry, while General Peter
G. T. Beauregard held Manassas Junction with 22,000 men. This
was too much for the people and the press in Washington, whose
eagerness to attack and whose slogan, "On to Richmond", forced
the hands of Lincoln and General Scott. On July 18 General
Irvin McDowell, after he had concentrated some 36,000 partially
trained men at Centerville, advanced to Bull Run near Manassas
Junction. On July 21 he was defeated and his men took panic and
broke back to Washington.

Although this battle had no strategical results, its influence on
the grand strategy of the war was profound. It imbued the
Southern politicians with an exaggerated idea of the prowess of
their soldiers, and so led them to underestimate the fighting
capacity of their enemy; and it so terrified Lincoln and his
Government that from then until 1864 the defence of Washington
coloured every Federal operation east of the Alleghanies.

The day after this battle Lincoln summoned to Washington
Major-General George B. McClellan, then commanding the
Army of the West in the Department of Ohio. On July 27
McClellan assumed control of the 50,000 troops in and about the
capital and soon replaced Scott as general-in-chief.

Born on December 3, 1826, he had served in Mexico, was
selected as one of the military commission sent to the Crimean
War, and in 1857 retired from the army to become chief engineer
of the Illinois Central Railroad. He was a man of great energy
and gifted with marked powers of organization as well as charm.
He soon won over the routed troops, whom he formed into the
Army of the Potomac, and raised their numbers to nearly 150,000
by October 27. On August 4 he set before the Government an
elaborate appreciation of the war,[1] which demanded an army
273,000 strong. A little later he found that so great a force could
not be raised, modified his ideas, and began to consider an advance
on Manassas or wherever the Confederates might be. But in
December he was taken ill and the operation he had in mind was
postponed until the early spring.

Although McClellan could win over his soldiers, he utterly
failed to win over the politicians, mainly because he never con-
descended to take them into his confidence. Yet the fault was not
altogether his, for, as John C. Ropes writes: "Few men at the head
of affairs during a great war have ever given such evidence of an

[1] See *W.R.*, vol. v, pp. 6–8.

entire unfitness to have any general direction over military men as Mr. Lincoln and Mr. Stanton [his Secretary of War]."[1]

Behind the politicians stood the public, who had forgotten Bull Run and again clamoured for an advance. Had McClellan possessed more perception he would have propitiated them by taking Norfolk[2] or by reducing one or more of the Confederate batteries on the Potomac. Instead, he drew too heavily on their faith when a little understanding and above all, action, would have drawn them to him.

While he was ill, Lincoln – apparently glad to be rid of him – took the unusual course of consulting his subordinate commanders, Franklin and McDowell. To the latter he said: "If something was not soon done, the bottom would be out of the whole affair; and if General McClellan did not want to use the army, he would like to *borrow* it, provided he could see how it could be made to do something."[3] When McClellan returned to duty on January 27, 1862, Lincoln, without consulting him, tried to terminate what he held to be an unwarranted delay by an order "for a general movement of the land and navy forces of the United States against insurgent forces", certainly one of the most extraordinary orders of the war.[4]

Of course, nothing happened. Then, on February 3, McClellan proposed to abandon the overland advance on Richmond because of the impassable condition of the roads[5] and to substitute for it a movement by water to Urbana on the lower Rappahannock, or should that spot be found unsuitable, then to Mob Jack Bay or Fort Monroe.[6]

At once the President and his Secretary of War took alarm, because such an operation would remove the army from before Washington, while the Confederates still held Manassas Junction. At length it was provisionally agreed, and on March 8 Lincoln issued another of his personal orders by which he directed that "no change of the base of operations of the Army of the Potomac"

---

[1] *M.H.S.M.*, vol. I, p. 77. For criticism of Stanton, see also *The Story of the Civil War*, John Codman Ropes (1894), vol. I, p. 225, and *Personal Memoirs*, U.S. Grant (1885–1886), vol. II, pp. 104–105.

[2] General Webb says, "The capture of Norfolk would have changed everything" (*The Peninsula: McClellan's Campaign of 1862*, 1882, p. 31), which we shall see is only too true. Writing to Mr. Stanton on April 24, 1862, Gideon Welles says: ". . . but the capture of Norfolk would, in my opinion, next after New Orleans, be the most decisive blow that could be struck for the suppression of the rebellion" (*ibid.*, pp. 170–171).

[3] Swinton, p. 80.   [4] See *W.R.*, vol. v, p. 41.

[5] *Ibid.*, vol. v, p. 45.   [6] *Ibid.*, vol. v, p. 42.

was to "be made without leaving in and about Washington such a force as in the opinion of the General-in-Chief and the Corps Commanders shall leave said city entirely secure."[1]

No objection was raised to this; but apparently in order to persuade McClellan to abandon his scheme, he was forbidden to transport his army to Urbana.[2]

Two events now occurred which in McClellan's mind made the Urbana scheme futile. The first was the memorable fight in Hampton Roads, on March 9, between the Federal *Monitor* and the Confederate *Virginia* – usually called by her former name, *Merrimac* – the first of the ironclad engagements. Although neither ship was seriously damaged the *Monitor* proved that she could match her rival and so protect the transports which were to carry the Army of the Potomac to Fort Monroe. The second event was Johnston's evacuation that same day of Manassas Junction and the Potomac batteries and his retreat to the Rapidan. Four days later McClellan summoned his four corps commanders – McDowell (Ist Corps), Sumner (IInd Corps), Heintzelman (IIIrd Corps) and Keyes (IVth Corps) – to a council of war, at which it was decided that the landing of the army could best be undertaken at Old Point Comfort or Fort Monroe, and that to protect Washington a force of 40,000 men would be sufficient.[3] These decisions were accepted by the President and the embarkation of the troops was at once put in hand; the first convoy sailed on March 17. Nevertheless, neither Lincoln nor Stanton troubled to ascertain what troops were to be left in Washington, and when McClellan suggested that one of his ablest officers – General Franklin – should be placed in command of its garrison, Lincoln appointed General Wadsworth, a volunteer officer of no experience. When McClellan objected, Stanton replied "that Wadsworth had been selected because it was necessary, for political reasons, to conciliate the agricultural interest of New York, and that it was useless to discuss the matter, because it would in no event be changed."[4]

Nothing further seems to have been done until April 1, when, as he was about to sail for Fort Monroe, McClellan wrote to

---

[1] *Ibid.*, vol. v, p. 50.
[2] See *McClellan's Own Story*, by George B. McClellan (1887), pp. 227–228.
[3] *W.R.*, vol. v, pp. 55–56.
[4] *McClellan's Own Story*, p. 226. Simultaneously, when McClellan was absent from Washington, Lincoln took the opportunity to issue an order relieving him from the command of all the armies and restricting him to the control of the Army of the Potomac (*W.R.*, vol. v, p. 54). McClellan first learnt of this through the newspapers (*McClellan's Own Story*, pp. 220, 224–225).

Stanton that "there would be left for the garrison and the front of Washington, under General Wadsworth, some 18,000, inclusive of the batteries under instruction",[1] or less than half the number decided upon on March 13 and agreed to by the President. However, as Swinton points out, besides this garrison there were in the neighbourhood of the capital the following troops: at Warrenton – 7,780; at Manassas – 10,859; in the Shenandoah Valley – 35,467, and on the lower Potomac – 1,350; in all, therefore, 73,456 officers and men.[2]

Although clearly McClellan must have known that he was contravening the President's order of March 8, Washington was in no danger; for no sooner had McClellan set out than Johnston was ordered to carry his army from the Rapidan to Richmond, where he was placed in command of the Confederate forces in the Peninsula and at Norfolk, which were under Generals Magruder and Huger.[3] When the Federals landed, Lee, who on March 13 had been made responsible for operations under the general direction of Jefferson Davis, recommended that Johnston's army should be sent south to reinforce Magruder. Davis agreed and Magruder and 13,000[4] men took up an entrenched position along the Warwick River.

Such was the Confederate position when, after he had landed his IInd, IIIrd, and IVth Corps, McClellan pushed forward the last, which at once came into contact with Magruder. He next intended to direct McDowell's Ist Corps on Gloucester, as soon as it arrived from Alexandria, in order to turn the strong Confederate works at Yorktown. But on April 6 he was informed by Stanton that, because of the defenceless state in which Washington had been left, the President had decided to retain this corps in the neighbourhood. McClellan stigmatized this as "the most infamous thing that history has recorded. . . . The idea of depriving a general of 35,000 troops when actually under fire."[5]

The occupation of Gloucester would have opened the York River to the fleet, which then could have turned the Yorktown defences. Since this was now impossible, McClellan went to work to besiege Yorktown. On May 3 Johnston carried his army back to Williamsburg, where two days later a bloody engagement was fought. On May 10 the Confederates destroyed the *Merrimac* and

[1] *W.R.*, vol. v, p. 61.   [2] Swinton, p. 92.   [3] *W.R.*, vol. XVIII, p. 846.
[4] *Narrative of Military Operations during the Late War between the States*, by Joseph E. Johnston (1872), p. 111.
[5] *McClellan's Own Story*, p. 308; see also   10.

evacuated Norfolk. This important event opened the James River to the Federal warships, which now could sail to within seven miles of Richmond. On May 16 McClellan established his headquarters at White House on the Pamunkey River – 20 miles east of the Confederate capital.

Although events proved that the establishment of the Federal base at White House was unfortunate, barely 60 miles to the north of it lay McDowell's corps, which had now been moved to Fredericksburg, where it awaited the arrival of Shield's division before marching south on Richmond. White House was, therefore, well secured against a flanking attack, and McClellan was well placed for a combined advance of all his four corps on his enemy's capital.

Meanwhile the Confederate situation had grown worse. "Stragglers", wrote Johnston to Lee on May 9, "cover the country and Richmond is no doubt filled with the 'absent without leave'. . . . The men are full of spirit when near the enemy, but at other times, to avoid restraint, leave their regiments in crowds. To enable us to gather the whole army for battle would require a notice of several days."[1] So desperate was the situation in the capital that preparations were made to remove all military papers,[2] and even Jefferson Davis, in a letter to Johnston, spoke of the "drooping cause of our country."[3]

This letter was written on May 10, the day Norfolk was lost, yet 10 days before this Johnston had written to Lee:

"We are engaged in a species of warfare at which we can never win.

"It is plain that General McClellan will adhere to the system adopted by him last summer and depend for success upon artillery and engineering. We can compete with him in neither.

"We must therefore change our course, take the offensive, collect all the troops we have in the East and cross the Potomac with them, while Beauregard, with all we have in the West, invades Ohio.

"Our troops have always wished for the offensive, and so does the country. . . . We can have no success whilst McClellan is allowed, as he is by our defensive, to choose his mode of warfare."[4]

When McClellan left for Fort Monroe, Lincoln, instead of placing the forces in and around the capital under a single

---

[1] *W.R.*, vol. XIV, p. 503.   [2] *Ibid.*, vol. XIV, p. 504.
[3] *Ibid.*, vol. XIV, p. 508.   [4] *Ibid.*, vol. XIV, p. 477.

command, divided that sub-theatre of war into three departments, each under an independent general – McDowell, Frémont and Banks. The first was responsible for the defences of Washington, the second and third were posted in the Shenandoah Valley. Similarly on the Confederate side the defence of Richmond also perturbed Jefferson Davis who, with General Lee, realized that the main threat to the capital lay in the almost certain move south of McDowell's corps. Their obvious move was, therefore, to play on Lincoln's fears, and an opportunity to do so arose on April 28 when Jackson, who faced Banks in the Valley, suggested that he should attack him.[1] Lee agreed because he considered that such a blow would result in McDowell being ordered north – that is, away from McClellan and Richmond. Soon after Jackson set out down the Valley and threw Lincoln and Stanton into such a panic that, on May 24, McDowell was ordered to lay "aside for the present the movement on Richmond" and "to put 20,000 men in motion at once for the Shenandoah moving on the line or in advance of the line of the Manassas Gap railroad."[2] Simultaneously McClellan was notified of this change.[3]

When McDowell received this order, he was eight miles south of Fredericksburg, waiting to make his own move on Richmond directly General Fitz-John Porter, at the head of a selected force 12,000 strong, had cleared the front by driving the Confederates out of Hanover Junction. There a sharp encounter took place on May 27, and the right of the Army of the Potomac established itself within 15 miles of McDowell's van.

This second withholding of McDowell – in circumstances far less justifiable than the first – threw McClellan's admirable combined operation out of gear. What Lincoln could not see was that the most certain protection of Washington lay in an immediate advance on Richmond, avoiding the trap set by the wily Jackson in the Valley. As Ropes writes: ". . . That this concentration of 150,000 men in the immediate vicinity of Richmond would have compelled its speedy evacuation is certainly very probable. It was, at any rate, obviously the true course for the Federal authorities to take. That this course was not taken was due entirely to the action of President Lincoln who, contrary to the urgent remonstrances of the generals charged with the conduct of operations against Richmond, broke up deliberately one of the most promising combinations for the defeat of the Confederates and the capture

[1] *Ibid.*, vol. xviii, p. 870.   [2] *Ibid.*, vol. xviii, p. 219.   [3] *Ibid.*, vol. xii, p. 30.

of their capital that fortune was ever likely to afford to the Federal cause."[1]

The recall of McDowell left the Army of the Potomac divided,[2] for between May 20 and 24 the IVth corps, followed by the IIIrd, had crossed the Chickahominy, while the IInd, Vth, and VIth corps[3] took position on the north side of that river. The latter were commanded respectively by Sumner, Porter, and Franklin.

Although this distribution had been decided upon in order to gain contact with McDowell, when McDowell was withdrawn McClellan made no change in it. Consequently his army remained divided by a treacherous river, which, though of no size, was a formidable military obstacle because of the boggy lands bordering it.[4] McClellan halted his forward movement and set to work to bridge the Chickahominy, while Johnston, in Richmond, when he realized the faulty situation McClellan was in, entrusted General Longstreet with the task of overwhelming Keyes and Heintzelman. The result was the muddled and bloody battle of Fair Oaks, or Seven Pines, fought on May 31 and continued throughout June 1. About seven o'clock that evening, Johnston was severely wounded. He was succeeded by General Gustavus W. Smith, who by order of the President handed the army over to General Lee on the following day.[5]

Although this battle was indecisive, there can be little doubt that, on June 2, McClellan should have launched a vigorous counter-offensive. Had he done so, the probabilities are that he would have routed his disorganized enemy. Instead, he returned to his bridge building, which, because of the rainy weather, occupied his army for the next three weeks. Changes he certainly did make in his distribution, for he withdrew all troops, except the Vth Corps – Fitz-John Porter's – from the north to the south of the Chickahominy, and began to build elaborate fieldworks from Golding's Farm to White Oak Swamp and also immediately to the east of Beaver Dam Creek, while the approaches from the south side were "strongly defended by intrenchments."[6] During this period, and in response to urgent demands for reinforcements, McCall's division, 9,500 strong, was sent to him and added to Porter's corps, as were 11,000 troops from Baltimore and Fort

---

[1] *The Story of the Civil War*, vol. II, pp. 132–133.
[2] White House had been selected as a base with a view to McDowell's cooperation.
[3] The Vth and VIth "Provisional" corps were organized on May 15. (See Webb, p. 84.)
[4] See Swinton, p. 130.   [5] *W.R.*, vol. XIV, p. 568.   [6] *Ibid.*, vol. XIII, p. 490.

Monroe. On June 20, the strength of McClellan's army was 105,445 officers and men.[1]

Once the bridges were finished there can be no possible doubt that McClellan should forthwith have assumed the offensive, if only because Jackson was still in the Valley and might at any moment descend upon his communications with White House, which, since the withdrawal of McDowell, were largely uncovered. He certainly realized this possibility[2] – which was all but confirmed by a hostile cavalry raid on his communications on June 11 – because, as we know, he took the precaution to send by water a quantity of his stores from White House to Harrison's Landing on the James river;[3] also he had the ground between the railway and White Oak Swamp and the roads leading to the James reconnoitred.[4]

Meanwhile Lee's position was a difficult one, for not only was the army badly demoralized by its failure at Fair Oaks, but his own reputation was not high. In August and September, 1861, he had failed in West Virginia, and since then until his summons to Richmond on March 13, 1862, he had been lost to sight among the coast defences of Georgia, South Carolina, and Florida. Therefore he was virtually unknown to his army and, as his military secretary – General Long – said, "lacked its confidence."[5]

As Lee saw that Richmond must be held at all costs, his first action was a wise one – namely, to secure it from the south by a line of works extending from "Chaffin's Bluff, on the James River . . . to a point on the Chickahominy a little above New Bridge."[6] Simultaneously he set out to reorganize his army, which consisted of six divisions – Longstreet's, Huger's, D. H. Hill's, Magruder's, Whiting's, and A. P. Hill's.

Once this work was in hand, on June 5 he reconnoitred the Federal position, and in the evening wrote to the President and suggested that, if Jackson could be reinforced, he might be able to "cross Maryland into Penn." Then he said: "I am preparing a line that I can hold with part of our forces in front, while with the rest I will endeavour to make a diversion to bring McClellan out."[7] It would seem that here we first touch upon the origin of

---

[1] *Ibid.*, vol. xiv, p. 238.   [2] *Ibid.*, vol. xii, p. 53.   [3] *Ibid.*, vol. xiii, p. 191.
[4] *Battles and Leaders of the Civil War* (1884–1888), vol. ii, p. 431.
[5] *Memoirs of Robert E. Lee*, by A. L. Long (1886), p. 163.
[6] *Ibid.*, p. 164. His A.D.C., Colonel Charles Marshall, tells us that for doing so Lee was abused by the Press for dawdling (*Papers of Colonel Charles Marshall*, p. 79).
[7] *Lee's Dispatches*, edited by Douglas Southall Freeman (1915), pp. 6–7.

the Seven Days Battle, because three days later and after another reconnaissance Lee wrote to Jackson:

"Should there be nothing requiring your attention in the Valley so as to prevent your leaving it in a few days, and you can make arrangements to deceive the enemy and impress him with the idea of your presence, please let me know that you may unite at the decisive moment with the army around Richmond. Make your arrangements accordingly, but should an opportunity occur of striking the enemy a successful blow, do not let it escape you."[1]

On June 11, Lee wrote to him again and informed him that he was sending him six regiments under Brigadier-General Lawton and eight under Brigadier-General Whiting to help to crush "the forces opposed to you." In this dispatch he added: Guard the passes and "move rapidly to Ashland by rail or otherwise . . . and sweep down between the Chickahominy and Pamunky, cutting up the enemy's communications, etc., while this army attacks General McClellan's in front."[2]

General Taylor writes of this reinforcement:

"To deceive the enemy, General Lee . . . sent to the Valley a considerable force under Generals Whiting, Hood and Lawton. The movement was openly made and speedily known at Washington, where it produced the desired impression, that Jackson would invade Maryland from the Valley. These troops reached Staunton by rail on the 17th and, without leaving the train, turned back to Gordonsville, where they united with Jackson."[3]

Simultaneously, in order to discover the exact situation of McClellan's right flank, Lee sent General J. E. B. Stuart and his 1,200 cavalry to reconnoitre toward the York River railway.[4] By June 13 Stuart had discovered that McClellan's entrenchments did not extend beyond Beaver Dam, and that there was no indication that McClellan intended to change his base. "But the most valuable and important information obtained by General Stuart was the fact that the enemy had neglected to fortify the ridge between the head waters of the Beaver Dam . . . and an affluent of the Pamunkey,"[5] for it was along this ridge that Lee hoped to strike at McClellan's communications.

---

[1] *W.R.*, vol. XVIII, p. 908. On June 6, Jackson had written to Johnston hinting that his command might be wanted at Richmond. Therefore, apparently, the same idea had occurred to him.

[2] *Ibid.*, vol. XIV, p. 589, and vol. XVIII, p. 910.   [3] *Destruction and Reconstruction*, p. 102.

[4] "You are desired to make a secret movement to the rear of the enemy" (*W.R.*, vol. XIV, p. 590).

[5] *Papers of Colonel Charles Marshall*, p. 82.

The value of this information was largely nullified by sending out so powerful a force and under so impulsive a leader as Stuart. Instead of returning after he had fulfilled his mission, he set out to ride round McClellan's entire army, and by attacks on its trains and rear services he opened McClellan's eyes to his danger.[1]

When he had circled McClellan, Stuart returned to Richmond on June 15, and when Lee received his report[2] he wrote to Jackson to suggest a meeting, after which, accompanied by Colonel Long, he rode out to reconnoitre the Federal position north of the Chickahominy.[3] Once he had made up his mind to bring Jackson down on McClellan's right, he mentioned it to Longstreet on his return. Meanwhile Jackson, on receipt of Lee's letter of June 15, moved his 18,500 men down the Virginia Central railway and arrived at Frederick's Hall ahead of them on Sunday, June 22. There he remained to attend religious meetings until the Sabbath was over,[4] and, at one o'clock on Monday morning, he rode the 52 miles to Lee's headquarters and arrived at 3 p.m. "Had he kept on the freight train to Richmond," writes General Alexander, "he would have arrived early Sunday morning. His brigades on the march also kept Sunday in camp. It was usually the general's custom to keep account of Sundays spent in fighting or marching and to make up for each by a week-day rest and sermons at the earliest opportunity."[5]

This loss of precious military time, as we shall see, was the initial cause that wrecked Lee's campaign.

On his arrival Lee at once assembled a conference, which Jackson, Longstreet, and the two Hills attended, and outlined his plan. The general idea was that, while Huger and Magruder held the entrenched lines east of Richmond and south of the Chickahominy, Jackson was to outflank McClellan's position north of the

[1] *Military Memoirs of a Confederate*, E. P. Alexander (1907), p. 114. A recent writer, Captain John W. Thomason, in his *Jeb Stuart* (1930), pp. 154-155, holds a similar though less outspoken opinion.
[2] *W.R.*, vol. XIV, p. 602, and vol. XVIII, p. 911.
[3] Long, p. 168.
[4] See D. H. Hill, in *Battles and Leaders*, vol. II, p. 349.
[5] Alexander, p. 115. "Jackson not only refrained from writing letters on Sunday: he would not read a letter on Sunday; he even timed the sending of his own letters so that they should not encumber the mails on Sundays" (*Memoirs of Stonewall Jackson*, Mary Anna Jackson, n.d., p. 75). "Had I fought the battle on Sunday instead of on Monday I fear our cause would have suffered" (*ibid.*, p. 249). Yet there was nothing of the New Testament about him, rather of the Old: he said, "No quarter to the violators of our homes and firesides" (*ibid.*, p. 310). And again, when someone deplored the necessity of destroying so many brave men, "No; shoot them all: *I* do not wish them to be brave" (*Life and Campaigns of Lieut.-Gen. Thomas J. Jackson*, by Prof. R. L. Dabney, 1866, p. 397).

river, to turn his right, fall on his rear and sever his line of communications, and so compel him to retire. Then Longstreet and
the two Hills were to advance on Beaver Dam Creek and assail
his front as it retired.[1]

Obviously, the success of this manœuvre depended on careful
timing between the advance of Longstreet and the two Hills and
Jackson's attack. It must have been equally obvious that, should
McClellan either before or after the action withdraw to the south
of the Chickahominy, break down the bridges over it and then
move on Richmond, the bulk of Lee's army would be completely
outmanœuvred. But Lee knew how cautious McClellan was and
was convinced that he would not seize such an opportunity, which
in any case would necessitate moving his base to James River, but
would instead retire down the Peninsula to Fort Monroe.[2]

According to Freeman, Lee's total effective strength was about
67,000 men, and Jackson's 18,500, which made a grand total of
85,500 men of all arms. His order of battle was as follows:

Defensive Force: Magruder's division, 12,000 men, and Huger's,
9,000.

Attacking Force: Jackson's division, 18,500 men, covered by
Stuart's cavalry division of 1,800 sabres.

Pursuit Force: Longstreet's division on the right, 9,000 men,
A. P. Hill's division in the centre, 14,000 men, and D. H. Hill's
division on the left, 9,000 men.

River James Defence Force: Holmes's division, 6,500 men, and
Wise's command, 1,500.

Reserve Artillery: General Pendleton, 23 batteries, 3,000 men.

Cavalry south of the Chickahominy: 1,200 men.[3]

To return to McClellan. Without counting the 10,000 men still
at Fort Monroe, he had under his command 117,000 officers and
men present for duty, of whom 105,500 were effectives. Therefore
he outnumbered his opponent by 20,000 in all.

On June 23 a rumour was picked up by McClellan's Secret
Service Corps, or "bureau of detectives", that a formidable combination was planned against him. On the following day he learnt
from a deserter that Jackson was marching from Gordonsville to
Frederick's Hall in order to fall upon his rear on June 28.[4]

---

[1] *W.R.*, vol. xiii, p. 490, 498.
[2] *Ibid.*, vol. xii, pp. 493–494, Lee's report. Also see *General Lee of the Confederate Army*,
by Fitzhugh Lee (1895), p. 162.
[3] *R. E. Lee: a Biography*, Douglas Southall Freeman (1934), vol. ii, pp. 116–117.
[4] *W.R.*, vol. xii, p. 49.

Nevertheless, he ordered a forward movement of his picket line on June 25, and a sharp engagement, known as the Skirmish of Orchard, or Oak, Grove followed. This advance was to be prepar-

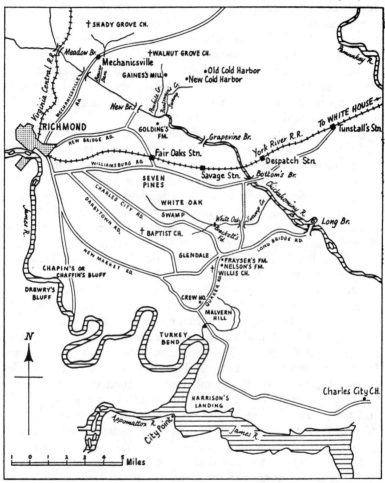

2.   THE SEVEN DAYS BATTLE, JUNE 25–JULY 1, 1862

atory to a general move on Richmond on June 26. But when he returned to his headquarters that evening he found that further rumours of Jackson's advance had been received; he accepted without question a report that Beauregard had joined Lee and telegraphed Stanton that he was faced by 200,000 Confederates.[1]

[1] *Ibid.*, vol. XII, p. 51.

Although both Lee and McClellan respectively believed themselves to be outnumbered two to one, the difference between their generalship is measured by the fact that the former decided to attack and the latter determined to retire. True, McClellan's communications were only weakly protected by Porter's 30,000 men, now the sole Federal force north of the Chickahominy; nevertheless, to attack them decisively Lee could not rely on Jackson alone, and this must have been clear to McClellan. Therefore, in order to overthrow the Federal right wing, Lee would have to strip his own right wing and risk its defeat by the Federal forces south of the Chickahominy.

As we have seen, Lee did strip his right and left with it Magruder and Huger in command of some 21,000 men to face more than three times their number. Once he had accepted this risk, largely because he had accurately measured McClellan's worth, he depended for success upon Jackson. If Jackson struck Porter before he could be reinforced, then, as General Alexander writes, "the game was Lee's for a great success – the greatest ever so fairly offered to any Confederate general."[1] Most unfortunately for Lee and the entire South Jackson failed him. Not only did Jackson's men, as we have seen, spend Sunday in prayer instead of on the march, but they made so poor an advance on Monday that by Tuesday morning they had arrived no farther than Beaver Dam Station, about 18 miles from Ashland where Jackson was expected to camp that night, and about 25 miles from the Virginia Central railway near the Stark Church, whence order No. 75 required Jackson to march at 3 a.m. on Thursday, June 26.[2] In fact, he crossed that railway at 9 a.m.[3] and marched only eight miles farther on, to go into bivouac at Hundley's Corner at about 5 p.m.; and this in spite of the fact that at the time he was within two miles of Porter's rear and could hear heavy firing in the distance.[4]

Meanwhile Lee waited. Noon came and went. About two o'clock a report was received that the Federals were evacuating certain gun positions. Lee, Longstreet, and D. H. Hill went forward to verify the report. Suddenly, heavy firing was heard to the

---

[1] Alexander, p. 112.
[2] *Ibid.*, p. 115. See also *Lee's Dispatches*, pp. 15–16.
[3] *W.R.*, vol. XIV, p. 620.
[4] Longstreet writes: "Jackson came up, marched by the fight without giving attention, and went into camp at Hundley's Corner" (p. 124). Page informs us that, on June 26, Jackson's guide lost his way because of the new roads cut by the Federals. The guide's name was Lincoln Sydnor (*General Lee, Man and Soldier*, by Thomas Nelson Page, 1911, p. 304).

north and it was assumed that at length Jackson had arrived. In fact it was not Jackson, but A. P. Hill's division; Hill had decided to wait no longer and had advanced without orders. The Federals then fell back through Mechanicsville to an all but impregnable position they had prepared behind Beaver Dam Creek. Hill attacked them fiercely and was repulsed with great slaughter.

As this premature attack caused the Federals opposing Longstreet and D. H. Hill to withdraw, their divisions were now ordered forward, and Hill launched Ripley's brigade "in a direct charge on perhaps the very strongest point of the whole Federal position." So writes General Alexander, who adds: "A more hopeless charge was never entered upon. . . . There they were killed until their bodies laid, as a Federal account described it, 'as thick as flies in a bowl of sugar'."[1] Thus Lee's first battle of the Seven Days ended in "a ghastly failure."[2] That evening he sent an urgent message to Huger: "Hold your trenches to-night at the point of the bayonet if necessary."[3] As his plan had now been disclosed, he feared that McClellan would withdraw Porter to the south of the Chickahominy, and from there with his united army break through Magruder and Huger, advance on Richmond and cut off the army from the capital.[4]

That McClellan should have done this is obvious; but as Swinton says: "The operation overlooked by its boldness the methodical genius of the Union commander."[5] Instead, as he had received a report from his Secret Service Corps that Lee now headed 180,000 men,[6] he decided to withdraw to the James and establish there a new base from which to reopen offensive operations.[7] To cover this retirement he should have either withdrawn Porter's command to the south side of the Chickahominy or have reinforced it. He did neither, and instead, at daybreak on June 27, in the knowledge that Jackson had joined Lee, he ordered Porter to withdraw to a prepared position along Boatswain's Swamp in the neighbourhood of Gaines's Mill. The retirement was successfully carried out.

While Porter consolidated his new position, Lee rode to Walnut

[1] Alexander, pp. 119, 121.   [2] Freeman, vol. II, p. 135.   [3] *W.R.*, vol. XIV, p. 617.
[4] Magruder, in his report to Lee, dated August 12, 1862, says: "Had McClellan massed his whole force in column and advanced it against any point in our line of battle . . . though the head of his column would have suffered greatly, its momentum would have insured him success, and the occupation of our works about Richmond, and consequently of the city, might have been his reward" (*W.R.*, vol. XIII, p. 686).
[5] Swinton, p. 147.   [6] *W.R.*, vol. XII, p. 269.
[7] See *McClellan's Own Story*, p. 412, and pp. 422–423.

Grove Church, which lay east of Mechanicsville, and there met
A. P. Hill and Jackson. The latter made no apologies for halting
at Hundley's Corner. Lee expected that the battle would be fought
on Powhite Creek, which flows immediately west of Boatswain's

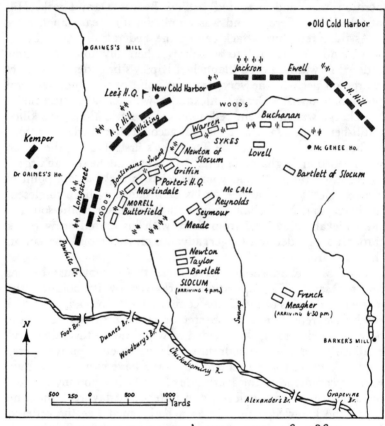

3.   BATTLE OF GAINES'S MILL, JUNE 26, 1862

Swamp, and his plan was that, while A. P. Hill, supported by
Longstreet on his right, assaulted Powhite Creek, Jackson and
D. H. Hill should advance against Porter's rear. In short, A. P.
Hill and Longstreet were to sweep the Federals into the arms of
D. H. Hill and Jackson. As usual, Lee's instructions were verbal.

At 2 p.m. the battle opened with a furious assault by A. P. Hill,
who expected that Jackson's whole army would simultaneously
be on the move. As he was repulsed, Lee ordered Longstreet to

come up on his right. Assault after assault followed, each shattered in turn. Although Lee continually sent messengers to Jackson to urge him to hurry forward, he had again lost his way, as Long informs us, and "being obliged to countermarch in order to gain the right road, caused a delay of several hours in the operations of General Lee and materially affected his plan of attack."[1]

He did more than this – he ruined it. At 4 p.m. Porter, who valiantly had held his own, was reinforced by Slocum's division of Franklin's corps, some 9,000 strong. At length, toward evening, Jackson came into line and Lee ordered a general assault all along the front. Porter s centre was broken and 22 guns and 2,800 prisoners – including 1,200 wounded – were taken. Thus Lee won the battle of Gaines's Mill at the cost of some 8,000 men killed and wounded, while his adversary, now reinforced by two brigades of Sumner's corps, fell back in good order. "Briefly it may be said of this battle," writes Alexander, "that it seems to have been left in the hands of the division commanders until it was nearly lost. Only at the last moment was the hand of the general in command revealed. But had Jackson's march that morning been pushed with the fierce swiftness natural to him on such occasions, and had he, during A. P. Hill's attack, thrown his whole force upon McClellan's right, a comparatively easy victory would have resulted."[2]

That night, while Porter withdrew in good order south of the Chickahominy, the Federal corps commanders were informed of McClellan's intention to fall back on Harrison's Landing on the James River.[3] The bridges over the Chickahominy were then destroyed.[4]

Lee's misuse of his cavalry, more than the burning of these bridges, delayed his advance. Instead of sending Stuart to work round McClellan's right, he ordered him to cooperate with Ewell's division in a wholly useless expedition against the York River railway, from which Jackson had already cut the Federal army. "Thus", as Sir Frederick Maurice writes, "he deprived himself of his eyes."[5] Not until June 30 did he order Stuart to recross the Chickahominy, which caused him to arrive too late to

---

[1] Long, p. 172.   [2] Alexander, p. 132.   [3] *W.R.*, vol. XII, p. 60.
[4] These bridges were, the Foot Bridge, Duane's Bridge, Woodbury Infantry Bridge, Woodbury and Alexander bridges, and Sumner's Upper (or Grapevine) Bridge. The Railroad bridges and Bottom's Bridge were burnt on the morning of June 28 (see *W.R.*, vol. XII, p. 118, and vol. XIII, pp. 192 and 200).
[5] *Robert E. Lee the Soldier*, by Major General Sir Frederick Maurice (1925), p. 115.

take part in the final battle of the Seven Days. The result was that Lee, without his cavalry, was unable to determine whether McClellan was withdrawing to Fort Monroe or to the James River.[1]

Meanwhile McClellan's army lay between the Chickahominy and White Oak Swamp, busily engaged on throwing two bridges over White Oak Swamp Creek. When the first was finished the IVth Corps, under Keyes, crossed to take up a position four miles to the south in order to block the Charles City, New Market, and Quaker roads. The reserve artillery next crossed, followed early on June 29 by a herd of 2,500 slaughter cattle and the army trains – 3,600 wagons and 700 ambulances. The whole was safely over White Oak Swamp by the afternoon.

The same day McClellan reported events to Stanton in one of the most extraordinary dispatches ever penned. It ended with the words: "If I save this army now, I tell you plainly that I owe no thanks to you or to any other persons in Washington. You have done your best to sacrifice this army."[2]

Not until a little after sunrise on June 29 did Lee learn that McClellan was falling back on the James. His spirits at once rose – "What fairer opportunity could any soldier ask than to attack his adversary in retreat and while changing base?"[3] Forthwith he issued orders, which he had every reason to assume would ensure his enemy's annihilation; but as usual they were verbal.

Ewell was to remain at Bottom's Bridge and come under the orders of Jackson, Stuart was to watch the lower crossings of the Chickahominy, while Jackson was to rebuild Grapevine Bridge and with all speed harass the enemy's rear. Simultaneously Magruder was to advance down the Williamsburg Road and Huger down the Charles City Road and attack his right flank, and Longstreet and A. P. Hill were to cross the Chickahominy at New Bridge, pass behind Magruder and Huger, gain the Darby-town Road and block the head of the Federal retreat to the James.[4] Much again depended upon Jackson, and with D. H. Hill and Ewell his command, which numbered 25,000 all told, was by far the strongest of these columns.

When he had issued his verbal orders Lee rode over to Magruder and then to Huger, with whom he remained. From then on he

[1] *W.R.*, vol. XIII, p. 494.   [2] *McClellan's Own Story*, pp. 424–425.
[3] Freeman, vol. II, p. 166.
[4] For these various movements see *W.R.*, vol. XIII, pp. 607, 517, 687, 494, 661, 679. Also Alexander, pp. 134–135.

lost all grip of the pursuit because his subordinate commanders utterly failed to cooperate with each other or to communicate with him. The result was a complete muddle.

To begin with, Magruder mistakenly thought that Huger had been ordered to take the Williamsburg Road and support him, and also that he was opposed in strength, and he called upon Lee for reinforcements. Lee's response was to send the two rear brigades of Huger's division, but authorized Huger to recall them should it appear that Magruder did not need them. In that case Huger was to move forward his whole division.[1] Because Huger decided that Magruder did not need the two brigades he recalled them, and this so delayed him that he advanced no more than six miles that day.

Meanwhile Magruder waited for Huger on his right and for Jackson on his left. When Huger failed to appear he got into touch with Jackson through General D. R. Jones, who commanded one of his brigades. He learnt from him that Jackson could not help him because he had "other important duty to perform."[2] Magruder then attacked the Federal rearguard opposing him and drove it back on Savage Station, which lay in the direct path of Jackson's advance.

When, late that evening, Lee heard of this, he wrote to Magruder: "I learn from Major Taylor that you are under the impression that General Jackson has been ordered not to support you. On the contrary, he had been directed to do so and to push the pursuit vigorously."[3]

Why had not Jackson complied with this order, and what was the "other important duty" he had to perform? Several reasons have been advanced; but the most likely one is that June 29 was a Sunday, and as General Alexander writes, "Jackson gave it strict observance. The greater part of his troops remained in camp all day and until after midnight Sunday night. Then they made a start at or before 2.30 a.m."[4]

The general result of these misunderstandings, coupled with

[1] *W.R.*, vol. xiii, p. 789.   [2] *Ibid.*, vol. xiii, p. 675. Incorrectly dated June 28.
[3] *Ibid.*, vol. xiii, p. 687.
[4] Alexander, p. 136. Henderson's account of Jackson's delay (*Stonewall Jackson and the American Civil War* (1927 edit.), vol. ii, pp. 56–58) is so misleading as to be almost fictitious. For other accounts, see *The Life and Campaigns of Major-General J. E. B. Stuart*, 1885, by H. B. McClellan, pp. 80–81; Longstreet, p. 150; *Destruction and Reconstruction*, p. 113; *Battles and Leaders*, vol. ii. pp. 402–403, 389 and 381, by Longstreet, D. H. Hill, and Franklin respectively; *Papers of the Southern Historical Society*, vol. xxv, p. 211; *The Army of Northern Virginia in 1862*, William Allan (1892), p. 121, and Alexander, pp. 146–153.

Jackson's devotions, was that McClellan was able to slip the bulk of his retiring army over the swamp on June 28 and 29, while Longstreet and Hill, who had advanced 13 miles down the Darbytown Road to Atlee's Farm (south of Baptist Church) were left undecided, with General T. H. N. Holmes and 6,000 men who had come down the New Market Road on their right flank.

That night Lee issued his orders for the following day.

"*1.* Holmes to advance down the New Market Road and take a strong defensive position at New Market Heights near the junction of his route and the Long Bridge Road.

"*2.* Magruder to return from Savage Station, enter the Darbytown Road by the shortest byway, advance down it, and take position as a general reserve.

"*3.* Longstreet and A. P. Hill to continue down the Darbytown Road to the Long Bridge Road and to prepare to attack the Federals when they were located.

"*4.* Huger to march down the Charles City Road and to open with his artillery when he established contact with the enemy.

"*5.* Jackson, with Whiting and D. H. Hill, to march to White Oak Swamp Bridge, cross there, and attack the enemy in rear.

"*6.* Stuart's previous orders to stand – to move to the main army and to cooperate as circumstances permitted."[1]

The fire of Huger's guns was to be the signal for the general advance.

Early the next morning Lee rode over to Savage Station, where he met Jackson, who had joined Magruder at 3.30 a.m. There Robert Stiles relates: "The two Generals greeted each other warmly. . . . They stood facing each other . . . Jackson began talking in a jerky, impetuous voice, meanwhile drawing a diagram on the ground with the toe of his right boot. He traced two sides of a triangle with promptness and decision; then starting at the end of the second line, began to draw a third projected toward the first. This third line he traced slowly and with hesitation, alternately looking up at Lee's face and down at the diagram, meanwhile talking earnestly; and when at last the third line crossed the first and the triangle was complete, he raised his foot and stamped it down with emphasis saying, 'We've got him', then signalled for his horse."[2]

Lee next sought out Magruder, explained to him his orders, and rode on and joined Longstreet, the head of whose column was

[1] Freeman, vol. II, pp. 177–178.   [2] Robert Stiles, pp. 89–99.

approaching the junction with Long Bridge Road. About noon the enemy was reported on the Willis Church Road; Longstreet's division was formed into line of battle and soon began skirmishing with the pickets of Heintzelman's corps. Next, at 2.30 p.m. gunfire was heard in the direction of Huger's division, which everyone supposed was the signal to launch the battle. Although it ceased at three o'clock, Longstreet's leading brigade had by then become engaged with the Federal infantry.

Simultaneously Lee received a report from Holmes – then moving down the New Market Road – that enemy columns could be seen withdrawing southward over Malvern Hill. If that were true, it meant that McClellan had nearly escaped the trap set for him. To verify it, Lee galloped down the Long Bridge Road to the New Market junction, and when he arrived there found the information to be correct.

While Lee was away, Longstreet instructed Magruder to march to the support of Holmes, but on Lee's return he was ordered back to reinforce Longstreet, for Huger's and Jackson's attacks still hung fire. It then became apparent to Lee that if Longstreet and A. P. Hill waited much longer the enemy would escape, and at 5 p.m. he ordered them forward through the woods and clearings about Glendale and Frayser's Farm. It was after this farm that the action was named. It is also called the battle of Nelson's Farm, another neighbouring settlement.

The attack now made was somewhat disjointed. Longstreet's leading brigade rushed the woods and clearings so impetuously that it outran those in support. The result was that although McCall's division, which held the centre of the Federal line, was driven back, Hooker's and Kearney's divisions of Heintzelman's corps on its flanks stood firm. These divisions, helped by Sedgwick's division and other troops who had been set free by Huger's and Jackson's inactivity, prevented Longstreet and Hill from reaching the Quaker Road, along which the Federal trains were moving to Malvern Hill. The attack accomplished little or nothing beyond the capture of 14 guns and several hundred prisoners.

Meanwhile Huger, in accordance with his orders, had set out down the Charles City Road. He advanced with extreme caution because he was afraid that, until Jackson's attack developed, his left flank might be turned. When he found the road obstructed by felled timber[1] he set to work to clear it and soon found himself

---

[1] *W.R.*, vol. xiii, p. 789.

opposed by detachments of Slocum's and Sedgwick's men. It was then that his guns opened, not as a signal of attack, but in order to clear the road. Instead of trying to flank the road by extending through the woods he continued along it, and the enemy felled the trees as fast as his men could remove them. In all, he advanced no more than two miles by nightfall, but for some unknown reason sent no message to Lee, nor received one from him.

In the meantime Jackson, with Ewell's division in support, spent so much time collecting discarded Federal rifles and equipment that he did not cover the seven miles to White Oak Swamp Creek until noon, when he found the bridge broken and a Federal battery – one of Franklin's – in action on its southern side.

We now come to the strangest incident in the campaign. It seems probable that Jackson's fanatical regard for the Sabbath accounted for his inaction on June 22 and 29. But this reason cannot hold good for June 30, which was a Monday, unless he was making amends for some previously violated Sabbath. Yet again, Jackson remained immobile.

Although the bridge was broken, the creek averaged no more than from 10 ft. to 15 ft. in width. Above the bridge were four fords – Chapman's, Jourdain's, Fisher's and Brackett's – and below it Carter's. Colonel Mumford without difficulty got the 2nd Virginian Cavalry over the creek, and General Hampton also crossed it. When he returned to Jackson he asked permission to build a bridge for infantry. This request was granted, and the bridge was built in "a few minutes". Next writes Hampton:

"On my return to our side of the swamp, I found General Jackson seated on a fallen pine alongside of the road that led down to the ford, and seating myself by him, I reported the completion of the bridge and the exposed position of the enemy. He drew his cap down over his eyes which were closed, and after listening to me for some minutes, he rose without speaking, and the next morning we found Franklin with the rest of the Federal troops concentrated on Malvern Hill. . . . I believe that if Franklin, who opposed us at White Oak, could have been defeated, the Federal army would have been destroyed."[1]

Dabney, who was with Jackson at the time, attributes this lethargy to "sleeplessness" and "the wear of gigantic cares". He writes: "After dropping asleep from excessive fatigue, with his

---

[1] Alexander, pp. 150–151. (See also *Battles and Leaders*, vol. II, p. 381, and *Papers of Colonel Charles Marshall*, pp. 110–112.)

supper between his teeth, he [Jackson] said; 'Now, gentlemen, let us at once to bed, and rise with the dawn, and see if to-morrow we cannot *do something!*' Yet he found time, amidst the fatigues of this day, to write to Mrs. Jackson, with a heart full of piety and of yearning for domestic happiness."[1]

During the evening and night of this day the Federal forces, which had maintained themselves at Frayser's Farm, fell back in good order to Malvern Hill. This skilful withdrawal was in no way due to McClellan's personal leadership; for on June 29, after he had issued his orders to his corps commanders, he left the battle in their hands and retired to Malvern Hill to lay out its defences. Well may Ropes write: "If his army had been beaten on that day, McClellan would have been cashiered, and justly. That the Federal corps commanders – although cordially and efficiently cooperating with each other – acted on this day without a head, is evidenced by the fact that, at night, Franklin (as he says himself) 'took the responsibility of moving' his 'command to the James River'."[2]

Thus ended the battle of Frayser's Farm which, in the opinion of Freeman, "was one of the great lost opportunities in Confederate military history."[3] Alexander writes:

"I have often thought that in his [Lee's] retrospect of the war no one day of the whole four years would seem to him more unfortunate than June 30, 1862. It was, undoubtedly, the opportunity of his life, for the Confederacy was then in its prime, with more men available than ever before or after. And at no other period would the moral or the physical effect of a victory have been so great as upon this occasion."[4]

Early on the morning of July 1 Magruder's division arrived at Frayser's Farm, and at once relieved Longstreet's and Hill's exhausted troops. Contact was soon established with Jackson, who at length had crossed White Oak Swamp Creek. Lee then issued his orders for the continuation of the pursuit.

Jackson was to move down the Willis Church Road[5] and Magruder along the Quaker Road,[6] while Mahone's and Ransome's brigades of Huger's division were to follow Jackson. Armistead's and Wright's were to advance along a track leading south from the Charles City Road across the Long Bridge Road

[1] Dabney, p. 467.   [2] Ropes, vol. II, p. 199.   [3] Freeman, vol. II, p. 199.
[4] Alexander, p. 155.   [5] *W.R.*, vol. XIII, pp. 495, 557.
[6] *Ibid.*, vol. XIII, p. 667. The Quaker Road was the same as the Willis Church Road, but apparently Lee thought they were two separate roads.

to Malvern Hill. Longstreet's and A. P. Hill's divisions were to remain in reserve and Holmes was to halt for the time being on the New Market Road. Lee, as usual, left the execution of his orders to his divisional commanders.[1]

In the meantime McClellan had united his entire army on Malvern Hill, a position of great natural strength, which had been carefully reconnoitred by Fitz-John Porter. It was a plateau a mile and a half long from north to south and about three-quarters of a mile wide, flanked on the south by Turkey Island Creek and also by the fire of the Federal gunboats in the James River, and on the north-east and east by a stream called Western Run. It was, Lee says, surrounded by country "broken and thickly wooded, and was traversed nearly throughout by a swamp, passable at but few places and difficult at those."[2]

According to McClellan, his general distribution was as follows:

"Porter's corps held the left of the line (Sykes's division on the left, Morell's on the right) . . . Couch's division was placed on the right of Porter; next came Kearney and Hooker; next Sedgwick and Richardson; next Smith and Slocum; then the remainder of Keyes's corps, extending by a backward curve nearly to the river. The Pennsylvania reserve corps was held in reserve, and stationed behind Porter's and Couch's position. One brigade of Porter's was thrown to the left on the low ground to protect that flank from any movement direct from the Richmond road."[3]

When he had issued his orders Lee rode out to examine his enemy's position. He found the Federal artillery massed "in a long crescent from west to north-east" with infantry in support. After a somewhat perfunctory examination he returned and adopted Longstreet's suggestion to attack under cover of a bombardment, the signal for which was to be a yell by Armistead's brigade. It was to be given directly it was found that the Confederate artillery fire had proved effective.[4] This order was issued at 1.30 p.m.

After some delay a feeble fire was opened by the Confederate cannon, to be at once smothered by the enemy's massed gunfire. ". . . this inefficient artillery service," writes Alexander, "so discouraged the prospects of an assault that before three o'clock Lee abandoned his intention to assault. Longstreet was informed, but

[1] Webb, p. 161.
[2] *W.R.*, vol. xiii, p. 496.
[3] *McClellan's Own Story*, p. 434.
[4] *W.R.*, vol. xiii, p. 677.

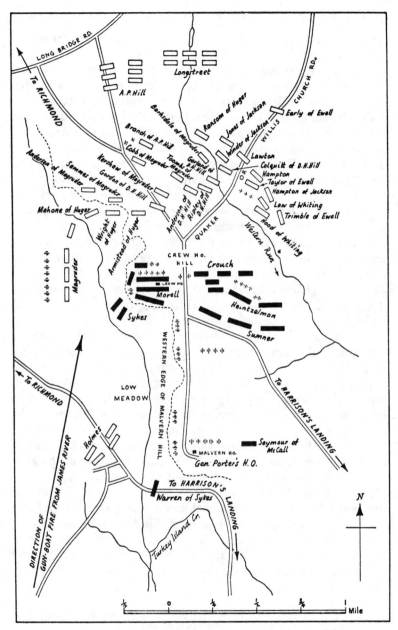

4. BATTLE OF MALVERN HILL, JULY 1, 1862

no notice was sent to the other generals, as there seemed no apparent need."[1]

Lee now determined on a turning movement. With Longstreet he rode eastward to find a suitable position, and after a hurried examination decided to seize the high ground in that quarter. As he did so, he received a report that the Federals were retiring, that Magruder had now arrived on the right, and that Armistead had driven back the enemy. Therefore he dropped the idea of outflanking McClellan, and instead sent through Captain Dickinson (Magruder's A.D.C.) the following order for Magruder:

"General Lee expects you to advance rapidly. He says it is reported the enemy is getting off. Press forward your whole command and follow up Armistead's success."[2]

Magruder had arrived on the right at about 4 p.m. and was hastily examining the ground when he received this order. Before he could complete his reconnaissance the 1.30 p.m. order arrived. As it was untimed he accepted it as current,[3] and forthwith decided to assault Crew House Hill. At 4.45 p.m. he advanced and was met by devastating gunfire.

"I never saw anything more grandly heroic than the advance after sunset of the nine brigades under Magruder's orders", writes D. H. Hill. "Unfortunately they did not move together, and were beaten in detail. As each brigade emerged from the woods, from fifty to one hundred guns opened upon it, tearing great gaps in its ranks; but the heroes reeled on and were shot down by the reserves at the guns, which a few squads reached. Most of them had an open field half a mile wide to cross, under the fire of field-artillery in front, and the fire of the heavy ordnance of the gunboats in their rear. It was not war – it was murder."[4]

Next, D. H. Hill heard a shout on his right followed by musket fire, which he took to be the signal for the attack – he did not know it had been cancelled – and he ordered his division to advance. It was met by blasts of canister. Magruder called for support from Longstreet and D. H. Hill appealed to Jackson. Thus more and more men were poured into the inferno until night put a stop to the carnage.[5]

---

[1] Alexander, pp. 160–161. See also Freeman, vol. II, p. 209. The mix-up of the Confederate units on the plan shows this confusion clearly.
[2] *W.R.*, vol. XIII, pp. 677–678.
[3] *Ibid.*, vol. XIII, p. 669.
[4] *Battles and Leaders*, vol. II, p. 394.
[5] For the chaos which reigned, see *M.H.S.M.*, vol. I, pp. 266–267.

Lee had failed. He rode through the bivouacs of his shattered army to find Magruder.

" 'General Magruder', he asked, 'why did you attack?'

"Magruder answered unhesitatingly: 'In obedience to your orders twice repeated.'

"Lee said nothing in reply, for there was nothing to say."[1]

That night Stuart returned from the Chickahominy.

Instead of counter-attacking Lee on July 2, as Porter, Hunt, and Sumner urged, McClellan decided to continue his retreat to Harrison's Landing. In pouring rain he finally changed his base from the Pamunkey to the James. Meanwhile Lee sent Stuart and his cavalry in pursuit and ordered Jackson (less D. H. Hill), Longstreet, and A. P. Hill to move south, while the rest of the army remained at Malvern Hill, except for Holmes, who was ordered back to Drewry's Bluff.

On July 2 only a two mile march was made. The following day Lee received a message from Stuart to inform him that he had reached Harrison's Landing and had discovered that an extensive plateau called Evelington Heights, which dominated it, had been left unoccupied. Once this dispatch had been sent in, Stuart, more noted for his dash than his brains, put the finishing touch to the many follies committed during the campaign. Instead of avoiding Evelington Heights, in order not to draw McClellan's attention to their nakedness, he sent forward his one and only howitzer, then "nearly out of ammunition", with some cavalry, and opened fire on the enemy's camp below. The result was that McClellan at once occupied the heights in strength.

On July 3 Longstreet missed his road and Jackson covered only three miles. On the following day, Lee rode forward to find his army in line of battle ready to regain Evelington Heights, but a rapid reconnaissance made it clear to him that these were now too strongly held to warrant an attack. On July 7 he published an order thanking his army, and two days later he carried it back to Richmond.

The price paid in the seven days following June 25 was a heavy one for both sides. Lee's army lost 19,739 in killed and wounded and McClellan's 9,796, to which must be added 6,053 men missing.[2]

[1] Freeman, vol. II, p. 218.
[2] *Numbers and Losses in the Civil War in America*, 1861-65 (1901), Thomas L. Livermore, p. 86.

Thus ended probably the most interesting and instructive campaign of the war.

That McClellan could have occupied Richmond is nearly certain, even in spite of the withdrawal of McDowell. That Lee could have routed the Army of the Potomac if the Jackson of the Seven Days had lived up to his recently gained reputation is also, as far as hypothesis allows, nearly certain. Why both men failed to achieve their desired ends is a question which hinges on their generalship, for Federal and Confederate fought with equal valour. McClellan, though an able staff officer, was a faint-hearted commander, and Lee, though an audacious commander, was an indifferent staff officer. This stricture on Lee may be reinforced by quoting the opinions of two Confederate generals. D. H. Hill writes:

"Throughout this campaign we attacked just when and where the enemy wished us to attack. This was owing to our ignorance of the country and lack of reconnaissance of the successive battlefields."[1]

General Richard Taylor says:

"Indeed it may be confidently asserted that from Cold Harbor to Malvern Hill inclusive, there was nothing but a series of blunders, one after another, and all huge. The Confederate commanders knew no more about the topography of the country than they did about Central Africa."[2]

Although Lee mentions this "ignorance of the country" in his report,[3] and throughout the campaign made use of a map that might have been drawn by a child of 10,[4] he never seems to have realized that it was his duty to overcome this ignorance by establishing a well-organized intelligence department and mapping service.

Nevertheless, in spite of the deficiencies of the two generals-in-chief and the bunglings of their as yet amateur armies, the greatest blunder of the campaign was not perpetrated by them, but by General Henry Wagner Halleck, who in Washington had replaced Stanton in the direction of operations. When at Harrison's Landing McClellan sought his permission to resume the

---

[1] *Battles and Leaders*, vol. II, p. 395.
[2] *Destruction and Reconstruction*, pp. 107–108. Jefferson Davis writes: ". . . we had no maps of the country in which we were operating; our generals were ignorant of the roads and their guides knew little more than the way from their homes to Richmond. . . ." (*The Rise and Fall of the Confederate Government*, 1881, vol. II, p. 142).
[3] *W.R.*, vol. XIII, pp. 496–497.
[4] See Freeman, vol. II, facing p. 138.

advance on Richmond – incidentally the operation by which, in 1865, General Grant ended the war – Halleck refused to give it. Accordingly on August 3, against its commander's will, the Army of the Potomac, in no way beaten and still full of fight, was compelled through the shortsightedness of a narrow-minded military pedant to abandon the campaign.

The importance of the Seven Days Battle lies in what it did not accomplish. Had McClellan lost his army, which except for Confederate blunderings he might well have done, the possibility is that the Union would have been temporally lost with it; and had Lee lost his army, and with it Richmond, which except for Federal blunderings might easily have happened, as two American historians point out: ". . . the horrors of reconstruction could not have occurred, slavery would not have been abolished by violence, or Southern society gutted, and the South would have had some voice in whatever means of gradual emancipation might subsequently have been adopted."[1] Therefore the political importance of this first of the great battles of the Civil War is that, instead of shortening the war it prolonged it by nearly three years, and by doing so it shaped its aftermath.

[1] *The Growth of the American Republic*, Samuel Eliot Morison and Henry Steele Commager (1942), vol. I, p. 686.

Progress of the American Civil War, 1862-1863

D uring the 12 months after McClellan's failure to occupy Richmond five major battles were fought in the eastern theatre of the war, and all were indecisive. First came the Second Battle of Manassas or Bull Run (August 29–30, 1862) in which the Federals, under General John Pope, were worsted by Lee. Within a month of this engagement Lee was repulsed by McClellan at the Battle of Sharpsburg, or Antietam (September 17, 1862). Next came the Battle of Fredericksburg (December 13, 1862) in which General Ambrose E. Burnside's assault was repulsed by Lee. Then followed the Battle of Chancellorsville (May 1–4, 1863) in which Lee outmanœuvred General Joseph Hooker and ruined his campaign. Lastly came the Battle of Gettysburg (July 1–3, 1863) when Lee was repulsed by General George G. Meade.

All these battles were based on a faulty strategy. Each side was so obsessed by the idea that the speediest way to win the war was to occupy the other's capital that both failed to appreciate that the strategical centre of gravity of the war lay not on the Potomac or James rivers, but in the region Chattanooga–Atlanta. As we have pointed out, if that region could have been occupied by the Federals, the Confederacy logistically would have been cut in halves and its north-eastern quarter opened to a simultaneous two-front attack. But as long as it was held by the Confederates, even if Richmond had been lost the war might have been prolonged indefinitely. All that these five battles accomplished was mutual attrition, and because the Federals could better afford their losses the gain was theirs.

While the war in the eastern theatre was being fought, in the west, by force of circumstances rather than by calculation, the importance of the strategical centre of gravity gradually impressed itself on the mind of a hitherto obscure soldier – Ulysses S. Grant (1822–1885).

Born on April 27, 1822, he had distinguished himself in the Mexican War, but in 1854 he had been retired from the army on a charge of drunkenness. When the Civil War broke out he was appointed to command the 21st Illinois Infantry, and on September 4, 1861 – by which time he had been promoted to the rank of brigadier-general – he opened his headquarters at Cairo. It was a point of great strategical importance because river communications ran from it to Vicksburg, New Orleans, Louisville, Pittsburg, Nashville, and Chattanooga. To block them the Confederates had erected strong works on the Mississippi and had built Fort Henry on the Tennessee and Fort Donelson on the Cumberland rivers, to the east of which they had pushed out forces under General Albert Sidney Johnston into southern Kentucky.

Grant appreciated the importance of Paducah on the Ohio River and occupied it on September 5. Two months later General Henry Wagner Halleck and General Don Carlos Buell respectively were placed in command of the departments of Missouri and Ohio.

In order to separate the Confederate forces in Missouri from those in Kentucky Grant obtained permission to move against Fort Henry and Fort Donelson. The former he took on February 6, 1862, which compelled Johnston to abandon Bowling Green, and the latter on February 16. These successes were of the greatest strategical importance because they forced the Confederates back towards their sally port, opened the road south towards Vicksburg, and by winning Kentucky and laying Tennessee open to invasion, deprived the Confederacy of 175,000 potential recruits.

Meanwhile Johnston fell back on Corinth, whereupon, on February 24, Buell occupied Nashville and suggested that a blow be struck against the Memphis–Charleston railway. Halleck agreed to this, but as he was jealous of Grant he placed General C. G. Smith in command of the expedition. Soon afterwards Halleck was given the command of all the Federal forces in the west, and as this appointment brought Buell under his orders, Halleck decided to move his combined armies on Corinth.

Meanwhile Smith established himself at Savannah and Grant – now again in favour – was sent by Halleck to take over command from him, but to remain on the defensive until the arrival of Buell, who was then at Columbia. On his arrival Grant concentrated the whole of Smith's army at Pittsburg's and Crump's Landings, near Shiloh, and awaited the coming of Buell, who informed him that he expected to arrive at Savannah before April 5.

In the meantime Johnston, at Corinth, was reinforced by two

divisions under General Beauregard and General Braxton Bragg, and now at the head of 45,000 men he determined to strike at Grant before Buell could join him. The result was the bloody battle of Shiloh, fought on April 6–7, in which, after an initial success, Johnston was routed. On April 11, Halleck took over field command from Grant and Buell and occupied Corinth on May 30. On June 10 Buell set out for Chattanooga, and on the following day Halleck was called to Washington and appointed general-in-chief of the entire land forces of the Union.

On July 30 Grant, now in command of the Department of West Tennessee, asked Halleck's permission to advance against Van Dorn, then at Holly Springs and Grand Junction, but it was not until September 18 that Halleck agreed. The move was then made and Grant won two brilliant engagements at Iuka and Corinth which compelled the Confederates to withdraw south.

Meanwhile, on May 1, Admiral David G. Farragut had opened the mouth of the Mississippi and General Benjamin F. Butler had occupied New Orleans, and on June 6, by his naval victory at Memphis, Admiral Davis had gained for the Federals the command of the Upper Mississippi. These actions left Vicksburg as the main link between the Confederate states east and west of the Mississippi. Grant, who realized its importance, pressed to be allowed to advance on it, and received permission to do so on November 6.

The situation which then faced Grant was as follows: Bragg, who had replaced Beauregard on June 27, opposed Buell in east Tennessee. Buell's danger lay in the exposure of his right flank, for even if he gained Chattanooga, a turning movement from the west – that is, from northern Alabama – might easily drive him out of the town. Grant saw that his own projected campaign depended on Buell's advance, and that Buell's advance depended for its security on his own army moving south on Vicksburg, because this move would draw Confederate reinforcements away from Buell. Because he realized that he and Buell must cooperate, Grant asked Halleck to inform him of the exact situation. The only answer he received was: "Fight the enemy where you please."

On the Southern side Bragg, when he succeeded Beauregard, found the bulk of his army at Tupelo. By that time Buell's van had reached Decherd. There, on July 13, General Nathan B. Forrest raided his communications at Murfreesboro and forced him to halt. Bragg then made up his mind to regain east Tennessee by invading middle Tennessee and southern Kentucky. His plan was to reinforce General Kirby Smith at Cumberland Gap and direct him on Louisville – Buell's base of operations – while he himself advanced from Chattanooga.

Again a raid, this time at Gallatin, on the railway between Nashville and Bowling Green, compelled Buell to halt; at once Kirby Smith advanced from Cumberland Gap, pushed back the weak enemy forces that confronted him, and on September 2 established his headquarters at Lexington, from where he threatened Louisville and Cincinnati. Meanwhile Bragg moved to Sparta, and Buell concentrated his army at Murfreesboro. A race north followed; Buell fell back on Bowling Green and Bragg advanced to Glasgow. But instead of following Buell and bringing Kirby Smith down on his rear, Bragg cast all strategy aside and decided to join up with Kirby Smith, not in order to fight a battle, but to inaugurate a secessionist state capital at Frankfort. Soon after, Bragg's left wing, under Hardee, advanced on Perryville, and on October 8 it attacked Buell. Although the battle was a drawn one, during the following night Bragg withdrew, and after an abortive pursuit Buell transferred his troops to Bowling Green and Glasgow. On October 30 he was replaced by General William S. Rosecrans, whose Army of the Ohio was renamed the Army of the Cumberland.

On December 26 Rosecrans moved out of Nashville, and on the last day of 1862 he fought Bragg at Murfreesboro. Although the battle was indecisive Bragg's losses were so heavy that he withdrew to Chattanooga, where he went into winter quarters.

Some time before this, General John A. McClernand, one of Grant's subordinates and a political soldier, had brought pressure to bear on Washington to place him in command of a force to be collected at Memphis, from where he intended to move down the Mississippi and operate against Vicksburg, then held by General John C. Pemberton. Grant, when he heard of this proposal, and uncertain whether McClernand was fit for an independent command, decided to hasten forward an operation he was preparing. On November 13 he had informed Halleck that his cavalry had entered Holly Springs, but that he did not intend to move farther south until his line of communications was in working order. Now he decided to move as soon as possible and to send General William T. Sherman by river from Memphis to Vicksburg, while he advanced from Grand Junction. His plan was to draw Pemberton, then at Jackson, toward Grenada, and thus to weaken the Confederate forces at Vicksburg and facilitate Sherman's attack.

On December 12, when Grant was 60 miles south of Grand Junction, Sherman set out at the head of 32,000 men and landed them at Milliken's Bend on Christmas Day. On December 29, he fought the battle of Chicksaw Bluff and was repulsed. On January 2, 1863, McClernand, who was of senior rank, arrived at Milliken's Bend and took over command of the expedition.

As Grant moved southward his supply difficulties increased. A general who realized the importance of supplies, he established a depôt at Holly Springs. Meanwhile Jefferson Davis had become thoroughly alarmed and appointed General Joseph E. Johnston to command all the Confederate forces between the Blue Ridge Mountains and the Mississippi. When he arrived at Chattanooga, Johnston ordered Bragg to send out a force of cavalry to fall upon Grant's communications. On December 20 this order was carried out. Van Dorn made a dash for Holly Springs, surprised Grant's depôt, and destroyed it.

This raid completely upset Grant's plan and went far to render Sherman's thrust abortive. Fearful of McClernand's incompetence, Grant asked Halleck's permission to withdraw to Memphis and take command of the river expedition. The request was granted; on January 10 Grant returned to Memphis, and on January 30 arrived at Young's Point at the mouth of the Yazoo River. There he took over command from McClernand.

CHAPTER 2

The Siege of Vicksburg and the Battle of Chattanooga, 1863

The capture of Vicksburg, which lay on the left bank of the Mississippi, demanded that Grant should establish a base of operations on that bank, either to the north or south of the fortress. Although he was fully aware of the superiority of the southern approach he could not attempt it until the winter rains were ended and the floods had subsided. But neither could he remain quiescent, for political conditions in the North were so precarious that he had to do something.[1] He was therefore compelled, as he says, to carry out "a series of experiments to consume time and to divert the attention of the enemy, of my troops, and of the public generally." And further: "I myself never felt great confidence that any of these experiments resorted to would prove successful. Nevertheless, I was always prepared to take advantage of them in case they did."[2]

The more important moves attempted were the opening of the Yazoo Pass; the approach by way of Steel's Bayou and Deer Creek; the digging of a canal from the Mississippi to Lake Providence, and the opening of Roundaway Bayou to the south of Milliken's Bend.

These various operations we do not intend to examine. All were extremely difficult and entailed immense labour, and although all failed in that none led to the reduction of Vicksburg, they undoubtedly provided admirable training for Grant's army.

The day after Grant took over command at Young's Point, General James H. Wilson proposed to General Rawlins, Grant's chief of staff, "to ignore all the canal schemes; run the gunboats and transports by the batteries under the cover of darkness; march the troops overland to the bank of the river below; and then use the fleet for transferring them to the east side of the river at the first point where they could find a safe landing with a dry road

---

[1] Lincoln and Halleck were urging him on. See *W.R.*, vol. xxxvi, p. 10,
[2] *Personal Memoirs of U. S. Grant* (1885–1886), vol. i, p. 446.

to the highlands back of it; that accomplished, to march inland, scatter the enemy, and take Vicksburg in rear."[1]

Rawlins explained this scheme to Grant, and although Sherman considered it impracticable Grant gave no indication whether he was for or against it. The truth is that he could not afford to take risks; he could not afford even to agree that it was the only sound scheme and the one he intended to adopt directly the floods began to subside. He could not do so because this was not only Wilson's plan but his own,[2] and should Pemberton, who was still in command of Vicksburg, learn that he intended to adopt this line of advance, then most certainly he would prepare to meet it. All this bayou warfare, and some of it was quite desperate, was a gigantic bluff to deceive the enemy, the politicians, and his own troops, so that, when he moved, Pemberton might be taken by surprise.

In the west clamours were raised against Grant's slowness; his soldiers, it was rumoured, were dying by thousands of swamp fever, and Badeau writes: "He was pronounced utterly destitute of genius or energy; his repeatedly baffled schemes declared to emanate from a brain utterly unfitted for such trials; his persistency was dogged obstinacy, his patience was sluggish dullness."[3] Yet he had one friend who unfailingly supported him, a man he had as yet never met – Lincoln. When urged to recall him, the President would turn round and earnestly reply: "I can't spare this man; he fights."[4]

By the end of March the political necessity for an advance on Vicksburg had become paramount, and as the waters on the Louisiana bank of the Mississippi began to recede Grant decided to move his army south of the fortress. On April 4 he wrote to Halleck:

"There is a system of bayous running from Milliken's Bend, and also from near the river at this point [Young's Point] that are navigable for barges and small steamers, passing around by Richmond to New Carthage. The dredges are now engaged cutting a canal from here into these bayous. I am having all the

---

[1] Letter of General Wilson, October 31, 1911, quoted by Colonel W. B. Livermore in *The Story of the Civil War* (1913), Pt. III, bk. I, p. 234.

[2] "I had in contemplation the whole winter the movement by land to a point below Vicksburg from which to operate, subject only to the possible but not expected success of some one of the expedients resorted to for the purpose of giving us a different base. This could not be undertaken until the waters receded. I did not therefore communicate this plan, even to an officer of my staff, until it was necessary to make preparations for the start" (Grant's *Memoirs*, vol. I, pp. 460–461).

[3] *Military History of Ulysses S. Grant*, A. Badeau (1868), vol. I, p. 180.

[4] *Lincoln and Men of War Times*, A. K. McClure, p. 179.

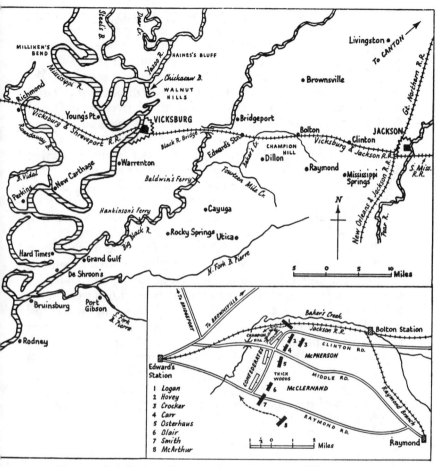

5. THE VICKSBURG CAMPAIGN, 1863

empty coal and other barges prepared for carrying troops and artillery, and have written to Colonel Allen for some more, and also for six tugs to tow them. With them it would be easy to carry supplies to New Carthage and any point south of that.

"My expectation is for a portion of the naval fleet to run the batteries of Vicksburg, whilst the army moves through by this new route. Once there, I will move either to Warrenton or Grand Gulf, most probably the latter. From either of these points there are good roads to Vicksburg, and from Grand Gulf there is a good road to Jackson and the Black River Bridge without crossing Black River. . . . I will keep my army together and see to it that I am not cut off from my supplies, or beat in any way, than in fair fight."[1]

When this plan became known to his subordinate commanders, Sherman, McPherson, and Logan opposed it; Sherman asserted that the only way to take Vicksburg was from the north, which meant a return to Memphis. But Grant saw that the political situation permitted no turning back. Although he had under his command some 97,000 officers and men,[2] only 51,000 were in the neighbourhood of Vicksburg. They were organized in three corps, each approximately 17,000 strong – the XIIIth under McClernand, the XVth under Sherman, and the XVIIth under James B. McPherson. Opposed to Grant was General Pemberton with an equal number,[3] distributed as follows: 13,000 at Vicksburg, 4,000 about Haines's Bluff, 9,000 between Vicksburg and Port Gibson, 5,000 at Jackson, 10,000 in the state of Mississippi and 11,000 at Port Hudson.

On April 6 New Carthage was occupied by McClernand's corps, to be followed by McPherson's and eventually by Sherman's. But in order to mystify the enemy Steele's division of Sherman's corps was sent 150 miles upstream to march through the Deer Creek country and lay waste the land, while Colonel Grierson at the head of 1,800 cavalry was sent on a 600-mile raid through the state of Mississippi with a similar object.[4]

---

[1] *W.R.*, vol. XXXI, p. 26.

[2] *Ibid.*, vol. XXXVIII, p. 249. As usual in this war it is most difficult to arrive at correct strengths. F. V. Greene, in *The Mississippi* (1909), p. 136, estimates Pemberton's force at over 50,000, and states that Grant began his campaign with about 41,000, and at no time before the siege had over 45,000. Grant in his *Memoirs* (vol. I, p. 481), says that, on May 7, he had 33,000, and that his enemy had nearly 60,000. In *Battles and Leaders* (vol. III, p. 549), it is stated that Grant's effective force varied from 43,000 at the opening to 75,000 at the close of the campaign.

[3] *W.R.*, vol. XXXVIII, p. 702.

[4] See Badeau, vol. I, p. 189.

These two feints completely bewildered Pemberton, who reported to Richmond that the enemy was in constant motion, that Grant's principal effort was directed against Deer Creek, and that the rumours that troops had moved south along the western bank of the Mississippi were not to be believed.

On the night of April 16 Admiral David D. Porter ran a convoy of river steamers towing barges, escorted by seven ironclads, past the Vicksburg batteries. On April 20 the final orders for the move south were issued; McClernand's corps was to form the right wing, McPherson's the centre, and Sherman's the left wing. Two days later a second convoy loaded with rations successfully passed the batteries.

On April 24 Grant reconnoitred Grand Gulf, and four days later McClernand's corps was assembled at Perkin's Plantation, from where, on April 29, it was transported to Hard Times. There it was landed, and re-embarked in readiness to move over to Grand Gulf. Porter then opened fire on the batteries, but as his bombardment had little effect, Grant decided to re-land his troops and move the transports past the batteries under cover of night. Early on the morning of April 30 McClernand's corps and one division of McPherson's re-embarked at De Shroon's and landed on the eastern bank of the river at Bruinsburg. Meanwhile Sherman with Blair's division and eight gunboats made a vigorous demonstration against Haines's Bluff in order to distract Pemberton.

When this landing was effected, Grant writes:

"I felt a degree of relief scarcely ever equalled since. Vicksburg was not yet taken it is true, nor were its defenders demoralized by any of our previous moves. I was now in the enemy's country, with a vast river and the stronghold of Vicksburg between me and my base of supplies. But I was on dry ground on the same side of the river with the enemy. All the campaigns, labors, hardships and exposures from the month of December previous to this time that had been made and endured were for the accomplishment of this one object."[1]

Four months of ruses and feints, of wrestling with swamps, bayous and forests, of labours seldom equalled in war, were the fog which covered this landing. Pemberton had been completely misled. His forces were distributed between Grand Gulf and Haines's Bluff; his left flank was but lightly guarded and was

[1] Grant's *Memoirs*, vol. I, pp. 480–481.

turned by the first flight of the invading army. By 2 a.m. on May 1 McClernand's leading division had advanced eight miles east of Bruinsburg. There it came into contact with the enemy, who tried to hold up Grant's advance on the Bayou Pierre until reinforcements could arrive from Vicksburg. But this was a vain hope, for the battle of Port Gibson opened at dawn and turned the Confederate right flank. The Confederates then retired northward with McPherson in pursuit. On May 3 McPherson drove the enemy forces over the Big Black River, with the result that Grand Gulf, now threatened in rear, had to be evacuated. A bridgehead was thus secured and Grant moved forward his depôts from Bruinsburg to Grand Gulf.

Grant now faced a difficulty exceptional in the history of war. He was operating in hostile country with his enemy's main forces located between his base of supply at Memphis and his base of operations at Grand Gulf. Although the fleet commanded the Mississippi his line of supply was uncertain, since every convoy had to pass the Vicksburg batteries. Vicksburg was not only exceedingly strong, but was connected by railway with Jackson – an important junction 45 miles to the east – and could be rapidly reinforced. There was also the danger that, should the Confederates concentrate an army at Jackson, Grant might easily be caught between two fires.

Although Pemberton was greatly outnumbered, according to all the rules of war his position was by no means hopeless; his enemy was operating in hostile country and presumably would have to make large detachments in order to protect his line of supply. Furthermore, the country was broken and wooded and therefore admirably suited to defensive warfare. To hold Grant at Vicksburg while forces concentrated at Jackson did not appear to Pemberton to be a difficult task.

Grant's difficulty was the reverse, in fact it would be hard to devise a more risky situation. The whole of his strategy pivoted on the question of supply. At first he proposed[1] to send 15,000 men to cooperate with General Banks in the capture of Port Hudson and then to shift his base of supply from Memphis to New Orleans. But when informed that Banks could not begin to move until May 10,[2] because of the importance of the time factor he says: "I therefore determined to move independently of Banks, cut loose from my base, destroy the rebel forces in rear of Vicksburg

---

[1] *W.R.*, vol. xxxviii, p. 192.   [2] *Ibid.*, vol. xxxvi, p. 30.

and invest or capture the city."[1] That is, he would attack the enemy from behind and simultaneously leave no rear to be attacked. This decision completely bewildered Pemberton who failed to grasp the audacity of Grant's strategy, for he could not believe that he would dare to advance without first securing his communications. Therefore he based his own operations on the assumption that Grant would act like a normal general.

Besides the strategical soundness of Grant's decision, as long as his army could be fed, the political situation demanded that not a minute should be lost. The battle of Chancellorsville had just been fought, and were Grant not to act at once he ran every chance of being recalled and his army broken up, for Washington had been thrown into panic by Lee's bold manœuvre. As it was, directly Halleck learnt of his move[2] he at once sent him orders to return and cooperate with Banks. Fortunately for Grant there was no telegraph line in operation south of Cairo and this order reached him only after his movement had begun; consequently it could not be obeyed. "Had the general-in-chief, however, been able to reach his subordinate, the Vicksburg campaign would never have been fought."[3]

Grant's position at this moment was as follows: He was opposed – so he believed – by a force double his own. He knew that the Government, reeling under Hooker's defeat at Chancellorsville, must be aghast at the news that he was not only about to plunge into the wilds of the Mississippi, but cut loose from his communications in face of two hostile armies, one based on a powerful fortress and the other on an important railway junction. Further, his army was without proper transport: ". . . the ammunition train was a curious assemblage of fine carriages, farm waggons, long coupled waggons with racks for carrying cotton bales – every vehicle, indeed, that could be found on the plantations which had been used either for work or pleasure. Those vehicles were a nondescript outfit, drawn by oxen and mules, wearing plough harness, or straw collars and rope lines."[4]

On April 29 Grant had ordered Sherman to cease his demonstration against Haines's Bluff and to march with all haste to Hard Times. On May 3 he directed him[5] to organize a supply

---

[1] *Grant's Memoirs*, vol. I, pp. 491–492.
[2] According to Grant, Halleck "was too learned a soldier to consent to a campaign in violation of all the principles of the art of war" (*Ulysses S. Grant*, W. C. Church, 1906, p. 163). See also Badeau, vol. I, p. 221, and *W.R.*, vol. cix, p. 406.
[3] Badeau, vol. I, p. 221.   [4] Church, p. 164.   [5] *W.R.*, vol. xxxviii, p. 268.

train of 120 vehicles and ferry them over to Grand Gulf, where they were to be loaded with 100,000 rations from the transports. This would give five days' rations for Sherman's corps and two days' for McClernand's and McPherson's,[1] which had already three days' rations with them. These were all the rations Grant intended to carry.

Sherman expostulated. It seemed to him quite impossible to supply the army over a single road. He urged Grant to "stop all troops till your army is partially supplied with waggons, and then act as quickly as possible, for this road will be jammed, as sure as life."[2] Grant replied: "I do not calculate upon the possibility of supplying the army with full rations from Grand Gulf. I know it will be impossible without constructing additional roads. What I do expect is to get up what rations of hard bread, coffee, and salt we can, and make the country furnish the balance."[3]

What was Grant's plan, once he was on dry ground at Port Gibson? The obvious course was to march direct upon Vicksburg, and a *bon général ordinaire* would undoubtedly have taken it. Not so Grant. He knew that a Confederate force under Gregg – of what strength he was uncertain – was collecting east and north-east of Vicksburg. Were he to advance on Vicksburg this force would certainly move there, and he might be outnumbered. Therefore he decided not to push between the two armies before they could cooperate, but to move against Jackson in order to draw the Confederate forces east of Vicksburg towards that important junction, defeat them in its vicinity before Pemberton could sally out of his fortress, and then destroy the railway at Jackson. This would protect his rear when the time came for him to advance against Vicksburg and would simultaneously cut off Vicksburg from its base of supply. In brief, his idea, rather than plan, was to manœuvre against the Vicksburg line of communications in order to isolate the fortress, and at the same time destroy those enemy forces which could operate against his own rear.

Success depended not so much upon boldness as upon rapidity of execution, hence we find Grant's dispatches teeming with urgency. To Sherman, on May 3, he wrote: "It is unnecessary for me to remind you of the overwhelming importance of celerity

---

[1] If this is correct it would appear that, as Grant says, his total force numbered 33,000: 55,000 rations for Sherman's corps, and 22,000 each for the remaining two, gives an average corps strength of 11,000.

[2] *W.R.*, vol. xxxviii, p. 285.   [3] *Ibid.*, vol. xxxviii, p. 285.

in your movements."[1] To Hurlbut, on May 5: "Send Lauman's division to Milliken's Bend. . . . Let them move by brigades, as fast as transportation can be gotten."[2] To the commissary at Grand Gulf: "There must be no delay on account of either lack of energy or formality"; load up "regardless of requisitions or provision returns." To an officer of his staff: "See that the commissary at Grand Gulf loads all the wagons. . . . Issue any order in my name that may be necessary to secure the greatest promptness in this respect. . . . Every day's delay is worth two thousand men to the enemy." And again on May 6: Rush "forward rations with all dispatch. . . . How many teams have been loaded with rations and sent forward? I want to know as near as possible how we stand in every particular for supplies. How many wagons have you ferried over the river? How many are still to bring over? What teams have gone back for rations?"[3]

Grant's tremendous energy electrified his men, until activity became contagious. McPherson was pushed up to Hankinson's Ferry to protect the left flank; reconnaissances were sent out daily to examine the roads and country, and forage parties swarmed over the cultivated areas to collect supplies.

Grant's plan was to keep the Big Black River on his left or strategic flank and use it as a shield; and to advance Sherman's and McClernand's corps under cover of it to the Vicksburg–Jackson railway between Edward's Station and Bolton, while McPherson's corps was to move by way of Utica to Raymond and thence on Jackson.

On May 7 the move forward began, and on May 12 Sherman and McClernand reached Fourteen Mile Creek. When McPherson encountered Gregg's brigade two miles west of Raymond, he drove it back and bivouacked on the outskirts of the town. Grant had now gained the position he wanted; his left flank rested on the Big Black and his right was secured by Gregg's defeat.

Although to Pemberton Grant's move south was not unexpected, it would seem that he believed it to be no more than another feint. When he heard that Grant had landed, on May 1 he telegraphed Johnston for reinforcements.[4] Johnston ordered him to unite all his troops against Grant, while Jefferson Davis, who believed that the movement was nothing more than a raid,[5]

[1] *Ibid.*, vol. xxxviii, p. 268.   [2] *Ibid.*, vol. xxxviii, p. 274.
[3] Badeau, vol. i, pp. 223–224.
[4] *W.R.*, xxxviii, pp. 807, 810 and 817; also *W.R.*, xxxvi, pp. 214 and 259.
[5] *Ibid.*, xxxvi, p. 327.

instructed him to hold on to Vicksburg and Port Hudson. These orders were contradictory, and because Pemberton was under the impression that Grant must within a few days fall back in order to replenish his supplies, he inclined to follow the second. He decided, therefore, to hold the line of the Big Black so that, when the opportunity arose, he could fall upon Grant's (nonexistent) line of supply and keep open the Vicksburg–Jackson railway, his own line of communications.

On May 3 Pemberton assembled the bulk of his forces between Vicksburg and the Big Black. On May 11 he ordered Gregg, if attacked, to retire toward Jackson; but should Grant move on Edward's Station, to fall upon his flank and rear. On May 12, as we have seen, Gregg was compelled by McPherson to adopt the former course. The next day Pemberton ordered three divisions – Bowen's, Loring's and Stevenson's – to advance on Edward's Station on May 14. On the night of May 13 Johnston arrived at Jackson from Tullahoma, but when he found the railway occupied by Sherman he telegraphed to Richmond: "I am too late."[1] He ordered Pemberton to attack Grant in rear. "I have arrived," he wrote, "and learnt that Major-General Sherman is between us. . . . It is important to re-establish communications that you may be reinforced. If practicable, come up on his rear at once. The troops here could cooperate. . . . Time is all important."[2] Pemberton, still believing that Grant must fall back were he to strike at his line of supply, set aside Johnston's order and informed him that, early on May 17, 17,000 men would move on Dillon. "The object is to cut the enemy's communications and force him to attack me. . . ."[3]

Meanwhile, on May 12, McPherson's corps was ordered to move on Clinton to destroy the railway, while Sherman and McClernand converged on Raymond. These movements were preparatory to the occupation of Jackson, for as Grant says: "As I hoped in the end to besiege Vicksburg, I must first destroy all possibility of aid. I therefore determined to move swiftly towards Jackson."[4] During the night of May 13 and on the morning of the next day it rained in torrents, nevertheless Grant pushed on at top speed.

On May 14 McPherson moved from Clinton towards Jackson, and Sherman also advanced on Jackson from Mississippi Springs,

---

[1] *The Rise and Fall of the Confederate Government*, Jefferson Davis (1881), vol. II, p. 404.
[2] *W.R.*, vol. XXXVIII, p. 870.　[3] *Ibid.*, XXXVI, p. 262.　[4] *Grant's Memoirs*, vol. I, p. 499.

while McClernand protected their rear by sending a brigade to Clinton and by occupying Raymond. The attack on Jackson was at first delayed by the rain, because it was feared that ammunition might be spoilt if the men opened their cartridge-boxes. At 11 a.m. the battle opened, and at 4 p.m. the town was carried.

Forced out of Jackson, Johnston withdrew up the Canton Road, and on May 15 wrote to Pemberton: "The only mode by which we can unite is by your moving directly to Clinton, informing me, that we may move to that point with about 6,000."[1]

The situation of the Confederate forces was ludicrous: Johnston was moving north to unite with Pemberton, and Pemberton was moving east and south-east from Edward's Station to cut Grant's imaginary communications. On the night of May 14 Pemberton had 9,000 men about Vicksburg, which was not threatened, and some 14,000 were moving on Edward's Station; Johnston–now about Calhoun–headed 12,000, with 10,000 reinforcements on their way to join him. Thus we see 45,000 men in three detachments faced by an equal force, concentrated and ready to strike at any one in overwhelming strength. Pemberton who, on the night of May 15, had arrived in the neighbourhood of Raymond, there received Johnston's second order to unite with him; he therefore abandoned his attack on Grant's imaginary line of communications and decided to turn north.

Unfortunately for both Johnston and Pemberton, Johnston's dispatch of May 13 was carried by three separate messengers, one of whom happened to be a Federal soldier enlisted in the Confederate Army. This man took his copy to General McPherson, who forwarded it to Grant on the evening of May 14. Grant assumed that Pemberton would obey the order given in it and would be on the move from Edward's Station to unite with Johnston, and at once issued orders for May 15: McPherson to move back to Bolton "and make all dispatch in getting there"; Sherman's corps, less Blair's division, to remain at Jackson and destroy the railway.[2] By evening Grant had concentrated in all about 32,000 men between Bolton and Raymond, and that night he opened his headquarters at Clinton.

Early on May 16 Pemberton informed Johnston that, as he considered he could not move on Clinton, he would return to Edward's Station and take the Brownsville Road. Meanwhile Grant, when he learnt from two men employed on the Vicksburg–

---

[1] *W.R.*, vol. xxxviii, p. 882.   [2] *Ibid.*, vol. xxxviii, p. 310–312.

Jackson railway that Pemberton with some 25,000 men had marched eastward the night before, ordered up Steele's division of Sherman's corps, which was on the road within an hour. McPherson's corps, on the right, he directed to advance by the Clinton Road on Champion's Hill; and McClernand's corps, on the left, to move by the Middle and Raymond roads on Edward's Station. By 7.30 a.m., when skirmishing had begun, Grant rode forward and joined McPherson's corps, and later ordered McClernand to push forward and attack.

Pemberton's position was a strong one. Not only did his front command the three roads along which Grant's leading divisions advanced, but his left was protected by Champion's Hill and Baker's Creek, as well as by some precipitous ravines, woodland and much undergrowth, "difficult," as Grant says, "to penetrate with troops even when not defended." This difficulty soon became apparent. An examination of it is illuminating as it explains many of the lost opportunities experienced a year later in the Wilderness of Virginia.

Although Smith's division on the Raymond Road was the first to encounter the enemy, its advance was painfully slow, and Osterhaus's on the Middle Road did no better. These divisions were confronted by a weak but well-placed force, and had McClernand ordered a charge he would have cleared his front in a few minutes. But the ground was thickly wooded, and unable to ascertain the strength of the enemy he groped his way forward with extreme caution. Throughout the day he never made his strength felt. Meanwhile, on the right, Hovey's division had become closely engaged, and to protect its right flank, Logan's division was pushed beyond it to attack Champion's Hill from the north. Still pressed in front, Hovey was reinforced by Crocker.

The situation was now as follows: Hovey, in spite of Crocker's assistance, could make little impression on Champion's Hill, and on Hovey's left, because McClernand failed to assault, the enemy's freedom of movement was in no way restricted. Logan, although neither he nor Grant was aware of it, had worked his way behind the enemy on Champion's Hill and was actually in line parallel to their rear and in command of the only road by which Pemberton could retreat. At the same time a brigade of McArthur's division, which a few days before had crossed over to Grand Gulf, was coming up on McClernand's left flank. Thus, although Grant had not realized it, Pemberton's army was to all intents and purposes surrounded, when Hovey again called for reinforcements. Because Grant feared that Hovey's front might be broken, he ordered McPherson to disengage part of Logan's division and move it round to Hovey's support. The assault which was then made was successful, principally because the enemy's line of retreat was now opened. Grant at once sent forward Osterhaus's and Carr's divisions in pursuit and ordered them to push on to the Big Black and to cross it if they could. That night McPherson's command bivouacked six miles west of the battlefield and Carr and Osterhaus at Edward's Station. The losses in this battle were: Grant's army, 2,438; Pemberton's, 4,082.[1]

Defeated at Champion's Hill, Pemberton abandoned his intention to move north and unite with Johnston. It is true that he could no longer move by the Brownsville Road, but he could have retired under cover of darkness across the Big Black, burnt the bridges and, by abandoning Vicksburg, have saved his army by moving north and then east toward Canton. Instead he fell back on the Big Black and reported to Johnston that he had about 60 days' rations in Vicksburg, but that, when Grant advanced, he would be compelled to abandon Haines's Bluff. Johnston replied: "If it is not too late, evacuate Vicksburg and its dependencies and march to the north-east."[2] This message was received by Pemberton at noon on May 18. He at once assembled a council of war which decided that, as Vicksburg was "the most important point in the Confederacy", it could not be abandoned.[3]

Early on May 17 Grant continued his pursuit, and about midday he broke the Confederate line. For the Confederates, as Pemberton says: "It very soon became a matter of *sauve qui peut*."[4] His army, greatly demoralized, he withdrew to Vicksburg.[5] Many stragglers had already made their way there; the bridge over the Big Black was burnt and Haines's Bluff abandoned.

On the morning of May 18, Sherman, by means of the sole pontoon train in Grant's army, crossed the Big Black at Bridgeport and that night, accompanied by Grant, reached Walnut Hills. The true goal of the campaign was won – namely, high, dry ground free from enemy interference upon which a supply base could be established. Sherman turned to Grant and exclaimed:

[1] Livermore, pt. III, bk. II, p. 310.
[2] *W.R.*, vol. xxxvi, p. 241, and vol. xxxviii, p. 888.
[3] *Ibid.*, vol. xxxviii, p. 890.   [4] *Ibid.*, vol. xxxvi, p. 367.
[5] General Loring's division, unable to cross the Big Black, retreated on Jackson to join up with Johnston.

"Until this moment, I never thought your expedition a success. I never could see the end clearly, until now. But this is a campaign; this is a success, if we never take the town."[1] Indeed an amazing success, the greatest in Grant's life, and from a strategical point of view one seldom equalled.

Grant handed Haines's Bluff over to the navy and re-established his line of supply. He then issued orders to carry the fortress by storm at 2 p.m. on May 19, "relying," as he says, "upon the demoralization of the enemy in consequence of repeated defeats outside of Vicksburg."[2] The assault failed, for though during the past two days the Confederates "had run like sheep . . . now they were in intrenchments which had been prepared long before . . . they felt at home. Their demoralization was all gone. . . ."[3] There was every excuse for attempting the first assault, but little or none for the second. Of it Grant says: "The attack was ordered to commence on all parts of the line at ten o'clock a.m. on the 22nd with a furious cannonade from every battery in position. All the corps commanders set their time by mine so that all might open an engagement at the same minute."[4] Every possible preparation was made and the attack might have succeeded had Grant concentrated on one point instead of ordering an assault all along the line.

"Suddenly . . . as if by magic every gun and rifle stopped firing. . . . The silence was almost appalling, at the sudden cessation of the firing of so many field guns [about 180] and the crackling of so many thousands of sharpshooters' rifles. But the silence was only for a short time. Suddenly, there seemed to spring almost from the bowels of the earth dense masses of Federal troops, in numerous columns of attack, and with loud cheers and huzzahs they rushed forward at a run with bayonets fixed, not firing a shot, headed for every salient advanced position along the Confederate lines. . . . As they came within easy range (almost as soon as they started) the Confederate troops, not exceeding 9,938 men, along the 3½ miles of assault, deliberately rose and stood in their trenches, pouring volley after volley into the advancing enemy; at the same time the troops in reserve advanced to the rear of the trenches and fired over the heads of those in the trenches. Every field gun and howitzer belched forth continuously and incessantly double-shotted discharges of grape and canister. . . ."[5]

[1] Badeau, vol. I, p. 281. [2] W.R., vol. xxxvi, p. 54. [3] Greene, p. 170.
[4] Grant's Memoirs, vol. I, p. 531.
[5] Publications of the Mississippi Historical Society, vol. III, p. 60.

This description of the assault, written by General S. D. Lee, speaks for itself. It failed because it was launched on so wide a front that no concentrated covering fire could support it. Unfortunately McClernand, who believed that his troops had gained a secure footing in the enemy's entrenchments, sent urgent appeals to Grant for aid. Another assault was ordered, which also failed.

Because the fortress could not be stormed Grant resorted to siege. The entrenched camp of Vicksburg was some four miles in length and two in breadth and its outer line of works extended over seven miles. Grant's lines were twice as long. Moreover he had to prepare his rear against attack because Johnston was assembling a powerful army in the neighbourhood of Canton. On May 29 Grant informed Halleck that unless Banks could come to his assistance large reinforcements would be required. These demands were promptly met by the general-in-chief, and a month later Grant's army numbered 71,141 men and 248 guns.[1]

The siege was prosecuted methodically. A line of contravallation was dug from Haines's Bluff to Warrenton, and one of circumvallation from the Yazoo to the Big Black River. The latter was held by Sherman and some 30,000 men.

On July 3 at 10 a.m. white flags appeared on the Confederate works and an aide-de-camp crossed to the Federal lines bearing a letter from Pemberton to ask for an armistice. In reply Grant sent a demand for "unconditional surrender." When Pemberton refused it, Grant modified his decision to a surrender on terms. There were several reasons for this. In the first place, had he insisted on unconditional surrender the prisoners could not have been paroled and would have had to be transported to Cairo at much inconvenience to the army. Secondly, the moral effect of a surrender on July 4[2] could not fail to be of considerable political significance.

At 10 a.m. on Saturday, July 4, the garrison of Vicksburg, some 31,000 men in all, stacked their arms in front of their conquerors, and when they had laid their colours upon them they returned to the town and proceeded to fraternize with the Federal soldiers.

On July 1 Johnston and 27,000 men were encamped between Brownsville and the Big Black. On July 4, immediately after Pemberton's surrender, Sherman, at the head of 40,000 men,

---

[1] Greene, p. 188.
[2] Pemberton also realized this. He says: "I believed that upon that day I should obtain better terms. Well aware of the vanity of our foes . . ." (*W.R.*, vol. xxxvi, p. 285).

moved out against him. Two days later he crossed the Big Black and Johnston retired to Jackson, in the hope that scarcity of water would compel his antagonist to assault, but as he did not do so he evacuated it on July 16. Sherman decided not to follow up his retreating enemy as he would have had to cross 90 miles of waterless country, and on July 25 he returned to Vicksburg.

The losses in this campaign are instructive because, quite unjustly, Grant has been called a butcher. Since April 30 he had won five battles, had taken Vicksburg, and had occupied Jackson at a cost to himself of 1,243 killed, 7,095 wounded and 535 missing, a total of 8,873 casualties.[1] He had killed and wounded about 10,000 Confederates, and had captured 37,000,[2] among whom were 2,153 officers, including 15 generals. Also 172 cannon fell into his hands.

The disparity between the losses of the contending forces was primarily due to Grant's strategy. He founded his plan on surprise and accepted risks which surprise alone justified. In the first 18 days after he crossed the Mississippi he defeated his enemy at Port Gibson, established a temporary base at Grand Gulf, marched 200 miles, and won the battles of Raymond, Jackson, Champion's Hill, and the Big Black River – the four within a space of six days. During all of this period his men had only five days' rations and for the rest had to live on the country. Well may Greene say: "We must go back to the campaigns of Napoleon to find equally brilliant results accomplished in the same space of time with such small loss."[3]

At 7 a.m. on July 9 Port Hudson surrendered unconditionally to General Banks, and a week later "the steamboat *Imperial* quietly landed at the wharf in New Orleans, arriving direct from St. Louis, laden with a commercial cargo, having passed over the whole course of that great thoroughfare of commerce undisturbed by a hostile shot or challenge from bluff or levee on either side."[4] The South had been cleft in two; Vicksburg and not Gettysburg was the crisis of the Confederacy.

Two days later, on July 11, Grant suggested to Halleck that an expedition should set out from Lake Pontchartrain with the object of taking Mobile,[5] from where a movement against the rear of

---

[1] Badeau, vol. I, p. 399. *W.R.*, vol. xxxvii, p. 167, gives 9,362.

[2] *W.R.*, vol. xxxvi, p. 58.

[3] Greene, pp. 170–171. Grant's losses during the first 18 days were about 3,500; Pemberton's, 8,000 and 88 guns.

[4] *Abraham Lincoln: A History*, J. B. Nicolay and J. Hay (1890), vol. vii, p. 327.

[5] *W.R.*, vol. xxxviii, pp. 529–530.

Bragg's army might induce Bragg to detach troops from Chattanooga and so facilitate a Federal advance on that town. As an alternative, Grant suggested an advance through Georgia with the aim of laying waste the country from which Lee in Virginia drew most of his supplies. Although he repeated this proposal during August and September Halleck would have none of it; once again his extreme caution held Grant back, as the year before it had done after the victories of Shiloh and Corinth.

Once the Mobile operation was forbidden, Grant's magnificent army was broken up. The IXth Corps was sent to Kentucky; 4,000 men went to Banks in Louisiana, 5,000 to Schofield in Missouri, a brigade to Natchez, while the remainder was employed in the thankless task of hunting down guerrilla bands.[1] On August 7 Grant was instructed further to deplete his army by sending the XIIIth Corps to General Banks. To arrange this move he went to New Orleans, where he met with a serious accident – his horse shied at a locomotive and threw him. On September 13 he received an urgent telegram from Halleck ordering him to send all "available forces to Memphis and thence to Corinth and Tuscumbia, to cooperate with Rosecrans."[2]

While Grant was operating against Vicksburg he had been anxious that Rosecrans – still at Murfreesboro – should advance against Bragg in order to prevent him from reinforcing Johnston. But on June 3 Burnside, with the Army of the Ohio, who was to advance from Lexington, Kentucky, and cooperate with Rosecrans, was ordered to send large reinforcements to Grant, and it was not until June 23 that Rosecrans resumed his long interrupted move against Bragg. On July 1 Bragg evacuated Tullahoma and crossed the Tennessee, and when on August 16 Burnside advanced on Knoxville and was able to cover Rosecrans's left flank, the latter decided to feint at Bragg's right and cross the Tennessee below Chattanooga. Bragg was completely deceived by this manœuvre and on September 9 Rosecrans took possession of Chattanooga.

Thus far Rosecrans's strategy left nothing to be desired, but as

[1] It must never be overlooked that throughout this war the difficulty of the guerrilla faced Grant and other Federal commanders. In the east this form of warfare was to a certain extent organized; in the west it was murder, robbery and terrorism. When caught, guerrillas were usually shot. General Crook and some cavalry once fell in with a party of 20 guerrillas. He shot 12 and the rest were captured. "He regrets to report that on the march to camp the eight prisoners were so unfortunate to fall off a log and break their necks." This was in Tennessee (*Papers of the Military Historical Society of Massachusetts* – cited as *M.H.S.M.* – vol. XIV, p. 81).

[2] *W.R.*, vol. LII, p. 592.

he believed Bragg to be in full retreat he pushed on in pursuit, and with his army in no way prepared to offer battle suddenly found himself confronted by a concentrated enemy. In order to extricate himself, on September 19–20 he was compelled to fight the battle of Chickamauga,[1] in which he was badly beaten and saved from complete destruction only by the gallant defensive action of General G. H. Thomas – the "Rock of Chickamauga." He retired on Chattanooga and abandoned Lookout Mountain which commanded the town. This battle was one of the most bloody of the war: 55,000 to 60,000 Federals met from 60,000 to 70,000 Confederates; the former lost 16,336 and the latter 20,950 in killed, wounded and missing.[2] At Chattanooga Rosecrans was besieged.

This disaster brought to the fore the immense strategical importance of Chattanooga, where Rosecrans was now locked up. Hitherto the departments of the Tennessee, Cumberland, and Ohio had been commanded respectively by Grant, Rosecrans, and Burnside, and Halleck in Washington was incapable of establishing cooperation between them. Now they were fused into the Military Division of the Mississippi.

On September 29 Halleck telegraphed Grant to send all possible reinforcements to Rosecrans, and on October 3 he wrote: "It is the wish of the Secretary of War that, as soon as General Grant is able to take the field, he will come to Cairo and report by telegraph."[3] Grant, still crippled, replied from Columbus: "Your dispatch of the 3rd, directing me to report at Cairo, was received at 11.30 a.m. the 9th inst. I left same day with my staff and headquarters, and have just reached here, *en route* for Cairo."[4] From Cairo he was ordered to Louisville, and on his way there, at Indianapolis, he met Stanton "pacing the floor rapidly in his dressing-gown." Stanton at once placed him in command of all troops between the Alleghanies and the Mississippi – a course suggested by Grant nearly a year before.

Grant forthwith assumed command, assigned the Department of the Cumberland to General Thomas, and on October 19 set out by rail for Chattanooga. The last 40 miles of this journey had to be made on horseback, and General Howard tells us that "at times it was necessary to take the General from his horse. The

---

[1] "The River of Blood," in Indian.
[2] *Battles and Leaders*, vol. III, pp. 673–676, and *The Army of the Cumberland*, H. M. Cist (1909), p. 228.
[3] *W.R.*, vol. LIII, p. 55.   [4] *Ibid.*, vol. LIII, p. 375.

soldiers carried him in their arms across the roughest places. Yielding to no weakness or suffering, he pushed through to Chattanooga, and reached General Thomas the evening of October 23rd.''[1]

Before Thomas took command the condition of the Army of the Cumberland can be described only as deplorable. Rosecrans had quarrelled with Halleck, and he now occupied a nearly untenable position. His back was against the Tennessee River, his left rested on Citico Creek, his front faced Missionary Ridge,[2] which rose to a height of some 300 ft. to 400 ft. above the plain. This ridge was separated from Lookout Mountain on his right by Rossville Gap, through which ran Chattanooga River. Lookout Mountain, 2,400 ft. high, dominated the town of Chattanooga and the railway which ran thence up Lookout Valley to Decatur and Trenton. The Confederate entrenchments began on the north end of Missionary Ridge, ran along the ridge, spanned Chattanooga Valley, and ended on Lookout Mountain, which commanded the railway. It had been abandoned by Rosecrans because he considered that his weakened army was not strong enough to hold it. General William F. Smith believed that he was right to abandon it, for had he not done so he would have "diminished his force in the front by about 8,000."[3] Rather would it seem that either Lookout Mountain should have been held or Chattanooga evacuated, because to remain there with the mountains in the hands of the enemy was to risk the loss both of the town and the army. Colonel Livermore agrees with this. His opinion is that Rosecrans abandoned the mountain because he exaggerated Bragg's strength. On October 1 Bragg had 41,972 men on a line seven miles long, and Rosecrans 38,928[4] "equal to 6,500 men per mile of a possible line of six miles from Citico Creek across the point of Lookout Mountain to Lookout Creek." Further, Livermore says: "The example of the Confederate defence for six weeks of seven miles of intrenchments at Vicksburg five months before with 22,000 effectives against a force as large as, or greater than Bragg's . . . would have amply justified Rosecrans in the attempt to hold the line from Citico to Lookout Creek."[5]

[1] Church, p. 199.
[2] Called so by the Indians who, in former times, allowed the missionaries to pass no farther west. Rossville was named after the Cherokee chief John Ross. Chattanooga is Indian for "The Eagle's Nest."
[3] W.R., vol. LIII, p. 721.
[4] Ibid. vol. LII, pp. 914–915.
[5] M.H.S.M., vol. VIII, pp. 285–286.

Although he lost his railway communications, which on September 30 were raided by Wheeler and his cavalry, who destroyed 400 wagons with their loads and teams[1] – a crippling blow to the transportation of the army – Rosecrans made no efforts to run boats down the river. There were two steamers at Chattanooga and these could have brought up 200 tons of supplies daily from Bridgeport to a point near William's Island, whence the wagon haul was only four or five miles to the town.[2] Instead, supplies were hauled over a circuitous and mountainous route north of the river, a distance of 60 to 70 miles. The result was that the troops could not be properly rationed nor the animals fed. Boynton informs us: "Thousands of horses and mules . . . died from want of food. There were Brigade headquarters where the officers lived chiefly on parched corn; there were regimental headquarters where the daily food was mush or gruel; there were officers of high rank who lived for days on sour pork and wormy mouldy bread."[3] This statement is corroborated by General W. F. Smith and by Grant.[4] The latter informs us that nearly 10,000 horses and mules died, and "not enough were left to draw a single piece of artillery or even the ambulances to convey the sick . . . the beef was so poor that the soldiers were in the habit of saying . . . that they were living on 'half rations of hard bread and beef dried on the hoof'."[5]

It would be difficult to find a more perfect example of an army paralysed by the inefficiency of its commander, who had completely collapsed under the shock of defeat. C. A. Dana, Assistant Secretary of War, on October 16 in a letter to the War Department said: "Nothing can prevent the retreat of the army from this place within a fortnight. . . . General Rosecrans seems to be insensible to the impending danger, and dawdles with trifles in a manner which can scarcely be imagined . . . all this precious time is lost because our dazed and mazy commander cannot perceive the catastrophe that is close upon us, nor fix his mind upon means of preventing it. I never saw anything which seemed so lamentable and hopeless."[6] Such was the state of affairs when Grant arrived at Chattanooga on the evening of October 23.

[1] *W.R.*, vol. LIII, pp. 114, 231.

[2] *Ibid.*, vol. LII, p. 890; vol. LIII, p. 102, and vol. LIV, pp. 67 and 74.

[3] *Sherman's Historical Raid*, by H. V. Boynton (1875), p. 69. This was written in 1875, and it is strange to find this same officer writing in 1892: "At no time did the men suffer, and at no time were the troops of the Cumberland either discouraged or demoralized" (*M.H.S.M.*, vol. VII, p. 381).

[4] *M.H.S.M.*, vol. VIII, p. 167.

[5] Grant's *Memoirs*, vol. II, p. 25, and *W.R.*, LVI, p. 216.

[6] *W.R.*, vol. L, pp. 218–219. See also pp. 202, 215.

Grant's immediate task was to establish a workable line of supply. He at once saw that the key to it lay in securing command of Lookout Valley. Had Bragg grasped this, he would have held it in force, as well as the passes over Raccoon Mountain, and Grant's problem would then have been all but impossible to solve.

Hooker was at Bridgeport, where on October 1 he had been ordered by Rosecrans to bridge the river. To bring him forward was useless unless a footing could be gained on the left bank of the Tennessee near Brown's Ferry and the enemy driven from the hills commanding that point. On October 19 General William F. Smith had reconnoitred Brown's Ferry and had come to the conclusion that it was the most suitable place at which to cross the river. Immediately after his arrival on October 23 Grant approved Smith's scheme, and after he had examined the ferry on the following morning he ordered Smith to force a crossing on October 27.

At 3 a.m. that day 1,500 men, under the command of Smith, left Chattanooga in 52 boats which hugged the right bank of the Tennessee until they reached a signal light. Then the men bent to their oars, crossed the river, landed, rushed the weak Confederate pickets, occupied the hills on the left bank and entrenched. So thoroughly was this work done that at 3.30 p.m. Smith was able to telegraph General Thomas's chief of staff: "This place cannot be carried now."[1] Thus Chattanooga was saved at a cost of four men killed and 17 wounded.

That night Hooker's advanced guard entered Lookout Valley, and at 3 p.m. on October 28 the head of the main body reached Wauhatchie. At 11 p.m. General Thomas telegraphed Halleck that "the wagon road is now open to Bridgeport. We have besides two steamboats, one at Bridgeport and one here, which will be started tomorrow. . . . By this operation we have gained two wagon roads and the river to get supplies by, and I hope in a few days to be pretty well supplied. . . ."[2] Within five days of Grant's arrival at Chattanooga the road to Bridgeport was opened, and within a week the troops were receiving full rations, clothes and ammunition, "and a cheerfulness prevailed not before enjoyed in many weeks. Neither officers nor men looked upon themselves any longer as doomed."[3]

[1] *Ibid.*, vol. LIV, p. 54.   [2] *Ibid.*, vol. LIV, p. 41.
[3] Grant's *Memoirs*, vol. II, p. 38.

On the night of October 28–29 Longstreet attacked Hooker at Wauhatchie, but was easily repulsed. The Federals were assisted by their mules which took fright and stampeded towards the enemy, who broke and fled, imagining that a cavalry charge was upon them. By 4 a.m. on the 29th the battle was over and the "Cracker Line" was never again disturbed.[1]

Once he had secured a workable line of supply Grant's next task was to bring up Sherman's corps from Corinth. On October 27 "a dirty black-haired individual, with a mixed dress and strange demeanour" approached Sherman's house in Iuka. It was Corporal Pike, who had paddled down the Tennessee under the enemy's fire with a message to Sherman which ordered him to move with all possible haste to Bridgeport. Sherman arrived there on November 13. Meanwhile Burnside's position at Knoxville was causing high alarm at Washington, and Grant was plied with dispatch after dispatch urging that action be taken to relieve the pressure on him.

Longstreet had quarrelled with Bragg, and either to put an end to this bad feeling or because he believed that Longstreet could move on Knoxville 100 miles away, destroy Burnside, and withdraw to Chattanooga before Grant was ready to attack, President Davis instructed Bragg to send him to Knoxville. Longstreet set out on November 4, and when Grant heard of this on the 7th he ordered[2] Thomas to attack Bragg, and so force Longstreet to return. Thomas replied that he could not comply with the order as he was unable to move a single gun. Grant directed him to take "mules, officers' horses, or animals wherever he could get them."[3]

Thomas, much perturbed by this order, rode out on November 7 with General Smith to examine the approaches which led from the mouth of the South Chickamauga toward Missionary Ridge. On this reconnaissance Smith pointed out to Thomas that the ground lent itself to a turning operation against Bragg's right flank. If successful, such a move would threaten his rear and separate him from Longstreet in east Tennessee. On their return they informed Grant of their conclusions, whereupon he at once countermanded his order.[4]

[1] On the 29th Grant inspected the pickets, and as he was under fire he took only a bugler with him. On passing a post, he heard a soldier shout: "Turn out the guard for the commanding general." He replied: "Never mind the guard." Barely had he uttered these words than a little way off a Confederate sentry called out: "Turn out the guard for the commanding general – General Grant!" Grant saluted and rode on.
[2] W.R., vol. LVI, p. 634.   [3] Ibid., vol. LVI, p. 73.
[4] Ibid., vol. LV, p. 29, and Battles and Leaders, vol. III, p. 716.

When he had studied the new proposal Grant ordered Smith to explore the country and to prepare material for a second bridge at Chattanooga or Brown's Ferry, as well as a bridge across the South Chickamauga. On November 14 Grant informed[1] Burnside that Sherman would cross South Chickamauga river in a few days' time and that a general attack would then be launched on Bragg. Two days later Grant took Thomas, Smith, and Sherman out to a position overlooking the mouth of the river, and Sherman, after he had carefully examined the ground, shut up his long glass with a snap and said: "I can do it."[2]

Grant's idea was to effect a double envelopment with the forces under Sherman and Hooker pivoted on Thomas's army. Sherman was to attack Bragg's right, envelop it, and threaten or seize the railway in Bragg's rear. This would compel Bragg either to weaken his centre or lose his base at Chickamauga Station.[3] Hooker was to advance from Lookout Valley to Chattanooga Valley, move on Rossville, and threaten Missionary Ridge from the south. Thomas was to hold the centre and move forward in conjunction with Sherman, travelling obliquely to the left to form a continuous battle front.[4]

Grant's main difficulty was that from Lookout Mountain and Missionary Ridge Bragg could watch every move in or around Chattanooga. In order to mislead Bragg and convince him that Grant's intention was to attack his left, Sherman was ordered to cross the river at Bridgeport, move his leading division by the Trenton Road, and then throw some troops on to Lookout Mountain. (This move was effected and a brigade was encamped on the mountain on November 18.)[5] Sherman's remaining forces were to take the Brown's Ferry Road, move towards South Chickamauga river as if their intention were to advance on Knoxville, and then hide themselves in the hills opposite the mouth of the river where they could not be observed from Lookout Mountain. One brigade was to move on to the North Chickamauga, where 116 pontoons were ready to be floated down the river in order to effect a landing on the left bank. "All things," said Sherman, were "prearranged with a foresight that elicited my admiration."[6]

[1] *Ibid.*, vol. LV, p. 30.
[2] *M.H.S.M.*, vol. VIII, p. 195, and Grant's *Memoirs*, vol. II, p. 58.
[3] Grant's *Memoirs*, vol. II, p. 55.
[4] *W.R.*, vol. LV, pp. 130, 131, 154, 184, and *Battles and Leaders*, vol. III, p. 716.
[5] *W.R.*, vol. LV, p. 583.   [6] *Ibid.*, vol. LV, p. 571.

These movements partially misled Bragg, and had not the rain and the shocking state of the roads delayed Sherman they might have completely succeeded. At 9.45 p.m. on November 20 Hardee, in command of Bragg's left, ordered the passes over Lookout Mountain to be blocked and said to a subordinate commander: "Direct your advanced brigade to make obstinate defense, so as to give time to send reinforcements. Be constantly on the alert. General Bragg is under conviction that a serious movement is being made on our left."[1] Unfortunately for Grant, Sherman's command was not ready to cross on the night of November 22,[2] and on the afternoon of the 21st the march of his division from Trenton toward Wauhatchie had been observed. As a result on the afternoon of the following day Bragg began to move troops to his right.[3]

On the night of November 22, a deserter came into the Federal lines and reported that Bragg was falling back. He stated that two divisions had been sent towards Sherman, who was expected to attack Steven's Gap – over Lookout Mountain – and that the greater part of Bragg's army was massed between his headquarters and the mountain. This move – assuming the information to be correct – exactly fell in with Grant's plan of drawing Bragg away from the point selected for Sherman's attack. Whether Grant realized this at the time is unknown, but he had received news[4] that Knoxville had been attacked, and as the authorities in Washington were appealing daily to him to assist Burnside, he apparently thought that Bragg's move was a ruse to cover the sending of more troops to Knoxville. Furthermore, on November 20 he had received the following cryptic message from Bragg: "As there may still be some non-combatants in Chattanooga, I deem it proper to notify you that prudence would dictate their early withdrawal."[5] Grant knew that this letter was meant to deceive him, but when he coupled it with the information furnished by the deserter and his anxiety about Knoxville,[6] as well as the fact that Sherman could not cross the Tennessee until the night of November 23–24, and that the flooded river was threaten-

---

[1] *Ibid.*, vol. LV, p. 668.
[2] Originally ordered for the 21st, see *ibid.*, vol. LV, p. 31.
[3] *Ibid.*, vol. LV, p. 671. [4] *Ibid.*, vol. LVI, p. 206. [5] *Ibid.*, vol. LV, p. 32.
[6] Grant says: "Hearing nothing from Burnside [the telegraph was cut], and hearing much of the distress in Washington on his account, I could no longer defer operations for his relief. I determined, therefore, to do on the 23rd, with the Army of the Cumberland, what had been intended to be done on the 24th." (Grant's *Memoirs*, vol. II, p. 62.)

ing the bridges, he ordered Thomas[1] to make a reconnaissance in force on the morning of the 23rd in order to verify Bragg's position. This was done; Thomas moved forward and established his lines

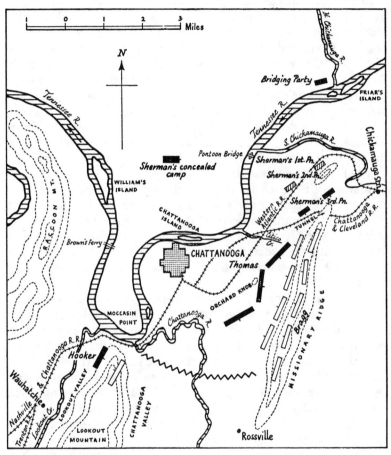

6. BATTLE OF CHATTANOOGA, NOVEMBER 23–25, 1863

parallel to Bragg's within a mile of the western flank of Missionary Ridge. This movement materially changed the task allotted to Thomas in Grant's order of November 18;[2] it also awoke Bragg to the danger threatening his right flank. On the night of November 23, Bragg ordered Walker's division to move from near

[1] *W.R.*, vol. LV, p. 32.   [2] *Ibid.*, vol. LV, p. 31.

Lookout Mountain to Missionary Ridge[1] and a brigade to occupy a position near the mouth of the South Chickamauga.[2]

By the night of the 23rd Sherman's command, with the exception of Osterhaus's division – still west of Brown's Ferry – was ready to move. Osterhaus was ordered to report to Hooker should he not be able to cross by 8 a.m. on the 24th. At midnight Sherman's landing force, under General Smith, advanced downstream from the North Chickamauga. At two o'clock the following morning a landing was effected near the mouth of the South Chickamauga and the work of ferrying over Sherman's infantry at once began. By daylight two divisions had crossed. A bridge 1,350 ft. long was then thrown over the Tennessee and another across the South Chickamauga, and a brigade of cavalry moved over under orders to proceed to the vicinity of Charleston and destroy the railway.

At 1 p.m. Sherman began his advance in three divisional columns with the left leading and covered by the South Chickamauga, while the right was echeloned back in order to refuse that flank. At 3.30 p.m. the heads of the columns reached a detached hill north of Missionary Ridge, when Sherman, instead of pushing on to the tunnel, ordered his division to halt and entrench for the night. "This," General Smith points out, "was the blunder of the battle."[3]

What was Sherman's difficulty? Although it has been debated by several historians, it has not been carefully analysed.

The date was November 24; therefore by half-past four it would be getting dark. Throughout the day drizzling rain fell and the clouds were low.[4] Even before four o'clock it was so dark on Lookout Mountain that Hooker had to suspend his advance.[5] Although we are told that the whole of Sherman's cavalry was over both bridges by 3.30 p.m.,[6] we do not know when his artillery began to cross. But it could not have been much before 2 p.m. – probably later – because during the night of November 23–24 Thomas, who had no artillery horses, had to borrow Sherman's in order to move forward 40 guns of the Army of the Cumberland on the north side of the Tennessee "to aid in protecting the approach to the point where the south end of the bridges was to rest."[7]

In short, Sherman's position would appear to have been as

[1] *Ibid.*, vol. LV, p. 718.   [2] *Ibid.*, vol. LV, pp. 745–746.
[3] *M.H.S.M.*, vol. VIII, pp. 202 and 228.   [4] Grant's *Memoirs*, vol. II, p. 68.
[5] *Ibid.*, vol. II, p. 72.   [6] *Ibid.*, vol. II, p. 69.   [7] *Ibid.*, vol. II, p. 66.

follows: Tunnel Hill was a mile and a half away; visibility was
poor; night was approaching, and only part of his artillery was up.
If he decided to advance to the tunnel, which might, so far as he
knew, be strongly held, he could not arrive there until dark. Once
there, his right would be a mile and a half to two miles from
Thomas's left flank and in advance of it. If attacked in flank his
force might be rolled up and thrown back into the South Chickamauga. In any case in the dark he would have found it extremely
difficult to select a tactically sound position to entrench. It is not
suggested that he should not have risked ▪an advance, but that
these circumstances should be carefully weighed before Sherman
is condemned. It would seem that Sherman's blunder was not that
he halted where he did, but that apparently he did not make it
clear to Grant that he was not on the northern end of Missionary
Ridge. That night Grant wrote to Thomas: "General Sherman
carried Missionary Ridge as far as the tunnel with only slight
skirmishing. . . ."[1]

While Sherman was advancing, Thomas stood fast. Brown's
Ferry bridge broke before Osterhaus's division could cross, and
at 12.30 a.m. on November 24 Thomas, under instructions from
Grant, ordered Hooker to "take the point of Lookout."[2]

Early on the 24th Hooker advanced, worked his way through
the mist, and climbed the mountain as far as the base of the
"upper palisade" – that is, to the foot of the precipitous wall of
rock which tops the mountain. During the night he pushed forward small parties of sharpshooters who drove the enemy off the
summit. "Just before sunrise a group of soldiers stepped out on
the rock which forms the overhanging point of the mountain.
They carried a flag but held it furled, waiting for the sun. The
instant the rays broke full upon them they loosened its folds, and
the waiting thousands below beheld the stars and stripes."[3]

That evening Grant reported his position to Washington, and
the following day he received replies from both Lincoln and
Halleck; the former bade him "Remember Burnside", and the
latter answered: "I fear that Burnside is hard pushed, and that
any further delay may prove fatal." This was scarcely encouraging
and shows how persistently Grant was pressed to move.

A little after midnight Grant ordered[4] Sherman to advance as

[1] *W.R.*, vol. LV, p. 44.   [2] *Ibid.*, vol. LV, p. 106.
[3] *M.H.S.M.*, vol. VII, p. 391. See also *W.R.*, vol. LV, p. 122.
[4] *W.R.*, vol. LV, p. 40.

soon as it was light, and to Thomas he wrote: "Your attack, which will be simultaneous, will be in cooperation. Your command will either carry the rifle-pits and ridge directly in front of them, or move to the left, as the presence of the enemy may require." Further: "If Hooker's present position on the mountain can be maintained with a small force, and it is found impracticable to carry the top from where he is, it would be advisable for him to move up the valley with the force he can spare and ascend (i.e. to the top of Lookout Mountain) by the first practicable road."[1] Obviously "top of Lookout Mountain" was a slip for "top of Missionary Ridge,"[2] and Thomas, who recognized this, at 10 a.m. on November 25 ordered Hooker to march "on the Rossville road towards Missionary Ridge"[3] – that is, toward its southern extremity. A little later on Grant, who then was with Thomas at Orchard Knob, decided that Thomas should not move forward with Sherman, but wait until Hooker had reached Missionary Ridge[4] – obviously in order to take advantage of Hooker's success of the 24th, if it were followed by an equal success that day.

One of the results of Thomas's reconnaissance of November 23 was that Bragg moved a division from Lookout Mountain to Missionary Ridge. Although this move facilitated Hooker's advance, it was destined to delay Sherman's. On the morning of the 23rd Cleburne's division and one brigade of Buckner's were at Chickamauga Station *en route* to join Longstreet. Directly after Thomas attacked, Bragg ordered Cleburne to place his division immediately behind Missionary Ridge. Early on November 24, when Sherman was still crossing the Tennessee, Bragg ordered Cleburne to send a brigade to the East Tennessee and Georgia Railroad bridge over the South Chickamauga in order to protect his line of retreat. Next, at 2 p.m., he ordered him to move his remaining three brigades to the northern end of Missionary Ridge near the railway tunnel, and "preserve the bridge in" his "rear at all hazards."[5] Actually, when Sherman arrived at the position he occupied on the night of November 24–25, Cleburne had only one brigade entrenched between him and the tunnel.[6] On the morning of the 25th Cheatham's division and a brigade from

---

[1] *Ibid.*, vol. LV, p. 44.
[2] See footnote, *M.H.S.M.*, vol. VIII, p. 232, and Grant's *Memoirs*, vol. II, p. 75.
[3] *W.R.*, vol. LV, p. 115.
[4] Grant's *Memoirs*, vol. II, p. 75, and *W.R.* vol. LV, pp. 34, 96, 112, and 113.
[5] *W.R.*, vol. LV, p. 745.
[6] *M.H.S.M.*, vol. VIII, p. 205.

Stevenson's arrived from Lookout Mountain, but the rear of
Stevenson's division did not come up until later in the day.[1]

The morning of November 25 was clear and bright, and Grant
from Orchard Knob had a full view of the left of the battlefield.
Sherman advanced at daylight as ordered, and after a two-hour
contest Grant from his observation post saw "column after column
of Bragg's forces moving against him." Forthwith he ordered
Thomas to send Baird's division to reinforce Sherman, but it was
not required. "Bragg at once commenced massing in the same
direction."[2] "This," says Grant, "was what I wanted. But it had
now got to be late in the afternoon, and I had expected before
this to see Hooker crossing the ridge in the neighbourhood of
Rossville, and compelling Bragg to mass in that direction also."[3]

Meanwhile Sherman could not understand what delayed
Thomas's advance. At 12.45 p.m. he asked, "Where is Thomas?"
To which Thomas replied: "I am here, my right is closing in
from Lookout Mountain toward Missionary Ridge."[4] Grant was
still holding Thomas back, for the circumstances of battle had
compelled him to modify his original plan. Because Sherman had
been checked there was now little hope left of turning Bragg's
right; but directly Hooker turned Bragg's left, Bragg would be
compelled to denude his centre in order to reinforce his left. This
was the movement Grant was waiting for before he launched
Thomas against the enemy's weakened centre.

Hooker had advanced early on November 25, but the retiring
Confederates had burned the bridge over Chattanooga Creek.
This delayed his crossing for several hours and prevented him from
reaching Rossville Gap until after 3 p.m. When he did, he carried
it immediately and swept on to Missionary Ridge. He did not,
however, report his success to Thomas.

As Grant considered that Sherman's position was critical, at
3.30 p.m. he ordered Thomas to advance and carry the "rifle
pits" at the foot of the ridge.[5] This, when related to Grant's instructions issued to Thomas a little after midnight on the 24th,
was obviously meant to be the first step toward carrying the ridge.
In spite of the quibbles raised over this order by a number of
historians, and more particularly by General Smith, the *Official
Records* of the war leave its meaning in no doubt. General Baird in

---

[1] *W.R.*, vol. LV, pp. 701, 726.   [2] *Ibid.*, vol. LV, p. 34.
[3] Grant's *Memoirs*, vol. II, p. 78.   [4] *W.R.*, vol. LV, p. 44.
[5] *Ibid.*, vol. LV, p. 34. Thomas, always slow, delayed to do so, and nearly an hour
later Grant himself ordered the advance. (Grant's *Memoirs*, vol. II, p. 79.)

his report says that an officer of Thomas's staff brought him a verbal order to carry the rifle pits and told him that "this was intended as preparatory to a general assault on the mountain, and that it was doubtless designed by the major-general commanding that I should take part in this movement, so that I would be following his wishes were I to push on to the summit."[1]

Dana says: "The storming of the ridge by our troops was one of the greatest miracles in military history."[2] It was nothing of the kind; it was an act of common sense. Missionary Ridge was protected by two entrenched lines, each held by men at one pace interval, and the artillery fire from the ridge was plunging, and therefore not fully effective. When the first line – that is, the line of rifle pits mentioned by Grant – was taken, its defenders fell back and many of them rushed through the second line. General Manigault, who commanded a brigade of Hindman's division (Confederate), says:

"All order was lost, and each striving to save himself took the shortest direction for the summit. . . .

"The troops from below at last reached the works exhausted and breathless, the greater portion so demoralized that they rushed to the rear to place the ridge itself between them and the enemy."[3]

Obviously Grant intended the ridge to be taken, but not foreseeing the demoralization of the garrison of the forward Confederate line, he ordered the line of rifle pits to be carried first. The attacking troops, when they saw their enemy run, instinctively ran after him, and thus carried the ridge in one bound instead of two. The difficulty of holding back a line of men when an enemy is flying before it is well known to every soldier who has taken part in such an engagement. The continued advance was caused not by a miracle, but by the fighting instinct. This in no way detracts from the gallantry of Thomas's superb assault, yet it does explain it.

Because the charge was successful Hooker's advance, which had already made itself felt, was the decisive act of the battle. Shattered in front, Bragg could not possibly meet this flank attack. Instead of winning the battle with his left as originally intended, Grant won it with his right. That he should have done so after his

---

[1] *W.R.*, vol. LV, p. 508. See also *Battles and Leaders*, vol. III, pp. 724–726, for Brigadier-General Joseph E. Fullerton's account.
[2] *W.R.*, vol. LV, p. 69.
[3] *Military Memoirs of a Confederate*, E. P. Alexander (1907), p. 478.

mistake of ordering a reconnaissance by Thomas on November 23 does not reflect adversely on his generalship; instead it shows that his plan and distribution were flexible – that is, that they could be adapted to circumstances.

The pursuit was at once taken up, but abandoned on November 28, for Grant's immediate duty was the relief of Burnside. On the 29th, when he had ascertained that Bragg was in full retreat, Grant ordered Sherman to march on Knoxville.[1] Sherman arrived there on December 6, to find that Longstreet had raised the siege on the 4th and retired to the Holston Valley. On November 30 Grant moved his headquarters to Nashville and left Thomas in command of the sally port – now firmly in Federal hands.

In this battle Grant's losses were 5,815 men out of a total force of about 60,000.[2] Bragg, who after Longstreet's departure had no more than 33,000 troops in line, lost 6,175 stands of arms, 40 guns, and 5,471 prisoners.[3] His killed and wounded numbered about 3,000.

Grant's victories at Vicksburg and Chattanooga sealed the eventual doom of the Confederacy. The one severed the States east of the Mississippi from those to the west of it, and the other blocked the main approach northward into Tennessee and opened the road to Atlanta – the back door of Lee's army in Virginia.

On March 3, 1864, Lincoln, who at length had found the type of general he had been seeking, called Grant to Washington and made him commander-in-chief. He arrived there on March 9 and at once set to work on the plan which was to bring the war to an end. This was to hold Lee in Virginia by relentless attacks while from Chattanooga Sherman seized Atlanta and then operated against Lee's rear. In brief, to open a two front attack on what remained of the Confederacy and pinch it out of existence.

In the east this dual campaign opened on May 4, 1864. After six weeks of desperate fighting in the Wilderness of Virginia – the wooded country south of the Rapidan – Grant drove Lee back on to the fortifications of Richmond; but as he found them too strong to attack frontally, in the middle of June he by-passed them and crossed the James River at Wilcox's Landing. From there he struck at Petersburg, through which ran Lee's main line of supply, but unfortunately, through the bunglings of his subordinates, he

---

[1] On the 27th, Grant instructed Thomas to send Granger's corps to Knoxville. On the 29th, finding that it had not yet started, he sent Sherman instead (Grant's *Memoirs*, vol. II, pp. 90–92).

[2] *Battles and Leaders*, vol. III, p. 711.   [3] H. M. Cist, p. 258.

failed to occupy "the Key to Richmond." From then until the end of March, 1865, the Army of the Potomac was mainly engaged in siege warfare.

Four days after Grant set out Sherman struck southward from Chattanooga against General Joseph E. Johnston. Historically his campaign is of particular interest, for Sherman was a general of a new kind. He broke away from the conventions of nineteenth-century warfare, took the public into his confidence, and waged war with steel as ruthlessly as Calvin had waged it with the word. After severe fighting, on September 1 he took Atlanta, "the gate city of the South", and bent on leaving no enemies behind him he evacuated its entire population. He explained to Halleck, who since Grant's promotion had been appointed chief of staff at Washington: "If the people raise a howl against my barbarity and cruelty, I will answer that war is war, and not popularity-seeking. If they want peace they and their relatives must stop the war."[1]

For the nineteenth century this was a new conception, for it meant that the deciding factor in war – the power to sue for peace – was transferred from government to people, and that peace-making was a product of revolution. This was to carry the principle of democracy to its ultimate stage, and with it to introduce the theory of the psychological attack, or what in the popular idiom of to-day is called "cold war". Of Sherman, Major George W. Nichols, one of his aides-de-camp, says: "He is a Democrat in the best sense of the word. There is nothing European about him. He is a striking type of our institutions."[2]

Later, when Sherman set out on his famous march through Georgia, he made this new concept of war his guiding principle and waged war against the people of the South as fully as against its armed forces.

Nothing like this march had been seen in the West since the maraudings of Tilly and Wallenstein in the Thirty Years War, although during the Napoleonic Wars it had parallels. Southern guerrillas, as Sherman notes, had shown and continued to show much brutality; but the atrocities they perpetrated were individual acts and not a matter of policy. With some justification Jefferson Davis calls Sherman "the Attila of the American Continent."[3]

---

[1] *Personal Memoirs of General W. T. Sherman* (1875), vol. II, p. 132.
[2] *The Story of the Great March* (1865), p. 80.
[3] Jefferson Davis, vol. II, p. 279.

Terror was the basic factor in Sherman's policy, as he openly says. Here are two quotations out of a number:

"Until we can repopulate Georgia, it is useless to occupy it; but the utter destruction of its roads, houses and people will cripple their military resources. . . . I can make the march, and make Georgia howl."[1]

"We are not only fighting hostile armies, but a hostile people, and must make old and young, rich and poor, feel the hard hand of war. . . . The truth is the whole army is burning with an insatiable desire to wreak vengeance upon South Carolina. I almost tremble for her fate."[2]

Sherman, like Nichols, believed that his army was "God's instrument of justice."[3] Hitchcock, another of Sherman's aides-de-camp, says much the same thing: "It is war now that it may not be war *always*. God send us peace – but there is no peace save in *complete submission to the Government*: and this seems impossible save through the terrors of war."[4] Also: "Sherman is perfectly right – the only possible way to end this unhappy and dreadful conflict . . . is to make it *terrible beyond endurance*."[5]

On December 21 Savannah fell to Sherman's pillaging horde, now followed by thousands of plundering Negroes. The next day he presented it as a Christmas gift to President Lincoln.[6] Then the Carolinas were devastated.[7] In Georgia Sherman estimated the damage done at $100,000,000 of which only $20,000,000 "inured to our advantage"; the remainder was "simple waste and destruction."[8]

While these events were unfolding themselves in the south, Grant in the north was waging ceaseless war against the Petersburg railways. At length on January 15, 1865, with the fall of Fort Fisher which protected the entrance to the port of Wilmington, Lee's supply difficulties became so desperate that he warned the Confederate Government that Richmond might have to be abandoned.[9] Soon after, when Grant learnt that Sherman would not be able to advance on the Roanoke until April 10, he decided not to wait for him and to strike at once.

[1] *W.R.*, vol. LXXIX, p. 162.   [2] *Ibid.*, vol. XCII, p. 799.   [3] Nichols, p. 101.
[4] *Marching with Sherman, Letters and Diaries of Henry Hitchcock* (1927), p. 53.
[5] *Ibid.*, p. 35.   [6] Sherman's *Memoirs*, vol. II, p. 231.
[7] Nichols, pp. 189–190. See also pp. 86, 93, 102, and 116.
[8] *W.R.*, vol. XCII, p. 13. "In nearly all his [Sherman's] dispatches after he had reached the sea, he gloated over the destruction of property" (Rhode's *History of the United States*, 1895, vol. V, p. 22).
[9] *W.R.*, vol. XCVIII, p. 1044.

On March 30, in order to turn the right of the Petersburg entrenchments, he instructed General Philip H. Sheridan and his cavalry corps to seize the road junction at Five Forks, which they did, and beat back General Pickett on April 1. This battle placed the South Side railway, which ran from Petersburg to Lynchburg, at Grant's mercy and sealed the fate of Petersburg. Next day Grant stormed the works south of Petersburg and cut Lee's army in two. Sheridan then drove all forces west of Lee's centre beyond the Appomattox, while Grant forced all those east of it into Petersburg. When the Federals entered the town on April 3, Lee abandoned Richmond and fell back along the Danville Railroad.

As the Army of Northern Virginia straggled on to its doom Grant ordered the IInd and VIth Corps to move north of the Appomattox and harry the enemy's rear. Sheridan, the Vth and Ord's corps were directed on Appomattox Station because information had been received that Lee intended to resupply his army at that place. On the evening of April 8 Sheridan reached Appomattox Station, from where he pushed Lee's advanced troops back towards the Court House. On the morning of the 9th Lee advanced to attack him, whereupon Sheridan's cavalry parted to right and left and disclosed the Vth and Ord's corps in line behind them. The white flag was then raised[1] and a little later, at McLean's house, in "a naked little parlor containing a table and two or three chairs," Robert E. Lee, at the head of 7,872 infantry with arms, 2,100 cavalry, 63 guns, and not a single ration, surrendered to Ulysses S. Grant. So ended

> The pastoral rebellion of the earth
> Against machines, against the Age of Steam –
> The Hamiltonian extremes against the Franklin mean.[2]

After four years of fratricidal war the Union was affirmed and a mighty empire born, which, moated by the Atlantic and Pacific Oceans, was virtually unattackable. Linking as it did Europe in the east with Asia in the west it held in its hands the eventual balance of world power.

Although the war brought ruin and chaos to the South, and although its ills were aggravated by the vengeance of the years of reconstruction, to the North it brought victory and unprecedented prosperity. "Never before," write Morison and Commager, "had the American people exhibited greater vitality, never since has

[1] *W.R.*, vol. xcv, pp. 1109–1110.
[2] *John Brown's Body*, Stephen Vincent Benét (English edit., 1929), p. 375.

their vitality been accompanied by more reckless irresponsibility. To the generation that had saved the Union everything seemed possible: there were no worlds, except the worlds of the spirit, that could not be conquered. Men hurled themselves upon the continent with ruthless abandon as if to ravish it of its wealth."[1]

The resources of the new empire were all but inexhaustible: iron, coal, oil, labour and individual energy abounded. Inventions flowed from drawing boards, goods from the factories and wheat from the fields, while hundreds of thousands of emigrants poured into the cities and over the land. Whereas, in 1865, there were 35,000 miles of railways in the United States, by 1900 there were 200,000, a mileage greater than that of all Europe.

It has been estimated that the war cost the belligerents twenty billion dollars, and as Marx has pointed out it "left behind it a colossal national debt, with the consequent increased pressure of taxation, the creation of a financial aristocracy of the meanest kind, the handing over of an enormous proportion of the public lands to speculative companies for exploitation by means of railways,[2] mines, etc. – in a word, the centralization of capital at a headlong pace."[3]

Within two generations from the ending of the war the United States became the greatest capitalist as well as the greatest industrial power in the world. Stephen Vincent Benét calls it, "The great metallic beast," and depicts its emergence from the Titanic struggle of the Civil War in these tremendous lines:

> Out of John Brown's strong sinews the tall skyscrapers grow,
> Out of his heart the chanting buildings rise,
> Rivet and girder, motor and dynamo,
> Pillar of smoke by day and fire by night,
> The steel-faced cities reaching at the skies,
> The whole enormous and rotating cage
> Hung with hard jewels of electric light,
> Smoky with sorrow, black with splendor, dyed
> Whiter than damask for a crystal bride
> With metal suns, the engine-handed Age,
> The genie we have raised to rule the earth. . . .[4]

The reverse of this urge and power to produce in peacetime is the urge and power to destroy in wartime, and because of this – to revert to a point already touched upon – for the first time in

---

[1] *The Growth of the American Republic* (1942), vol. II, p. 9.
[2] "Altogether the Federal Government gave to the railroads 158,293,377 acres – almost the area of Texas" (*ibid.*, vol. II, p. 112).
[3] *Capital* (Everyman's Lib.), vol. II, pp. 857–858.   [4] *John Brown's Body*, p. 376.

modern history the aim of war became not only the destruction of the enemy's armed forces, but also of their foundations – his entire political, social and economic order. Lee, as Rhodes says,[1] in all essential characteristics resembled Washington, and resembling him mentally he belonged to the eighteenth century – to the agricultural age of history. Sherman, and to a lesser extent Grant, Sheridan, and other Northern generals, spiritually and morally belonged to the age of the Industrial Revolution. Their guiding principle was that of the machine which was fashioning them – namely, efficiency. And as efficiency is governed by a single law – that every means is justified by the end – no moral or spiritual conceptions or traditional behaviour must stand in its way. Sherman must rank as the first of the modern totalitarian generals. He made war universal, waged it on his enemy's people and not only on armed men, and made terror the linchpin of his strategy. To him more than to any other man must be attributed the hatred that grew out of the Civil War.

In tactics, because the rifle made the defensive the stronger form of war, the offensive became more and more difficult and costly. This is noted by Colonel Theodore Lyman, who says: "Put a man in a hole, and a good battery on a hill behind him, and he will beat off three times his number, even if he is not a very good soldier."[2] And Frank Wilkeson wrote: "Before we left North Anna I discovered that our infantry were tired of charging earthworks. The ordinary enlisted men assert that one good man behind an earthwork was equal to three good men outside it."[3] This gave rise to a progressive increase in the strength of armies.

Other changes – and many for years after the war remained unnoticed – were that the cavalry charge had become impotent; that the rifled-cannon was coming more and more to the fore, and that the dethronement of the bayonet was complete. "I don't think a single man of them was bayonetted,"[4] writes one eyewitness. General John B. Gordon says: "The bristling points and the glitter of the bayonets were fearful to look upon as they were levelled in front of a charging line; but they were rarely reddened with blood. The day of the bayonet is past."[5] And Surgeon-Major G. Hart writes that he saw few bayonet wounds "except

---

[1] *History of the United States*, vol. III, p. 413.
[2] *Meade's Headquarters, 1863–1865* (1922), p. 224.
[3] *The Soldier in Battle, or Life in the Ranks of the Army of the Potomac* (1896), p. 99.
[4] *Life in the Confederate Army*, William Watson, p. 217.
[5] *Reminiscences of the Civil War* (1904), pp. 5 and 6. See also *Memoirs of the Confederate War of Independence*, Heros von Borcke (1886), vol. I, p. 63, and vol. II, p. 50.

accidental ones. . . . I think half-a-dozen would include all the wounds of this nature that I ever dressed."[1]

It is easy to criticize the tactical ability of Grant, Lee, and other generals of this war, but it should be remembered that they had few precedents to guide them. To all intents and purposes the rifle was a new weapon. When we do criticize we should remember that in 1914 – 50 years after the Civil War – seven out of eight professional soldiers still believed in the bayonet.

The war fought by Grant and Lee, Sherman and Johnston, and others closely resembled the first of the World Wars. No other war, not even the Russo-Japanese War of 1904–1905, offers so exact a parallel. It was a war of rifle bullets and trenches, of slashings, abattis, and even of wire entanglements – an obstacle the Confederates called "a devilish contrivance which none but a Yankee could devise" because at Drewry's Bluff they had been trapped in them and "slaughtered like partridges."[2] It was a war astonishing in its modernity, with wooden wire-bound mortars, hand and winged grenades, rockets, and many forms of booby traps. Magazine rifles and Requa's machine gun were introduced and balloons were used by both sides, although the Confederates did not think much of them.[3] Explosive bullets are mentioned[4] and also a flame projector,[5] and in June, 1864, General Pendleton asked the chief ordnance officer at Richmond whether he could supply him with "stink-shells" which would give off "offensive gases" and cause "suffocating effect." The answer he got was: "stink-shells, none on hand; don't keep them; will make if ordered."[6] Nor did modernity end there; armoured ships, armoured trains, land mines and torpedoes[7] were used, together with lamp and flag signalling and the field telegraph. A submarine was built by Horace L. Huntly at Mobile. It was 20 ft. long, 5 ft. deep, and $3\frac{1}{2}$ ft. wide and was "propelled by a screw worked from inside by seven or eight men."[8] On February 17, 1864, she sank the U.S.S. *Housatonic* off Charleston and went down with her.

Had the nations of Europe studied the lessons of the Civil War and taken them to heart they could not in 1914–1918 have perpetrated the enormous tactical blunders of which that war bears record.

[1] *M.H.S.M.*, vol. XIII, p. 265.   [2] *Battles and Leaders* vol. IV, p. 212.
[3] *The Times* Special Correspondent, January 1, 1863.
[4] *Campaigns and Battles of the Army of Northern Virginia*, George Wise (1916), p. 160.
[5] *Meade's Headquarters*, Colonel Theodore Lyman, p. 284.
[6] *W.R.*, vol. LXIX, pp. 888–889.   [7] *Battles and Leaders*, vol. II, p. 636.
[8] *M.H.S.M.*, vol. XIV, pp. 450, 453.

The expansion of Prussia

W hile the semi-independent American states were being fused by friction into a federal empire, central Europe became the scene of another gestation. It arose out of the void created by the dissolution of the Holy Roman Empire, which the Congress of Vienna, in 1815, had hoped to fill by calling into being a Germanic Confederation of 38 sovereign States. Its object was to guarantee the external and internal peace of Germany and its organ was a Diet, permanently established at Frankfort-on-Main, in which each State was represented. Actually, the Diet remained impotent because it was a Senate without a House of Representatives – a conference and not a parliament.

More important than the Germanic Confederation was the creation of the Prussian *Zollverein* or Customs' union. In idea it originated with Friederich List, who saw that until the tariff barriers which separated the various States were removed British goods must continue to inundate Germany, whose own restrictions would prevent her from becoming industrialized. In order to put an end to this absurd situation all customs duties within Prussia, of which there were 67 affecting nearly 3,000 different articles, were abolished in 1818, and in October the following year the first tariff treaty was signed between Prussia and the small sovereign State of Schwarzburg-Sonderhausen. This soon gave birth to two Customs' unions, a northern and a southern, which in 1829 agreed to suspend all duties on the mutual exchange of products until 1841. In that year the *Zollverein* was reaffirmed, and three years later it included the whole of Germany less the Austrian dominions. Inevitably commercial unity led in the direction of political control, and therefore towards mutual military security.

Although we hear much of the *Pax Europa*, the 40 years after Waterloo was a period of nightmares and delirium in which reaction and revolution chased each other. No sooner was Louis XVIII re-established in Paris than reaction climbed back into the saddle. In France the *Tricolore* was abolished and so was divorce; in Spain the Church demanded and obtained the restoration of the Inquisition; in Austria the Emperor would go neither backward nor forward, and Prince Metternich, his chief Minister, looked upon the unification of Germany as an "infamous object." In England Whig and Tory, oblivious of the onrush of the Industrial Revolution, demanded protection for the agricultural interests and close trade within the Empire; and at the same time Alexander of Russia, a religious fanatic, persuaded the Emperor of Austria and the King of Prussia to sign with him in the name of "The Indivisible Trinity" a treaty called "The Holy Alliance," which was well suited to provide occasions for further Russian expansion. Later, all the leading monarchs, except the Prince Regent of England, subscribed to this treaty, and the only potentates not asked to do so were the Sultan and the Pope.

Although the 20 years which followed this "loud-sounding nothingness," as Metternich called it, witnessed no single great battle, the surge of nationalism against reaction made them some of the most bloody in Western history. The Spanish-American colonies revolted against Spain and Brazil against Portugal; Spain and Portugal were swept by revolution, and in the name of the Holy Alliance France invaded Spain. The Greeks revolted against the Turks, and in Russia the Decembrist Revolt followed the death of Alexander. In 1827 England, France and Russia intervened on behalf of the Greeks and on October 20 annihilated the Turkish fleet at Navarino. Russia invaded Persia and in 1828 declared war on the Porte and invaded Bulgaria. At length, in 1830, came the reckoning. Paris was rocked by revolution, Charles X was dethroned and Louis Philippe called to power; Belgium revolted against Holland; Poland against Russia; Hanover and Hesse Cassel boiled over in turmoil, and disturbances rent Austria, Hungary, Switzerland and Italy. In 1831 the Poles were defeated at Ostrolenka and their constitution abolished, and the Papal states, which revolted against Austria, were crushed. In 1832 the French laid siege to Antwerp; in 1833 Sir Charles Napier, with extraordinary audacity, destroyed Don Miguel's fleet off Cape St. Vincent, and in 1834 the Carlist War opened in Spain and for seven years drenched the Peninsula with blood. At length, in 1837, with the accession of Queen Victoria to the throne of England, a period of relative quietude set in for 10 years.

The next revolutionary outburst occurred in 1848. Its aim was no longer to change the form of government but the national structure, in the bottom strata of which living conditions had steadily worsened as industrialism deepened. In 1847 the Communist League was founded in London under Marx and Engels, and from its inauguration the *Marseillaise* passed to the bourgeoisie and a more formidable battle-song – the *Internationale* – vibrated from the throats of the workers:

> *Debout! les damnés de la terre!*
> *Debout! les forçats de la faim!*
>
> . . . .
>
> *Le raison tonne en son cratère,*
> *C'est l'éruption de la fin.*
> *Du passé faisons table rase,*
> *Foule esclave, debout, debout!*
> *Le monde va changer de base:*
> *Nous ne sommes rien, soyons tout!*

On February 22, 1848, Louis Philippe and his Queen slipped out of a back door of the Tuileries and fled to England as Mr. and Mrs. Smith.

Seldom had a revolution started with so little bloodshed. The right to work was established as the leading principle of reform, and to guarantee it the National Guard was suppressed and the workers were armed. In June General Cavaignac was appointed dictator; he led the west-end of Paris against the industrial east-end under Pujol and crushed the revolt with his cannon. "The combatants," writes Mr. C. A. Fyffe, "fought not for a political principle or form of government, but for the preservation or overthrow of society based on the institution of private property." Nevertheless France was so badly shaken that the Duke of Wellington wrote: "France needs a Napoleon! I cannot yet see him. . . . Where is he?"

In England there was much excitement, but the Chartists' demonstrations fizzled out. In 1849 the Corn Laws were repealed and Great Britain slid into free trade. Meanwhile revolution broke out in Vienna and was followed by a general upheaval throughout the Empire. Charles Albert of Piedmont with all Italy, except the Pope, behind him and urged on by Cavour decided on war to his cost. Defeated at Santa Lucia and Custozza, on March 23, 1849, he was finally crushed at Novara and compelled to abdicate in favour of his son Victor Emmanuel (1849–1878). Hungary in the meantime burst into flames; the Czechs rose in Bohemia and the Serbs and Croats took up arms. These revolts led to a recurrence of revolution in Vienna and to the abdication of Ferdinand I in favour of his nephew Francis Joseph (1848–1916), a boy of 18. Nevertheless, Hungary refused to acknowledge him, and since the Austrian Government was unable to suppress the revolt, Russia was called in, in the name of the expiring Holy Alliance, and on August 9, 1849, the Hungarians were routed at Temesvár and the rebellion ruthlessly suppressed.

Although in Germany the workers, who followed the lead set by the French, clamoured for a greater share in the profits of their masters, rebellion took on a national rather than a social form. In February, 1847, Frederick William IV (1840–1861) had been compelled to summon a united Prussian Diet, which at once suspended the old Diet of 1815 and authorized the assembly of a German National Parliament at Frankfort in order to construct a new Germany out of the States. In the middle of its debates Schleswig and Holstein revolted against the Danish Crown and a Prussian army was sent to support the Holsteiners. Russia supported the Danes and Frederick William, taking fright, flouted the National Parliament by agreeing to an armistice. In spite of this setback the National Parliament next offered to make him Emperor of Germany, and with Austria in turmoil had Frederick William accepted the offer it would probably have been unopposed. But as he loathed the democratic policy of the National Parliament he declined it unless the sanction of the Princes and free cities was first obtained. This was a death-blow to the hopes of the German patriots.

To offset this blunder Frederick William concluded a treaty with the Kings of Hanover and Saxony so as to agree on a new constitution. The suggestion was that, instead of an Emperor, a supreme chief aided by a College of Princes should be established. The proposal was accepted and assumed the name of "The Union." But unfortunately for Frederick William the propitious moment had passed, for Austria had now recovered and, on her detaching Saxony and Hanover from the Union, Germany was split into two hostile parties – one supporting Prussia and the other Austria. A disturbance in Hesse Cassel brought them to the verge of war; but as Frederick William was in no way prepared to wage one, on November 29, 1850, at Olmütz, he yielded virtually everything to Austria; the Union was dissolved and Prussia was compelled to recognize the old Frankfort Diet. Never since the black day of Jena had Prussia suffered such an eclipse.

Meanwhile in France, after the "June Days," Cavaignac

reigned as dictator, but because he failed to establish a stable government he was defeated on December 10, 1848, by Louis Napoleon in the presidential elections. At length there had appeared the man for whom less than a year before Wellington had looked vainly.

He was the third son of Louis Bonaparte and Hortense Beauharnais, daughter of Josephine, and therefore nephew and stepgrandson of Napoleon I. Because he was an astute opportunist politician he had every intention of investing in the glory of his great uncle. When in May, 1850, the Assembly blindly reduced the number of electors from nine million to six – a highly unpopular act – Louis Napoleon saw his opportunity. Although a year or two before he had posed as a vindicator of universal suffrage, he now sided with the Assembly in order to precipitate its ruin. When a friend said to him: "But you will perish with it," he replied: "On the contrary, when the Assembly is hanging over the precipice, I shall cut the rope."

After he had discredited the Assembly he flattered the clergy, promised prosperity to the bourgeoisie and wealth to the workers, and distributed cigars and sausages to the soldiers, until in the eyes of the people from a simple *citoyen* he became *notre prince*. Once he had carefully prepared everything, he overthrew the government on December 2, 1851, and a year later was elected by popular vote Emperor of the French with the title of Napoleon III.

While he was scheming the Great Exhibition was held in London. "It seemed," writes Mr. Fyffe, "the emblem and harbinger of a new epoch in the history of mankind, in which war should cease. . . . Yet the epoch on which Europe was then about to embark proved to be pre-eminently an epoch of war. In the next quarter of a century there was not one of the great Powers which was not engaged in an armed struggle with its rivals."

The first of these conflicts was the war in the Crimea, and although the pretext for its outbreak was Louis Napoleon's revival of the claims of France to the guardianship of the holy places in Palestine, the hidden cause was the expansionist policy of Russia and the craving by Nicholas I (1825–1855) to obtain control of the Dardanelles. Once she felt assured of the support of the western Powers, Turkey declared war on Russia in October, 1853, and early in 1854 was joined by France and Great Britain, and later by Sardinia.

This war ended the 40 years peace which followed Waterloo and its results were fatal to the peace of Europe. From 1856 to 1878 Europe was afflicted with five great wars, all of which found their roots in the Crimean conflict.

Immediately after the Crimean War, when Russia was helpless and Great Britain had her hands full with the Indian Mutiny, a plot to assassinate Louis Napoleon was hatched in London by the revolutionist Felice Orsini. This not only caused acute friction between France and Great Britain, but so terrified the Emperor that he persuaded himself that, unless he took up arms in favour of the liberation of Italy, other attempts on his life would follow. The result was the Franco-Austrian War in 1859, which, after the French victory of Solferino, terminated on November 10 with the Treaty of Villafranca. By its terms France gained Savoy and Nice, and with the exception of Venetia and Rome, all Italy was united under Victor Emmanuel.

In these two wars the following military developments are of interest. In the Crimea, chloroform was first used; the Press began to exert a decisive influence and for the first time newspaper correspondents accompanied armies. James Cowen, a philanthropist, proposed the use of armoured traction engines fitted with scythes to mow lanes through the enemy infantry; Bauer, a German, built a submarine – the *Diable Marin* – for Russia, and Lord Dundonald revived his project of 1812 to use burning sulphur to suffocate the garrisons of naval fortresses. Although his scheme was not tried out, he predicted that poison gas as a weapon "would ultimately become a recognized means of warfare." In 1859 for the first time in war the railway was extensively used; rifled-cannon were employed in numbers, and on account of the sufferings of the wounded at Solferino, the first Geneva Convention came into being in 1864.

Since her humiliating surrender at Olmütz Prussia had been recuperating, and a rapid revival followed the accession of William I (1861–1888) on January 2, 1861.

William was born in 1797 and in 1814 had taken part in the battle of Arcis-sur-Aube. He was a soldier by instinct and education, and in his first speech from the throne proclaimed: "The Prussian Army will, in the future, also be the Prussian Nation in Arms" – words which were to change the destiny of Europe, and with it that of the world. He at once set about reorganizing the Prussian army with the aim of creating an effective war force of

371,000 men, backed by a reserve of 126,000, and a *Landwehr* of 163,000. He appointed Count von Roon as Minister of War, Count von Moltke as Chief of the General Staff, and in 1862 he made Otto von Bismarck his President-Minister.

Bismarck's policy was simple and direct – to drive Austria out of Germany – and because Russia had not recovered from the Crimean War and France, though formidable, was engaged in a wild-goose chase in Mexico, his road was clear, and he determined to travel along it at the first opportunity. It came in 1863, when on the accession of Charles IX to the Danish throne, Saxon and Hanoverian troops marched into Holstein. On the pretext of restoring peace, Bismarck persuaded Austria to join Prussia. In 1864 came the Schleswig-Holstein War, and in October it was concluded by the Treaty of Vienna, which put the two duchies under the joint control of Austria and Prussia.

Bismarck calculated correctly that Schleswig-Holstein would become a bone of contention and lead to war with Austria. Therefore, in order to isolate her, he promised Louis Napoleon a free hand in Belgium or part of the Rhinish Provinces if in his turn he would persuade Austria to sell Venetia to Italy. This he knew Austria would refuse to do. At the same time, in order to annoy Austria, he reopened the question of German federation. As Austria would not part with Venetia, an offensive and defensive treaty of alliance was signed by Italy and Prussia on April 8, 1866; and Louis Napoleon, who was watching the gathering storm and who believed that the time was opportune to erase the treaties of 1815, offered to join Prussia with 300,000 men in return for the Rhinish Provinces. Bismarck, however, had no intention of parting with them, and now that Italy was in the Prussian knapsack, he ordered troops into Holstein to precipitate the conflict. On June 12 Austria broke off diplomatic relations.

The war which was now fought was not a war of aggression in the common meaning of the word, nor a war of conquest, but a war of diplomacy – of rectification. The aim of Prussia was not to humiliate Austria or even to weaken her, but to persuade her that nationalism in Germany was a living, growing force which demanded unity. On no account did Bismarck want to make Austria a vindictive enemy, because he knew that one day Germany would have to contend with France for the hegemony of Europe, and when that day came he wanted a neutral Austria.

When he learnt that the Austrians were concentrating in

Moravia in order to advance into Bohemia, Moltke decided to invade the latter with two armies, the First, under Prince Frederick Charles, and the Second under the Crown Prince. One was to advance on Müchengrätz and the other on Trautenau-Nachod, from where they would move forward and unite at Gitschin. When Prince Frederick Charles neared Müchengrätz, the Austrians, under Clam-Gallas, fell back on Gitschin, and when the Crown Prince defeated Ramming at Nachod and Skalitz, Field-Marshal Benedek, the Austrian commander-in-chief, ordered a general withdrawal on Sadowa. On June 30 the two Prussian armies were sufficiently close to unite at short notice, and on July 3 the battle of Königgrätz (also called Sadowa) was fought. The First Army engaged the Austrians during the morning, and in the afternoon the Second fell upon their right flank and crumpled it up. Although the victory was decisive – the Austrians lost nearly 45,000 men in killed, wounded and prisoners – Benedek with some 150,000 got away, because the two Prussian armies were in such a state of confusion that pursuit was out of the question. On July 18 Moltke issued orders for an advance on Wagram, 10 miles north-east of Vienna, and on the 21st the Austrians asked for an armistice, which was conceded.

On the Austrian defeat at Königgrätz the Emperor Francis Joseph telegraphed to Louis Napoleon to intervene. But his escapade in Mexico made him unwilling to embark on a war, and moreover the rapid Prussian victories were entirely contrary to his expectations. Peace with Prussia had to be made, and in accordance with the treaties of Prague, Berlin and Vienna, although the integrity of the Austrian monarchy was respected, Italy received Venetia and Prussia Hanover, Schleswig-Holstein, Hesse, Nassau and the free city of Frankfort-am-Main. Saxony was left intact and the States north of the Main were formed into a North German Confederation under Prussia, and those to the south into a separate Southern Union.

To placate liberal sentiment, William, on his triumphal return to Berlin, established a Federal Parliament, and a new party called the National Liberals was formed with the main object of securing a union between southern and northern Germany. Such a fusion, in spite of the Customs Parliament (*Zollparlament*) now agreed upon by the two groups of States, would have taken a long time to effect had not the French Emperor brought such pressure to bear on the whole of Germany as to make it inevitable. He did what Bismarck calculated he would do. Even before the Treaty of Prague was signed he had claimed the left bank of the Rhine in compensation for Prussia's gain in power, and he now claimed it again. Fear of France threw the Southern Union into the arms of the Northern Confederation, and a secret offensive and defensive alliance under the King of Prussia was agreed. All that was now required was a common war against a common enemy in order to weld together the severed halves of Germany, and for this Bismarck steadily prepared.

CHAPTER 3

The Battle of Sedan, 1870

The causes of the Franco-Prussian War were, on the one hand the determination of Prussia to unite all Germany under her leadership, and on the other the determination of France to prevent this union. Added to these was the age-old animosity between Gaul and Teuton. Few nations have had so bad a neighbour as Germany has had in France. Between 1675 and 1813 she had invaded her on no fewer than 14 occasions – on the average once every 10 years. Besides, France for centuries had been *la grande nation*, the dominant power in Europe, and the secret fear that her glory was fading awoke in her a touchy and irascible temper. Ever since 1789 the political foundations of Europe had been in flux; power was passing from kings and courts to demagogues and parliaments to become the shuttle-cock of Press and people and the battledore of the great financial and industrial interests.

The immediate cause – the spark which exploded these well-tamped animosities – was little more than an extraneous accident; nevertheless, it is of sufficient interest to be described in some detail because it is a classic example of how wars are detonated in the democratic age.

In September, 1868, a mutiny in the Spanish fleet led to the expulsion of Queen Isabella II and the appointment of Marshal Prim as regent. Because the mass of the people did not favour a republic Prim offered the Spanish crown to one foreign prince after another, but with no success. At length in February, 1870, he entered into secret negotiations with Bismarck, who suggested as a possible candidate Prince Leopold of Hohenzollern-Sigmaringen, a distant relative of the Prussian royal house. Prim communicated with the Prince, who welcomed the suggestion provided the consent of Louis Napoleon and the King of Prussia could first be obtained. Prim then wrote to William, who was profoundly surprised by his letter, for he had no knowledge of the secret negotiations. He strongly opposed the suggestion and informed Prim accordingly. Further negotiations between Prim and

Bismarck followed, and suddenly, on July 3, 1870, the secret was revealed by the Spanish newspaper *Epoca*. Even more surprised than William was Louis Napoleon, who at once dispatched strongly worded protests to Spain and Prussia. The Paris newspapers published violent articles and talked of the revival of the Empire of Charles V. So hysterical did Paris become that on July 5 Edouard Vaillant (a French politician) wrote in his diary: "It seems to me that this is war, or very nearly so." The next day the French Emperor summoned his Council of State; mobilization was discussed, and on the suggestion of the Duke of Gramont, the French Foreign Minister, it was decided to instruct Count Benedetti, the French ambassador at Berlin, to go to Ems, where the King of Prussia was taking the waters, and request him to persuade Leopold to withdraw his candidature.

On July 9 William saw Benedetti and told him that he had no intention of encouraging Leopold and that the question concerned Madrid alone. As this did not satisfy Louis Napoleon, Gramont telegraphed Benedetti: "We demand that the King forbids the Prince to persist in his candidature." When he was informed of this William was exceedingly annoyed; nevertheless, he gave Benedetti permission to telegraph to Leopold direct. At the time Leopold was in Switzerland and the telegram was received by his father, who at once replied that he withdrew the candidature in the name of his son. This he had every right to do as head of his princely house. When he heard of this William was delighted and considered the matter closed. Not so the French Emperor, who told Gramont to instruct Benedetti to see the King again and obtain his personal assurance that he would forbid Leopold to revive his candidature at a later date.

On July 13 at 9 a.m. Benedetti met William in the park at Ems and was cordially greeted by him. The King said that he was delighted to see that Leopold's renunciation had been published in the German Press. Benedetti then put forward Louis Napoleon's new demand, on which William replied: "My cousins are honourable people; as they have withdrawn the candidature it is not with the intention of reviving it later." He then broke off the conversation.

When he learnt what had taken place, Bismarck, through his representative at Ems, begged the King to cease these irregular personal interviews and revert to the normal procedure of negotiating through ambassadors and ministers. The King agreed, but

Benedetti, urged on by Gramont, asked for another audience. William refused to see him, sent Bismarck a report on what had taken place, and left it to him to decide whether it should be communicated to the embassies and the Press.

Bismarck received the King's dispatch on the evening of July 13, took advantage of the King's permission to publish it, and reduced it to a précis which read: "Because the French ambassador has requested the King at Ems to authorize the dispatch of a telegram to Paris stating that he pledges himself never to allow a revival of the candidature, his Majesty has refused to see the ambassador again, and through an aide-de-camp has informed him that he has nothing further to communicate to him."

That Bismarck falsified the "Ems telegram" is a pure invention. What he did was to condense the King's dispatch into telegraphic form; in any case the original was not meant for publication as it stood. He knew that the French were bent on war, and as he said later: "It is essential that we should be attacked. . . . If I communicate this draft to the Press and telegraph it to the embassies it will soon be known in Paris . . . and its effect on the Gallic bull will be that of a red rag."[1]

No sooner was this telegram published in Paris than the Emperor assembled his Council, and while it was deliberating a dispatch from Benedetti was handed in. It was more moderate than Bismarck's; Gramont, in order to avoid war, proposed that a European Conference should be called to forbid reigning families to permit their members to accept foreign crowns. Although the Emperor approved of this proposal the Empress did not; it was laid aside, and no alternative was suggested. Next, the mob in Paris took charge; the *Marseillaise*, hitherto forbidden, was sung, and "*Vive la guerre, à Berlin!*" was shouted. In spite of the warnings of Thiers and Gambetta the French Assembly lost all balance and, urged on by the popular outcry, rapidly slid into war, which officially was declared on July 19.

France had hoped to have Austria and Italy as her allies, and in 1869 approaches had been made to both, but only vague replies were received. Not until the storm was about to break did Louis Napoleon send a personal representative to Vienna to discuss an alliance, and on July 20 – the day after war was declared – back came the answer – "neutrality!" Denmark also decided to remain

[1] The above account of the "Ems incident" is taken from *Histoire de France Contemporaine* (edit. Ernest Lavisse, 1921), vol. VII, pp. 209–219.

neutral, and England, who all along had been opposed to war, was in no way encouraged to support France, especially when, on July 25, Bismarck had a letter published in *The Times* divulging the French Emperor's project of 1866 to annex Belgium.

Thus France stood alone. Worse still, since 1815 she had been living spiritually on the Napoleonic legend of French invincibility. This illusive dream obscured from the public view what actually existed – a divided, profit-seeking people, a *bric-à-brac* government, "a corpse upon which, like vultures, a swarm of contractors gathered to divide between themselves the budget."[1] "While the soldier held firm to his ancient courage, innate among the French, in the government, the administration, the command, direction, preparations, science, artillery and the furnishing of the arsenals all had been degraded and neglected. . . . *Voilà le matérialisme. Il raille la terre et blasphème le ciel!*"[2] General Trochu says much the same: each revolution since 1815 had "excited ambitions, provoked competitions, confused in the mind of the masses the idea of the true and the false, of the just and the unjust, and had substituted for patriotism and public interest self-profit."[3]

That the Emperor and his councillors should have been living in such a fool's paradise is all but incomprehensible, for they had been kept fully informed by Lieutenant-Colonel Baron Stoffel, the exceptionally observant French Military Attaché in Berlin, of conditions in Prussia, and he had not been afraid to compare them with those prevalent in France. His reports are so illuminating that they warrant quoting at some length.

May 26, 1868. "During divine service it is upon the King and the army the minister calls down, before all others, the blessing of the Most High. The great bodies of the State are only named afterwards. . . . What a contrast with the position filled by the army in France, where it is but a mass of men, the outcasts of fortune, who lose every day more and more discipline and military spirit."

August 12, 1869. "The principal points that I seek to make are clear:

"(1) War is inevitable, and *at the mercy of an accident.*

"(2) Prussia has no intention of attacking France; she does not seek war, and will do all she can to avoid it.

---

[1] *Un Ministère de la guerre de vingt-quatre jours*, le Général Cousin de Montauban, Cte de Palikao (1871), p. 78.
[2] *Les Deux Abimes*, le Comte Alfred de la Guéronnière (1871), pp. 19, 25.
[3] *Une page d'histoire contemporaine devant l'Assemblée Nationale*, Général Trochu (1871), p. 18.

"(3) But Prussia is far-sighted enough to see that the war she does not wish will assuredly break out, and she is, therefore, doing all she can to avoid being surprised when the fatal accident occurs.

"(4) France, by her carelessness and levity, and above all by her ignorance of the state of affairs, has not the same foresight as Prussia.

. . . .

"What, on the contrary, do we see in France? A Chamber that boasts itself as representing the people and which is its reflection, so far as levity and inconsistency are concerned . . . whose patriotism consists of spiteful recrimination or premeditated malice; who hide their incapacity and impotence under flowers of rhetoric, who pretend that they alone are anxious for the well-being of the country, and who, to gain a factious popularity, dispute with the Government over one soldier, one franc . . . they seek to weaken France, they betray her into the hands of her most formidable enemy . . . a Press always vain and empty, whose leading journals descant on the most important subjects without in the least comprehending them, seeking to serve parties, not France. . . . France has laughed at everything; the most venerable things are no longer respected; virtue, family ties, love of country, honour, religion, are all offered as fit subjects of ridicule to a frivolous and sceptical generation. . . . Are not these things palpable signs of real decay?"[1]

Such was the state of the French nation, depicted not by foreigners but by Frenchmen, and this state was reflected by the army, which in Algeria, the Crimea, China, Italy and Mexico had learnt to despise its officers and to hypnotize itself into believing that the *élan* of the French soldier would prove irresistible. In 1859 the saying "*C'est le général soldat qui a gagné la bataille de Solferino*" implied that generals were of little account, and its spirit was fostered by the democratic Press.[2]

Conditions in Prussia were totally different. The army was aristocratic and not democratic, and since William's accession it had become what he had determined it should become – the Prussian Nation in Arms. Since the humiliating Convention of

---

[1] *Military Reports*, Lieut.-Colonel Baron Stoffel, French Military Attaché in Prussia, 1866–1870 (English edit., 1872), pp. 93, 142.
[2] *Tactical Deductions from the War of* 1870–71, A. von Boguslawski (English edit., 1872), p. 8.

Olmütz, the General Staff had accepted Clausewitz's *On War* as its military gospel, and because from 1866 onward it profoundly influenced the theory and practice of war, we shall here summarize its leading doctrines:

"War is only a continuation of State policy by other means" . . . "War is not merely a political act, but also a real political instrument, a continuation of political commerce" . . . "War is only a part of political intercourse, therefore by no means an independent thing in itself" . . . "Is not war merely another kind of writing and language for political thought?" . . . "If war belongs to policy, it will naturally take its character from thence. If policy is grand and powerful, so will also be the war."

Secondly, as to the nature of war:

"War is nothing but a duel on an extensive scale" . . . "Let us not hear of Generals who conquer without bloodshed" . . . "War is an act of violence pushed to its utmost bounds" . . . "Our aim is directed upon the destruction of the enemy's power" . . . "Destruction of the enemy's military forces is in reality the object of all combats" . . . "The more is war in earnest, the more is it a venting of animosity and hostility."

This leads, thirdly, to the offensive:

"There is only one form of war – to wit, the attack of the enemy" . . . "The combat is the single activity in war."

Which, fourthly, demands numerical superiority:

"The best strategy is always to be strong" . . . "A war" should be "waged with the whole weight of the national power" . . . "A people's war in civilized Europe is a phenomenon of the nineteenth century."

And, fifthly, war demands moral and intellectual superiority:

"Courage is the highest of virtues" . . . "The chief qualities are the talents of the Commander; the military virtue of the army; its national feeling" . . . "There is nothing in war which is of greater importance than obedience."

Sixthly, as regards tactics:

"The destructive principle of fire in the wars of the present time is plainly beyond measure the most effective" . . . "The defensive form of war is in itself stronger than the offensive . . . but has a negative object" . . . "The attack is the positive intention, the defence the negative" . . . "Only great and general battles can produce great results."

Lastly, organization:

"War is divided into preparation and action" . . . "Everything is very simple in war, but the simplest thing is difficult" . . . "War belongs not to the province of Arts and Sciences, but to the province of social life."[1]

Although Moltke was saturated with Clauzewitz's ideas he did not blindly follow him, but adapted his theories to the conditions of his own day, which were very different from those of Napoleon, on whose campaigns *On War* had been based. The railway was now revolutionizing logistics, and with it armies were growing in size, which demanded more and more a highly trained General Staff. Besides, the chaos of Königgräts had terrified Moltke as much as the success of the great flank attack had electrified him. As early as 1861 he had considered that infantry were frontally unassailable, and he had compared an open plain to a wet ditch which cannot be rushed. After 1866 he realized that a man who shoots at rest has the advantage over a man who fires when advancing; and therefore that the Napoleonic principle of concentration before battle could be supplemented by that of concentration during battle. Further, that the Napoleonic grand tactics of penetration must give way to that of the decisive flank attack.

In 1869 he issued a series of *Instructions for Superior Commanders of Troops*, in which we read:

"Very large concentrations of troops are in themselves a calamity. The army which is concentrated at one point is difficult to supply and can never be billeted; it cannot march, it cannot operate, it cannot exist at all for any length of time; it can only fight.

"To remain separated as long as possible while operating and to be concentrated in good time for the decisive battle, that is the task of the leader of large masses of troops. . . . Little success can be expected from *mere frontal* attack, but very likely a great deal of loss. *We must therefore turn towards the flanks of the enemy's position.*"[2]

One serious matter which Moltke never tackled was the provision of the Prussian infantry with a more effective rifle than the Dreyse needle gun, which, although improved, had been retained

[1] *On War*, Carl von Clausewitz (English edit., 1908). The quotations in order will be found in: Vol. I, p. 33; vol. I, p. 23; vol. III, p. 121; vol. III, p. 122; vol. III, p. 123; vol. I, p. 1; vol. II, p. 288; vol. I, p. 4; vol. I, p. 42; vol. I, p. 253; vol. I, p. 16; vol. I, p. 40; vol. I, p. 207; vol. I, p. 231; vol. II, p. 341; vol. I, pp. 20–21; vol. I, p. 179; vol. I, p. 187; vol. II, p. 9; vol. II, p. 135; vol. III, p. 254; vol. I, p. 285; vol. I, p. 93; vol. I, p. 77, and vol. I, p. 121.
[2] Quoted from *The Development of Strategical Science during the 19th Century*, Lieut.-General von Cämmerer (English edit., 1905), p. 214.

since 1841. In the 1866 war it had been badly outranged by the Austrian muzzle-loading Lorenz rifle, but because of its quicker loading in the prone position it had proved itself the superior weapon. Nevertheless, much of its superiority could have been discounted had the Austrians made better use of the rifled field gun they had adopted in 1863, for it had an effective case shot range of 500 yards, which was as great as the effective range of the needle gun. This was appreciated by Moltke, and as he knew that the French infantry were armed with the *Chassepot* breech-loading rifle, which was sighted to 1,200 m., that is twice the sighting of the needle gun, he hoped to make good the deficiency of the latter by means of the superiority of the Prussian iron breech-loading field gun over the French bronze muzzle-loader. The latter had been retained by the French because they had a secret weapon up their tactical sleeve. It was Reffeye's *mitrailleuse*, a machine gun of 25 barrels, axis grouped, which was sighted to 1,200 m., and could fire 125 rounds a minute. It was planned to use it to replace case shot, but it was kept so secret that it was not issued to the army until a few days before the outbreak of war, and according to Reffeye was then used "in a perfectly idiotic fashion."

The main weakness and strength of the two armies lay not in their armaments, but in their respective General Staffs. In the French, as we have seen, the lack of an efficient General Staff was one of the main causes of Napoleon I's ultimate ruin. This was little appreciated in France after 1815, and when war broke out in 1870 we find that the officers of the General Staff of the Second Empire were mere popinjays and clerks, either young "bloods" out of touch with the army or greybeards overwhelmed by the minutiae of routine. So far did Marshal Bazaine distrust his General Staff that he forbade its officers to appear on the battlefield, and instead of them he used his Personal Staff, as Napoleon had done 60 years before. And this in spite of the fact that, on February 25, 1868, Stoffel had reported:

"But of all the elements of superiority which Prussia, in case war broke out, would possess, the greatest and the most undeniable will be that she will obtain from the composition of her corps of staff officers . . . ours cannot be compared with it. . . . The composition of the Prussian staff will, in the next war, constitute the most formidable element of superiority in favour of the Prussian Army."[1]

---

[1] *Military Reports*, pp. 48, 56.

Since the days when Scharnhorst and Massenbach first organized an intelligence staff and systematized staff duties, the Prussian General Staff had developed so rapidly that by 1866 its authority had become paramount. Thus in 1870 we find that, in order of responsibilities, Moltke, the Chief of the General Staff, took precedence over the Commander-in-Chief – the King. From this it followed that, as the supreme command became less personal, more and more initiative was transferred from the Commander-in-Chief to the subordinate army and corps commanders, with the result that unity of doctrine became all-important in order to harmonize the actions of these subordinate officers. In brief, the art of war became mechanical and doctrinaire.

The routine character of staff command is explained as follows by General von Verdy du Vernois.[1] Every morning, under the chairmanship of the Chief-of-Staff, a staff conference was held at which the situation was discussed and decisions were made. These were then taken to the King and, if approved by him, were dispatched to the subordinate commanders concerned.

This clockwork system of command had an important defect: it took little or no account of the unexpected; it left local decisions in the hands of those on the spot, which at times was apt to throw the general plan out of gear.

The Prussian General Staff plan of war was first prepared in 1867, since when it had been constantly revised. It was in character highly offensive and in idea simplicity itself – general direction, Paris; objective, the enemy wherever met. Three armies were to be employed:

First Army, General von Steinmetz, the VIIth and VIIIth Corps and one cavalry division; 60,000 men.

Second Army, Prince Frederick Charles, the IIIrd, IVth and Xth Corps, Guards and two divisions of cavalry; 131,000.

Third Army, Crown Prince of Prussia, the Vth and XIth Prussian and Ist and IInd Bavarian Corps, the Württemberg and Baden Divisions, and one cavalry division; 130,000.

Reserve, under the King of Prussia, the IXth Corps and XIIth Saxon Corps; 60,000 at Mainz.

Besides these, the Ist, IInd and IVth Corps, one Regular

---

[1] See *With the Royal Headquarters in 1870–1871*, J. von Verdy du Vernois (English edit., 1897), vol. I, pp. 30–31. A full account of the Prussian General Staff is given in *The German General Staff*, Walter Görlitz (English edit., 1953).

division and four *Landwehr* divisions were held back to watch the Danish coast and the Austrian frontier.

Moltke reckoned correctly that the French would not be able to bring into the field more than 250,000 men against his 381,000, and that, because of railway communications, they would be compelled to assemble their forces about Metz and Strasbourg, which meant that they would be separated by the Vosges. He decided therefore to assemble his three armies behind the fortresses of the middle Rhine; the First about Wittlich, the Third near Landau and Rastatt, and the Second between Homburg and Neuenkirchen to act as a connecting link between the First and Third. Then, should the French attempt an *attaque brusquée* before they were completely mobilized, which he suspected they would do, he reckoned that, because their two army groups would be separated by the Vosges, he would be in a position to reinforce either his centre or flanks more rapidly than these two groups could be brought together either in Lorraine or in Alsace. Of his intention he says:

"But above all the plan of war was based on the resolve to attack the enemy at once, wherever found, and keep the German forces so compact that a superior force could always be brought into the field. By whatever special means these plans were to be accomplished was left to the decision of the hour; the advance to the frontiers alone was pre-ordained in every detail."[1]

Opposed to this plan was the French Emperor's, which may be described as bastard Napoleonic, for though it looked well on paper it was so highly speculative as to be in fact suicidal. Marshal Leboeuf, Minister of War, had calculated – or rather guessed – that on the ninth day of mobilization 150,000 men could be assembled in Lorraine and 100,000 in Alsace, and that this total could rapidly be brought up to 300,000. Because the Emperor knew that the Prussian army would outnumber him by approximately 100,000, he decided on an *attaque brusquée* before his own mobilization was completed. Fixed in his mind was the idea that a sudden attack eastward would force the south German States to desert Prussia and would bring Austria and possibly also Italy to his support. He decided therefore to assemble 150,000 men at Metz, 100,000 at Strasbourg and 50,000 at Châlons, move forward the first two, unite them, cross the Rhine, force neutrality upon

[1] *The Franco-German War of 1870–71*, Field-Marshal Count Helmuth von Moltke (English edit., 1891), pp. 10–11.

the south German States, link up with Austria, and then move *via* Jena on Berlin, while his fleet threatened the Elbe and the Baltic.

This grandiose scheme obviously demanded the most careful preparation and timing; yet directly war was declared complete chaos reigned while Prussian mobilization worked like a well-regulated clock. Nothing had been arranged; camps were not pitched because no one knew where the tents were; railway time tables had not been made out; some formations had no guns, others no transport, still others no ambulances; magazines were found unstocked and fortresses unsupplied. On August 10, the day Count Palikao was called to Paris to be Minister of War,[1] he received a letter from a general at the front informing him:

"In the supply depôts no camp-kettles, dishes or stoves; no canteens for the ambulances and no pack-saddles; in short no ambulances neither for divisions nor corps. Up to the 7th it was all but impossible to obtain a mule-litter for the wounded. That day thousands of wounded men were left in the hands of the enemy; no preparations had been made to get them away. . . . If for four days our soldiers lived on the charity of the inhabitants, if our roads are littered with stragglers dying of hunger, it is the administration which is to blame. . . . On the 6th an order was given to blow up a bridge, no powder could be found in the whole army corps, nor with the engineers, nor with the gunners!"[2]

As confusion became worse confounded the idea of invading southern Germany was abandoned and the fleet sailed for the Elbe without troops. The scattered state of the corps[3] finally persuaded the Emperor to form them into two armies – the Ist Corps and a division of the VIIth, 35,000 men under Marshal MacMahon about Strasbourg; and the IInd, IIIrd, IVth, and Vth with the Guard, 128,000 men known as the Army of the Rhine, about Metz under his own control. The VIth Corps, of 35,000 men, under Marshal Canrobert, was to remain in reserve at Châlons, and the remainder of the VIIth was left at Belfort to watch the exits of the Black Forest. When, on July 28, the Emperor took over the supreme command, not a single corps was ready to take the field.

[1] Marshal Leboeuf had gone forward with the Emperor.
[2] *Un ministère de la guerre de 24 jours*, Palikao, pp. 57–59.
[3] There were nominally seven army corps and the Guard, but the VIth and VIIth Corps were never united. They were Ist (MacMahon) at Strasbourg; IInd (Frossard) at Forbach; IIIrd (Bazaine) at St. Avold; IVth (Palikao) at Lyons; Vth (de Failly) at Bitche; VIth (Canrobert) at Châlons; VIIth (Félix Douay) at Belfort and Colmar; and the Guard (Boubaki) at Metz.

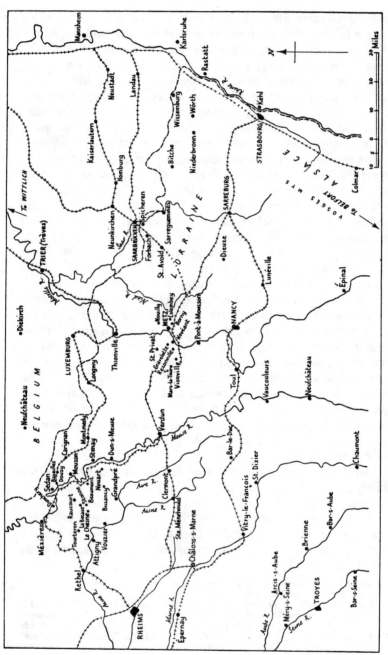

7. THE FRANCO-PRUSSIAN WAR, 1870–1871

Hesitation at once handed strategy over to the Paris mob. The boulevards were thronged, and shouts were raised demanding the instant invasion of Germany. This clamour forced the Emperor's hand, and on August 1 he initiated a movement on the Saar, which was entrusted to Marshal Bazaine. Besides his own corps, the IIIrd, Bazaine had under his orders the IInd and Vth. He pushed the Vth (de Failly) forward, and on August 2, when it came up against a detachment of the VIIIth Corps of the First Prussian Army at Saarbrücken, the latter fell back. Thereupon Moltke instructed Steinmetz to concentrate his army toward the Second Army, and at the same time he ordered the Third Army to cross the frontier and prevent the French from transferring troops from Alsace to Lorraine.

On August 3, Marshal MacMahon occupied Weissemburg with one division under Abel Douay who, unconscious of the approach of the Third Prussian Army, was surprised on the following day while in bivouac. Douay was killed, and his division fell back to join MacMahon near Wörth, where MacMahon was able to assemble some 32,000 infantry and 4,500 cavalry. On the 5th, the Third Army, with 72,000 infantry and 4,500 cavalry, came up with him. Vaguely informed of his enemy's strength, MacMahon planned an advance on the 7th, and the Crown Prince, whose army was scattered, decided to postpone his attack until he had concentrated his corps. This was not to be, for a clash between outposts early on August 6 involved the IInd Bavarian and Vth Prussian Corps and precipitated the battle of Wörth. It was the first major engagement of the war, and although the German attacks were disjointed, the French, after they had displayed their traditional valour, were unable to withstand the superiority of numbers brought against them, were forced back, and hurriedly withdrew through the Vosges to Neufchâteau, which they reached on August 14. From there by rail MacMahon's group was sent to Châlons, where it arrived on August 19. In this unlooked for battle each side lost between 10,000 and 11,000 in killed and wounded, and the Third Army was so unprepared to fight it that there was no pursuit.

Before the battle of Wörth was fought, Moltke's intention was that the First and Second Armies should concentrate behind the Saar on August 6 and pause there until the Third Army had secured the passages of the Vosges. But when he learnt of the action at Saarbrücken, the impetuous Steinmetz pushed ahead towards it, as also did the leading troops of Prince Frederick Charles's Second Army. At the time Saarbrücken was occupied by Frossard's IInd Corps, but when Frossard learnt of Douay's disaster at Weissemburg he considered his position too exposed and, on August 5, fell back to the heights of Spicheren, a few miles to the south-west. Early on August 6 the advanced cavalry of the Second Army drew fire from Frossard's outposts, and shortly afterwards General von Kameke's 14th Division came up. As Kameke felt sure of support and believed that he was faced by no more than a rearguard, he did not wait for orders but sent a single brigade forward to storm the Rotherberg in the centre of Frossard's position. This it did and, again as at Wörth, the battle started before the Prussians were ready. Nevertheless, as successive bodies of troops arrived on the field, Kameke was able to hold fast to the Rotherberg and Frossard, who believed that he was outnumbered – which he was not – ordered a retreat. Again there was no pursuit, because the Prussian cavalry were far behind. Spicheren cost the French nearly 4,000 killed and wounded and the Prussians about 5,000.

These two disasters, Spicheren and Wörth, threw the Imperial headquarters at Metz into panic, and an order was issued to fall back on Châlons. When this became known in Paris the Government, under the regency of the Empress, declared that, should the army retire, the capital would revolt. Accordingly, on August 9 the plan was changed, and all troops east of Metz were ordered to halt, while Metz was to be held at all costs. This caused a separation of forces, for whereas Bazaine halted, MacMahon was in the process of falling back.

The same day the Ollivier Ministry fell and the Imperialist Party, headed by the Empress, handed over the Government to General Count Palikao, who at the outbreak of the war had been in command of the IVth Army Corps at Lyons. On the following day, August 10, he took over the direction of the war, and from then onward strategy became the creature of politics. His "Apology", published in 1871, is illuminating, for it shows the total incapacity of a weakly led democratic assembly to conduct a war. For instance, he tells us that each morning at eight o'clock a Council of Ministers was held at which interminable discussions took place. On August 9 it was agreed to raise 500,000 soldiers in eight days, and on the 10th fear was expressed that, should they be armed, they might prove more dangerous than the Prussians.

On the 11th a resolution was passed to sacrifice the last *écu* and the last man, and on the 18th and 23rd M. Jules Favre was still shouting: "It is weapons we need!" Whereupon the Left yelled: "Arms! Arms!" for their sole aim was to overthrow the Government.[1] Such was the political instrument directing operations.

On August 12 the Emperor, although he remained with the army, handed over the supreme command to Marshal Bazaine. This change was made at a critical moment, because on the 13th Steinmetz's First Army, on the Prussian right, reached the river Nied, east of Metz; Frederick Charles's Second Army secured a bridgehead over the Moselle at Pont-à-Mousson, and the advanced guards of the Crown Prince's Third Army were approaching Nancy and Lunéville. All three armies were converging on Bazaine from the east and south, and although he was far from fully aware of this, he decided, when he learnt that Metz was badly provisioned, to abandon the line of the Moselle and fall back to the Meuse about Verdun.

To facilitate this withdrawal he ordered bridges to be thrown over the Moselle, but unfortunately for him heavy rain flooded the river and swept away several, with the result that on August 14 the greater part of his army was still east of Metz. There it was attacked at Colombey and Borny by Steinmetz's VIIth Corps, but under cover of night it succeeded in crossing the Moselle and in taking up a position astride the Metz-Verdun road facing south-west. This meant that, unless the Prussians were defeated, the withdrawal to Verdun would have to be abandoned and that the only line of retreat left open would be by way of the Metz-Briey-Montmédy road, which led either to Rethel or to Sedan. The truth is that Bazaine was already more than half cornered, although at the time he was unaware of it; he could not continue his withdrawal without a fight and to attempt to withdraw by the Metz-Montmédy road, which would entail a flank march in face of a victorious enemy, was to say the least a most hazardous operation.

While Bazaine marshalled his army, the 5th Cavalry Division of Frederick Charles's Second Army crossed the Moselle at Pont-à-Mousson and on August 15 came into contact with French cavalry near Vionville and Rezonville. By nightfall the Xth Corps was also across the Moselle at Pont-à-Mousson and the IIIrd Corps at Novéant. On the following day at 9 a.m. a violent

[1] *Ibid.*, pp. 68, 138, 141, 142, and 144.

attack by von Alversleben's IIIrd Corps precipitated the battle of Vionville, also called Mars-la-Tour. It was a desperately fought engagement, in which at times the Prussians were hard pressed, and though it ended in a draw it was for Moltke strategically

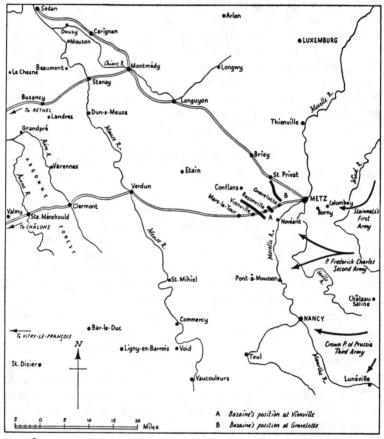

8. BATTLES OF VIONVILLE AND GRAVELOTTE, 1870

decisive, because it compelled Bazaine to abandon all further idea of withdrawing to the Meuse. Instead, he ordered his army to fall back on a strong position between St. Privat and Gravelotte, to the north-west and west of Metz. The losses in the battle were about 16,000 on either side.

On August 17 Bazaine's withdrawal was carried out without interference. Moltke was engaged in bringing up the whole of his

First and Second Armies, less the IVth Corps, which was on its way towards Toul to form a connecting link with the Third Army. On the next day the great battle of Gravelotte, also called St. Privat, was fought between 200,000 Prussians and 140,000 French. As at Valmy in 1792 each army faced its base, which meant disaster for the defeated. The action was hotly contested, but in the late afternoon the Prussians succeeded in turning the French right by storming St. Privat and Bazaine was forced to retire within the fortifications of Metz. He thus separated his army from Paris and MacMahon who, on the 16th, had been joined by the Emperor. Gravelotte was the most bloody battle of the war; the Prussians lost more than 20,000 in killed and wounded, and the French about 13,000 besides 5,000 prisoners.

The original Prussian plan of campaign had not provided for the withdrawal of the main French army to Metz, only the invest-ment of the fortress by a number of *Landwehr* divisions. As this unexpected withdrawal demanded the formation of an army of investment, the whole of the First Army and the bulk of the Second, 150,000 troops in all, were placed under the command of Prince Frederick Charles, who was instructed to pin Bazaine down to his fortifications.

The Third Army, now 85,000 strong, remained under the Crown Prince of Prussia; and the Guard, IVth and XIIth (Saxons) Corps, of 138,000 men, were formed into the Army of the Meuse under command of the Crown Prince of Saxony. On August 20 the latter, on a broad front between Briey and Com-mercy, advanced on Verdun and the advanced guards of the former crossed the Meuse at Void and pushed forward toward Ligny-en-Barrois and Bar-le-Duc. Both were moving on Paris in order to compel the French to accept battle east of their capital. On the 23rd the Army of the Meuse reached the right bank of the Meuse about Verdun, failed to seize that fortress by a *coup-de-main*, and pushed out its advanced cavalry to Clermont and Ste. Ménehould.

Meanwhile at Châlons Marshal MacMahon was instructed to form a new army, to be known as the Army of Châlons, and this he did on August 18–20. It was a heterogeneous force consisting of the Ist Corps (Ducrot) 32,000 men; the Vth (de Failly) 22,000; the VIIth (Félix Douay) 22,000; the XIIth (Lebrun) 41,000, and two divisions of cavalry. Besides these there were some newly formed infantry divisions, a corps of marines, refugees from Wörth and a number of Parisian *Gardes Mobiles*, then in a state of mutiny. In all this army comprised 166 battalions, 100 squadrons and 380 guns and totalled 130,000 men. Many of its units were so untrained that General Lebrun informs us he allotted five rounds to each of his men to enable the officers and non-commissioned officers to show them how to load and sight their rifles.[1]

At Châlons MacMahon decided to fall back on Paris, and in this he was supported by General Trochu, who arrived there on August 16 to take over command of the XIIIth Corps, then forming. On August 10 Trochu had written to a confidant of the Emperor that Bazaine's army ought to fall back on Paris, and although the Emperor agreed, Palikao had cancelled the movement.[2] On the 17th, the day after the Emperor arrived from Metz, a conference was held at which it was decided that, as he had handed over the supreme command to Bazaine, he should return to Paris and take charge of the government. This he agreed to do, and appointed Trochu Governor of Paris. Next he ordered him to return to the capital and announce his own arrival, while MacMahon fell back on Paris. Trochu then set out on his return journey.[3]

He arrived in Paris on the night of August 18 and was at once received by the Empress who, when she had learnt the import of his mission, exclaimed: "General, only the enemies of the Emperor can have counselled him to return to Paris; he will not enter the Tuileries alive. . . . No, General, the Emperor must not enter Paris, he must remain at Châlons . . . and you will defend Paris; you will fulfil your mission without the Emperor."[4]

After some hesitation Trochu agreed. He presented himself to Palikao, but was badly received. He was informed that his strategical ideas were absurd, and that under no consideration would Palikao agree to MacMahon retiring on Paris.[5] From then on every obstacle was placed in Trochu's way.

While Trochu was on his mission, MacMahon prepared to withdraw, and on August 21 fell back to Rheims, his men straggling over the countryside and antagonizing the inhabitants. On the 22nd the army remained at Rheims, and during the halt M. Rouher, President of the Senate and an envoy of Palikao's,

[1] *Bazeilles-Sedan*, le Général Lebrun (1884), p. 9.
[2] *Une page d'histoire contemporaine*, Trochu (1871), pp. 28–29.
[3] *Ibid.*, pp. 31–33. See also *Bazeilles-Sedan*, Lebrun, pp. 3–4.
[4] *Une page d'histoire contemporaine*, Trochu, pp. 34–35.
[5] *Ibid.*, pp. 36–37 and 42–45.

arrived at Imperial Headquarters to persuade the Emperor not to return to Paris and to urge him to instruct MacMahon to move on Metz. When this became known to MacMahon he telegraphed Paris: "How can I move towards Bazaine when I am in complete ignorance of his situation, and when I know nothing of his intentions?"[1]

As ill fortune would have it, no sooner had this message been dispatched than two telegrams came in. One, from Bazaine, said that he expected to retire in a northerly direction; the other, from the Regency Council, addressed to the Emperor, read: "Unanimous decision, more pressing than ever. . . . Not to support Bazaine will have the most deplorable consequences in Paris. Faced by this disaster, it is doubtful whether the capital can be defended." To this the Emperor replied: "Tomorrow we leave for Montmédy."[2] Therefore on August 23 the army moved to Bethiniville, its men scouring the countryside for supplies, and on the 24th to Rethel, where it remained over the 25th. On August 26 MacMahon advanced to Tourteron, and the next day to le-Chesne-Populeux, where he received information that the Crown Prince of Saxony had crossed the Vosges, advanced on Nancy and turned north-west. MacMahon ordered the following movements for the 28th: the XIIth Corps on La Becase, the Vth on Nouart or Buzancy, the VIIth on Stonne and the Ist on Raucourt.

While MacMahon was making his wide detour eastwards in order to slip past the right flank of his enemy and join hands with Bazaine, the Army of the Meuse and the Third Army advanced westward under orders to reach the line Vitry-St. Ménehould on August 26. The Prussian cavalry scoured the countryside in front of them and on August 24 entered Châlons to discover that it had been evacuated. Letters were picked up intimating that MacMahon was about to relieve Metz and that he was at Rheims with 150,000 men. This news surprised Moltke because he could not believe that his adversary would commit so flagrant an error as to uncover Paris and march across a hostile front with the Belgian frontier close to his left flank. But the next day the information was corroborated by a telegram from London, as well as by the Paris newspapers – particularly *Temps*, which kept nothing secret,[3] and on the 26th orders were issued to both armies to wheel northward. The same day the Prussian General Headquarters

---

[1] *Bazeilles-Sedan*, Lebrun, p. 39.   [2] Lavisse, vol. VII, p. 238.
[3] See *The Franco-German War*, Moltke, vol. I, p. 95.

moved from Bar-le-Duc to Clermont, and on the 27th the foremost corps, the XIIth (Saxons) of the Army of the Meuse was directed on Stenay and adopted a non-offensive attitude until the Third Army arrived. Two days later a French staff officer was captured while carrying MacMahon's orders to two of his corps. These furnished the Prussian Headquarters "with a complete confirmation of the movements of the French Army as they had been conjectured."[1] The four corps of the Third Army had now closed up; the 5th Cavalry Division was pushed forward to Attigny across the enemy's lines of communication, while the 6th followed on the heels of the French. The royal headquarters were moved to Grandpré and the decision was taken to attack the French the following day before they could cross the Meuse.[2] The Army of the Meuse was directed on Beaumont and the Third Army to between Beaumont and Le Chesne.

When he learnt that Bazaine had not moved from Metz and that two enemy armies were moving towards his communications, MacMahon abandoned his advance and ordered his army to withdraw to Mézières. On August 28 another urgent dispatch from Paris persuaded him to resume his march on Montmédy. By now these orders and counter-orders had completely demoralized his men. On the 30th, when contact was established with the enemy, de Failly's Vth Corps was surprised at Beaumont by the Prussian IVth Corps as its men were drawing their rations and its artillery horses were at water.[3] This surprise cost MacMahon some 5,000 men and 42 guns. He felt that he could no longer make headway and between eight and nine o'clock in the evening he ordered Lebrun to move his XIIth Corps to Sedan. He said to him: "This has been an unfortunate day . . . nevertheless the situation is not desperate. The German army which is before us numbers at most from sixty to seventy thousand men. If we are attacked so much the better, I expect to be able to drive them into the Meuse."[4] This miscalculation of his enemy's strength was to lead to his ruin.

That night Moltke issued the following orders:

"The forward movement is . . . to be continued tomorrow as early as possible, and the enemy to be vigorously attacked wherever he stands on this side [west] of the Meuse; he is to be squeezed

---

[1] See *With the Royal Headquarters*, Verdy du Vernois, vol. i, p. 116.
[2] *The Franco-German War*, Moltke, vol. i, p. 102.
[3] See *Bazeilles-Sedan*, Lebrun, p. 62.   [4] *Ibid.*, p. 74.

into the narrowest possible space between that river and the Belgian frontier.

"The army detachment of H.R.H. the Crown Prince of Saxony has the special task of preventing the enemy's left wing from escaping to the east. For this purpose it is advisable that, if possible, two corps should push forward on the right bank of the Meuse and attack in flank and rear any enemy posted opposite Mouzon.

"In the same way the Third Army is to deal with the enemy's front and flank. Artillery positions as strong as possible are to be taken on this bank so as to disturb the marching and encamping of enemy columns in the valley plain on the right bank from Mouzon downwards.

"If the enemy should pass on to Belgian territory without being at once disarmed he must be pursued thither without more ado."[1]

Meanwhile, in Algeria, Fate had placed her finger on the man destined to seal the French downfall.

At 8.35 p.m. on August 22 General de Wimpffen, in command of the troops at Oran, received a telegram from Palikao ordering him forthwith to Paris. He left by boat on August 24, disembarked at Marseilles on the 27th, and the next day at 8 p.m. arrived in the capital. He found Palikao engaged until midnight and did not see him until 1 p.m. the following day, when he was informed that Bazaine was attacking Prince Frederick Charles in front, while MacMahon had fallen on his rear![2] Palikao suggested that, as General Trochu *"cherche trop à grandir sa personnalité,"*[3] he wished de Wimpffen to replace him. De Wimpffen refused and instead was appointed to succeed de Failly in command of the Vth Corps. He was then handed a roll of maps of the wrong locality and, on the morning of August 29, as he was about to enter his railway carriage and leave for the front, a messenger rushed up and thrust into his hand the following letter signed by Palikao:

"In the event of Marshal MacMahon being incapacitated, you will take over the command of the troops actually placed under his orders. I will send you an official letter regulating this, which you will make use of as occasion demands."[4]

General de Wimpffen arrived at Rheims at midday. At Rethel, as the line was unsafe, he left for Mézière by carriage at 7 p.m.

[1] Moltke's *Military Correspondence*, Précis by Spenser Wilkinson (1923), p. 122.
[2] *Sedan*, le Général de Wimpffen (1871), p. 121.
[3] *Ibid.*, p. 122.   [4] *Ibid.*, p. 124.

and arrived there at 8 a.m. on August 30. From Mézières he took a train to Bazeilles, where complete chaos reigned. At 9 p.m. he heard that MacMahon was falling back on Sedan. At 1 a.m. on the 31st he entered Sedan to find it blocked with transport, and at 9 a.m. reported to MacMahon, who received him coldly. There followed a fracas with de Failly, who had heard nothing about his demission. De Wimpffen took over the command of his corps, but made no mention of the all-important letter.

As the two Prussian armies pushed on in accordance with the instructions already quoted, the Army of Châlons straggled into Sedan. The Emperor had arrived there the previous evening and, without consulting MacMahon, had fortunately counter-ordered the advance of the newly formed XIIIth Corps from Mézières to Sedan. When MacMahon's corps entered the fortress the XIIth (Lebrun) was instructed to hold Bazeilles and the hills facing La Moncelle and Daigny, with the Ist (Ducrot) on its left, facing Givonne; while the VIIth (Félix Douay) occupied Illy and the Vth (de Failly) was held in reserve.

Sedan was badly supplied. There were no more than 200,000 rations in store and a train which brought in 800,000 more encountered shell fire and was ordered back to Mézières before it could be unloaded.[1] The truth would appear to be that only MacMahon imagined that the Army would remain in Sedan, for as Lebrun says, it was a "*nid à bombes.*" Verdy du Vernois describes it as follows:

"The town itself lay before us as on a tray, so that we could even look into its streets. Several very large buildings and churches gave it quite an important look, while the clearly defined lines of the fortifications around it enclosed the whole as in a frame. Behind the town there rose gradually from the plain a line of hills, on the slopes of which a large French encampment was visible, in which there was much stir; on its crest, which descended to the left of the plain, was a wood. The lines of the distant hills beyond formed part of the neighbouring state."[2]

On the morning of August 31 Bavarian troops of the Third Army, imbued with the spirit of the offensive, crossed the Meuse by a pontoon as well as by the railway bridge south of Bazeilles, but were driven back by Lebrun's XIIth Corps. The second of

---

[1] *Histoire de la Guerre de 1870–1871*, Pierre Lehautcourt (Palat) (1907), vol. VI, p. 492.
[2] *With the Royal Headquarters*, Verdy du Vernois, vol. I, p. 127.

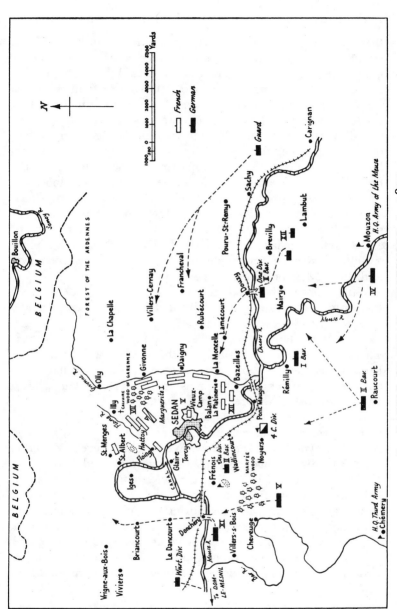

9. BATTLE OF SEDAN, SEPTEMBER 1, 1870

these bridges had not been blown, apparently because MacMahon intended to use it in his proposed advance on Metz; but when at 5 p.m. he finally ordered Lebrun to demolish it, the powder proved to be wet, and before more could arrive from Sedan the bridge was reoccupied by the enemy.[1] Much the same thing happened with the bridges at Douzy and Donchéry. Orders were issued for the demolition of the former, but no one carried them out; a party of engineers were sent out from Sedan to destroy the latter, but while they were inspecting it the train which had brought them steamed off to Mézières with their tools and powder![2] Everywhere confusion reigned. When General Douay set about to entrench his position, MacMahon stopped him and said: "What, entrenching! But I do not intend to shut myself up as in Metz, I mean to manœuvre." To which Douay replied: "Will they give you time to do so?"[3] MacMahon then rode away and spent hours on inspections and routine.

Little wonder that that evening Ducrot was in despair. He turned to Dr. Sarazin and exclaimed: "*Nous sommes dans un pot de chambre et nous y serons emmerdés.*"[4] At 8 p.m. General Douay asked General Doutrelaine: "Well, what do you think of the situation?" To which Doutrelaine replied: "I think, General, we are lost." Douay was silent for a moment, then rejoined: "That is my opinion . . . nothing now remains, my dear Doutrelaine, but to do our best before we are overwhelmed."[5]

That night Paul Déroulède, a private soldier in the 3rd Zouaves, wrote a brief pencil note to his mother: "Sedan, August 31, 1870. A battle will be fought tomorrow. Eve of Jena, or eve of Waterloo, which? God alone knows. I kiss and love you, Paul."[6]

Moltke could not believe that MacMahon intended to accept battle in so unfavourable a position and thought that he would either fall back on Mézières during the night, or advance on Carignan, or retire over the Belgian frontier. Yet he issued no orders and left it to his two army commanders to continue their advance on the lines laid down in his directive of the 30th. The Crown Prince decided upon the following arrangements for his Third Army:

---

[1] *Bazeilles-Sedan*, Lebrun, pp. 88–89. See also *Belfort, Reims, Sedan*, le Prince Bibesco, p. 128.
[2] *Histoire de la Guerre de 1870–1871*, Palat, vol. VI, p. 484.
[3] *Ibid.*, p. 496.
[4] *Récits sur la dernière guerre franco-allemande*, Docteur Sarazin (1887), p. 115.
[5] *Belfort, Reims, Sedan*, Bibesco, p. 132.
[6] *1870–Feuilles de Route*, Paul Déroulède, pp. 175–176.

XIth and Vth Corps to move at dawn *via* Donchéry on Vrigne-aux-Bois.

The Württemberg Division to cross the Meuse at Dom-la-Mesnil and come into reserve.

The IInd Bavarian Corps to advance one division to the south of Douzy and the other to between Frénois and Wadlincourt.

The Ist Bavarian Corps to remain at Remilly and cooperate with the left of the Army of the Meuse.

The Crown Prince of Saxony's orders for the Army of the Meuse were:

One division of the Guard to move on Villers-Cernay and the other on Francheval.

The XIIth Corps to move by Lamécourt on la Moncelle.

The IVth Corps to send one division to Remilly to cooperate with the Ist Bavarian Corps, and the other to be held in reserve at Mairy.[1]

The Army of Châlons had by now fully occupied the triangle between the rivers Meuse, Floing and Givonne. The XIIth Corps (right wing) occupied Balan, Bazeilles, la Moncelle and la Platinerie; the VIIth Corps (left wing) stretched from Floing to Illy; and the Ist Corps (centre)-linked these two wings together, while the Vth was held in reserve at Vieux-Camp. Unfortunately for the French, during the night of August 31, and contrary to orders, the outposts of the XIIth Corps had fallen back from the Meuse and Bazeilles. This enabled General von der Tann, commander of the Ist Bavarian Corps, to cross by the railway bridge at 4 a.m. on September 1, under cover of a dense fog, and penetrate as far as Bazeilles.[2] There the French gallantly counter-attacked and his Bavarians were driven back. Meanwhile, the Saxons advanced on la Moncelle, only to be checked by the French skirmishers, and at 8 a.m. the Saxon artillery, by then reinforced, silenced their opponents' batteries.

At about 7 a.m.,[3] as this action was being fought, Marshal MacMahon was so severely wounded by a shell fragment while visiting the XIIth Corps that he relinquished his command and appointed General Ducrot to succeed him. About 8 a.m. Ducrot received this information, and as he knew nothing of MacMahon's plan, nor had received any instructions from him, he at once took

---

[1] See *The Franco-German War, 1870–1871* (German Official Account, English trans. 1881–1884), vol. II, part I, pp. 307–309.
[2] *Ibid.*, p. 312.   [3] *Bazeilles-Sedan*, Lebrun, p. 100.

action. From the first he had been opposed to accepting battle in so unfavourable a position, and when the news of his appointment reached him he was watching strong enemy columns moving north-west to turn the left flank of his corps. He turned to his Staff and exclaimed: "Gentlemen, I have been placed in supreme command. We have not a moment to lose. We must at once withdraw to the plateau of Illy. When we are there our retreat will be assured, and we can then make up our minds what to do."[1] His chief of staff suggested that the Emperor should first be informed of this change, whereupon Ducrot turned on him and shouted: *"Que l'Empereur aille se faire f—— ou il voudra,* it is he who has put us in this mess."[2]

At once he sent orders to his own corps, the Ist, and to Lebrun's, the XIIth, to disengage and fall back on Illy, preparatory to a withdrawal on Mézières. Lebrun at first demurred, and then, at 9 a.m., began to evacuate Bazeilles. By 10 a.m. the Bavarian advance was eased, and before 11 o'clock the village was in their hands.

Now took place an event rare in history. The Army of Châlons had had two commanders-in-chief within three hours of the opening of the battle; now it was about to have a third – General de Wimpffen, at the time in command of the Vth Corps at Vieux-Camp. At 7.15 a.m. he had heard that Marshal MacMahon was wounded[3] and a little over an hour later that Ducrot was in command;[4] yet he had made no use of Palikao's letter. At about 8.30 a.m. he visited General Lebrun, and as he believed that the repulse of the Bavarians meant a French victory he was furious to learn soon after that Ducrot had ordered a withdrawal. Pulling out his letter of commission he proclaimed himself commander-in-chief, turned to Lebrun and exclaimed: "Stop forthwith the movement General Ducrot has ordered you to carry out. . . . I will not have a retirement on Mézières. If the army is to retire it is to be on Carignan and not on Mézières."[5] He then wrote a hasty note to Ducrot informing him that he was superseded.[6]

---

[1] *Sedan,* Ernest Picard (1912), p. 33 (Déposition Ducrot). In *La Journée de Sedan,* Ducrot (1871), a slightly different version is given.
[2] *La Guerre de 1870–71* (French Official History, 1901), vol. III, p. 55.
[3] *Sedan,* Wimpffen, p. 158.
[4] *La Guerre de 1870–71* (French Official History), vol. III, p. 66, and *Bazeilles-Sedan,* p. 110.
[5] *Bazeilles–Sedan,* Lebrun, pp. 111–112.
[6] See *La Journée de Sedan,* Ducrot, pp. 28–29, and *Sedan,* Wimpffen, p. 162. The latter is unreliable, several words in the original document are changed.

Ducrot, on receipt of it, galloped to de Wimpffen's corps and in conversation with him discovered his ignorance of the field of battle to be so profound that he did not know what Illy was.[1] De Wimpffen counter-ordered the withdrawal and at 10.30 a.m. met the Emperor who, when informed of its cancellation, became greatly agitated. "Your Majesty need have no fears," said de Wimpffen. "Within two hours from now we shall have thrust the enemy into the Meuse."[2]

The Crown Prince of Saxony was engaged on the Givonne. At 7.30 a.m. King William and his Staff rode over to the small hill south-west of Frénois to watch the advance of the Third Army, which had marched out of its bivouacs at 3 a.m. The XIth Corps had crossed the Meuse at Donchéry and was marching on the sound of the guns. The road was good and its advanced guard, meeting no opposition, passed through the defile of St. Albert and occupied St. Menges. At 10 a.m. seven of its battalions began to form front against Illy and these were soon supported by 62 guns from the rise of Hattoy. So devastating was their fire that General Marguerite ordered General Galliffet to charge the enemy infantry then approaching Illy. He most gallantly did so, and was driven back at great loss.

When this advance was reported to General de Wimpffen he began to realize his danger, but worse was to follow. The Crown Prince's Vth Corps, which had advanced close on the heels of the XIth, brought up 60 guns to the wood of Hattoy to support the 84 of the XIth Corps then in action. The fire of these two groups crossed that of the guns of the Army of the Meuse and demolished the French batteries. Half an hour later the left of the Third Army and the right of the Army of the Meuse made contact near Illy and the French forces were surrounded.

The King, Bismarck, Moltke, Roon, princes, dukes, gunners and aides-de-camp now gathered on the hill by Frénois. They were joined by Colonel Walker, the English military plenipotentiary, and General Sheridan of Five Forks fame.

"About 11 o'clock," writes Moritz Busch, "there rises from the fortress, which, by the way, is not firing, a black, grey pillar of smoke, edged with yellow. Beyond it the French are firing furiously, and above the wood of the gorge rise unceasingly a

[1] *La Journée de Sedan*, Ducrot, pp. 30–31.
[2] *Ibid.*, p. 32. See also *Histoire de la Guerre de 1870–71*, Palat, vol. VI, p. 546, for a slightly different version.

number of little white clouds from bombs, whether German or French we know not; sometimes also the cracking and snarling of a *mitrailleuse*."[1]

While the Third Army was enveloping the French left, the Prussian Guard, who had entered Villers-Cernay at 8 a.m., moved round the left of the French Ist Corps and brought into action 120 guns on the enemy batteries west of the Givonne. Once again this concentration of fire proved overwhelming; it drove the French infantry into the wood of Garenne, already crowded with fugitives. At 10 a.m. the Saxons carried Daigny and brought up 29 batteries at the gallop. At this phase of the battle, writes Prince Hohenlohe, "the effect of their combined fire at such a short range was truly terrible. . . . The spectacle of the carnage was horrible; the fearful cries of the victims of our shells reached as far as where we stood . . . our superiority over the enemy was so overwhelming that we suffered no loss at all. The batteries fired as if at practice."[2]

"It was now one o'clock," continues Busch. "Our line of fire by this time swept the larger half of the enemy's position on the heights on the other side of the town. . . . Between two and three o'clock by my watch, the King came close past the place where I was standing, and said to the people about him, after looking for some time through a glass towards the suburb: 'They are pushing great masses forward there to the left – that, I think, must be an attempt to break through'."[3]

He was right: General Marguerite's cavalry division was preparing to attack Floing. At about 2 p.m. Ducrot, who realized that the position was desperate, rode over to Marguerite and implored him to blaze a trail through the enemy for his infantry to follow. He at once agreed but was mortally wounded while reconnoitring. Galliffet took over command and three charges were made. In spite of the heroism shown, each failed, but Galliffet, accompanied by a few officers and chasseurs, penetrated to the enemy reserves. On their return, when they were within pistol-shot of a Prussian battalion, its commander was so filled with admiration that he ordered the cease fire. The French troopers shouted "*Vive l'Empereur!*" at which the German officers saluted as they galloped past.[4]

---

[1] *Bismarck in the Franco-German War*, Busch (1879), vol. I, p. 97.
[2] *Letters on Artillery*, Prince Kraft zu Hohenlohe-Ingelfingen (English edit., 1890), pp. 93, 94.
[3] *Bismarck in the Franco-German War*, vol. I, pp. 98–99.
[4] See *Sedan*, Ernest Picard, pp. 108–109.

Although the doom of the Army of Châlons was now sealed, General de Wimpffen seemed oblivious of the true situation; at the moment when the enemy was storming the Calvaire d'Illy he sent the following message to General Douay:

"I have decided to smash my way through the enemy and reach Carignan in order to gain Montmédy. You are to cover the retreat. Rally around you all troops now in the wood [of Garenne]."[1]

The situation confronting Douay's VIIth Corps is described by Prince Bibesco as follows:

"The wrack of the rout is rolling towards the moats of Sedan, which are to swallow up the débris of our unfortunate army, consisting of fractions of all corps and all arms. From every point on the horizon shells are being fired which smite the maddened masses in front, in flank and in rear. Amidst shouts of fear mingled with groans, on our right an ambulance bursts into flames and is pulverized by shells. Around us artillery limbers explode to add to the number of the victims. Everywhere one can see singly and grouped together the riderless horses of our heroic cavalry – exhausted and bleeding."[2]

Between noon and 1 p.m. Lebrun's XIIth Corps held its own and the Bavarians failed to push beyond Bazeilles. In order to cut his way to Carignan, de Wimpffen decided to throw in the Vth Corps and hurl the enemy into the Meuse. To cover this desperate attempt he had sent his order to Douay and at the same time had instructed Ducrot to assemble his corps and march by way of la Moncelle on Bazeilles. At 1.30 p.m. he sent the following note to the Emperor:

"Sire, I have decided to force the line facing General Lebrun and General Ducrot rather than be taken prisoner in Sedan.

"I beg your Majesty to place yourself in the midst of your soldiers, so that they may have the honour of opening a way for your retreat."[3]

Louis Napoleon was in Sedan when this note was handed to him; he read it and rightly set the proposal aside. Instead, he considered reassuming the supreme command and capitulating.

While he pondered this last act of his reign Ducrot's corps dissolved and huddled in and around Sedan. As Ducrot entered the moat of the citadel an officer shouted: "The white flag is hoisted!"

[1] *Belfort–Reims–Sedan*, Bibesco, p. 154.
[2] *Ibid.*, p. 155.   [3] *Sedan*, Wimpffen, p. 170.

At that moment Ducrot received de Wimpffen's orders. He writes:

"Within Sedan the situation was indescribable: streets, open places and entrances were blocked with wagons, carts, cannon and and all the impedimenta and débris of a routed army. Bands of soldiers without rifles or equipment rushed here and there seeking refuge in the houses and the churches, while at the gates of the town they crushed each other to death. Athwart this rabble galloped troopers *ventre à terre*, and gunners on limbers lashed their way through the maddened mob. Such as were not completely insane had set to work to pillage, and others shouted: 'We have been betrayed, we have been sold by traitors and cowards!' "[1]

Ducrot presented himself to the Emperor, who exclaimed: "Why is the firing going on? I have hoisted the white flag." He bade Ducrot write a note ordering all fire to cease. Ducrot did so, but refused to sign it as de Wimpffen was commander-in-chief, and General Faure, chief of staff, also refused to sign.[2] The Emperor dictated another letter, this time for de Wimpffen, and gave it to Lebrun to take to him,[3] but the commander-in-chief refused to read it. Lebrun pointed out that the white flag had been hoisted. "No! No!" cried de Wimpffen, "I will have no capitulation. Haul the flag down. I intend to continue the battle."[4]

De Wimpffen hurried to Sedan, not to see the Emperor but to collect such men as he could for his counter-attack. With the idea of rousing the terror-stricken fugitives he shouted: "Bazaine approaches! Bazaine approaches!"[5] but although a few rallied round him, many skulked away. At length, when he had gathered some 1,200 men and two guns he headed them for Balan. It was the act of a madman. The band of heroic or demented men met a hail of bullets from both sides and ran howling back to the fortress. Whereupon de Wimpffen exclaimed to Lebrun: "I resign my appointment as general-in-chief; you will take my place!"[6]

Naturally Lebrun refused the honour, and at 6 p.m. the Emperor informed General Ducrot that he wished him to take over command. He refused, and so did General Douay. Thereupon de Wimpffen, wildly gesticulating, shouted: "Sire, if I have lost the battle, if I have been beaten, it is because my orders have not been carried out, it is because your generals have refused to obey me."[7]

[1] *La Journée de Sedan*, p. 46.　　[2] *La Journée de Sedan*, Ducrot, p. 48–51.
[3] *Bazeilles-Sedan*, Lebrun, p. 133.　　[4] *Ibid.*, p. 135.
[5] See *Sedan*, Picard, p. 147.　　[6] *Bazeilles–Sedan*, Lebrun, p. 141.
[7] *La Journée de Sedan*, Ducrot, p. 52.

Ducrot sprang to his feet and contradicted him and a wordy dispute followed. At length de Wimpffen accepted the inevitable and agreed to proceed to the enemy's headquarters and surrender the army.

Some time before this scene a Bavarian officer galloped up the hill of Frénois, where the royal headquarters were still established, and informed the King that the French had decided to capitulate. "About half past six, a guard of honour of cuirassiers appeared a little way off, and the French General, Reille, the bearer of Napoleon's flag of truce, rode slowly up the hill. He dismounted 10 paces from the King and went up to him, took off his cap and presented him with a letter bearing a large red seal."[1] The King opened it and read:

Monsieur mon Frère,

    N'ayant pu mourir au milieu de mes troupes, il ne me reste qu'à remettre mon epée entre les mains de Votre Majesté.

Je suis de Votre Majesté,
le bon Frère,
Napoléon.

Sédan, le 1er Septembre, 1870.

He conferred with his Chancellor, and then wrote a reply. General Reille, accompanied by an officer, and a Uhlan trumpeter carrying a white flag, then rode back to Sedan in the twilight. "The town was still blazing in three places, and the red lights flashing in the pillar of smoke rising over Bazeilles showed that the conflagration there was still raging. But for these signs the tragedy of Sedan was played out, and the curtain of night fell on the scene."[2]

The next morning, at about six o'clock, a voice called out in the passage of Doctor Jeanjot's house in Donchéry: "Your Excellency! Your Excellency! there is a French general [Reille] down here at the door; I don't understand what he wants." Bismarck leapt out of bed, hastily dressed and rode to Sedan. As soon as he could, Dr. Busch followed him to a solitary house, some 800 paces from the bridge over the Meuse at Donchéry: "a one-storied house, painted yellow, with four windows in front, white shutters on the ground floor, and on the first floor white venetian blinds." Busch then writes: "Soon afterwards a little thick-set man came

---

[1] *Bismarck in the Franco-German War*, Busch, vol. I, p. 101.
[2] *Ibid.*, vol. I, p. 102.

forward, behind the house, who wore a red cap with a gold border, a black patelot lined with red, with a hood, and red trousers. He spoke, first to the Frenchmen, some of whom were sitting on the bank near the potatoes. He wore white kid gloves, and was smoking a cigarette."[1]

It was the Emperor. He had surrendered himself to Prussia, but the capitulation of his army was left to General de Wimpffen. After a lengthy argument this resulted in an all but unconditional surrender.[2]

The losses in the two German armies were about 460 officers and 8,500 men killed and wounded,[3] and the French lost 3,000 killed, 14,000 wounded, and 21,000 prisoners;[4] which with 83,000 prisoners at the capitulation and 3,000 disarmed in Belgium made a total of 124,000. Also one eagle and two colours, 419 field guns and *mitrailleuses*, 139 garrison guns, 1,072 carriages and 6,000 serviceable horses were surrendered.

"The victory of Sedan," writes the German official historian, "crowns the united efforts of the German leaders and their men with a success almost unprecedented in history." These words are not exaggerated. He continues:

"With the defeat of an entire army the Napoleonic dynasty in France crumbles for the third time to the dust. Instantaneously as the lightning's flash, the startling intelligence spreads throughout the realms of Germany and through the whole of Europe, where it is received partly with sparkling enthusiasm and partly with incredulous astonishment. The German Army, however, in ignorance at first of the *political* consequences of the victory, casts, with the captive adversary at its feet, an anxious glance towards the French Capital."[5]

What went on in Paris on that fateful day?

At 10.35 a.m. the commander of the 1st Division of the XIIIth Corps at Mézières telegraphed to Palikao: "I am informed at this very instant that King William and his son, who slept last night at Clermont in Argonne, are in full retreat." Later came in a dispatch from Brussels, timed 7.25 p.m.: "MacMahon has this morning defeated the Prussians; this morning Bazaine was pur-

---

[1] *Ibid.*, vol. I, pp. 103–104.
[2] For the capitulation see *The German Official History* (1881–1884), vol. II, part I, pp. 402–409, and *The French Official History*, vol. III, pp. 242–273.
[3] For detail see *The German Official History*, Appendix I.
[4] *Ibid.*, vol. III, part I, p. 408. The official French figures are 799 officers killed and wounded, and 23,689 men killed, wounded and disappeared.
[5] *German Official History*, vol. II, part I, p. 416.

suing them towards Sedan"; which report was confirmed from London at 12.30 a.m. on September 2.[1]

Apparently the exchanges were busy rigging the stock-markets.

Then came de Wimpffen's letter to Palikao, beginning: "*Mon général,* – I can say: I came, I saw and I was defeated. . . ."[2] which threw Paris into revolution. On September 4 the Assembly was stormed by a rabble shouting "*Vive la sociale!*" Palikao fell, and Trochu, whom he had persistently frustrated, replaced him as head of the Government: the last lap and the longest of the war was now entered.

By the end of September Paris was surrounded, and while Metz, Belfort, Strasbourg, Toul, Verdun and Mézières held out, the Defense Nationale raised new armies. Then all the fortresses fell one by one, except Belfort, and on December 17 the bombardment of Paris was opened. On January 29, 1871, Paris capitulated. For over 200 years it had been the centre of European politics, Berlin took its place until 1918.

An event which preceded the capitulation by 11 days was equally important. On January 18, 1871, in the Hall of Mirrors in the Palace of Versailles, in the centre of which is painted "*Le Roi Gouverne Par Lui-Même,*" William I of Prussia was proclaimed Emperor of Germany. Thus did Wallenstein's dream of 240 years before come true. Equally historic, when the French garrison in Rome was withdrawn during the war, the Papal mercenaries laid down their arms before Victor Emmanuel. Thus was the national union of Italy accomplished, a task urged by Machiavelli upon the Italian princes three and a half centuries earlier.

Disorder followed on the surrender of Paris, and on March 18 came the Commune, in which 30,000 men, women and children perished in fratricidal strife. Finally, on May 10, the treaty of Frankfort was signed, and ratified by the National Assembly on the 18th. Its terms were moderate and in no way vindictive.[3]

---

[1] *Un Ministère de la Guerre*, etc., Palikao, pp. 74–75.   [2] *Ibid.*, p. 121.

[3] When in September, 1870, the *National Zeitung* complained of the considerate treatment accorded to the captive French Emperor, Bismarck by no means shared this view. "Popular feeling, public opinion," he said, "always take that line. People insist that, in conflicts between States, the conqueror should sit in judgment upon the conquered, moral code in hand, and inflict punishment upon him for what he has done, not only to the victor himself, but to third parties as well. This is an altogether unreasonable demand. Punishment and revenge have nothing to do with policy. Policy must not meddle with the calling of Nemesis, or aspire to exercise the judge's office. . . . In such a case as the one referred to, the question would be, 'Which of the two will be most useful to us – a badly-used Napoleon or a well-used Napoleon?' It is by no means impossible that he may one day rise to the surface again" (*Our Chancellor*, Moritz Busch, English edit., 1884, vol. I, pp. 98–99).

(*1*) The payment of an indemnity of £200,000,000.

(*2*) The right of Germany to be treated by France as the most favoured nation.

(*3*) The annexation of Alsace and Eastern Lorraine.

Although Leopold von Ranke and most Germans at the time justified the annexation of Alsace – an essentially German province – and of Eastern Lorraine – mainly French – it would have been wiser for Prussia to have foregone their strategical advantages and to have considered the political implications of their seizure. It not only humiliated a proud nation, but mortgaged the future, because from the Peace of Frankfort onward every foreign enemy of the German Empire would be able to count upon France as a potential if not an actual ally. Thus the annexation of Alsace-Lorraine became a festering sore in the peace of Europe.

What were the influences of this war on history?

The first was that, by humbling France – a humiliation from which she never recovered – it made Germany "Queen of the Continent."[1] The second was her upsurge of strength unhinged the balance of power in Europe and directly challenged the *Pax Britannica*, which had prevented the war from developing into a general European conflict. The third was that Britain was compelled to bring to an end her centuries old quarrel with France in order to re-establish the balance of power in regard to Germany. The fourth was that, when after the war Germany set out to become a leading industrial country, a quarrel with Great Britain over the markets of the world became inevitable. Henceforth there were to be only two really great military and commercial Powers in Europe proper, Britain who commanded the sea, and Germany who commanded the land, and, as in the days of Napoleon, although there was room enough in Europe for half-a-dozen great Powers to live in concord, there was insufficient room for two although neither desired war with the other. This ineluctable fact, which has dogged European history since the fall of Rome, established a general fear which through industrialization led to the militarization of Europe, until before the end of the nineteenth century all her continental nations, in varying degrees of efficiency, had become nations in arms. And because henceforth the words "military" and "political" were to become interchangeable, it is of no little importance briefly to consider the influences of the Franco-Prussian conflict on the art of war.

[1] Thomas Carlyle in a letter to *The Times*, November 11, 1870.

The first is the growing preponderance of artillery over infantry, which is seen throughout the war, and is well expressed by a French officer taken prisoner at Sedan, when he ascribed the German success to "five kilometres of artillery."[1] The preponderance of the cannon and all the technical requirements which followed in its wake gave a tremendous stimulus to science and industry, which began to become the material bases of war. As the cavalry age in war had given way to the infantry, so now was the infantry age giving way to that of artillery. War was to become more and more industrialized and industrial civilization demanded its military counterpart.

The second is the increasing influence of railways on military organization, and because of them the rapid development of mass-armies. Though the idea of the nation in arms dates back to Guibert and was expanded by Clausewitz, it was unrealizable until railways were built. It was the locomotive which regimented the nations, democratized their armies, and made peace a preparatory period for war.

The third is the increasing importance of the Staff system (business management). In so complex an instrument as a modern army its advantages are obvious; yet its dangers and defects were not appreciated, or at most very superficially so, once the war was at an end.

Guglielmo Ferrero in his essay *The Problem of Peace* points out that, between 1870 and 1914, war-making power and peace-making power, which formerly had been in the same hands, became separated; the one became the exclusive province of the General Staff and the other of civilians and diplomats. "But what could civilians and diplomats do," he writes, "when the old rules of the art of making peace were made inoperative by the new methods of making war? The soldiers perfected the technique of war; the diplomats lost the art of making peace. . . . Being unable to make peace, the diplomats in their turn began to prepare the way for war by making and unmaking alliances. Two Powers had signed the armistice of 1871, but when it was repudiated in 1914 it was two formidable groups of Powers that confronted one another, armed to the teeth."[2] In other words, the more perfect the technical side of war grew, the less possible did it become politically to limit

---

[1] Quoted from *Decisive Battles Since Waterloo*, Thomas W. Knox (1889), p. 358.
[2] *Peace and War* (1933), p. 132. To Ferrero the period 1870–1914 was an armistice and not a peace.

its radius, until the whole world became so explosive that a pistol shot in some obscure corner of it was sufficient to detonate a global war. In its turn, this foretold that national wars would give way to wars between coalitions, and that in the future, unless a nation was a partner of a coalition, its resources would prove insufficient to conduct successfully a war single-handed.

One point – the defects in the Prussian Staff system – introduces the question of generalship and command.

Moltke's famous maxim was "First reckon, then risk," and in this war the risks were not great, yet had he been faced by a normally good general assisted by a normally efficient staff, they might easily have become startling. As it was, the Prussian Staff system displayed many defects, obscured only by the utter rottenness of the French. For instance, the insubordination of General Steinmetz ("the Lion of Nachod"), whom Bismarck called "a blood-spendthrift", and the precipitated way such battles as Spicheren, Wörth, and Colombey were fought. Of the first two, Verdy du Vernois says: "Both battles are peculiar, in so far as they were fought against the will of the Commander-in-Chief"[1] – an extraordinary confession.

Moltke may be described as a general on rails, for his system of war was both direct and rigid. He was a supremely great war organizer, who relied on logic rather than on opportunity. For success his art depended on adherence to a somewhat static doctrine set in motion by *directives* rather than by orders. To him a war of masses was a war of accidents in which genius was subordinate to the offensive spirit. Whereas Napoleon I led and controlled throughout, Moltke brought his armies to their starting points and then abdicated his command and unleashed them. On August 31 and September 1 he never issued an order except for a few suggestions to General Blumenthal, chief of staff of the Third Army. He never foresaw the encirclement of the French, which was due to their stupidity, the initiative of the Prussian army commanders and the superb handling of the Prussian artillery. Moltke is not a general to copy but to study. His reckonings were wonderful, yet his risks against an able opponent might easily have proved damnable; for he was apt to be run away with by his subordinates.

Finally, this war showed, as Thiers said, "that in the great duel of peoples, unless accidents or material means are disproportion-

[1] *With the Royal Headquarters in 1870–71*, vol. I, pp. 56–57.

ate, victory remains with the nation which holds ascendency in science and moral force."[1] The will to win and the means to fight were the pillars of might which only emerged from the fogs and mists of doctrinaire soldiership into clear daylight during the First and Second World Wars.

[1] Quoted from *Les Deux Abimes*, Alfred de la Guéronnière, p. 16.

The rise of Japanese imperialism and the expansion of Russia in the Far East

When the Americans and Prussians were laying the foundations of their respective empires, Japan emerged from behind her bamboo curtain, and soon after set out to follow in their footsteps.

The causes which precipitated this violent change were biological and industrial. Japan, over populated, did not produce sufficient rice to feed her people and over-production of industrial goods upset her balance of trade. Both causes dictated oversea expansion: the conquest of foreign lands to absorb the excess population and the conquest of foreign markets to absorb Japanese trade goods. Because of the ever-increasing competition between industrial nations it was only a matter of years before an un-westernized Japan would have been sucked into the capitalist vortex.

Since 1638, when throughout Japan Christianity and foreign trade – with the exception of a minute Dutch trading post on the island of Deshima (near Nagasaki) – were suppressed by the Shogunate (or Tycoonate), all contact with the West had been severed. Then, in July, 1853, President Fillmore sent Commodore Perry and four warships to Japan to negotiate in the name of the United States a treaty of friendship with the Tenno (Mikado). Though the request was refused, in March the following year Perry returned with seven warships, and as the Shogun could not resist his cannon, the treaty was signed and Shimoda and Hako-daté were opened to American trade. Thus, after more than two centuries of undisturbed tranquillity, the bamboo curtain was pierced, and immediately the aperture was widened into a yawning gap when Great Britain, Russia, Holland, France, and Prussia, demanded and obtained similar privileges.

To appreciate what followed, it is necessary to say a word or two on the system of government which then prevailed in Japan. Since the opening of the seventeenth century, supreme authority had passed from the Tenno (King of Heaven), who was the divine head of the theanthropic Shinto State, into the hand of the Shogun (Barbarian-quelling Generalissimo) his Master of the Troops, who became an absolute dictator over a feudal country in which the barons of medieval Europe were duplicated by the daimios. Each daimio had his body of retainers called samurai, professional soldiers who followed certain rules of knightly conduct called *Bushido*. They lived in the traditions of the past and violently opposed all contact with Europeans, whereas the merchant class welcomed it because it increased their trade. The result was that the people were split into two factions, those who wanted free intercourse with the West and those who were determined to prevent it, and when in 1858 the American Consul-General in Japan, without the consent of the Tenno – who still possessed the power to ratify foreign treaties – forced a new trade treaty on the Shogun, the daimios and their followers began to murder Europeans, which only led to further exactions. Thus the situation steadily grew worse until February, 1867, when the reigning Tenno died and was succeeded by Mutsuhito (Meiji Tenno, 1867–1912), a boy of 15. The daimios seized upon the chance a minority rule offered to them and rose against the Shogun and compelled him to abdicate. The outcome was the revolution of 1868, which abolished the Shogunate and restored the Tenno to power as Emperor of Japan.

When the backwardness of the country is taken into consideration, the changes which followed the overthrow of the Shogunate border on the miraculous. They can only be accounted for by the intense resentment aroused in the country by the dictated trade treaties with their clauses of extraterritorial rights. If the white man, backed by his cannon, could accomplish such things, what could not the Japanese, an ancient, proud and intelligent people, do with cannon of their own? This vision of future deliverance through gunpowder was the dynamo of the Japanese Reformation.

In 1869, all 237 daimios returned their fiefs to the Tenno. In 1870, the first daily newspaper was published in Yokohama, and the first section of the national railway between Yokohama and Tokyo was opened. In 1871, feudalism was abolished and two million samurai were pensioned off. Other reforms followed, and of these the most important was the establishment of a national army in 1873. The profession of arms, hitherto the privilege of the samurai, was extended to the people. Conscription was introduced; the army and fleet were modernized; French and German methods were adopted by the former and British methods by the latter; and the Tenno became the godhead of the armed forces. Although, in 1889, a superficial and limited parliamentary system was introduced, the army and navy were placed outside its control.

Meanwhile, generously financed by European and American capitalists and able to call upon unlimited cheap labour, the Japanese rapidly changed from an agricultural into an industrial nation. Revenue increased by leaps and bounds, half of it to be spent on the fighting forces, and population increased from 32 million in 1868 to 45 million by 1903. British yards built warships for Japan, liners and tramp steamers for her merchant navy, and provided machine tools for her arsenals; the Germans sold her armaments; the Australians supplied her with wool; South America provided fertilizers; Malaya, tin and rubber; Scandinavia, wood pulp; and India and the United States, cotton and scrap iron. Thus the West became the wet nurse of the Farthest East, and by the time the century had run its course Japan had accomplished in a generation what Europe had taken 20 generations to effect. From a feudal polity, such as had existed in the West in the fourteenth century, she stepped over the threshold of the twentieth century a fully equipped industrial, military and naval power. Nevertheless, though outwardly she had become westernized, in her heart lived the memories of *Bushido*.

This amazing transformation, with its emphasis on military power, was bound to lead to expansion, which inevitably meant both a clash between Japan and China and friction with those European States which, like vultures, battened on the decaying Manchu Empire.

Among the latter, and because of her contiguity with China, Russia was most to be feared. Besides, she was largely an oriental Power, whose contact with China dated back to 1567, when Ivan the Terrible opened an embassy in Pekin. But after 1689, when in the early years of Peter the Great's reign Moscow entered into a treaty with China, which extended the Muscovite Empire to the borders of Manchuria, Russian expansion eastward halted until 1847. That year the great Russian administrator Count Muraviev was appointed Governor-General of Eastern Siberia. In 1849 he built the fortress of Petropavlovsk (bombarded during the Crimean War) on the eastern shore of Kamchatka, and in the following year he established the port of Nicholaievsk at the mouth of the Amur. Next, in 1851, he set out to gain the line of that river. After he had founded the towns of Blagoveshchensk and Kharbarovsk on its banks, in 1858, by the Treaty of Aigun, he obtained from China the surrender of the vast territory on the left bank of the Amur, which covered an area of 715,000 square miles – three and a half times the size of France.

China was convulsed by the Taiping rebellion and General Ignatiev took advantage of the turmoil, a procedure at which Russia is adept. General Ignatiev so skilfully worked on the fears of the Chinese Government that in 1860 he obtained a further surrender of 173,000 square miles – the maritime province of Manchuria, with its 600 miles of coast line. Soon after this the port of Vladivostok was built.

Next, Russia set out to acquire the island of Sakhalin, and although its southern half belonged to Japan, she was too weak to resist Russian pressure, and in 1875 an agreement was arrived at whereby the whole island was ceded to Russia in return for her recognition of Japan's title to the Kurile Islands.

Japan took her first step toward expansion at this time. Because of the ill treatment of some shipwrecked Japanese sailors in Formosa – part of the Chinese Empire – she invaded the island, and, in 1875, agreed tó withdraw from it on payment of an indemnity and Chinese recognition of her rights to the Ryukyu Islands. The first Korean incident followed. A Korean fort opened fire on a Japanese warship, and as Japan by now had learnt the white man's trick of using the threat of war as a diplomatic weapon, in 1876 a fleet was sent to Korea which compelled the Korean Government to sign a treaty of amity and to open three ports to Japanese trade. This was an important concession because Korea was Japan's natural gateway to the Asiatic mainland and the possibility of its eventual seizure by Russia had long been a nightmare to the Japanese. They knew that Russia hoped to gain a harbour on the Korean coast, and they were fully aware that the corrupt and decrepit Korean Government was incapable of resisting the slightest Russian pressure.

The second Korean incident came in 1884, when an attack was made on the Japanese legation at Seoul. Although the affair was settled without strife, Russia was casting such longing eyes on Korea that, in 1885, Great Britain intervened and occupied the island of Port Hamilton (Kyobunto) off the southern coast of Korea and held it for two years. But no sooner had she relinquished it than, in 1888, Russia concluded a treaty with Korea which opened Chemulpo, Seoul, Pusan and other towns to Russian trade.

Six years later followed the third Korean incident. Since 1884 the country had been in turmoil, and in 1894, when it culminated in revolution, the Korean Government appealed to China for help. She sent 2,000 troops to Seoul. So did Japan, and the outcome was the first Sino-Japanese war. Japan won an unbroken succession of triumphs. On September 15, the Chinese army was routed at Payong-yang by General Nodzu, and two days later the Chinese fleet was defeated by Admiral Ito in the battle of the Yalu. On November 21, Marshal Oyama stormed Port Arthur. Its loss compelled China to sue for peace, which was signed at Shimonoseki on April 17, 1895.

By its terms China surrendered to Japan the Liao-tung peninsula, Formosa and the Pescadores, and agreed to recognize the independence of Korea and pay an indemnity of 200 million *taels* (£25 million). But scarcely was the ink of this treaty dry when Russia, Germany and France objected to China's cession of the Liao-tung peninsula, and as Japan was not powerful enough to resist their combined pressure she agreed to abandon it for a payment of 30 million *taels*.

Immediately after this concession the Russian Minister at Peking entered into treaty with Li Hungchang, the Emperor of China's chief minister. In 1891 Russia had begun to build the Trans-Siberian Railway and by 1895 it had reached Chita, near the Manchurian border. As its terminus was to be Vladivostok, 600 miles of line could be saved if a short cut were taken across Manchuria. Li Hungchang now agreed to this diversion.

Next, in 1897, Russia secured from China the lease of the Liao-tung peninsula and permission to build a railway from Harbin, on the main Moscow-Vladivostok line, to Port Arthur and Talien, which was renamed Dalny (Darien). About the same time Germany obtained from China the lease of Kiao-chow; Great Britain that of Wei-hai-wei; and France that of Kwang Cho Wan.

Trouble was not long delayed, for the rivalry between the Western Powers and their utter disregard of the interests of the Chinese led, in 1900, to the outbreak of the Boxer rising, so named because it was fomented by a secret society known as the *Iho Cu'üan* ("Patriotic Harmonious Fists"). Massacres of Europeans followed and the foreign legations in Pekin were besieged. From Berlin Kaiser William II ordered his troops in China to fight in such a way that for a thousand years no Chinaman would dare to look a German in the face. At the same time an obscure Russian refugee in Switzerland, Vladimir Ilyich Ulyanov, later to become known as Lenin, called upon enslaved humanity in China to break its chains. In the middle of July, after an eight-week siege, the Pekin legations were relieved by an international force which included a contingent of Japanese, and on September 7, 1901, peace was restored and China was compelled to pay an indemnity of 450 million *taels*.

Two subsidiary results of this rising and suppression were of exceptional importance. The first was that the Japanese were able to measure the inefficiency of the Russians and their difficulties in maintaining large forces in the Far East, difficulties so great that the Russians were little to be feared. The second result was that the English were so impressed by Japanese efficiency that, in order to guarantee peace in the Far East, on January 30, 1902, they broke away from their policy of isolation and entered upon a defensive alliance with Japan.

Two months later a treaty was signed between Russia and China according to which the former undertook to withdraw her troops from Manchuria in stages. But the Tsar had no intention of doing so, and this was made clear when, in 1903, he created the Vice-Royalty of East Asia to control Russian affairs in what was claimed to be Russia's sphere of influence in China. When it became known to the Japanese that Korea was included in this sphere, they offered to recognize Russia's position in Manchuria, provided that Russia extended similar recognition to Japan's position in Korea, and further they proposed that all nations should be granted equal commercial rights in both countries. While negotiations proceeded, a Russian speculator, Bezobrazov, obtained a concession from the Korean Government to cut timber on the Yalu and Turmen rivers, a project in which the Tsar's *entourage* was financially interested. To protect this undertaking pressure was brought on the Russian Government not only to strengthen the Manchurian garrison and the Eastern Fleet, but also to send troops to the Yalu to protect the lumberjacks. In view of this, the Japanese ambassador at St. Petersburg was instructed to press for a settlement of the negotiations by February 4, 1904. As on that date no answer was received, on the following day diplomatic relations were severed with Russia and an order issued for the mobilization of the Japanese army and fleet.

CHAPTER 4

The siege of Port Arthur, 1904-1905

The Russo-Japanese War of 1904–1905 is one of the great turning points in Western history, for not only was it a trial of strength between an Asiatic and a semi-European power, but above all it was a challenge to Western supremacy in Asia. When, on February 5, 1904, the Japanese bugles blared forth war, simultaneously they resounded a reveille throughout the East and Asia began to stir in her ancient sleep.

From a European point of view no theatre of war could have been more distant than Manchuria and the Yellow Sea, and few theatres could have been more unsuited to a struggle between highly organized armies. Manchuria was a primitive and roadless country and, though mountainous, its plains and valleys were highly cultivated. The main crop was kao-liang (tall grain) which grows to a height of from 12 ft. to 15 ft., and in season converted vast tracts into dense jungle. The summer is hot, reaching at times 112 deg. in the shade, and in winter it is bitterly cold. In July and August, and often in September, the rainfall is high, when the ground becomes a sea of mud. Captain Soloviev, who took part in this war, writes: "The mud reaches the breasts of the horses, covers the spokes of the wheels of heavy wagons sinking in the soil. . . . Only Chinese *arbas* (mere platforms on two enormous wheels) survive the swamps and holes of the impassable Manchurian roads."[1] Before and after the rains the country is swept by clouds of blinding dust, and between November and March it is ice-bound.

Nevertheless, for military operations the main difficulty was not climate, but lack of communications, and this more particularly affected the Russians, who were compelled to fight 5,500 miles from their main base – the distance between Moscow and Port Arthur. This vast stretch was spanned by the Trans-Siberian Railway and its extension from Harbin to Dalny, which was skirted by the Mandarin Road from Mukden to Port Arthur – 262 miles in length.

[1] *Actual Experiences in War*, Captain L. Z. Soloviev (1906), p. 34.

The railways were poorly built; neither permanent way, which was single track, nor sidings, stations and rolling-stock were suited to the heavy traffic demanded by a great army. Worse still, when the war began there was a gap of over 100 miles around Lake Baikal, which was 30 miles in breadth. Between November and April, when the lake was frozen over, stores could be hauled across it, at other seasons they had to go by road. To show how slow movement could be it is only necessary to state that normally it took over a month to transport a battalion from Moscow to Port Arthur.

Besides these two lines of communication, which determined the direction of all the main land operations, there was the sea, the command of which was vital to the Japanese. Korea, which offered a comparatively safe line of supply leading into Manchuria, as well as a convenient base for a Japanese withdrawal in the event of defeat, was also vital to them. Beyond Korea lay Port Arthur, which as long as the Russian fleet sheltered there commanded the sea communications to Japan. Therefore the Japanese were compelled to attack it, and in consequence to divide their land forces. For the Russians this was a tremendous advantage, because their one great problem was how to gain time to assemble sufficient troops in Manchuria to meet their enemy.

Yet the moral value of Port Arthur, as a symbol of Japanese superiority, was as important as the destruction of the Russian fleet. In 1894 Japan had taken Port Arthur and then had been deprived of it because she was too weak to hold it. To regain it would not only justify the war, but above all it would proclaim the superiority of Japan over Russia, and, incidentally, of Asia over Europe. In short, whether strategy demanded it or not, the conquest of Port Arthur was for Japan the spiritual pivot of the conflict.

The main factors which governed the strategy of the war can be summarized thus: the gap in the Siberian railway and the Russian naval base at Port Arthur. As long as the gap existed, the reinforcement of the Russian troops in Manchuria would be slow; and as Vladivostok was ice-bound in winter and Port Arthur ice-free, could the latter be secured by the Japanese before the next winter set in, not only would warships at Vladivostok be cut off from Port Arthur, but should the Russian Baltic Fleet be sent east, without Port Arthur it would be denied an ice-free base of operations. What the Baikal gap was to the Russian land operations, ice was to their sea operations. Lastly, once Port Arthur had been wrested from the Russians the Japanese would be in a position to concentrate the whole of their land forces in a great decisive battle, the loss of which it was hoped would persuade the Russians to abandon the war. Be it noted that Japan fought for a compromise and not for a total victory – which lay beyond her reach.

Once the Japanese aim had been decided on, the next question was – how best could it be attained?

Firstly, it was obvious that, to reduce Port Arthur, it would have to be attacked on its landward side; secondly, that to its north the attacking army would have to be protected by a covering force; and thirdly, as both these armies were based on Japan, command of the Yellow Sea must be guaranteed. This introduces the naval problem.

When war was declared (February 10) the opposing fleets in the Far East were:

	Russia	*Japan*
Battleships, 1st Class	7	6
Battleships, 2nd Class	—	1
Cruisers, 1st Class	9	8
Cruisers, 2nd Class	—	12
Cruisers, 3rd Class	2	13
Destroyers	25	19
Torpedo boats	17	85
Sloops and Gunboats	12	16

Of the Russian ships four first class cruisers were stationed at Vladivostok and one at Chemulpo; therefore the Port Arthur Fleet, under Vice-Admiral Stark, was in fighting power inferior to the Japanese, commanded by Vice-Admiral Togo. Nevertheless, this disadvantage was mitigated by the fact that whereas Russia possessed a powerful fleet in the Baltic, which should it unite with the Port Arthur Fleet would decidedly outnumber its enemy's, Japan had no reserves of armoured vessels, nor did she "possess a single yard in which they had ever been built."[1] Therefore it was imperative that the Port Arthur Fleet should be captured or destroyed before the Baltic Fleet could arrive from Europe. This meant a land attack.

---

[1] *Official History (Naval & Military) of the Russo-Japanese War*, prepared by the Historical Section of the Committee of Imperial Defence (1910), vol. 1, p. 41.

Although the total number of trained soldiers in Russia numbered 4,500,000 and in Japan about 800,000, this disproportion was largely offset by the fact that on the outbreak of war Japan could rapidly place the bulk of her entire standing army of 283,000 men and 870 guns in the field; but in the immense area east of Lake Baikal the total Russian field troops numbered no more than 83,000 and 196 guns, supported by 25,000 fortress troops and some 30,000 railway guards, and these could only be slowly reinforced because of the low carrying-power of the Siberian railway.

Both armies were conscript forces. Service in Japan was on a three-year footing and in Russia on five, after which the Russian soldier was relegated to the reserve until his forty-third year. In illustration of the astonishing military progress in Japan since conscription was first introduced, Colonel Teruda, who commanded a regiment during the war, "had once fought in chain armour and carried a battle axe."[1] And, to show the little advance which had been made by their antagonists, it is only necessary to quote that, instead of amalgamating their reservists with their active soldiers, they formed the former into separate corps which proved almost useless. Captain Soloviev writes of the reservists: "As a general rule, these uncouth, heavy bearded men look discontented, are clumsy, slothful and cowardly. Their propensities are anything but warlike; they like to sleep well, eat their fill, raise a fuss behind one's back, while in battle they are too quiet."[2]

Since the Franco-Prussian War there had been a steady development in armaments. The most radical were the introduction and general adoption of the small bore magazine rifle and smokeless powder, first used on an extensive scale in the South-African War of 1899–1902. In this war the old terror of a visible foe gave way to the paralysing sensation of advancing on an invisible one, which fostered the suspicion that the enemy was everywhere. A universal terror, rather than a localized danger, now enveloped the attacker, while the defender, always ready to protect himself by some rough earth or stone-work, was enabled through the rapidity of rifle-fire to use extensions unheard of in past fighting, and in consequence to overlap every frontal attack. Thus, at the battle of the Modder River, the Boers extended 3,000 men on a

---

[1] *Port Arthur: The Siege and Capitulation*, Ellis Ashmead Bartlett (1906), p. 265.
[2] *Actual Experiences in War*, p. 46. See also *The Russian Army and the Japanese War*, General Kuropatkin (English trans., 1909), pp. 280 and 289.

frontage of 7,700 yards; at Magersfontein, 5,000 on 11,000; and at Colenso, 4,500 on 13,000. Yet in spite of this human thinness, these fronts could not be penetrated. This spelt the end of successful frontal rifle attacks.

The general lesson of the Boer War is well put in the *German Official History*, which said: "In South Africa the contest was not merely one between the bullet and the bayonet, it was also between the soldier drilled to machine-like movements and the man with a rifle working on his own initiative. . . . Fortunate is that army whose ranks, released from the burden of dead forms, are controlled by natural, untrammelled, quickening common-sense."[1]

Besides the magazine rifle, the crude *mitrailleuse* of 1870 had given way to a number of improved machine-guns – the Gatling, Gardener, Nordenfeldt, Hotchkiss, Colt, and Maxim. The last named was designed by Hiram S. Maxim in 1884, and in the First World War it became the queen of the battlefield. Probably it has killed and wounded more men than any other weapon, yet in its youth it was little considered by soldiers.

Since the introduction of rifled cannon, the field-gun had steadily forged ahead. In the Russo-Turkish War of 1877–1878 the Russian General Oukanov had said: "Artillery will become the scourge of mankind. . . . The day cannot be much longer delayed when artillery shall raise itself from being an auxiliary to the rank of the principal arm." A decisive step toward this end was taken when the proposals put forward by General Wille in Germany and Colonel Langlois in France in 1891–1892 a few years later led to the invention of the quick-firing field gun, which by absorbing its recoil on discharge enabled the non-recoiling gun carriage to be introduced; it permitted a bullet-proof shield to be attached to it, and thus reintroduced armour on the battlefield. Until this improvement was made, the magazine rifle was the dominant weapon, but after its introduction it was challenged by the quick-firing gun, which not only outranged it and could be fired with equal rapidity, but which by indirect laying could also be made invisible.

Though in armaments the opposed armies did not differ widely, between their men there was a vast gulf. In Japan loyalty, patriotism and self-sacrifice were looked upon as the highest of civic and soldierly virtues; in Russia they were unknown. As we are told,

[1] *The War in South Africa*, German Official Account (English edit., 1906), vol. II, pp. 336, 344.

the result was that the Japanese soldier "obeyed the dictates of honour and duty,"[1] and Tadayoshi Sakuri calls his brother soldiers "human bullets", and "the essence of *Yamato Damashii* (the spirit of Old Japan)."[2] On the other hand, Kuropatkin writes of the Russian army: "To maintain discipline in an army is impossible when the mass of the nation has no respect for authority, and when the authorities actually fear those under them."[3] On the moral differences he is highly illuminating. "Though our information," he writes, "as to the material points of the enemy's strength can hardly be described as good, we very much underestimated – if we did not entirely overlook – its moral side. We paid no attention to the fact that for many years the education of the Japanese people had been carried out in a martial spirit and on patriotic lines. We saw nothing in the education methods of a country where the children in the elementary schools are taught to love their nation and to be heroes. The nation's belief in the deep respect for the army, the individual willingness and pride in serving, the iron discipline maintained among the ranks, and the influence of the *Samurai* spirit, escaped our notice, while we attached no importance to the intense feeling of resentment that we aroused when we deprived the Japanese of the fruits of their victories in China."[4]

An army of unbelievable inefficiency encompassed this moral vacuum. For instance, while at Port Arthur "officers were strictly forbidden to make themselves acquainted with the topography of the fortress . . . numbers of officers of the Japanese General Staff, disguised as washermen, coolies, etc., were permitted to move about the batteries without hindrance"; private and military telephone lines "were all together, so that, owing to the induction, anyone could overhear the most secret military message," and after the battle of the Yalu, an urgently needed party of reinforcements which was sent there in "serviceable" instead of "first-year" tunics, a breach of regulations, was sent back 200 miles "for better coats."[5]

The tactics and training of the two armies kept step with their moral differences. Whereas the Japanese closely followed the

---

[1] *Human Bullets*, Tadayoshi Sakuri (1907), p. xi.   [2] *Ibid.*, p. 138.
[3] *The Russian Army and the Japanese War*, General Kuropatkin, vol. II, p. 124.
[4] *Ibid.*, vol. I, pp. 214-215.
[5] *The Truth about Port Arthur*, E. K. Nojine (1908), pp. 8, 9, 14, and 39. We are also told that when after considerable trouble a balloon was made in Port Arthur, it was discovered "there was no means of producing hydrogen" (*My Experiences at Nan Shan and Port Arthur*, Lieut.-General N. A. Tretyakov, 1911, p. 259).

German pattern, the Russians were incredibly archaic. General de Négrier comments on them: "The cult of the bayonet has been pushed to such an extreme that, under all circumstances, it remained fixed to the rifle. The officers try by every means to persuade their men that they ought above everything to place confidence in the bayonet. They keep on repeating the words of Souvaroff: 'The bullet is a mad thing; only the bayonet knows what it is about'. As regards fire, their notions are equally heretical. Down to the end of August, 1904, the Russians fired salvoes as in the days of Apraxine [1671–1728]."[1]

"Our men," writes General Tretyakov, "are not accustomed to act on their own initiative, and a long skirmishing line does not permit of the officers directing their men by voice and example. It was lucky that we were the defenders and not the attackers!"[2] E. K. Nojine informs us that Russian officers would shout: "Front rank, tell me why the Japanese are fools." The soldiers would reply in chorus: "Because, when attacking, their firing-line extends widely."[3]

In the higher direction of the war the contrast is equally marked. Whereas the Japanese command and General Staff were modelled on those of Germany, many of the Russian generals had never, according to Kuropatkin, held an independent command and the Staff was filled with office soldiers and bureaucrats. When war was declared, Admiral Alexiev, Viceroy of the Far East and a favourite of the Tsar, was made generalissimo of all the Russian sea and land forces in the Far East in spite of his military inexperience. And when, on March 27, General Kuropatkin[4] arrived at Liao-yang to command the army, a dual system of command was established until after the fall of Port Arthur, when Alexiev was recalled and Kuropatkin made the Tsar's supreme representative. It was a fatal combination, because the two men seldom saw eye to eye and Alexiev's constant interference in military matters, which he was incapable of understanding, led to one disaster after the other.

In 1903, when Minister of War at Petersburg, Kuropatkin's

---

[1] *Lessons of the Russo-Japanese War* (1906), p. 57.
[2] *My Experiences at Nan Shan and Port Arthur*, p. 27.
[3] *The Truth about Port Arthur*, p. 13.
[4] Kuropatkin was born on March 17, 1845. In 1876 he served on Skobelev's staff and in the Russo-Turkish war of 1877–1878 as chief-of-staff. He was a fine character and a good staff officer, but as a general he lacked boldness and audacity, in spite of the fact that he once said: "Generally speaking, the man who conquers in war is the man who is least afraid of death."

idea was that the soundest course in the event of war was to evacuate the Liao-tung peninsula, and on August 6 he submitted a memorandum to the Tsar in which he pointed out that a defensive policy should be adopted. "We cannot," he wrote, "hold our ground in Southern Manchuria in the first period of the war if that region be invaded by the whole Japanese army. We should, therefore, still count upon Port Arthur being cut off for a considerable period, and in order to avoid defeat in detail, should withdraw towards Harbin until reinforcements from Russia enable us to assume the offensive."[1]

These suggestions clashed with the views held by the Naval Staff, which were: "Our plan of operations should be based on the assumption that it is impossible for our fleet to be beaten, taking into consideration the present relationship of the two fleets, and that a Japanese landing at Newchuang [Ying-chou], and in the Gulf of Korea is impracticable."[2]

In brief, before the war started two plans were in opposition; one sought the decisive battle on land, and the other at sea. The former was backed by Kuropatkin and the latter by Alexiev, and the outcome was a series of half-measures.

Once in command of the army in Manchuria, Kuropatkin put his plan into operation. But because it had been decided to hold the fleet at Port Arthur – which to him was what Bazaine's army at Metz had been to MacMahon – he modified it. Instead of concentrating his forces at or near Harbin – that is, well back – he selected Liao-Yang – 350 miles to its south – as his point of concentration and pushed out detachments from there toward Port Arthur.

This modification in no way satisfied Alexiev. Because he considered it unlikely that the Port Arthur Fleet would gain command of the sea, he thought it vital to hold fast to Port Arthur – the only ice-free port in Russian hands – until it had been reinforced. He was then in Port Arthur, and when on May 5 he left it for the north he was so impressed by the precarious state of affairs that he ordered Kuropatkin to abandon his defensive plan. When the latter hesitated to do so, he persuaded the Tsar to lay on Kuropatkin's shoulders the responsibility for the fate of Port Arthur. Kuropatkin should then have resigned his command.

Meanwhile the Japanese considered their plan. They saw that

---

[1] *The Russian Army and the Japanese War*, vol. II, pp. 29–30.
[2] *Ibid.*, vol. I, p. 224.

the whole issue of the struggle hinged on naval supremacy, but they also realized that no fleet, however powerful, could by itself expel the Russians from Manchuria, and until they were expelled

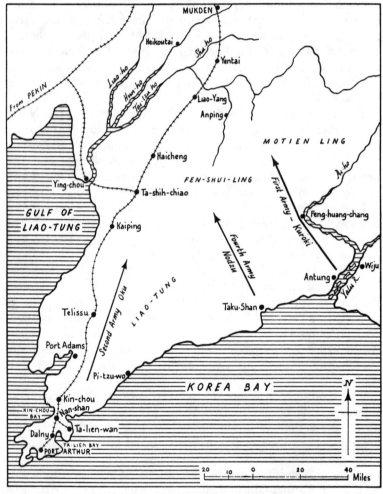

10.　THE RUSSO-JAPANESE WAR, 1904–1905

or decisively defeated on land, there was little chance of winning the war. Therefore their plan was as follows:

(1) At once to bring the Russian fleet to action, and should it refuse to fight, then to blockade it and reduce Port Arthur by land attack before it could be reinforced.

(2) To land three armies on the northern shore of the Bay of Korea under protection of the fleet, and as soon as possible a fourth army in order to attack or invest Port Arthur. The first three to move on Liao-Yang and act as a covering force to the fourth, which, directly Port Arthur was occupied, would move north and reinforce them, when the aim of all four combined would be to "win a Sedan" before the Russians could gain numerical superiority.

As will be seen later, the fly in their strategical ointment was that they underestimated the strength of the Russian naval base; they expected to rush it as they had done in 1894. Further, they considered that it was of such strategic importance that its fall would be equivalent to that of Plevna, the capitulation of which had ended the Russo-Turkish War of 1877-1878.

The Japanese did not even wait for the formal declaration of war. Immediately after diplomatic relations were severed they put their plan into execution. On February 6, 1904, Togo and his fleet lay with steam up at Sasebo off the Strait of Tsushima, and on the following day he stood out to sea to attack the Russian fleet while a torpedo boat flotilla escorted three transports of troops to Chemulpo. On February 8, at 6 a.m., Togo was off Round Island, 60 miles east of Port Arthur, and that night he launched a torpedo attack on his enemy's ships, hit three and drove them to port. The next day the Russian battle fleet put to sea and an engagement was fought which, though it lasted only forty minutes and proved indecisive, vindicated Japan's claim to be considered a first-class naval power and broke the spell of Russia's naval supremacy. Henceforth the Russian fleet was forced to act defensively. Next, on February 12, followed a second attack, and from then on to May 3 a series of harbour-blocking and mine-laying operations took place, during which, on April 12, the Russian flag-ship, the *Petropavlovsk*, struck a mine and went down with Admiral Makarov, the brain and heart of the fleet.[1]

Meanwhile, on February 9, a landing was effected at Chemulpo, where a base of operations was established for the First Army under General Kuroki. On February 27 Pingyang was occupied, and a fortnight later so was Anju. On May 1, the first battle of the war was fought on the Yalu River between Kuroki and General Zasulich, in which the latter was compelled to withdraw. It was

[1] Makarov had succeeded Admiral Stark on March 8. In this disaster perished the celebrated painter Vereshchagin.

an important victory, because it lowered the prestige of Russia in the eyes of the world. The news that a comparatively small eastern nation had in its first encounter defeated a great western Power, flashed like a meteor over the Asian sky.

Because this victory made Japan paramount in Korea, the next step taken was to isolate Port Arthur. On May 5 the Second Japanese Army, under General Oku, which consisted of the 1st, 2nd, 3rd, 4th Divisions, and later also the 5th, began landing at Pi-tzu-wo. This was a risky operation, for Pi-tzo-wo was only forty miles north-east of Port Arthur. The disembarkation was nevertheless successfully carried out although it took some three weeks. As soon as his leading troops had landed, Oku pushed them across the peninsula to Port Adams, left the 5th Division to guard his rear, and with the remaining four moved toward Kin-chou, to find himself face to face with a Russian detachment at Nan-Shan. In the meantime, on May 19, General Kawamura landed with the 10th Division[1] at Taku-Shan to establish there a connecting link between the First and Second Armies.

Strange as it may seem, the landing of the Second Japanese Army took the Russians by surprise, and worse still for them, General Stössel, in command at Port Arthur, was in no way ready to meet his unexpected enemy. On April 14 Admiral Alexiev had arrived at the fortress to organize its defence, and on the very day the first echelon of the Second Army began to disembark he left it to hasten north. Once in sole command, Stössel proved to be unbelievably incompetent, even for a Russian. He was a petty-minded man, whose stupidity and active ignorance were worth many a soldier and gun to his enemy. The following order of his, No. 187, gives some idea of his military capabilities:

"To-day, near the church, I met two officers with a lady; she was wearing an officer's rifle forage-cap . . . I do not think that I need dwell upon how out of place it seems for one of the female sex to wear a military cap with a cockade, when even retired officers and reserves are not allowed by regulations to wear them."[2]

On February 28 he issued a proclamation in which he declared that "there will be no retirement", and ended by stating that

---

[1] This detachment was later on reinforced and formed into the Fourth Army under General Nodzu, who took over its command on July 16.

[2] *The Truth about Port Arthur*, Nojine, p. 48. "To march out of step he considered such a crime that he thought it necessary even to make a special report on the subject to the Viceroy" (p. 195).

"there was no place to retreat to". Yet, in spite of this and that
the population of the fortress numbered some 55,000 in all, he
allowed tons of preserved foods to be exported, and when at the
railway station a "mountain of packing-cases . . . which served
as a landmark – a sort of triumphal arch by the entrance of the
Old Town" – was examined, it was found to be "composed
entirely of – vodka!"[1]

Under him came General Smirnov, the Fortress Commander,
a competent soldier, whom he obstructed at every turn until, on
June 18, Kuropatkin sent him an order to hand his command over
to him, and to leave Port Arthur by cruiser. He pocketed the
telegram and took no notice of it. As will be seen later, it was a
case of Palikao's famous letter in reverse.

While Stössel, through his muddling, prepared eventual disaster, Oku made ready to attack the position on Nan-Shan which,
though the Russian defences were indifferent, was by nature
formidable. It stood at the narrowest part of the peninsula, in
width at high tide 3,500 yards from shore to shore. Looked at
from the Japanese advanced posts it appeared well-nigh impregnable, and it would probably have proved to be so had its garrison
been fully employed, for though between 16,000 to 18,000 men
were assembled there, in the forthcoming battle only 3,500 were
engaged against Oku's 38,500.

The orders for the attack were issued on May 24, when, according to Nojine, Stössel's subordinates, instead of carrying out
his instructions, "wrote long-winded memoranda and proceeded
to do the opposite. . . . The day before the battle was a nightmare of confusion: no one knew what was being done or why it
was done."[2] The next day Kin-Chou was stormed, and the
following morning, at 5 a.m., as the summit of Nan-Shan crept
out of the mist, the bombardment opened, and an hour later a
Japanese flotilla steamed into Kin-Chou bay and joined in the
cannonade. By 11 a.m. the attack had failed, but when it was
renewed the Russian gun ammunition began to run short. At
4 p.m., the 4th Division, on the Japanese right, pushed breast-high
through the sea, turned their enemy's left flank, and uncovered
his centre and right. The Russians then broke back as "In the
dim light the flashes of the enemy artillery showed up against the
dark mass of gigantic Mount Samson like long threads of fire, like
golden chains swaying up and down, rocking to and fro."[3] When

[1] *Ibid.*, p. 48.   [2] *Ibid.*, p. 58.   [3] *Ibid.*, p. 67.

at 7.20 p.m. the Rising Sun floated over Nan-Shun, the Russian firing line, unsupported as it had been, collapsed and spread panic in its rear. General Tretyakov says: "The din and confusion were awful, and from the bivouacs behind us shots and volleys were heard. Together with the other officers near me I rushed to the rear . . . to restore order. I also ordered our band to strike up a march, and, thank God, its martial strains restored confidence among the fugitives. . . ."[1]

The Japanese losses in this first battle for Port Arthur were heavy; they numbered 4,885 killed and wounded, and those of the Russians in proportion to men engaged were devastating, namely 1,416, or over 40 per cent., which suggests that there was little wrong with the Russian private soldier as a fighter. Heavily though the Japanese had paid for their victory, it was an insignificant price for the port of Dalny which fell into their hands. There they found the docks intact,[2] and without them it would have been nearly impossible to carry out their ultimate operation – the siege of Port Arthur.

Once Dalny was in Japanese hands, the 11th Division was landed, and with the 1st Division was formed into the Third Army under General Nogi, who was instructed to push the Russians southward into Port Arthur, while Oku with the 3rd, 4th and 5th Divisions moved northward against General Stackelberg, who moved to the relief of the fortress. On June 14 and 15 Oku met Stackelberg at Telissu and drove him back. Meanwhile Nogi, who, in 1894, with one brigade and at the cost of 18 men killed had captured Port Arthur, maintained a defensive attitude until reinforced by the 9th Division and other troops, who began to land at Dalny on July 7. On July 26, he launched his first attack, and after desperate fighting took Hsi-Shan, and on the 30th occupied Feng-huang-Shan (Hozan). With its loss the Russian resistance collapsed, and, except for Ta-ku-Shan and Hsiao-ku-Shan, the last line outside the permanent defences of Port Arthur was evacuated. This ended the field operations of the Port Arthur garrison, and also, for over a month, the Japanese offensive.

Port Arthur was isolated, and until Kuropatkin could relieve it, or help came from Europe, Stössel's task was to withstand a siege. It was governed by three factors – men, food, and fortifications.

---

[1] *My Experiences at Nan Shan and Port Arthur*, p. 62.
[2] *The Russo-Japanese War* (Official Reports), compiled by M. Kinai (English trans., 1907), vol. I, p. 296.

On May 14, without counting the ships' crews, he had under his command 41,899 men and 506 guns, no mean force with which to hold back his opponent's army, which, when reinforced by the 7th Division, was brought up to a strength of 63 battalions, three squadrons, 17 companies of engineers, and 474 field and siege guns; in all between 80,000 to 90,000 men.

His supplies were less satisfactory. In the middle of July, for a garrison of 42,000 men and 4,500 horses, they were estimated to be: "flour, 180 days; oatmeal, 37 days; meat, 18 days (13 days salt, 5 days on the hoof); pickles, 15 days; sugar, 190 days; tea, 320 days; forage, 150 days."[1] But from time to time these supplies were augmented by ships which ran the blockade.

The defences consisted of three main lines:

(*1*) A formidable entrenchment encircling the old town, but of little tactical value.

(*2*) Following along the Chinese Wall, about 4,000 yards from the centre of the Old Town, was a chain of permanent concrete forts linked together by subsidiary works and entrenchments. This line was continued on the west of the Lun-Ho in order to enclose the New Town and the harbour.

(*3*) Beyond this main line of defence lay a series of fortified hills and positions. The two most important groups were: Ta-ku-Shan and Hsiao-ku-Shan to the east of the fortress; and 174 Metre Hill, Namako Yama, Akasaka Yama, 203 Metre Hill and False Hill to the west of it.

Many of the works in these groups were incomplete and blinded by fields of kao-liang. Barbed wire was scarce and worth its weight in gold,[2] and vehicles were lamentably deficient.[3]

Nogi's task was to reduce the fortress as soon as possible so that command of the sea might be assured, and then to move north and join Marshal Oyama, who had been appointed to the supreme command of the Japanese land forces in Manchuria on July 6.

The Japanese line of investment ran from Louisa Bay (north of 174 Metre Hill) to Ta-Ho Bay (mouth of the Ta-Ho), and once Ta-ku-Shan and Hsiao-ku-Shan were occupied, the Third Army would be well placed to prevent a sortie from any quarter. Nogi therefore decided to make the capture of these two fortified hills his first operation.

[1] *Official History*, etc., vol. I, p. 324.
[2] *My Experiences at Nan Shan and Port Arthur*, Tretyakov, pp. 126 and 152.
[3] *Ibid.*, p. 148.

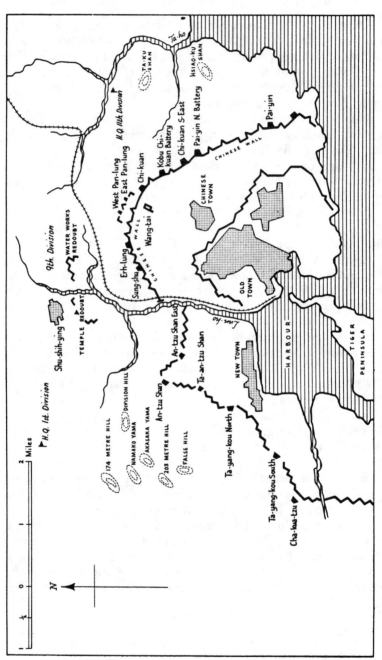

II. SIEGE OF PORT ARTHUR, 1904–1905

To prepare the way for an assault on these hills, the former of which rose nearly 600 ft. above sea level, a bombardment was opened at 4.30 a.m. on Sunday, August 7, and was continued until 7.30 p.m., when the infantry advanced. But because of heavy rain and darkness they succeeded only in establishing themselves on their lower slopes. "The powder-smoke covering the whole scene was like surging waves, and the dark shower of rain may be likened to angry lions. Above us the steep mountain stood high, kissing the heavens – even monkeys could hardly climb it."[1] Such is Tadayoshi Sakuri's description of the situation that night.

On the following day the rain continued until 3.30 p.m., at which hour the artillery bombardment was reopened. It was so effective that many of the defenders were driven out of their hastily dug trenches; yet, when the Japanese infantry advanced, those who remained put up a desperate resistance. At length, at 8 p.m. Ta-ku-Shan fell, and Hsiao-ku-Shan was taken at 4.30 o'clock on the following morning.

When he learnt of the loss of these hills, the Tsar ordered Admiral Vitgeft, who on the death of Admiral Makarov had succeeded to the command of the fleet, to break out of Port Arthur and join the Vladivostok squadron. On August 10 he attempted to do so at 8.30 a.m., and with six battleships, five cruisers, and eight destroyers he steamed out under cover of a low-lying mist. At 11.30 a.m. he was sighted by the Japanese destroyers, and at 12.10 p.m. action was opened. He broke away and manœuvred for nightfall; but at 4.14 p.m. was again brought to action and an hour and a half later was killed on his flagship, the *Tsarevich*, by the explosion of a 12-in. shell. His death was followed by a confusion of orders, which resulted in five of his battleships, one cruiser and three destroyers regaining Port Arthur, while the rest of his fleet, under cover of darkness ran for Chinese and other ports and was eventually interned, except the *Novik* which was sunk. Thus ended the first real sea fight of the war, and it gained for Japan absolute command of the sea until the arrival of the Baltic Fleet. As this fleet was far from ready, Nogi believed that if he could storm Port Arthur before it set out, it might never sail. He decided to rush the fortress.

Though such a decision is understandable, for this was the first attempt in history to storm a fortress held with magazine rifles, machine guns, and quick-firing artillery, there was little

[1] *Human Bullets*, p. 184.

justification for General Nogi to suppose that it was likely to succeed against so determined an enemy as the Russians had proved themselves to be.

On August 16, in accordance with the customs of war, a flag of truce was sent to Port Arthur with a summons to surrender, and, when this was refused, Nogi ordered the first general assault for the 19th. The front of attack selected ran from Chi-Kuan Battery to Fort Sung-shu; at the same time a separate assault was to be made against 174 Metre Hill. As most of the fighting took place during night time and often at close quarters, the confusion was so great that it will be left to an observer and a participant to describe it.

On August 22, writes Frederick Villiers, an English Correspondent with the Third Army, "it is 1 a.m. and still the fighting rages furiously. Three of the nine searchlights that the Russians appear to possess are playing incessantly on this section of the battle-field, and star bombs or rockets are bursting continually, their incandescent petals spreading fanlike and falling slowly to the ground. So brilliant are these lights that the moon, now nearing the horizon, is but a faint slip of silver in the sky. The colour of this night warfare is what Whistler would have revelled in. The deep purple of the mountain against the nocturnal blue, the pale lemon of the moon, the whitish rays of the searchlights, the warm incandescent glow of the star bombs, the reddish spurt from the cannon's mouths, and the yellow flash from the exploding shell, all tempered to a mellowness by a thin haze of smoke, ever clinging to hill-top and valley, make the scene the most weird and unique I have ever looked on during all the many wars I have witnessed."[1]

On the next night Nojine describes the battle from the opposite side:

"At 11 p.m.," he writes, "Nogi gave the sign, and a living avalanche of men rolled irresistibly up towards us, and from valley, ditch and ravine the Japanese appeared. Rifles cracked, machine guns spluttered, guns boomed and boomed again and

---

[1] *Port Arthur, Three Months with the Besiegers*, Frederick Villiers (1905), pp. 26–27. On the use of searchlights, Ashmead Bartlett writes: "This was the first occasion on which the searchlight as a weapon of defence has been used in actual warfare in land operations, and its results excelled the most sanguine expectations. I have been told by survivors that it blots out everything in front, causing the men to wander aimlessly about seeking shelter from this terrible enemy; but all their efforts are in vain, for the rays follow their every movement, and the machine gun follows the rays" (*Port Arthur: the Siege and Capitulation*, p. 265).

the air was turned into an inferno of shrieking missiles. The rays of the searchlights flashed up and down, rockets shot up into the sky like enormous fiery snakes and burst, and hundreds of large brilliant balls, eclipsing the light of the eternal stars and blinding the heroic little infantry-men who were attacking us. They ran forward, fell, jumped up again and pressed on, in groups together. In the shimmering rays of the searchlights, the flashes of bursting shells seemed almost blood-red. The noise became a horrible blur of sound – shouts, moans, cheers – clash of arms and detonations. But at last it ended; the clamour gradually died away; the attack had been repulsed. In front of us not a living soul remained – only dead – piles of dead and wounded men. Never shall I forget that night."

A second assault took place at 2 a.m. It failed, and an hour later it was followed by a third:

"The signal was given," writes Nojine, "and a fresh wave of living flesh and blood rolled forward. This time it was the attack, the spring of a maddened, wounded, blood-drunk herd of tigers, not men. Our truly awful fire was of no avail; the mass roared forward with the strength of a tidal wave. On it came, though lit up by rockets and search-lights, on, on, it rolled irresistibly on, right through the breached Chinese Wall. . . ."[1]

Nevertheless it was repulsed, and thus the first general assault ended at dawn on August 24. Its fruits were the capture of West and East Pan-lung and 174 Metre Hill; all other objectives remained in Russian hands.

This desperate fighting cost the Russians some 3,000 in killed and wounded and the Japanese over 15,000. It was an expensive lesson, and it convinced Nogi that the north-east front of the fortress could only be reduced by regular siege operations, which might last for several months. As this meant that Marshal Oyama could no longer reckon on Nogi reinforcing him with the Third Army, on August 25 – that is, the day after Nogi's final assault failed – Oyama launched his three armies into the great battle of Liao-Yang, which, had Nogi's 80,000 men been available, would in all probability have ended in a decisive Japanese victory. Instead, on September 3, Kuropatkin slipped away north after he had lost 16,500 killed and wounded to Oyama's 23,615.

During this battle and up to September 19 nothing of importance occurred on the Third Army front. A request was sent to

[1] *The Truth about Port Arthur*, pp. 183–184.

Japan for heavy howitzers capable of demolishing permanent fortifications, and systematic sapping was begun.

As this work proceeded, General Nogi selected as his next objectives Waterworks Redoubt and Temple Redoubt in the eastern sector, and Namako Yama and 203 Metre Hill in the western. When it is remembered that he had occupied Port Arthur in 1894, it is strange that so far he had taken so little notice of the last of these positions, for he must have known that from its summit a complete view of the harbour could be obtained, and that therefore it was the key to the whole Russian defensive system.

By September 13 siege works had been pushed to within 80 yards of the first of these objectives, which, on the 19th, was assaulted and carried on the following day, as also was the Temple Redoubt. Simultaneously, an assault was made on Namako Yama and 203 Metre Hill, and though the former was carried on September 20, each attack on the latter was repulsed at fearful loss because the Japanese persisted in advancing in dense columns. Even when these assaults were successful, the gains were incommensurate with the losses sustained, and when they failed they only raised the enemy's *morale*. If the character of the siege operations had not been changed toward the end of the month by the arrival of the first 28-centimetre howitzers, the probability is that starvation alone would have reduced the fortress.

As it was, artillery now became the dominant arm, and in all 474 guns and howitzers, as well as many 6-in. and 8-in. wooden trench mortars, were brought into action. Of these weapons the most powerful were the 28-centimetre (11-in.) howitzers – 18 in all – which were supported by 16 5.9's and 28 4.7s. The whole of this artillery was linked up by telephone to artillery headquarters and was supplied from Dalny. The 11-in. howitzer had a range of 10,000 yards and threw a shell weighing 550 lb. In all 1,500,000 shells were fired into Port Arthur, including 36,000 of 11 in., which were called "train shells" from the noise they made in flight. The first 11 in. bombardment was opened on October 1, and is described by Nojine as follows: ". . . a pillar of smoke, sand and stones rose up out of Chi-Kuan-Shan Fort, as if a gigantic tree had sprouted up and been thrown down. Then, with clockwork regularity, fantastic trees grew up every few minutes in different directions along the north-east front, and we heard the roars of dreadful explosions. Eight of them occurred in Erh-Lung-

Shan and Chi-Kuan-Shan Forts this day and did great damage to the casemates."[1]

The effect of these formidable weapons on the siege may be compared with that of Mahomet II's giant bombards in 1453. At once the permanent defences began to crumble, and, equally important for the Japanese, because part of the harbour could be observed from Namako Yama, several of the enemy's warships were hit.

On 203 Metre Hill sapping was begun, while on the eastern front, upon which Nogi's attention was still fixed, preliminary operations were carried out in preparation for a second general assault on October 30. On October 16, Erh-lung advanced trench was taken, and so was that of Sung-Shu on the 26th, as well as the glacis trench of Erh-lung. Next, at 4.30 a.m. on October 30, a mine was sprung under Fort Erh-lung, and at 9 a.m. a simultaneous assault was launched on all works from Chi-Kuan Battery to Fort Sung-Shu. Again it was made in mass formations, and again it was repulsed with slaughter. Swept by case shot fired from smooth-bore pieces, rained upon by hand grenades and caught in flank by bursts of machine-gun fire the Japanese were swept back at heavy loss, and though the assault was renewed on the 31st it was again repulsed.

In spite of the Russian resistance, the situation within Port Arthur deteriorated rapidly. Food ran short; the sick list mounted; jealousies and intrigues between the higher command were rife; and the news of Kuropatkin's retreat after the battle of the Shaho, fought between October 12–14, gave little encouragement to the defenders. Such was the situation when, on October 15, and after innumerable delays, the Baltic Fleet, under the command of Admiral Rozhestvenski, set sail from Libau. It consisted of eight battleships, four armoured and eight protected cruisers, nine destroyers, and some auxiliary vessels. Although many of these ships were out of date, because the Japanese battleships had been reduced from seven to five – two had been sunk by mines – should Rozhestvenski succeed in joining the Port Arthur Fleet, it was possible that Togo might be defeated. Therefore it became essential, at whatever cost, to destroy the ships in the harbour. As this meant the capture of 203 Metre Hill, a third general assault was ordered for November 26, on which day the Baltic Fleet left Dakar in Senegal for the Indian Ocean.

[1] *Ibid.*, pp. 206–207.

The interval between the failure of the second general assault and the launching of the third, on November 26, was devoted mainly to underground fighting. "For an entire month," writes Ashmead Bartlett, "in the fetid atmosphere of narrow concrete cellars, with the ever-present danger of mines, amid the bursting of dynamite hand-grenades, and exposed to death from bullet and bayonet, the Japanese sapper struggled, unobserved by the world to drive his equally stubborn opponent out of these underground works."[1]

The same objectives were selected for the third assault as had been for the second, and, on the 26th, on the eastern front the same desperate struggles were repeated to end in the same costly failures. It was now that General Nogi decided to take 203 Metre Hill, cost what it might, and to prepare the way it was bombarded throughout November 26 and 27.

203 Metre Hill was a position of great natural and artificial strength. On it "was a huge redoubt, with two keeps, completely surrounded by wire entanglements. The interval between" it "and False Hill was covered by several rows of fougasses," and "Akasaka Yama was encircled with a well-built line of trenches, and had a strong redoubt on the top, with two weaker ones on the right flank."[2] All three hills were under the command of Colonel Tretyakov, who had at his disposal nearly 2,200 men.

The bombardment was continued until 5 p.m. on November 27, by when the position resembled a volcano in eruption. At that hour fire lifted and the assault on 203 Metre Hill and Akasaka Yama was launched. Under the cover of darkness the attackers reached the entanglements and held them throughout the following day. "They fought and fought like fiends," writes Nojine, "fought till exhausted, till they lost consciousness, one of their battalions being literally swept from the face of the earth."[3] Throughout the night the bombardment was maintained, and at 8.30 a.m. on November 29, another assault was made, which was hurled back by a counter-attack led by Colonel Tretyakov. On Akasaka Yama a similar struggle took place.

On November 30 fighting was renewed and was continued until December 4. The weather was bright and frosty, and Nojine tells us that "it was hardly a fight between men that was taking place on this accursed spot; it was the struggle of human flesh against

[1] *Port Arthur, etc.*, p. 233.   [2] *My Experiences, etc.*, p. 218.
[3] *The Truth about Port Arthur*, p. 244.

iron and steel, against blazing petroleum, lyddite, pyroxyline, and mélinite, and the stench of rotting corpses."[1] At length, on December 5, by when Nogi had completed his preparations, another assault was hurled at the stubborn hills. One regiment stormed up Akasaka Yama while a brigade rushed 203 Metre Hill.

The assault began between 10 and 11 a.m. and at 1.30 p.m. a company entered the 203 Metre Hill redoubt to find only a handful of defenders left alive. Soon before 5 p.m. the struggle ended, and over the rubble on the top of the hill the Rising Sun of Japan was seen flapping in the dusty air.

This mountain, writes Ashmead Bartlett, "would have been an ideal spot for a Peace Conference. There have probably never been so many dead crowded into so small a space since the French stormed the great redoubt at Borodino. . . . The Japanese are horrible to look at when dead, for their complexion turns quite green, which gives them an unnatural appearance. . . . There were practically no bodies intact; the hillside was carpeted with odd limbs, skulls, pieces of flesh, and the shapeless trunks of what had once been human beings, intermingled with pieces of shells, broken rifles, twisted bayonets, grenades, and masses of rock loosed from the surface by the explosions."[2]

What was the cost in human flesh? Four hundred Russians killed and 10,000 to 11,000 Japanese killed and wounded.

High though the cost was, the dividend paid on this investment of death was the Russian fleet, which, from the summit of 203 Metre Hill could be seen in the harbour. On December 6 its ships were bombarded and in the following days they were reduced to wrecks. Thus was Admiral Togo freed to steam home and refit so that he might be ready to meet the Baltic Fleet, which was approaching Madagascar.

The end of the siege was in sight, even if it were to be decided by starvation. All fishing had ceased, £40 was refused for a pig, eggs cost 6s. 6d. apiece, and 36 pound of garlic sold for £64. "On the 8th December the scale of rations in Port Arthur was fixed as follows: ½ lb. biscuit (in addition to the bread ration), ¼ lb. of horseflesh, and ⅛ pint of vodka, daily."[3]

---

[1] *Ibid.*, p. 252.
[2] *Port Arthur, etc.*, pp. 328–330. A similar description is given by David H. James in *The Rise and Fall of the Japanese Empire* (1951), p. 137.
[3] *Official History*, vol. II, p. 601.

This lack of food and the general situation caused General Stössel to summon a council of war on December 12, which decided that in spite of the destruction of the fleet it was premature to consider surrender. So the siege continued, and the phase now entered was devoted almost entirely to sapping and mining. Galleries were run under the forts, and on December 15 General Kontratenko, a soldier of energy and character in whom the garrison had the greatest confidence, was killed when an 11-in. shell entered a casemate. With his death the hope of the besieged began to flicker.

The main efforts of the besiegers were now directed against Forts Chi-Kuan, Erh-lung and Sung-shu. At 2.30 p.m. on December 18 two mines were exploded under the first, "when an immense cloud rose above the escarpment . . . completely hiding the fort from view." As the smoke cleared, writes Ashmead Bartlett, "On the north-west angles where had formerly stood the high yellow-coloured escarpment, a V-shaped crater lay exposed to full view. Through this hollow hundreds of black-coated figures were rushing to the attack. The Japanese infantry had wasted no time; hardly had the smoke lifted before they were in the breach. . . ."[1] Nevertheless fighting continued until early on December 19, when the garrison surrendered. On the 28th Erh-lung was also blown up, and, on the 31st, Sung-shu met with a similar fate; the entire garrison was annihilated by the explosion of about a thousand grenades stored in one of its chambers. Lastly, on January 1, the Chinese Wall in the vicinity of Fort Chi-Kuan was evacuated and the defenders fell back to Wang-tai; but they were speedily driven out of it.

The capture of Wang-tai sealed the fate of the fortress, and when he heard of it, without consulting Smirnov General Stössel dispatched a *parlementaire* to General Nogi with proposals of capitulation. When he received the answer that he was willing to negotiate, the white flag was hoisted on the morning of January 2. The representatives met at noon, English was used in their conversation, and at 9.45 p.m. the terms of surrender were signed. When they became known large numbers of the Russians threw down their arms and began to loot the town.

On January 4 the uncaptured fortifications were handed over to the Japanese, as well as 546 guns, 82,000 shells, 2,250,000 rounds of rifle ammunition and a considerable quantity of food.

[1] *Port Arthur, etc.*, Ashmead Bartlett, p. 352.

Then 878 Russian officers and 23,481 men marched out of the fortress as prisoners of war.

The losses during the siege were: Russian killed, wounded and missing, 31,306; Japanese killed, wounded and missing, 57,780, to which must be added 33,769 sick. Of the latter no less than 21,023 were victims of beriberi.[1]

The immediate result of the capitulation was that Nogi and the Third Army were set free to reinforce Marshal Oyama, who was enabled to assemble some 300,000 men against Kuropatkin's 310,000. On February 23, the greatest battle of the war was launched at Mukden. Its frontage was 40 miles in extent and both sides were entrenched. It lasted until March 10, when, as Mukden was occupied by the Japanese, Kuropatkin fell back on Harbin. The Russians lost 60,000 in killed and wounded as well as 25,000 prisoners, and the Japanese casualties numbered 71,000.

Meanwhile the doomed Baltic Fleet had slowly steamed eastward, encumbered by a large number of supply ships. On May 9 it entered the China Seas, and on May 27 it was attacked by Admiral Togo in the Strait of Tsushima and annihilated. "Far from assisting our army," writes Kuropatkin, "Rozhestvenski brought it irreparable harm. It was the defeat of his squadron at Tsushima that brought about negotiations and peace at a time when our army was ready to advance – a million strong."[2] The truth is that both sides were exhausted, the Japanese physically and the Russians morally – strikes and riots were already taking place in St. Petersburg. Thus it came about that, when on June 10 the President of the United States intervened, negotiations were opened which led to the signing of the Treaty of Portsmouth on August 29. Russia agreed to evacuate Manchuria, cede to Japan the Liao-tung peninsula – including Port Arthur and Dalny – and also the southern half of the Island of Sakhalin. Further, Russia agreed to recognize Japanese preponderance in Korea.

These were indeed small gains and losses when compared with the length and intensity of this war, and with the numbers of men killed and wounded and the wealth expended. Yet to measure its results by these alone, which unfortunately for them European nations did, would be to overlook the revolutionary character of the war. Not only did it establish a tactical revolution, but it reoriented world affairs.

[1] For details of casualties, see *Official History*, vol. II, Appendices 21 and 22.
[2] *The Russian Army and the Japanese War*, vol. I, p. 241.

When the war began the Russian tactics were still those of the early nineteenth century, and although those of the Japanese were founded on the latest European manuals, from the beginning they were proved to be only a few degrees less obsolete, as the following quotation supports:

"You are doubtless astonished," said a Japanese officer to a French attaché after the battle of Liao-Yang, "at the difference between what you see here and anything you may have witnessed at home in times of peace. We were not less astonished ourselves. Our regulations, as you know, are identical with those of the European armies. We, too, began by manœuvring according to the drill-books, and thus it was that we continued to carry the lines of Nan-shan on May 27 in a single day. But at what terrible sacrifice! . . . We have profited by that lesson, and, thanks to the experience we have acquired, we have now learnt not only not to go ahead so fast, but also to keep under better cover."[1]

The reason for this was the ever-increasing power of the bullet and the shell; in other words, the dominance of the projectile,[2] which deepened the no-man's-land which separated the combatants and so made a decision increasingly difficult. This, in its turn, prolonged the battle, compelled both attacker and defender more and more to depend upon the spade, and accentuated the moral and physical exhaustion of both.

Compared with the warfare of 1870 and 1878, the differences were radical. Though tens of thousands of men might be engaged, battlefields appeared empty, yet the air was full of bullets, each one sapped the moral strength of the fighters. Consequently intelligent discipline, in contradistinction to automatic, grew in importance. From 1905, not only had the soldier to obey, but also to think; to know how to live as well as how to fight, not for hours only, but for days on end. This urge to live made the spade as complementary to rifle as once shield had been to sword, and increasingly accentuated the importance of entanglements, of machine-guns (portable case-shot artillery) and of grenades – hand howitzers.

Nevertheless, after the war the machine-gun was at once side-

---

[1] *Lessons of the Russo-Japanese War*, p. 62.
[2] As regards casualties, see *Étude sur les caractères généraux de la guerre d'extrême-Orient*, Captain F. Culmann, 1909. The following figures are taken from this book: Losses from *armes blanches* and projectiles – Russians 1·7% to 98·3% and Japanese 3% to 97%. Losses from shell and bullet – Russians and Japanese both 15% to 85%. Proportion of killed to wounded – Russians 1 to 4.9 and Japanese 1 to 3·7 (see pp. 33, 34, 50).

tracked, as it had been after the Anglo-Boer war of 1899–1902. The Russians called it "the devil's spout",[1] and Tadayoshi Sakuri says of it: Its "belt is loaded into the chamber of the gun; it works like the film of a vitascope. And the sound it makes! Heard close by, it is a rapid succession of tap, tap, tap; but from a distance it sounds like a power loom heard late at night when everything else is hushed. It is a sickening, horrible sound! The Russians regarded this machine-gun as their best friend. . . . Whenever an army attacked the enemy's position, it was invariably this machine-gun that made us suffer and damaged us most severely."[2] Kuropatkin says much the same; "The value of machine-guns is now so great that we cannot afford to be without them. In my opinion each company should have one gun, and six men should be detailed to carry it and its ammunition."[3]

As bullets, trench and wire made fronts more and more un-attackable, the importance of artillery grew and grew, and indirect laying completely ousted direct fire. General Tretyakov says of this:

"Events here made it clear to every one what preponderance in artillery really means. The side that silences the enemy's guns can capture his positions without particularly hard fighting, for, having once got the enemy's fire under control, one can choose a point of attack, concentrate the whole of one's artillery on it, and then take it by storm with comparatively small numbers."[4]

It should be borne in mind in this regard that during this war field defences consisted of a single line of trenches, which could be overwhelmed by massed artillery fire, and not of deep zones of entrenchments, which could not be so treated as the range of the field gun was insufficient to cover them. Therefore, so long as this condition prevailed, Major J. M. Home, a British eye-witness, was right when he wrote:

"The great impression made on me by all I saw is that artillery is now the decisive arm and that all other arms are auxiliary to it. The importance of artillery cannot be too strongly insisted upon, for, other things being equal, the side which has the best artillery will always win. . . .

"So strongly am I convinced of the immense importance of artillery that it seems almost a question for deliberate consideration

[1] *Actual Experiences in War*, Soloviev, p. 33.
[2] *Human Bullets*, pp. 152–153.
[3] *The Russian Army and the Japanese War*, vol. II, p. 134.
[4] *My Experiences at Nan Shan and Port Arthur*, p. 113.

whether artillery should not be largely increased even at the expense of the other arms. Infantry can, if necessary, be trained in about three months, whereas artillery cannot be so improvised.

"With the extraordinary development of artillery it begins to appear as though infantry fire action cannot usefully be employed at ranges beyond 600 yards, as beyond that distance the hostile guns ought to be able to prevent infantry from using their rifles."[1]

But after the war little notice was taken of these tactical changes; the need for more and more artillery in the field battle was overlooked, nor was the delaying power of the machine-gun, when coupled with wire entanglements and entrenchments, recognized, and as for the use of arsenical smoke[2] by the Japanese in their last attack on Fort Chi-Kuan, no one even noticed it or dreamt what it implied.

More important than these tactical changes were the influences of Japan's victory on world affairs. It disrupted Russia by stimulating the virus of revolution which for long had eaten into her bowels. By liberating Germany from fear of war on her eastern flank it freed her to concentrate on her western border, and thereby upset the balance of power in Europe. This caused Great Britain to abandon her policy of isolation, which had been the backbone of the *Pax Britannica*, and, in order to re-establish the balance, it drew her away from Germany toward France. Further, by challenging the supremacy of the white man over the coloured, it awakened Asia and Africa and dealt a deadly moral blow to every colonial empire. Though this was little appreciated at the time, in his treatise *The Problem of National and Colonial Policy and the Third International*, M. Pavlovich points out that "The Russian Revolution of 1905 played the same great part in the life of the Asiatic people as the French Revolution had formerly played in European countries. It gave the impulse in Turkey to the revolutionary activities which led to the fall of Abdul Hamid. It made an overwhelming impression upon Persia, which was the first Asiatic nation to start a simultaneous struggle against its own despots and against the rapacity of European governments. The same is true of China. But everywhere European intervention frustrated the fulfilment of dreams of national liberty."[3]

[1] *The Russo-Japanese War, Reports from British Officers* (1908), vol. III, pp. 209–210.

[2] General Tretyakov says: "The Japanese tried to drive us out of the caponier of this fort by burning in it material soaked in arsenic. Our men were stifled by the fumes, and the sentries in the casemates had to be relieved every few minutes. Fort Ehr-lung was in a similar plight" (p. 287).

[3] Quoted from *A History of Nationalism in the East*, Hans Kohn (1929), p. 130.

In Africa the influence was equally profound. Dicey, an Englishman, who had lived in that continent for 40 years, writes: "Suddenly and unexpectedly, the conviction that native forces, however brave, were bound to be worsted by Europeans, was shaken to its base by the discovery that Russia, which was regarded in the East as the greatest military power in Europe, had been driven from pillar to post by the victorious Japanese, that her armies had been put to flight, her navy destroyed, her fortresses captured by a comparatively diminutive and feeble Power, whose people, whatever else they might be, were certainly not Caucasians or Christians. It may be said with truth that the native Africans . . . knew nothing . . . about Japan. But yet I should doubt whether there was a town or village in the whole of Africa where the inhabitants did not learn directly or indirectly that the Russian invaders of the Far East had been scattered like sheep by an unknown non-European race."[1]

But it was in India – the pivot of British imperial power – that this world revolution took surest form. There "A stir of excitement passed over" the northern provinces, writes C. F. Andrews. "Even the remote villages talked over the victories of Japan as they sat in their circles and passed round the *huqqa* at night. . . . A Turkish consul of long experience in Western Asia told me that in the interior you could see everywhere the most ignorant peasants 'tingling' with the news. Asia was moved from one end to the other, and the sleep of the centuries was finally broken. . . . A new chapter was being written in the book of the world's history. . . . The old-time glory and greatness of Asia seemed destined to return."[2]

In corroboration of this, Mr. Pradhan writes: "It is impossible to exaggerate the effects of the Japanese victory on the Indian mind."[3] Indian students began to study the history of Japan to discover what had enabled her to wound so deeply one of the greatest European Powers. They found the answer in Japanese patriotism, self-sacrifice and national unity. Here were miraculous powers beyond the might of armaments. The rise of Japan was looked upon as "a divine dispensation". Indian students flocked to the Rising Sun, and in the years 1907, 1908 and 1909 they returned haloed with knowledge, both true and spurious, to take

---

[1] *The Egypt of the Future*, Edward Dicey (1907), pp. 139–140.
[2] *The Renaissance in India*, C. F. Andrews (1912), p. 4.
[3] *India's Struggle for Swaraj*, R. G. Pradhan (1930), p. 75.

part in the *Swadeshi* movement, and to help a cause which the Japanese victories had endowed with a vigour undreamt of before the war.

All these stupendous happenings were fertilized by this conflict, fought on the far eastern flank of Asia, as over 450 years before an equally great conflict had been fought on the far eastern flank of Europe: The fall of Port Arthur in 1905, like the fall of Constantinople in 1453, rightly may be numbered among the few really great events in history.

The foundations of the First World War

With the fulfilment of "Manifest Destiny" in America; the emergence of the Second Reich in central Europe; the rise of Japanese imperialism in the Far East; the ever-expanding empires of Britain, France, and Germany;[1] and the vast outpouring of South African gold,[2] an age is entered comparable with that of the Diadochi, in which the rivalries and alliances between Germany, France, Great Britain, and Russia precipitated an epoch of world-wide conflict.

As is usual in history, its immediate origins are to be sought in the results of the preceding war – that of 1870–1871. From its close until his dismissal in 1890, Bismarck's policy was to stabilize and secure the peace Germany had won. This he set out to do by the isolation of France and the maintenance of friendly relations with Russia. In order to achieve the former aim, on October 2, 1879, he concluded with Austria a defensive treaty known as the Dual Alliance. Two years later France played into his hands by occupying Tunisia. This annexation so irritated Italy that she joined the Dual Alliance and thereby converted it into a triple alliance. Thus things stood until June 15, 1888, when on the death of his father, Frederick III, William II of Hohenzollern (1888–1918), grandson of Queen Victoria, became Emperor of Germany.

He was an excitable, impulsive and headstrong man; industrious, pious, and patriotic. Vain and theatrical, he fancied himself as an autocrat, and soon after his accession he declared: "There is only one master in the country, and I am he." He delighted to pose as supreme war lord, and though he kept his country out of war for 26 years, his intemperate language, flaming orations and unmeasured ambitions made him the Spanish fly of international politics. In 1890 he dismissed Bismarck, and in the following

---

[1] Between 1870 and the end of the century Great Britain acquired 4,754,000 square miles of land; France 3,583,580; Germany 1,026,220; Belgium 847,000; and the United States the remnants of the old Spanish empire.

[2] Between 1850 and 1853 the annual world output of gold rose from 1,819,600 oz. to 6,350,108, then remained steady until 1892, when it rapidly rose to 21,529,300 oz. in 1908.

year France, thoroughly alarmed by Germany's new master, entered into negotiations with Russia which, in 1893, led to a defensive alliance between the two countries. Two years later Tsar Nicholas II (1894–1918) visited Paris and received a tremendous ovation.

Thus two opposing alliances were born; nevertheless, as long as Great Britain was not a party to either, the peace of Europe was little threatened, and even were their antagonisms to lead to war, without British participation it was unlikely to spread beyond Europe. Unfortunately, this situation was not to last, because in 1895 a period of German expansion opened. It was heralded by the German emperor in a speech delivered on the twenty-fifth anniversary of the founding of the empire, in which he said that the German empire had ceased to be merely continental, and had become world-wide. Though it would have been wiser to have left this unsaid, the Kaiser's new *Weltpolitik* was the inevitable result of Germany's rapid industrialization since the Franco-Prussian war. Between 1870 and 1895 her population had increased from 41 million to 55 million, and its subsistence had become increasingly dependent upon foreign trade. To support her traders in all parts of the world, it was therefore imperative for Germany to assume the position of a world Power. Unfortunately, this meant commercial rivalry with Great Britain.

Next, in 1898, to guarantee the Kaiser's policy of expansion, a Bill was passed by the Reichstag which increased the size of the German navy, and in the memorandum which accompanied it his voice was clearly heard in the boastful statement that the navy was to be such that "even for the greatest sea power, a war with it would involve such risks as to jeopardize its own supremacy." It was a shot aimed at Britain, on the brink of war with France over the Fashoda incident. Then, in 1899, came the Anglo-Boer war, which raised all but universal hostility against England, who found herself isolated. Its outbreak was speedily followed by another German naval Bill, in which it was laid down that the permanent establishment of the fleet was to be 38 battleships and 20 armoured cruisers, and that each ship would be replaced once in every 25 years. Such was the situation when, on January 22, 1901, Queen Victoria died and was succeeded by her son Edward VII (1901–1910).

The hostility shown by Germany toward England during the South African war, coupled with her naval expansion and the

Kaiser's policy of brag, gave rise to violent anti-German propaganda in Britain, which was reciprocated in Germany. This propaganda obscured the real bone of contention between the two countries: it was not that Germany deliberately looked forward to forcing a war with England, let alone to invading her – a popular British illusion – but that the enormous expansion of German oversea trade and the growth of her merchant navy increasingly ousted British commerce. Between 1894 and 1904 the value of German trade rose from £365 m. to £610 m., and in the same period the tonnage of her merchant shipping increased by 234 per cent. So acute grew the struggle for trade that in 1907, when Mr. Henry White, American Ambassador in Italy, was sent by the State Department to London to ascertain the views of the British Government toward the second Hague Conference, the following conversation between him and Mr. Arthur Balfour is recorded by Allan Nevins in his *Henry White, Thirty Years of American Diplomacy*:

Balfour (*somewhat lightly*): "We are probably fools not to find a reason for declaring war on Germany before she builds too many ships and takes away our trade."

White: "You are a very high-minded man in private life. How can you possibly contemplate anything so politically immoral as provoking a war against a harmless nation which has as good a right to a navy as you have? If you wish to compete with German trade, work harder."

Balfour: "That would mean lowering our standard of living. Perhaps it would be simpler for us to have a war."

White: "I am shocked that you of all men should enunciate such principles."

Balfour (*again lightly*): "Is it a question of right or wrong? Maybe it is just a question of keeping our supremacy."

The point to note in this conversation is not whether Mr. Balfour was or was not an unprincipled cynic, but that the Industrial Revolution had led to the establishment of an economic struggle for existence in which self-preservation dictated a return to the ways of the jungle. The primeval struggle between man and beast had been replaced by the industrial struggle between nation and nation in which all competitors were beasts. On September 11, 1919, in an address given at St. Louis, President Woodrow Wilson laid bare the heart of the problem when he said: "Why, my fellow-citizens, is there any man here, or any woman – let me say, is there any child here – who does not know that the seed of war in the modern world is industrial and commercial rivalry? . . . This war, in its inception, was a commercial and industrial war. It was not a political war." And at about the same time John Maynard Keynes wrote in his *The Economic Consequences of the Peace*: "The politics of power are inevitable, and there is nothing very new to learn about this war or the end it was fought for; England had destroyed, as in each preceding century, a trade rival. . . ."

The isolation in which England found herself during the South African war was broken by Edward VII in 1903. In the spring of that year he visited Paris, was hissed on his arrival and cheered on his departure: his charm, as well as his antipathy for his nephew, the Kaiser, had broken the ice. His visit was followed by a series of agreements between the British and French governments which, in April, 1904, led to the establishment of an Anglo-French entente, a treaty of friendship which was to grow into a secret military alliance and change the whole course of British history. Lloyd George records in his *War Memoirs* that, soon after it was agreed, Lord Rosebery said to him: " 'Well, I suppose you are just as pleased as the rest of them with the French agreement?' I assured him that I was delighted that our snarling and scratching relations with France had come to an end at last. He replied: 'You are all wrong. It means war with Germany in the end'." Four years later, Admiral Sir John Fisher, First Sea Lord, was even more foresighted. "I hazarded a prophecy (but, of course, I was only doing the obvious!)" he writes, "that should we be led . . . into a sort of tacit pledge to France to land a British Army in France in a war against Germany, then would come the biggest blow to England she would ever have experienced – not a defeat, *because we never succumb* – but a deadly blow to our economic resources and by the relegation of the British Navy into a 'Subsidiary Service'."

In accordance with the Anglo-French entente, the two governments settled their outstanding colonial differences; while Britain was given a free hand in Egypt, France was to be allowed a free hand in Morocco as long as the integrity of that country was respected. Nevertheless, in October a convention was drawn up between France and Spain for the partition of Morocco, and a copy of this secret treaty was sent to Lord Lansdowne, the British Foreign Secretary, who, although it flatly contradicted the first treaty, accepted it. This shady transaction was to prove a veritable Pandora's box of trouble.

Nor was trouble long delayed. In March, 1905, the Kaiser, who knew nothing of either of these treaties, suspected that Morocco might become a second Tunis and visited Tangier. So violent a campaign of abuse was launched against him that in order to prevent the outbreak of war President Theodore Roosevelt stepped into the international arena and suggested a conference. In January, 1906, it met at Algeciras and confirmed the pledges of the Powers to uphold the independence of Morocco. Although it allayed the storm, it left Europe divided into two hostile camps – the German and the anti-German – and to fortify the latter, Sir Edward Grey, who had succeeded Lord Lansdowne as Foreign Secretary, agreed with the French Government on secret conversations between the British and French military and naval General Staffs. Already, in 1904, Admiral Sir John Fisher had persuaded the British Government to shift the centre of gravity of the British fleet from Gibraltar to the North Sea, and in the following year, when he laid down the first *Dreadnought* battleship, he completely unhinged the German naval programme, because the *Dreadnought* made all existing battleships obsolescent.

Soon after the Algeciras Conference the British Government came to an understanding with the Russians, and among other things it was agreed to divide Persia – an independent country – into three zones: a Russian and a British zone of influence, with a neutral zone in between. This settlement relieved Russia of perils in the Far East and enabled her, as Mr. Gooch in his *History of Modern Europe* writes, to turn "her undivided attention to the even more dangerous game of European politics." Thus a Triple Entente came into being to face the Triple Alliance, which meant that in the event of war Germany would have to fight on two fronts.

While the Morocco crisis shocked international relations, in England a naval panic, started by a Mr. Mulliner of the Coventry Ordnance Company, shocked the Government, the Opposition, and the people, and so unreasonable did it become that Sir John Fisher decided to inform the King of the true situation. Late in 1907 he wrote to him:

"In March this year, 1907, it is an absolute fact that Germany has not laid down a single 'Dreadnought', nor has she commenced building a single Battleship or Big Cruiser for eighteen months

. . . half of the whole German Battle Fleet is only equal to the English Armoured Cruisers. . . . Now this is the truth: England has seven 'Dreadnoughts' and three 'Dreadnought' Battle Cruisers (which last three ships are, in my opinion, far better than 'Dreadnoughts'); total, ten 'Dreadnoughts' built and building, while Germany, in March last, had not begun even one 'Dreadnought'. . . . We have 123 Destroyers and 40 Submarines. The Germans have 48 Destroyers and 1 Submarine. . . . Admiral Tirpitz, the German Minister of Marine, has just stated, in a secret official document, that the English Navy is now four times stronger than the German Navy. Yes, that is so, and we are going to keep the British Navy at that strength. . . . But we don't want to parade all this to the world at large."

Later, on March 21, 1909, in a letter to Lord Esher, Fisher wrote: "The unswerving intention of 4 years has *now* culminated in *two* complete Fleets in Home Waters, each of which is incomparably superior to the whole German Fleet mobilized for war. . . . This can't alter for years. . . . *So sleep quiet in your beds!* . . . The Germans are not building in this feverish haste to fight you! *No!* it's the daily dread they have of a second Copenhagen, which they know a Pitt or a Bismarck would execute on them!"

Although Mr. Balfour, leader of the Opposition, must have been aware of this, in the General Elections of January, 1910, he let loose a cyclonic attack on Germany in order to terrify the people into voting for the Conservatives. He declared that England was in danger and that her naval power was inadequate. He said: "I am perfectly confident that you will find among" the lesser powers "an absolute unanimity of opinion that a struggle sooner or later between this country and Germany is inevitable." Mr. Winston Churchill replied: "The attitude of the Conservative party with regard to the navy has been a disgrace . . . it was a policy of trying to raise a panic without reason, a policy of trying to raise ill-will between two great nations without cause."

The crux of the naval question was that it had been the policy of successive British governments to concentrate popular attention on British and German naval expansion alone; they did not take into account the fact that Germany had other naval considerations than war against England. Her naval situation in a war against France and Russia was overlooked, yet it was this situation which was, and had been, the governing factor in her naval policy since 1900, when Admiral Tirpitz said: "We should be in a position to blockade the Russian fleet in the Baltic ports, and to prevent at the same time the entrance to that sea of the French fleet." The following figures, which are those of new construction from 1909 to 1914, speak for themselves.

	Great Britain	France	Russia	Germany
1909	£11,076,551	£4,517,766	£1,758,487	£10,177,062
1910	14,755,289	4,977,682	1,424,013	11,392,856
1911	15,148,171	5,876,659	3,215,396	11,701,859
1912	16,132,558	7,114,876	6,897,580	11,491,187
1913	16,883,875	8,093,064	12,082,516	11,010,883
1914	18,676,080	11,772,862	13,098,613	10,316,264

When the cost of Austrian and Italian new construction for 1914, respectively £4,051,976 and £3,237,000, is added to the last of the above German figures, it will be seen that when war broke out the Triple Entente was spending on new construction two and a half times the amount spent by the Triple Alliance, and France and Russia approximately two and a half times as much as Germany. How anyone could say that German naval expansion threatened England is difficult to understand; yet from 1909 on it was said again and again. Why? The reason was, not that the German navy threatened England, but that, as Mr. Balfour had said to Mr. White, her merchant navy was increasingly taking away England's trade and that German industrial production was ousting her own. Were these changes to continue the collapse of British economy became possible.

On May 6, 1910, Edward VII died and was succeeded by his son, George V; but before his coronation, on June 22, 1911, another violent incident exploded in Morocco. The French Government, bent on complete control over Morocco, and urged on by the *Comité du Maroc*, occupied Fez under the pretext of protecting French nationals. Though still without knowledge of the secret treaty of 1904, the German Government seized upon this as a violation of the Treaty of Algeciras and sent a gunboat, the *Panther*, to Agadir to protect German commercial interests and subjects in Morocco. Thereupon Mr. Lloyd George, then British Chancellor of the Exchequer, delivered a violent speech at the Mansion House which nearly precipitated a general war. By November a settlement was reached, under which France obtained a free hand in Morocco and Germany a slice of the French Congo. This did not satisfy Italy, and fearful that France would next seize Tripoli, on the now normal pretext of securing trade and nationals, she declared war on Turkey, invaded Tripoli, and occupied Rhodes and other of the Dodecanese Islands.

It is time to turn from western to eastern Europe, for there imperialism followed an equally dangerous road.

Frustrated in the Far East by Japan, Russia turned westward to take up again the task she had been forced to drop after Plevna, and because she was now in alliance with France and a member of the Triple Entente, her prospects of expansion in that direction were more propitious than they had been in 1877. Her aim was to gain the balance of power in Europe, firstly by the liquidation of Turkey; secondly by morally weakening Austria; and thirdly, through this, physically weakening Germany. The instrument she intended to use was the Balkan States, more particularly Serbia and Bulgaria. The former had gained her independence in 1878, but the latter was still a tributary of the Sultan, and as this anomalous position had for long rankled with the Bulgarians, on October 5, 1908, Prince Ferdinand publicly proclaimed his country an independent kingdom. Immediately after this Austria annexed Bosnia and Herzegovina.

This was an opportunity Russia did not miss. Her Government set out to unite the Balkan States by the promotion among them of the belief that unless they dropped their respective antagonisms and combined in mutual defence they would be swallowed piecemeal by the Austro-Hungarian empire. The outcome was the formation of the Balkan League, which in the Italo-Turkish War saw an opportunity of expansion at the expense of the Turks.

On October 8, 1912, as the Italo-Turkish War was about to end, Montenegro declared war on Turkey, and was joined forthwith by Bulgaria, Serbia and Greece. Macedonia was overrun by the Serbs, Salonika occupied by the Greeks, and, after they had defeated the Turks at Kirk Kilisse and Lula Burgas, the Bulgars were held up on the Chatalja lines a few miles west of Constantinople. On December 3 an armistice was agreed, but it was not until May 30, 1913, that peace was signed in London. No sooner had it been signed than a quarrel arose over the spoils. Without a declaration of war, the Bulgars fell upon the Serbs and Greeks. The Rumanians then entered the conflict, and the Turks – since January under Enver Pasha – retook Adrianople. The Bulgars were overwhelmed, and when on August 10 the second Balkan War was ended by the Treaty of Bucharest, Turkey in Europe was reduced to Adrianople and Constantinople and the country around them, including the Gallipoli peninsula.

Although the two Balkan wars nearly drove Turkey out of Europe, for Russia the second war was a setback because it fractured the Balkan League. Nevertheless, it left Europe in such tension that another incident was bound to occur which might enable St. Petersburg to pursue its policy against Austria. This was sensed by Colonel E. M. House – President Woodrow Wilson's roving ambassador. In the spring of 1914 he visited Berlin, and in a dispatch to the President reported: "The whole of Germany is charged with electricity. Everybody's nerves are tense. It only requires a spark to set the whole thing off." Further, he wrote: "Whenever England consents, France and Russia will close in on Germany and Austria."

Russia was fearful that England's consent might be withheld. From London, Benckendorff, the Russian Ambassador, wrote to Sazanov, the Russian Foreign Minister: "It is impossible for the Anglo-Russian entente to be maintained if the estrangement between Britain and Germany ceases." This was with reference to German attempts to dissipate the estrangement. The one thing Russia feared was delay; the Emperor Francis Joseph was 84, and the Archduke Francis Ferdinand, the heir apparent, was opposed to the Greater Serbia movement. At all costs Russia was determined that the Yugoslavs should look to St. Petersburg and not to Vienna. This was the position when on June 28, 1914, the Archduke and his wife were assassinated in Serajevo and the Age of the Contending States became a reality.

According to Mr. Bogitshevich, the Serbian Chargé d'Affaires in Germany, "Serbia had already received the assurance of Russia that this time she would not desert Serbia." Further, he writes: "And what is more important still, Serbia must have been assured that war against Germany and Austria had been resolved upon, and the assassination of the Austrian heir to the throne furnished a favourable pretext for the war only because England and France had allowed themselves to be drawn into this conflict by Russia (which in and of itself was but a local conflict between Austria and Serbia). . . . If Sir Edward Grey," Bogitshevich writes, "had . . . simply declared to Russia and France (Germany need not have heard a word of it) that England was uninterested in this conflict – retaining entire freedom of action as regards what might subsequently arise – the European war would in that case certainly not have broken out. But all this is of course on the supposition that England had not already so bound herself that retreat was no longer possible."

Unfortunately, not only for England but for the world in general, this is what had happened. Shrouded in secrecy, the Entente of 1904 had grown into an irrevocable secret military alliance.

On July 23, an Austrian ultimatum was presented to Belgrade with a time limit of 48 hours, and to prevent action by Russia Sir Edward Grey urged Serbia to promise full satisfaction. But Sazanov thought differently. He declared the ultimatum to be an unparalleled act of aggression and that the only way to avert war with Germany was to let Berlin know that she would be confronted by the united forces of the Entente. Russia then ordered partial mobilization. In her turn Germany urged that the question should be settled by Austria and Serbia alone, and that any interference of any other Power would be followed by incalculable consequences. Wedged between France, England, and Russia, she was badly placed to enter a general war, but as the German *White Book* points out: "If the Serbs continued with the aid of Russia and France, to menace the existence of Austria, her gradual collapse and the subjection of all the Slavs under the Russian sceptre would result, thus rendering untenable the position of the Teutonic race in central Europe. A morally weakened Austria under the pressure of Russian Pan-Slavism would be no longer an ally on whom we could count in view of the ever more menacing attitude of our eastern and western neighbours." Germany therefore decided to stand by her ally.

On July 25 Serbia replied to the Austrian ultimatum, and although the answer was conciliatory, because it was incomplete it was rejected; full Austrian mobilization was ordered, and on the 28th Austria declared war on Serbia. At once Russia ordered full mobilization. On the 29th, the German Chancellor sent for Sir Edward Goschen, British Ambassador in Berlin, and said that if Great Britain remained neutral, in the event of a successful war against France Germany would respect the integrity of France. The offer was refused.

Next, on July 31, the German Ambassador in St. Petersburg was instructed to present an ultimatum to the Russian Government to demand the cessation of mobilization within 12 hours, failing which Germany would mobilize. As this demand was unanswered, on August 1 Germany and Russia were at war, and France ordered general mobilization.

On August 2, Italy declared her neutrality[1] and Sir Edward Grey informed France that should the German fleet attack France in the Channel Great Britain would intervene with her fleet. Meanwhile, early on August 2, German cavalry patrols had crossed the Luxemburg frontier, and at 7.20 p.m. the German Minister in Brussels delivered a note to the Belgian Government which demanded free passage of German troops through Belgium. If this were granted Germany would undertake at the end of the war to leave Belgium with her independence and territories un-impaired. An answer was required within 12 hours – it was negative.

On August 3, the King of the Belgians made a personal appeal to the King of England to safeguard his country. At 6.45 p.m. Germany declared war on France, and nine hours later on Belgium also. Lastly, at 3 p.m. on August 4, Sir Edward Goschen was instructed by the Foreign Office to obtain assurance from Germany that Belgian neutrality, which was guaranteed by treaty, would be respected. It was then that von Bethman-Hollweg said in reply: "Just for a scrap of paper Great Britain is going to make war on a kindred race." At midnight on August 4, Britain declared war on Germany.

Much play has been made of the Chancellor's words, yet they were largely true of the Treaty of 1839 which, if not a "scrap of paper," was little more than a "holy relic".[2] Under its terms British obligations were not defined, and there was no provision which necessitated England sending troops to Belgium to make war on any Power that should violate her territories. As later (March 8, 1915) *The Times* pointed out: Even had Germany not violated Belgian neutrality British "honour and interest" must have compelled England to join France and Russia against Germany. Had its editor substituted for these words "secret diplomacy and secret obligations, about which Parliament knew nothing," he would have been more correct.

---

[1] Austria did not declare war on Russia until August 6.

[2] Queen Victoria's outlook on treaty obligation of this type is worth comparison. With reference to the treaty of 1852 which guaranteed the integrity of Denmark, when trouble arose over Schleswig-Holstein she wrote to Lord Granville: "The only chance of preserving peace for Europe is by not assisting Denmark. . . . Denmark is after all of less vital importance than the peace of Europe, and it would be madness to set the whole Continent on fire for the imaginary advantages of maintaining the integrity of Denmark."

CHAPTER 5

The Battles of the Marne and Tannenberg, 1914

The war which leapt out of the Serbo-Austrian brawl rapidly assumed the shape of a world conflict. The reason was that all the greater Powers involved, including Japan and Turkey, who respectively joined the Triple Entente and the Central Powers on August 23 and October 29, and Italy, who joined the former on May 4, 1915,[1] were empires whose frontiers for the most part clashed with each other. Eventually, when on April 6, 1917, the United States declared war on Germany and was followed by some South American and other States, the war became global and not a single greater Power was left free to act as its arbiter.

It is manifestly impossible in so vast a conflict, within the limits of this book, to touch upon circumferential campaigns, although most of them had vast historical consequences. Further, it is considered more to the point to use some of the space which might be devoted to these operations to the pre-war military theories held by the leading belligerents, particularly those of the French and Germans – who set the tactical pace – before the first decisive battle is described. Unless these theories are appreciated, it is impossible clearly to fathom the reasons why, in spite of the disastrous defeat sustained by the Germans within six weeks of the start of the war, the war dragged on until November, 1918; it was the complications arising out of the length of the war which fundamentally changed the course of history.

The 40 years before the war were prolific in military theories, for they were years of advancing industrial development, and if they were not the cradle, they were the nursery of the present scientific age. Among the many military theorists who appeared during these years, one was outstanding, namely I. S. Bloch, because he got down to the roots of the war problem. He was a

---

[1] Later Rumania and Portugal joined the Allies and Bulgaria the Central Powers. Greece tried to remain neutral, but when the Allies occupied Salonica she was forced to join them.

Polish banker and economist. In 1897 he published an elaborate analysis on modern warfare, entitled *The War of the Future in its Technical, Economic and Political Relations*, and in 1899 an abridged edition, edited by W. T. Stead, appeared in English under the title *Is War now Impossible?*

Bloch's thesis was that war is shaped by civilization, and because at the end of the nineteenth century civilization had nearly passed out of its agricultural into its industrial phase, the character of war had changed with it. "What is the use," he wrote, "of talking about the past when you are dealing with an altogether new set of considerations? Consider for a moment what nations were a hundred years ago and what they are to-day. In those days before railways, telegraphs, steam ships, etc., were invented each nation was more or less a homogeneous, self-contained, self-sufficing unit. . . . All this is changed. . . . Every year the interdependence of nations upon each other for the necessaries of life is greater than it ever was before. . . . Hence the first thing that war would do would be to deprive the Powers that made it of all opportunity of benefiting by the products of the nations against whom they were fighting. . . . The soldier is going down and the economist is going up." Therefore war is no longer a profitable court of appeal. The old conception of war as a business is absurd; to-day it is a mad kind of burglary – the plundering of one's own house.

"The outward and visible sign of the end of war," he said, "was the introduction of the magazine rifle. . . . The soldier by natural evolution has so perfected the mechanism of slaughter that he has practically secured his own extinction."

His description of the modern battle is exact, for it is exactly as it was fought 17 years later. And his prediction of the war is no less accurate:

"At first there will be increased slaughter on so terrible a scale as to render it impossible to get troops to push the battle to a decisive issue. They will try to, thinking that they are fighting under the old conditions, and they will learn such a lesson that they will abandon the attempt for ever. . . . The war, instead of being a hand-to-hand contest in which the combatants measure their physical and moral superiority, will become a kind of stalemate, in which neither army being able to get at the other, both armies will be maintained in opposition to each other, threatening each other, but never being able to deliver a final and decisive attack. . . . That is the future of war – not fighting, but famine, not the slaying of men, but the bankruptcy of nations and the break-up of the whole social organization. . . . Everybody will be entrenched in the next war. It will be a great war of entrenchments. The spade will be as indispensable to a soldier as his rifle. . . . All wars will of necessity partake of the character of siege operations . . . soldiers may fight as they please; the ultimate decision is in the hand of *famine*."[1]

He pictured that in a war between the Triple and Dual Alliances 10 million men would take the field; that battle fronts would be so enormous that command would become impossible; that cavalry would be useless; the day of the bayonet gone, and that artillery would be the dominant arm.

Although this picture exactly depicted the next war, Bloch failed to follow his thesis to its logical conclusion. If granted to be correct, then it followed that the sole thing impossible was for warfare to stand still. The validity of his forecast depended on the conditions of his day remaining static, and the turn of the century witnessed an outburst of inventiveness which was destined to revolutionize war even more completely than had the introduction of the horse in the third millennium B.C.

Of the many inventions of this period, the two most fateful for war were the internal combustion engine and wireless telegraphy.[2]

As a commercial proposition the gas engine was first introduced by Dr. N. A. Otto in 1876.[3] Nine years later Gottlieb Daimler improved upon it; he fitted a small petroleum spirit internal combustion motor to a bicycle and produced the first petrol driven vehicle.[4] Next, it was adapted to four-wheeled carriages, and in 1895 the first automobile race was held. It was from Paris to Bordeaux and back, and the winner covered the 744 miles at a mean speed of 15 miles an hour. Lastly came the most revolutionary of its triumphs. On December 17, 1903, at Kill Devil Hill, Kitty Hawk, North Carolina, Orville Wright in a power-driven aeroplane flew for 12 seconds. Six years later Blériot in a monoplane spanned the English Channel in 31 minutes. After 3,000

[1] Quoted from the Preface ("Conversations with the author, by W. T. Stead") of *Is War Impossible?* (1899).
[2] Others were: Bell's electric telephone, 1876; Parson's steam turbine, 1884; Dunlop's pneumatic tyre, 1888; Batter's endless chain track tractor, 1888. Also, at the opening of the present century, Rutherford and Soddy were at work on the nuclear atomic theory, which was to lead to the invention of the atomic bomb.
[3] In idea it was old, and dates from Christian Huygens in 1680.
[4] In the same year (1885) Butler, in England, propelled a tricycle by means of a benzoline engine exploded electrically.

years the legend of Daedalus came true. A power had been born which within half a century was destined to change the face of war.

The second invention – wireless telegraphy – was first given theoretical form in 1887 by Rudolf Hertz. He proved that under certain conditions an electrical spark creates an effect which is propagated into space as an electric wave. This drew the attention of Guglielmo Marconi to the invention of a practical device which could detect these waves, and so successful was he that in 1897 he transmitted a wireless message over a distance of nine miles, and in 1901 over 3,000 miles.

These two inventions introduced warlike possibilities which went far beyond anything as yet accomplished by either gunpowder or steam power. The former not only led to a revolution in road transport, and consequently in land warfare, but as it solved the problem of flight it raised war into the third dimension. The latter virtually raised it into the fourth dimension; for to all intents and purposes the wireless transmission of energy annihilated time as well as space. Thus two new battlefields were created – the sky and the ether.

These changes, as well as others which resulted from scores of less prominent inventions, when coupled with the strides made in the metallurgical, chemical, electrical, biological and other sciences, set in motion forces very different from those released by coal and steam. Mind more than matter, thought more than things, and above all imagination, struggled to gain power. New substances appeared, new sources of energy were tapped and new outlooks on life took form. The world was sloughing its skin – mental, moral and physical – a process destined to transform the industrial revolution into a technical civilization.

Divorced from civil progress, soldiers could not see this. They could not see that as civilization became more technical, military power must inevitably follow suit: that the next war would be as much a clash between factories and technicians as between armies and generals. With the steady advance of science warfare could not stand still. Even the far-sighted M. Bloch failed to see this.

Few soldiers and sailors were as clear-sighted as he, and those who did see clearly, like him, failed to see that industry and science had already placed in their hands weapons of such power that if rightly combined they could prevent a war of pure attrition. Most were hostile to novelty, nevertheless faith in a war of movement abounded, and in this respect most military opinion was in opposition to that of Bloch. For instance, in 1912, a French soldier of distinction wrote: "In a war between France and Germany we do not anticipate a battle of such a nature [*i.e.*, an entrenched battle]. . . . Battles in entrenched camps as occurred at Plevna or Mukden will never take place in a war with the French army."[1]

The godhead of this heresy was formed by General Foch, General Grandmaison, and General Langlois, who established a school of thought rivalled only by the dervishes of the Sudan.[2] Their leading principle was that morale was the infallible answer to the rifle bullet – pure witchcraft. Foch quoted approvingly the words of Joseph de Maistre: "A battle lost is a battle one thinks one had lost; for a battle cannot be lost physically." Foch added: "Therefore it can only be lost morally. But, then, it is also morally that a battle is won, and we may extend the aphorism by saying: 'A battle won is a battle in which one will not confess oneself beaten'."[3]

Coupled with this sophistry, he believed that "any improvement of firearms is ultimately bound to add strength to the offensive." Therefore in battle there is only one principle to follow – namely, attack![4] He appears to have overlooked that to make attack profitable a return must be made to the essence of the Napoleonic offensive, which was – "it is with artillery that war is made."[5]

Count von Schlieffen, Chief of the German General Staff, 1891–1905, partly realized this,[6] and to make the attack superior to the defence he increased the number of the German heavy guns; but

[1] Quoted in *A Critical Study of German Tactics*, Major de Pardieu (1912), p. 117. The outlook of the French on the approaching war is summarized by General Herr in his *L'Artillerie* (1923), pp. 4–5. Among other things he says: "The war will be short and of rapid movements, where manœuvres will play the predominant part; it will be a war of movement. The battle will be primarily a struggle between two infantries . . . the army must be an army of personnel and not of material. The artillery will only be an accessory arm. . . . The necessity for heavy artillery will seldom make itself felt. . . . It will serve no useful purpose to encumber oneself with an over-numerous artillery. . . ."
[2] They drew their inspirations from Colonel Ardant du Picq's *Études sur le combat*, which exaggerated the value of the moral factor in war. His theory was sound enough for the hand-to-hand combat of classical times; moderately sound for musket and bayonet warfare, but most misleading for rifle warfare. After 1871 his book cast a spell on the French army.
[3] *The Principles of War* (English edit., 1918), p. 286.
[4] *Ibid.*, p. 32.
[5] *Correspondance*, vol. xxx, p. 447.
[6] So did Admiral Sir John Fisher in England; hence the laying down of the first *Dreadnought* battleship in 1905.

he did not see that this in itself was insufficient, and that true superiority could only be gained when a new fighting organization was built round the gun. This was the leading tactical problem which faced all armies after the Russo-Japanese War, and it was by no means an obscure one.[1]

Such was the unseen tactical background of the war of 1914–1918; the apparent background was this:

After the Franco-Prussian war the French and German General Staffs periodically revised their training manuals, and after 1905 the tactical doctrines expressed in them were almost exclusively based on the offensive; the bayonet assault remained the accepted goal of the attack. Such differences as existed between them arose mainly out of national and traditional characteristics. Intellectually, the German is heavy and methodical and the Frenchman quick and cautious. The French followed Napoleon, and believed in attack in order to uncover, and then, when information had been gained, to manœuvre against the point selected *during* battle for the decisive blow. The Germans did not. They believed in marching direct upon the enemy once he had been located, and then to attack him *au fond* in front and simultaneously to envelop his flanks. Their system was Spartan, an advancing wall of men without a general reserve; that of the French was Roman, a lighter front supported by a heavy rear. The Germans recognized that fronts were inviolable, but must always be attacked in order to fix them. The French believed that a flank attack can always be anticipated, whereas a frontal one cannot be. In brief, because the Germans were methodical they believed in plan supported by brute force, and because the French were individual they believed in skill adapted to ground. The Germans considered that the French method would lead to disorder, they pinned their faith on the general and his plan; the French, because they believed that the German method would lead to excessive slaughter and blunt the attackers, pinned their faith on the initiative of their private soldiers.

As regards infantry tactics, the German believed in opening an attack with a dense firing line; to advance it until the enemy's fire was felt; then to smother the enemy's position with bullets; next to crawl forward to between 800 and 400 yards of the enemy; to gain fire superiority, and lastly to advance again and at 100 yards assault with the bayonet. Should this last advance prove

[1] See *Memoirs of an Unconventional Soldier*, J. F. C. Fuller (1936), pp. 23–26.

impossible, the final forward movement was to be made by night and the assault carried out at dawn. The French theory was based on the doctrines of Ardant du Picq; to move forward under controlled fire to 400 yards range, at which point it was held that, because aimed fire would become impossible, losses would diminish, and then to advance and take the position with the bayonet.

Both general staffs studied the artillery tactics of the Manchurian war. The French considered the reports on the preponderance of the Japanese artillery exaggerated, and the Germans learnt that the artillery duel and the infantry attack were one and not two separate acts of battle. Both accepted the advantages of indirect laying for all guns not immediately supporting the infantry attack; but on the whole the Germans disliked defiladed fire, and held that, as their artillery was numerically superior to the French, by simultaneously opening fire with all guns from uncovered positions they could more rapidly crush their antagonist. The main difference lay in their respective outlooks on the howitzer. After Plevna the Germans had adopted the light howitzer; after Mukden they adopted the heavy. The French did not like howitzers; they considered their 75 mm. field guns all-sufficient. The heavy howitzer, they said, was a cumbersome weapon unsuited for mobile warfare, and though the Germans acclaimed the tremendous effect on morale of its heavy shells the French answer was: that German troops required to be stimulated by noise, but French troops did not – they were too intelligent.

Such were the theories propounded between 1905 and 1914, and of the two armies it was certainly the German which had learnt most from the Manchurian struggle. But both sides missed its main lesson: the preponderance of the projectile, bullet and shell *in the defensive*, and its logical consequence – field entrenchments. Both failed to see that unless the next war could be won in the first shock, because of the bullet a conflict between millions, instead of hundreds of thousands of men, must become a war of entrenchments, and that a war of entrenchments must result in an enormous increase of artillery and of shell ammunition.

On the outbreak of war the strengths of the belligerent armies were as follows:

	France	Britain	Russia	Belgium	Serbia	Germany	Austria
Inf. Divs.	62	6	114	6	11	87	49
Cav. Divs.	10	2	36	1	1	11	11

Although armaments varied in design, generally speaking they were on the same scale. Almost all transport was still horse-drawn; lorries were only just coming into use, and on the declaration of war the British War Department owned no more than 80 of them. Motor cars, however, were used freely by higher commanders and their staffs. Aircraft was on a very limited scale: the German army had 384 aeroplanes and 30 dirigibles; the French, 123 aeroplanes and 10 dirigibles; and the British 63 aeroplanes; these machines were mainly used for reconnaissance. Compared with armies in the past, probably the most important difference was that those of 1914 had well-organized divisional cable companies for inter-communication, which were also provided with wireless sending and receiving sets.

The French and German plans of campaign had nothing in common except that both were based on the offensive, and as regards that of the French, it is necessary to enter into some extraneous detail, for it is a classic example of how a plan should not be devised.

On June 29, 1911, General Messimy became Minister of War in the Caillaux Government; he was the fourth to hold that appointment within four months. Three days later, for the first time he met General Michel, vice-president of the Supreme War Council (*Conseil Supérieur de la Guerre*) and general-in-chief designate in the event of war, and Colonel de Grandmaison, head of the operations branch of the General Staff (*3e Bureau*). These two did not see eye to eye, and behind Michel's back one of those politico-financial intrigues which are the curse of French democracy was brewing.

General Michel's views were that in the event of a war with Germany the probabilities were that the Germans would do two things: (*1*) simultaneously mobilize their reserve with their active troops, and (*2*) direct their main line of advance through Belgium. Therefore, in his opinion, it was essential that the French reserves should be similarly mobilized and that the plan of war should pivot on frustrating this advance. The distribution he suggested was: 490,000 men between Lille and Avesnes; 280,000 between Hirson and Rethel; 300,000 between Montmédy and Belfort; and a reserve of 220,000 about Paris, which could reinforce any one of these groups directly the German plan was disclosed.[1]

---

[1] For General Michel's scheme in full see *1914 Les erreurs du haut commandement*, Général Percin (1922), pp. 42–49.

For various reasons this project was anathema to the General Staff. The more important one was that to mix reserve with active formations would delay offensive operations; yet it cannot have been overlooked that ever since 1813 the Germans, the originators of the reserve system, had never failed to mix them. Messimy knew of this, also he knew that three members of the Supreme War Council – General Galliéni, General Dubail and General Durand – were hostile to Michel. In order to get rid of the latter, on July 19 he summoned a meeting of the Council, and when the question of reserves was vetoed by a majority of its members, he said to Michel that as his colleagues had lost confidence in him, he must ask for his resignation. Thus it came about that the sole member of the Council who saw clearly what was ahead, and as clearly understood how to meet it, was dismissed. Messimy looked around for a successor.

First he thought of General Galliéni, but as he had voted against Michel he set him aside and asked General Pau, who refused. Then he turned to General Joffre, who had never commanded an army – not even on paper – and who had no knowledge whatever of General Staff work. Joffre accepted, and asked for General Foch to be his chief of staff;[1] but this was not allowed, because Foch was a Catholic. Messimy informs us that he selected Joffre because he possessed "a strong, powerful and lofty personality . . . a clear though slow wit . . . power of decision, though not very quick . . . and imperturbable sang-froid."[2] Be this as it may, because Messimy was only the tool of the General Staff camarilla which controlled the army, it would appear that the truth was that this irresponsible body had pushed Joffre forward because, as General Percin says, he knew nothing about what he would have to do, and that therefore it would be easier to make him do all that the General Staff required.[3] In other words, from the General Staff point of view Joffre would make a good ventriloquist's dummy.

Joffre was the son of a cooper of Rivesaltes, born in 1852. He was a typical French peasant – slim though unimaginative, stubborn, astute, secretive and practical. He knew his own defects and he hid them. He seldom wrote a memorandum or read one. A

---

[1] *The Memoirs of Marshal Joffre* (English edit., 1932), vol. I, p. 12. These Memoirs were not written by Joffre, but by one of his staff officers.
[2] Quoted from *Les lois éternelles de la guerre*, Général Arthur Boucher (1925), vol. II, pp. 144–145.
[3] *Les erreurs du haut commandement*, p. 121.

man of simple mind, he liked simple solutions and his Staff fed him on simple précis of the subjects he had to deal with. As a general he was a strategical vacuum within which buzzed his General Staff. Nevertheless, as the fighting peasant he saved France, because he did not shirk responsibility, and because he was a man of great courage and also of great brutality. Though before the war he selected his own subordinates, once war was declared and they failed him he dismissed them in droves. In one month – August 2 to September 6 – two army commanders, 10 corps commanders and 38 divisional commanders were retired, that is, about half the superior generals placed under his orders.[1]

The theory of "mass plus velocity", then held by the General Staff, exactly fitted Joffre's bull-like understanding. The offensive became his one and only aim, as it became that of his political master, President Fallières, who, in 1912, had asserted: "We are determined to march straight against the enemy without hesitation. . . . The offensive alone is suited to the temperament of our soldiers."[2] Thus Joffre became the instrument of a school of military occultism, a Bergsonian society, as Pierrefeu calls the General Staff, "whose doctrine was founded on the discredit of intelligence and favoured the cult of the intuitive."[3] These military occultists, backed by the Comité des Forges de France, were Joffre's brain, out of which percolated the plan of war. It was of pathetic simplicity, "reposant", as Jean de Pierrefeu says, "tout entier sur l'idée mystique de l'offensive",[4] as well as on the ideas of General Bonnal, who had been responsible for the previous two plans – Nos. XV and XVI.

Bonnal was a profound though blind student of Napoleon; a copyist whose slavish erudition had gained for him the reputation of being the leading strategist of his day. Saturated in Napoleonic lore he failed to equate his knowledge with changed conditions. He thought in "lozenges" of men and in "battalions carrées", but not in railways, magazine rifles and quick-firing artillery. His leading idea was simplicity itself. Because, as he assumed, the Germans would marshal some 10 corps on a frontage of 60 to 80 kilometres between Toul and Épinal, the sole thing necessary was to confront them with a "battalion carrée" of 800,000 men – three lines of armies, one in first line, three in second, and one in fourth.

[1] Mes Souvenirs, Général Adolphe Marie Messimy (1937), pp. 349–350.
[2] The Memoirs of Marshal Joffre, vol. I, p. 30.
[3] Plutarque a menti, Jean de Pierrefeu (1922), p. 38.
[4] Ibid., p. 55.

A head-on collision between the first line army and the enemy would then take place, under cover of which the second and third line armies would manœuvre. This was the Jena manœuvre in elephantiasis; yet "Bonnal was convinced that he had discovered the secret of victory."[1]

Joffre's young intellectuals adopted Plan XVI as a foundation, and then set to work to build on to it Plan XVII. It was based on two postulates. The first was that the Germans would not at first bring into line reserve formations as well as active ones; therefore they would not be numerically strong enough simultaneously to advance through Belgium as well as Lorraine. The second was that as the French soldier is irresistible in attack the sole thing to do was to concentrate the French armies between Mézières and Épinal and move forward. Behind this was the insistance of the *Comité des Forges* that the Lorraine iron fields must be protected.

Joffre accepted these ideas blindly, and though he informs us that he was convinced that the Germans would not use their reserve troops[2] or move through Belgium, he nevertheless says in his *Memoirs*: "We were acquainted with their plan of mobilization bearing the date of October 9, 1913; we knew that in this plan it was set down that 'reserve troops will be employed in the same way as active troops'."[3] He further states that he had in his hands a map of an exercise "executed by the German Great General Staff in 1905, in which the movement of the German right wing across Belgium was studied"; also a plan of "a big war-game carried out in 1906" which showed the same move.[4] In order to prove that the General Staff was right, things were carried to such a pitch that, in 1913, Lieutenant-Colonel Buat forged a document, *La Concentration Allemande*, which he pretended he had found in a railway carriage. It showed that the German reservists would *not* be in first line, and that the German advance would be by the *right bank* of the Meuse on Mézières.

In spite of the fact that Joffre & Co. were intent upon playing the rôle of Napoleon, so far as he was concerned it would appear that he never had a plan at all. He says: "there never was any

[1] *Les lois éternelles de la guerre*, Boucher, vol. ii, p. 126.
[2] *The Memoirs of Marshal Joffre*, vol i, pp. 61 and 64.
[3] *Ibid.*, vol. i, p. 145.
[4] *Ibid.*, vol. i, pp. 63 and 46. It is of interest to note that Jaurès, in his *L'armée nouvelle* (1899), p. 537, predicted that the Germans would use their reserve formations and would move through Belgium.

plan of operations set down in writing. . . . I adopted no pre-conceived idea, other than a full determination to take the offensive with all my forces assembled. . . . I, therefore, decided to limit our studies to a concentration capable of lending itself to any possible plan of operations."[1]

Nevertheless, as we shall see, this is exactly what the concentration he accepted did not do. It was:

(*1*) *First Army* (Dubail): Charmes – Arches – Darney; head-quarters Épinal; five active corps, four divisions and two cavalry divisions: total 256,000 men.

(*2*) *Second Army* (de Castelnau): Pont St. Vincent – Mirecourt; headquarters Neufchâteau; five active corps, three divisions and two cavalry divisions: total 200,000 men.

(*3*) *Third Army* (Ruffrey): St. Mihiel – Damvillers; head-quarters Verdun; three active corps, three divisions and one cavalry division: total 168,000 men.

(*4*) *Fourth Army* (de Langle de Cary): Vavincourt – Bar le Duc – Void; headquarters St. Dizier: three active corps and one cavalry division: total 193,000 men.

(*5*) *Fifth Army* (Lanrézac): Grandpré – Suippes – Chaumont – Porcien; headquarters Rethel: five active corps, five divisions and one cavalry division: total 254,000 men.

(*6*) *Cavalry Corps* (Sordet): Mézières, three divisions.

(*7*) *Right Flank Guard:* Vesoul, three divisions.

(*8*) *Left Flank Guard:* Sissonne, three divisions.

Such was the distribution decided upon by the French General Staff and accepted by Joffre, whose idea, when war was declared, was to advance the First Army on Baccarat – Sarreburg, and the Second Army on Château Salins – Sarreburg, and overwhelm his enemy.

His opponent's plan, though equally offensive, was very different. In 1905 Count von Schlieffen, who as Chief of the General Staff had succeeded von Moltke in 1891, recast the then existing plan by turning it round. Moltke's idea was an offensive against Russia and a defensive against France; but as the defeat of the Russians in the Russo-Japanese War had altered the balance of

[1] *Ibid.*, vol. 1, p. 69. When in 1919 he was called before the Briey Commission and asked, "Who elaborated the war plan?" he replied: "The General Staff", and when pressed to state which officers were concerned, his answer was: "I no longer remember. . . . A plan of operations is an idea carried in one's head and not set down on paper. . . . You ask me a heap of things to which I cannot reply. I know nothing" (*Les erreurs du haut commandement*, see Appendix, pp. 179–278, in which the minutes of the Commission are given in full).

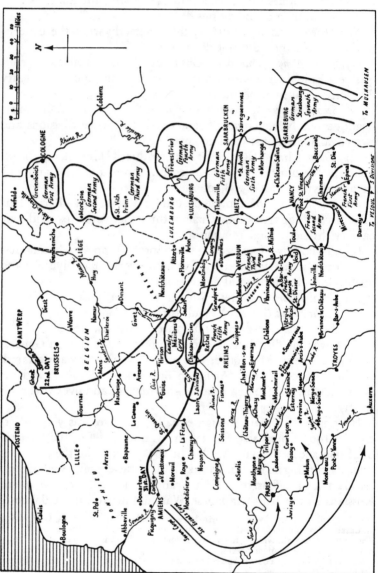

12. FRENCH AND GERMAN DISTRIBUTIONS, AUGUST, 1914

power, Schlieffen determined to oppose the Russians with only 10 divisions and local troops and to concentrate everything else against France. The grand tactics he decided upon were not those of Cannae, as so many writers suggest, but of Leuthen. He antici- pated that the French would assemble their forces where they actually did, and decided to deploy seven armies on the line Krefeld–Mulhausen, centred on Thionville–Metz; five to the north of Metz and two to the south of it. The former was to com- prise thirty-five and a half corps, supported by seven cavalry divisions, 16 brigades of Landwehr and six Ersatz divisions, and the latter five corps supported by three cavalry divisions.

Next, he planned to advance in oblique order pivoted on Metz. The left wing was first to gain contact with the French main forces, pin them down, or if this were not possible, then to retire and draw them toward the Rhine. At the same time the right wing was to move through Belgium, swing south-west around Paris, and thence move eastward and fall on the rear of the French and drive them pell-mell into Germany and Switzerland. To make certain that this wing should be strong enough, he decided, directly this gigantic wheel was on its way, to withdraw two corps from the left wing and with them reinforce it.

When we consider the plan which was eventually adopted by his successor, it is important to remember the factors which governed Schlieffen's grand tactics:

(*1*) The right wing was to operate through good offensive country and be strong enough to besiege Antwerp, Namur, etc., and Paris, which was the rail centre of France and the base of supply of the French armies.

(*2*) The left wing was to operate in good defensive country, and to be only just strong enough to mislead the French and make it worth their while to attack it. Its rôle was *defensive*.

In 1906 Schlieffen handed over this plan to his successor Count von Moltke, who had been selected by the Kaiser to replace him because he imagined that his name would have a terrifying effect on neighbouring countries. In this we discover the key which unlocks the whole system of the German Higher Command, which was as royally rotten as the French was politically corrupt. After 1870, as after 1763, the German army rested on its laurels, and when William II succeeded to the throne he set out to create a parade army, a toy which he loved to play with. Unable to tolerate soldiers of real worth he set them aside and filled the higher army appointments with royal princes – figurehead generals who knew little or nothing of war. General von Moltke was one of his creatures; he had not passed through the Staff College, and most of his service had been spent as aide-de-camp to his uncle and the Kaiser. In 1914 he was 68 years old, out-of-date and soused in the staff ideas of his uncle, which he copied slavishly. To him the army was commanded by the staff, and as commander-in-chief, for that is what he was in all but name, he looked upon his rôle as that of the starter of a race: all he had to do was to lower the flag, and then to leave operations to his generals. He did not believe in executive control, nor even in contact, and his system of communication with his subordinates, as we shall see, was about as defective as it could be.

Though Moltke accepted Schlieffen's plan, he entirely changed its character, notwithstanding that several new corps were raised between 1906 and 1914. On the Russian front he left things much as they were, and allotted to it four active and reserve corps, one reserve division, one cavalry division, and some Landwehr formations; in all about 200,000 men. But on the French front he not only radically altered the proportional strengths of the two wings, but by reinforcing the left he set out to win a Cannae instead of a Leuthen.[1] Colonel Tappen, Chief of Operations, says that this change was forced upon him by technical reasons – railways, etc.[2] This is to be doubted, for the real reason would appear to have been the pressure brought to bear upon him by the royal princes to strengthen their armies.

In 1910 he cancelled the withdrawal of the two corps from the left wing, and concentrated the six Ersatz divisions in the neighbourhood of Metz. Lastly, when nine new divisions became available, he allotted one, as well as one withdrawn from the Russian

---

[1] Sir James Edmonds (*A Short History of World War I*, 1951, p. 16) says that "In 1912, owing to changed conditions and the necessity to cover the Rhineland industrial area, Schlieffen (who in the interval had written a book on Cannae, a battle which he regarded as a model of a battle of annihilation) himself suggested the alteration of his 1905 plan to the one which was put into force. This was revealed in 1934, under the Hitler régime, by the officer who examined the papers of General von Moltke." If this is correct, then Schlieffen's strategical sense must have sadly degenerated in his seventy-ninth year, for the region of the Vosges is some of the best defensive country in Western Europe, and to attempt a rapid envelopment through it would be an act of madness. On this question, Görlitz (*The German General Staff, 1657–1945*, 1953, p. 142) writes: "Even as late as 1912 he [Schlieffen] was still busy with his theoretical planning, and in that year – he had come to recognize the growth of the offensive spirit in France – he began to develop the idea of attacking along the whole front all the way from Belgium to Switzerland. But even in the hour of death, the great plan continued in his thoughts. His last words were: "See you make the right wing strong."

[2] *Jusqu'à la Marne en 1914*, Général Tappen (French edit.), p. 97.

front, to the right wing, and the remaining eight to the left. The initial distribution of the seven German armies then became:

(*1*) *First Army* (General von Kluck): headquarters Grevenboich; seven corps, three cavalry divisions and three Landwehr brigades. To march on Aix-la-Chapelle and thence on Brussels. Total 320,000 men.

(*2*) *Second Army* (General von Bülow): headquarters Montjoie; six corps, two cavalry divisions and two Landwehr brigades. To capture Liége and thence advance with its right flank on Wavre and its left on Namur. Total 260,000 men.

(*3*) *Third Army* (General von Hausen): headquarters Prüm; four corps and one Landwehr brigade. To march westward with its right on Namur and its left on Givet. Total 180,000 men.

(*4*) *Fourth Army* (Duke of Württemberg): headquarters Trèves; five corps and one Landwehr brigade. To march westward with its right on Framay and its left on Attert, north of Arlon. Total 180,000 men.

(*5*) *Fifth Army* (The Crown Prince): headquarters Saarbrücken; five corps, one division, two cavalry divisions and five Landwehr brigades. To keep its left on Thionville and to move its right on Forenville. Total 200,000 men.

(*6*) *Sixth Army* (Prince Rupprecht of Bavaria): headquarters St. Avold; five corps, three cavalry divisions and four Ersatz divisions. To advance on the Moselle and attack the French and pin them down. Total 220,000 men.

(*7*) *Seventh Army* (General von Heeringen): headquarters Strasbourg; three corps, one division, two Ersatz divisions and four Landwehr brigades. To advance on the Meurthe or to counterattack in Lorraine. Total 125,000 men.

Although the shadow of the Schlieffen plan remained, its substance was altered completely by the change in balance between the weight of the two wings hinged on Thionville–Metz. The one allotted 59 Active, Reserve and Ersatz divisions to the northern wing and nine Active and Reserve divisions to the southern. In the other, the proportion was 55 Active and Reserve divisions to 23 Active, Reserve and Ersatz divisions. In percentages the Schlieffen plan represented 100: 15, and the Moltke plan 100: 42. Further, as Schlieffen intended to shift two corps from the left to the right wing directly the French forces in Alsace and Lorraine were entangled, the proportion of 100 : 15 was to fall to 100 : 9 *in order that the southern wing might be pushed back.*

Now we see two offensive wings, of which the southern, instead of enticing the enemy eastward so that the northern wing might the more easily wheel round his rear, pushed him westward – that is, away from the manœuvre against his rear. This was no Cannae, nor Leuthen. To call it either would make Hannibal or Frederick turn in his grave.

While the enormous German phalanx, strong in form yet weak in structure, formed up, and while far away in East Prussia General von Prittwitz with his comparatively minute force made ready to block the onrush of the Russian hordes, futility and discord reigned in Paris. In May, General Messimy had again become Minister of War, and was, so we are told, "constantly at the end of the telephone asking for information or giving meaningless orders and not in the least conscious of the greatness of his task."[1] On July 31 "Nothing was discussed except . . . financial measures. . . ."[2] On August 2 came mobilization and, on the 3rd, Joffre assembled his army commanders. Secretive as usual, he vaguely sketched for them the "broad line of manœuvre" he would "probably execute." This was "a combination of two attacks, one in Lorraine and the other north of the line Verdun–Toul."[3] On the 4th he established his General Headquarters at Vitry-le-François; meanwhile Moltke remained in Berlin, from where he later moved to Coblenz.

The day Joffre assembled his army commanders, the advanced guard of General von der Marwitz's Cavalry Corps crossed the Belgian frontier at Gemmenich, and, on August 5, the surrender of Liége was demanded and refused by General Leman. On the following day the German assault failed. General Ludendorff, Quartermaster-General of the Second Army, then took charge of the attack, and on the 7th his men penetrated between the forts and entered the city. On August 12 some 420 mm. howitzers were brought forward; the forts were pulverized, and, on the 16th, Liége was in German hands.

Meanwhile a detachment of Dubail's First Army had entered

[1] *Britain and the War: A French Indictment*, General Huguet (English edit., 1928), p. 31.
[2] *The Memoirs of Marshal Joffre*, vol. I, pp. 124–125.
[3] *Ibid.*, vol. I, p. 135. It is extremely difficult to discover what did happen. In the Briey enquiry Joffre says he never assembled his generals as they all knew exactly what to do. Throughout the war these contradictions occur.

Mulhausen, and on August 7, as five German corps had by then been identified on the Belgian front,[1] Lanrézac informed Joffre that the probability was that the Germans intended to operate along the left bank of the Meuse. The answer he received was, "so much the better."[2] Still convinced that the main German forces were in the Thionville–Metz area, on the 8th Joffre ordered the First and Second Armies to prepare to attack.[3] This meant that one-third of his total forces was to penetrate Lorraine. The attack was launched on August 14, when, according to plan, Prince Rupprecht's Sixth Army fell back.

In the meantime Lanrézac continued to warn Joffre that the main German forces were in Belgium, but with no effect until August 15, when Joffre informs us that "for the first time this hypothesis began to take actual shape."[4] By the 18th he was sufficiently perturbed by it to create a new army, the Army of Lorraine, under General Maunoury, to protect the left flank of the Second Army from "forces which might debouch from the entrenched camp of Metz."[5] The right of the First Army was already protected by the Army of Alsace, under General Pau, which had been formed on August 9.

Although Joffre little realized it, the position of his First and Second Armies was critical, and would have become more so had Rupprecht only continued to fall back. Instead, urged on by his ambitious Chief of Staff, Colonel von Dellmensingen – the real commander of the Sixth Army – he obtained permission to draw in the six Ersatz divisions, and with the Seventh Army, which had already been placed under his command, he counter-attacked the French on August 20; pushed the French First and Second Armies out of the trap they had unwittingly entered, and beat them back to the Grand Couronné of Nancy and the Meurthe. The first nail had been driven into the Schlieffen-Moltke plan and it so unbalanced Moltke that he abandoned the idea that the left wing was a reservoir for the right, and substituted the idea of a double envelopment. Thus it came about that from August 25 to

---

[1] See: *La préparation de la guerre et la conduite des opérations*, Maréchal Joffre (1920), p. 32, and *The Memoirs of Marshal Joffre*, vol. I, p. 141.

[2] *Historie illustrée de la guerre de 1914*, Gabriel Hanotaux (1920–1927), vol. VIII, p. 246.

[3] See *La préparation de la guerre*, etc., p. 68, and *La conduite de la guerre jusqu'à la bataille de la Marne*, Lieut.-Colonel Grouard, p. 5.

[4] *The Memoirs of Marshal Joffre*, vol. I, p. 159. It would appear that this *hypothesis* took form on the 17th and not the 15th, because on the 16th an official *communiqué* stated: "the *attaque brusquée* by Belgium had lamentably failed" (see Percin, p. 117).

[5] *Ibid.*, vol. I, p. 166.

September 7, the Sixth and Seventh Armies dashed themselves to pieces in the defensive region Schlieffen had warned them against attacking.

While Rupprecht and Dellmensingen emasculated the German plan of war, Joffre "assassinated" his generals. Because the attack had failed, victims had to be found in order to propitiate General Messimy. *"Donnez-moi la guillotine, je vous donnerai la victoire!"*[1] he shouted, and, on August 24, Messimy wrote to Joffre: "I consider that, as in 1793, there are only two punishments, dismissal and death. You want to win; to do so use the most rapid, brutal, energetic and decisive methods."[2] Fortunately for France, on August 27, Messimy was dismissed.

Two days before Rupprecht launched his attack the First, Second, and Third German Armies set out on their advance through Belgium and the bulk of the Belgian forces fell back upon Antwerp. Then the second nail was driven into the Schlieffen-Moltke plan, because General von Kluck was ordered to detach the 3rd Reserve Corps to cover Antwerp, which meant a reduction in strength of some 35,000 men. When Namur was reached the third nail was driven home, because its reduction forced the Second Army to detach the Reserve Corps of the Guard, and the Third Army to detach the XIth Corps as well as one division of the 7th Reserve Corps. On August 21 the Second Army came into contact with the French Fifth Army and Kluck, now under Bülow's orders, was instructed to move south-westerly instead of westerly. Thus was the fourth nail hammered home, because, had he continued on his original course, instead of a head-on collision with the British Expeditionary Force at Mons, he would have outflanked it and quite possibly have annihilated it. On August 22, the river Sambre was reached.

Two days before this happened, Joffre suddenly saw daylight; "the German manœuvre was clear to my eyes," he said.[3] Yet was it? From the action he took he would seem to have had only a hazy idea of the formidable nature of the great German wheel through Belgium. Instead of trying to smash the advancing German right wing he launched the Third and Fourth Armies into the difficult country of the Ardennes to sever it from its base, and ordered the Fifth Army on their left, in cooperation

[1] *Mes Souvenirs*, Messimy, p. 350.
[2] *The Memoirs of Marshal Joffre*, vol. I, p. 184.
[3] *Ibid.*, vol. I, p. 170.

with the British Expeditionary Force – the last units of which were about to land – to hold back the head of the onrushing flood.

The initial objective given the French Third and Fourth Armies were Arlon and Neufchâteau, and their advance on them led to a head-on collision with the Fourth and Fifth German Armies. The battle of the Ardennes followed, or, as the Germans call it, the battle of Longwy and Neufchâteau, in which the French Fourth Army was severely repulsed and on August 24 the Third forced to retire behind the Meuse. Like the offensive in Lorraine, this attack was a complete failure.

Meanwhile the French Fifth Army, under Lanrézac, advanced on the Sambre. On August 22 it was met in front by Bülow's Second Army and attacked on its right flank by Hausen's Third Army. The outcome was the battle of Charleroi, called by the Germans the battle of Namur, in which Lanrézac was forced back, and Sir John French withdrew on Mons. There, when isolated, he was attacked by Kluck's First Army, and on the 24th forced to continue his retreat. On this day the general situation was that the whole of the French left wing was in retreat, and the whole of the German left wing was battering itself to pieces on the lower Moselle, from Toul to Nancy, and thence to St. Die.

To understand what now followed on the western front it is first necessary to examine events on the eastern front.

The aim of the original Russian plan was to hold back the Germans with the First Army, while the Third, Fourth, Fifth and Eighth, with the Second in reserve at Warsaw, assumed a vigorous offensive against the Austrians, and the Ninth remained at Petrograd to repel a possible German invasion. Immediately after mobilization this plan was changed in order to help the French; the Second Army was moved toward East Prussia to cooperate with the First, and the Ninth took its place as a reserve. Thus two groups of armies were formed, the North-Western, under General Jilinski, consisted of the First Army under General Rennenkampf and the Second under General Samsonov; and the South-Western, under General Ivanov, which included the Third, Fourth, Fifth and Eighth Armies. The whole was under the command of the Grand Duke Nicholas Nikolaievich.

The First and Second Armies were respectively deployed in the Vilna district and on the Narew; the First consisted of the IIIrd, IVth and XXth Corps, supported by five cavalry divisions, and the Second of the IInd, VIth, XIIIth, XVth and XXIIIrd Corps and three cavalry divisions.

Though numerically these two armies – the First Army 200,000 strong and the Second Army 250,000 – were vastly superior to the German Eighth Army, which then held East Prussia, in quality and command they could not compare with it. Further, the German railway system was in every way superior to that of the Russians.

Though improvements had been made since the Russo-Japanese War, the Russian remained what he always had been, a big-hearted child who thought out nothing and was surprised by everything. The generals were incapable, and what made things worse was that they thirsted for a fight. The Staff was grotesquely inefficient, and the worth of that of the Second Army may be judged from the fact that it "had a compass but no maps." General Knox, British Military Attaché with this Army, says that on one occasion "An eccentric youth travelled with me, the son of a chocolate manufacturer of Warsaw, who is on the Staff of the 2nd Army simply because he can draw caricatures."[1]

The original Schlieffen plan had been worked out in 1905 when Russia was weak. It was based on the formation of the Vistula, which describes in its course an immense "S". Its centre is Warsaw, with Danzig at its northern extremity and Cracow at its southern, and at the bends of the "S" are the fortresses of Thorn in the north and Sandomir in the south.

On this skeleton Schlieffen worked out his plan. As he expected that the main Russian forces would assemble between Warsaw and Sandomir, he decided to deploy against them a weak front which rested between two powerful groups: an Austro-Hungarian army in the south, which was to move on Lublin, and a German army in the north which was to move on Pultusk. Because he reckoned that the Russian deployment would take between six and seven weeks he considered he would be able to dispense with the northern army until after he had crushed France, and then, by a rapid transfer of troops from the western theatre of war to build it up and carry out a true Cannae operation.

By 1913 this situation had changed, for the Russians had largely recovered from their defeats in 1904–1905. Further, they had strengthened their western railways. Therefore Moltke rightly

[1] *With the Russian Army, 1914–1917*, Major-General Sir Alfred Knox (1921), vol. I, pp. 78 and 86.

13. BATTLE OF TANNENBERG, AUGUST 26–31, 1914

assumed that their mobilization would take less time and decided that a properly constituted army would be required – namely, the Eighth. He allotted to it the following formations: Ist Corps (General von François), XVIIth Corps (General von Mackensen), XXth Corps (General von Scholtz), Ist Reserve Corps (General Below), 3rd Reserve Division (General von Morgen), 1st Cavalry Division (General Brecht) and three Landwehr brigades as well as all the fortress troops in East Prussia. The whole was commanded by General von Prittwitz, who in the event of an advance of greatly superior Russian forces was instructed to withdraw to the left bank of the Vistula.[1]

Directly war was declared, General Conrad, Chief of the General Staff of the Austro-Hungarian Armies, launched an offensive on Lublin and was driven back upon Lemberg. Meanwhile von Prittwitz deployed his 160,000 men (without counting Landsturm), as follows:

(*1*) From Angerburg to the Baltic, on the river Angerapp and south of the Pregel, he held his front with the Ist Reserve Corps, the XVIIth Corps and the Ist Corps, and to the area north of the Pregel, along the Deime, he allotted the Königsberg garrison.

(*2*) From Johannisburg to Thorn and based on Deutsch-Eylau he deployed the XXth Corps. Its object was to protect the railway which supplied his army. It was supported by the garrisons of Thorn and Graudenz.

When General von Prittwitz held this line, Rennenkampf, in true Russian fashion, did not wait to complete mobilization of his rear services and crossed the frontier on August 17; he drove back the German advanced troops at Stallupönen and defeated the left of the Eighth Army at Gumbinnen. Then his supply system broke down and the gauge of the railway changed from broad to narrow.[2] Four days later Samsonov crossed into East Prussia. He occupied Willenberg on August 22 and Ortelsburg and Neidenburg on the 23rd. His advance was even more chaotic. A German description of it reads:

"Whole army corps advanced from Byelostok without bread or oats, and had to have recourse to their reserve rations. Even before the Narew the march discipline was bad, and from that river to the Prussian frontier the Russian columns had to wade through

[1] See *The War of Lost Opportunities*, General von Hoffmann (English edit., 1924), p. 12.
[2] See *Memoirs and Impressions of the War and Revolution in Russia, 1914–1917*, General Basil Gourko (1918), pp. 31, 62.

sand. Nerves were so shaky that the troops fired at every airman, occasionally even at their own automobiles. The Higher Command was ignorant of the enemy's movements. Corps commanders were only informed of the immediate objectives of the neighbouring corps; they were told nothing, for instance, of the task of Rennenkampf's army. . . ."[1]

There was no cooperation either between the units of the Second Army or between that army and the First. The IInd Corps, which was directed to advance between these two armies, kept contact with neither, and it has been hinted that this lack of solidarity was due to the personal dislike of Samsonov for Rennenkampf. A better reason would appear to be the inherent inefficiency of the Russian cavalry, more especially the Cossacks, who were little more than brigands.

The repulse of the Eighth Army at Gumbinnen, although no more than a tactical incident, led to the most astonishing strategical results. Firstly, Rennenkampf – who very nearly had been defeated – sat down to enjoy his escape, and to show how strange Russian mentality can be, we will quote General Knox, an eyewitness:

"B—— asked the General if he might go to bed, and was told that he might, but that he should not undress. He lay down for an hour and was awakened by Rennenkampf, who stood beside his bed, smiling, and said: 'You can take off your clothes now; the Germans are retiring'."[2]

As Knox remarks, surely it was precisely the time to exert every effort to keep in touch with the retiring Germans, and certainly not the moment to undress.

Secondly, because Samsonov believed the Eighth Army to have been routed, he cast precaution to the winds; lost contact with Rennenkampf, and he pushed on toward Deutsch-Eylau to cut off Prittwitz from his base. Thirdly, Prittwitz, when he learnt of this advance, panicked and ordered a retirement to the Vistula. On the advice of General Grünert and General Hoffmann, he cancelled this order, which was fortunate for the Germans, for the Russian Second Army was nearer to that river than his own. He then decided to attack Samsonov's left wing, and on the evening of August 20 issued the following orders: The XXth Corps to concentrate at Hohenstein; the Ist Corps and 3rd Reserve

---

[1] Quoted from *With the Russian Army*, Knox, vol. 1, p. 84.
[2] *Ibid.*, vol. 1, p. 88.

Division to move by rail to the right wing of the XXth; the Königsberg garrison to hold the line Pregel–Deime, and the Ist Reserve Corps and XVIIth Corps to fall back directly west.

Strangely enough the repulse at Gumbinnen, coupled with Prittwitz's nervousness, led to events which were destined to change the whole course of the campaign, not only in the east, but also in the west.

When the news of Gumbinnen was received in Coblenz and was followed by a copy of Prittwitz's order to fall back on the Vistula, which, though according to plan, would, as Ludendorff says, "have spelt ruin,"[1] two changes were decided upon. The first was to find a new commander for the Eighth Army, and the second to reinforce it – which will be dealt with later. A telegram was sent to General Paul von Hindenburg, an old soldier born in 1847 and a veteran of the 1866 and 1870–1871 wars, then in retirement at Hanover, to ask him to take over Prittwitz's appointment. His answer was: "I am ready."[2] On the same day (August 22) a letter was sent to General Ludendorff to appoint him Hindenburg's Chief of Staff. It found him between Wavre and Namur, and when he received it he got into his car and sped to Coblenz. He reported himself to Moltke, who explained to him the situation in the east in detail, after which, at his request, the following instructions were sent to Prittwitz:

"The 1st Reserve Corps, the 17th Army Corps and the Main Reserve of the Königsberg garrison were to call a halt. The 1st A.C. was not to be detrained at Gosslershausen, but near General von Scholtz's position, somewhere east of Deutsch-Eylau. Any available troops from the garrisons at Thorn, Kulm, Graudenz and Marienburg, were to go to Strasburg and Lautenberg. . . . Thus, in the south-west part of East Prussia a strong group was formed which could undertake an offensive, while the northern group either continued its retreat in a south-westerly direction, or could be brought straight south to assist in the action against the Narew (Second Russian) Army."[3]

Unknown to Ludendorff, on the suggestions of General Grünert and General Hoffmann, almost identical moves were being made.

Once these orders had been sent Ludendorff hastened to Hanover; met Hindenburg, and with him went to Marienburg,

---

[1] *My War Memories*, General Ludendorff (English edit., 1920), vol. I, p. 45.
[2] *Out of my Life*, Marshal von Hindenburg (English edit., 1920), p. 81.
[3] *My War Memories*, Ludendorff, vol. I, p. 46. See also Hindenburg's *Out of my Life*, pp. 87–88.

where they arrived on the afternoon of August 23. There they learned that "The situation had changed and the decision to retire behind the Vistula had been abandoned."[1] They also learned that Rennenkampf's army was still inactive; that the 37th Division on the left wing of the XXth Corps had been furiously attacked and was in retreat; that Samsonov's order of pursuit, which had been sent out in clear, had been intercepted; and more important still, that Jilinski's plan of operations had been found on a captured Russian officer. "It told us," writes Hindenburg, "that Rennenkampf's Army was to pass the Masurian Lakes on the north and advance against the Insterburg–Angerburg line. It was to attack the German forces presumed to be behind the Angerapp, while the Narew Army was to cross the Lötzen–Prtelsburg line to take the Germans in flank."[2]

Meanwhile Samsonov slowly moved westward on a frontage of some 60 miles. From left to right his distribution was: Ist, XXIIIrd, XVth, XIIIth, and VIth Corps. The IInd had by now been replaced by the Ist Corps and transferred to the First Army. This widened the gap between the two Armies and this was increased by Samsonov who to ease his supply directed his left on to the Nowo Georgiewsk–Mlawa–Soldau railway, which pulled his right away from Rennenkampf.

Ludendorff's quick eye at once noticed this gap and he determined to turn it to his advantage. He decided to leave a thin screen of troops to amuse Rennenkampf and to concentrate everything else against Samsonov. He writes:

"Gradually during the period from 24th to 26th August, the battle plan took shape in all its details. The great question was whether it would really be possible to withdraw the 1st Reserve Corps and the 17th Army Corps from their position facing Rennenkampf, so as to unite them with other units of the 8th Army, for a blow against the Narew Army. It depended solely on Rennenkampf himself, for if he knew how to make the most of his success of Gumbinnen and advance quickly my plan would be unthinkable. . . .

"We discovered by degrees that Rennenkampf was advancing only slowly. The two Army Corps could therefore be gradually deflected . . . in a sharp southerly direction to Bischofsburg–Neidenburg.

"Next, the 17th A.C., protected by the 1st Cavalry Division

[1] *My War Memories*, Ludendorff, vol. i, p. 47.   [2] *Out of my Life*, p. 87.

and the 1st R.C., was moved south *via* Schippenbeil to Bischofstein. As soon as it had passed behind the 1st R.C., and on the
26th advanced from Bischofstein to Bischofsburg, the 1st Army
Corps itself moved, south of Schippenbeil, in the direction of
Seeburg. Only the 1st Cavalry Division remained facing Rennenkampf, near, and to the south of Schippenbeil. Of this division,
also on the 26th, the 1st Cavalry Brigade received the order to
draw out *via* Rössel on Sensburg. Accordingly from the 27th of
August onwards, only two cavalry brigades stood between Lake
Maur and the river Pregel, facing twenty-four very strong and
several cavalry divisions of Rennenkampf's. . . .

"On this line the two Corps were marching in rear of the Narew
Army from Neidenburg to Allenstein. In this way they exposed
their rear without adequate protection to Rennenkampf's Army,
which was only two or three days' march away. When the battle
began in real earnest on the 27th . . . Rennenkampf's formidable
host hung like a threatening thunder-cloud to the north-east."[1]

It was a plan of supreme daring and good judgment, which
resulted not only in the most brilliant campaign of the war, but
in one of the most tactically decisive.

"A general," writes Ludendorff, "has much to bear and needs
strong nerves. The civilian is too inclined to think that war is only
like the working out of an arithmetical problem with given
numbers. It is anything but that. On both sides it is a case of
wrestling with powerful, interwoven physical and psychological
forces, a struggle which inferiority in numbers makes all the more
difficult. It means working with men of varying force of character
and with their own views. The only quality that is known and
constant is the will of the leader."[2]

These are true words, and they carry with them the great truth
that generalship in its highest form is a combination of will and
idea, and not merely a matter of calculations.

The battle which was fought on August 26 may be divided into
two operations. While half the XXth Corps, supported by General
von der Goltz's Landwehr, held back Samsonov's main forces in
the centre, (*1*) the Ist Corps and the remaining half of the XXth
attacked the Russian left at Usdau and drove back the Russian
Ist Corps; (*2*) from the north the Ist Reserve Corps with the
XVIIth on its left struck at the Russian VIth Corps and drove
back one of its divisions on Bischofsburg. The flanks were now

---

[1] *My War Memories*, vol. i, pp. 47–49.   [2] *Ibid.*, p. 53.

cleared for the envelopment of Samsonov's centre – the XIIIth, XVth, and XXIIIrd Corps.

While these converging movements were made, Samsonov, with the XVth Corps, watched its advance though "Destitute of any information concerning the other troops under his control."[1] He was worried, so General Knox informs us, "because he had not yet received a letter from his wife,"[2] and when he heard of the attack on his Ist Corps he buckled on his sword and set out to see what was happening.

The next day, as Rennenkampf slowly moved toward Königsberg, the attack continued. On Samsonov's left the greatest confusion set in: the troops at Niedenburg panicked, and in his centre many of the men of the XIIIth Corps when they reached Allenstein were under the impression that they had entered Berlin.[3]

That evening, on the German left, the Ist Reserve Corps occupied Wartenburg, some eight miles north-east of Allenstein. The XVIIth Corps on its left approached Bischofsburg, and the XXth, in the centre, much exhausted, held its ground, while on its right, the Ist Corps, still in the neighbourhood of Usdau, prepared to advance on Neidenburg. Samsonov's centre slowly pushed forward between Allenstein and Gilgenburg.

For August 28 Ludendorff's orders were: The Ist Corps to occupy Neidenburg; the Ist Reserve Corps and the XVIIth Corps to abandon the pursuit of the Russian VIth Corps and to move south-west on Passenheim against the right flank of the Russian XIIIth Corps, while the XXth Corps assumed the offensive and Goltz's Landwehr stormed Hohenstein. His idea was that, while the German centre attacked, the two wings, by closing in on Willenburg, would encircle the Russian centre.

Though the morning of August 28 started badly for the Germans, during the afternoon Hohenstein was occupied, and a little later the Ist Reserve Corps reached a position south of Allenstein, while the Ist Corps held the left flank of the Russian centre north of Neidenburg. The next day the Ist Russian Corps again appeared on the field and caused a critical situation on the German right when it launched a rear attack on the German Ist Corps. It was driven back as the double envelopment closed in on Samsonov's doomed centre.

[1] *Memories and Impressions*, etc., Gourko, p. 64.
[2] *With the Russian Army, 1914–1917*, vol. I, p. 68.   [3] *Ibid.*, vol. I, p. 84.

The end was near. On August 30 the Russian centre was surrounded and on the 31st, "the day of harvesting", as Hindenburg calls it, Hindenburg sent the following dispatch to the Kaiser:

"I beg most humbly to report to Your Majesty that the ring round the larger part of the Russian Army was closed yesterday. The 13th, 15th, and 18th [XXIIIrd] Army Corps have been destroyed. We have already taken more than 60,000 prisoners, among them the Corps Commanders of the 13th and 15th Corps. The guns are still in the forests and are now being brought in. The booty is immense though it cannot yet be assessed in detail. The Corps outside our ring, the 1st and 6th, have also suffered severely and are now retreating in hot haste through Mlawa and Myszaniec."[1]

While from the German bivouacs scattered among the forest rose the hymn of the Battle of Leuthen, Samsonov accompanied by five staff officers hastened on foot through the darkness toward the Russian frontier. At length, exhausted, he began to lag behind and ultimately disappeared. What his fate was is unknown, but it is believed that he shot himself.[2]

Thus ended this great battle, which Ludendorff named the Battle of Tannenberg after a village which lies to the north of Usdau as an answer to the victory won there by the Poles and Lithuanians over the Teutonic Knights in 1410. Although it had no decisive influence on the war, had the Germans lost it, it would have changed its course completely. As it was, its indirect influence on the western theatre was profound.

In that theatre, of all the days during this war, probably the most fateful for both the French and the Germans was August 25. On that day the French commander-in-chief made a decision, and the German commander had one forced upon him by a subordinate officer – Colonel Tappen, chief of the operations section at Coblenz.

Tappen believed that a great and decisive victory had already been won in the west,[3] and, perturbed by events in East Prussia, he believed that reinforcements should be sent there immediately. This suggestion fitted Moltke's original intention to withdraw six corps from the western front once they could be spared and to

---

[1] *Out of my Life*, p. 99.

[2] A dramatic account of his last hours is given by General Gourko, see *Memories and Impressions*, etc., pp. 65–67.

[3] *Jusqu'à la Marne en 1914*, Général Tappen, p. 112. (See also *Documents Allemands sur la bataille de la Marne*, 1930.)

send them to East Prussia. Two were to be taken from the left wing, two from the centre, and two from the right wing. Urged by Tappen that the moment was now opportune, Moltke approached Rupprecht and the Crown Prince, but both protested so vigorously against the withdrawal that he decided to take only one from the Second Army and one from the Third. Tappen then telephoned Ludendorff and informed him that three (*sic*) army corps and one cavalry division had been ordered to reinforce the Eighth Army. Ludendorff replied that they were not wanted; Tappen answered "that the troops could be spared." The next day he telephoned again and explained "that only the XIth and Reserve Guard Corps [both then besieging Namur] and also the 8th Cavalry Division would come, but that the Vth Army Corps . . . was wanted in the West." Once again General Ludendorff assured him "that the corps would arrive too late for the battle that was then being fought," and therefore it was unnecessary to send them.[1]

It would appear that this conversation was never reported to Moltke, and the result was that the Second Army was ordered to withdraw the Guard Reserve Corps and the Third Army the XIth Corps and the 8th Cavalry Division. There can be little doubt that these armies were selected because their commanders were not royal princes, and in spite of the fact that they already had provided the following detachments: the IIIrd and IXth Reserve Corps to Antwerp and the VIIth to Maubeuge, as well as some minor detachments to watch Givet and Brussels. In all, the decisive right wing was now reduced from 34 to 25 divisions, that is, with casualties added, by a third of its original strength.

While, all unknown to the French, this destruction of the Schlieffen-Moltke plan took shape, the complete breakdown of Plan XVII as well as the successive defeats of the French armies had thrown Paris into panic. Nevertheless, on August 25, when a

---

[1] *The War of Lost Opportunities*, Hoffmann, pp. 34–35. General Hoffmann says the first of these calls took place "On one of the last days of the battle of Tannenberg", Ludendorff says "The telegram announcing the proposed reinforcements arrived just at the commencement of the battle of Tannenberg" (vol. I, p. 58), which is probably correct. Further, he says: "The decision to weaken the forces on the Western Front was premature. . . . But it was particularly fateful that the reinforcements destined for the Eastern Front were drawn from the right wing, which was fighting for a decision" (vol. I, pp. 58–59). And again: "If Moltke had not sent the Guard Reserve Corps and the XI Corps . . . all would have gone well. If he wished to send something, he should have taken the Corps from the left wing" (see *Army Quarterly*, vol. III, p. 50). General von Kluck says the same thing (see *The March on Paris*, English edit., 1920, p. 77).

Council of Ministers was assembled, Viviani, its President, made a long discourse on finance, and Doumergue upon Italian-Albanian relationships. In the middle of this fatuous debate Messimy very rightly sprang to his feet and shouted: "*Je me f——de l'Albanie.* What only matters is that within ten days of now the Germans may appear before Paris."[1] It was therefore decided to create an army to cover the capital and to replace General Michel, whom Messimy loathed, by General Galliéni as Governor of Paris. Two days later Messimy was dismissed and was succeeded by Millerand as Minister of War.

Who it was who first thought of creating a defence force for the capital is not easy to decide. Galliéni says he suggested it toward 3 p.m. on August 25,[2] and Joffre says that the order was dated 7 a.m. that day.[3] In all probability the order was dispatched before the meeting of the Council of Ministers, for such councils do not generally meet at so early an hour. The order read:

"If victory does not crown the success of our armies, and if the armies are compelled to retire, an army of at least *three active corps* should be moved to the entrenched camp of Paris, to assure it protection."[4]

This order, it appears, was received at 11.30 a.m.[5]

Meanwhile Joffre, according to his *Memoirs*, thought on somewhat similar lines, for "on the evening of August 25th" he decided to create a new army "outside of the British and in a position to outflank the German right." It was to consist of "the VIIth Army Corps and one division coming from Alsace, two divisions taken from the entrenched camp of Paris, and two divisions withdrawn from the Army of Lorraine." Next, he tells us that at 9 p.m. he received the Minister of War's 7 a.m. order, and "that there was no actual connection between the idea of constituting an army of manœuvre in the region of Amiens, which was my thought, and that of sending three active corps to defend the entrenched camp of Paris, which was what the Ministers' decision amounted to."[6]

---

[1] *Mes Souvenirs*, 368–370.
[2] *Mémoires du Général Galliéni* (1926), p. 21.
[3] *The Memoirs of Marshal Joffre*, vol. I, p. 193.
[4] *Les Armées Françaises dans la Grand Guerre* (French Official History), Tome I, vol. II, Annexes vol. I, Annexe No. 372, p. 263.
[5] *1914 Les erreurs du haut commandement*, Percin, p. 276.
[6] *The Memoirs of Marshal Joffre*, vol. I, pp. 190–193. The writer of Joffre's Memoirs is frequently unreliable. On p. 146 he makes Joffre say that, on August 23, he became aware the Germans were using reserve formations, and, then, on August 25, he writes: "Believing as I still did that the Germans were engaging only active army corps in their offensive operations," etc.

Be this as it may, that evening he issued "*Instruction Générale No. 2*" (it is untimed) and it reads:

"As it is impossible to carry out the offensive manœuvre which had been projected, future operations will have as their objective to form on our left a mass capable of resuming the offensive. This will consist of the Fourth, Fifth and British Armies, together with new forces drawn from the Eastern Front, while the other armies contain the enemy for as long as is necessary.

. . . .

"A new group, comprising formations transported by rail (VIIth Corps, four divisions and perhaps in addition another active corps) will be formed between the 27th August and the 2nd September in front of Amiens, between Domarten–Ponthieu and Corbie, or behind the Somme between Picquigny and Villers-Bretonneux. This group will be in readiness to assume the offensive in the general direction of St. Pol–Arras or Arras–Bapaume."[1]

This army, known as the Sixth Army, was created on the following day and was placed under the command of General Maunoury.[2]

The day this army was created, Kluck attacked the British Army at Le Cateau, drove it from its position, yet failed to pursue. Joffre then realized that were Sir John French's two corps destroyed, the projected manœuvre of the Sixth Army would become impossible, so he ordered Lanrézac's Fifth Army, which on August 27 was immediately south of the river Oise, to relieve the pressure upon the English by launching a counter-attack. Meanwhile Moltke, who still blindly rested in Coblenz – 200 miles from the scene of action – issued the following directive for the 28th:

The French Army is fighting to gain time in order to facilitate the offensive of the Russian Armies. "The objective of the German Army, therefore, must be to advance as rapidly as possible on Paris, not to give the French Army time to recover, to prevent it from forming fresh units, and to take from France as many of her means of defence as possible."

The First Army to advance on the lower Seine, marching west of the Oise.

The Second Army to march on Paris.

[1] *Les Armées Françaises*, etc., Tome I, vol. ii, Annex vol. i, Annex 395, pp. 278–280. See also text Tome i, vol. ii, pp. 116 and 580–581.
[2] *Ibid.*, Annexe 619, p. 421.

The Third Army to march on Château-Thierry.

The Fourth Army to march on Épernay.

The Fifth Army to move on Verdun and invest that fortress.

The Sixth and Seventh Armies to oppose an advance of the enemy into Lorraine and Alsace.

"If the enemy puts up a strong resistance on the Aisne and later on the Marne, it may be necessary to abandon the south-western direction of the advance and to wheel south."[1]

Thus the Schlieffen-Moltke plan was retained, but it was inoculated with doubt.

Simultaneously Kluck, when he found that the French left wing was retreating in "a southerly and south-westerly direction", came to the conclusion that it was of decisive importance "to find the flank of this force" and drive it away from Paris. He proposed to Bülow that the Second and the First Armies should "wheel inwards", and no sooner had he done so than Moltke's directive of August 27 arrived, in which it was found that such a move was not excluded.[2] No change, however, was made, and, on the 29th, while the First Army came into contact with General d'Amade's detachment of Territorials on its right flank, and simultaneously learnt of enemy detrainments at Amiens and Moreuil, the battle of Guise-St. Quentin was fought between Bülow and Lanrézac. It was indecisive; the French slipped back and no pursuit followed. Meanwhile the British Army continued to retire. Joffre met Sir John French but to no good purpose,[3] for General Berthelot, Joffre's Chief of Staff, "even at this hour . . . did not appreciate fully the importance of the German threat to" the French "left flank."[4]

Neither did Kluck appreciate the importance of the French threat from Amiens to his right wing. So certain was he of victory that it seems he never even reported it, and he reverted to his idea of an inward wheel. At 9.30 a.m. on August 30 he prepared to carry it out, and at 5.55 p.m. he heard by wireless from Bülow that he had beaten the French, that they were in retreat and that, on the 31st, the Second Army would rest.

At 6.30 p.m. another message came in from Bülow to ask for the cooperation of the First Army. "To gain the full advantages of

[1] Quoted from *Liaison, 1914*, Brigadier-General E. L. Spears (1932), pp. 533–534. Also see *The Campaign of the Marne, 1914*, Sewell Tyng (1935), pp. 371–374.

[2] *The March on Paris*, von Kluck, pp. 75–76.

[3] See *Memoirs of Marshal Joffre*, vol. 1, pp. 213–214.

[4] *Britain and the War*, Huguet (1928), p. 75.

the victory," it read, "a wheel inwards of the First Army pivoted on Chauny toward the line La Fère–Laon is urgently desired." As this fitted his own ideas, he at once complied, and informed the Supreme Command: "The First Army has wheeled round toward the Oise and will advance on the 31st by Compiègne and Noyon to exploit the success of the Second Army."[1]

Moltke, now established at Luxemburg, agreed to this. His message reads: "The Third Army has converged toward the south against the Aisne . . . and will pursue a southerly direction. The movements undertaken by the First and Second Armies conform to the intention of the High Command."[2] As Bülow points out: "This order was of the highest importance. To all appearances it ignored that since the 29th enemy troops had detrained at Amiens, Moreuil, Montdidier and Roye, and that important forces had already attacked the right wing of the First Army at Villers-Bretonneux east of Amiens."[3]

The fault, therefore, rests with Kluck, who never reported this attack; also with Moltke who, 150 miles away to the north-east, might as well have been in Berlin.

While this vital change was made, which meant the end of the Schlieffen-Moltke plan in shadow as well as in substance, in London Lord Kitchener, who had been appointed Secretary of State for War on August 6, was alarmed to hear from Sir John French that he intended to retire to the south-west of Paris, which was tantamount to an abandonment of the campaign. A telegraphic battle followed which ended when Kitchener hurried over to France. Then, on August 31, the wheel of the German First Army was spotted by a British aeroplane, and its position was confirmed by a captured order. At once Joffre was informed of this momentous news.

It was on the following day, September 1, that the fast approaching series of battles, to become known to history as the Battle of the Marne, finds its origin, and though it is true that if the Sixth Army had not been created it could not have been fought, it is equally true that had Kluck not wheeled eastward, its four divisions – two of the VIIth Corps and the 55th and 56th divisions – would in all probability easily have been swept aside.

On this day Joffre asked the Minister of War to place the

[1] *The March on Paris*, von Kluck, pp. 82–83.
[2] *Mon rapport sur la Bataille de la Marne*, von Bülow (French edit., 1920), p. 51.
[3] *Ibid.*, p. 51.

capital directly under his command. He then ordered Maunoury to retire on Paris, moved his headquarters to Bar-sur-Aube, and issued "*Instruction Générale No. 4*", in which he said:

"As soon as the Fifth Army has escaped the menace of envelopment against its left, the Third, Fourth and Fifth Armies will resume the offensive. . . .

"If circumstances permit, parts of the First and Second Armies will be recalled in due course to participate in the offensive. Finally the mobile troops of the fortified camp of Paris may also take part in the general action."[1]

Vague though this order was, it carried with it a definite hint of a counter-attack from Paris, and its vagueness may have in part been due to Joffre's uncertainty about the British, for Sir John French was still in full retreat. Meanwhile, on the German side, though it was known that the French were hurrying troops to Paris,[2] Bülow was instructed by Moltke to move his left wing eastward in order to support the Third Army.[3] This drew him away from the First Army.

The next day, September 2, the British continued their retreat, and Kluck abandoned the pursuit and moved the IIIrd and IXth Corps on Château-Thierry to help Bülow.[4] No sooner had he done so than he received this order from Moltke: "The intention is to drive the French in a south-westerly direction from Paris. The First Army will follow in echelon behind the Second Army and will be responsible for the flank protection of the Armies."[5] Kluck comments in his book: "The Supreme Command, however, seemed to be firmly convinced that the garrison of Paris need not be taken into account for any operations outside the line of forts of the capital,"[6] and instead of halting and assuming his new rôle of flank guard – he was already a day's march ahead of the Second Army – he set Moltke's order aside and pushed on to Château-Thierry – that is, away from Paris.

Meanwhile, while General Maunoury fell back on Paris, Joffre dispatched a secret note to his Army Commanders in which he ordered them to establish themselves on the general line Pont-sur-Yonne – Méry-sur-Seine – Arcis-sur-Aube – Brienne-le-Château – Joinville, and then:

[1] *La préparation de la guerre*, etc., Joffre, pp. 95–96.
[2] *Jusqu'à la Marne en 1914*, Tappen, p. 115.
[3] *Mon rapport sur la Bataille de la Marne*, von Bülow, p. 54.
[4] *The March on Paris*, von Kluck, p. 91.
[5] *Ibid.*, p. 94.   [6] *Ibid.*, p. 95.

"To reinforce the right-hand army by two corps drawn from the armies of Nancy and Épinal.

"At that moment to assume the offensive on the whole front.

"Cover our left wing with all available cavalry between Montereau and Melun.

"Ask the British Army to participate in the manœuvre,

(*1*) – by holding the Seine from Melun to Juvisy,

(*2*) – by debouching from that front when the Fifth Army assumes the offensive.

"Simultaneously the garrison of Paris will act in the direction of Meaux."[1]

The extraordinary point in this order is that a retirement to Joinville meant the abandonment of Verdun, the pivot upon which the whole of the left of the French Army swung. Had that fortress been abandoned, Joffre's front would have been cut in two, and no sortie from Paris could have saved the situation. Fortunately for Joffre, General Sarrail, who on August 30 had replaced Ruffrey, set this order aside, and instead of withdrawing his right he held fast to Verdun and swung back his left some 15 miles until it faced due west. This made a gap between his army and the Fourth Army, into which the Crown Prince entered and was attacked in flank.

It is obvious from the secret note of September 2 that Joffre's mind was befogged. Nevertheless, while Moltke sat in monastic seclusion at Luxemburg, Joffre acted. At least he did something, and thanks to Sarrail it was something worth while, and something which gradually began to clear the mists which surrounded him. It was that, so long as his right held fast to Verdun and his centre was not driven in, might not it be possible to swing his left forward?

Thus it came about that he was attracted toward that flank. Two things next happened: firstly, he replaced General Lanrézac by Franchet D'Espérey – probably the ablest of the French generals – and secondly he began to pay some attention to Galliéni. Strange as it may seem, thus far Joffre had left him in ignorance of his intentions, and for some unexplained reason Galliéni only received his General Instruction No. 4 this day.[2] He then at once considered the problem of advancing Maunoury's army on Meaux.[3] Toward noon, for the first time he learnt of Kluck's

[1] Quoted from *Liaison, 1914*, Spears, pp. 365–366.
[2] *Mémoire du Général Galliéni*, p. 77.   [3] *Ibid.*, p. 81.

wheel eastward,[1] and he asked for instructions regarding Maunoury, and suggested that he be moved north of the Marne toward the river Ourcq. Joffre replied that part of his active troops "can be pushed to the north-east at any moment from now on, so as to threaten the right flank of the Germans" and encourage the British.[2] Then, suddenly, the clouds of doubt thicken again and Joffre wrote to Millerand:

"As one of the allied powers our duty is to hold out, gain time and contain the strongest possible German forces. . . . My decision therefore is to wait several days before launching the battle . . . rest our troops and prepare an eventual offensive with the British Army and the mobile garrison of Paris."[3]

This meant a wearing battle followed by an eventual attack at some uncertain future date. Meanwhile General von Kluck plunged on. His order for September 4 reads: "The First Army will continue its march across the Marne tomorrow, so as to force the French away eastwards. If the British offer opposition they are to be driven back."[4] At the same time Bülow believed that the French Fifth Army was in rout.[5]

In spite of this rosy outlook, on the following day nervousness began to show itself at Luxemburg. It was decided to move the headquarters of the Seventh Army and two corps from the left flank to the right.[6] Meanwhile Kluck continued his advance, and such skirmishes as his IVth Corps – on his right flank – had with Maunoury's patrols led him to believe that there was little behind them.

On the Allied side, far from the battle being several days distant, as Joffre supposed, it was imminent, and it emerged chaotically out of a confusion of conferences. Joffre, who still thought in terms of the defensive, created a new army, the Ninth, under General Foch, between his Fourth and Fifth Armies, and then returned to his offensive idea and at 12.45 p.m. telegraphed Sir John French, and asked him whether his army would be ready "to deliver battle tomorrow."[7] Simultaneously he sent an identical message to Franchet d'Espérey.[8]

---

[1] *Ibid.*, pp. 93–94. See also *Les Carnetos de Galliéni* (1932), pp. 58–59.
[2] *Memoirs of Marshal Joffre*, vol. I, p. 241.
[3] *Plutarque a menti*, Pierrefeu, pp. 98–99. See also *Liaison*, Spears, pp. 372–373.
[4] *The March on Paris*, p. 100.
[5] *Mon rapport sur la Bataille de la Marne*, p. 56.
[6] *Jusqu'à la Marne en 1914*, Tappen, pp. 106, 116.
[7] *Liaison, 1914*, Spears, p. 399.
[8] *Memoirs of Marshal Joffre*, p. 246.

When Galliéni and Maunoury were told by Joffre to get into touch with Sir John French, they visited his headquarters at Melun at 3 p.m., but as they found him absent they provisionally arranged with Sir Archibald Murray, French's chief of staff, that while on the 5th the Sixth Army was to advance on Meaux, the British Army would fall back to make room for it, and on the 6th or 7th "pivot on its right wing . . . so as to face east, its left joining the Sixth Army." Then both were to attack the right flank of the German First Army while held by the French Fifth Army.[1]

On his return Sir John French approved this plan; but a little later General Sir Henry Wilson, his sub-chief of the General Staff, arrived with a totally different plan. What had happened?

Franchet d'Espérey, who wished to meet Sir John French, set out for Bray-sur-Seine. There, at 3 p.m., he was met by Wilson – Sir John French was out. He explained to Wilson that the First German Army was "in the air", with its communications exposed, and that it was not in contact with the Second Army. He then proposed:

(*1*) On September 5 the Fifth Army should take up the line Sézanne–Provins in readiness to attack on the front Sézanne–Courtaçon.

(*2*) The Sixth Army should advance to the Ourcq and fall on the flank and rear of the First German Army.

(*3*) The British Army should cooperate by filling the gap between the Fifth and Sixth Armies with its axis directed on Montmirail and its right covered by Conneau's Cavalry.

These proposals he at once telegraphed to Joffre, and Wilson took them to Sir John French, who, now quite bewildered, did nothing. When this telegram arrived Joffre was telephoned by Galliéni, who told him that he was ready to move, but that British cooperation was essential. Half an hour later – at 10 p.m. – Joffre issued General Instructions No. 6; according to which an attack was to be launched against the exposed wing of Kluck's Army on September 6. Its main items were:

(*1*) The Sixth Army to cross the Ourcq and move in the direction of Château-Thierry.

(*2*) The British Army, on the front Changis–Coulommiers, facing east, to be ready to attack in the direction of Montmirail.

(*3*) The Fifth Army, on the front Courtaçon–Esterney–Sézanne, to be ready to attack from south to north.

[1] See *Liaison, 1914*, Spears, pp. 406–407, and Galliéni's *Mémoires*, pp. 119–128.

(*4*) The Ninth Army to cover the right of the Fifth Army and hold the boundaries of the marshes of St. Gond.

(*5*) The Fourth Army to stand fast and maintain contact with the Third Army.

(*6*) The Third Army, while it held back its right, to advance its centre and left and attack the left of the enemy forces marching west of the Argonne.[1]

Strangely enough, in idea this was a Cannae plan. While the French centre – the Fifth, Fourth, and Ninth French Armies – held the Second, Third, and Fourth German Armies in a great pocket, the two French wings – the French Sixth Army and British on the left flank and the Third French Army on the right – were to operate toward Rheims, the one to advance eastward against the German First Army and the other westward against the German Fifth Army.

This night Galliéni ordered Maunoury to be ready to attack directly Sir John French decided to cooperate.[2]

While at the French G.H.Q. all was activity, Moltke, who thus far had rigidly followed the non-interference theory of his uncle, began to doubt its wisdom as report after report was received of French rail movements towards Paris. At length, anxious about the safety of the right flank of his armies, at 7 p.m. on September 4 he ordered Tappen to telegraph the following message:

"The First and Second Armies are to remain facing the eastern front of Paris: The First Army, between the Oise and the Marne, is to occupy the Marne crossing west of Château-Thierry; the Second Army, between the Marne and the Seine, is to occupy the Seine crossing between Nogent and Méry inclusive."[3]

This order was received by the First Army at 7.15 a.m. on September 5. At 11 a.m., General von Gronau, in command of the IVth Reserve Corps, which acted as flank guard to the First Army, and who was suspicious of enemy concentrations west of him, attacked the heights of Monthyon, surprised the advanced guards of the Sixth French Army, which that morning had moved forward, and drove them back. Thus opened the Battle of the Marne; prematurely so far as the French were concerned because the Allied forces were not yet ready.

A stubborn fight followed, and Gronau, when he found himself

---

[1] *La préparation de la guerre*, etc., Joffre, pp. 108–110.
[2] *Mémoires du Général Galliéni*, p. 112.
[3] *The March on Paris*, Kluck, p. 105.

outnumbered, fell back some six miles, but was not pursued. When he heard of this action, Kluck at once turned about his IInd Corps (General von Linsingen) and hurried it to Gronau's support.

Shortly before this decision was made, Lieutenant-Colonel Hentsch, one of Moltke's staff officers, had arrived at Kluck's headquarters. Kluck was then under the impression that the armies on his left were advancing victoriously and he was amazed to learn that the Fifth, Sixth, and Seventh Armies had been held up, and because the French were moving troops by rail from the east toward Paris[1] a general retirement of the German front might become necessary.

Meanwhile Joffre's anxiety about Sir John French's intentions had become so unbearable that, at 2 p.m. he visited him at Melun; explained to him the vital necessity for British cooperation, and ended by exclaiming: "*Monsieur le Maréchal, c'est la France qui vous supplie.*" Sir John French tried to reply in French, but words failed him and he turned to an English officer and exclaimed: "Damn it, I can't explain. Tell him that all that men can do our fellows will do."[2] Thus at last cooperation was established, and Joffre issued the following proclamation to his troops:

"We are about to engage in a battle on which the fate of our country depends and it is important to remind all ranks that the moment has passed for looking to the rear; all our efforts must be directed to attacking and driving back the enemy. Troops that can advance no farther, must, at any price, hold on to the ground they have conquered and die at the spot rather than give way. Under the circumstances which face us, no act of weakness can be tolerated."[3]

The Battle of the Marne – opened on September 5 by Gronau's surprise attack on the leading troops of General Maunoury's army – was destined for seven days to rage up and down the western front from Verdun to Senlis, and it comprised so many engagements that they will be here restricted to those fought on the vital right flank of the German phalanx. They may be divided into the battle of the Ourcq, the battle of the two Morins, and the "battle" of the Gap.

As regards the battle of the Ourcq, the fighting on September 5 was continued on the following day by Linsingen, who arrived at

---

[1] *Ibid.*, p. 107.
[2] *Liaison, 1914*, Spears, p. 417. See also *Memoirs of Marshal Joffre*, vol. I, pp. 253–254.
[3] *The Memoirs of Marshal Joffre*, vol. I, p. 255.

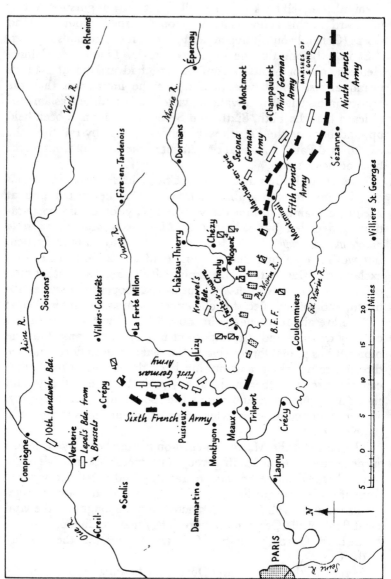

14. BATTLE OF THE MARNE, SEPTEMBER 8, 1914

Trilport at 5 a.m. In spite of the long march his corps had made, six hours later he launched it into the fight, which soon spread northward along the whole front of the Sixth French Army.[1]

In spite of the severe fighting, von Kluck was as yet in no way convinced of the seriousness of the situation; nevertheless, on an urgent call from von Linsingen, he sent forward General von Arnim's IVth Corps, which arrived early on September 7. But during the day the situation grew so precarious that Kluck was persuaded to order back his two remaining corps – the IIIrd and the IXth.[2] This decision, as will be seen, led to the most fateful results, because, in order to secure the right flank of the Second Army, these two corps were at the moment of recall engaged with the Fifth French Army, and their withdrawal not only uncovered that flank, but simultaneously increased the already wide gap between the Second Army and the First. Further, as Bülow points out, their withdrawal raised the morale of Franchet d'Espérey's men.[3]

Kluck's decision to withdraw the IIIrd and IXth Corps was taken without consulting either Bülow or Moltke, not only because he was no longer under Bülow's control, but also because Moltke had lost all power to intervene. From September 5 to 8, not a single order was sent either to the First or Second Army by the Supreme Command.[4]

On this day Maunoury's position was also precarious and Galliéni collected some 1,200 Paris taxi-cabs to rush reinforcements to him.[5] On September 8, Maunoury attempted to outflank his enemy's right, but without success, and Kluck, as the IIIrd and IXth Corps came up, planned to turn the French left on the following day. He felt certain of a speedy victory, but fate decided differently, and on another part of the 300-mile long battle-front.

When the battle of the Ourcq opened, as General von Kluck's IIIrd Corps (General von Lochow) and IXth Corps (General von Quast) were in the process of conforming to Moltke's order to

---

[1] In all, General Maunoury appears to have had under his command some 150,000 men. See *Mémoires du Général Galliéni*, pp. 110–111.

[2] On the evening of September 6 an order of Joffre's was found on a prisoner which revealed the seriousness of the attack (see *Jusqu'à la Marne in 1914*, Tappen, p. 116).

[3] *Mon rapport sur la bataille de la Marne*, Bülow, p. 68.

[4] In *La direction suprême de l'armée pendant la bataille de la Marne* (Documents Allemands), p. 133, Lieut.-Colonel Muller-Löbnitz writes: "Even during the battle the Supreme Command abstained from all intervention." He informs us that General Tappen said to him: "The Supreme Command considered best to give the Army Commanders a free hand."

[5] See *La véritable histoire des taxis de la Marne*, Commandant Henri Carré (1921).

protect the right flank of the Second Army, suddenly a violent and unexpected bombardment burst on them. All unknown to them the tide of battle had turned. The Fifth French Army, which was considered beaten, was upon them. Lochow and Quast rushed their corps forward and soon all along the front a battle raged between these two corps and the three left-wing corps – the XVIIIth, IIIrd, and Ist – of Franchet d'Espérey's Army, while his Xth Corps was engaged on their right. The French advanced about one mile that day, but by nightfall they were held up and ordered to entrench. The next day their attack was continued in the direction of Montmirail.

Although Bülow had held his own, the situation was sufficiently serious to warrant a retirement behind the Petit Morin; this he carried out during the night of September 7–8, which meant the end of Moltke's order of September 4. Thus it was that not until September 8 did the French regain contact, by when the IIIrd and IXth Corps were on their way to the Ourcq in response to Kluck's urgent call. During the day several French frontal attacks were repulsed, and, on the night of September 8–9 General de Maud'huy, Commander of the XVIIIth Corps, carried Marchais-en-Brie, to the west of Montmirail. This success, as Mr. Tyng points out, was an event of supreme importance, because its capture rendered Montmirail indefensible, and since that town was now completely dominated from the west, "Bülow ordered his VIIth and Xth Reserve Corps to fall back to the line Margny-le-Thoult, a position running from north to south. It was a retreat of ten kilometres towards the east, which left the right wing of the German Second Army facing west instead of south, and it ended all further possibility of closing the breach between Bülow and Kluck."[1]

For the Germans the best chance of victory that remained was to break through the front of Foch's Ninth Army, which extended from Villeneuve to Sommesous along the marshes of St. Gond; to turn the right wing of the Fifth and force it to retire. On September 6, General von Hausen had launched his Third Army against Foch, and on the 8th, at 3 a.m., he surprised his right, drove it back and carried Fère Campenoise, but failed to penetrate. Though it is related that Foch reported to Joffre, "Hard pressed on my right. My centre is yielding. Impossible to manœuvre. Situation excellent. I am attacking," it is not true; it is true how-

---

[1] *The Campaign of the Marne, 1914*, Sewell Tyng (1935), p. 251.

ever that he ordered attacks and counter-attacks in rapid succession, but to no avail, for his men had as much as they could do to hold on by the skin of their teeth.

While Maunoury compelled Kluck to draw the whole of his Army to the Ourcq, and Franchet d'Espérey forced Bülow to retire north-eastward, Sir John French and his three corps[1] cautiously crept into the gap between Kluck and Bülow, unwittingly to conjure forth from a situation created for them "the miracle of the Marne", or, as Pierrefeu describes it: "How Sir John French saved the situation without understanding it."[2]

On the morning of September 6 French had set out against what was a near vacuum, because on the night before Kluck had withdrawn his IInd Corps, which early on the 6th was followed by his IVth. All that remained in front of the British Army were two divisions of General von der Marwitz's Cavalry Corps and some Jäger and cyclist battalions. French slowly felt his way as he advanced with the IIIrd Corps (Pulteney) on his left, the IInd (Smith-Dorrien) in the centre, and the Ist (Haig) on his right, and when on the following day Bülow fell back and the IIIrd and IXth Corps of the First German Army were ordered north, the IInd and IIIrd British Corps crossed the Grand Morin while the Ist was delayed near Rozoy. Seldom in the history of war was speed more necessary; yet Sir John French, although a cavalry officer, did little or nothing to urge on his corps. On September 8 the Petit Morin was crossed after some opposition and the advance was continued to the Marne. In three days the British Army had moved forward 25 miles, and because it stood at the entrance of the gap between the First and Second German Armies, all it had to do was to step forward and sever the head of the invading phalanx from its body.

Joffre saw this, and that evening, at 8.7 p.m., he ordered his Sixth Army to hold on to the Germans on the Ourcq, while the British crossed the Marne between Nogent-l'Artaud and la Ferté-sous-Jouarre and advanced against Kluck's left and rear. Also, he instructed the Fifth Army to cover the right flank of the British.

Meanwhile what of Moltke at Luxemburg? With only just sufficient information to fill him with the gravest anxiety, he sent for Lieutenant-Colonel Hentsch and instructed him to visit the

---

[1] The IIIrd Corps, commanded by Lieut.-General Sir W. Pulteney, came into being on August 30.
[2] *Plutarque a menti*, p. 121.

five right-wing armies and ascertain the exact situation. At that moment neither he nor any of his staff dreamt that a general retirement would be necessary;[1] nevertheless the situation was of sufficient importance for written instructions to have been given to Hentsch, but he received only verbal ones. He says: "The Chief of the General Staff empowered me, should it be necessary, to order the five armies to fall back behind the Vesle along the heights north of the Argonne," and "I was given the mission, if it were necessary, to order the retreat of the armies on the line Sainte–Ménehould–Rheims–Fismes–Soissons. I was given full powers to give orders in the name of the Supreme Command."[2]

Hentsch, who was no optimist, left Luxemburg at 11 a.m. on September 8. First he visited the Fifth, Fourth, and Third Armies, and arrived at Montmort, the headquarters of the Second Army, at 7.45 p.m. There he found that Bülow believed a retreat of the First Army to be inevitable and that he had decided to withdraw his own army.[3]

At 7 a.m. on September 9, Hentsch set out for Chézy, the First Army headquarters, and although it was no more than 25 miles away, because of troop movements along his road he did not arrive there until noon. Every mile he travelled he witnessed confusion and disorder[4] – conditions no more than normal in rear of a retiring army – which accentuated his pessimism and must have suggested to him that the situation was desperate. As he found Kluck out, he talked the situation over with his chief of staff, General von Kuhl, and while he did so a message came in from the Second Army that Bülow was falling back. Hentsch, who knew that the gap between the First and Second Armies had widened to over 30 miles, and that the British had entered it, then invoked the power given him by Moltke, and ordered the First Army to retire. This was done without the approval of Kluck and in spite of the fact that he was not far off.[5]

That Hentsch was empowered to give the order is undoubted, but it was of such supreme importance that he had no right to give it to anyone other than Kluck himself, and that he did not do so goes to show how far the presumptions of the General Staff had replaced the authority of the commanding generals. It would

[1] *La direction suprême de l'armée*, etc., Muller-Löbnitz, p. 137.
[2] *Ibid.*, pp. 138–139.
[3] *Mon rapport sur la bataille de la Marne*, p. 66.
[4] *La direction suprême de l'armée*, Muller-Löbnitz, p. 161.
[5] See *The March on Paris*, Kluck, p. 137.

appear that Kluck never saw Hentsch, and when he heard of the order he accepted it against his better judgment,[1] probably because of his awe for the Great General Staff. Although he did not know that the French on his right were contemplating retreat, he must have been aware of the inordinately slow and cautious advance of the British in the gap between him and Bülow. Had he ignored Hentsch's verbal order and acted on the principle "when in doubt hit out", not only might he have driven back Maunoury, but by doing so have paralysed the British and carried Bülow along with him. As Görlitz points out, this is what Seydlitz did at Zorndorf, and adds, "but this kind of thing was not in the mode of the era of William II."[2]

Thus the Schlieffen-Moltke plan, created and directed by the staff, was liquidated by the staff, because generalship was bankrupt. On the morning of September 11, for the first time during the campaign Moltke went forward and visited the headquarters of his armies. On his return he was taken seriously ill[3] and soon after was replaced by General von Falkenhayn.

Tannenberg and the Marne were both decisive battles – the one tactically and the other strategically. The former led to no strategical results other than exalting Hindenburg and persuading the German General Staff to assume that a rapid defeat of Russia was a comparatively easy task. Yet, had the battle been won by the Russians, its effects on both Germany and Europe might have been appalling. On the contrary, the latter battle, which was only a partial tactical success, led to such overwhelming strategical results that Sir James Edmonds is unquestionably right when he classes Joffre's victory "as one of the decisive battles of the world."[4] It meant that Germany had lost her one and only chance to defeat France before she engaged Russia *au fond*.

One reason for this was that, as Bloch had foreseen, mobile warfare rapidly degenerated into siege. Under the cover of innumerable entrenchments the initiative passed from the General Staffs to the industrial potentials of the contending nations. Where these potentials were weak, as in Russia, mobile warfare, though attenuated, was still possible; but where they were strong, as they were in France and Great Britain, it ceased altogether. Henceforward decision in the West was more and more sought in

[1] *The German General Staff*, Walter Görlitz (English edit., 1953), p. 162.
[2] *Ibid.*, p. 162.   [3] See *Jusqu'à la Marne en 1914*, Tappen, p. 121.
[4] *History of the Great War, France and Belgium, 1914*, vol. 1, p. 295.

factories than in armies, and also in sea power, which could either safeguard or strangle industrial supplies. As Bloch had foretold, the ultimate arbiter was to be famine.

Deeper than this, there was a fundamental misjudgment in the Schlieffen plan, which had it been appreciated might, and probably would, have deterred Germany from going to war unless supported by England or assured of her neutrality. This misjudgment arose out of the composition of the German two-front war. Had it been restricted to a conflict with France and Russia, the probability is that, had the Schlieffen plan been adhered to, France would have been hurled into the dust within six weeks of the start of the war and that a compromise peace with Russia would have followed. But, as things stood in August, 1914, the western front included England as well as France, and though the British Army would, in the circumstances stated, have shared the fate of the French, the integrity of England would nevertheless have remained inviolate. The question therefore arises, however successful the Schlieffen plan might have been, would it have led to a conclusion of the war? The historic answer is "No!" As in the days of Napoleon, England would have continued at war until she had built up another coalition, or until both she and Germany were faced with economic collapse, when a negotiated peace on traditional British lines would have ended it.

Time and again in the past, when England was involved in a continental war the historic lesson had been that as long as she commanded the seas, because her frontiers were un-attackable and her maritime communications secure, no continental nation, however powerful its land forces, could wrest the initiative from her. This was the governing factor, not only in the collapse of Germany in 1918, but also in her still more overwhelming collapse in 1945, and in both World Wars Germany failed to appreciate it.

Tactical stalemate and change of objectives

The operations which immediately followed the battle of the Marne led to a radical change in the orientation of the war. Each side first attempted to outflank the other's northern wing by reinforcing its own northern wing from its southern. But the race was so close that it ended in a dead-heat at Nieuport on the Channel. Then it was discovered that the magazine rifle had made the defensive so much stronger than the attack that when near the enemy, in order to exist, let alone fight, entrenching became imperative. Thus, as Bloch had predicted, the outcome was siege warfare.

But neither side was prepared to wage it, least of all the British, who were so ill-equipped for the task that they made hand grenades out of jam tins and converted field-gun cartridge cases into trench mortars. Catapults again came into use and wooden cannon were bored out of logs, from which oil drums filled with explosives were fired. Soon lines of entrenchments began to supplement each other, and though it was still possible at great cost to carry a front line entrenchment by assault, the ever-growing depth of trench systems, coupled with entanglements, soon prohibited complete penetration. Thus, until the advent of the tank, spade and barbed wire beat rifle and gun; mobility ceased on the western front and gave way to stalemate.

Meanwhile in the east, because of the disastrous retreat of the Austrians to the Dunajec, on September 15 Hindenburg was ordered to hold East Prussia with a minimum of his forces and transfer the bulk of his army to the Austrian left wing. This he did, and on November 1 was appointed commander-in-chief of the eastern front. But he was still too weak to force a decision, and when the Russians advanced again, their near approach to Silesia and their reoccupation of part of East Prussia so alarmed the Kaiser that pressure was brought on Falkenhayn to stop operations in the west and reinforce Hindenburg. This he was able to do in November, when the fighting in the Ypres area bogged down in the Flanders mud.

To save Austria, it was imperative to dislodge the Russians from the Carpathians, and on the suggestion of Field-Marshal Conrad von Hötzendorf, the chief of the Austrian General Staff, it was decided to break through the Russian front between Gorlice and Tarnow and wheel eastward behind the Russian left flank and sever its communications. In the east this was a feasible plan, because the Russian front was weakly entrenched, almost entirely unwired and held by little more than outposts.

At 6 a.m. on May 2, 1915, after four hours of bombardment, the German and Austrian infantry advanced, broke through the Russian front and captured 140,000 prisoners. But as the roads were rivers of mud, the pursuit was so slow that it was not until August 5 that the Russians were compelled to abandon Warsaw. Kovno and Grodno fell next, and by the end of September, after they had lost 325,000 men in prisoners alone and more than 3,000 guns, the Russians were forced back on the line Riga–Dvinsk–Pinsk–Tarnopol–Czernowitz. Although not driven out of the war, they were so weakened[1] that the armies of the Central Powers were free to select what objective they liked in 1916.

Meanwhile the Russian situation was made worse because Turkey had joined Germany, and to understand how this came about it is necessary to step back into pre-war history.

In 1883, in order to strengthen the Dual Alliance, General von der Goltz was lent by Germany to Turkey to reorganize her army, and two years later the defences of the Dardanelles were modernized. Twenty years later, when the Anglo-French entente was agreed, Admiral Sir John Fisher, then First Sea Lord, studied the Dardanelles problem and came to the conclusion that to force their passage, even with military support, would be "mighty hazardous". Next, in 1906 and again in 1911, the newly created British General Staff examined the question and decided "that owing to the impossibility of effecting a surprise, an attempt to disembark an army on the Gallipoli peninsula would be too hazardous to be recommended". In the meantime the British entente with Russia had drawn Turkey toward Germany, and to propitiate the Turks a British naval mission was sent to Constantinople. In order to counteract its activities, in 1913 a German military mission of 70 officers headed by General Liman von

---

[1] "Even before the end of the campaign in 1914," writes Mr. Lloyd George, "the Russian Army's resistance threatened to break down through lack of equipment" (*War Memoirs*, 1933, vol. I, p. 441).

Sanders was sent to Turkey, and on August 2, 1914, a secret defensive and offensive alliance was signed by Germany and Turkey. It was followed immediately by the mobilization of the Turkish Army and the mining of the Dardanelles. No sooner was this treaty made than an unlooked-for event gave it life. Two warships, then being built in English yards for the Turkish Navy, were requisitioned by the British Government, and two German warships – the *Goeben* and *Breslau* – which were in the Mediterranean, after a series of adventures in which they successfully eluded the French and British fleets, entered the Dardanelles on August 10 and steamed for Constantinople. But they were not interned; instead they were nominally bought by the Turks to replace the two ships seized. This event more than any other determined the destiny of the war in the Mediterranean. Because of it, in September a British squadron was sent to watch the Dardanelles, and as this made the position of the British naval mission intolerable, the latter was withdrawn. This left the German military mission master of the field and it became obvious to the Allied Powers that war with Turkey was probable. It did not take long to come. On October 29 a Turkish squadron, under German command, entered the Black Sea and shelled Odessa, Sebastopol, and Theodosia. The following day the Russian Ambassador in Constantinople asked for his passports, and the British Government demanded the withdrawal of the German military mission within 12 hours. As this ultimatum was ignored, war with Turkey was declared by Russia on November 2, and by Britain and France on the 5th. This meant that all hope of the British and French to gain a southern approach to Russia was blocked.

The Turkish Army consisted of 36 divisions headed by Liman von Sanders, with General Bronsart von Schellendorf as his chief of staff. Its distribution was:

First Army, 13 divisions, based on Constantinople with one division on the Gallipoli peninsula. Second Army, six divisions on the coast of Asia Minor with one on the Asiatic side of the Dardanelles. Third Army, 11 divisions in Asia Minor, earmarked for the Caucasus. Two divisions in Yemen, two in Mesopotamia, and two in the Hejaz. Eventually, 70 new divisions were raised.

Although short of arms and ammunition, neither of which had been fully replenished since the Balkan wars, Enver Pasha decided on two campaigns – one against the Russians in the Caucasus and the other against Egypt. The aim of the first campaign was to secure possession of the Baku oilfields, and in December Enver Pasha headed the advance of the Third Army on Kars. Although nominally it totalled 190,000 men, it could only provide 66,000 combatants; it was ill-provisioned and without organized transport, and therefore had to live on the country through which it advanced. Before he set out, Enver Pasha told von Sanders that once he had occupied Baku he intended to march through Afghanistan on India. Instead, he was caught in the mountains by the Russians and the snow, and, on January 5, 1915, was forced to retreat. By January 23, through frost and famine his army was reduced to 12,400 men. Nevertheless, his advance had so perturbed the Grand Duke Nicholas that on January 2 he asked the British military mission attached to his headquarters to suggest to Lord Kitchener that if he could arrange for either a naval or military demonstration against Turkey it might compel the Turkish Government to withdraw troops from the Caucasus front and thereby ease the Russian situation. It was a modest request; but it was to lead to a muddled campaign, one of the most costly ever waged by the British Empire.

CHAPTER 6

The Battles of Sari Bair and Suvla Bay, 1915

W hen the race between the British and Germans to the Channel ended at Nieuport, the mobile war both had set out to fight was so abruptly halted by the spade that Lord Kitchener exclaimed: "I don't know what is to be done – this isn't war." Unfortunately it was war, as every private soldier knew.[1] But ministers are not private soldiers, and the stalemate so shocked them that blame for it was heaped on the generals. Mr. Churchill, First Lord of the Admiralty, exclaimed: "Confronted with this deadlock, military art remained dumb; the Commanders and their General Staffs had no plan except the frontal attack which all their experience and training had led them to reject; they had no policy except the policy of exhaustion."[2] And on December 31, Mr. Lloyd George said: "I can see no signs anywhere that our military leaders and guides are considering any plans for extricating us from our present unsatisfactory position."[3]

Thus it came about that the more silent the soldiers became, the more vociferous grew the politicians. But because there was no organ of strategical direction within or behind the Government at that time, no minister had any idea of what his colleagues were doing. "The men at the head of affairs," wrote Admiral Wemyss, "are ignorant of all technique; they think they have only to say 'Do it' – and it is done – wrong."[4] What was the result? General Sir William Robertson supplies the answer: "The Secretary of State for War, was aiming at decisive results on the Western front; the First Lord of the Admiralty was advocating a military expedition to the Dardanelles; the Secretary of State for India was devoting his attention to a campaign in Mesopotamia . . . the Secretary for the Colonies was occupying himself with several small wars in Africa; and the Chancellor of the Exchequer, Mr.

[1] "The enemy rose up and started to advance. They were stopped at once: with the parapet as a rest for our rifles it was impossible to miss. The attack was over before it had hardly commenced . . . ten men holding a trench could easily stop fifty who were trying to take it" (*Old Soldiers never Die*, Private Frank Richards, 1933, p. 36).
[2] *The World Crisis, 1915*, The Rt. Hon. Winston S. Churchill (1923), p. 20.
[3] *War Memoirs of David Lloyd George* (1933), vol. I, p. 356.
[4] *The Life and Letters of Lord Wester Wemyss*, Lady Wester Wemyss (1935), p. 194.

Lloyd George, was attempting to secure the removal of a large part of the British Army from France to some Eastern Mediterranean theatre."[1] This was at the time when the British Army in Flanders had lost half its men, and when there were no trained replacements at home to reinforce it.

Of these many political solutions, strange to say, the Dardanelles proposal pre-dated the Battle of the Marne. On August 20 Mr. Venizelos, the Greek Prime Minister, with the full approval of King Constantine, placed all the military and naval resources of Greece at the disposal of the Entente Powers; but Sir Edward Grey, who feared that acceptance would antagonize Turkey, rejected the offer.[2] In spite of this, on August 31 Mr. Churchill discussed the problem with Lord Kitchener, and on the following day "Mr. Churchill asked the Chief of the Imperial General Staff to appoint two officers to examine and work out, with two officers from the Admiralty, a plan for the seizure of the Gallipoli peninsula, by means of a Greek army of adequate strength, with a view to admitting a British fleet to the Sea of Marmora."[3] Thus the Dardanelles venture was born. It was challenged by Lord Fisher, who urged a landing in the Baltic. But as his operation required troops, and Kitchener had none to spare, the Dardanelles project gained in favour, although the Greeks refused to budge unless Bulgaria agreed to declare war on Turkey. This caused the proposal to be shelved, but when two Australian divisions arrived in Egypt late in November, Mr. Churchill revived it by ordering the transports which had carried them to remain in Egypt "in case they are required for an expedition."[4] Meanwhile, on his authority, a senseless operation of war had been carried out. On November 3, two days after the British Ambassador left Constantinople, the Admiralty ordered the bombardment of the Dardanelles forts. This bombardment, says Jevad Pasha, commandant of the fortresses, "warned me and I realized that I must spend the rest of my time in developing and strengthening the defences by every means."[5]

After this Mr. Churchill became increasingly obsessed by the idea of occupying Constantinople, where the sole munition factory in Turkey was located. As a problem of pure strategy the idea was

[1] Quoted in *Gallipoli, The Fading Vision*, John North (1936), p. 83.
[2] *War Memoirs*, Lloyd George, vol. 1, p. 390.
[3] *Military Operations Gallipoli* (British Official History), Brig.-General C. F. Aspinall-Oglander (1929), vol. 1, p. 41.
[4] *The World Crisis, 1915*, p. 47.   [5] *Official History*, vol. 1, p. 35.

brilliant. But without a powerful Greek army to back it, it was amateurish, because England was not capable of fighting on two fronts, and the British Army was neither equipped nor trained to fight in a theatre such as Gallipoli. Hypnotized by the glittering prize, "the shortest paths to a triumphant peace,"[1] as Churchill called it, the inadequacy of the means never disturbed his vision. We cannot but agree with John North, who wrote that "the responsibility for the inauguration of the Dardanelles campaign rests upon Mr. Winston Churchill,"[2] and with Admiral Keyes, who wrote: "But if he had not committed the Government to the enterprise, they would never have looked at it."[3] Against the opinion of Sir William Robertson,[4] who became Chief of the Imperial General Staff in December, Mr. Churchill forced his Dardanelles card on the Government, and the Government was incapable of playing the hand. The result was that the British Empire not so much drifted, but was pushed into a campaign which in the end proved as disastrous as that of Saratoga.

On January 1, 1915, two papers were submitted to the recently constituted War Council; the first by Lieutenant-Colonel Maurice Hankey (later Lord Hankey) Secretary of the Council, and the second by Mr. Lloyd George. In the former it was suggested that Germany could be struck more easily through Turkey, and that should the Black Sea be reopened the price of wheat would fall and 350,000 tons of shipping would be released. The latter considered that the eastern operation should be directed against Austria and be based on Salonika;[5] but this suggestion was set aside because it demanded a considerable number of troops.

The Grand Duke Nicholas's momentous request was received the following day through the British Ambassador at Petrograd and the Cabinet was notified of the critical position of the Russian forces in the Caucasus when, in fact, the crisis there was nearly over. Without further consideration, Kitchener telegraphed in reply: "Please assure the Grand Duke that steps will be taken to make a demonstration against the Turks."[6] At the same time Fisher set before Churchill a grandiose plan. He strongly supported

---

[1] Quoted from *The Dardanelles Campaign*, Henry W. Nevinson, p. 23.
[2] *Gallipoli, the Fading Vision*, p. 54.
[3] *The Naval Memoirs of Admiral of the Fleet Sir Roger Keyes* (1934), vol. I, p. 344.
[4] "This scheme had often been mentioned before the war and as often opposed by the General Staff. From a military standpoint it was not a practicable proposition" (*Soldiers and Statesmen*, Field-Marshal Sir W. Robertson, 1926, vol. I, p. 83).
[5] See *War Memoirs*, Lloyd George, vol. I, pp. 374-380.
[6] *Official History*, vol. I, p. 52.

an attack on Turkey if it could be carried out immediately; 75,000 men from France were to land at Besika Bay; another landing was to be made at Alexandretta, and a demonstration against Haifa. "Simultaneously," wrote Fisher, "the Greeks should be landed on the Gallipoli peninsula, the Bulgarians should be induced to march on Adrianople, and the Rumanians to join the Russians and Serbs in an attack on Austria. Finally, Admiral Sturdee should at the same time force the Dardanelles with ships of the *Majestic* and *Canopus* class."[1]

Churchill blew the froth off this tankard of strategic ale and gulped down the idea of forcing the Dardanelles with old battle-ships, and telegraphed to Vice-Admiral Carden, at the Darda-nelles: "Do you consider the forcing of the Dardanelles by ships alone a practicable operation?"[2] On January 5, Carden replied: "I do not consider Dardanelles can be rushed. They might be forced by extending operations with large numbers of ships."[3]

This was good enough for Mr. Churchill, and though Lord Fisher,[4] Admiral Sir Henry Jackson,[5] and Mr. Lloyd George[6] were vehemently opposed to this proposal because it did not entail the use of troops,[7] he saw in it the means to win over Kitchener. "So Lord Kitchener swung round to the Dardanelles plan," writes Mr. Lloyd George, "and that settled it."[8]

On January 13 Churchill brought his project before the War Council and pointed out that if progress were not made "the bombardment could be broken off and the fleet could steam away." This won over the Government.[9] Two days later he tele-graphed to Carden: "The sooner we can begin the better. . . . Continue to perfect your plan";[10] and on January 19 he sent a cable to the Grand Duke Nicholas and informed him that the Government had determined to force the Dardanelles. At length, on January 28, when the War Council met again, though Fisher opposed the project and urged the greater value of his Baltic

---

[1] *Ibid.*, vol. 1, p. 54. See also *The World Crisis, 1915*, pp. 95–96.
[2] *The World Crisis*, 1915, p. 97.   [3] *Ibid.*, p. 98.
[4] Lord Fisher stated that he was "instinctively against" the Carden plan because he knew it must be a failure (*Dardanelles Commission*, First Report, 1917, para. 68).
[5] He said: "It would be a very mad thing to try and get into the sea of Marmora without having the Gallipoli Peninsula held by our own troops or every gun on both sides of the Straits destroyed" (*The Dardanelles Campaign*, Nevinson, p. 31).
[6] See his *War Memoirs*, vol. 1, p. 226.
[7] "He [Churchill] kept on saying he could do without the army." Sir Arthur Wilson's evidence, *Dardanelles Commission*, First Report, para. 88.
[8] *War Memoirs*, vol. 1, p. 395.   [9] *Official History*, vol. 1, p. 59.
[10] *The World Crisis*, 1915, p. 111.

scheme, Kitchener considered the naval attack of vital importance; Mr. Balfour could not imagine a more helpful operation; and Sir Edward Grey thought it would settle the attitude of the whole of the Balkans. Not a soldier was to be used, the navy alone was to force the Dardanelles and seize Constantinople.[1]

Thus the proposal passed into the realm of action and apparently became public property, for Lord Bertie, then British Ambassador in Paris, writes: "The Dardanelles Expedition was known only to the inner ring: Louis Mallet heard of it at a dinner from Leo [Leopold] de Rothschild, who had learnt it from Alfred de R. [Rothschild] who may have picked up the information in the course of his daily visit to Kitchener at the War Office, and 10 Downing Street. There is no such thing as a secret nowadays."[2]

No sooner had the naval attack been agreed than the Salonika project was revived, and though it was rejected, the old question emerged whether the ships should not be supported by a military force. So, on February 16, the War Council met again to review this question and a decision was made to send out the 29th Division. Thus the foundations of the military attack were laid. Then, three days later, Kitchener said he could not spare the 29th Division, so in its stead were substituted the Australian and New Zealand Divisions in Egypt. But Churchill now considered that at least 50,000 men would be required, and for the first time insisted that it "would be impossible for the fleet to keep the Dardanelles open for merchant shipping."[3] On February 24, Mr. Lloyd George asked him whether, should the naval attack fail, the Army would carry out a land attack, and his answer was "No."[4]

When it is considered how hazardous was the operation and how completely it depended upon surprise for its success, the next step taken was suicidal. The fleet was ordered to bombard the Dardanelles forts, and did so on February 19 and 25. Sufficient damage was done to allow small parties of 50 and 100 sailors and marines to land on February 26 and leisurely blow to pieces all the guns in Sedd-el-Bahr, as well as in the two forts on the Asiatic side,[5] at a cost of one killed and six wounded.[6] Meanwhile, on February 23, the island of Lemnos was occupied by marines, and

---

[1] See *Official History*, vol. I, p. 61. See also *Dardanelles Commission*, Memorandum by Mr. Roch, para. 25.
[2] *The Diary of Lord Bertie of Thame, 1914–1918* (1924), vol. I, p. 134, under March 27, 1915.
[3] *Official History*, vol. I, p. 71.   [4] *War Memoirs*, vol. I, p. 418.
[5] *The World Crisis*, 1915, p. 193.   [6] *Naval Memoirs*, Keyes, vol. I, 198.

when the Greeks objected to this the British Government pleaded military necessity; incidentally, the same plea put forward by the Germans when they invaded Belgium. When the bombardment opened, only the Turkish 9th Division was on the Gallipoli Peninsula, and the 3rd Division on the Asiatic side. But thoroughly alarmed by the impending danger, by April 4 they were respectively reinforced by the 5th, 7th, and 19th, and the 11th divisions.

Thus it came about that no sooner had the Government made up their mind not to use troops than they decided to use them, and then, after they had arrived at this decision, they decided to carry out the naval attack without them. Instead of waiting until the army was ready to follow up the naval barrage, on the day after the bombardment Lord Kitchener warned General Maxwell, General Officer Commanding Egypt, to hold in readiness 30,000 Australian and New Zealand troops, under Lieutenant-General Sir W. R. Birdwood, "to embark about the 9th March, in transports sent from England to assist the navy . . . and to occupy any captured forts."[1] Then, suddenly, on February 24, the War Council realized that because of Mr. Churchill's impetuosity they had precipitated the operation into a bottomless bog, or as the official historian writes: "If a success at the Dardanelles could win the Balkans to the Entente, a failure would have the opposite effect. The opening of the bombardment had attracted such world-wide attention that, for the sake of British prestige, the enterprise must be carried through, no matter what the cost. . . . Mr. Churchill argued that the country was absolutely committed to seeing the Dardanelles attack through."[2]

On March 4 further landings were attempted, but they were faced by strong opposition and each effort to sweep the minefields was met by heavy fire directed by searchlights. On the 5th the *Queen Elizabeth* and other warships opened an indirect bombardment on the forts in the Narrows, and continued to do so until March 12; each shell brought home to Turkey the impending danger.

While the bombardment was in progress, the next blunder was made, but this time by Russia, for whose benefit the operation had so largely been undertaken. On March 1 Venizelos informed the British Government that he was ready to land three divisions on the Gallipoli peninsula, which, in the circumstances, was as miraculous an offer as Abraham's ram. It was communicated at

[1] *Official History*, vol. 1, p. 73.　　　　[2] *Ibid.*, vol. 1, p. 75.

once to the Tsar who, on March 3, replied: "The Russian Government could not consent to Greece participating in operations in the Dardanelles, as it would be sure to lead to complications. . . ."[1] These centred on who should gain Constantinople, which the British Government had promised to Russia as her share of the booty once the war was won. On the 7th the Venizelos Government fell, and, on March 12, the day the bombardment ceased, this piece of political backshish was made public.

On the day this suicidal refusal was made the War Council met again, and once more Kitchener refused to release the 29th Division. Then, on March 5, he received a telegram from General Birdwood which stated: "I am very doubtful if the Navy can force the passage unassisted."[2] Kitchener changed his mind, assumed full responsibility for the military attack, and took over the Royal Naval Division at Port Said. On March 16, the 29th Division sailed.

This decision – three weeks too late – was followed by another blunder. Once his mind had been made up to send out the 29th Division, Kitchener next looked for a general-in-chief. He selected General Sir Ian Hamilton, a soldier of considerable war experience, loyal, chivalrous, imaginative and journalistic, yet a man of little drive and one who may be described as an R. B. Cunningham Graham in uniform. When he discussed the situation with him, Kitchener said: "If the fleet gets through, Constantinople will fall of itself and you will have won not a battle, but the war."[3] Nevertheless he gave him no instructions, instead he gave him an out-of-date map and hurried him off on March 13.

On his arrival at Mudros (port of Lemnos) on March 17, General Hamilton found that Admiral J. M. de Robeck had that day replaced Admiral Carden, and that, when the 29th Division had left England, the embarkation authorities had loaded the ships in such a way that the troops could not disembark in fighting order. The transports would have to be discharged and reloaded, and as this could not be done at Mudros, it had to be done at Alexandria, which meant another three weeks of delay.

The day Lord Kitchener selected Sir Ian Hamilton to command the expedition, Mr. Churchill, instead of waiting for a combined operation to be elaborated, telegraphed Admiral Carden: "We suggest for your consideration that a point has now

[1] *The World Crisis*, 1915, p. 201.   [2] *Ibid.*, p. 188.
[3] *Gallipoli Diary*, General Sir Ian Hamilton (1920), vol. 1, p. 16.

been reached when it is necessary . . . to overwhelm the forts at the Narrows at decisive range by the fire of the largest number of guns. . . ."[1] Thus the blunder of February 19–25 was repeated. The attack was made on March 18 and three battleships were lost by running into an unswept minefield. De Robeck then informed the Admiralty that he intended to postpone his next effort until about the middle of April, when the army would be ready to act. The truth would appear to be, as Admiral Keyes comments: "He never really wished to risk his ships again in another naval attack, after the losses of the 18th March, and he welcomed the opportunity of combining with the Army in an operation which promised success without hazard to the Fleet."[2]

While the Turks dug for their lives, the 29th Division disembarked at Alexandria. It was then found that it had been equipped for mobile warfare in a well-roaded country, and was deficient of guns, gun and rifle ammunition, hospital requirements and trench stores. Of secrecy there was none: one of Sir Ian Hamilton's staff received "an official letter from London, sent through the ordinary post, and addressed to the 'Constantinople Field Force'."[3]

On March 22 a conference was held on the *Queen Elizabeth*. General Hamilton writes: "The moment we sat down de Robeck told us he was quite clear he could not get through without the help of all my troops . . . the fat (that is us) is fairly in the fire."[4] The idea of landing at Bulair was set aside because it was known to be entrenched. Instead, it was decided to land on the toe of the peninsula, which meant that the British forces would have to advance up a defile – a pass flanked not by mountains but by the sea.

The strength of the force to be employed in this most difficult operation was:[5]

	Ships	Men	Animals	Vehicles
29th Division (Alexandria)	15	17,649	3,962	692
Anzac Corps (Alexandria)[6]	30	25,784	6,920	1,271
Anzac Corps (Mudros)	5	4,854	698	147
French, 1st Colonial Division (Alexandria)	22	16,762	3,511	647
Royal Naval Division (Port Said)	12	10,007	1,390	347
	84	75,056	16,481	3,104

---

[1] *The World Crisis*, 1915, Churchill, p. 218.
[2] *Naval Memoirs*, Keyes, vol. I, p. 274.   [3] *Official History*, vol. I, p. 110.
[4] *Gallipoli Diary*, Hamilton, vol. I, p. 41.   [5] *Official History*, vol. I, p. 127.
[6] Anzac = A. and N.Z.A.C. – Australian and New Zealand Army Corps.

Meanwhile, between March 18 and April 25 – when the first British landing was made – the Turks were given ample time to entrench and prepare the more likely beaches against invasion. Yet only on March 26 was Field-Marshal Liman von Sanders appointed commander-in-chief of the Turkish forces in the peninsula; and that day he landed at Gallipoli and took over his command. When he found his troops strung out *en cordon*, he formed them into three groups – "The 5th and 7th Divisions were stationed on the upper Saros (Xeros) Gulf; the 9th and newly organized 19th Divisions were ordered to the southern part of the peninsula, and the 11th Division was stationed on the Asiatic side together with the 3rd which soon arrived by boat."[1] Although his men were miserably equipped[2] he appreciated their fighting value, which the British did not; they had forgotten Plevna and its lessons. General Kannengiesser writes:

"The Turkish soldier, the 'Askar,' was the Anatolian and Thracian, slightly educated, brave, trustworthy. . . . Content with little, it never entered into his mind to dispute the authority of those above him. He followed his leader without question. . . . The Turks are glad to feel an energetic leader's will, they feel supported in the consciousness that they are being led by a strong hand against a definite objective."[3]

Although the ultimate aim of the campaign was the occupation of Constantinople, the immediate task was to force the Narrows between Kilid Bahr on the European side of the Dardanelles and Chanak on the Asiatic bank. Here the strait shrinks to 1,600 yards in width, and it was a little north of this waist, at Nagara (Abydus), where the current is not so strong, that, in 480 B.C., Xerxes built his bridge, Alexander crossed in 334 B.C., Barbarossa in 1190, and Orkhan in 1356. It was here that Hero swam the Hellespont and, centuries later, Lord Byron.

On the western flank of this narrow strip of water lies the Gallipoli Peninsula. At Bulair in the north it is no more than 4,600 yards in breadth; then it widens out to about 12 miles between Suvla Point to a little north of Ak Bashi; narrows again to four and a half miles between Gaba Tepe and Maidos; widens

---

[1] *Five Years in Turkey*, Liman von Sanders (English edit., 1927), pp. 60–61.

[2] When sandbags were sent them "there was danger of their being used by the troop leaders for patching the ragged uniforms of their men" (Liman von Sanders, p. 74).

[3] *The Campaign in Gallipoli*, Hans Kannengiesser Pasha (English edit., 1927), pp. 146–147.

once more and finally tapers off to Cape Helles. Most of this tongue of land is hilly and broken, cut by sharp valleys, cliffs and ravines which end in the eminence of Achi Baba, 700 ft. above sea level.

When war was declared, the sole fortifications were at Bulair, at the entrance to the Dardanelles and at the Narrows. The last two were defended by over 100 guns, of which 14 were modern, and all were short of ammunition. The forts Kilid Bahr and Chanak, built by Mahomet II in 1462, were so well built that during the bombardment of March 18 the 15-in. shells of the *Queen Elizabeth* did them little damage. There was only one road, which ran from Gallipoli to Maidos; therefore the main communications with Constantinople were by sea, a journey of about 12 hours. Such, in brief, was the theatre of war.

Sir Ian Hamilton's plan was, under cover of feints at Bulair and Kum Kale, (*1*) to effect landings on Cape Helles at five points, from east to west beach S in Morto Bay, V and W beaches on each flank of Cape Helles, and X and Y beaches on its western shore; (*2*) simultaneously to land another force just north of Gaba Tepe, the object of which was to advance on Maidos and to take in rear such Turkish forces as might oppose the Helles landings.

The plan was an able one, but more than is usual, its success depended upon execution, which demanded the highest leadership and audacity. Had these been forthcoming the operation might have proved successful; for later it was learnt that the Turkish coastal garrisons were insignificant. On April 25, the day the landings were made, south of Achi Baba there were only two infantry battalions and one company of engineers; at Y beach, not a man; at W and V beaches, two companies; at S beach, one platoon; and at X beach, 12 men. Further, only W and V beaches were protected by wire and machine-guns.[1]

Unfortunately, though courage was conspicuous, leadership was not. At W and V beaches disastrous delays occurred, and at X the landing party was too weak. At V beach disembarkation from the s.s. *River Clyde*, which was beached, was so fiercely opposed that the landing was held up until April 26. At Y beach, where 2,000 men stepped ashore without a shot fired and where for 11 hours they remained undisturbed, there was a complete muddle. Although unopposed the men did not advance on Krithia but were re-embarked and withdrawn.

[1] *Official History*, vol. 1, p. 221.

Meanwhile the Australians and New Zealanders landed north of Gaba Tepe, one mile north of the selected beach, at a spot later named Anzac Cove. Their landing was a complete surprise, and a penetration of three and a half miles was made to a spot from where the gleaming Narrows could be seen, the nearest point to

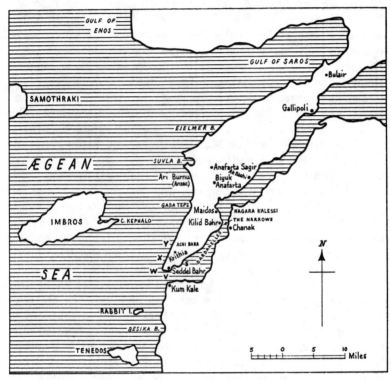

15. GALLIPOLI AND THE DARDANELLES, 1915

them reached during the campaign. There they were attacked by Mustafa Kemal and driven back in such disorder that General Birdwood suggested a complete withdrawal; a request very rightly refused by Sir Ian Hamilton, who replied: "You have got through the difficult business. Now you have only to dig, dig, dig, until you are safe."[1] Ominous words, for digging meant that surprise was at an end and, therefore, that the whole operation had failed. Thus the foundations of one of the greatest tragedies in British

[1] *Ibid.*, vol. I, p. 270.

history were scraped into the stony soil of the Gallipoli peninsula, near where Alexander had set out to conquer the Oriental world.

The landing had succeeded, though its object had not been attained, and the second phase of the invasion was entered; a series of wasteful frontal attacks, as hopeless and costly as any seen on the western front. At Anzac, where the total area held was barely 400 acres, no offensive was attempted until August 6; but at Helles three costly battles, based largely on the unwarranted optimism of General Hunter-Weston, commander of the 29th Division and G.O.C. troops in the Helles area,[1] were fought – namely, the First, Second, and Third Battles of Krithia.

The first, waged between April 27–30, was badly conceived and ended in chaos and a loss of some 3,000 officers and men. This failure was followed by a determined Turkish attack on May 1. It was beaten back, and on May 6–7 the Second Battle of Krithia followed. On the 8th it ended like the first, the casualties numbered 6,500 – about 30 per cent of the numbers engaged. Next, on May 19, the Turks attacked again, this time against Anzac, and lost some 10,000 men and the Australians and New Zealanders only 600. Then followed the third Battle of Krithia. Covered by the fire of 78 guns, supplemented, as in all these attacks, by the guns of the fleet; the VIIIth Corps advanced and again was slaughtered; it lost 4,500 officers and men of 16,000 engaged, and the French lost 2,000. In the 2nd Naval Brigade 60 officers of 70 became casualties and more than 1,000 men out of 1,900. The objective of all these attacks was Achi Baba, because it was supposed to dominate the Narrows, which it did not, as was discovered after the war by Captain Keyes, Commodore to Admiral de Robeck.[2] Exhausted, military operations came to a standstill.

Meanwhile, the day after the first landing, Italy renounced the Triple Alliance and, in accordance with the Treaty of London, threw in her lot with the Allied Powers. On May 23 she was at war with Austria.

On June 2, Sir Ian Hamilton telegraphed Lord Kitchener, and said that "the movement of a quarter of a million men against us seems to be well under way."[3] This exaggerated figure sent a shudder through the government, and on June 7 the newly con-stituted Dardanelles Commission was assembled to consider three

---

[1] On May 24 they were constituted the VIIIth Corps.
[2] *Naval Memoirs, 1910–1915*, vol. I, p. 325.
[3] *Official History*, vol. II, p. 42.

alternatives: to leave things as they were; to abandon the enterprise and evacuate the peninsula; or to send out large reinforcements. Under pressure from Lord Kitchener and Mr. Churchill the third course was adopted, and eventually it was decided to dispatch five new divisions, and Mr. Churchill suggested that they should be used to occupy the Bulair isthmus.[1] This proposal was rejected because Admiral de Robeck considered the threat of German submarines in the Gulf of Saros too great a risk.

General Birdwood was also against a landing so far north; instead he favoured a big attack from Anzac, where conditions were such as to persuade anyone to fight. The Official Historian – an eye witness – writes:

"The heat of the noon-day sun was intense; and there was little or no shade; and the scanty water supply in the trenches was rarely sufficient for men with a parching thirst. The sickening smell of unburied corpses in No Man's Land pervaded the front areas; dense clouds of infected dust were incessant; and despite the preventive care of the doctors there was such a loathsome plague of huge flies (known to the troops as 'corpse flies') that it was difficult to eat a mouthful of food without swallowing the pests. A tin of beef or jam, as soon as opened, would be covered with a thick film of flies, and amongst the troops in the trenches small pieces of veiling, to throw over their faces at meal times or when trying to sleep, were almost beyond price."[2]

When it was agreed to organize three of the five divisions into a new corps – the IXth – Sir Ian Hamilton requested that either General Byng or General Rawlinson – both able officers then serving in France – should be given its command. There was an objection to this because both were junior to General Mahon, the commander of the 10th Division of the IXth Corps, and instead Lieutenant-General Sir Frederick Stopford was selected. No worse choice could have been made. He was 61 years old, kindly, affable and incompetent, and during the war in South Africa had been Military Secretary to Sir Redvers Buller. He had never commanded troops, and was a sick man.

While these arrangements were in hand, General Hamilton did not conserve the energies of his army, but launched three wasteful attacks, on June 21, June 28, and July 12–13, in the Helles area.

[1] *The World Crisis, 1915*, pp. 396–397.
[2] *Official History*, vol. II, pp. 72–73. See also *The Dardanelles Campaign*, Nevinson, p. 207.

He lost 7,700 British and 4,600 French officers and men – that is, approximately the effective strength of an entire division.

Once the above reinforcements had been promised, Hamilton began to consider his next plan. First, it was obvious to him that Anzac Cove was too restricted in breadth and depth to allow five new divisions to be deployed there. In order to gain more room he determined to extend his base of operations by landing a force at Suvla Bay, which lay five miles to the north of the Australians and New Zealanders, and then launch two closely affiliated attacks with the object of occupying the high ground from Kiretch Tepe to Koja Chemen Tepe and thence to Gaba Tepe.

On paper this plan was an able one, for not only was it known that the Suvla Bay area was lightly defended, but that, should the Turks be surprised, only four miles of open plain would have to be crossed in order to seize the surrounding hills; to the north-east, the Tekke Tepe, 900 ft. above sea level; to the east, the Anafarta Spur (350 ft.) or ridge, and to the north the Kiretch Tepe (650 ft.). Could these heights be occupied within 24 hours, the right flank of the Turkish forces opposing the Anzac Corps would be turned, which almost certainly would enable General Birdwood to occupy Koja Chemen Tepe (Hill 971) – the key to the Narrows.

For this dual attack Sir Ian Hamilton had at his disposal two corps, the Anzac and the IXth. The former consisted of the 1st and 2nd Australian divisions and the New Zealand and Australian Division, and the second of the 10th, 11th, 13th, 53rd, and 54th divisions, the last two attached. Further, in the Helles area he had the VIIIth Corps, which consisted of the 29th, 42nd, 52nd, and Royal Naval divisions, as well as the *Corps Expéditionnaire d'Orient*, now two divisions – in all 13 divisions. He selected Mudros, Imbros, and Mitylene as his advanced bases, and established his G.H.Q. on the second of these islands.

He fixed on August 6, because it was a moonless night, as the day of attack, and decided on the following operations:

While the VIIIth Corps by attack held the Turkish forces which opposed it, Birdwood was first to feint at Lone Pine, in order to draw his enemy away from the Sari Bair heights, and then to assault those heights and carry Hill 971, Hill Q, and Chunuk Bair; all three were to be occupied by dawn on August 7. For these attacks the 13th Division was added to the Anzac Corps.

Next, to land the 11th and 10th Divisions during the night of the 6th–7th south of Nibrunesi Point. The former was to occupy

Lala Baba, Suvla Point, and Kiretch Tepe, as well as Chocolate and W Hills and Tekke Tepe, all to be gained by daylight on the 7th; while two brigades of the 10th Division were to advance at dawn on the 7th and make straight for the Anafarta gap so as to threaten the right rear of the Turks on and about Hill 971.

This plan was radically faulty. The Anzac Corps was physically worn out and the area over which its men would have to fight their way was indescribably difficult. Secondly, the 10th and 11th Divisions were half trained, and the country was covered with scrub; only highly trained light infantry led by skilful officers could have carried out a successful night advance over it. Sir Ian Hamilton did not possess such men and officers; his plan, however well it looked on paper, was a gamble.

Not until July 22 was General Stopford informed of the plan, when it was impressed upon him that Chocolate and W Hills "should be captured by a *coup de main* before daylight,"[1] and that bold and vigorous leadership were imperative. At first he accepted the plan, next he began to doubt it, possibly because General Mahon quite rightly considered it too intricate. He pointed out his deficiency in artillery, and when he found that all his troops were to be landed at A, B, and C beaches, which were situated south of Nibrunesi Point, against naval advice he[2] persuaded General Hamilton to shift A beach to within the Bay and immediately north of the Cut. This was, as will be seen, a mistake.

The next mistake must be attributed to Sir Ian Hamilton – it was over secrecy. No unit was given any idea of what was required of it: maps were not handed out until the evening of August 6, and no one, except the generals and admirals, was informed of the destinations.[3] Physically and mentally the operation was a plunge into the dark.

The landing arrangements were carefully worked out, including the carriage of 400 tons of water; but they seem so to have monopolized the attention of Stopford and his staff, that the landing itself, and not the advance from the beaches, dominated their minds, with the result that the importance of capturing Chocolate and W Hills was forgotten. This is also true of Sir Ian Hamilton, for in his final instructions, issued to the IXth Corps on July 29, we read:

"Your *primary objective* will be to secure Suvla Bay. . . . Should,

---

[1] *Official History*, vol. II, p. 148.   [2] See *Naval Memoirs*, Keyes, vol. I, p. 378.
[3] *The Dardanelles Campaign*, Nevinson, p. 298.

however, you find it possible to achieve this object with only a portion of your force, your next step will be to give such direct assistance as is in your power to the General Officer commanding Anzac in his attack on Hill 305 [Hill 971] by an advance on Biyuk Anafarta. . . . He, however, directs your special attention to the fact that the Hills Yilghin [Chocolate] and Ismail Oglu Tepe [Green] are known to contain guns which can bring fire to bear on the flank and rear of an attack on Hill 305. . . . If, therefore, it is possible *without prejudice to the attainment of your primary objective*, to gain possession of these hills at an early period of your attack, it will greatly facilitate the capture and retention of Hill 305.''[1]

This insistence that the landing was the objective was the greatest error of all, and the root cause of the eventual disaster; for in itself it was a means and not an end.

The last error was that Stopford had no conception of what generalship meant. He did not land with his troops and establish his G.H.Q. on shore, but decided to maintain them on board the *Jonquil*, where, incidentally, he remained throughout the 7th.

If Sir Ian Hamilton's task was a difficult one, and it certainly was, that of Liman von Sanders was far more difficult. Although always afraid of a landing at Bulair, he nevertheless suspected that the British object was to occupy Koja Chemen Tepe, and that therefore a landing at Suvla Bay was possible. Equally possible was a landing south of Gaba Tepe, where he sent the 9th Division under Colonel Kannengiesser. In August his distribution was: three divisions at Kum Kale, three at Bulair, three on the Anzac front, under Essad Pasha, two south of Gaba Tepe, and five in the Helles area. To Suvla he sent a small body of troops, known as the Anafarta Detachment. It was commanded by a Bavarian officer, Major Willmer, and it consisted of three battalions, one pioneer company, one squadron of cavalry, 19 guns and a labour battalion. Willmer, an exceptionally able officer, at once realized that his detachment was too weak to repulse a landing, and that all he could hope to do was to delay an invader for 36 to 48 hours from gaining the Anafarta spur, after which he might expect to be reinforced. He threw out a forward screen of posts, and held the following localities:

Kiretch Tepe – two companies Gallipoli Gendarmerie.

Hill 10 – three companies Broussa Gendarmerie.

Chocolate and Green Hills – three companies 1/31st Regiment.

---

[1] *Official History*, vol. II, Appendix 3. Italics added.

Lala Baba – one company 1/31st Regiment with a sentry post on Nibrunesi Point.

His reserve he placed at Baka Baba–W Hills, astride a track leading from the Bay to Anafarta Sagir.

In all he had some 1,500 men with whom to face his enemy's 25,000.

At 2.30 p.m. on August 6, the combined battle, which was to decide the campaign and much more besides, opened on the Helles front. But the VIIIth Corps Commander did not carry out a holding attack as ordered, but foolishly attempted to capture Krithia and Achi Baba. He failed to do so at a cost of nearly 2,000 men out of 4,000.

Two hours later the Anzac battle opened by an attack on the Turkish position of Lone Pine. Though successful, it led tó an unfortunate event. It frightened Essad Pasha, who called to his support two regiments of Kannengiesser's 9th Division, which on arrival were well placed to reinforce Chunuk Bair when it was attacked the next morning.

Directly Turkish attention was concentrated on Lone Pine, two columns of troops under General Johnston and General Cox set out at 7.30 p.m. to seize the Sari Bair ridge between Hill 971 and Battleship Hill. The operation was complicated, if not impossible. Ashmead Bartlett writes:

"It was launched against positions the like of which had never been attacked before under modern conditions of warfare. The men were expected to climb mountains during the night over un-explored ground, so tortuous, broken and scrubby that, had the advance taken place during peace manœuvres, it would have been an extremely arduous task for troops to reach the summit of the Sari Bair Ridge in the prescribed time."[1]

The right column (Johnston's), obscured by the shadows cast by the ships' searchlights, moved on Table Top to gain Chunuk Bair by dawn. Part of the column lost its way, and the remainder was thrown into confusion. Meanwhile the left column (Cox's) moved up the coast, swung right and set out to gain Hill 971 and Hill Q. It took the wrong track, was sniped at and delayed, and the men became exhausted. Thus the entire initial operations ended in fiasco; 650 officers and men out of the 1,250 engaged became casualties.

While these operations were under way, at 5.30 a.m. on August

---

[1] *The Uncensored Dardanelles* (1928), p. 222.

7, Mustafa Kemal, when he learnt that British troops were establishing themselves on Rhododendron Spur – immediately west of Chunuk Bair – called up his reserve division, the 19th, and ordered

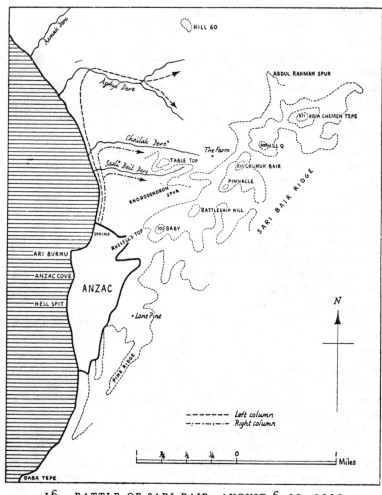

16. BATTLE OF SARI BAIR, AUGUST 6–10, 1915

it to occupy the main ridge. Simultaneously, Kannengiesser's two regiments were sent by Essad Pasha to hold the same ridge from Chunuk Bair to Hill 971. Kannengiesser hurried forward with a patrol and reached Chunuk Bair at about 7 a.m. Meanwhile Liman von Sanders, who realized that the critical hour had struck, yet still fearful that the main blow would be directed against Bulair, telegraphed Feizi Bey, in command there, to be vigilant, and next, he decided that Sari Bair must be reinforced and at 1.30 a.m. he ordered him with all possible speed to send three battalions south.

Meanwhile Johnston's right column shook itself into some order, and at 10.30 a.m. on the 7th sent forward five companies to attack Chunuk Bair under cover of a land and sea bombardment; but almost immediately fire was opened on them by Kannengiesser's men and the attack collapsed. This, and the fact that Cox's left column was too exhausted to accomplish anything, induced General Godley, in command of the operation, to call off the attack until August 8, when Johnston was to occupy Chunuk Bair and Cox Hill Q and Hill 971.

In all Cox's force consisted of 13 battalions, which he divided into four columns. Their objectives were:

1st Column, Northern slopes of Chunuk Bair.
2nd Column, Southern peak of Hill Q.
3rd Column, Northern peak of Hill Q.
4th Column, Abdul Rahman spur and Hill 971.

While the fourth column advanced at 3 a.m. and was almost instantly checked, and the third and first columns were too scattered to advance at all, the second column moved forward to link up with the 1/6th Gurkhas, who had occupied a position far out to the front; but its men were too exhausted to reach them. Major C. J. L. Allanson, O.C. 1/6th Gurkhas, waited in vain for them, and at length decided to attack Hill Q on his own. After a fierce fight he gained a lodgement 100 ft. below its crest and there he dug in; then, at 2 p.m., General Godley, who knew nothing of this fine advance, suspended operations until the following day.

Meanwhile Johnston ordered an advance at 3.30 a.m. which, though it started late, to his surprise was not opposed, and the top of the ridge was gained. Lieutenant-Colonel W. G. Malone with two companies of the Wellington Battalion then started to dig in. "The men," we are told, "were in high spirits. Away on their right the growing daylight was showing up the paths and tracks in rear of the enemy's lines at Anzac, now at last outflanked. Straight to their front were the shining waters of the Narrows—the goal of the expedition. Victory seemed very near."[1]

Why the Turks had abandoned Chunuk Bair is not known; but

[1] *Official History*, vol. II, p. 213.

as they still held firm on Battleship Hill and Hill Q, when dawn broke a devastating fire was opened on the flanks of Malone's small force. The two Wellington companies fought grimly and maintained their exposed position on the top of the ridge until nearly every man was killed, among them their gallant leader. Thus Chunuk Bair was lost because Hill Q had not been taken.

Nevertheless General Godley determined to renew the attack on the 9th. He abandoned all idea of occupying Hill 971 and limited his objective to the main ridge from Chunuk Bair to Hill Q. Johnston was to assault the former and Cox the latter, while in between these vital points General A. H. Baldwin, in command of the 38th Brigade of the 13th Division, was to attack. All three forces were to work in close cooperation.

As night fell Baldwin advanced along an unreconnoitred track. Long halts and delays followed; confusion set in, and as the track ended in a precipice the advance was counter-marched. While this muddle went on, Johnston's forward troops became heavily engaged, and because Baldwin did not appear his attack and Cox's were abandoned. Meanwhile Allanson's reinforcements had gone astray, so again he attacked on his own, and directly the bombardment lifted he gained the top of the crest, when a second bombardment started and this time fell upon his small force and drove it back to its original position. His description of this unfortunate event is as follows:

"The roar of the artillery preparation was enormous; the hill, which was almost perpendicular, seemed to leap underneath one. I recognized if we flew up the hill the moment it stopped, we ought to get to the top. I put the three companies into the trenches along my men, and said that the moment they saw me go forward carrying a red flag, everyone was to start. I had my watch out, 5.15. I never saw such artillery preparation; the trenches were being torn to pieces, the accuracy was marvellous, as we were only just below. At 5.18 it had not stopped, and I wondered if my watch was wrong. 5.20 silence; I waited three minutes to be certain, great as the risk was. Then off we dashed all hand in hand, a most perfect advance and a wonderful sight. . . . At the top we met the Turks; Le Marchand was down, a bayonet through the heart. I got one through my leg, and then for about what appeared 10 minutes, we fought hand to hand, we bit and fisted, and used rifles and pistols as clubs, and then the Turks turned and fled, and I felt a very proud man; the key of the whole peninsula was ours, and our losses had not been so very great for such a result. Below I saw the Straits, motors and wheeled transport, on the roads leading to Achi Baba. As I looked round I saw we were not being supported, and thought I could help best by going after those (Turks) who had retreated in front of us. We dashed down towards Maidos, but had only got about 100 feet down when suddenly our own Navy put six 12 in. monitor shells into us, and all was terrible confusion. It was a deplorable disaater; we were obviously mistaken for Turks, and we had to get back. It was an appalling sight; the first hit a Gurkha in the face; the place was a mass of blood and limbs and screams, and we all flew back to the summit and to our old positions just below."[1]

Thus ended the battle for the Sari Bair ridge, a battle of valour run waste, and of muddle exceeded only by the landing at Suvla Bay. This operation, as Liman von Sanders says, was "the political-military summit of the campaign,"[2] yet, unlike Sari Bair, it was a feasible operation, for it was faced by no insuperable obstacles. Nevertheless, this operation also was ruined by indifferent leadership and the rawness of the troops engaged.

At 9.30 p.m. on August 6 the 32nd and 33rd brigades of the 11th Division (General F. Hammersley) in pitch darkness approached B beach to find it undefended. By 10 p.m. four battalions had landed without a man killed; but they were dog-tired, for the men had been on their feet for 17 hours. Lala Baba was occupied and the way opened to the capture of Hill 10, but as no one knew its exact position, nothing was done. Meanwhile the 34th Brigade, under General W. H. Sitwell, entered Suvla Bay, but as the lighters headed for A beach, when 50 ft. from shore they struck a reef, which so delayed the landing that dawn broke before the bulk of the men could disembark. To make matters worse, the 10th Division (General Sir B. T. Mahon), which should have landed at A beach in order to occupy Kiretch Tepe, was in part disembarked on C beach and on a new beach discovered north of A beach. Thus its organization was broken up and confusion set in.

Orders and counter-orders followed each other in rapid succession, while the Turkish sharpshooters, like the American riflemen of 1777, picked off the invaders by scores. Thus the situation remained from hour to hour. Not until daylight faded did an

---

[1] Quoted from *The World Crisis, 1915*, Churchill, p. 442. This account was written 48 hours after the event. The Navy deny that the second bombardment was theirs; it is said to have killed 150 men.
[2] *Five Years in Turkey*, p. 90.

attack on Chocolate Hill begin to develop, and as darkness set in
the hill was carried, as also was the western half of Green Hill.
Meanwhile, on the left little was done except that a foothold was
gained on Kiretch Tepe. All the encircling hills remained in
Turkish hands, yet more than half the IXth Corps – 22 battalions
in all – had not been engaged; nevertheless, those which had been

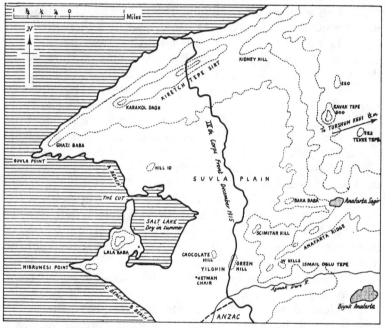

17.   BATTLE OF SUVLA BAY, AUGUST 6–10, 1915

engaged had lost 100 officers and 1,600 men, "or rather more than
the total strength of the Turks arrayed against them."[1]

Not only had the whole military plan collapsed, but also the
naval plan, for the unloading of guns, ammunition, water, supplies, carts, and transport animals was delayed by the general
confusion. Water, though it existed in abundance, was not found;
and those men who had emptied their water-bottles went nearly
mad with thirst. Mobs of soldiers collected on the beaches and
were "sucking water through holes they had made in the hoses
with their bayonets."[2]

[1] *Official History*, vol. I, p. 261.   [2] *Naval Memoirs*, Keyes, vol. I, p. 396.

Kannengiesser writes of the landing, as seen by the Turks: "Suvla Bay lay full of ships. We counted ten transports, six warships, and seven hospital ships. On land we saw a confused mass of troops like a disturbed ant-heap. . . . Nowhere was there fighting in progress."[1]

Throughout August 7, writes the Official Historian, "General Headquarters exercised no influence over the course of the Suvla operations, and their inactivity on this day, which in the light of after events, may be regarded as one of the crises of the World War, can only be explained as the result of over-confidence." When he heard that even Hill 10 had not been captured, why did not Sir Ian Hamilton at once proceed to Suvla? "Had he done so," adds the historian, "and insisted upon an immediate advance, the duration of the World War might have been very considerably shortened."[2]

As the commander-in-chief sat on his island and fretted for news, General Stopford sat in his ship vastly pleased that his men had got on shore, and a visit to him nearly drove Commodore Keyes "to open mutiny."[3] Both generals waited for victory or defeat as if the whole operation were a horse race. Such general-ship defies definition; yet it was part and parcel of the Moltke staff theory that generals-in-chief cease to command the moment they are most needed, that is, when battle begins.

While Sir Ian Hamilton and Sir Frederick Stopford still waited for their telephone bells to ring, on the Turkish side there was intense activity. At 6 a.m. Willmer telegraphed Liman von Sanders that the enemy, covered by numerous warships, had landed at Nibrunesi Point. The Turkish commander-in-chief made up his mind when he heard this that Bulair was safe and that his enemy's objectives were Hill 971 and Chunuk Bair, and instructed Feizi Bey to lead south two of his three divisions – namely, the 7th and 12th. At the same time he ordered every available man on the Asiatic side of the Dardanelles to march on Chanak and cross into Europe. He also ordered the 8th Division from Krithia to move north. His anxiety was great, because none of these reinforcements could reach him under 36 to 48 hours. In the meantime could Willmer's minute force hold back the inva-sion? – that was the problem. Definitely the answer appeared to be "no!" Then came a morsel of relief; at 7 p.m. Major Willmer

---

[1] *The Campaign in Gallipoli*, p. 205.   [2] *Official History*, vol. ii, pp. 263–264.
[3] *Naval Memoirs*, vol. i. p. 397.

reported: "The landing of hostile forces has continued all day. Estimate their present strength as at least 1½ divisions. No energetic attacks on the enemy's part have taken place. On the contrary, the enemy is advancing timidly."[1] This meant a probable gain of 24 hours.

At 1 a.m. on August 8, Willmer's command was disposed as follows: Three companies of Gallipoli Gendarmerie on the Kiretch Tepe ridge; 1,100 men and five mountain guns between Baka Baba and W Hill, and two batteries on the eastern side of the Tekke Tepe ridge. His nearest reinforcements were the three battalions from Bulair, then exhausted and bivouacked two miles east of Turshun Keui.

August 8 – the most critical day of the whole campaign – was a Sunday, and so far as the IXth Corps was concerned it was to be a day of rest, and so completely out of touch was the commander-in-chief that, at 10.50 a.m., he sent Stopford the following message: "You and your troops have indeed done splendidly. Please tell Hammersley how much we hope from his able and rapid advance."[2]

"Splendid" and "rapid"! Why, outside the muddled landing itself practically nothing had been done, and, worse still, Stopford was incapable of doing anything; for as the Official Historian writes: As on the 7th, "the basic cause of inaction on the 8th was the absence of resolute leadership, not only on shore but at corps headquarters and even at G.H.Q." He continues:

"Following a quiet night, the morning of the 8th was absolutely still. Out of a cloudless sky, the sun was shining fiercely. The enemy's guns were silent. Apart from an occasional rifle-shot on Kiretch Tepe there was not a sound of war. The sand-dunes near the Cut were crowded with resting troops. The shores of the bay were fringed with naked figures bathing. General Stopford and his chief staff officer were still on board the *Jonquil*, and had not yet been ashore."[3]

As no news was received at G.H.Q., it was decided to send Colonel Aspinall (later the Official Historian) ashore to ascertain what was taking place. At 9.30 a.m. he set out and found the whole bay at peace. When he boarded the *Jonquil* he met General Stopford who was "in excellent spirits" . . . "Well Aspinall," he

[1] *Official History*, vol. ii, p. 266.
[2] *Dardanelles Commission*, Final Report, p. 41, and *Gallipoli Diary*, Hamilton, vol. ii, p. 59.
[3] *Official History*, vol. ii, p. 268.

said, "the men have done splendidly, and have been magnificent."
"But they haven't reached the hills," replied Aspinall. "No,"
answered Stopford, "but they are ashore."[1] Then he added that
he intended to order a fresh advance *next day*. Whereupon Aspinall
sent the following wireless message to G.H.Q.: "Just been ashore,
where I found all quiet. No rifle fire, no artillery fire, and apparently no Turks. IX Corps resting. Feel confident that golden
opportunities are being lost and look upon the situation as
serious."[1]

While Aspinall was ashore, news was received at G.H.Q. that
Turkish troops were advancing east of Tekke Tepe, and Stopford
was urged to push on. He transmitted this order to his divisional
commanders, but added to it that "in view of want of adequate
artillery support I do not want you to attack an entrenched
position held in strength."[2] In consequence nothing was done.

At length Sir Ian Hamilton decided to go ashore, but he was
unable to do so until 4.30 p.m., because his destroyer was having
her fires drawn. First he proceeded to the *Jonquil*, to find Stopford
"happy," for in that general's opinion "everything was quite all
right and going well." Further, Stopford informed him that "he
had decided to postpone the occupation of the ridge [Kiretch
Tepe] (which might lead to a regular battle) until next morning."
Then Sir Ian Hamilton writes: " 'A regular battle is just exactly
what we are here for' was what I was inclined to say; but did not."
Next, he decided to visit Hammersley's headquarters, but Stopford asked to be excused from accompanying him . . . "he had
not been very fit: he had just returned from a visit to the shore
[400 yards away] and he wanted to give his leg a chance."

At Hammersley's headquarters General Hamilton found a
chaotic peace. "Here," he writes, "was a victorious Division rested
and watered, said to be unable to bestir itself, even feebly, with
less than twelve hours notice! This was what I felt and although I
did not say it probably I looked it."[3] He ordered an immediate
attack on the Tekke Tepe ridge, which resulted in a search for
units, and when they were found they were marched and counter-
marched; during which manœuvre the first Turkish reinforcements from Bulair – exhausted – occupied the crest of the ridge.

[1] *Ibid.*; vol. II, p. 277. Lieut.-Colonel Maurice Hankey, who accompanied Colonel
Aspinall, when he saw "dug-outs" being built, said to a staff officer: "You seem to
be making yourselves snug." He received the reply: "We expect to be here a long
time!"
[2] *Gallipoli Diary*, Hamilton, vol. II, pp. 61–64.   [3] *Ibid.*, vol. II, p. 67.

Thus surprise vanished, equal forces were to face each other in the field.

"During the whole of the 8th August," writes Kannengiesser, "the goddess of victory held the door to success wide open for Stopford, but he would not enter . . . nobody advanced. In short a peaceful picture, almost like a boy scouts' field day.

"At the same time under the same sun on the other side the panting troops of the 7th and 12th Divisions were straining forward over the hills from Bulair: from the Asiatic side along the shadeless Sultan's Way: over Erenkoi the Turkish battalions and batteries were pressing towards the embarkation stations in Tchanak Kale [Chanak]. Will they arrive in time? This thought feverishly occupied the mind . . . of the Marshal who waited there by Anafarta."[1]

While the British commander-in-chief looked ferocious and thought what he was inclined to say and yet remained dumb, Marshal Liman von Sanders was all fire and activity. Before daybreak he mounted his horse; searched for his reinforcements and found the staff officer of the 7th Division, who informed him that both that division and the 12th were still far behind. Anxiously he looked over the battlefield at the invading horde. Between the enemy and where he stood were 400 men on W Hills, 300 on Kiretch Tepe, and not a man in between. That evening he heard from Willmer that Feizi Bey had not arrived. He summoned the latter to him and when Feizi Bey told him that his troops were too exhausted to attack before the morning of August 9, what did von Sanders do? He dismissed him on the spot and placed Mustafa Kemal Bey in command of all troops in the Anafarta section, because, as he says: "he was a leader that delighted in responsibility."[2]

August 7 and 8 were days of crisis, August 9 and 10 were days of decision. After a series of orders and counter-orders, Hammersley was instructed to carry the Anafarta spur at 5 a.m. on the 9th, and Mahon to occupy Tekke Tepe. The attack of the 11th Division opened in confusion and ended in chaos. As the leading battalion of the 32nd Brigade moved forward Turkish reinforcements poured up the other side of the ridge; then a clash took place and the battalion was thrown back in confusion. "Despite the 48 hours delay, the race for Tekke Tepe" was "lost by rather less than half an hour."[3]

---

[1] *The Campaign in Gallipoli*, p. 220.   [2] *Five Years in Turkey*, p. 85.
[3] *Official History*, vol. II, p. 288.

The attack of the 33rd Brigade was only a little less chaotic. It was met as it advanced by crowds of demoralized stragglers; on the Asmak Dere it was stopped, held its own and dug in. Meanwhile at Kiretch Tepe, after a short advance, the attackers of the 10th Division also dug in, and so did General Stopford, who had now established his headquarters ashore. "Walking up the lower slope of Kiretch Tepe Sirt," writes Sir Ian Hamilton, "we found Stopford, about four or five hundred yards east of Ghazi Baba, busy with part of a field Company of Engineers supervising the building of some splinter-proof headquarters huts for himself and Staff. He was absorbed in the work, and he said that it would be well to make a thorough job of the dug-outs as we should probably be here for a very long time."[1]

The following day the 53rd Division – now landed – was thrown into the battle to retake Scimitar Hill, lost on the 9th, and to assault the Anafarta Spur. Two attacks were made, and both failed.

Ashmead Bartlett comments on these two days' fighting: "No one seemed to know where the headquarters of the different brigades and divisions would be found. The troops were hunting for water, the staffs were hunting for their troops, and the Turkish snipers were hunting for their prey. . . . Where I had seen one Turk yesterday there seemed to be ten today. . . . Leaving comparatively few in the trenches, large numbers descended into the unburnt scrub, and there, almost immune from artillery fire, awaited our attack. . . . Their snipers crept from bush to bush, from tree to tree, from knoll to knoll, picking off our men wherever they saw a favourable target, and were themselves left almost unmolested."[2]

On this day Mustafa Kemal Bey also attacked. On August 9 he had checked the IXth Corps, and on the 10th had moved against Chunuk Bair. Now he reconnoitred the latter and decided to recapture Rhododendron Spur. At 4.45 a.m. dense waves of Turks poured across the skyline; they swept over their enemy's advanced trenches and captured the Pinnacle and the Farm. The attack then lost its momentum. Thus, on August 10, ended the Battles of Sari Bair and Suvla Bay. What were their cost to the invader? Of 50,000 British troops, 18,000 were killed, wounded and missing. On the 12th Ashmead Bartlett jotted down: "We have landed again and dug another graveyard."[3]

[1] *Gallipoli Diary*, vol. II, p. 72.   [2] *The Uncensored Dardanelles*, pp. 190–192.
[3] *Ibid.*, p. 197.

The remainder of the campaign must be told briefly. Stopford was dismissed and replaced by General Sir Julian Byng, who originally had been asked for. "This is a young man's war," now wrote Lord Kitchener, just six months too late; yet Sir Ian Hamilton, as responsible as Stopford was for the disaster, remained to carry out on August 21–22 a wasteful frontal attack at Suvla which cost 5,300 in killed, wounded and missing out of 14,300 engaged.

The immediate result of the British failure was the mobilization of the Bulgarian Army on September 25. Next, on October 14, Bulgaria declared war on Serbia and Lord Kitchener decided to withdraw two divisions from the Dardanelles for service at Salonika. Then the storm burst, Mackensen at the head of nine German and Austrian divisions crossed the Danube. Uskub fell on October 22, Nish on November 2, and Monastir was entered on December 2. Serbia was reduced to ruin and German guns and ammunition were poured into Constantinople.

On October 14 Sir Ian Hamilton was recalled to England and replaced by Sir Charles Munro, who landed on October 28. Two days later he recommended the total evacuation of the British forces. This threw Mr. Asquith into panic, and, on November 2, he decided to entrust the conduct of the war to a War Committee of not less than three and not more than five members, a change he should have initiated a year or more before. On November 4, Lord Kitchener was sent to the Dardanelles to give a second opinion and to get rid of him, as Asquith informed Lloyd George.[1] His answer was that evacuation was inevitable; but Mr. Churchill – long superseded by Mr. Balfour as First Lord of the Admiralty – pressed for a renewal of the naval attack on the Narrows, though its strategic purpose had vanished. In this vain attempt to spoon up spilt milk, he was strongly supported by Commodore Keyes, who rushed this idea here, there, and everywhere, like a tactical bull in a strategical china shop. To him, the forcing of the Narrows meant that the "whole business" would be finished. He could not see that Germany and Turkey were now without a dividing frontier, and that once the fleet had bombarded Constantinople nothing further could have been done. Nor did he know at the time that on the German-Turkish side "A large-scale offensive with the assistance of gas was in course of preparation."[2] This, however, he might have guessed.

[1] *War Memoirs*, vol. 1, p. 520.   [2] *The Campaign in Gallipoli*, Kannengiesser, p. 238

On November 27, a terrific blizzard swept the peninsula for 72 hours, in which hundreds of men died of exposure. "At Suvla alone in the course of three days' storm there had been more than 5,000 cases of frostbite, and over 200 men had been drowned or frozen to death."[1] This storm hastened the crisis; for though General Munro had estimated that the probable losses involved in evacuation would total between 30 and 40 per cent. of the men and materials then on the peninsula, after much wrangling the War Committee at first decided to evacuate Anzac and Suvla only, but later it decided to evacuate Helles as well. The evacuation of the first two was carried out by December 20, and of the last by January 9, 1916, without a single soldier killed. Thus were concluded the sole successful operations of the campaign. In all, 410,000 British and 70,000 French soldiers had been landed, of whom 252,000 were killed, wounded, missing, prisoners, died of disease or evacuated sick.[2] The Turkish casualties amounted to 218,000 men, of whom 66,000 were killed.[3] The booty left behind was immense: "It took nearly two years to clean up the ground."[4]

Thus ended one of the greatest disasters in British history, and one comparable with the siege of Syracuse in 415 B.C., because its root cause was the inability of a democracy to conduct a war. As Mr. Churchill has pointed out: "No man had the power to give clear, brutal orders which would command unquestioning respect. Power was widely disseminated among the many important personages who in this period formed the governing instrument."[5] Therefore, as Mr. Lloyd George said: "There was no co-ordination of effort. There was no connected plan of action. There was no sense of the importance of time."[6] But worst of all, there was no judgment; no clear strategical analysis of the initial problem; no proper calculation of its tactical requirements; and no true attempt to balance the means in hand with the end in view. Had there been, it would have become apparent that the only practical solution was not to make the obvious frontal assault but to rely on surprise. This might have been done by unexpectedly landing a comparatively small, well-trained force under a bold commander at or near Bulair – the back door – and immediately after this to have set out to force the Dardanelles – the front door – and

[1] *Official History*, vol. II, p. 434.   [2] For detail see *Official History*, vol. II, p. 484.
[3] *Five Years in Turkey*, Liman von Sanders, p. 104.
[4] *Ibid.*, p. 103. See also *The Gallipoli Campaign*, Kannengeisser, p. 253.
[5] *The World Crisis*, 1915, Churchill, pp. 498–499.
[6] *War Memoirs*, Lloyd George, vol. I, pp. 422–423.

bombard Constantinople. Although such an operation would have been a gamble, as surprise operations so frequently must be, in the circumstances it would have been legitimate, and had it failed at the outset it could have been stopped immediately and with only a fraction of the loss of prestige the actual failure entailed.

To revert to the operation which was decided on, could not a bolder generalship have mitigated the disaster, even if it could not have annulled it? This is an important question, because its answer reveals the radical fault in the system of command then prevalent.

Like Burgoyne in 1777, Sir Ian Hamilton was asked to carry out a most difficult task. Like the former, his master was a debating society whose members were ignorant of war. And also, like his predecessor, he was an unlucky general; yet it should be remembered that luck and ill-luck are largely the by-products of character.

In the initial landings, it was no fault of Sir Ian Hamilton's that there was a lack of surprise, nor was he responsible for the lack of naval support. Had the Admirals risked their battleships as many a lieutenant-commander risked his submarine, there is little doubt that the Narrows could at a cost have been forced any time between April 25 and August 7. It is all very well for Lord Fisher to exclaim: "Can the Army win the war, before the Navy loses it?"[1] but once the naval attack was decided upon, however much he objected to it, like a good staff officer he should have backed his chief. It is only necessary to read his *Memories* to realize that he was a better democrat than admiral. What was lacking was Churchill's authority to say: "Do it!" and "Do it again!" But, unsupported by the Admiralty, none but a man of Napoleonic determination could have uttered these words. It was in the subsequent operations in which generalship was at so parlous a discount.

As a soldier, Sir Ian Hamilton was a typical product of pre-South African War days, when to the English wars were looked upon as gentlemanly affairs; when the team spirit killed initiative, and soldiership was the equivalent of sportsmanship. On top of this, when after that war a general staff was created, it was largely modelled on the German. The Moltke idea that the initiative should be surrendered to subordinate commanders once an operation had been launched was accepted. While Liman von

[1] *The World Crisis*, 1915, p. 514.

Sanders, the Turkish commander-in-chief, was always on the spot and eagerly accepted responsibilities, Sir Ian Hamilton sat at his G.H.Q., commented on the war and wrote: "So wrapped in cotton-wool is a nowadays Commander-in-Chief that this was the first musketry fire I could claim to have come under since the beginning of the war,"[1] at that time nearly four months old! Well may it be asked, why did he not unwrap himself? Why did he not assume command and impose his will on his subordinates as Liman von Sanders did? Imagine the latter writing: "Saw Stopford. Wrestled with him for over an hour; Braithwaite [his Chief of Staff] doing ditto with Reed."[2] And again: "Were not my hands tied by Mahon's seniority?" Were Sanders's hands tied by Feizi Bey, when he replaced him by Mustafa Kemal? At Y beach Sir Ian Hamilton took no action though he saw that things were going wrong. ". . . Roger Keyes started the notion that these troops might be diverted to Y where they could land unopposed. . . . Braithwaite was rather dubious from the orthodox General Staff point of view as to whether it was sound for G.H.Q. to barge into Hunter-Weston's plans. . . . But to me the idea seemed simple commonsense"; yet, "it was not for me to force his hands; there was no question of that. . . ."[3] No question? – when victory trembled in the balance?

Again at Suvla Bay, as John North writes: he became a prisoner on his island[4] while Liman von Sanders and Mustafa Kemal were activity itself. Of the latter, the Official Historian remarks: "Seldom in history can the exertions of a single divisional commander have exercised, on three separate occasions, so profound an influence not only on the course of a battle but perhaps on the fate of a campaign and even the destiny of a nation."[5] Inversely, this is as true of Sir Ian Hamilton's self-imposed lethargy.

What the campaign might have accomplished, had it been based on surprise and had it succeeded, has been pointed out by many – namely, the relief of Russia; the neutrality or active co-operation of the Balkan States; the salvation of Serbia; the defeat of Turkey; and the encirclement of Germany from the east while

---

[1] *Gallipoli Diary*, vol. II, p. 74.   [2] *Ibid.*, vol. II, p. 92.
[3] *Ibid.*, vol. I, pp. 132–133.   [4] *Gallipoli, the Fading Vision*, p. 256.
[5] *Official History*, vol. II, p. 486. Admiral Keyes writes: "It seems that in modern war, the Staff consider that the Commander-in-Chief should not be subject to any risk . . . there must be occasions when the personal touch and leadership are nine-tenths of the battle" (*Naval Memoirs*, vol. I, p. 319).

she was firmly gripped in the west. In all probability, not only could Russia have held her own, but in the opinion of Kannen-giesser, "without Gallipoli" the Russians "would have had no revolution."[1] Further, there would have been no prolonged campaigns in Macedonia, Mesopotamia, Egypt, and later in Palestine, and the vast numbers of troops absorbed by these subsidiary theatres of war, supported by the armies of the Balkan States, would have enabled the Allied Powers to have launched two million men, if necessary, against the Austro-Hungarian Empire. Because that empire was already engaged on two fronts, it is probable that it would have collapsed before the autumn of 1916.

Although these are hypothetical possibilities, they are in no way improbable, for Constantinople was to Germany what Chatta-nooga had been to the Confederacy in the American Civil War. On August 8, 1915, the day after General Stopford landed at Suvla Bay, Admiral von Tirpitz wrote: "Heavy fighting has been going on since yesterday at the Dardanelles. . . . The situation is obviously very critical. Should the Dardanelles fall, the world-war has been decided against us."[2] It was because all these things were possible that no one will quarrel with Sir Edward Carson when he said in the House of Commons that the withdrawal from Gallipoli was "the most vast disaster that had happened in the course of the war."[3]

[1] *The Campaign in Gallipoli*, p. 269.
[2] *Erinnerungen*, Alfred von Tirpitz (1918), p. 491.
[3] Quoted from *Official History*, vol. II, p. 385.

Progress of the War, 1915-1918

England was the strategical centre of gravity of the allied coalition; to win the war it was imperative for the Central Powers to drive her out of it. This demanded the defeat of France and Russia and the winning over of neutral support, so that, after the defeat of their allies, the British Government would be unable to raise another coalition. The British problem was to sustain the coalition. In the past this had been done by blockading the enemy, by subsidizing allies, and by employing the small British army in diversionary and distracting operations. Now, although Britain became the banker and arsenal of the coalition, she did not resort to full blockade from the outset and the army was not used as a diversionary force, but was transported to the western theatre of the war. Nevertheless, once stalemate was reached the British Government did not adhere to this new continental policy, but returned to the traditional policy of distraction.

Even before the Dardanelles diversionary venture had been decided on, two subsidiary campaigns were initiated, one in Egypt to protect the Suez Canal, and the other in the Persian Gulf to secure the Anglo-Persian oil installations at Abadan, and later, as we have seen, yet another expedition was sent to Salonika. These diversionary operations rapidly grew into major campaigns, and during 1917, when Russia was in death throes and the allied man-power problem reached its crisis, the first had grown into the Palestine campaign, in which the British ration strength was 340,000 men; the second into the Mesopotamia campaign, in which it was approximately 400,000; and the third into the Macedonian campaign in which, of 600,000 allied troops, 202,000 were British. These three campaigns cost the British Empire 174,500 men in killed, wounded, and dead of disease, to which must be added the 214,000 casualties sustained in Gallipoli.

This wastage of man-power was one of the main causes which prolonged the war; an even more important cause was the delay in establishing a full blockade of the Central Powers. This was because the British Government had in 1909 shackled themselves by the Declaration of London, which was based on the Declaration of Paris of 1856. This divided contrabands into two classes; one absolute, covering military stores, and the other conditional, which included foodstuffs and fodder destined for the enemy's armed forces. Because it was impossible to prove that the latter were not destined for Germany by way of neutral countries, the British blockade was hamstrung from the start, and on August 20, 1914, the first British Order in Council revising the Declaration of London was issued, and followed by the second on October 29. In reply to these revisions, which seriously curtailed supplies entering Germany and Austria, on February 4, 1915, the German Government declared that all waters surrounding Great Britain and Ireland would from the 18th be blockaded by submarine. It was a foolish decision politically, because the British Orders in Council had antagonized neutrals – particularly the United States – and the submarine blockade would inevitably modify neutral hostility toward Britain by embroiling Germany with every neutral Power trading with Britain. Events soon proved this to be so. On May 1 a United States merchantman was sunk and a week later the neutral world was shocked when the *Lusitania* was torpedoed.

In order to exploit the revulsion caused by the loss of this great vessel, on May 15 the British Government issued another Order in Council by which goods of any kind entering or leaving Germany were declared contraband. Thus full blockade was established. At the same time the Kaiser became so alarmed over American feelings that he ordered all attacks on passenger and neutral ships to cease. Had the United States then placed an embargo on munitions of war probably it would have brought the Allies to book, for their own factories were quite unable to supply the enormous demands of their armies.

When the German right wing was halted at Nieuport, the western front assumed the shape of a great salient that bulged westward between the Channel and the Vosges, with its apex near Compiègne. For 1915, Joffre's plan was to cut this salient off by a dual offensive; the British were to attack eastward from Artois, and the French northward from Champagne, the axes of their attacks to meet west of St. Quentin. Throughout the war this plan remained the norm of French strategy, and in accordance with it the following battles were fought in 1915: The First Battle of Champagne (December 20–March 17); the Battle of Soissons

(January 8–14); the Battle of Neuve-Chapelle (March 10–13); the Battle of Festubert (May 15–25); the Second Battle of Artois (May 9–June 18); the Battle of Loos (September 25–October 15), and the Second Battle of Champagne (September 25–November 6). None did more than dent the great salient.

Faced with winter on the Russian front, and aware that the abortive allied attempts to break through the western front had created in France a spirit of defeatism, toward the end of 1915 Falkenhayn decided once again to shift the main German effort to the west. His plan was to reopen the submarine campaign and simultaneously to strike at Verdun, which he selected as his objective because the French considered it impregnable. Could he wrest it from them, its loss might so lower their declining morale that it would lead to their collapse and the consequent isolation of England.

On February 21, 1916, the battle of Verdun was opened. Although, like all previous attacks against entrenched fronts, it failed to break through, it dragged on until July 11, by when the Germans had suffered 281,000 casualties and the French 315,000. A week after the battle began, the submarine campaign was launched, and with such startling success that at first it appeared that the Germans had at length discovered the weapon which would enable them to force their implacable enemy to terms. But on March 24, when the Folkestone–Dieppe packet, *Sussex*, was torpedoed without warning, the United States Government threatened to sever diplomatic relations with Germany unless she modified her submarine warfare. This so frightened the Kaiser that he agreed to restrict his submarines to purely military targets. Next, on July 7, the British Government rescinded the Declaration of London.

Though the battle of Verdun upset the allied spring offensive, a combined operation between Russia, France, and Britain was agreed, and on June 5 it was opened on the Russian front by General Brusilov. It came as welcome news to the English after their abortive naval battle off Jutland on May 31 and the loss of Lord Kitchener at sea five days later. Although by June 20 200,000 Austrians had surrendered to the Russians, between June 16 and 23 Brusilov was heavily counter-attacked by the Germans and pressed back. Nevertheless, this offensive continued until August 17, by when the Russians had lost over a million men and were bled white.

When the Brusilov offensive was at its height, on July 1, after enormous preparations and a seven-day preliminary bombardment, the French and British – the latter now under Sir Douglas Haig – opened their delayed offensive on the Somme, and again a battle of mutual attrition followed. It lasted until November 18 and each side lost more than 600,000 men in killed, wounded, and prisoners. Meanwhile, on August 27, the Rumanians declared war on the Central Powers, and two days later Falkenhayn was superseded by Hindenburg as Chief of the General Staff. On December 6 Bucharest capitulated to the Germans.

With the battle of the Somme the stalemate on all fronts became so complete that neither group of combatants appeared to have a chance of forcing a decision in the field, and the question of peace negotiations began to be considered in London, Berlin, and Vienna. On November 14, Lord Lansdowne, Minister without Portfolio in the Asquith coalition Government, laid a memorandum before the Cabinet in which he suggested that the possibilities of peace should be examined. The Asquith administration was tottering, and on December 7 it fell and Lloyd George, who was pledged to a more vigorous prosecution of the war, succeeded Asquith. Five days later Germany and her allies put forward four identical notes in which they stated their willingness to consider peace proposals. But whether Germany was sincere appears doubtful from what followed immediately. On December 18, President Woodrow Wilson indented a note to all belligerents asking them to state "the precise objects which would, if attained, satisfy them and their people that the war had been fought out," and, on January 22, 1917, in an address before the Senate, he declared for "peace without victory". Instead of courting the President, or offering to cede Alsace-Lorraine to France which, according to M. Viviani, French Minister of Justice, would have bought France out of the war, on January 31 the Kaiser commanded that the submarine campaign should from February 1 be placed on an unrestricted footing. To add to this folly, at the same time it became known in the United States that Germany had been urging Mexico to conclude an offensive alliance with her and Japan against the Americans should they enter the war. These things so exasperated the United States that, on February 3, diplomatic relations between Washington and Berlin were severed, and though peace conversations were continued, they were now bereft of all reality.

The reason why this stupidity was committed was that in Berlin it was considered that Russian morale had reached breaking point, and that if the havoc the submarine campaign had already caused were accentuated it would bring England to terms before the Americans could make their military influence felt. Clearly, what Germany should have done was to wait until Russia had collapsed, and then, when all was ready for an assault on the western front, to have opened the submarine campaign in full strength.

German prognostications about Russia were correct. In Petrograd 1916 had ended with a foreboding event. On December 29 the monk Rasputin, confidant of the Tsarina and the Svengali of the court, was assassinated, and from then on the situation in Russia slumped. On March 8, 1917, riots broke out in Petrograd and the bakers' shops were sacked. On the 11th, the troops were called out; they did not fire on the rioters but shot their officers and joined the mob. There were 190,000 soldiers in the capital and the mutiny, which started in the Imperial Guard, spread like wildfire. On the 12th revolution was in full swing, the Winter Palace was invaded, public buildings were burnt, and the prisons, including the fortress of St. Peter and St. Paul – the Russian Bastille – were opened and their inmates released. On March 15 Nicholas II abdicated and three days later a provisional Government, under Prince Lvov, was formed. Brusilov was appointed commander-in-chief and Kerensky Minister of Justice. In May, the latter became Minister of War, and in July Prime Minister. On March 22 the provisional Government was formally recognized by the allied Powers.

The March revolution was followed immediately by an extension of the conflict. On Good Friday, April 6, the United States declared war on the German Empire, and at about the same time the German Government sent Lenin (Vladimir Ilyich Ulyanov, 1870–1924) in a sealed train to Petrograd. These were the two most portentous events of the war, and they were destined to change the political axis of the world.

April 6, 1917, was the most fateful day in European history since Varus lost his legions, and in a mysterious way the American President sensed it to be so. On the night of April 1 – the day before he delivered his war message to Congress – in a conversation with Frank Cobb of the New York *World*, he is reported by the latter to have said:

". . . war would overturn the world we had known; that so long as we remained out there was a preponderance of neutrality, but that if we joined with the Allies the world would be off the peace basis and onto a war basis.

" 'It would mean that we should lose our heads along with the rest and stop weighing right and wrong. It would mean that a majority of the people in this hemisphere would go war-mad, quit thinking and devote their energies to destruction.' The President said a declaration of war would mean that Germany would be beaten, and so badly beaten that there would be a dictated peace, a victorious peace.

" 'It means,' he said, 'an attempt to reconstruct a peacetime civilization with war standards, and at the end of the war there will be no bystanders with sufficient peace standards left to work with. There will be only war standards' . . .

" 'Once lead this people into war,' he said, 'and they'll forget there ever was such a thing as tolerance. To fight you must be brutal and ruthless, and the spirit of ruthless brutality will enter into every fibre of our national life, infecting Congress, the courts, the policeman on his beat, the man in the street.' Conformity would be the only virtue, said the President, and every man who refused to conform would have to pay the penalty."

Had not public opinion, raised by propaganda to white heat, forced Wilson to take this fateful step, now that Russia was four-fifths out of the war and Germany thereby free to concentrate her forces against France, it is nearly certain that, without American support, France and Great Britain would have been forced on the defensive, that Germany would have failed to break their front decisively, and that because in May the British Admiralty by introducing convoying at sea,[1] began to master the submarine, a negotiated peace would have been agreed with the United States as referee before Lenin could have got into the saddle.

The wisdom of America's entry into the war was questioned by Mr. Ramsay Macdonald, leader of the British Labour Party. On August 17 he addressed a statement to Colonel House and the President, in which he wrote: "The majority of our people welcomed America's entry into the war, but a minority, much larger than newspapers or vociferous opinion indicates, regard it not

---

[1] After the convoy system was introduced, in which the United States Navy lent assistance, against the loss of 169 ships in April, between then and the end of the year, on the average losses were reduced by 75·5 ships a month, and not a single troopship was sunk.

with any hostile feelings but with regret. They come to that view because (a) they do not think that American military help was required in order to compel any of the Powers to make a reasonable peace; and (b) they think that America, out of the war, would have done more for peace and good feeling than in the war, and would also have had a better influence on the peace settlement." Further he wrote: ". . . whilst you can have peace without victory, history shows that as a rule nations have had victory without peace. . . . It would also compel them to welcome political activities parallel with military activities."

Years later – in August, 1936 – Mr. Churchill in a statement to William Griffen, editor of the New York *Enquirer*, is reported by the latter to have said that "America should have minded her own business and stayed out of the World War. If you hadn't entered the war the Allies would have made peace with Germany in the Spring of 1917. Had we made peace then there would have been no collapse in Russia followed by Communism, no breakdown in Italy followed by Fascism, and Germany would not have signed the Versailles Treaty, which has enthroned Nazism in Germany. If America had stayed out of the war, all these 'isms' wouldn't to-day be sweeping the continent of Europe and breaking down parliamentary government, and if England had made peace early in 1917, it would have saved over one million British, French, American, and other lives."

With Russia virtually out of the war and America as yet only nominally in it, the wisest course for the French and British to have adopted would have been to hold their front defensively, economize their man-power, and wait until America could develop her strength. Instead, they decided on a joint spring offensive eastward from Arras and northward from Rheims. When from the preparations the Germans gauged what was in hand, and in order better to hold their western front until reinforcements could arrive from Russia, they withdrew from the nose of the great western salient to what they called the *Siegfried Stellung*, and the allies called the Hindenberg Line. It was a vast system of entrenchments that stretched from near Arras to a few miles east of Soissons. This withdrawal threw the allied joint offensive out of gear and led to two separate battles – the battle of Arras (April 9–May 15) and the second battle of the Aisne (April 16–20). The former cost the British 158,000 casualties, and the latter, under the direction of General Nivelles, who had succeeded Joffre in December, 1916, ended in fiasco and cost the French 187,000 men. Worse, extensive mutinies followed, which meant that for the time being all further thought of a French offensive had to be abandoned. On May 15, Nivelles was replaced by General Pétain. Next, in the east, what was known as the Kerensky offensive was launched on June 29, and by July 18 was so crushed that no further Russian offensive was possible.

Before the battle of the Somme, Sir Douglas Haig had urged that the decisive battle should be sought in Flanders, and now, in order to draw the Germans away from the demoralized French, as well as to seize the German submarine bases at Ostend and Zeebrugge, he decided first to gain the Messines ridge, and next to break through the Ypres front and advance on Bruges and Ghent.

On May 21, under cover of 2,266 guns and nineteen mines, packed with a million pounds of explosives, the battle of Messines was launched, and by June 14 the ridge was successfully occupied. Next, on July 31, after a 13-day bombardment, a series of battles known as the "Third Battle of Ypres" was opened. The battle field was reclaimed swampland, and under the bombardment it reverted to a vast bog in which the attacking troops fought and wallowed until November 20, when the battle ended with a loss of 244,897 men.[1] To persist after the close of August in this tactically impossible battle was an inexcusable piece of pigheadedness on the part of Haig, because on the 20th of that month the French had recovered sufficiently to mount an attack at Verdun, which was continued until December 15 with the usual heavy losses.

Meanwhile in Italy, between October 24 and November 4, the Italians had suffered a catastrophic defeat in the battle of Caporetto, in which they lost 305,000 men, of whom 275,000 were captured. In order to prevent the Italians from being driven out of the war, British and French troops were rushed to Italy, and, on November 20, Haig attacked the Germans at Cambrai, a battle in which there was no preliminary bombardment and in which tanks for the first time were employed in mass. It opened with a startling success, and, on December 5, through lack of reserves, ended in failure and a loss of 45,000 men. By the close

[1] These are Sir James Edmonds' figures (*A Short History of World War I*, 1951, p. 252). According to the British *Official Strategical Abstract* (1920) between July 31 and December 31, the losses in the Third Battle of Ypres were 380,335, and in the Battle of Messines, 108,882.

of 1917, the British were bled white, the French were morally exhausted, the Italians nearly out of the war, and the Americans not yet sufficiently involved to make good a fraction of the enormous losses sustained.

Meanwhile on November 7 (old style October 25 – hence "the October Revolution") Lenin and Trotsky (Lev Davidovich Bronstein) seized power in Petrograd and overthrew the Kerensky Government. A month later, when hostilities between Russia and Germany were suspended, the Tsarist empire began to disintegrate. On January 22, 1918, the Ukraine declared its independence, which, on February 9, was recognized by Germany under the terms of the first Treaty of Brest-Litovsk. Next, between February 16 and May 30, Lithuania, Latvia, Estonia, Bielorussia, Georgia, Azerbaijan, Armenia, North Caucasia and Cossakia (Don and Kuban Cossacks) proclaimed their independence. Then, in order to bring the Bolshevik Government to heel and call a halt to Trotsky's interminable propaganda arguments, on February 18 the Germans recommenced hostilities, and immediately the Bolsheviks declared their readiness for peace. This led to the signing of the second Treaty of Brest-Litovsk on March 3, by the terms of which the Bolshevik Government recognized the independence of Finland and the Ukraine; surrendered Courland, Lithuania, Poland, Batum and Kars (the last two to the Turks); demobilized its army and fleet; and refrained from all propaganda in Germany. On May 7 followed the Treaty of Bucharest with Rumania.

While Russia was in anarchy, President Wilson considered peace, and on January 8 he outlined before Congress his settlement of the war in 14 points, and added four others later. Highly idealistic in character, they caught the imagination of a war-weary world and offered Germany an opportunity to end the war by a negotiated peace. This the Kaiser and his advisers refused to consider, in part at least because while Wilson waved his olive branch suggestions were voiced in America that the harshest possible terms should be imposed on the Germans and peace dictated in Berlin. Therefore, now that the war had been reduced to one front, the German Supreme Command decided to knock out the French and British before the Americans could get into their stride. Other than accepting the Fourteen Points, this was the only practical course open; for as Ludendorff has pointed out, the collapse of Russia had caused such an intensive relief within

Germany that everyone was eager for the offensive and dreaded a defensive campaign in face of the ever-mounting *matériel* of the enemy. Further, the stranglehold of the blockade was choking Germany to death, and only an offensive could break it rapidly.

The error committed by the Supreme Command was not that it decided on the offensive, but that it selected as its target the stubborn British instead of the war-weary French.

Once the western front had been reinforced by 70 divisions from Russia, the German plan was to break through the British Third and Fifth Armies north and south of Péronne, and directly penetration had been effected, to wheel the right attacking wing northward and drive the British away from the French.

On March 21 the *Kaiserschlacht* (Emperor Battle) was opened under cover of fog and gas shells, and it proved so successful that on the 26th, in order to meet the situation, General Foch was appointed co-ordinator of the allied armies. Nevertheless, by April 5 the momentum of the attack had exhausted itself and the Germans were left in an extensive salient with its apex nine miles east of Amiens. Frustrated in the Somme area, on April 9 a powerful attack was launched on the British First Army astride the Lys. On April 30 it petered out and left the Germans in yet another salient.

Only after these two abortive battles did the German Supreme Command decide to turn against the French on the Aisne. At one o'clock in the morning of May 27 the third great offensive opened; the ridge of the Chemin des Dames was stormed, and by the night of the 28th a large salient was pushed southward between Rheims and Soissons. On June 3 the Marne at Château Thierry was reached and a pause followed until the 9th, when the attack was renewed, but only to die out again on the 14th. On July 6 came the last German attack, this time east and west of Rheims, but the allies held fast and little progress was made.

In order to prevent a continuance of the offensive toward Paris, Foch decided to counter-attack the western flank of the salient, and on July 18 he struck eastward from Villers Cotterets, and by August 2 had forced the Germans back to the line Rheims–Soissons. By then, each side since March 21 had suffered about a million casualties. For the Germans these losses were absolute, because they could not be made good; but by now more than a million Americans had been landed in France, and they arrived at the rate of a quarter of a million each month. Thus the Americans, as Ludendorff said, "became the deciding factor in the war". Yet it was not the Americans who were to win the battle which decided it.

CHAPTER 7

The Battle of Amiens, 1918

The battle of Amiens, known to the French as the battle of Montdidier, was the most decisive battle of the First World War. It led not only to the collapse of the German armies on the western front, but also to the solution of the stalemate, and in solving this it established a tactical revolution. Nevertheless, had the German armies in 1914 been organized round the quick-firing field-gun and the machine-gun – the dominant weapons of the early twentieth century – instead of round the magazine rifle – the dominant weapon of the late nineteenth century – the probability is that there would have been no stalemate and that France would have been overrun almost as rapidly as she was in 1940 by two very different dominant weapons – the tank and the aeroplane. But they were not so organized, nor were their opponents, and, as we have seen, the result was that the rifle bullet was able to gain sufficient time for the spade to throw up bullet-proof entrenchments and neutralize the power of the gun. Only then did all armies set about to multiply their artillery and machine-guns, either in order to hold or to break an entrenched front, and because trenches and entanglements impeded the offensive and aided the defensive, as Bloch had foreseen, the latter became the stronger form of war.

To overcome this difference, the first solution was sought in the obliteration of trenches and entanglements by intense preliminary artillery bombardments,[1] and though, generally speaking, they guaranteed an initial success, they converted the battlefield into a cratered area and created as formidable an obstacle to forward movements of wheeled vehicles, without which the attackers could not be supplied, as the trenches and entanglements they demolished.[2] Besides, even when these artillery battles were successful they invariably left the attacker in a salient – that is, in a tactically

[1] The growth of the British preliminary bombardments was rapid: in the battle of Hooge (1915) 18,000 shells; in that of the Somme (1916) 2,000,000; at Arras (1917) 2,600,000; at Messines (1917) 3,500,000; and at Ypres III (1917) 4,300,000.
[2] During the third battle of Ypres the forward troops and guns had, as in mountain warfare, to be supplied by pack horses.

disadvantageous position. Thus, although the gun came into its own, because its destructiveness rendered it static it was unable to play a decisive part in a war of movement. Further, the cratered area favoured the machine-gun on the defensive. The outcome was that, instead of stalemate being liquidated by artillery fire, it became more and more consolidated.

Since the gun failed to solve the problem, on April 22, 1915, the Germans in the Ypres area resorted to discharges of chlorine gas.[1] But in spite of its initial success, because gas was easily neutralized by the box respirator, the problem remained unsolved.

Late in the war, in order to force a decision through demoralization, both sides resorted to aircraft attacks on civil populations. But they were no more than sideshows, for though they pointed to a deplorable future, throughout the war air power was not sufficiently developed to warrant decisive results.[2]

All these solutions were spurious, because the problem was not clearly understood. It was not to remove trenches and entanglements, but to neutralize the bullet; the question was how to disarm the mass of the enemy's riflemen and machine-gunners, not gradually but instantaneously. Obviously the answer was bullet-proof armour and not an increase in projectiles – whether bullets, shells, bombs, or even gas. Quite early in the war this was seen by Colonel E. D. Swinton[3] and others in England, and by General Estienne in France. Further, they saw that though the soldier could not carry bullet-proof armour, he could be carried, as the sailor was, in a bullet-proof armoured vehicle, and as this vehicle would have to travel across country it would have to move on caterpillar tracks instead of on wheels. Thus the tank, a self-propelled bullet-proof landship, was conceived. On September 15, 1916, it first went into action on the shell-blasted battlefield of the Somme.

Actually this solution was an exceedingly old one,[4] and in

---

[1] Toward the end of 1915 the Germans introduced phosgene gas shells, and in the summer of 1917 sneezing gas (diphenylchloroarsine, or Blue Cross), and mustard gas (dichloroethyl, or Yellow Cross). The last was a highly volatile vesicant liquid and a formidable weapon. The American gas casualties in the war were 74,779 (mostly due to mustard gas) or 27·3 per cent of the total; of these only 1·87 per cent were fatal.

[2] One hundred and eleven air attacks were made on England, in which 8,500 bombs weighing about 300 tons were dropped; 1,413 people were killed, 3,407 injured, and £3,000,000 worth of property was destroyed. In Germany 720 people were killed, 1,754 injured, and damage to property amounted to £1,175,000.

[3] See his book *Eyewitness* (1932).

[4] See *Tanks in the Great War*, J. F. C. Fuller (1920), chap. 1.

recent times had been examined with remarkable understanding by Colonel C. B. Brackenbury in an article entitled "Ironclad Field Artillery," which appeared in *The Nineteenth Century Review* of July, 1878. It is worth quoting at some length, for in it is clearly foreshadowed the "tank idea".

In condensed form, Brackenbury's argument ran: The leading lesson of the Plevna operations was "that troops of any kind under cover are practically invincible so long as the enemy is in front of them"; that the effect of artillery fire "increases as the range diminishes"; "that the destructive power of artillery at close quarters is practically annihilating"; but that, as the power of infantry "has immensely increased", it is not possible to advance the guns to annihilating range. Therefore the problem was how to protect the guns from bullets, and Brackenbury's suggestion was to carry forward "thin iron shields (in sections) capable of protecting the gunners against infantry fire" in "one or possibly two carriages to each battery". "Then the artillery might calmly await any attack whatever, certain to destroy an enemy long before he could reach the guns. All anxiety as to capture would be extinguished, and we might proceed to build up a system of tactics based upon the supposition that artillery will not need to run away from anything in front of it. . . . If two lines of artillery were contending against each other, surely the side which was safe from shrapnel bullets and the infantry fire of the other side ought to overwhelm its antagonist. . . . If we can prevent nine-tenths of the loss in killed and wounded, and nearly all the risk of capture, we can afford to disregard accidents. . . . As surely as ships of war can carry iron plates sufficient for defence against heavy guns, so surely can field artillery carry sufficient protection against the fire of infantry and shrapnel bullets. . . . The fire of infantry has become so formidable of late years that defensive measures must inevitably be adopted sooner or later by field artillery. . . . If we add the use of defensive armour which can be carried by artillery and cannot be carried by cavalry and infantry, a power will be created which must seriously modify the tactics of the battlefield. The development is as sure to come as the day to follow the night. We may hope that England will set the example instead of following other nations."[1]

[1] This was not to be. His idea was adopted by Colonel Schumann and tested in the 1899 and 1890 German autumn manœuvres. Also it was adopted by the Rumanian army (*Journal of the Royal United Service Institution*, vol. XXIV, pp. 867–889 and 1029–1035).

What is remarkable in Brackenbury's proposal is that he realized that "Moral effect is the object aimed at in a battle, for the killed and wounded have no influence on the final retirement" – this is the soul of the "tank idea". He saw as Frederick had seen, "that to advance is to conquer" because of the terrifying moral effect of a *continuous* advance. This was the underlying idea of the "bayonet school" of thought, an idea preeminently sound, but under the conditions that prevailed in 1914 – impossible. The "shell school" of 1914–1917 never grasped this idea; it could not, or did not, see that the problem was not to reduce the enemy's position to rubble, but *to advance the guns* under hostile rifle and machine-gun fire, and that could such an advance be sustained it would prove not *overwhelmingly destructive*, but *overwhelmingly demoralizing*. This is exactly what the tank – self-propelled armoured artillery – accomplished. It solved the two outstanding difficulties which had faced armies since the introduction of firearms – namely, how to harmonize movement and fire power and movement and protection. It increased mobility by substituting mechanical power for muscular; it increased security by neutralizing the bullet with armour plate; and it increased offensive power by relieving the soldier from the necessity of carrying his weapons and the horse from hauling them. Because the tank protected the soldier dynamically, it enabled him to fight statically; it superimposed naval tactics on land warfare.

The first occasion upon which tanks were used correctly was in the Cambrai attack on November 20, 1917. In this battle no preliminary artillery bombardment was employed. Instead, grouped in threes, tanks operated like a chain of mobile armoured batteries in advance of the infantry. With certain modifications these tactics were maintained until the end of the war and they vastly reduced casualties to ground gained. But although this battle showed that a true solution of the stalemate had been discovered, lack of reserves led to tactical failure, and it was not until the battle of Amiens that on a grand scale the same solution led to complete success.

Concurrent with the introduction of what was to become known as "armoured warfare", was the development of air warfare – the most mobile form of war – and this also was largely fostered by the stalemate. First, we see the aeroplane almost exclusively devoted to the direction of artillery fire; next, to air photography in order to produce special artillery trench-maps. These tasks stimulated fighting in the air, but it was not until the introduction of the German Fokker monoplane in the summer of 1915, which fired a fixed machine-gun between its propeller blades, that systematic air fighting began. Bombing of artillery positions and other targets was tentatively initiated during the battle of Loos; contact patrols were first introduced in the battle of the Somme; low flying attacks on trenches and artillery positions were developed in the battles of Messines and Cambrai; and, on April 1, 1918, the Royal Air Force was created as a separate arm to supersede the Royal Flying Corps. So enormous was the progress made that, whereas in 1914 the R.F.C. consisted of 165 officers and 1,264 other ranks, and took with it to France 63 aeroplanes, in the summer of 1918 the R.A.F. comprised 291,175 officers and men and 22,000 aircraft, of which 3,300 were in first line. It was the greatest air force in the world.

These preliminary tactical developments should be borne in mind when considering the great decisive battle fought east of Amiens between August 8 and 11.

Toward the end of June, when the British position on the Amiens front was much improved, General Sir Henry Rawlinson, in command of the Fifth Army, which since its defeat had been renumbered the Fourth, decided that the 4th Australian Division should occupy the village of Hamel and a neighbouring wood east of Corbie. On July 4, in cooperation with the 5th Tank Brigade, these objectives were taken so completely to plan and at so low a cost[1] that on the following day Rawlinson suggested to Haig a similar operation, but on a more extended scale. With this operation in mind, on July 12 Haig suggested to Foch – who two days before had been created a marshal of France – an offensive which would advance the allied front east and south-east of Amiens and disengage the town as well as the vital Amiens–Paris railway, both of which were under German gun-fire. Foch agreed, and on the following day Rawlinson was instructed to draft his plan. He submitted it on July 17, and on the 23rd it was approved by Foch and Haig.

The plan was that of Hamel enlarged, and its aim was a limited advance to the old Amiens outer defence line, lost in the previous

---

[1] It was the battle of Hamel more than the battle of Cambrai which made the reputation of the British Tank Corps (see *Tanks in the Great War*, Chap. XXVII, and *Memoirs of an Unconventional Soldier*, J. F. C. Fuller (1936), pp. 287–290.

April, and which on the Fourth Army front ran from le Quesnel on the Amiens–Roye road, through the village of Caix to a little east of Méricourt on the Somme.

While he waited for Haig's approval, Rawlinson had on July 21 assembled a conference at his headquarters in Flexicourt. It was attended by his three corps commanders, Lieutenant-General Sir Arthur Currie, Canadian Corps; Lieutenant-General Sir John Monash, Australian Corps, and Lieutenant-General Sir Richard Butler, IIIrd Corps, as well as by Lieutenant-General Sir Charles Kavanagh, commanding the cavalry, and representatives of the R.A.F. and Tank Corps. The original idea was somewhat enlarged at this conference and the number of tank battalions required raised from eight to twelve. Next, on July 26, Foch issued his formal orders for the operation, which began:

"1. The object of the operations is to disengage Amiens and the Paris–Amiens railway, also to defeat and drive back the enemy established between the Somme and the Avre.

"2. To do so, the offensive, covered in the north by the Somme, will be pushed as far as possible in the direction of Roye."[1]

Though the aim remained the same, the objective was pushed well beyond the Amiens outer defences, for Roye lies eight miles south-east of le Quesnel. At the same time zero day was fixed for August 8, and on July 28 the project was extended by Foch, who placed the French First Army, commanded by General Debeney, under Haig with instructions to employ it offensively on Rawlinson's right flank. Finally, on August 5, at a conference presided over by Haig, the aim of the operations was radically changed. Not only was the French Third Army, which stood on the right of the First, to be included in the attack, but Rawlinson was instructed to arrange for an advance eastward of the Amiens outer defence line, and, in order to facilitate the advance between Montdidier and Noyon of the French Third Army, he was further ordered to capture the line Roye-Chaulnes and thrust the enemy back on Ham – 15 miles south-east of Chaulnes. To assist him in this the Cavalry Corps was placed at his disposal.

To double the depth of penetration three days before the attack was due meant that corps commanders would not have time enough to change the intricate administrative detail which all offensive plans in this war demanded. It followed that the plans

[1] *Military Operations France and Belgium, 1918* (British Official History, edit. Sir James E. Edmonds, 1947), vol. IV, p. 3.

as they stood would have to be fitted to a situation for which they had never been contemplated. Further, it would seem that neither Foch nor Haig took into account the change in the character of the battlefield this extension carried with it.

North of the Somme the ground was cut up by gullies and spurs, which were serious obstacles for tanks, but the distance to be attacked over was short, because the Amiens outer defence lines were under 5,000 yards east of the starting line. South of the Somme and up to the Amiens outer defences lay perfect tank country, and the German works were indifferent. But beyond it lay the French part of the Somme battlefield of 1916; a jumble of decayed trenches, entanglements and shell holes. Not only was it difficult for tanks and infantry to fight over, but it constituted an ideal defensive area for enemy machine-gunners. Therefore, now that the depth of the attack had been extended to the line Roye–Chaulnes–Somme, the attackers were faced with two operations: as planned, how to advance up to the Amiens defence lines, and, as not planned, how to carry on the advance from there across the old Somme battlefield to the line Roye–Chaulnes. As the latter could not be rushed, strong infantry and tank reserves would be required to win it, and since they had not been budgeted for, as we shall see, like the battle of Cambrai, the battle of Amiens was virtually a one-day operation.

On August 8 General Rawlinson had under his command the following: on the left the IIIrd Corps, with the 12th, 18th and 58th Divisions in line, the 47th on the extreme left to secure the corps' left flank, and the American 33rd Division in reserve; in the centre the Australian Corps, with the 2nd, 3rd and 4th Divisions in line, and the 1st and 5th in reserve; and on the right the Canadian Corps, with the 2nd and 3rd Divisions in line, and the 1st and 4th in reserve. Also he had the Cavalry Corps, which consisted of the 1st, 2nd and 3rd Cavalry Divisions; the 5th Brigade R.A.F. – six corps squadrons, eight scout squadrons and three bomber squadrons – and the 3rd, 4th and 5th Brigades and the 10th Battalion of the Tank Corps. As a general reserve, the 17th, 32nd and 63rd Divisions were placed at his disposal.

The frontage of attack extended from Moreuil in the south to the river Ancre in the north. From Moreuil to the Amiens–Roye road it was held by the French XXXIst Corps; from the Amiens–Roye road to the Villers Bretonneux–Chaulnes railway (both inclusive) by the Canadian Corps; from this railway to the river

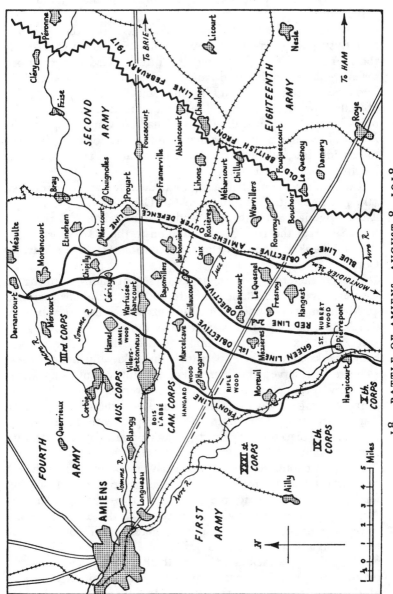

18. BATTLE OF AMIENS, AUGUST 8, 1918

Somme by the Australian Corps; and thence to the Ancre by the IIIrd Corps.

For the first day's battle the general idea was that the Canadian and Australian Corps were to carry out the main attack, while the French XXXIst Corps and the British IIIrd Corps formed defensive flanks on their right and left. The battlefield was divided into three objectives: Green Line, first objective, Red Line, second objective for all corps, and Blue and Blue Dotted Lines, third objective for the Australian and Canadian Corps respectively. A halt of two hours was to be made on the first objective, in order to provide time for the second wave of the attack to come up and leapfrog over the first.

Tank units were allotted as follows: the 4th Tank Brigade (1st, 4th, 5th and 14th Battalions) to the Canadian Corps; the 5th Tank Brigade (2nd, 8th, 13th and 15th Battalions) to the Australian Corps; the 10th Tank Battalion to the IIIrd Corps; and the 3rd Tank Brigade (3rd and 6th Battalions) to the Cavalry Corps.

The characteristics of the tanks these battalions were armed with are given in the table. The 3rd and 6th Battalions each had 48 Medium A (Whippet) tanks, and except for the 1st and 15th, which each had 36 Mark V Star tanks, the rest had 36 Mark V's apiece, and six in reserve to make good breakdowns. In all, 324 heavy tanks and 96 Whippets took the field, and besides them 42 were in reserve; also there were 96 supply tanks (converted Mark IV's) and 22 gun-carriers, also converted for supply; in all a grand total of 580 machines. In addition there was the 17th Tank (Armoured Car) Battalion, equipped with 12 armoured cars. It was placed under the 5th Tank Brigade, to operate with the Australians.

These distributions and allotments were more than sufficient to guarantee an advance to the Amiens outer defence lines; but for an advance beyond them to the Roye–Chaulnes line on August 9 they were insufficient, because all divisions and tanks were to be engaged on the 8th, and, therefore, all would require to be reorganized before a co-ordinated advance could be made on the 9th. The attacking forces on the 8th were over-strong and over-condensed. Divisional frontages averaged from 2,250 yards at the start to 3,000 at the finish. Had time permitted, these frontages could have been extended, and had this been done, probably two divisions and two tank battalions could have been

CHARACTERISTICS OF ARMOURED VEHICLES USED ON AUGUST 8, 1918

Characteristics	Mark IV		Mark V		Mark V Star		Medium Mark A	Gun-carrier
	Male	Female	Male	Female	Male	Female		
Length	26 ft. 5 in.	26 ft. 5 in.	26 ft. 5 in.	26 ft. 5 in.	32 ft. 5 in.	32 ft. 5 in.	20 ft. 0 in.	30 ft. 0 in.
Weight	28 tons	27 tons	29 tons	28 tons	33 tons	32 tons	14 tons	34 tons
Crew	1 Ofr. 7 O.R.	1 Ofr. 7 O.R.	1 Ofr. 7 O.R.	1 Ofr. 7 O.R.	1 Ofr. 7 O.R.	1 Ofr. 7 O.R.	1 Ofr. 2 O.R.	1 Ofr. 3 O.R.
Armament	2 6-pdrs. 4 Lewis guns	6 Lewis guns	2 6-pdrs. 4 Hotchkiss guns	6 Hotchkiss guns	2 6-pdrs. 4 Hotchkiss guns	6 Hotchkiss guns	4 Hotchkiss guns	1 Lewis gun
Engine	105 h.p.	105 h.p.	150 h.p.	150 h.p.	150 h.p.	150 h.p.	Two 45 h.p.	105 h.p.
Max. Speed	3·7 m.p.h.	3·7 m.p.h.	4·6 m.p.h.	4·6 m.p.h.	4·0 m.p.h.	4·0 m.p.h.	8·3 m.p.h.	3·0 m.p.h.
Average Speed	2·0 m.p.h.	2·0 m.p.h.	3·0 m.p.h.	3·0 m.p.h.	2·5 m.p.h.	2·5 m.p.h.	5·0 m.p.h.	1·75 m.p.h.
Radius of Action	15 miles	15 miles	25 miles	25 miles	18 miles	18 miles	40 miles	15 miles
Spanning Power	10 ft. 0 in.	10 ft. 0 in.	10 ft. 0 in.	10 ft. 0 in.	14 ft. 0 in.	14 ft. 0 in.	7 ft. 0 in.	11 ft. 6 in.

The Mark V Star tank could carry 20 men in addition to its crew.

Gun-carriers were originally designed to carry a 6-inch howitzer or a 60-pdr.

The Gun-carrier and Mark IV converted could transport 10 tons of stores.

Radii of Action approximate, depended on the nature of the ground.

added to the three divisions in reserve. Further, had the Cavalry Corps and its tank battalions been held back until August 9, five fresh infantry divisions, three fresh cavalry divisions, and four fresh tank battalions could have continued the battle on that day. This continuance of the forward movement was all important, because in order to maintain the momentum of the attack it was not only necessary to rout the enemy front line divisions, but to keep them routed before his reserve divisions could move up; for to throw back routed troops on unrouted ones is the surest way to disorganize and demoralize the latter.

Two German armies were involved, the Second and Eighteenth, the former commanded by General von der Marwitz and the latter by General Hutier. The front of the former extended from near Méaulte, on the left flank of the IIIrd Corps, to St. Hubert Wood, three and a half miles south of Moreuil, and the front of the latter from St. Hubert Wood to Noyon, which coincided with the right flank of the French Third Army. The Second Army had 10 divisions in line and four in reserve, and the Eighteenth Army 11 and four respectively.

On the Fourth Army front, the battle tactics were those of Cambrai. The tanks were to assemble 1,000 yards behind the infantry starting line, and before zero hour, which was fixed at 4.20 a.m., they were to move forward under an aircraft noise barrage to the starting line, from where at zero hour they were to lead the infantry forward under cover of a creeping barrage[1] fired by one-third of the guns of the army, while the remaining two-thirds bombarded the enemy's battery positions. Because the French First Army had few tanks, at zero hour a standing barrage was to be put down on the enemy trenches and batteries and maintained for 45 minutes, when the advance of the XXXIst Corps was to begin. The aircraft at the disposal of the Fourth Army numbered 800, and of the French First Army 1,104. As before the battle the opposing German armies had only 365 machines, the allies held the mastery in the air. Besides attempting to hold it during the battle, other tasks of the R.A.F. were to co-operate with the attacking troops, to bomb and machine-gun enemy ground targets; to supply ammunition to the forward attackers, and to bomb the rail centres at Chaulnes, Roye, Nesle and Péronne, as well as the crossings over the Somme.

The task given to the Cavalry Corps and the 3rd Tank Brigade

[1] The creeping barrage was introduced in 1916 during the battle of the Somme.

was to push through the leading infantry of the Canadian and Australian Corps at the first opportunity and to secure the Amiens outer defences and hold them until relieved. They were then to advance south-eastward on Roye–Chaulnes, cut the enemy communications and ease the advance of the French.

It was a fantastic task and strongly criticized by the Commander and General Staff of the Tank Corps, who held that tanks and horses could not work together successfully, because tanks were bullet-proof and horses were not. It was suggested that a better way to help the advance of the French would be to hold the two Whippet battalions back until the infantry and Mark V tanks had broken through, and then to move them forward from Villers-Bretonneux towards Rosières, swing right and sweep southward on a wide front through the rear of the German Second and Eighteenth Armies, and eventually emerge south-east of Montdidier. General Rawlinson considered this manœuvre too risky and it was decided to keep to the original task.[1]

Finally, secrecy and surprise were to be the soul of the attack. Troops were to remain unacquainted with the aim and attack orders until 24 to 36 hours before zero hour; all movements were to be made by night; forward reconnaissances and artillery registration were prohibited; normal work was to be carried on; the *pavé* roads were to be strewn with sand or straw; dumps were to be camouflaged; and a strong air barrage maintained to restrict enemy observation into rear areas. In spite of these precautions, early on July 29, the 5th Australian Division, then occupying the sector north of the Somme, carried out an asinine raid and captured 138 prisoners. On August 6 the all but inevitable retaliation followed. The German 27th (Württemberg) Division launched a violent attack on a 4,000-yard front against the inner flanks of the 18th and 58th Divisions of the IIIrd Corps – now in line – penetrated to a depth of 800 yards, and captured 236 prisoners. This attack completely upset IIIrd Corps preparations, and, as will be seen, led to serious consequences on August 8.

Between July 29 and early on August 8, without a hitch 14 infantry divisions, three cavalry divisions, three brigades of tanks and more than 2,000 guns were concentrated east of Amiens on a front of some 10 miles and within striking distance of an unsuspecting enemy. It was a triumph of organization and staff work.

[1] See *Memoirs of an Unconventional Soldier*, p. 299.

The night of August 7–8 was moonless and fine, but at 3 a.m. a ground mist began to rise, and when a little after four o'clock the tanks slowly moved forward from their assembly positions to the infantry starting line, it had grown so dense that visibility fell to nil. Exactly at 4.20 a.m., in one resounding crash, 2,000 guns opened fire. A hurricane of shells swept down on the Amiens outer defences and enemy batteries, while the creeping barrage fell 200 yards ahead of the leading tanks and infantry, to move forward at first at the rate of 100 yards every three minutes.

Although the mist compelled the attacking troops to break up into groups, and prevented air operations until 9 a.m., south of the Somme the surprise was complete. Led forward, because of the mist, by the first wave of skirmishers, the leading tanks advanced, and were followed by small columns of infantry in single file, behind which came the supports in company groups. No-man's-land, some 500 yards wide, was rapidly crossed, and the first line of the enemy swept back in rout.

On the right flank the French were late in starting, but when they did, the Germans were surprised by this extension of the battle front. Moreuil was occupied by 9.30 a.m. Then a fresh bombardment was opened for three hours and twenty minutes, and the French IXth Corps, on the right of the XXXIst, began to advance, but soon after was held on the Avre. Later, the XXXIst took Mézières, then halted for a further bombardment, and at 5.30 p.m. advanced again. At about nine o'clock this corps occupied Fresnoy, but failed to take le Quesnel. When we remember that the French had few tanks, they did not do so badly; for at a cost of 3,500 casualties they captured over 5,000 of the enemy and 161 guns.

Meanwhile, on the left, the advance of the IIIrd Corps was at once met by a barrage of gas shells, which compelled the attackers to move forward in their gas masks – a most exhausting task. Yet, in spite of heavy casualties, by 7.40 a.m. the first objective was reached in places; but from then on further attempts to advance were frustrated, and the result was that the left flank of the Australians, south of the Somme, suffered severely from the enfilade fire of the enemy batteries posted about Chipilly. This failure by the IIIrd Corps to fulfil its task was largely, if not entirely, due to the Australian raid on July 29.[1]

On the Canadian front, the leading brigades of the 3rd, 1st,

[1] See British Official History, 1918, vol. IV, p. 154.

and 2nd Canadian Divisions occupied the first objective at 7.45 a.m., and the second at about 11 a.m., when the 4th Canadian Division came up to move through them. Few German guns were then firing, and the rout of the enemy infantry was so complete that many officers present "thought that armoured vehicles could have gone anywhere."[1] This was true, for, as will be related, one was fortunate enough to break away from the cavalry and prove it to be so. From the second objective the Mark V Star tanks,[2] which carried machine-gun teams, were sent forward with the 4th Canadian Division to occupy the third objective. At the same time the 3rd Cavalry Division and the 3rd Tank Brigade were ordered to push ahead and seize Rosières. The final Canadian advance began at 12.40 p.m., and by 3.30 p.m. the third objective was reached along its whole front, except at le Quesnel. Undoubtedly this village would also have been taken if the French had not been held at le Fresnoy.

In the meantime, on the Australian front,[3] the 2nd Australian Division on the right and the 3rd Division on the left swept forward, and by 6.20 a.m. had captured the whole of the first objective. A halt was then made to allow the 4th and 5th Divisions to come up and push through to the second and third objectives. When these divisions moved forward at 8.20 a.m. they were accompanied by the 15th Tank Battalion, and the 1st Cavalry Brigade and 16 Whippet tanks were sent ahead, as well as the 17th Tank (Armoured Car) Battalion, whose cars had been towed over the broken roads by tanks. By 9.15 a.m. the second objective was reached by the 5th Division, but the 4th, on its left, was delayed by the German batteries on the Chipilly ridge, and did not occupy their part of the second objective until 10.30 a.m. The leading brigades of the 5th Division pressed on and reached the third objective between 10.30 a.m. and 11 a.m.; but again because of German enfilade fire the 4th Division was delayed, and only after it had suffered heavy casualties and had lost many of its tanks was it able to gain its final objective, except on the extreme left.

Throughout the Canadian and Australian advance the tanks

---

[1] *Ibid.*, p. 52.
[2] They were under-engined, slow, cumbersome and conspicuous. The teams carried suffered severely from exhaust gas and often were quite unfit for action when disembarked.
[3] The 1st Australian Division only arrived from the north on August 7, and was held in corps reserve.

proved of the utmost value in overcoming enemy machine-gun resistance. Nevertheless, as at Cambrai, their main effect was on morale. Faced by a weapon which they could not halt, the German infantry felt disarmed and instinctively took to their heels. They did so not because the fire of the tank six-pounders and machine-guns slaughtered them—it was too erratic to do so—but because the continuous forward movement of the tanks created a feeling of irresistible power. When tanks were faced with artillery, it was a different question, for during the day 109 tanks were knocked out by gunfire.[1] This was approximately 25 per cent. of the total engaged, a percentage which remained fairly constant for each day's tank action during the remainder of the war. But concerning the future rôle of tanks, the most instructive lesson on August 8 was the conspicuous failure of the attempt to combine them with cavalry.

As was foreseen by the Tank Corps General Staff, this combination proved impossible. They did not help each other; they impeded each other. Because the horsemen could move faster than the Whippets, the latter were left behind during the approach march, and because the cavalry could not face rifle and machine-gun fire, the Whippets forged ahead during the attack. The result was a continuous shuttle movement in which tanks advanced, cavalry retired, and tanks turned back to bring forward the cavalry. Also, because the Whippets were given no fixed objectives, they became little more than armoured guerrillas roaming from one enemy machine-gun to another. Although on the 8th glowing reports were received of cavalry charges[2] and actions around Rosières and Chaulnes, the bulk of the horsemen never crossed the Blue Line, although they did round up considerable numbers of the enemy left in rear by the impetuous attack. Long before dusk they were compelled to retire in order to water their horses, and with them went the Whippets!

It was apparent at the time that had the 3rd and 6th Tank Battalions been followed by infantry in lorries, which, like the armoured cars, could have been towed forward near to the Blue Line by the Whippets, and then had the infantry advanced on foot behind the tanks, it is probable that the high ground about Lihons and Chaulnes would have been occupied during the

---

[1] Nearly all, however, were repairable.
[2] There was one near Harbonnières, but the enemy turned out to be a German transport column. Forty-six of its men were killed and captured by the 1st Cavalry Brigade.

afternoon of the 8th. Had this ground been occupied, then, because the sole railway which fed the German Second and Eighteenth Armies ran from Chaulnes, *via* Roye, southward, the whole of the German forces facing the French First Army would almost certainly have fallen back.

Two incidents during the battle support this possibility. The first was the action of the 17th Tank (Armoured Car) Battalion, commanded by Lieutenant-Colonel E. J. Carter, and the second the action of a single Whippet which became detached from the cavalry and carried out a raid on its own.

The first incident occurred after the armoured cars had been towed to Warfusée-Abancourt – a little to the west of the Green Line – and unaccompanied by other troops had moved forward to Foucaucourt, some four miles east of the Blue Line, the third and final objective. There they surprised a German headquarters and threw it into panic. Under cover of this confusion the cars turned north and south of the Amiens–Brie road. Those which turned south met large columns of transport, and mounted officers and teams of horses, presumably belonging to the German corps headquarters at Framerville. These were fired on at short range – four officers were shot down by a single burst of fire. Soon after this the German headquarters was reached and the Australian Corps flag run up over the house which a few minutes before had been occupied by the German corps commander. About the same time one of the cars sighted a German train on the Amiens–Chaulnes railway and put it out of action. Later it was captured by the cavalry.

The cars which had turned northward entered Proyart and Chuignolles; two moved up to the Somme. At Proyart, German troops were found at dinner; the cars shot them down and scattered them in all directions. Next, they moved westward and saw in the distance masses of the enemy driven from their trenches by the Australians. To surprise them the cars hid in the outskirts of Proyart, and when they approached they rapidly moved forward and shot great numbers. The enemy scattered before the cars at Proyart, and made across country toward Chuignolles, but there the Germans were met by other cars and again fired on and dispersed. Near Chuignolles, one car obtained "running practice" with its machine-guns at a lorry full of troops until it ran into a ditch. Other cars followed German transport without being suspected until they opened fire at point-blank range.

Although more than half the armoured cars were out of action by the evening of the 8th, there were no casualties among their crews sufficiently serious to require evacuation.

The second incident was equally dramatic. "Musical Box" was a Whippet tank of B Company of the 6th Tank Battalion, and was commanded by Lieutenant C. B. Arnold. On the morning of the 8th it passed through the 2nd Australian Division, moved on parallel with the Amiens–Brie railway, and lost touch with its accompanying cavalry. Its first adventure was between Warfusée-Abancourt and Bayonvillers, where it attacked a German battery in the rear and put it out of action. It then moved on toward Guillaucourt; advanced eastward along the railway and helped two cavalry patrols; and then, as it approached Harbonnières it opened fire on a party of the enemy packing kits and killed and wounded some 60 of them. Next, at ranges of from 200 to 600 yards, it fired on lines of Germans as they retired, and after shooting up several columns of enemy transport, it caught fire and was put out of action.[1]

The confusion caused by these 12 armoured cars and one Whippet tank was phenomenal, and should it be multiplied by the number of Whippets which took the field on the 8th, it is probably no exaggeration to assume that, had they been concentrated around Chaulnes, they would have ruined the whole German command and administration from Albert to Montdidier and from Montdidier to Noyon, a front of some 50 miles.

In spite of this might-have-been, the battle of August 8 was the greatest allied triumph since the Marne. At a cost of some 12,000 men the two attacking armies had killed and wounded 13,000 of their enemy; captured 15,000; taken 400 guns; and had driven right through the German front. All that remained for the allies to do was to follow up their initial success with relentless exploitation.

This was the one thing for which they were not prepared. Also, the old Somme battlefield dictated that mobile warfare should give way to trench warfare. Although the tank had been designed as a trench warfare weapon, its true rôle lay in mobile warfare, and of the 300 tanks which still remained operative, the crews of those which had been engaged were exhausted, and all tanks which had been in action required repairs, munitions, and fuel. The result was that only 145 could be made ready for the

[1] For Arnold's full report, see *Tanks in the Great War*, pp. 230–235.

9th. Meanwhile, because Ludendorff was opposed to a withdrawal to the Hindenberg Line – which probably would have been the wisest course – six German reserve divisions had been rushed forward to reinforce the Second and Eighteenth Armies, and seven other reserve divisions were on their way.

For the 9th, General Rawlinson's orders were for the Fourth Army to advance to the line Roye–Chaulnes–Bray sur Somme-Dernancourt, while the French came up to Roye. But as his Chief of Staff writes: "Owing, however, to the difficulties of communication and other causes, the general movement did not begin till 11 a.m., and in the case of some brigades not until 1 p.m. As a result, the fighting was of a very disjointed nature throughout the day, the attacks of the various divisions and brigades starting at different times. Some of the attacks were covered by artillery or supported by tanks; others were carried out by infantry without support of the other arms."[1] Further, on the right flank the French attack showed little life.[2] Nevertheless, by nightfall, the battle front had been advanced to approximately the line Bouchoir-Rouvroy–Méharicourt–Framerville–Méricourt–Dernancourt.

On the night of the 9th–10th the Australian Corps was ordered to extend its left north of the Somme, and the 32nd Division was moved up to support the 3rd Canadian Division. On the 10th the objectives of the three British corps were to be the same as on the previous day.

On August 10 the battle front was extended by the French Third Army, on the right of the First, which joined in the offensive. As on the 9th, there was little co-ordination on the Fourth Army front and brigades moved forward piecemeal. German resistance had stiffened considerably, and more reserve divisions were thrown in. On the French First and Third Army fronts, because the German Eighteenth Army was now falling back, the advance was rapid; but on the Fourth Army front the Canadian Corps advanced no more than two miles, the Australians less, and the IIIrd Corps gained the whole of its first day's objective.

It was apparent to Haig and Rawlinson that along the whole of the Fourth Army front the offensive was petering out, and early on the 10th, in order to end it and reopen it further north, Haig sent a staff officer to General Sir Henry Horne, commanding the

[1] *The Story of the Fourth Army*, Major-General Sir Archibald Montgomery (n.d.), p. 52.
[2] *La Bataille de Montdidier*, Commandant M. Daille (1922), p. 197.

British First Army, to hasten the plan of an operation already in hand to capture La Bassée and the Aubers' ridge in conjunction with an advance of the Second Army against Kemmel and of the Third Army against Bapaume.

Soon after these instructions had been sent, Marshal Foch arrived at Haig's advanced headquarters at Wiry with a directive to push the offensive eastward in the direction of Ham. Because this would mean the continuance of a wholly frontal battle of attrition against ever-increasing odds, Haig proposed to slow the attack east of Amiens, and while his First and Second Armies made ready, to transfer the offensive to Sir Julian Byng's Third Army, which was in line on the left of the Fourth, with the right flank of the Germans opposing the Fourth Army and the French First Army as its target. But Foch was confident that the Germans were so demoralized that little resistance was to be expected from them. He had arrived at this conclusion because of the little resistance then offered to the French First and Third Armies. It would appear that he was unaware that the German Eighteenth Army and part of the Second were in retreat. Haig also would appear not to have known this, and half convinced by Foch, he ordered the directive to be carried out–much to Rawlinson's annoyance.

On the evening of August 10 the Fourth Army orders were for the IIIrd Corps to remain on the defensive on the 11th while the Canadian and Australian Corps pressed on to the Somme between Ham and Péronne and established bridgeheads on its right bank. At the same time the left of the French First Army was ordered to occupy Ham.

It became apparent on the 11th that both Haig and Rawlinson had been right and that Foch had misjudged the situation. "Owing to the increase of hostile artillery fire, the lack of tanks and sufficient artillery support," writes General Montgomery, "the Canadian attacks were cancelled by Sir Arthur Currie early on the 11th."[1] The Australians, after severe fighting, captured Lihons, and about noon, on the heels of a heavy bombardment, the Germans launched a series of determined counter-attacks against Chilly and between Damery and Fouquescourt on the old British front line of February, 1917. Although all were beaten back, they were a sure sign that it was time to end the battle.

At 3 p.m. Rawlinson held a conference of corps commanders

[1] *The Story of the Fourth Army*, p. 61.

at Villers-Bretonneux, at which it was decided to postpone offensive operations until August 15, and on the 12th the Cavalry Corps was withdrawn into reserve.

Thus, officially, the battle of Amiens was ended. Nevertheless, when Haig visited Foch at Sarcus on the 14th, again the latter pressed him to attack the enemy on the Chaulnes–Roye front. Haig writes in his diary: "I declined to do so because they could only be taken after heavy casualties in men and tanks. . . . I spoke to Foch quite straightly and let him understand that *I was responsible to my Government and fellow citizens for the handling of the British forces.* F's. attitude at once changed and he said all he wanted was early information of my intentions. . . . But notwithstanding what he now said, Foch and all his Staff had been most insistent for the last five days that I should press on along the south bank and capture the Somme bridges above Péronne, regardless of German opposition, and British losses."[1]

The casualties of this great battle were: French, 24,232; British, 22,202; and German estimated at 75,000. The French captured 11,373 men and 259 guns, and the British 18,500 and 240 guns. In killed and wounded, the losses of the Allies and the Germans were almost identical.[2]

Although neither Foch nor Haig realized then how decisive the battle had been, the events of the 8th alone were sufficient to convince not only the German generals, but also their soldiers, that it was a catastrophe. Whereas the former were already engaged upon preparations for a spring offensive, including the use of several thousand tanks, General Ludendorff acclaimed the 8th to be "the black day of the German Army in the history of this war."[3] Nor was he alone in this. The author of the German official monograph on this battle thus describes the situation on that fateful day: "As the sun set on 8th August on the battlefield the greatest defeat which the German Army suffered since the beginning of the war was an accomplished fact."[4] These expressions were not the mere afterthoughts of peacetime reflection; they were the heartfelt outbursts of the moment. As General von Cramon, German Military Plenipotentiary at the Austrian G.H.Q. records: "The turn of events on the Western Front had

[1] *The Private Papers of Douglas Haig, 1914–1919* (edit. Robert Blake, 1952), pp. 313–324.
[2] *British Official History, 1918*, vol. IV, pp. 154–155.
[3] *My War Memories*, vol. II, p. 679.
[4] Quoted in *British Official History, 1918*, vol. IV, p. 88.

a devastating effect upon Austria. The belief that German might could accomplish miracles was so deeply rooted in the mass of the Austrian people, that disillusionment struck them like a sledge-hammer. The Emperor himself was profoundly affected. He summoned me to his presence and informed me that the repulse on the Piave had not produced on his people an impression so overwhelming as the change in the situation on the Western Front."[1]

The nearly universal reason alleged for the German defeat was the employment of tanks in masses by the Allied Powers. But although the tank played a leading part in the German *débâcle*, had there not been deeper reasons, in all probability the results of the battle would have been not much greater than those after the battle of Cambrai.

Of the many causes of the German collapse, first and foremost stood the blockade. By the summer of 1918, if it had not been for the wheat of Rumania and the Ukraine the Central Powers would have been starved into capitulation. As it was, even with these extraneous supplies, their peoples were reduced to starvation level, and as their stomachs shrank their hearts sank. Further, although the German soldier was better fed than his civilian brother, his morale was shattered by the realization that the succession of offensives since March 21 had been in vain, and that their result was a defensive which could see no offensive dawn. Wedged as the German soldier was between his starving family and a hopeless future, it is little wonder that Ludendorff should record that during the battle the retiring troops shouted at the advancing reinforcements: "Blacklegs, you're prolonging the war!"[2]

Such was the gloomy background of Germany against which the power of the tank scintillated, and although Sir James Edmonds correctly points out that the material effect of the tank was small, because its moral effect was great – so he writes – "It has pleased the Germans to attribute their defeat in the field to the tank. The excuse will not bear examination."[3] What is missed here is what Colonel Brackenbury saw so clearly 40 years earlier: "moral effect is the object aimed at in battle." It was not the killing power of the tank which caused the author of the German

---

[1] *Quatre ans au G.Q.G. Austro-Hongrois*, p. 285.
[2] *My War Memories*, vol. II, p. 683.
[3] *British Official History, 1918*, vol. IV, p. iv.

monograph to entitle it *"Die Katastrophe des 8 August, 1918,"* it was the terror it instilled; it precipitated not the final retirement, but the initial rout. Without the tank there would have been no surprise commensurate with the one achieved on the morning of the 8th, and it was the suddenness of the attack which detonated the panic. Added to this, the feeling of utter powerlessness of the soldier on foot when faced by an antagonist that no rifle or machine-gun bullet could halt instinctively led him to exaggerate the danger in order to mitigate the ignominy of immediate surrender or flight.

These exaggerations flooded the German Press. As an example, Baron von Ardenne wrote in the *Berliner Tageblatt*: "An attack by tanks has something appalling and demoniacal about it. It might terrify the superstitious . . . in the battle now raging the enemy made use of 500 armoured monsters. In addition to these there were numerous Whippet tanks which broke through our lines more quickly than an express train"(!) In a German Second Army order of August 25 we read: "People with anxious temperaments [usually every soldier under fire] saw everywhere squadrons of tanks, masses of cavalry and thick lines of infantry." A German prisoner said: "The officers and men in many cases come to consider the approach of tanks a sufficient explanation for not fighting. Their sense of duty is sufficient to make them fight against infantry, but if tanks appear, many feel they are justified in surrendering."[1] As will be seen, in the Second World War identical psychological incidents abound.

Ludendorff made no mistake over the situation the tank created. "Everything I had feared, and of which I had so often given warning," he writes, "had here, in one place, become a reality. Our war machine was no longer efficient. Our fighting power had suffered, even though the great majority of divisions still fought heroically.

"The 8th of August put the decline of that fighting power beyond all doubt and in such a situation as regards reserves, I had no hope of finding a strategic expedient whereby to turn the situation to our advantage. On the contrary, I became convinced that we were now without that safe foundation for the plans of G.H.Q., on which I had hitherto been able to build, at least so far as this is possible in war. Leadership now assumed, as I then stated, the character of an irresponsible game of chance, a thing

[1] *Weekly Tank Notes*, 10th August–2nd November, 1918, pp. 9, 14, 25, 26.

I have always considered fatal. The fate of the German people was for me too high a stake. The war must be ended."[1]

On August 11, the German Emperor summoned a conference of the senior army leaders. It assembled at Avesnes, Hindenburg's headquarters, and there he uttered the historic words: "I see that we must strike a balance. We have nearly reached the limit of our power of resistance. The war must be ended."[2] Two days later another conference assembled at Spa, at which Ludendorff reviewed the military situation and explained that "as it was no longer possible to force the enemy to sue for peace by an offensive," and "as the defensive alone could hardly achieve that object . . . the termination of the war would have to be brought about by diplomacy." The Emperor instructed the Secretary of State, von Hintze, "to open up peace negotiations, if possible, through the medium of the Queen of the Netherlands."[3]

Meanwhile the explosion of August 8–11 had detonated "the final battle of the world war," as Ludendorff calls it. It comprised a series of battles directed against the two sides of the great western salient; because of this a return was made to the strategy of Marshal Joffre.

On August 20 battle was opened simultaneously by the French Tenth and Third Armies between Soissons and Roye and by the British Third Army north of Albert. Immediately after this the front was extended south of the Somme by the British Fourth Army. In rapid succession battle followed battle, and on September 12 the American First Army joined in the fray and set out to reduce the St. Mihiel salient. The war in the west had entered its final phase; to use Foch's expression, it was until November 11 to be "*Tout le monde à la bataille.*"

On September 26, between the Meuse and Rheims, the American First Army and the French Fourth Army attacked. On the 27th, between Epéhy and Lens, the British Third and First Armies attacked. On the 28th, from Armentières to the Channel, the British Second Army, the Belgian Army, and the French Sixth Army attacked. And on the 29th, between La Fère and Epéhy, the French First Army and British Fourth Army attacked. Meanwhile, in Macedonia the Balkan front was broken by the allied armies under General Franchet d'Espérey, and

---

[1] *My War Memories*, vol. II, p. 684.
[2] Quoted in *British Official History*, vol. IV, p. 140.
[3] *My War Memories*, vol. II, pp. 684–687.

Bulgaria asked for a suspension of hostilities; on September 19 the battle of Megiddo was opened by General Sir Edmund Allenby, Damascus was entered on October 1, and on the 30th Turkey was out of the war.

Overwhelmed by defeat, at six o'clock on the afternoon of September 28, Ludendorff entered Field-Marshal Hindenburg's room and suggested that an armistice could no longer be delayed. "We did not consider any abandonment of territory in the East," he writes, "thinking that the Entente would be fully conscious of the dangers threatening them as well as ourselves from Bolshevism."[1] In this he was mistaken; nevertheless, on October 5, President Wilson's Fourteen Points were accepted as the basis for armistice negotiations.

[1] *Ibid.*, vol. II, p. 721.

CHRONICLE 8

The struggle between Italy and Austria

When the pistol shot in Serajevo detonated the war, Italy was in no way prepared to enter it, either as a member of the Triple Alliance, or on the side of the Entente. She was disorganized militarily by her recent war against the Turks in Tripolitania and distraught politically by Socialists, Republicans, and other anti-monarchists and through force of circumstances neutrality was imposed upon her. There were some who held that if she stayed out of the war she would forfeit her prestige as a first-class Power, and among them were two forceful men, the poet Gabrielle d'Annunzio and a journalist then rising to fame – Benito Mussolini. The former appealed to the intellectuals, the latter to the masses; together they formed a powerful partnership.

When the war began Mussolini was editor of *Avanti*, the official organ of the Socialist party. He was the son of a blacksmith, and was born in the province of Forli on July 29, 1883. On November 15, 1914, he resigned his editorship of *Avanti*, founded his own paper *Il Popolo d'Italia*, and 10 days later was expelled from the Socialist party. He then grouped his followers into the *"Fasci rivoluzionari d'azione,"* and thereby planted the seed of a new political theory, which within 10 years was to challenge both liberal-democracy and Communism, not only in Italy but throughout Europe.

It was the energy and drive of these two men more than other factors which awakened a war spirit in the people of Italy, and coupled with English pressure, the imminent attack on the Dardanelles, and the offer of a loan of £50 million to be negotiated in London, Italy was persuaded on April 26, 1915, to throw in her lot with the Allied Powers and declare war on Austria.

Although better prepared in the spring of 1915 than they had been in the autumn of 1914, the Italians were still far from ready to wage a war of the first magnitude. Also, the frontier with Austria was an exceedingly difficult one to use as a springboard for attack, not only because of the Trentino salient, the apex of which lay only 15 miles north of Verona, but because for 300 of its 350 miles it was mountainous country. The remaining 50 miles ran through the Carso, immediately north of the Gulf of Venice, which was also girt about with hilly land. The outcome was that the Italian commander-in-chief, General Luigi Cadorna, born in 1850 and a soldier of considerable ability, was compelled by strategical circumstances to attack this narrow and open front; he trusted that the Austrians would meanwhile be held by the Russians in the north and by the Serbians in the south. Once war was declared these possibilities vanished; not only did Russia give way before the onslaughts of Mackensen, but Serbia was soon rendered helpless.

On June 23 Cadorna opened his offensive with the first battle of the Isonzo, and from then until the summer of 1917, 11 battles of the Isonzo were fought in all, as well as a number of engagements in the Trentino. In 1915 these operations cost the Italian armies 280,000 casualties, in 1916 they cost 483,000, and in 1917, 323,000; yet little or nothing was gained beyond killing, wounding and capturing an equivalent number of Austrians. This butchery was bound to lead to disaster, and especially in Italy where the civil population was morally ill-prepared to withstand the stresses and strains of war. One million casualties in a little over two years' fighting appalled the people, and it was not ignored by the Socialists and other non-interventionalists. Every man killed and every man wounded sent up their stock and steadily brought toward bankruptcy that of the attrition-mongers. What the latter could not grasp was that the validity of their theory of weighing victory in tons of human flesh depended upon which side was morally the better able to endure. The moral effect of the attrition theory more than its physical effect was the determining factor. Here Italy was at a discount.

As this question of national morale forms the background of the greatest Italian military disaster in modern history, which in its turn formed the background of the greatest Italian military success – the Battle of Vittorio-Veneto – it should be examined.

First and foremost, it was a question of government. Since the opening of the war no steps had been taken to consolidate or invigorate the people. The government retained a policy of *laisser faire* – a government of hoping for the best. No attempts were made to suppress subversive propaganda. For instance, though a Press censorship was established, the Socialist *Avanti*, which daily contained articles to insinuate that the war was a war of the *signori* and the plutocrats, was not only distributed among the troops, but was also thrown or dropped into the trenches by the enemy; while according to Villari, Giolitti's (the former Prime Minister) organ "*La Stampa* of Turin . . . systematically pursued an insinuating, carefully guarded defeatist policy, daily instilling anti-patriotic poison into the minds of its numerous readers."

The more aggressive the Socialists grew, the more did the Government hope to kill them with kindness; as if vermin could be destroyed by petting. What was the result? The audacity of subversion startled the people into believing what they were told. When the deputy Treves proclaimed: "Next winter not another man in the trenches," his words thundered through city, village and homestead, and when coupled with the rising cost of living and food scarcity, they rotted the morale of the people. Added to this, when the Government roused itself, its action was almost invariably as disastrous as its lethargy. For instance, when in 1917 an organized riot among the munition workers occurred at Turin, thousands of these men as a punishment were sent to the front in the vicinity of Caporetto. George M. Trevelyan says of this: "I know from what I have been told by those who were in Caporetto . . . that the soldiers made no secret of their intentions, and that many of their officers lived in fear of their own men, locking themselves up carefully at night."

Two other forces, both international in character, helped to accentuate this moral rot. These were the Catholic Church and Bolshevism, now in its first stage of aggressiveness. The priests, led by the Pope, preached defeatism; the last thing the papacy wanted was a really united Italian nation. The Bolsheviks, intent upon the disruption of all organized peoples, aimed at a somewhat similar end. Signor Villari writes:

"The Socialist and Communist organizers at once proceeded to encourage the belief that if the Russian revolution, which had practically put an end to the war on the Eastern Front long before Brest-Litovsk, were imitated in Italy, peace would be obtained on the Italian front as well. They hoped to bring about this result by means of a military mutiny, and looked forward to unlimited plunder and power for themselves. Some of them, no doubt, were in the pay of the German and Austrian secret service, as was proved by certain documents discovered by the Italian secret service in the Austrian Consulate at Zurich, but most of them were inspired merely by personal ambitions, while perhaps a few may have been sincere in their convictions. . . . At a meeting of the Socialist party directorate in Florence, in the summer of 1917, a group representing a minority decided on a policy of whole-minded solidarity with the Russian Bolshevists and undertook to try to destroy the fighting spirit of the Italian Army. . . ."

This was comparatively easy, because in mountain warfare formations and units are usually split into small groups and these can readily be influenced by secret agents. Also, as the war dragged on, officers of the old army were killed off and many of those who replaced them failed to understand the necessity of maintaining human touch with their men. Besides, General Cadorna was a mediocre psychologist who never seems to have grasped the demoralizing influences of static warfare.

1917 was a year of moral attrition for all the Allied Powers: Russia was in a state of anarchy; the German submarine campaign was at its height; the British Army in France was submerged in the swamps of Flanders; and the discipline of the French Army was so deeply fissured that it did little during the summer of that year.

In this general picture of collapse, Italy and Austria stood in the fore rank. Both their armies had been bled white by incessant attacks; yet their intense tactical activities had been so far no more than the marking of time on one corpse-strewn battlefield until, like the skidding wheels of two great Juggernaut cars, they failed to grip the solid soil of victory and dug themselves deeper and deeper into the mud of a helpless hopelessness. At length, on August 25, while a bloody battle still raged on the Bainsizza plateau, Austria appealed to Germany for aid, and four days later General von Waldstatten submitted a plan of campaign to General von Arz, Chief of the Austrian General Staff, for a combined Austro-German attack on the Plezzo–Tolmino–Gorizia front.

This front was already held by 23 Austrian divisions and 1,800 guns. Von Waldstatten suggested that 14 more divisions should be added – seven Austrian and seven German – and a further 1,000 guns; and that the main attack should be made between Plezzo and Tolmino against the Italian Second Army in order to drive it and the Italian Third Army on its left over the Taglia-mento and thence toward Padua.

This plan was accepted by Field-Marshal von Hindenburg

and he placed General von Below in charge of the operation. The attack was to open on October 24, and was to be preceded by a short, sharp and intense artillery bombardment, such as that which had been so successful at Riga against the Russians. Although between October 16–20 General Cadorna received full information of this from Austrian deserters, against his orders the Italian front line was strongly reinforced instead of thinned out. Further, the reserve lines had been dug much too far forward; they were so close to the front line that an initial bombardment could strike both simultaneously.

At 2 a.m., on October 24, the Austro-German bombardment was opened and a deluge of gas shells fell upon the Italian front and reserve lines. At 9.30 a.m. the front of the IVth Corps of the Second Army was penetrated at Fornace, and at 4 p.m. the village of Caporetto – after which the battle was named – was occupied by the Germans.

It is not necessary here to examine in detail what followed; instead the results of this penetration will be outlined. On October 26 Cadorna ordered the whole of his Second Army to fall back on the Tagliamento; the next day he instructed the Third Army, commanded by the Duke of Aosta, to do likewise, which it did in good order in spite of the rout of the Second Army.

On October 31 the Austro-German forces reached the Tagliamento; on November 4 their right wing swung round to face Poredenone; on the 6th the river Livenza was gained; on the 7th another swing round was made by the right wing, this time on Conegliano; and on the 9th and 10th the left bank of the river Piave was reached. There the attack petered out within 20 miles of Venice.

Though many of the Italian columns had fought staunchly during the disastrous retreat, Socialist propaganda accomplished its end in the Second Army. Its results were catastrophic, for although the killed and wounded in the battle numbered no more than 10,000 and 30,000 respectively, 265,000 men surrendered as prisoners, and 3,152 guns, 3,000 machine-guns and 1,732 trench mortars were lost as well as vast quantities of army stores.

When the news of this disaster was made known, which it was immediately, for General Cadorna in his rage issued a *communiqué* to tell the truth about the betrayal, the Italian people were stunned. Then occurred the miracle of the war – Italy arose from the ashes of her defeat.

"Suddenly," writes Trevelyan, "as by a flash of lightning, men and women in Turin and Florence, and in the remotest villages of north and south, saw what they had done by their murmurings, their cryings for peace when there was no peace. . . ." And in this startling moment the moral decay of a generation was pulled from the shoulders of the nation and Italy girt herself for the final battle of the *Risorgimento*. By right of prestige, the first Italian to sound this national rally was King Victor Emmanuel who, on November 19, proclaimed: "As neither My House nor My People, united in a single spirit, have ever wavered in the face of danger, so even now We look adversity in the face without flinching. . . . Citizens and soldiers, be a single army. All cowardice is treachery, all discord is treachery, all recrimination is treachery."

D'Annunzio also spoke, so did Mussolini, until in every city and village arose a Peter the Hermit. Thus the whole nation fell into line, while France and England at length realized that Venetia was a vital part of the theatre of war, rushed 11 divisions southward, and at Rapallo laid the foundations of that unity of command which, strange to say, demanded yet another allied catastrophe – that of March, 1918 – for its creation. Cadorna was replaced by General Armado Diaz, a man of lesser ability but of greater human understanding who, supported by his sub-chief of staff, General Pietro Badoglio, began to organize a new army of stronger moral character than the one that had been lost.

CHAPTER 8

The Battle of Vittorio-Veneto, 1918

When he assumed his appointment as Chief of the General Staff, General Diaz's intention was to open an offensive, but when toward the middle of May, 1918, he learnt that the Austrians were preparing to do the same, he decided not to forestall their attack but to wait.

The Austrian plan was a compromise, and like most compromises it was bad. Field-Marshal Conrad von Hötzendorf, former Austrian chief of general staff and in command of the Tenth and Eleventh Armies on the Trentino front, strongly urged that the attack should be made on the Asiago plateau while Boroevic, in command of the Sixth and Isonzo Armies on the lower Piave, carried out a demonstration. But as Boroevic did not intend to play second fiddle to Conrad he demanded the opposite. The outcome was that General Arz, the Austrian chief of general staff, who was more of an aide-de-camp to the Emperor than a chief of staff, solved the problem by accepting both plans, but without the demonstrations.[1] Because of this we are told that the offensive was to consist of "a single attack, carried out on two fronts."[2] While Conrad's attack was to be made astride the Brenta to force a rapid passage through the mountain front and encircle such portions of the Italian forces as were found behind the Piave, Boroevic's attack was to be directed toward Treviso-Mestre, with the line of the river Bacchiglione as its immediate objective.

No sooner was this offensive agreed, than the usual flow of deserters began from the Austrian to the Italian lines. General Gathorne-Hardy, chief of staff to Lord Cavan, who commanded the XIVth Corps, tells us that: "Shortly before the offensive of June, 1918, three Austrian officers entered the British lines, accompanied by their servants carrying their portmanteaus. Further and detailed information was always available through

---

[1] See *Quatre ans au G.Q.G. Austro-Hongrois*, General A. von Cramon (French edit.), pp. 270–272. Cramon was the German military plenipotentiary at the Austro-Hungarian Supreme Command Headquarters.
[2] *The Battle of the Piave*, issued by the Supreme Command of the Royal Italian Army (English edit., 1924), p. 17.

the British listening sets. Experience had in no way restricted the enemy in the use of his field telephones. From the latter source alone, the most minute details of the coming bombardment and assault were in the hands of the Italian Command previous to the attack. . . ."[1] Nevertheless, Arz was confident of success, and to Field-Marshal Hindenburg he wrote: "I am confident that, as a result of our offensive which must bring us to the Adige, we shall achieve the military dissolution of Italy."[2]

At 3 a.m. on June 15, the battle, to become known as the battle of the Piave, opened with a short and intense bombardment; briefly it may be summarized as follows: Conrad's attack on the Asiago plateau was checked almost at once, while Boroevic's thrust in the Montello sector gained little headway. Next day deluges of rain greatly impeded the Austrians in their attempt to cross the Piave, and although violent attacks were made on the 17th, they broke down on the 18th. Then, on the following day, the Italians launched their counter-attack, which was pressed until July 6, when not an Austrian soldier remained on the western bank of the Piave. In short, the Austrian attack was a complete fiasco which cost them 150,000 men in killed, wounded and prisoners.[3]

Trevelyan is of opinion that this defeat "may be added to the long list of 'decisive battles of the world'."[4] In a way he is right, for not only was it the first great allied victory of 1918, but Vittorio-Veneto was founded on it. In his turn Mr. Lloyd George considered that, "it came at the most fateful hour of the whole year,"[5] which is also right, because it deprived Germany of hoped-for Austrian support on the western front. Although Hindenburg asked for six Austrian divisions, Arz at first refused to send any, then he consented, and lastly he referred decision to the Emperor, who informed Ludendorff that he could do nothing about it until he had "discussed the question with his wife."[6]

In Cramon's opinion, "The June battle had the gravest consequences both for the internal situation of the Monarchy and for the general situation, not only on account of the defeat itself, but

[1] *The Army Quarterly*, vol. III, p. 26.

[2] See *The War on the Italian Front*, Luigi Villari (English edit., 1932), pp. 197–198.

[3] *Quatre Ans au G.Q.G. Austro-Hongrois*, Cramon, p. 282. In *The Battle of the Piave*, the figures given for prisoners are 524 officers and 23,951 men (p. 81).

[4] *Scenes from Italy's War*, G. Macaulay Trevelyan (1919), p. 215.

[5] See *Italy's part in Winning the World War*, Colonel Girard Lindsley McEntree, p. 99.

[6] *Quatre Ans au G.Q.G. Austro-Hongrois*, Cramon, p. 276.

also for the losses suffered by the Austrian Army. . . . In the Hungarian Parliament the bitterest reproaches were levelled against the High Command. The cry of the 'Forty-eighters,' demanding the liberation of the Hungarian army from the hands of conscienceless Austrian generals, had the widest repercussions among parties of all colours. . . . Both the Emperor and the Empress were publicly accused of treason and collaboration with the enemy."[1] It was the beginning of the end of the Austro-Hungarian Empire.

Although comparative quiet reigned on the Venetian front during the remaining months of the summer of this titanic year and well into the autumn, the Italian counter-attack on the Piave was, as already recorded, immediately followed by a series of terrific allied offensives in France, in Macedonia, and in Palestine. Although they spelt final defeat for the Central Powers, one more great battle was to be waged which, although it in no way hastened this end, nevertheless had a profound influence on the future of Europe. This was the battle of Vittorio-Veneto.

Soon after the battle of the Piave, both Lord Cavan and General Graziani[2] urged a vigorous resumption of the offensive because they held that in the demoralized state of the Austrian armies it would lead to a collapse of the Dual Monarchy. But General Diaz would not risk it. He was an extremely cautious soldier, and although Marshal Foch, who since July 1 had been invested with the power to coordinate the actions of all the allied armies, urged him on, he remained obdurate until the final great allied offensive was launched in France on September 26. Only then did he and Signor Orlando, the Italian Prime Minister, listen to Foch; yet it seems doubtful whether they would have acted on his advice, had not the German proposal for an armistice – with which Austria was associated – been addressed to President Wilson on October 5. This, it would appear, ended their hesitation, not that they wanted to attack, but because they were fearful that, were hostilities to end before Italy could claim a resounding victory, her position at the peace conference would be jeopardized.

According to Villari,[3] the idea upon which the offensive was

---

[1] *Ibid.*, p. 282.

[2] See *Military Operations, Italy, 1915–1919* (British Official History), compiled by Sir James E. Edmonds and Maj.-Genl. H. R. Davies (1949), p. 247, and *The Army Quarterly*, vol. I, p. 16.

[3] *The War on the Italian Front*, p. 248.

to be based was suggested by Colonel Nicolosi, director of military operations of the Third Army, and in accordance with this idea General Badoglio elaborated in great detail the plan of attack. Its general intention was to break through on the lower Piave and separate the Austrian armies which held that sector of the front from those in the Trentino, and then to wheel westward and roll up the mountain front. The objective of the break-through was to be Vittorio-Veneto, which when occupied would lead to the severance of the Austrian railway communications which led to the Piave, and, therefore, would paralyse most of the enemy's left wing at the moment the westward wheel against his right wing was made.[1]

To help to carry out these operations, on October 6 two new armies were created – the Tenth and Twelfth. From right to left the Italian order of battle became:

Third Army (Duke of Aosta): four divisions.

Tenth Army (Lord Cavan): British XIVth Corps (7th and 23rd Divisions) and Italian XIth Corps (23rd and 27th Divisions).

Eighth Army (General Caviglia): 14 divisions.

Twelfth Army (General Graziani): four divisions, including one French.

Fourth Army (General Giardino): nine divisions.

Sixth Army (General Montuori): six divisions, including one French and one British.

First Army (General Pecori-Giraldi): five divisions.

Seventh Army (General Tassoni): four divisions.

In general reserve, Ninth Army (General Morrone): six divisions, one Czecho-Slovak division, one American infantry regiment; and the Cavalry Corps (Count of Turin): four cavalry divisions.

Opposed to these were the two Austrian Army groups, the Piave and the Trentino, respectively commanded by Field-Marshal Boroevic and the Archduke Joseph. The boundary between them was the Cismon river. The first group consisted of the Isonzo Army ($14\frac{1}{2}$ divisions), the Sixth Army ($7\frac{1}{2}$ divisions) and the Belluno Group (12 divisions). These faced the Italian Third, Tenth, Eighth, Twelfth, and Fourth Armies. The second group comprised the Eleventh (nine divisions) and Tenth (nine divisions) Armies. They faced the Italian Sixth, First, and Seventh Armies.

---

[1] See *Vittorio-Veneto*, "Report of the Comando Supremo on the Battle of Vittorio-Veneto" (English Trans., n.d.), p. 11.

In all, 57 allied divisions, four cavalry divisions, and 7,700 guns faced 52 Austrian divisions, six cavalry divisions and 6,030 guns.[1]

The tasks allotted to the Italian armies which faced the Austrian Piave group were: The Tenth and Eighth to penetrate in the sector Grave-di-Papadopoli–the Montello; the former protected the right flank of the Eighth Army until it had advanced to the line Sacile–Vittorio and cut the communications of the Austrian Sixth Army. The Twelfth Army was to support the Eighth on its left, and the Fourth, on the left of the Twelfth, was to support the Twelfth's advance by an advance in the Monte Grappa sector. The Third, on the right of the Tenth, was to wait until the latter was over the Piave, and only then was it to advance eastward. The task of the Sixth, First, and Seventh Armies was to hold the Austrians on the Trentino front until the capture of Vittorio-Veneto, and then, in the second phase of the battle, they were to push northward against the Austrian Eleventh and Tenth Armies, while the Eighth Army, supported by the Fourth, wheeled westward against the left flank of the Belluno Group.

The first of these two closely related operations was to be preceded by a preliminary operation which entailed the occupation of the Grave-di-Papadopoli and the gaining of a bridgehead on the left bank of the Piave by the Tenth Army and certain units of the Eighth. Only when these two aims had been attained was the general attack to start. October 16 was to be Z-day, but because of the rain and the consequent rise of the river it was put forward to the 24th and the preliminary operation was scheduled to take place on the preceding night. It is of peculiar interest, not only because it entailed the crossing of a wide river in flood, but because, as will be seen, the failure of the Eighth Army to fulfil its principal task caused the Tenth Army's attack to develop into the decisive operation of the battle.

The Grave-di-Papadopoli was the largest of a lozenge-shaped group of islets and shingle banks, each separated from the next by a channel. In all, this group was four-and-a-half miles in length, and in the centre about two miles wide. Between the right bank of the river and Papadopoli ran the main channel, its width varied from 280 to 780 yards, and the island, which was only a few feet above water level, was about four miles in length with an average breadth of one mile. When in flood, as it was at the time,

---

[1] See *British Official History*, pp. 264–265, and Villari, p. 252.

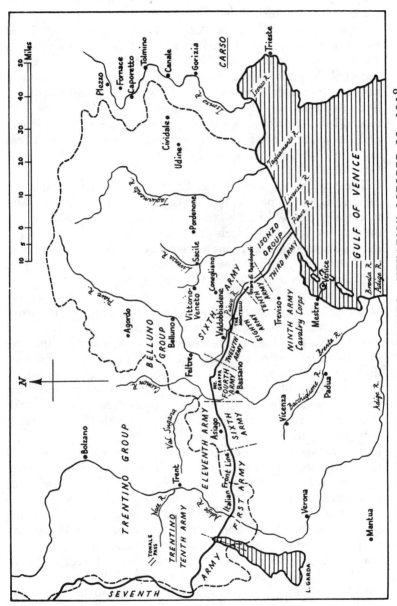

19. BATTLE OF VITTORIO-VENETO. SITUATION OCTOBER 23, 1918

the current is swift enough to carry a man off his feet, and the main channel unfordable.

In this sector the Austrian defences consisted of two belts of entrenchments. The first, known as the *Kaiserzone*, some 2,000 yards in depth, fronted on a *levée*, called the Bund, which skirted the whole length of the eastern side of the lozenge. The Bund was about 10 ft. in height, was entrenched and wired, and its outpost line was pushed forward on to Papadopoli and other islands. The second belt – the *Königzone* – lay about six miles east of the Piave, and ran along the left bank of the Monticano river, which rose south of Vittorio-Veneto and joined the Livenza to the east of Oderzo.

The preliminary operation of Cavan's Tenth Army was to be carried out in two phases; first the occupation of Papadopoli, and next the gaining of a lodgment on the left bank of the Piave, in order to establish a bridgehead: this meant the storming of the Bund. These two operations were to be made on the night of October 23–24, under cover of darkness, and the crossing to Papadopoli was to be effected by means of boats and footbridges.

The first flight of the crossing was entrusted to the 22nd Brigade of the 7th Division, and as only 12 Italian scows – punts with pointed ends – were available, each of which could carry seven men besides two Italian pontoneers (*pontieri*), no more than 84 men could be carried on each trip. At 8.15 p.m. on October 23 the first small flotilla pushed off, and though the river was a swirling flood of water, the *pontieri* handled their craft with amazing skill. Mr. E. C. Crosse, senior chaplain of the 7th Division, says: "It is impossible to speak too highly of the assistance rendered by the Italian boatmen. . . . Their skill was perfectly uncanny. At first we doubted it, then we couldn't believe it, finally we knew it. In their hands a boat in that stream was as tame as a tabby cat, and, quite apart from the skill they displayed, their unremitting toil and courage were equally conspicuous."[1]

Once a footing on Papadopoli had been gained, the leading platoons of the 22nd Brigade rushed several small Hungarian posts, and then they wheeled to the right and advanced southward down the island. As they did so the Austrian distress rockets[2] went up. While the ferry crossing was made, two footbridges resting on scows were built, but as in daylight they would be exposed to

---

[1] *The Defeat of Austria as seen by the 7th Division* (1919), p. 48.
[2] The signal that an enemy attack has been made.

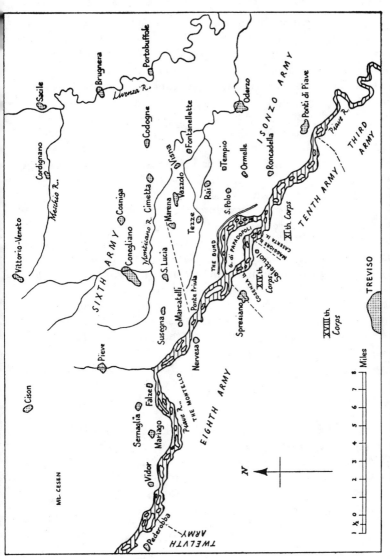

20. BATTLE OF VITTORIO-VENETO, THE BREAK-THROUGH ON THE PIAVE, OCTOBER 23–29, 1918

enemy machine-gun fire, they were dismantled after two battalions had crossed. By 5 a.m. on the 24th all the 7th Division's objectives were secured, but nothing was seen of the Italian 37th Division, which had been detailed to cross farther down the Piave. Six of its battalions had crossed to Caserta island, but had been held up there by machine-gun fire.

Soon after this success on the right, another preliminary operation was undertaken in the centre. In a dense fog an artillery bombardment was opened between the Piave and the Brenta, and at 7.15 a.m., when the fog had given way to a deluge of rain, units of the Fourth Army, supported on their right by units of the Twelfth, stormed down the slopes of Monte Grappa. Monte Asolene was carried and then lost; such intense machine-gun fire was met with everywhere that each subsequent advance was beaten back. Both sides fought with the greatest courage. Cramon praises the Austrians, and Lord Cavan their opponents. A few days later, when the Fourth Army carried this formidable position, the latter writes: "their final victory there was one of their most heroic achievements, especially when it is remembered that their attacks began before any attempt was made to cross the river. Their duty, therefore, of attracting the enemy's main forces to Mount Grappa and away from the threatened point, was accomplished with a devotion worthy of a great place in their military history."[1] On October 25 their attack was continued, and although no progress was made it drew in the Austrian reserves on the 26th and 27th, and thereby helped the general operations.

Meanwhile, because of the rain and the swollen state of the river, General Diaz had postponed a further advance of the XIVth Corps until the following day, when the rain ceased, and the crossing was resumed. "In order to screen the operation from the enemy," we read, "the beam of the Austrian searchlight on the opposite bank was blanketed by a beam of light established by the 3rd Italian Searchlight Company (attached to the 23rd Division) from a point on the river bank some 500 yards up stream. This threw its beam parallel to, and in front of, the scene of the crossing, and formed a perfect screen."[2]

[1] *The Army Quarterly*, vol. i, p. 17.
[2] *British Official History*, p. 277. In the previous August searchlights had been used: "In the 7th Division sector two searchlights were used to light up the area of the objectives; experiments had shown that if the beam was directed sufficiently high, the downward glow enabled the attackers to see without being seen, and that the best results were obtained by directing the beam immediately above the point to be raided" (*ibid.*, p. 257).

The task of clearing the island was fixed to start at 9.30 p.m., when the moon would provide sufficient light. By 9 a.m. on the 26th the whole island was in British and Italian hands. The Italian 37th Division had before then crossed over from Maggiore island.

On October 26 a pontoon bridge was built 300 yards above Salettuol, and at 6 p.m. Diaz ordered the Tenth, Eighth, and Twelfth Armies to begin the postponed operation of crossing the river. On the 27th, the Twelfth Army established a bridgehead on the left bank, opposite Pederobba, and the Eighth Army gained a foothold south of Sernaglia. The Tenth Army attacked with the 23rd and 7th Divisions of the XIVth Corps on the left, and the 37th, followed by the 23rd Division of the Italian XIth Corps attacked on the right. Under cover of a thin barrage, which opened at 6.25 a.m., the assault troops of the first two divisions crept through the scrub, and then, because the water was waist deep and flowed at 10 knots, they linked arms and entered the eastern channel of the river. The barrage then lifted, and the Bund, which had been under enfilade artillery fire from the left, was rushed. By 7 a.m. the whole of its right half was in British hands; but again on the right nothing was seen of the Italian 37th Division. It had failed to cross, but did so soon after. Diaz then placed the Italian XVIIIth Corps (33rd and 56th Divisions) –the reserve of the Eighth Army–at Cavan's disposal, so that he might have troops enough to protect his left flank, as the Eighth Army was unable to do so.

Immediately after the Bund had been taken the advance of the British 23rd and 7th Divisions was continued, and at 8.10 a.m. the next objective was taken. Again there were no signs of the 37th Division, but Cavan pushed ahead and by noon the whole of the *Kaiserzone* was in his hands.

On the night of the 27th–28th, troops still west of the Piave were pushed forward, but the bridging difficulties were so considerable that of the XVIIIth Corps only two brigades were able to cross the river to take their place on the left of the XIVth Corps. In spite of their numerical weakness, they were ordered to attack, and at 9 a.m. on the 28th, under cover of a barrage provided by the guns of the British 23rd Division, one brigade advanced on Santa Lucia to link up with the left of the 23rd Division, and the other on Marcatelli–north of Nervesa–to take in flank the Austrian infantry and artillery which so far had prevented the

VIIIth Corps of the Eighth Army from establishing a bridgehead at Ponte Priula. Though Santa Lucia was not occupied, the threat offered to Marcatelli compelled the Austrians to fall back and thereby enabled the Eighth Army to bridge the river the following night.

While these attacks were under way, at 12.30 p.m. on October 28 the XIVth Corps moved forward, the 23rd Division on Vazzola–Santa Lucia, and the 7th on Vazzola–Rai. Both objectives were gained and, under cover of night, companies from the two divisions were ordered forward to seize the bridges over the Monticano, but as they approached the bridges were blown up by the enemy. Thus, by early morning on the 29th, both the 23rd and 7th Divisions were beyond the objectives set them on the previous day. On the 28th, the Italian XIth Corps advanced its left flank to Tempio, and thence formed a defensive flank back to the river a little west of Ponte-di-Piave. On the right of the Tenth Army the Third Army did not move on the 28th, and on its left, the Eighth Army was engaged on bridging throughout the night.

In spite of his now exposed flanks, on the afternoon of the 28th Lord Cavan issued his orders for a continuation of the Tenth Army's advance on the following day. The objectives were: Marcatelli–Conegliano–Cosniga for the XVIIth Corps; Cosniga–Cadogne–Fontanellette for the XIVth Corps, and Fontanellette–Tempio for the XIth Corps. The first two objectives were not reached because Boroevic, affected by the increasing number of mutinies in his group, had on the evening of the 28th decided to retire to the Austrian frontier and to cover the withdrawal he had brought forward fresh troops to form a strong rear guard. The XVIIIth and XIVth Corps therefore met with stubborn resistance on the line of the Monticano, and although the Austrians were bombed heavily by the R.A.F., they maintained their position throughout the day and not until nightfall were the attackers able, except on the right, to cross the Monticano. Meanwhile, R.A.F. observers had reported that the roads in rear of the river were packed with troops in retreat.

While the Tenth Army was engaged with Boroevic's rear guard, the VIIIth Corps of the Eighth Army crossed the Piave at Ponte-Priulo, and unopposed moved forward its leading two divisions, which came up on the left of the XVIIth Corps beyond Susegna on the Susegna–Conegliano road. From there, as night fell, a column of Lancers and Bersaglieri cyclists was sent forward to seize Vittorio-Veneto. This it did early on October 30, and blocked the retreat of the Austrian Sixth Army and threw it into wild confusion. Meanwhile the Twelfth Army found it difficult to maintain its communications across the Piave near Pederobba, and its left was hampered by the failure of the Fourth Army in its attack in front of Monte Grappa on the 29th.

According to the Austrian official historians, October 29 was the decisive day of the campaign. "On 29th October," they write, "in view of the confusion in the interior of the Monarchy and the increasing dissolution of the Army and Navy, the Imperial and Royal High Command had come to the conclusion that it was impossible to continue the struggle. At evening, therefore, instructions were sent to Field-Marshal Boroevic from Baden to evacuate Venetia and to offer only such resistance as was necessary to the enemy who followed up. When this order reached Udine, the Sixth Army and the northern wing of the Isonzo Army were already in full retreat. After three days' heavy fighting, in order to withdraw the troops, whose moral power of resistance was already much shaken from enemy pressure, these forces retired during the night of 29th/30th October on the edge of the mountains north of Vittorio, on Sacile, and behind the Livenza to beyond Brugnera in the south."[1]

As all air reports received on the 29th pointed to a general Austrian withdrawal on the Piave front, General Diaz ordered the Third Army, which so far had remained stationary on the right of the Tenth, to advance on the 30th. Further, he brought forward his four cavalry divisions, one of which was moved up between the Eighth and Tenth Armies, and it was given as its objective the Livenza, north of Sacile.

At 9 a.m. on the 30th the pursuit of the Tenth Army began, but, in spite of little opposition until the Livenza was approached, progress was slow. By nightfall the Meschio and Livenza were reached, but as all bridges had been demolished and neither river was fordable, a halt had to be made until bridging material was brought forward. During the day only one division of the Third Army crossed the Piave; the advance of the Eighth met with little opposition; the Twelfth moved forward a short distance into the mountains; and the Fourth continued to be held up. Throughout the 30th the offensive was transferred to the air. The retiring

---

[1] Quoted from *British Official History*, pp. 315–316.

Austrian columns on the roads which lead out of Conegliano offered tremendous targets to the R.A.F., and were mercilessly bombed and machine-gunned with terrible effect, which may be gauged from the following two eyewitness reports:

"It is doubtful," writes General Gathorne-Hardy, "whether in any theatre during the Great War the Royal Air Force obtained such targets as those which were offered to them in Italy on the 29th and 30th October. It is certain that they took full advantage of the opportunities presented to them. On these two days the Conegliano–Pordenone road was black with columns of all arms hurrying eastwards. On to these the few British squadrons poured 30,000 rounds of S.A.A. and 3½ tons of bombs from low altitudes. Subsequent examination of the road almost forced the observer to the conclusion that this form of warfare should be forbidden in the future."[1]

The Rev. E. C. Crosse writes:

"What, however, was most noticeable as the Division passed along the Sacile–Pordenone–Udine road on the morning of November 2 were the remains of the awful carnage caused on it by aeroplanes a few days before. Apparently our aeroplanes had swept down on the road when the Austrian Army was in full retreat along it, and nowhere, even in France, do we recollect so grim a reminder of the horror of war. Judging from the casualties the road must have been crowded at the time, and the deep ditch on either side of the road had made it impossible for the horses, at any rate, to escape. Dead horses, abandoned guns, and many dead Austrians lay, all unburied on the road, whilst the horror of the situation was in no way lessened by the frequent spectacle of an almost starving civilian cutting slices of horseflesh for food."[2]

General Diaz issued the following orders for October 31: The Third and Tenth Armies were to close up on the Livenza and bridge it; the Eighth, in order to cut off the Austrians on the Monte Grappa front, was to advance on Feltre and Belluno; and the Twelfth and Fourth were to continue their forward movement, while the Sixth attacked in the Asiago sector. Because of the retreat of the Austrian Belluno Group, the Eighth, Twelfth, and Fourth Armies made considerable progress, but no large captures, as had been hoped. On the southern front, the Tenth spent the day bridging the Livenza, while the Third came up on its right.

---

[1] *The Army Quarterly*, Vol. III, p. 34.
[2] *The Defeat of Austria as seen by the 7th Division*, pp. 91–92.

For November 1 the tasks were as follows: The Cavalry Corps was to push to the Isonzo; the Third and Tenth Armies to the Tagliamento; the Eighth to beyond Belluno; the Twelfth, now pinched out by the Eighth and Fourth, was to come into reserve at Feltre; and the Fourth was to move on Bolzano. The Sixth, First, and Seventh Armies were to pursue the enemy in the direction of Trent-Bolzano; the Sixth directly northward, the First up the valley of the Adige, and the Seventh north-eastward down the valley of the Noce.[1] None of these advances was opposed, and everywhere signs of the enemy's disorderly retreat were to be seen; the roads and mountain tracks were encumbered with discarded impedimenta. The pursuit was pressed until November 4, and Villari states that in prisoners alone the Austrians lost 387,000 men.[2] This would appear to be an exaggeration, since the Austrians claimed that "there were no more than 260,000 combatants on the Italian front,"[3] and the Tenth Army, which did the brunt of the fighting, took less than a tenth of this figure. Villari places the Italian losses at 38,000, of whom 24,000 fell on the Monte Grappa front. The losses of the XIVth Corps were 1,622.

The armistice of Villa Giusti was the climax of a long series of attempts by Austria to get out of the war. Ever since his accession on November 21, 1916, the Emperor Karl's one idea had been to end the struggle, not only because of the defeats his armies had suffered, but above all because of the internal situation of the Dual Monarchy caused by the stranglehold of the blockade. Want of food was the deciding factor, and as far back as the spring of 1917 only "four-fifths of the minimum amount of corn was available, and nearly half of this came from Rumania, a source which was lacking in the next twelve months."[4] The British official historians quote that since August, 1914, cattle in Austria and Hungary had decreased from 17,324,000 to 3,518,197, and pigs from 7,678,000 to 214,000.

When, on October 9, President Wilson's reply to the joint German, Austrian, Turkish, and Bulgarian note to request an armistice was received, it was found to demand as evidence of good faith that no negotiations could be considered until all occupied country had been evacuated. When he learnt this, Karl at once instructed Field-Marshal Boroevic and the Archduke

---

[1] *Vittorio-Veneto*, pp. 28–29.   [2] *The War on the Italian Front*, p. 274.
[3] *British Official History*, p. 355.   [4] *Ibid.*, p. 379.

Joseph to prepare to withdraw from northern Italy. Then, in order to propitiate the American President, on October 16 Karl issued a Manifesto to his people based on point 10 of the President's Fourteen Points, which read: "The peoples of Austria-Hungary, whose peace among the nations we wish to see safeguarded and assured, should be accorded the freest opportunity of autonomous development." The most important pronouncements of the Manifesto were:

"Austria, in accordance with the will of its peoples, will become a Federal state (*Bundesstat*) in which each nationality will form its own state community on the territory on which it is settled.

"This reorganization . . . is intended to secure independence to each of the single national states. It will at the same time protect the common interests.

"I call upon the peoples, on whose self-determination the new *Reich* will be founded, to cooperate in the great work by forming national councils (*Nationalrathe*) which, drawn from the members of the [existing] *Reich* Parliaments of each nation, will serve to further the interests of the various nations in their relation to each other and to maintain communication with my Government."[1]

This was political dynamite, for instead of binding together the people of the Austro-Hungarian Empire, the Manifesto blew them apart and led to the complete disintegration of the Dual Monarchy. On October 29, by the Emperor's orders, an Austrian *parlementaire* entered the Italian lines to open conversations. And then, on the 31st, Wilson, to add more dynamite to his wrecking policy, insisted that the complete satisfaction of the Austrian and Hungarian Slavs should be a condition of the armistice – already he had recognized the Czecho-Slovak National Council as an allied belligerent government. Hungarian regiments then began to desert; the Austrian fleet handed itself over to the Croats; autonomous governments were formed in Budapest, Prague, Laibach, Serajevo, Cracow, and Lemberg, and a neutral government was set up in Vienna to liquidate the central administration. On November 2, the Italian armistice conditions were accepted; on the 3rd Austria ceased hostilities; and on the 12th the Emperor Karl renounced his share in the government, after which a republic was proclaimed in Vienna and the ancient Austro-Hungarian monarchy ceased to exist.

Meanwhile in Germany a parallel situation had developed.

[1] *Ibid.*, pp. 361–362.

When, on October 9, Wilson's reply was received, the German Government was quite prepared to agree to a withdrawal of its troops from the occupied countries. Then, a week later, in addition to this demand, Wilson called for the abandonment of submarine warfare; this also was agreed. Next, on October 23, in a third note he stated that if he were compelled to negotiate with the military rulers and monarchist autocrats of Germany he would demand, not peace negotiations, but a general surrender. As compliance with this meant the abdication of the existing German Government and its replacement by a revolutionary Socialist assembly, Ludendorff urged that negotiations should be broken off. But the political leaders refused to do so, and on the 27th Ludendorff resigned.

On November 3, the German crews at Kiel mutinied and Berlin was swept by revolution. On the following day soldiers' and workmen's councils on the Bolshevik model began to spring up, and the cry that the Kaiser should abdicate grew so loud that on November 9 Prince Max of Baden, the German Chancellor, without consulting the Emperor, proclaimed his abdication and that of the Crown Prince; a German republic was then formed. On November 10 William II crossed the Dutch frontier and the next day, at Rethondes Station in the forest of Compiègne, an armistice was concluded between the Allied and Associated Powers and Germany.

Of this calamity for Germany Ludendorff writes: "All that we had lived for, all that we had bled four long years to maintain, was gone. We no longer had a native land of which we might be proud. Order in state and society vanished. All authority disappeared. Chaos, Bolshevism, terror, un-German in name and nature, made their entry into the German fatherland. . . . We lived through scenes no Prussian had thought possible since 1806."[1]

In this overwhelming tragedy, the battle of Vittorio-Veneto played no part, for long before it was fought the death knell of Germany had been sounded at Amiens. Nor did Vittorio-Veneto hasten the collapse of Austria, for bound as she was to Germany, German defeat meant her downfall. In what, then, is the importance of Vittorio-Veneto to be found?

Firstly, there is its moral influence on the Italian people. Following as it did the Austrian defeat on the Piave, it capitalized

---

[1] *My War Memories*, vol. II, p. 766.

the national spirit awakened after Caporetto, and without the myth which emerged from it, Italy would almost certainly have succumbed to Bolshevism. In its turn, this myth was capitalized by Mussolini and woven into a witchery which awakened the spirit of the *Risorgimento*. The day after the armistice was signed he had written in the *Popolo d'Italia*:

"It is the great hour of divine joy, when the tumult of emotion suspends the beating of hearts and gives us a lump in the throat. The long passion, crowned at last by triumph, draws tears even from eyes which have seen much and have wept much.

"We are at Udine.

"More, we are at Trieste. We are at Trento. Who is the Italian, worthy of the name, who does not grasp the immense historic significance of what has been accomplished in these days by our heroic armies?

"Let a rending shout arouse the *piazze* and the streets from the Alps to Sicily.

"Viva, viva, viva l'Italia!"[1]

This was more than a paean of victory; it was a battle cry that challenged all those forces of subversion and corruption which decomposed the national spirit in Italy.

Without Vittorio-Veneto, Mussolini would have remained an obscure scribbler and the first great victory over Bolshevism would never have been won. Instead he became an oracle inspired with a new faith, and the secondary importance of Vittorio-Veneto is not whether his philosophy of Fascism was good or evil, but that it heralded the coming of the epoch of ideological wars which were to perplex and distract the entire world, for with Lenin's triumph over Tsarism a new crusading age was born, and Mussolini was the first western crusader.

Italy had lost half a million men killed and twice as many disabled. Made bankrupt by the war and with millions of her people on starvation level, she was ripe for revolution.

"The example of Russia," writes Villari, "exerted immense influence, and was made the most of; the extreme Socialist leaders . . . were in close touch with Moscow, and, by depicting the conditions of Russia, as those of an earthly paradise, they convinced large numbers of workers that if a similar régime were introduced into Italy everyone would be happy without any

---

[1] Quoted from Villari's *The War on the Italian Front*, p. 274.

necessity for work."[1] An epidemic of revolutionary strikes and disorders followed, and when in June, 1919, Signor Francesco Nitti became Prime Minister he allowed the Socialists and Communists a free hand, and afraid to resist the Bolshevik madness he tried to win their support.

Because he disliked the army, he opened a savage campaign against all who served or had served in it. Soldiers were insulted in the streets, their medals were snatched from their breasts, and not a few were murdered by gangs of ruffians in political pay. Deserters and military criminals were liberated, discipline was scouted. . . . "Landowners, large and small, farmers, and peasants who refused to obey the injunctions imposed upon them were boycotted, starved, robbed, and not infrequently murdered. Milk was refused to the children of boycotted parents, medical aid to the sick, and even the dead could not be buried. No Tricolour flag could be exposed from a window without the house being wrecked and inmates brutally outraged."[2]

The man who strove most ardently against this return to the spirit of Caporetto was Mussolini. On March 23, 1919, in his small editorial office he recruited his first *Fascio di Combattimento*, a group of young men who would work for Italian regeneration. Soon group after group was added, each composed mainly of ex-soldiers, men who remembered the self-sacrifice of the war and who had learned that without discipline and comradeship nothing worth while could be accomplished. These *fasci* focussed on themselves the spirit of Vittorio-Veneto, and it was due to them that the whole Communist-Socialist dominion collapsed, first in the valley of the Po and then throughout Italy.

On November 8, Mussolini formed his followers into the Fascist Party. In his own words, its aim was to foster the "integral vision of that Italy which at Vittorio-Veneto inaugurated a new period in her history." This he explained as follows: "The nation is an organism comprising an unlimited series of generations, of which individuals are merely transient elements: it is the supreme synthesis of all the material and non-material values of the race. . . . Political institutions are efficient in so far as national values find in them expression and protection."[3]

Such was to be the seed of the new way of life in Italy; a challenge not only to Bolshevism, which was to be trampled into

[1] *The Awakening of Italy*, pp. 50–51.
[2] *Ibid.*, pp. 158–159.   [3] *Ibid.*, p. 166.

the dust, but also to the materialism which had begotten the war, and through which it had ruined the nations economically, socially, and morally.

In 1922, on the anniversary of Vittorio-Veneto, Mussolini ordered four columns of his followers to march on Rome, "an event of deeper significance for Europe," writes Francis Neilson, "than Brunswick's retreat from Valmy,"[1] and on Salandra's advice the King made Mussolini his Prime Minister.

Once in power, he cleaned out the Italian Augean stable. "Poverty, discontent and disease were everywhere. Unemployment was increasing, and in Britain the dole had to be given to keep the people from revolt. The contrast between the state of Italy and other European countries, after two years of Mussolini's rule, was so startling that he was hailed one of the greatest men of Europe."[2] In 1927, when Winston Churchill visited Rome, he is reported to have said to him: "If I had been an Italian, I am sure that I should have been wholeheartedly with you from the start to finish in your triumphant struggle against the bestial appetites and passions of Leninism."[3]

The influences of the first of the world wars on vanquished and victors, and through them on history, were cataclysmic. Most of the Europe of a thousand years was shattered and the balance between its nations destroyed. Three empires were tumbled into the dust. Germany was reduced to economic ruin and slices of her frontier territories were amputated; Alsace-Lorraine was returned to France, and parts of Silesia and Posen were given to a resuscitated Poland. Russia ceased to be a Christian country, and the autocracy of Marx was substituted for the autocracy of the Tsars. The Austro-Hungarian Empire was split into a congeries of squabbling states bereft of economic foundations, and Turkey was almost reduced to her original sultanate of Rum. Nor did the victors emerge much better. France, bled white, was left a demoralized, second-rate Power; Great Britain, who before the war had been the banker of the world, ended a debtor country, and for the *Pax Britannica* was substituted the League of Nations – a sham to replace a reality. The United States was left to pay for the war she had so blindly entered in order to disencumber herself of the consequences she had failed to foresee. Japan, who had played a minor part, alone emerged triumphant. Her empire was

[1] *The Makers of War* (1950), p. 138.
[2] *Ibid.*, p. 138.   [3] *Ibid.*, quoted from p. 139.

extended and the war raised her to a dominant position in the Far East and the western Pacific. Such were the sorry products of bankrupt statesmanship.

Of these many disasters, the Russian Revolution and the replacement of the *Pax Britannica* by the League of Nations – the Wilsonian brand of a sovietized world – were, historically, the most momentous. Because the aim of the former was world revolution, and that of the latter world peace, and because no arbiter was left to judicate between them, the world was split ideologically in twain by a political Manicheism – it was not a struggle between the powers of Light and Darkness, but between a world to be made safe for American democracy and a world to be secured by Russian autocracy. This meant the inversion of Clausewitz's dictum that war is a continuation of peace policy. In other words, because both policies were global, it led to the establishment of a global state of "wardom."

Although the *Pax Britannica* had not prevented the outbreak of continental wars, it prevented them from spreading to world-wide dimensions and so had played the part of international arbiter. And although the *Pax Britannica* was destroyed by the war, it was because of the inept statemanship of Great Britain and America that the war engulfed the entire world. This ineptness is worth investigation, for the passing of the *Pax Britannica* was as catastrophic an historical event as had been the passing of the *Pax Romana*.

When, in *King Richard the Second*, Shakespeare compares England to a "fortress built by Nature for herself against infection and the hand of war," and calls her "This precious stone set in the silver sea, which serves it in the office of a wall," he summed up the foundations of the *Pax Britannica*. And when, in his day, Napoleon acclaimed that "England can never be a continental power and in the attempt must be ruined," he did no more than accentuate Shakespeare's dictum. In brief, the sea dictated England's foreign policy, and of all her statesmen Chatham saw this the most clearly; he realized that as a colonial empire, and not as a continental power, England could go from strength to strength.

Later Canning saw it. "I do not say (God forbid I should!)," he declared, "that it is no part of the duty of Great Britain to protect what is termed the balance of power and to aid the weak against the strong. I say, on the contrary, that it is her bounden duty; but I affirm also, that we must take care to do our duty to ourselves. The first condition of engaging in any war . . . is that the war must be just; the second that, being just in itself, we can also with justice engage in it; and the third . . . that we can so interfere without detriment or prejudice to ourselves."[1]

Disraeli also understood. "The abstention," he said, "of England from any unnecessary interference in the affairs of Europe is the consequence, not of her decline of power but of her increased strength. England is no longer a mere European power; she is the metropolis of a great maritime Empire, extending to the boundaries of the farthest ocean. It is not because England has taken refuge in a state of apathy that she now almost systematically declines to interfere in the affairs of the Continent of Europe, England is as ready and as willing to interfere as in old days when the necessity of her position requires it."[2]

Finally, Winston Churchill at the opening of his political career held the same idea in mind. When on May 13, 1901, the question of defence was being debated in the House of Commons he said: "Whereas any European Power has to support a vast army first of all, we in this fortunate, happy island, relieved by our insular position of a double burden, may turn our undivided efforts and attention to the Fleet. Why should we sacrifice a game in which we are sure to win to play a game in which we are bound to lose?"[3]

In spite of this enormous initial blunder – the jettisoning of the *Pax Britannica* by Britain herself – if the United States had not entered the war on the side of the Entente, it is probable that in 1917 the war would have ended in a negotiated peace and most of the calamities which followed its American extension would not have befallen Europe. Therefore, and unquestionably, April 6, 1917, was the blackest of all days in modern European history. Although, as has been recorded in Chronicle 7, President Wilson foresaw the calamities that would follow American participation in the war, his propaganda-demented people could not see that the power of the United States was potentially so enormous that, as long as she refrained from participation in the war, it would make her the arbiter of the world. They also failed to see that although in all probability United States participation would

[1] Quoted from *The Foreign Policy of Canning*, 1822–1827, Harold Temperley (1925), p. 463.
[2] Quoted from *The Cambridge History of British Foreign Policy*, vol. III, pp. 9–10.
[3] *Parliamentary Debates* ("Hansard"), vol. XCIII, Fourth Series, May 13, 1901, cols. 1574–1575.

decide the war, when it ended there would be no arbiter of peace left in the world.

Had it not been for the octopus of propaganda, whose tentacles gripped him like a vice, there can be little doubt that Wilson would not have jettisoned the foreign policy which, in 1794, Washington outlined to Gouverneur Morris, and which since then had carried the United States from strength to strength.

"Peace," he said, "has been the order of the day with me since the disturbance in Europe, first commenced. My policy has been, and will continue to be, while I have the honor to remain in the administration of the government, to be upon friendly terms with, but independent of, all the nations of the earth; to share in the broils of none; to fulfil our own engagements; to supply the wants and to be carrier for them all; being thoroughly convinced that it is our policy and interest so to do. Nothing short of self-respect, and that justice which is essential to a national character, ought to involve us in war."[1]

The outstanding calamity of the war was that Wilson could not heed these words; it towered above all others, including the Russian revolution, because his war policy rendered Europe receptive to the Bolshevik contagion. What he did not, or could not, see, was that once involved in the war the only sane way to contain the contagion was to salve what remained of European stability; to prop up the tottering governments; to hold fast to the frontiers of 1913; to veto all territorial annexations; and to fight revolution by reinvigorating the existing European governments and in no way weaken them.

Ever since the days of Charlemagne, who established the East Mark (Austria) as an outwork to secure Christendom against Slavonic and other barbarians of the east, the Germanic peoples began to form two great bastions – the northern eventually centred in Brandenburg–Prussia and the southern in Austria – which protected Europe against Asia. Wilson set out to weaken the northern bastion by refusing to treat with William II and his Government except on terms of total surrender, and the southern bastion he utterly destroyed in spite of the dictates of history.

On October 17, 1805, a few weeks before the battle of Austerlitz, Talleyrand wrote to Napoleon: "The Austrian Monarchy is a combination of ill-assorted States. Such a power is necessarily

[1] Quoted from *The Growth of the American Republic*, S. E. Morison and H. S. Commager (1942), vol. I, p. 358.

weak, but it is an adequate bulwark against the barbarians [Russians] and a necessary one. In the future the Habsburg Empire will stand with its back towards Europe and its front to the East, thus protecting Western civilization from the aggression of Russia." And in 1848, the Czech historian, Frantisek Palanky, wrote: "If Austria did not exist she would have to be invented. The disintegration of the Austrian State into small republics would be an invitation to German and Russian Imperialism."[1]

What Wilson did not realize was that, as the Kremsier resolution put it, the old Austria was a valiant attempt "to unite all lands and races of the monarchy into one great body politic," and that under Francis Joseph nine nationalities learned to live and let live, and if they did not love one another, at least they respected each other and fought as a united army. Instead, he listened to the voices of the *émigrés*, and more particularly to that of T. G. Masaryk – the future Czech President – and was brought to believe that the Habsburg monarchy was a reactionary survival from the Middle Ages and the gaoler of enslaved peoples.

According to R. W. Seton-Watson, a close friend of Masaryk, Wilson's exchange of notes during the battle of Vittorio-Veneto "bore down the diplomatic defences of Vienna and Budapest, killed the Emperor's project of Austrian federation at birth, and wrested from him and his Government recognition of Czecho-slovak and Jugoslav as an essential part of the foundation of the new settlement. The Dual Monarchy crumbled before the impact of Wilsonian diplomacy . . . no one factor contributed more to this result than the Presidential thunderbolts."[2]

Besides faulty statemanship, another cause, this time military, underlay the many catastrophies the war begot. It was the tactical stalemate which, as Bloch had foreseen, followed the initial onrush, and, as he had predicted, led to a final decision through famine, bankruptcy, and the break-up of the whole social order.

Had there been no stalemate, the blockade would not have been effective, and it was the allies' blockade – sea and not land power – which finally broke the will of their enemies; it struck every man, woman and child, every factory, and every farm in the enemy countries. Only if the Central Powers at the outset had been able to penetrate their enemies' fronts – that is, shorten the range of the blockade – and thereby extend their food areas, would

---

[1] Both quoted from *Danubian Federation*, Lieut.-Col. F. O. Miksche (n.d.), p. 30.
[2] *Masaryk in England* (1943), pp. 113-114.

the blockade have been broken. A parallel was the breaking of the submarine counter-blockade by the convoy system which, so to speak, penetrated it. As it was, it has been calculated that, during the last two years of the blockade, "800,000 non-combatants died in Germany from starvation or diseases directly attributed to under-nourishment – about fifty times more than were drowned by submarine attack on British shipping."[1]

The character of the war was as revolutionary as its results, and this was mainly because of the ever-increasing use of propaganda. Morality and common decency were cast to the winds, and in this respect the war differed markedly from both the Napoleonic and Franco-Prussian wars, in which, generally speaking, the contenders guarded against fostering revolution.[2] The use of alleged atrocities as a weapon became universal, and as the war lengthened people became more credulous and savage until all reason was lost in a primitive animalism; a frantic hysterical endeavour to injure the enemy by every means foul and damnable.

When he wrote on the influence of British propaganda between 1914 and 1917 upon the American people, James Duane Squires said:

"Fired by such notions [that German soldiers cut the hands off Belgian children] about the behaviour of the enemy and by others equally absurd,[3] the American people launched themselves into the war with an emotional hysteria that can only be understood by realizing the power of propaganda in generating common action by a nation under belligerent conditions. Those who did not accept the war ideology were usually few in number and always quite impotent. The almost primitive ecstasy that could sometimes grip the American people has been recently summarized in unforgettable fashion.

" 'We hated with a common hate that was exhilarating. The writer of this review remembers attending a great meeting in New England, held under the auspices of a Christian Church – God save the mark! A speaker demanded that the Kaiser, when captured, be boiled in oil, and the entire audience stood on chairs

---

[1] *Unfinished Victory*, Arthur Bryant (1940), p. 3. See also pp. 9 and 10.

[2] Napoleon could to his advantage have unleashed the "pent-up animality" of the Russian serfs and Ukrainians in 1812, and have stirred up a revolution in France during the Hundred Days, but he refrained (*Napoleon*, Eugene Tarle (1936), pp. 289, 381). The Duke of Wellington had a horror of fomenting revolution in any country, and, in 1871, Bismarck did not befriend the Paris Commune.

[3] For a vast number of other alleged atrocities see *Falsehood in War-Time*, Arthur Ponsonby (1936).

to scream its hysterical approval. This was the mood we were in. This was the kind of madness that had seized us.' "[1]

The means of fighting were also revolutionary, because for the first time in the history of war battles were as much tussles between factories as between armies. The production of weapons was more of a deciding factor in battles than the conscription of men. God had marched with the biggest industries in preference to the biggest battalions, and more often with tank and gun than with rifle and bayonet. As J. T. Shotwell says: "During the years 1914 to 1918 . . . war definitely passed into the industrial phase of economic history . . . the industry of war combines two techniques; the technique of peace which supplies war with its resources, and the technique of destruction."[2] The pecuniary profits of war shifted from plunder by the generals and troops to the gains made by financiers, war contractors, and manufacturers.

Of the many changes which germinated in the war, probably the most ominous was that, contrary to common acceptance, the war *did* make the world safe for democracy in its several forms. From 1918 on, even more than in the Wars of Religion, the emotions of mass-man were to dominate human relations. Wresting reason from statecraft and strategy ". . . Demos rose a Demon, shriek'd and slaked the light with blood," and set a seal of madness and savagery on peace and war.[3]

[1] *British Propaganda at Home and in the United States from 1914 to 1917*, James Duane Squires (1935), pp. 67–68. In the appendix is listed 277 publications and books of British propaganda sent to the U.S. between the above dates. Also see *Spreading Germs of Hate*, George Sylvester Viereck (1931).

[2] *War as an Instrument of National Policy* (1929), pp. 34–35.

[3] For the bellicosity of democracies see Hoffman Nickerson's books: *Can We Limit War?* (1934) and *The Armed Horde* (1940).

The Russian revolution

W hen the nineteenth century opened, all the leading
nations had changed from an agricultural to an industrial economy, and the progress made was so startling
that it seemed to industrialized man that the new dispensation
to which steam power had given birth made archaic all that had
preceded it. Material progress was equated with happiness, and
economic determinism accepted as the new religion. "The
machine and the universe," writes Lewis Mumford in *Technics
and Civilization*,[1] "were identified, linked together as they were
by the formulae of the mathematical and physical sciences; and
the service of the machine was the principal manifestation of faith
and religion: the main motive of human action, and the source
of most human goods." Man, who in the Age of Faith had been
looked upon as only a little lower than the angels, was reduced
to the status of an economic animal – the "beast of prey" of
Oswald Spengler. For capitalist and socialist alike the worship of
Mammon replaced the worship of God, and as it led to class-war,
the socialists propounded the falsehood that classes could be extinguished, and thereby introduced a contradiction in the mammonic
creed, because economic determinism leads to diversity and not
uniformity of social status.

This contradiction was seized upon by Marx, who set out to
do for the proletariat – the industrial workers – what Calvin had
done for the elect, for his apocalypse gave them, as it has been
well said, "the certainty of a triumph predestined by the majestic
laws of the universe itself." The social world was not to be readjusted or reformed, but instead to be turned upside down, for
according to his dialectics the new gospel was to be associated,
not with amity but with enmity, not with charity but with violence.
The whole Christian order was to be reversed; the principle of
hate one another was to be substituted for that of love one another,
and not until war on behalf of the proletariat had been made
total – that is, world-wide – would the gates of his material paradise

[1] Published by George Routledge and Sons, Ltd., London, 1934.

open to the elect. Because, as Mumford has pointed out in *The Conditions of Man*, Marx believed "that material conditions and technical inventions were self-created entities, existing in and by themselves: prime movers, original sources of social power . . . he accepted the machine process as an absolute, imagined that the proletariat would simply take up capitalist production at the point that capitalism left off," and step straight into the social Eldorado. To Marx the proletariat was the new messiah and the organizer of an earthly kingdom in which the spiritual had no place.

Lenin accepted Marx's interpretation of the "dictatorship of the proletariat" and so became as much the victim of a theological obsession with doctrine as Luther and Calvin had been in their days. The process was simplicity itself. Through revolution the proletariat would become the governing class, and in the guise of a transitional state it would overthrow the bourgeoisie, wrest from it all means of production, exchange and distribution, and by centralizing them in its own hands would develop them for its own benefit until, after victory had been won and the entire people had been proletarianized, the State would die away into a self-sufficing and self-operating classless society.

This simplification was accepted by Lenin. Like Marx, he had never soiled his hands with a day's manual labour and knew nothing of the human side of the worker's life. Also like Marx, his views on national and industrial administration were naive. He declared that "we must break the old, absurd, savage, despicable and disgusting prejudice that only the rich [*i.e.*, the educated] can administer the State," since "every rank and file worker who is able to read and write can do organizational work." That "under Socialism all will administer in turn and will quickly become accustomed to nobody administering." Blindly he believed that "electrification plus socialism" was the highroad to the Communist New Atlantis, and was oblivious of the self-evident contradiction in Marx's gospel. Because everyone would own everything, nobody would own anything, and as this carried with it the elimination of individual incentive, who would keep the proletariat at work? This demanded the creation of a new class of taskmasters, which meant that the assumption that the proletariat could become the governing class was nonsense.

When, on November 7, 1917 (the October Revolution), Lenin, thanks to Trotsky's abilities as an organizer, began his struggle for power, he was almost unknown. But as everybody in Russia knew of the Social Revolutionary Party which had great influence with the peasants, he entered into coalition with its left wing, and between November 8 and December 31 issued 193 decrees. On November 9 he decreed that the property of the landlords was to be distributed among the peasants, and though this had nothing to do with Marxism, for Marx looked upon the peasants as "the barbarians of civilization," Lenin thereby gained the support of 80 per cent. of the Russian people. Little did the Social Revolutionaries and the peasants suspect at the time that Lenin's motive was to use the peasants to liquidate the bourgeoisie, and then in turn to liquidate them.

Later, on November 27, by another decree all industry was transferred to the workers, who became the governing class, and the Soviet of People's Commissars became their form of government, the task of which was to organize production and direct Communist affairs. The immediate result was that because the workers were incapable of organizing and directing anything, industry came to a standstill, factories were turned into debating clubs, and as the workers had nothing to exchange for food, the peasants ceased to cultivate the land, except for themselves. Thus the Marxian experiment was proved to be an illusion; it created nothing but confusion, and this because of its omission to take into account human nature. Yet it did prove something of inestimable future value – that the most certain way to wreck a potential enemy's economy is to plant Marxian communism in his realm.

Lenin was compelled to take his first decisive step away from Marx. On December 20 he formed a special police force, the Tcheka, on the lines of the old Tsarist Okrana. Ostensibly it was to fight counter-revolution; its real purpose was to compel the new governing class to cease misgoverning and to work. Since first of all food had to be provided for the workers, it was wrested from the peasants, and because of this the Social Revolutionaries broke away from Lenin. It was too late, a terror was at once unleashed by the Tcheka and the Marxian experiment drowned in blood. Lenin then formed a Political Bureau of five prominent members of the Bolshevik Party under his own leadership, which governed by means of the Tcheka and the Red Army Trotsky had created. The result was civil war. As this stimulated foreign intervention, it is opportune here to examine Lenin's foreign policy.

From the earliest days of the revolution there was one assumption upon which all the Bolshevik leaders were agreed; the revolution could not survive unless it became world-wide. It challenged the existing order of society, socially, politically, and economically. It not only offered to the world a new way of life, but its adherents held that it could not be established permanently until the old way was destroyed. As early as April 14, 1917, Lenin had proclaimed that "World Imperialism cannot live side by side with a victorious Soviet Revolution," and on March 12, 1919, in the name of the Central Committee he placed a report before the eighth congress of the Russian Communist Party in which he said:

"We are living not merely in a State, but in a system of States, and the existence of the Soviet Republic side-by-side with Imperialist States for a long time is unthinkable. One or the other must triumph in the end. And before that end supervenes a series of frightful collisions between the Soviet Republic and the Bourgeoise States will be inevitable."

Later, Stalin reiterated these words again and again, and summarized Soviet international policy as follows:

"The tasks of the Party in foreign policy are: (*1*) to utilize every contradiction and conflict among the surrounding capitalist groups and governments for the purpose of disintegrating imperialism; (*2*) to spare no pains or means to assist the proletarian revolutions in the west; (*3*) to take all necessary measures to strengthen the national liberation movement in the east; and (*4*) to strengthen the Red Army."

In order to make this subversive war world-wide, in March, 1919, Lenin founded the Third International, or Comintern; an instrument to unite all communist parties outside Russia in the struggle for world revolution, and its first task was to establish a communist régime in Germany. On the insistence of Poincaré, Clemenceau, Foch, and Klotz in France, and others in Great Britain, Germany was still under blockade, and out of desperation many Germans had turned to Bolshevism. So completely did the Paris peacemakers play into Lenin's hands that, in his own words, his plan was "To unite the proletariat of industrial Germany, Austria and Czechoslovakia with the proletariat of Russia, and thereby create a mighty agrarian and industrial combination from Vladivostok to the Rhine, from the Finnish Gulf to the blue waters of the Danube, capable of feeding itself and confronting the reactionary capitalism of Britain with a revolutionary giant, which with one hand would disturb the tranquillity of the East and with the other beat back the pirate capitalism of Anglo-Saxon countries. If there was anything that could compel the English whale to dance, it would be the union of revolutionary Russia with a revolutionary Central Europe."

One of the few men who realized this danger was Lloyd George who, on March 25, 1919, set forth his views:

"The greatest danger I perceive in the present situation is the possibility of Germany uniting her destiny with the Bolshevists, and placing her wealth, intellect and great organizing capacity at the disposal of the men who dream of conquering the world for Bolshevism by force of arms. This danger is no idle fancy. If Germany goes over to Spartacism [then being fostered by France] she will inevitably link her fate with that of the Bolshevists. If that takes place, all Eastern Europe will be drawn into the maelstrom of the Bolshevist Revolution, and a year hence we shall find ourselves opposed by nearly 3,000,000 men who will be welded by German generals and German instructors into a gigantic army equipped with German machine-guns and ready to undertake an offensive against Western Europe."

Because world revolution was Lenin's strategical goal, his tactics also had to be revolutionary. Their aim was not to persuade the enemy to change his mind by force of arms, but by force of ideas – in other words, to rot him internally and bring him to destroy himself. Before the Treaty of Brest-Litovsk he had said, "Let us give way in space, but gain time," because he saw that, once revolution was kindled in the west it would give back to Russia the space she had bartered, and without a fight.

He said: "We must be able to resort to all sorts of strategems, manœuvres, illegal methods, evasions and subterfuges only so as to get into the trade unions, to remain in them, and to carry Communist work within them at all costs. . . . The Communist Party enters such institutions not in order to do constructive work, but in order to direct the masses to destroy from within the whole Bourgeois State machine and Parliament itself."

Germany was the hub of the world revolution for Lenin and Trotsky because she was the strategical centre of gravity of Europe. Once she was won, the rest of Europe would become untenable and could be conquered. And when Europe was reduced to the position of a Soviet satrapy, the Mediterranean would also become untenable, and the Middle East could be

Bolshevized and Africa subverted. Finally, when the whole of the Old World was sovietized, the psychological conquest of the New World could be undertaken and the Soviet Republic of the World established.

The composition of the Russian empire prevented Lenin from launching out on this grandiose scheme. It was a mosaic of sub-jugated peoples held together by the centripetal autocracy of the Muscovite Tsar, which alone prevented the explosion of the centrifugal forces of discontent. Because of this, the overthrow of the Tsarist government in March, 1917, at once led to national uprisings among the non-Muscovites, with the result that at various dates – mostly following the October Revolution – 15 groups of subjugated peoples declared their autonomy. The first to do so was the Ukraine, the most populous of them, in which a Central Council of Liberation was formed on March 17, 1917. Next, on November 20, 1917, the Ukrainians formally proclaimed themselves to be a National Republic, and because Lenin could not prevent this, he acknowledged Ukrainian independence, and immediately began to establish a Communist shadow government at Kharkov. On December 17 it came into the open. It proclaimed the Ukraine a Soviet Republic and in accordance with Lenin's technique, appealed to the Soviet Government for aid. This was granted, and the Ukrainian War of Independence, which was to last until 1921, was started.

Meanwhile, immediately after the October Revolution, General Alexeyev in south Russia raised a volunteer army of White Russians (Imperialists) to fight the Bolsheviks, and was soon joined by General Kornilov and General Denekin. The former was killed in March, 1918, and when Alexeyev died the following September Denekin took over supreme command of the White Russian forces in the south. Two months later Admiral Kolchak raised his standard of counter-revolution at Omsk. At the moment when the Central Powers collapsed, civil war raged over most of Russia.

In the meantime foreign intervention had made confusion worse confounded. It was begun when the French supported the Czech prisoners captured by the Russians and formed by them into a corps to fight the Central Powers. After the Treaty of Brest-Litovsk the Czechs had elected to come under French command, and as they could not pass through Germany, they set out to reach France by way of Vladivostok.

By the close of 1918 the interventionist forces in Russia had reached a total of nearly 300,000 men – French, British, Americans, Italians, Japanese, German Balts, Poles, Greeks, Finns, Czechs, Slovaks, Estonians and Latvians – in Archangel, Murmansk, Finland, Estonia, Latvia, and Poland, as well as on the Black Sea, on the Trans-Siberian railway, and at Vladivostok. In April, 1919, Kolchak reached Kazan and Samara on the Volga, while Denekin advanced northward from the Black Sea. As Kolchak was considered the more dangerous, Trotsky sent General Tukhachevski against him. Tukhachevski won the battle of Busulug, set out from the Volga, crossed the Urals, and pursued his enemy to Vladivostok, 5,000 miles away. Next, in October, an offensive was opened against Denekin, who had advanced to Orel. He was pushed back, and once in retreat, because of the bandits and partisans who infested his rear communications, was unable to halt his demoralized men until they reached Novorossisk on the Black Sea. From there the remnants of his army were sent to General Wrangel in the Crimea. About the same time, General Yudenich, then advancing on Petrograd, was driven over the Estonian border, and intervention began to collapse. Two Powers were unwilling to give in; Japan, who had her eyes on territorial expansion in eastern Siberia, and France.

Because the French feared to lose the credits they had advanced Tsarist Russia, and that, in revenge for the Treaty of Versailles, the Germans would link up with the Bolsheviks, their policy was contradictory. One aim was to restore the Tsarist régime, which would be grateful to France, and the other was to create an enlarged Poland which as a French ally would threaten Germany from the east.

On November 5, 1916, the independence of Poland had been sanctioned by the Central Powers, and when on November 11, 1918, they collapsed, the Regency Council established by them appointed Joseph Pilsudski (1867–1935) to the supreme command of all Polish troops. His first act was to declare himself head of the National Government, and his second to notify all belligerent and neutral Powers that Poland was an independent state.

Pilsudski, assured of French good will, credits, and munitions, needed little encouragement to make enormous territorial claims, for the key-note of his foreign policy was to restore the Polish frontiers of 1772 – roughly the line of the Dvina and Dnieper – and to make Poland the head of an anti-Bolshevik confederation.

In April, 1919, he invaded Lithuania, stormed Lida and occupied Vilna. In May he invaded east Galicia, which had been proclaimed a West Ukrainian Republic by General Petliura who, in November, 1918, had become head of the Ukrainian National Government, and so began the Polish-Ukrainian War.

Because the Supreme Council of the Allied Powers took little heed of these campaigns and failed to appreciate what manner of man Pilsudski was, on December 8, it fixed the eastern frontier of Poland along the line of the river Bug, and in the following year it became known as the "Curzon Line". It in no way satisfied Pilsudski, and soon after it was suggested the situation in the Ukraine grew so critical that, in the spring of 1920, Petliura came to terms with Pilsudski, and on April 22, peace between them was signed at Warsaw. Poland recognized the independence of the Ukraine and undertook to support the Ukrainians against Russia.

CHAPTER 9

The Battle of Warsaw, 1920

The civil war in Russia threw up one remarkable general – Mikail Tukhachevski. An able soldier, his outlook on civilization so closely reflected the Asiatic side of Bolshevism that to understand the future trend of the Russian Revolution it is worth while to examine it.

Born in 1892 of a noble family which traced its descent back to the Counts of Flanders, although his mother was an Italian, in character he was Tartar. From her he inherited his Latin looks, black hair, and the quick wit which enabled him to probe the Russian within him and the Tartar within the Russian. In 1914 he was gazetted a sub-lieutenant in the Imperial Guard, and in the following year was taken prisoner by the Germans.

By instinct he was a romantic barbarian who abhorred western civilization. He had the soul of Genghis Khan, of Ogdai and of Batu. Autocratic, superstitious, romantic and ruthless, he loved the open plain lands and the thud of a thousand hoofs, and he loathed and feared the unromantic orderliness of civilization. He hated Christianity and Christian culture because they had obliterated paganism and barbarism and had deprived his fellow countrymen of the ecstasy of the god of war and the glamour of "the carnival of death". Also he loathed the Jews because they had helped to inoculate the Russians with "the pest of civilization" and "the morale of capitalism." He said: "The Jew is a dog, son of a dog, who sows his fleas in every land."[1]

When he was incarcerated at Ingolstadt, he said to Fervacque, a fellow prisoner: "A demon or a god animates our race. We shall make ourselves drunk, because we cannot as yet make the world drunk. That will come."[2] Once Fervacque found him painting in discordant colours on a piece of cardboard the head of an atrocious idol. What is that? he asked him. "Do not laugh," replied Tukhachevski, "I have told you that the Slavs are in want of a new religion. They are being given Marxism; but aspects of that

[1] *Le chef de l'armée rouge, Mikail Tukachevski*, Pierre Fervacque (1928), p. 24.
[2] *Ibid.*, p. 67.

theology are too modern and too civilized. It is possible to mitigate that disagreeable state by returning to our Slav gods, who were deprived of their prerogative and strength; nevertheless they can soon regain them. There is Daschbog, the god of the sun; Stribog, the god of the storm; Wolos, the god of human arts and of poetry; and also Pierounn, the god of war and of lightning. For long I have hesitated to choose my particular god; but, after reflection, I have accepted Pierounn, because once Marxism is thrust upon Russia, the most devastating wars will be let loose. . . . We shall enter chaos and we shall not leave it until civilization is reduced to total ruin."[1]

This was no sudden, imaginative whim caused by the boredom of imprisonment; when Tukhachevski was a small child he and his brothers scandalized their French governess by "baptising" three cats, amid dreadful howlings, in the name of "The Father, the Son and the Holy Ghost."[2] Every western virtue terrified him. "Honour, what is that," he cried? "Out-of-date word, which henceforth must be left to Occidentals."[3]

In his eyes, destruction justified everything because it unlocked the door which led to the road back to Seljuk, Tartar and Hun. "Seriously," he said, "it would be good for humanity were all books burnt, so that we could bathe in the fresh spring of ignorance. I even think that it is the sole means of preventing humankind becoming sterile." What he yearned for was a return to the days of Ivan the Terrible; "then Moscow will become the centre of the world of barbarians." "Had Nicholas II but followed in the footsteps of Peter the Great and Catherine II, how docile the Russians would have been, for they love a despot." "If Lenin is able to disencumber Russia from the old scrap iron of prejudices and de-westernize her, I will follow him. But he must raze all to the ground, and deliberately hurl us back into barbarism."[4]

In 1937 Stalin shot him, and in goodly company; for with Uborevitch, Primokov, Putna and others he returned to his god —Annihilation.

This strange volcanic man, whose soul was in revolt with civilization, was destined to cross swords with Pilsudski, who was as violently anti-Russian as he was violently anti-European. Of the latter, Lord D'Abernon, who had exceptional opportunities to watch him, says: "An ardent patriot and a man of immense courage and force of character. A pronounced sceptic about

---

[1] *Ibid.*, pp. 73-75. [2] *Ibid.*, p. 20. [3] *Ibid.*, p. 111. [4] *Ibid.*, p. 62.

orthodox methods, whether applied to military affairs or politics; he loves danger, his pulse only beating at a normal rate when he is in imminent personal peril. . . . Next to danger, he is said to love intrigue – a revolutionary by temperament and circumstances, his ingrained proclivity is to the secret and indirect."[1]

It was these characteristics – courage, unorthodoxy, and secrecy – coupled with success, which made Pilsudski a legendary figure. The day before his death, on May 12, 1935, he turned to General Smigly-Rydz and said to him: "To be vanquished and not surrender is victory, to vanquish and rest on laurels is defeat."[2] The first half of this saying sums up his generalship.

Before we describe the campaign which immediately followed the signing of the Treaty of Warsaw, it is as well to look at the opposing forces. Both were improvised, chaotically equipped and suffered from over-rapid growth. In November, 1918, when Pilsudski assumed command, the Polish army consisted of 24 battalions, three squadrons and five batteries; yet by January, 1919, these had respectively been raised to 100, 70, and 80, in all comprising some 110,000 men. A year later this figure had risen to 600,000 men, organized in 21 divisions and seven brigades of cavalry; but most were still in formation. Though manpower was sufficient, Poland possessed no arsenals and lacked munitions. A greater difficulty was an adequate supply of horses, because during six years of war the country had been searched repeatedly for remounts, and, as will shortly be seen, deficiency in the cavalry arm was Pilsudski's greatest weakness.

What of his opponent's army? Tukhachevski once said to Fervacque: "The Russian Army is not like yours – the French. It is a horde, and its strength is that of a horde."[3] Though these words were spoken during the World War, they are equally applicable to the campaign of 1920, because the army which faced Pilsudski was nothing more than a horde of peasants – whose sole idea was to get home[4] – leavened with a comparatively small number of fanatical revolutionaries. Though it was better equipped than the Poles – the rounding up of Denekin's and Kolchak's forces had supplied it with millions of pounds worth of French and British armaments – it was lamentably short of military

---

[1] *The Eighteenth Decisive Battle of the World*, Viscount D'Abernon (1920), pp. 38-39.
[2] Quoted from *Pilsudski Marshal of Poland*, Eric J. Patterson (1935), p. 127.
[3] *Le chef de l'armée rouge*, p. 36.
[4] See *The Eighteenth Decisive Battle of the World*, D'Abernon, p. 77.

transport and trained officers. The former consisted of thousands of peasants' carts, and the deficiency in the latter was made good by commissioning hundreds of officers of the old Imperial Army. But as their loyalty was suspect, Trotsky attached commissars to each formation. Most of these men were Jews, and, according to Lord D'Abernon, "they did everything in their divisions – commandeered food – gave orders—explained objectives."[1]

Both Poles and Russians desperately wanted peace, yet only on their own terms, which were: for the former, the old frontier of 1772; for the latter, the continuance of world revolution. So it came about that, when on December 22, 1920, the Soviet Government invited the Polish Government to negotiate a peace, though the proposal was accepted, nothing came of it.

At length, on April 25, diplomatic fencing was brought to an end by a sudden offensive launched by Pilsudski west of Zhitomir. His aim was to seize Kiev, and then to turn northward against Tukhachevski, who faced his left wing. Led by Pilsudski the Polish army, supported on its right by two divisions of Ukrainians under the Hetman Petliura, as well as by some Rumanians, swept towards the Dnieper, and, on May 7, occupied Kiev.

The forces faced each other as follows:

Russian: North of the Pripet, the Army of the West, under Tukhachevski, consisted of the Fourth, Fifteenth, Third and Sixteenth Armies, and the IIIrd Cavalry Corps (Gay Khan); and south of the Pripet the Army of the South-West, commanded by Yeḡorov, comprised the Twelfth and Fourteenth Armies, and five divisions of cavalry under Budienny. In all – possibly – 200,000 men.

Polish: North of the Pripet, the First and Fourth Armies, with a Reserve Army in rear near Vilna in process of formation; and south of the Pripet, the Third, Second and Sixth Armies. In all, some 120,000 men.[2]

Though the Russian numerical superiority was important, more especially as the bulk of it was opposed to the far weaker Polish left flank, what was more important was that the area between the Bug and the Dnieper was cut in half by the swamps of Polesia, a dead-level country practically impassable by large bodies of troops. This meant that a general action on the whole

---

[1] *Ibid.*, pp. 68, 76.
[2] Correct strengths for both sides are impossible to give. Throughout the campaign they changed constantly.

front of the two armies would at once develop into two separate actions which could not cooperate. When Comrade Sergei Kamenev, the commander-in-chief of all the Soviet armed forces,

21. POLISH-SOVIET CAMPAIGN, 1920

realized this, he ordered Tukhachevski to attack the Polish left wing. This he was eager to do, for frantic with revolution he dreamt of watering his horses on the Rhine[1] and of carrying the

---

[1] *Le chef de l'armée rouge*, Fervacque, p. 123.

war over the corpse of Poland into western Europe. At this time, Trotsky referred to Pilsudski as "a third rate Buonaparte", and, on May 2, he made the following forecast:

"There can be no doubt that the war of the Polish bourgeoisie against the Ukrainain and Russian workers and peasants will end with a workers' revolution in Poland. It would be a pitiful lack of spirit to be frightened at the first successes of Pilsudski. They are unavoidable. They were foreseen. They were a result of the earlier development of our relations with Poland. The deeper the right wing of the Polish troops penetrates into Ukrainia, turning against itself Ukrainian insurgents of all kinds, the more fatal for the Polish troops will be the concentrated blow which the Red troops will give them."[1]

Strategically this was correct, and when, on May 15, Tukhachevski selected as his objective the railway junction of Molodechno, and launched his Fifteenth Army against it, his aim was to drive it into the Pinsk swamps. Though the attack failed, it shook Pilsudski; but before he could reinforce his left wing, a formidable attack was launched against him in the south. There Budienny, who had served in the ranks during the Russo-Japanese War, at the head of 16,700 Cossacks, accompanied by 48 cannon, five armoured trains, eight armoured cars and 12 aeroplanes, struck at Pilsudski's right wing in the neighbourhood of Elizavetgrad on May 18. Next, he moved northward; attacked the Polish forces south and south-west of Kiev; broke through near Gaisin; raided west of Kiev; and swept into Berditchev and Zhitomir. On June 5 the Polish Third Army was nearly surrounded, but on the 13th it broke away and retired westward while Budienny's horsemen swept onward, crossed the Horyn on July 3, and two days later occupied Rovno. From there they pressed forward to Lutzk, Dubno, and the outskirts of Lvov (Lemberg).

As Pilsudski informs us, panic followed, and "the work of the State itself began to crack." He writes: "For our troops who were not prepared to meet this new offensive instrument, Budienny's cavalry became an invincible, legendary force. And it should be remembered that the farther in rear one goes, the more does such an obsession escape all reason – to become all-powerful and irresistible. Thus for me began to be created that most dangerous of all fronts – the inner one."[2] At the time, all he could do to meet

---

[1] *History of the Russian Revolution*, Trotsky (1932–35), vol. III, book 2, p. 102.
[2] *L'Année 1920*, Joseph Pilsudski (1929), p. 51.

this critical development was to save his left wing, the right flank of which had been turned by the defeat of his right wing; he therefore ordered its withdrawal.

When Pilsudski's left was in retreat, Tukhachevski set about to reorganize his chaotic army. During June he collected and incorporated nearly 100,000 deserters,[1] and though he complained bitterly of lack of equipment, the idea upon which he based his forthcoming attack was political rather than military. He considered that "the situation in Poland was favourable to revolution," and that a powerful rising of the city proletariat and peasants only awaited his arrival "on the ethnographical frontier of Poland." Further, he thought that Europe was ripe for revolution and that "a rapid and victorious offensive would hypnotize the peoples and draw them eastward." He arrived at these conclusions from exaggerated accounts of the conditions then prevalent: in Germany, where the people only awaited "the signal of revolt"; in England, where the situation resembled that in Russia in 1904; and in Italy, where the workers had occupied the factories and industrial establishments. He launched an advanced guard of propagandists to blaze a trail for his horde.[2] On this strategy, Lord D'Abernon writes:

"Moscow disposed of a host of spies, propagandists, secret emissaries and secret friends, who penetrated into Polish territory and undermined the resistance of certain elements of the Polish population . . . the services rendered by the unarmed were not less effective than those brought about by military pressure. The system adopted was to avoid frontal attack whenever possible, and to turn positions by flank marches, infiltration and propaganda."[3]

Though a cunning general, as an administrator Tukhachevski was, like most Russians, hopelessly inefficient. A Tartar at heart, he intended to live on the land and his system of supply closely resembled that of Attila or Genghis Khan. Fervacque probably exaggerates when he says that his 200,000 warriors were followed by a horde of 800,000 politicians, police, and pillagers, whose duty it was to bolshevize the conquered territories, by laying low the

[1] *Ibid.*, Annexe I, "La marche au dela de la Vistula," M. Tukhachevski, p. 215.
[2] *Ibid.*, pp. 231–232.
[3] *The Eighteenth Decisive Battle of the World*, p. 28. This propaganda cut both ways. Chamberlin points out its discouraging effect on the Red soldiers, when on reaching the outskirts of Warsaw they "learned that there were some workers among the volunteers who were increasing the numbers of the Polish forces against them" (*The Russian Revolution* (1935), vol. II, p. 317).

wealthy and shooting the bourgeois and aristocrats.[1] Yet his exaggeration is not so great as it appears, because Tukhachevski tells us that his Fourth, Fifteenth, Third, and Sixteenth Armies were followed by 33,000 farm carts, and somewhat ironically adds: "It was a heavy burden for the local inhabitants."[2] This number of carts, at six men a cart approximately adds up to 200,000, and while these men devastated the Soviet rear, propaganda cleared the way on the Soviet front.

What the opposing strengths were at the end of June is problematical. The Polish armies would appear to have numbered approximately 120,000 men and the Soviet 200,000. Tukhachevski gives the figure of 150,188, made up of 80,942 rifles, 10,521 sabres, and 68,715 oddments;[3] and Pilsudski states that the total number placed under Tukhachevski's orders was 794,645 men and 150,572 horses, of which figure fighters numbered 200,000.[4] Whichever figures are correct, the Soviet forces constituted a magazine-rifle horde.

When the way had been cleared by propaganda, Tukhachevski launched his four armies into attack between the rivers Dvina and Pripet at dawn on July 4; the axis of their advance was the Smolensk–Brest-Litovsk railway. It was met by a stout resistance by the First and Fourth Polish armies, but confronted by a four to one superiority they were forced back. No attempt had been made to entrench,[5] because Pilsudski realized the uselessness of field works when fronts are long and forces are in comparison small. Besides, trenches could always be turned by the enemy's cavalry.

On July 7 the whole Polish front was in full retreat. On the 11th, a battle for Vilna opened. Vilna fell to the Soviet Fourth Army on the 14th, and the Polish situation became still more critical when the Lithuanian Army joined the Bolsheviks. By now, writes Pilsudski, Tukhachevski's continuous advance produced "the impression of something irresistible, a monstrous and heavy cloud which no obstacle could halt. . . . Under the threat of this cloud, munitioned with hail, the State settled down to sink; men trembled, and the hearts of our soldiers began to yield."[6] Everywhere around him he felt despair and impotence grow; the complete dissolution of Poland seemed imminent.

---

[1] *Le chef de l'armée rouge*, p. 124.
[2] *L'Année 1920*, Annexe I, p. 218.   [3] *Ibid.*, p. 217.
[4] *Ibid.*, p. 16, quoting Froloff's *Approvisionnement de l'armée rouge sur le front occidental* (in Russian).
[5] *Ibid.*, p. 78, 84.   [6] *Ibid.*, pp. 113–114.

While Pilsudski clutched his retreating armies together, Tukhachevski moved on. On July 18 the latter ordered his Fourth Army to force the Niemen south of Grodno on the 21st; the Fifteenth to cross it on the 22nd; and the Third and Sixteenth to force the Shara river, north and south of Slonim. But the advance moved more rapidly than his orders; on the 19th Gay Khan and his horseman occupied Grodno and on the 21st Tukhachevski sent the following message to Moscow:

"Grodno was occupied on the 19th and Slonim yesterday. These two successes are witness to the fact that the line of the Niemen and Shara are forced and that the retreating enemy possesses no further positions upon which he can hope to hold us. We can now expect to complete our task in three weeks time."[1]

Kamenev was so thrilled by this that he imagined the Poles beaten beyond redemption and suggested the withdrawal of one of Tukhachevski's four armies in order to build up a reserve.

While north of the Pripet the Poles fell back, south of it the Polish Third Army, under General Smigly-Rydz, was so harassed by Budienny's Cossacks that it rapidly lost both energy and fighting spirit. Pilsudski says: "In the south the cavalry of Budienny were the motor of the war."[2]

When Grodno fell, Tukhachevski ordered Warsaw to be occupied on August 12. The reason he gives why he did not halt and reorganize his rear services and wait for 60,000 reinforcements to catch up with him is that, as his enemy was in rout, all that was necessary was to push on with the utmost energy.[3] This he did, while Pilsudski planned to hold the line of the Bug and counterattack Tukhachevski's left flank. But, on July 22 and 23, this line fell as well as that of the Niemen, and, on August 1, the Poles were driven out of Brest-Litovsk. Pilsudski's position was desperate, and because the Polesian swamps had been turned he expected that the two Soviet armies – Tukhachevski's and Yegorov's – would unite and crush his demoralized forces. Fortunately the situation was not so bad as it appeared, for Wrangel had emerged from his lair in the Crimea and so threatened Yegorov's rear that Tukhachevski agreed to detach part of the Twelfth Army[4] to help him. Although this did not relieve the immediate Polish situation, in the middle of August it had an important influence upon operations.

[1] *Ibid.*, Notes, p. 286.   [2] *Ibid.*, p. 120.
[3] *Ibid.*, Annexe I, p. 234.   [4] *Ibid.*, Notes, pp. 298–299.

On August 2 Pilsudski entered Warsaw to learn that the Narew was in his enemy's hands. On the following day Lomza was lost and the whole of the Polish First Army fell back on the capital. Annihilation seemed imminent; yet again the situation was not without hope, for the rapidity of the Bolshevik advance, nearly 300 miles in 30 days, had so disordered Tukhachevski's supply system that it was near dissolution. The situation was such that Tukhachevski could neither stand still nor retire; to halt and reorganize was out of the question for it would mean starvation. All he could do was to push on.

Further, the political situation favoured a continuation of the attack. In Austria, Czechoslovakia, and Germany the workers refused to allow munitions to pass through their countries to Poland. "On August 6 the British Labour Party published a pamphlet which stated that the workers of Great Britain would take no part in the war as allies of Poland." In Paris the French Socialists, through their organ L'Humanité, spoke of a "war against the Soviet Republic by the Polish Government on the orders of Anglo-French Imperialism, and cried 'Not a man, not a sou, not a shell for reactionary and capitalist Poland. Long live the Russian Revolution. Long live the Workman's International' ";[1] while in Danzig the dockers refused to unload munitions. Of all European peoples the Hungarians alone were friendly to the Poles, because under the hideous régime of Bela Kun they had tasted the fruits of the Bolshevik revolution.[2]

This dark political background to the Polish retreat of 375 miles convinced both Great Britain and France of the imminence of a Soviet victory – "Nothing could appear more certain than that the Soviet forces would capture Warsaw."[3] As early as July 12 this spirit of defeatism had already gripped the British Government. On that day, Lord Curzon, British Foreign Minister, who believed in the heresy that peace with Bolsheviks was possible, addressed a note to the Soviet Government, not only to propose a truce, but also that the frontier between Poland and Russia should be the line of the Bug. Five days later Chicherin suggested a conference, and, on August 10, Mr. Lloyd George in the House

---

[1] The Poland of Pilsudski, Robert Machray, pp. 112–113.
[2] On May 27, 1919, Lenin had written to the Hungarian Communists as follows: "Be firm. If there are waverings among the Socialists who came over to you yesterday, or among the petty bourgeoisie, in regard to the dictatorship of the proletariat, suppress the waverings mercilessly. Shooting is the proper fate of a coward in war" (Collected Works, Lenin, vol. XVI, p. 229).
[3] The Eighteenth Decisive Battle of the World, D'Abernon, p. 15.

of Commons advised Poland to accept the Bolshevik peace terms. These included among other things that the Polish army should be limited to 60,000 men supported by an armed militia of urban industrial workers "under the control of the labour organization of Russia, Poland, and Norway."[1]

As this meant the complete Bolshevization of Poland they were rejected by Pilsudski who, as will be seen, four days before Mr. Lloyd George gave his fearful advice, when in the solitude of the Belvedere Palace an idea flashed into his mind which was to change the whole course of the war.

Meanwhile, the Bolshevik typhoon swept westward, and as something immediate had to be done by Great Britain and France, they decided to send a Mission to Warsaw. Lord D'Abernon, British Ambassador in Berlin, was instructed to proceed to Paris, where he was to be joined by General Weygand and others, and then hasten to Warsaw. When the Mission arrived there on July 25 it found that Pilsudski wanted shells, not advice.

To return to the war. On his arrival in Warsaw Pilsudski was confronted by the following situation. The bridgehead was well entrenched and wired, and was defended by 43 batteries of heavy guns. Further, it was flanked by the strong places of Deblin (Ivangorod) in the south and of Modlin (Novo-Georgievsk) to the north, as well as Plock, on the Vistula, further westward. Satisfied that the position was strong, he left it as it was, avoided the diplomatists, now busy considering the Soviet peace terms, and like Joffre before the battle of the Marne, he demoted many of his subordinates, placed General Haller in command of Warsaw, and raised a new Army, the Fifth, under General Sikorski.

The situation on the 200-mile battle front was: The Polish army was distributed in two groups – one around Warsaw and the other around Lvov – linked together by a weak centre. The northern group consisted of the Fifth Army (34,000), First Army (38,000), and Second Army (12,000), and the Fourth Army (23,500) – still falling back from the river Bug. The southern group consisted of the Sixth Army (22,000) about Lvov, with the Seventh Army, Ukrainians and Rumanians (24,000), to its south, and it was linked to the northern group by the Third Army (25,000). From

---

[1] *The Russian Revolution, 1917–1921*, William Henry Chamberlin (1935), vol. II, p. 208. See also *The Soviets in World Affairs*, Louis Fischer (1930), p. 267, and *The Eighteenth Decisive Battle of the World*, pp. 70–71.

north to south, in face of this long line stretched the Army of the West under Tukhachevski and the Army of the South-West under Yegorov. The former consisted of the Fourth Army (28,000), supported by Gay Khan's IIIrd Cavalry Corps (4,700), the Fifteenth Army (26,000), Third Army (20,000), Sixteenth Army (20,700), and the Mozyr Group (8,000); and the latter of the Twelfth Army (22,500), Fourteenth Army (18,000), and Budienny's First Cavalry Army (30,000). In all, 178,500 Poles and Ukrainians faced 177,900 Bolsheviks.

As the bulk of both armies was in the neighbourhood of Warsaw, Weygand's advice to Pilsudski was to defend the line of the Vistula – while a deliberate counter-offensive was prepared behind that river. In this he was supported by many of the Polish generals, who favoured a counter-attack based on Modlin with its right hinged on the Vistula. Their idea was to smash the Soviet right and drive it south of the river Bug and cut it off from the Warsaw–Bialystok railway.

While Weygand and the Polish generals talked, Pilsudski listened. He neither agreed nor disagreed, and seemingly their discussions left his mind blank. Then, on the night of August 5–6, he retired to his study in the Belvedere Palace, and his account of this inner struggle is so self-revealing that we will quote it in full.

"There is on record," he writes, "an admirable expression made by the greatest authority on the human soul in war time – Napoleon – who said of himself that, while about to take an important decision, he was like a girl on the point of giving birth to a child. Since that night I have often been reminded of the profound subtlety of this thought. He, who despised the weakness of the fair sex, compares himself, a giant in will and genius, to a frail young woman on her bed, a prey to the pains of labour. He used to say to himself that in those moments he was pusillanimous. I, myself, a prey to the same pusillanimity, could not overcome the absurdity of the problem of this battle, which condemned the bulk of the forces gathered at Warsaw to passive resistance. In my opinion, the counter-attack could not be launched from Warsaw nor from Modlin. This would mean a frontal attack against the main forces of the enemy, which, as I believed, were concentrated before Warsaw, and up to that time neither our forces nor our command had been able to hold the victorious enemy. Besides, the nightmare of defeat and the excuses of poltroons were sweeping over the whole town."

Pilsudski's meditations brought him to realize that to hold Warsaw was not enough, and if only to reinstate the morale of his army an offensive was imperative. But where was he to obtain the necessary troops for a counter-attack? – this was the question which perplexed him. Were he to withdraw them from either wing, the civil population of Warsaw or Lvov would almost certainly fall into a panic which might spread to his troops. He turned to his reports and his map, and was struck by the slow retreat of the Fourth Army. "The natural direction in which the enemy was pushing it," he writes, "was bringing it onto the Vistula between Warsaw and Deblin. Now, in that direction, there were neither bridges nor any other means of crossing. In the event of the enemy pushing vigorously in the centre, this army might be driven into a corner on the Vistula and find itself in an extremely critical position. It was, therefore, necessary to incline it either towards Warsaw or Deblin, or divide it into two sections, one diverted to the north and the other to the south."[1]

At length he made up his mind; he decided to order the bulk of the Fourth Army to fall back on Deblin, and as Budienny's cavalry had been driven back, at the same time to withdraw two divisions – the 1st and 3rd of the Legion – from the southern wing to Deblin. This he decided in spite of the risk that should Budienny learn of this he would again advance. Lastly, because the success of the counter-attack was so doubtful, he decided to command it in person.

When we look at the situation as it faced him, it will be seen that his basic idea was to take advantage of the separation of his enemy's forces: Tukhachevski's army was massed about Warsaw, and Yegorov's and Budienny's cavalry were in the vicinity of Lvov. The entire enemy front ran diagonally from north-west to south-east, the two armies were linked together by a weak centre about Lublin near the river Wieprz. Could the enemy about Warsaw and Lvov be held back, Pilsudski was convinced that, were he to interpose his counter-attack force south of the Wieprz between Deblin and Lublin – that is, at a right angle to the enemy's weak centre – he might well be able to attack Tukhachevski's Sixteenth Army in rear and simultaneously prevent that army penetrating his own weak centre between Warsaw and Deblin. Further, he knew that the Mozyr Group, which lay between the

[1] *L'Année 1920*, pp. 136–141.

Soviet Sixteenth and Twelfth Armies, was too weak and over-extended to offer much resistance; therefore, as he writes: "It was on that base [*i.e.*, the Wieprz] upon which the order of August 6, regulating the strategical distribution of the troops for the battle of Warsaw, was directed,"[1] and this in spite of the fact that on that day and the day following the three divisions (14th, 16th, and 21st) of the Fourth Army were still engaged. Also, not only did he realize that the withdrawal of the Fourth Army would entail a flank march in face of the enemy, but that the withdrawal of the 1st and 3rd Divisions of the Legion would open the door to Budienny.[2]

Could he carry out this counter-attack with extreme rapidity, and it must be remembered that he had little cavalry, then it was possible, once the Mozyr Group was dispersed, to fall on the rear of the Soviet Sixteenth Army, which he knew was already in a state of dislocation because of the ever-growing confusion in Tukhachevski's supply system.[3] To accentuate that confusion was the moral arrow he intended to fire from his strategic bow – the Wieprz. If it struck home, the rear of the Soviet Sixteenth Army would recoil on the rear of the Third, Fifteenth and Fourth Armies around Warsaw, and with their supply paralysed his own armies at Warsaw – the First and Fifth – would be able to advance to the counter-attack. In brief, his grand idea was to counter-attack with the bulk of his forces – a physical counter-attack detonated by the moral counter-attack of his Fourth Army. General Camon says that, taken as a whole, the manœuvre was Napoleonic, because it favoured a rear attack. It would be more apt to call it Alexandrian, because it more closely resembles the field strategy employed at the battle of Arbela. There, it will be remembered, the great Macedonian held his enemy's right, charged through the Persian weak left centre, and attacked the Persian right in rear, and this is what Pilsudski intended to do.

Once Pilsudski had formulated his plan, it was severely criticized by his generals and his general staff. His boldness winded them, for like mice they were hypnotized by the cat-like Tukhachevski, and instead of urging their chief to strengthen his counter-attacking forces, they could think of nothing better than

---

[1] *Ibid.*, p. 142.   [2] *Ibid.*, p. 146.
[3] For the state of Tukhachevski's army at this time, see Camon's *La Manoeuvre Liberatrice* (1929), p. 109.

to supplicate him to strengthen Warsaw.[1] Pilsudski held firm to his idea, and on August 6 the order for the assembly was issued.[2] He settled on August 17 as the day for his counter-attack, and on the 12th he left Warsaw for Deblin.

What was Tukhachevski's plan?

He was well aware that Lenin[3] attached the highest importance to the fall of Warsaw, and now that he stood before its gates, what course should he take? In reply he says that lack of troops prevented him from delivering a central attack or simultaneously attacking both his enemy's flanks, and that he was forced to choose between either a right or a left flank attack. To attack the Polish right would, so he says, have required a complicated regrouping of his army and the changing of its line of communications which ran through Kleshcheli (Kleszczele) and Brest-Litovsk. He decided to turn the Polish left and cut its communications with Danzig, and this in spite of the fact that he recognized that the outflanking army would have its back to East Prussia, which would place it at a disadvantage should the operation fail. He expected his left wing to be covered by Yegorov's army.

On August 8 he issued his instructions for an attack on the 14th. They were to be carried out as follows:

The Fourth Army to move north of Warsaw; to cover itself from the direction of Thorn, and force the Vistula at Plock. The Fifteenth Army to move on Plonsk; the Third on Wyszograd–Modlin; the Sixteenth on Nowo-Minsk–Garwolin and to force the Vistula south of Warsaw while the Mozyr Group forced the river in the neighbourhood of Deblin. He ended his project by saying: "Because of the high morale of our troops, we had the absolute right to count upon victory."[4] He said this although a copy of Pilsudski's order of August 6 had fallen into his hands; but fortunately for his enemy he believed it to be a bluff.

When we examine these instructions, it will at once be seen

---

[1] See Sikorski's *La campgane Polono-Russe de 1920*, pp. 70–77. Commenting on this, General Camon writes: "In the Polish G.H.Q., like the German in 1914, and also in other G.H.Qs. of the same period, the Operations Branch considered itself superior to the General-in-Chief – after all only an amateur – and G.H.Q. again and again returned to the idea of halting the Bolshevik advance by a counter-attack launched from the left flank of the front" (*La Manoeuvre Liberatrice*, p. 31), which was also General Weygand's idea.

[2] See *La Campagne Polono-Russe de 1920*, Sikorski (1929), pp. 53–56, and *La Manoeuvre Liberatrice*, Camon, pp. 34–41.

[3] In his *Collected Works*, vol. XVII, p. 308, we read: "All Germany boiled up when our troops approached Warsaw."

[4] *L'Année 1920*, Annexe I, pp. 244–245.

that they entail a general advance of the bulk of the Soviet forces directed north of Warsaw. The weakness of this attack did not lie in lack of numbers, but in lack of unity of command. Kamenev was in Moscow, Tukhachevski remained in Minsk, and Yegorov was in the neighbourhood of Lvov – over 200 miles distant from him. Worse still, he and Yegorov were at daggers drawn.

On August 10 Kamenev sent Yegorov an order to transfer Budienny and his cavalry to Tukhachevski's command, but as his message could not be deciphered, there was a three-day delay before it was re-transmitted. Then, on the 13th, when it became understandable, Yegorov started to argue. He was not interested in the Warsaw operations, and was intent upon taking Lvov, Przemysl and Sambor, and once he had forced the Dniester, to carry the war into Rumania. The result was that Kamenev's order was set aside and Budienny marched on Lvov as formerly had done the Tartar horde of Chmielnicki.

Meanwhile, what of Pilsudski? He tells us that August 6 to 12 were days of great anxiety while he watched his enemy creep round his left flank. On the 11th Tukhachevski launched an attack on Pultusk, garrisoned, as Sikorski informs us, by worn-out troops who looked like "living corpses" in rags and with naked feet.[1] This old fortress blocked the crossing of the Narew, and when, as they did, the Bolsheviks carried it, the sole remaining line of defence between it and the Vistula was the Wkra river, which joins the Bug near Modlin. The loss of Pultusk was in part compensated by General Smigly-Rydz's skilful withdrawal of the 1st and 3rd Divisions of the Legion from the Bug. Next, on the 13th, Tukhachevski's final orders for a general attack on the following day, sent out in clear by wireless, were intercepted, and the foreign diplomatists hastily retired from Warsaw to Lodz.

As we have seen, Tukhachevski's plan was to turn Warsaw from the north and, once its communications were cut, to fall upon its rear. On the 13th his Sixteenth Army advanced on the southern flank of the city, and his Third Army on its northern flank, while his Fifteenth Army moved on the Wkra, its centre on Nasielsk, and his Fourth swung round its right flank on to Plock. That day the Third Army launched an attack on the outer defences of Warsaw, which ran through Radzymin. These were held by the First Polish Army, while the Fifth, under Sikorski, occupied the line of the Wkra.

[1] *La Campagne Polono-Russe de 1920*, Sikorski, p. 79.

Pilsudski, accompanied by five staff officers, established his G.H.Q. at Pulawy, a little to the south of Deblin, and on this day – August 13 – he visited the units of his Fourth Army, to be in no way encouraged by what he saw. The troops were so ill-equipped that, as he says, "Throughout the entire campaign I had as yet never seen such ragamuffins."[1] He visited unit after unit, spoke to the men, and did all he could to raise their confidence and morale.

On August 14, Radzymin was lost by the Poles; this brought the Bolsheviks to within 15 miles of Warsaw. Simultaneously a fierce attack was launched against Sikorski on the Wkra and the situation became so critical that General Haller urged Pilsudski to start his counter-attack a day earlier than the date fixed. He agreed to do so, although another 24 hours would have been invaluable to him.

On August 15 the battle of the Wkra continued and a group of eight Polish armoured cars operated with signal effect in the area Raciaz–Drobin–Bielsk. Sikorski says: "With great skill they insinuated themselves in between the enemy units, attacked out-posts and destroyed supply columns and communications, and rendered the highest service. They doubled their strength by their mobility; sowed confusion in the rear of the Russian divisions, and produced the impression that they were preparing the way for a formidable offensive."[2] The next day violent Bolshevik assaults were beaten back at Nasielsk; but under cover of these attacks Tukhachevski's Fourth Army wheeled round southward on to Plock, Wloclawek, Bobrowniki, and Nieszawa, all on the Vistula; the last-mentioned town was some 18 miles south-east of Thorn. The Polish situation grew worse and worse, for although the First Army held firm to Warsaw, Sikorski's left was turned, and in the vicinity of Plonsk a strong attack developed in his rear. Then from the Wieprz came salvation. That morning Pilsudski launched his counter-attack and during the next few days it was to advance to a depth of 150 miles.

On the Day of the Virgin, August 16, 1920, the Rubicon of Poland – the river Wieprz – was crossed, and the Polish Fourth Army was given as its objective the Warsaw–Brest-Litovsk road. Unlike Tukhachevski, who during his attack had remained at Minsk, Pilsudski passed the whole of this day in his motor-car and went from flank to flank to encourage his men and rapidly

[1] *L'Année 1920*, p. 147.   [2] *La Campagne Polono-Russe de 1920*, p. 181.

to estimate the situation. What astonished him most was the total absence of enemy forces. On the left Garwolin was occupied and passed without opposition; therefore for the 17th Pilsudski decided to swing forward the right wing of the counter-attack "and search for traces of the phantom enemy and for any signs of a trap." Again on the 17th he toured round his rapidly advancing front.

At the important railway station of Lukow, on the Brest-Litovsk line, he lunched with the headquarters staff of the 21st Division. Everyone affirmed "that there was no enemy in strength, and told him with enthusiasm that the whole of the civil population had risen in assistance, with the result that the few hostile groups met with were attacked by peasants armed with pitchforks accompanied by their wives carrying flails."[1] Of this day Pilsudski writes:

"Was I dreaming? But a few days back a veritable nightmare had obsessed me: a continuous movement of irresistible power, a movement in which I felt monstrous claws twining round my throat and suffocating me. Was it really true that my five divisions, freely and without any show of resistance, were boldly advancing over those self-same regions which but recently in the mortal agony of the retreat they had abandoned to the enemy? In spite of the joy of this dream, it seemed impossible that it could be real. A whole month of suggestions, suggestions of the superiority of the enemy refused to vanish. This happy dream could not be true. Thus I felt as I arrived that evening at Garwolin."[2]

A few hours later, as he sat by his bed drinking a cup of tea, away to the north he heard the distant thunder of cannon. "Then there was an enemy! It was not an illusion!" he exclaimed. "The shame which I had felt for the shock and my former terror, when engulfed in that monstrous nightmare which had all but conquered me by its savage illusive images, was not the dreamings of a madman and had been real. The enemy did exist, and the proof was the music of battle which rolled toward me from out the north."[3]

The next morning the cannonade had ceased, and although the countryside swarmed with Red Cossacks, again he set out in his car and drove to Kolbiel in order to catch up with the rear of his 14th Division, which had taken the town during the night and was then well on its way toward Nowo-Minsk. When he arrived there he found that the entire Soviet Sixteenth Army was in rout,

---

[1] *L'Année 1920*, p. 152.   [2] *Ibid.*, p. 152.   [3] *Ibid.*, pp. 152–153.

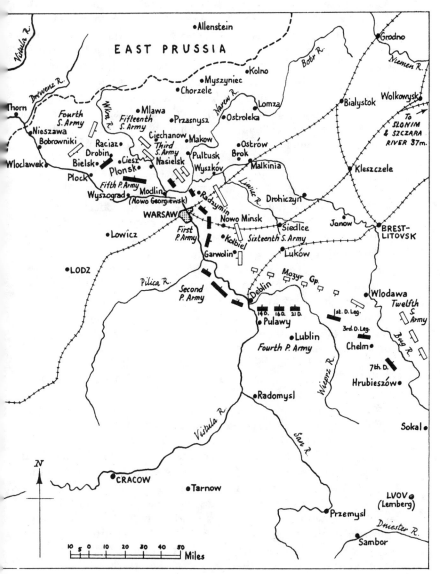

22. BATTLE OF WARSAW, AUGUST 16–25, 1920

so he ordered his driver to head for Warsaw, to co-ordinate the advance of the First and Fifth Armies with the counter-attack. This was unfortunate, as he acknowledges, for once his powerful presence was not felt on the battlefield, the pursuit slackened, with the result that much of August 18 was wasted. Also he blames himself for not having assumed the direct command of the First and Fifth Armies, for had he done so he would have been better placed to impose his will on their commanders, who were still gripped by the terror which had so long obsessed them. He writes: "There everyone seized upon the most minute manifestation of activity on the part of the enemy in order still to believe in the possibility of disaster instead of believing in victory."[1]

On August 18 he issued the following orders:

Third Army: To hold fast to the area Lublin–Chelm and push back all fractions of the Twelfth Soviet Army met with.

Second Army: To occupy Brest-Litovsk and pursue the enemy toward Bialystok.

Fourth Army: To advance by forced marches northward to the Malkinia–Bialystok railway; to occupy Brok and Wyzskov, and to push the enemy toward the German frontier.

First Army: To advance north-east, axis on Warsaw–Wyzskov–Ostrow–Lomza, with its cavalry on the left front, and to work toward the German frontier.

Fifth Army: To annihilate Gay Khan's Cavalry Corps; advance on Mlawa-Przasnysz and cut off all fractions of the Soviet Fifteenth Army west of those towns.

Unfortunately the Polish First Army had been too split up to enable it to carry out its orders. This prevented the total annihilation of Tukhachevski's forces.

When Pilsudski launched his counter-attack, Tukhachevski was still at Minsk, 300 miles from Warsaw, and twice the distance Moltke had been from Paris during the battle of the Marne. There he would seem to have lost all contact, not only with his enemy, but with his own armies; and he tells us that it was not until the 18th that he received a telephone call from the Commander of his Sixteenth Army to inform him that an attack had been launched. He was then told that the attack by the "White Poles need not be taken seriously."[2] Tukhachevski was too good a general to view the situation in this light and at once issued the following orders:

[1] *Ibid.*, pp. 165–166.   [2] *Ibid.*, Annexe 1, pp. 250–251.

The Fourth Army was forthwith to fall back and concentrate in the area Ciechanow–Przasnysz–Makow, and *en route* help the withdrawal of the Fifteenth Army. The Fifteenth was to hold back the enemy and assist the concentration of the Fourth; while the Sixteenth withdrew behind the Liwiec river, protected by the Mozyr Group on its left flank. The Twelfth Army was ordered to halt the enemy who had crossed the Wieprz by attacking him in flank. Lastly, the Third and Sixteenth Armies were each instructed to send a division to Drohiczyn and Janow to form a reserve for the whole front.[2]

Tukhachevski informs us that he had foreseen the necessity for a general retirement to the line Grodno–Brest-Litovsk; but this may be discounted as an afterthought, for the truth is that, apparently unknown to him half his army was already in rout, while the remaining half – the Fourth Army and most of the Fifteenth – was so trapped that his orders to them were inoperative. As it happened, those dispatched to the Fourth Army were long delayed in transmission, and when they were received, because its commander had been told nothing of the general situation and considered it favourable, he set his instructions aside and continued to cross the Vistula in order to attack Warsaw in rear.

By August 21 the rout of Tukhachevski's right wing was complete. First, the Soviet Sixteenth Army, then the Third, and lastly the Fifteenth had been struck in flank more by terror than by fighting. As they broke eastward in panic, the whole countryside became the scene of pandemonium; units, fractions of units and innumerable stragglers, mixed pell-mell with thousands of supply carts, swept toward the Niemen; while Pilsudski's bare-footed and tattered men pressed the pursuit mile after mile without firing a shot.

To the north and north-west of Warsaw, the right of the Soviet Fifteenth Army put up a desperate fight at Ciechanow; but driven out of it on August 19, and out of Mlawa on the 20th, it carried away with it in its flight the supply train of the Fourth Army, which faced the crossings of the Vistula at Wloclawek and Plock.

The sole Soviet force which distinguished itself in the disaster was Gay Khan's Cavalry Corps. On the 20th he fell back on Mlawa, launched a night attack on Konopki and cut up a Polish battalion, and then was pursued eastward to Chorzele, where he

[2] *Ibid.*, Annexe I, pp. 251–252.

cut his way through two regiments at Myszyniec. Next, he headed for Kolno, where he came up against the Polish Fourth Army, which a few hours earlier had occupied it. Although greatly outnumbered and short of ammunition he again attacked and, on August 25 was driven pell-mell over the German frontier, as was the Soviet Fourth Army.

Eventually, on August 25, the remnants of the Soviet Army of the West reached the line Grodno–east of Brest-Litovsk–Wlodawa, where the pursuit ended. The booty taken was immense: 66,000 prisoners besides 30,000 to 40,000 disarmed in Germany; 231 guns, 1,023 machine-guns and 10,000 ammunition and supply wagons. During July and August the total Polish casualties numbered about 50,000 and the Soviet 150,000.

In spite of this great victory the campaign was not ended and two separate operations followed, one in the south and the other in the north. The first was carried out by Sikorski, who opened his offensive on September 12 and occupied Kovel, Lutzk, Rovno and Tarnapol on the 18th and Pinsk on the 20th. The second was led by Pilsudski who, after a masterful manœuvre, attacked Tukhachevski on September 20, destroyed the Soviet Third Army in the Battle of the Niemen, and occupied Grodno on the 26th. This victory was at once followed by the battle of the Shara (Szczara),[1] in which the remnants of the Soviet Armies were driven back to Minsk. In these two battles Pilsudski took 50,000 prisoners and 160 guns. On October 10 an armistice was agreed, and on March 18, 1921, by the Treaty of Riga the eastern frontier of Poland was fixed as it stood until 1939.

This marked the end of a remarkable campaign, fought between improvised armies of limited size in a vast theatre of war. It was a campaign of mobility and surprise, totally different from most of those fought during the World War. It was a contest between armies led mostly by young generals, and in which cavalry played an important part and field trenches no part at all, and above all, it was a war in which men were more important than *matériel*, and generals more important than their staffs.

The influence of this decisive battle on history was fully appreciated by Tukhachevski, who lost it, and by Lord D'Abernon, who watched it. Yet, strange to say, its importance was little

---

[1] For these two battles see articles by General Faury (French) in the *Revue militaire française* of February and March, 1922, and March, 1929. Faury was in 1920 attached to General Skierski, who commanded the Fourth Polish Army.

grasped by western Europe, and since has remained little noticed. Soon after his defeat Tukhachevski wrote:

"In all European countries Capitalism was staggering; the workers were lifting their head and rushing to arms. There is not the slightest doubt that, had we been victorious on the Vistula, the revolution would have set light to the entire continent of Europe. . . . Exported revolution is possible . . . and had it not been for our strategical mistakes and our defeat on the field of battle, perhaps the Polish war would have been the link which would have united the revolution of October to the revolution of Western Europe. . . . There cannot be the slightest doubt that had we succeeded in disrupting the Polish Army of bourgeois and lords, the revolution of the Polish class workers would have been a *fait accompli*, and the conflagration would not have halted on the Polish frontiers. Like an overwhelming torrent it would have swept into Western Europe. The Red Army will never forget this experiment in exported revolution, and if ever the bourgeoisie of Europe invites us to new struggles, the Red Army will succeed in destroying it and fomenting revolution in Europe."[1]

Later, in an article published in the *Gazeta Polska* of August 17, 1930, Lord D'Abernon set down his judgment as follows:

"The history of contemporary civilization knows no event of greater importance than the Battle of Warsaw, 1920, and none of which the significance is less appreciated. The danger menacing Europe at that moment was parried, and the whole episode forgotten. Had the battle been a Bolshevik victory, it would have been a turning point in European history, for there is no doubt at all that the whole of Central Europe would at that moment have been opened to the influence of Communist propaganda and a Soviet invasion, which it could with difficulty have resisted. . . . The events of 1920 also deserve attention for another reason: victory was attained, above all, thanks to the strategical genius of one man and thanks to the carrying through of a manœuvre so dangerous as to necessitate not only genius, but heroism. . . . It should be the task of political writers to explain to European opinion that Poland saved Europe in 1920, and that it is necessary to keep Poland powerful and in harmonious relations with Western European civilization, for Poland is the barrier to the everlasting peril of an Asiatic invasion."[2]

[1] *L'Année 1920*, p. 255.
[2] Quoted from *The Poland of Pilsudski*, Machary, p. 118.

Further, by shielding Central Europe from the full blast of Marxist contagion, the battle of Warsaw set back the Bolshevik clock. It deprived Russia of the plunder she badly needed to stem her desperate economic crisis and dammed the outward flow of discontent and almost drowned the Bolshevik experiment.

In 1920, life in the U.S.S.R. had reached bedrock. Transport was at a standstill. Compared with 1914, the number of locomotives in working order had been reduced from 17,000 to 4,000, and nearly 4,000 bridges had been destroyed during the civil war. The town dwellers starved; typhus daily claimed thousands; fodder for horses was unobtainable in the towns, wooden houses were pulled down for fuel, and in their thousands the workers abandoned the factories to seek food in the villages. In February, 1921, violent strikes broke out in the Petrograd factories, and again the Kronstadt sailors mutinied. The situation grew so critical that Lenin ceased to harbour the illusion that the proletariat was the governing class by right of birth. On March 8 he convoked the tenth congress of the Party and, in order to obtain bread, he revoked all Socialist decrees that affected agriculture, and allowed the peasants to return to private enterprise and to employ wage earners. Further, he authorized private internal trading, but kept in his hands finance, heavy industry, much of light industry, transport and foreign trade. Thus, according to his new economic policy, everyone became reasonably free except the proletariat. Yet it was not a return to capitalism, but a retreat in order to gain time – "one step back", as Lenin was wont to say, "to gain two steps forward". Nevertheless, the results were startling: the peasants began to sell, shops opened and private trading again appeared. Between October, 1921, and October, 1922, production increased by 46 per cent., and in the following year it was 44 per cent. higher than in the previous year.

On October 17, 1921, Lenin openly admitted his failure. To a congress of the political storm troops of the Party he said: "We supposed that it would be possible to change the old Russian economy into a State economy on a communist base. Unfortunately we made a great mistake in trying to do this. . . . Being so uncultured as we are, we cannot destroy capitalism by one attack. . . . In the civil war we were able to win because we established in the army the severest discipline. We have yet to establish the most brutal discipline in our working army in order to secure our country, our republic. . . ."[1] Necessity and not Marx turned Russia back to Peter the Great and Ivan the Terrible.

On January 21, 1924, Lenin died at Gorky, near Moscow, and power passed to Stalin (Joseph Dzhugashvili, 1879–1953), who, because of his unbridled brutality, had been made secretary-general of the Party by Lenin. What remained of Marxism was grafted by him to the Russian Asiatic-Byzantine tradition, totalitarian State Capitalism was rapidly developed and everyone reduced to a proletarian level. The Political Bureau became dictator, with the secret police as its instrument of rule, and the ever-growing bureaucracy emerged as the new middle class. Oswald Spengler wrote in 1931: "What the Soviet régime has been attempting for the last fifteen years has been nothing but the restoration, under new names, of the political, military, and economic organization that it destroyed."[2] An observation proved correct to the letter, when the Russia of Stalin is compared with what the Marquis de Custine has to say of the Russia of Nicholas I in 1839.[3]

The State, instead of withering away, was established as an object of worship with Stalin as its omniscient prophet. Marxist terminology was retained as a liturgical language. "In this language," writes Borin, "totalitarian state capitalism would be called Communism. The dictatorship of the Political Bureau of the Communist Party would be named the dictatorship of the proletariat. The prosperity of the new governing class would be known as the prosperity of the working people. While preserving Marxist terminology the State Communistic bureaucracy pronounced the spirit of Marxism as reactionary, counter-revolutionary and Fascist. Marxism in Russia meant Political Bureau and State Police. Anybody who thought otherwise must die."[4]

As Tukhachevski had foreseen, Marxism was found to be a theology too modern and too civilized for the Russians and a return was made to their old Slav gods. The U.S.S.R. reverted to the historic Russia of the "Third Rome," and Tukhachevski's defeat by Pilsudski at Warsaw was not the least of the factors which brought her back on to the old, traditional Tsarist path.

[1] Quoted from *Civilization at Bay*, V. L. Borin (1951), p. 91.
[2] *Man and Technics* (English edit., 1932), p. 99.
[3] See *Journey for our Time*, trans. Phyllis Perm Kohler (English edit., 1953).
[4] *Civilization at Bay*, p. 103.

The rise of the Third Reich and the origins
of the Second World War

War alliances against a common enemy are proverbially
ephemeral, for once the enemy has been defeated the
alliance's centre of gravity is destroyed. There was little
reason to suppose that the entente between America, France, and
Great Britain, which won the First World War, would be more
durable than the Holy League after Lepanto, or the congress of
victorious powers after Waterloo. But when compared with the
latter there was a profound difference: whereas after the final defeat
of Napoleon, for 100 years the *Pax Britannica* maintained a balance
of power between the squabbling nations of Europe, during the
First World War it was destroyed and after it, thanks to American
participation in the war, it was replaced by the League of Nations,
an instrument designed neither to remove the causes which had
precipitated the war, nor to re-establish the balance of power
which had perished in it. Instead it rigidly imposed a peace on
the world on lines which conformed neither to history, nor to
geography, nor to economics. Instead of being designed as a
permanent conference of sovereign Powers for the settlement by
discussion of disputes between its members, it was fashioned as an
autocratic instrument which legalized war against any Power
which threatened its members' territorial integrity and political
independence, and outlawed all other forms of war. It was a
covenant of words without the sword, which caused ever-increasing discontent and friction and, as a reaction to its futile and
disingenuous efforts, led to an outcrop of tyrants who challenged
its authority and exploited its impotence.

Among these artists of power were two men possessed of a new
philosophy – Benito Mussolini and Adolf Hitler. They challenged
the myth of Economic Man, the fundamental factor in Capitalism,
Socialism, and Communism, and exalted in its stead the myth of
Heroic Man. This myth has been clearly defined by that remarkable French soldier René Quinton, in his *Maximes sur la guerre*:[1]

[1] Translated into English by Douglas Jerrold under the title *Soldier's Testament*
(1930), from which the quotations are taken.

"The hero is the man who forgets himself for others. . . . Nature created the hero not to live but to serve. . . . The hero is unique among men because his life is the apotheosis of devotion and not of effort. . . . Wars give back religion to men who have lost it. . . . It is security of life that has killed the gods. . . . By death man saves the life of the world. . . . Ideas, not men, are the founders of races."

In Hitler's eyes the aims of international Capitalism and Marxism were one and the same. Both, he said, repudiated "the aristocratic principle of Nature"; both were destroyers of quality, not of things but of life. He held that both lacked the self-justification of sacrifice, fought against Nature, and were destroyers of the race. Hence his creed of the blood, cryptically embalmed in his dogma *"ein Volk, ein Reich, ein Führer"*, which perversely he adulterated with confused ideas on Aryanism and Teutonic superiority, mixed with vitriolic hatred for the Jews. Like Cromwell, he created an Association, not of tapsters and decayed serving men, but of men of spirit who "made some conscience of what they did." And when we turn to his autobiographical bible – *Mein Kampf* – we find remarkable parallels to the maxims of René Quinton:

"Men do not die for business but for ideals. . . . He who would live must fight. He who does not wish to fight in this world, where permanent struggle is the law of life, has not the right to exist. . . . To recover Germany's power you must not ask 'How are we to manufacture arms?' but 'How are we to breed the spirit that makes a people capable of bearing arms?' . . . The greatness of the Aryan is not based on his intellectual powers; but rather on his willingness to devote all his faculties to the service of the community. . . . This mental attitude, which forces self-interest to recede into the background in favour of the common weal, is the first pre-requisite of any kind of really human civilization. . . . The renunciation of one's own life for the sake of the community is the crowning significance of the idea of all sacrifice. . . . Posterity will not remember those who pursued only their own individual interests, but it will praise those heroes who renounced their own happiness."

The comments of Peter F. Druker on this creed are illuminating. "It is a common and stupid mistake," he writes in *The End of Economic Man*, "to look at this exaltation of sacrifice in totalitarianism as mere hypocrisy, self-deception, or a propaganda stunt. It grew out of deepest despair. Just as nihilism in the Russia of 1880 attracted the noblest and bravest of the young people, so in Germany and Italy it was the best, not the worst representatives of the post-war generation who refused to compromise with a world that had no genuine values worth dying for and no valid creed worth living for."

Unless the struggle between these two myths – Economic Man and Heroic Man – is accepted and understood, the cataclysm which in 1939 submerged the world is almost incomprehensible and the age to which it gave birth little more than the plaything of chance.

Hitler, an Austrian by parentage, was born at Braunau-am-Inn on April 20, 1889, and when on the outbreak of war in 1914 he enlisted into the 16th Bavarian Infantry Regiment, no other recruit had a better claim to be called "the complete proletarian." Through sheer merit, he won the Military Service Cross with Swords, the Regimental Diploma for Gallantry, and the first-class order of the Iron Cross. Yet, strange to say, he never rose above the rank of corporal.

While the victors of the war inscribed their triumph on the memorial they erected at Rethondes in the forest of Compiègne, which read: "*Ici le 11 Novembre 1918 succomba le criminel orgeuil de l'empire Allemand, vaincu par les peuples libres qu'il prétendait asservir*", Corporal Hitler lay in hospital at Pasewalk in Pomerania half-blinded by poison gas. Little did they suspect that a day would dawn when this obscure soldier would at the foot of that same monument receive the surrender of the eagles of France and carry his swastika flag from the Atlantic to the Volga.

What was the power which enabled him to achieve this? In part his political genius, also in part his remarkable gift of leadership, but above all that he believed himself to be the divinely appointed regenerator of the Germanic peoples. He was a god-intoxicated man, the spiritual precipitate of the law of retribution, that he who soweth iniquity shall reap calamity.

The demons that exalted him were the Treaty of Versailles, which bore no resemblance to Wilson's Fourteen Points – "*Quatorze commandements! C'est un peu raide!*" had cried Clemenceau, "*Le bon Dieu n'en avait que dix!*" – the invasion of the Ruhr by Poincaré in 1923, which debauched the German currency and wiped out the German middle classes; the influx of £750 m. in foreign loans between 1924 and 1930, which debauched the German people, and lastly the crash on the American stock exchange, which begat the world-wide monetary depression of 1929–1931.

In 1930, 17,500,000 Germans were supported by the State, and in 1931 the Communist electorate in Germany rose to over five million. In that year the American journalist H. R. Knickerbocker in his book *Germany – Fascist or Soviet?* estimated that at least 15 million Germans were partially starving; that two-thirds of the voters were hostile to Capitalism, and more than half were hostile to the existing political system called democracy. In the following year these calamities led to Hitler's triumph. In 1919 – a "human-nothing", as he called himself – he had become the seventh member of an obscure political group the six members of which called themselves "the German Workers' Party". In 1932, this party, renamed the "National Socialist German Workers' Party", gained 13,779,017 votes out of 36 million votes in the July Reichstag elections, and on January 30, 1933, President Hindenburg called upon Hitler, leader of the largest political party in Germany, to fill the appointment of Chancellor and form a government. A year later, on June 30, Hitler purged his party in a series of hideous assassinations in which Ernst Röhm, General von Schleicher and General von Bredow, Gregor Strasser, and many hundreds of others were murdered. Lastly, when on August 2, Field-Marshal Hindenburg died, the office of President was abolished, and Hitler became Führer of the German people.

Save by those who witnessed it, the exultation of the masses on Hitler's advent to power is unbelievable, and when early in 1934 Rudolf Hess swore in the entire party to Hitler in a mass spectacle which brought millions of people to the microphone the words he spoke were those which echoed in every German heart. He said: "By this oath we again bind our lives to a man, through whom – this is our belief – superior forces act in fulfilment of Destiny. Do not seek Adolf Hitler with your brains; all of you will find him with the strength of your hearts. Adolf Hitler is Germany and Germany is Adolf Hitler. Germany is our God on earth."

Whether this extraordinary man was devil or madman, as his enemies proclaimed him to be, in no way belittles the fact that he stamped out Bolshevism in Germany and accomplished astonishing things. The truth would appear to be that he was a Jekyll and Hyde,[1] at one moment a normal being and at another an

---

[1] The writer, who met Hitler on a number of occasions, is of opinion that he possessed a dual-personality. At one moment he was Adolf, like any normal man, and at another *Herr Gott*, when to argue with him was, of course, absurd.

inspired paranoic. If that is not the truth it is difficult to explain how so intelligent a man as Lloyd George, on his return to England after a visit to Hitler in 1936, could say: "I have never seen a happier people than the Germans. Hitler is one of the greatest of the many great men I have ever met"; and that Winston Churchill in *Step by Step* could write of him: "If our country were defeated, I hope we should find a champion as indomitable to restore our courage and lead us back to our place among the nations."

Hitler's goal was Napoleonic: to establish a German Continental System under the aegis of Germany. Also, his means were not far removed from those of the great emperor: to liberate Germany from the shackles of international loan-capitalism, to unite all Germanic peoples into the Third Reich, and to establish in eastern Europe what he called the German *Lebensraum* (living space) which he considered as essential to the economic security of Germany as Napoleon had considered the Confederation of the Rhine essential to the strategic security of France.

Hitler held that, as long as the international monetary system was based on gold, a nation which cornered gold could impose its will on those who lacked it. This could be done by drying up their sources of exchange, and thereby compelling them to accept loans on interest in order to distribute their wealth – their production. He said: "The community of the nation does not live by the fictitious value of money, but by real production which in its turn gives value to money. This production is the real cover of the currency, and not a bank or a safe full of gold."[1] He decided: (*1*) To refuse foreign interest-bearing loans, and base German currency on production instead of on gold. (*2*) To obtain imports by direct exchange of goods – barter – and subsidize exports when necessary. (*3*) To put a stop to what was called "freedom of the exchanges" – that is, licence to gamble in currencies and shift private fortunes from one country to another according to the political situation. And (*4*) to create money when men and

---

[1] Mr. Churchill, who, as Chancellor of the Exchequer, reintroduced the gold standard in Britain in 1925, in 1931 held identical views. He said: "Is the progress of the human race in this age of almost terrifying expansion to be arbitrarily barred and regulated by fortuitous discoveries of gold mines? . . . Are we to be told that human civilization and society would have been impossible if gold had not happened to be an element in the composition of the globe? . . . These are absurdities; but they are becoming dangers and deadly absurdities. . . . I therefore point to this evil and to the search for the methods of remedying it as the first, second and the third of all the problems which should command and rivet our thoughts."

material were available for work instead of running into debt by borrowing it.

Because the life of international finance depended upon the issue of interest-bearing loans to nations in economic distress, Hitler's economics spelt its ruination. If he were allowed to succeed, other nations would certainly follow his example, and should a time come when all non-gold-holding governments exchanged goods for goods, not only would borrowing cease and gold lose its power, but the money-lenders would have to close shop.

This financial pistol was pointed more particularly at the United States, because they held the bulk of the world's supply of gold, and because their mass-production system necessitated the export of about 10 per cent. of their products in order to avoid unemployment. Further, because the brutalities meted out to German Jews by Hitler understandably had antagonized American Jewish financiers, six months after Hitler became Chancellor, Samuel Untermyer, a wealthy New York attorney, threw down the challenge. He proclaimed a "holy war" against National Socialism and called for an economic boycott of German goods, shipping, and services. Cordell Hull, American Secretary of State, under the terms of the Trade Agreement Act of 1934, insisted that American foreign trade should not be undercut by exchange controls, government monopolies, and the barter system.

Between 1933 and 1936, Hitler had reduced German unemployment from six millions to one, and prosperity had so far returned that, like Arthur Balfour in 1907, in 1936 Winston Churchill is reported to have said to General Robert E. Wood of America: "Germany is getting too strong and we must smash her." Then in September, 1937, a new American depression set in and developed with such startling rapidity that, on October 19, the stock market collapsed, and in the following month the census of unemployment showed about 11 million totally unemployed and 5,500,000 partially so. Something had to be done to divert public attention from this desperate internal situation – especially as the presidential elections were impending – and on October 5, at Chicago, President Roosevelt delivered his notorious "Quarantine Speech". He spoke of "a haunting fear of calamity . . . the present reign of terror . . . the very foundations of civilization are seriously threatened . . . let no one imagine that America will escape, that the Western Hemisphere will not be attacked", and that the easiest measure to enforce moral standards was an international quarantine against aggressors. Soon after this the main aggressor was named. Mr. Bernard Baruch told General George C. Marshall that "We are going to lick that fellow Hitler. He isn't going to get away with it". With what? Presumably his barter system, for in September, 1939, Baruch released a report of an interview he had with the President in which he said: "If we keep our prices down, there is no reason why we shouldn't get the customers from the belligerent nations that they have had to drop because of the war. In that event Germany's barter system will be destroyed."

In Great Britain a similar challenge to the barter system was in full blast, and on March 9, 1939, the Polish Ambassador in London reported to his Government that Mr. R. S. Hudson, the Parliamentary Secretary for Overseas Trade, had said to him: "The British Government were . . . determined not to abandon a single European market and not to renounce their economic advantages in favour of the German Reich. . . . Today we are making negotiations in the economic sphere and shattering the German barter system." So fiercely was the economic war waged that Robert E. Sherwood records in *The White House Papers of Harry L. Hopkins* that, in April, 1939, the acting military attaché in the American embassy at Berlin reported: "The present situation when viewed in the light of an active war which Germany is now in the process of waging becomes clear. It is an economic war in which Germany is fighting for her very existence. Germany must have markets for her goods or die and Germany will not die."

When we consider these economic causes of the Second World War it must be borne in mind, like with those of the first, that the struggle between the two economic systems is not a question of right and wrong, but of survival values. It was no more right or wrong for loan-capitalism to fight for its supremacy than it was for Hitler to fight for his barter system. Each was vital to the party concerned; both were the product of trade competition – the curse born of the Industrial Revolution.

Besides this cause of war, between 1933 and 1939 others helped to inflame the international situation, and of these the most important was the violence with which Hitler set out to carry out his programme of German regeneration. Firstly, on October 19,

1933, in order to clear his political decks, he withdrew from the League, and secondly, to secure Germany's eastern flank, on January 26, 1934, he entered on a 10 year peace pact with Poland, which in September was in part neutralized when the Soviet Union joined the League. Next, once the Saar plebiscite had gone in favour of Germany, on March 16, 1935, Hitler repudiated the arms provisions of the Treaty of Versailles and reintroduced conscription, which he justified by pointing at the enormous Soviet army. On May 2 this was countered by the Franco-Soviet Pact of Mutual Assistance, which made nonsense of the League, as also did the Anglo-German Naval Agreement of June 18, by which the strength of the German fleet was fixed at 35 per cent. of the British fleet.

The next crisis was further to increase Hitler's power and to bankrupt the League. In accordance with the secret treaties of the World War, Italy had been promised economic control in Abyssinia and, in order to purchase peace in Tunisia, in January, 1935, France had made a deal with Mussolini over Abyssinia – a member of the League. When Mussolini failed to obtain satisfaction at Geneva, on October 3 he invaded Abyssinia, and on November 18 the League, headed by Great Britain, enforced economic sanctions against Italy. Although they in no way impeded her, they threw Mussolini into Hitler's arms. In the end the 50-odd nations of the League were irretrievably discredited, and on March 7, 1936, Hitler declared the Franco-Soviet pact, which was then about to be ratified, a violation of the Treaty of Locarno, and reoccupied the demilitarized Rhineland.

The next crisis followed immediately. Since February, 1936, the misrule of the Popular Front Government in Spain had led to such chaos that, in order to quell anarchy, on July 18 General Francisco Franco raised his standard of revolt; he was supported by Italian troops, and the Republicans by Russian. Here again was an opportunity not to be missed by Hitler. On November 25 he entered into an Anti-Comintern Pact with Japan, and directly it became apparent that Franco was winning, on March 13, 1938, he annexed Austria.

A fortnight later the Sudeten Germans in Czechoslovakia demanded a restricted form of self-government, and were at once supported by Hitler, not only because of his racial principle, but because Czechoslovakia was a Franco-Soviet air pistol pointed at

Germany. He had not forgotten that, in 1919, the Allies had agreed that should Germany refuse to sign the peace treaty, she would be bombed from the Bohemian airfields. This crisis simmered until September 1, when Henlein, leader of the Sudeten Germans, visited Hitler at Berchtesgaden. The European atmosphere then grew so explosive that, on September 15 and again on the 22nd, the British Prime Minister, Mr. Neville Chamberlain, visited Hitler. On the 24th, Sir Eric Phipps, British Ambassador in Paris, informed Lord Halifax, British Foreign Minister, that "All the best in France is against war, almost at any price," and that the sole group in favour of war was that of the Communists, who were "paid by Moscow." Finally, on September 29, with M. Daladier and Signor Mussolini, for the third time Chamberlain flew to Germany and met Hitler at Munich, and, in order to avert war, he agreed to the secession of the Sudetenland to Germany. Mutinies had broken out in the French army and, according to Sir Neville Henderson, the British Ambassador in Berlin, England "did not possess any Spitfires . . . had only one or two experimental Hurricanes, and only seven modern A.A. guns for the defence of London."

These never-ending crises generated a violent propaganda against Hitler. Foreign affairs lost all objectivity and became wrapped in an explosive animosity which so perturbed Dr. Goebbels, the German Minister of Propaganda, that he appealed to the American Ambassador in Berlin, who replied that the "most crucial thing that stood between any betterment of American Press relationships was the Jewish question."

It was in no way improved when, on November 7, 1938, a young Polish Jew assassinated the third secretary at the German Embassy in Paris, because the murder at once precipitated a pogrom against the Jews in Berlin which added fuel to anti-German sentiment in America. The situation as it was at the end of the year is so illuminatingly described by the Polish Ambassador at Washington, Count Jerzy Potocki, in a report to the Polish Foreign Office, dated January 12, 1939, that we will quote from it fully:

"Public opinion in America nowadays," he wrote, "expresses itself in an increasing hatred of everything . . . connected with National Socialism. Above all, propaganda here is entirely in Jewish hands . . ." and "when bearing public ignorance in mind, their propaganda is so effective that people here have no real knowledge of the true state of affairs in Europe. . . . It is interesting to observe that in this carefully thought-out campaign – which is primarily conducted against National Socialism – no reference at all is made to Soviet Russia. If that country is mentioned, it is referred to in a friendly manner and people are given the impression that Soviet Russia is part of the democratic group of countries. Thanks to astute propaganda, public sympathy in the U.S.A. is entirely on the side of Red Spain. Side by side with this propaganda an artificial war-panic is created. . . . No effort is spared to impress upon the American mind that in the event of a world war the U.S.A. must take an active part in a struggle for freedom and democracy. President Roosevelt was first in the field to give expression to this hatred of Fascism. He had a two-fold purpose in mind: firstly, he wanted to divert American public opinion from difficult and complicated domestic problems. . . . Secondly, by creating a war-panic . . . he wanted to induce Americans to endorse his huge program of armaments. . . .

"Furthermore, the brutal treatment meted out to the Jews in Germany as well as the problem of the refugees are both factors which intensify the existing hatred of everything connected with German National Socialism. In this campaign of hatred, individual Jewish intellectuals such as Bernard Baruch, Lehman, Governor of New York State, Felix Frankfurter, the newly appointed Supreme Court Judge, Morgenthau, the Financial Secretary, and other well-known personal friends of Roosevelt have taken a prominent part in this campaign of hatred. All of them want the President to become the protagonist of human liberty, religious freedom and the right of free speech. . . . This particular group of people, who are all in highly placed American official positions and who are desirous of being representatives of 'true Americanism', and as 'Champions of Democracy', are, in point of fact, linked with international Jewry by ties incapable of being torn asunder. For international Jewry – so intimately concerned with the interests of its own race – President Roosevelt's 'ideal' role as a champion of human rights was indeed a godsend. In this way Jewry was able not only to establish a dangerous centre in the New World for the dissemination of hatred and enmity, but it also succeeded in dividing the world into two warlike camps. The whole problem is being tackled in a most mysterious manner. Roosevelt has been given the power to enable him to enliven American foreign policy and at the same time to create huge reserves in armaments for a future war which the Jews are deliberately heading for."[1]

Two days after Count Potocki penned this dispatch, he was assured by William C. Bullitt, American Ambassador to France, that, in the event of war, the United States would be prepared "to intervene actively on the side of Britain and France." Then came the next crisis, for soon after this assurance was given Hitler decided to complete the subjugation of Czechoslovakia. He fomented a *coup d'état* which liberated Slovakia, and on March 15, 1939, he occupied Prague and proclaimed the Protectorate of Bohemia and Moravia. Not content with these aggressions, he had moved toward his final one. On October 24, 1938, Joachim von Ribbentrop, his Foreign Minister, suggested to the Polish Ambassador in Berlin that the Polish Government should agree to a "reunion of Danzig with the Reich" and should consent to the building of "an extraterritorial motor road and railway line across Pomorze" – that is, across the Polish Corridor – which 20 years earlier Mr. Lloyd George had declared, "must sooner or later lead to a new war in the east of Europe." Arguments followed, during which Mr. Chamberlain produced a formula whereby Britain, France, Poland, and Russia would sign a declaration that they "would act together in the event of further signs of German aggressive ambitions". Strangely enough, Josef Beck, the Polish Foreign Minister, rejected the proposal and, equally inexplicable, when in its stead Beck suggested a bilateral agreement between Britain and Poland, Chamberlain agreed to it, and on March 27 the British Foreign Office informed Beck that if the Poles would undertake to defend themselves in event of a German attack, Britain would pledge "all her forces and resources to their assistance." This agreement was made public on March 31.

The effect Chamberlain's Polish guarantee had on Hitler was immediate; for though the latter was aware that an attack on Poland was likely to involve him in a war on two fronts, on April 3 he issued a directive to prepare an invasion of Poland after

---

[1] *German White Paper of Polish Documents*, New York (1940), pp. 29–31. Addressing the Reichstag on January 30, 1939, Hitler said: "I want to-day once again to make a prophecy: if the international Jewish financiers within and without Europe succeed once more in hurling the people into a world war, the result will be, not the Bol-shevization of the World and with it a victory of Jewry, but the annihilation of the Jewish race in Europe." This was to be only too true, for according to Goebbels: "About 60 per cent. of them will have to be liquidated; only 40 per cent. can be used for forced labour" (*Diaries*, p. 103).

September 1, and on April 17, in order to avoid a two-front war, he opened negotiations with the Kremlin.

That by now war had been decided on by others besides Hitler is clear; for Karl von Weigand, the doyen of American journalists in Europe, informs us that, on April 25, he was called to the American Embassy in Paris and told by Bullitt, " 'War in Europe has been decided upon. Poland', he said, 'had an assurance of the support of Britain and France, and would yield to no demands from Germany. America,' he predicted, 'would be in the war after Britain and France entered it.' "[1] This statement is corroborated by *The White House Papers of Harry Hopkins*, in which their editor says that, about this time, Winston Churchill told Bernard Baruch: "War is coming very soon. We will be in it and you (the United States) will be in it. You (Baruch) will be running the show over there, but I will be on the sidelines over here."

Throughout the summer the crisis fluctuated, and both Chamberlain and Hitler bid for Russian support; the one to enable him to honour his Polish pledge, and the other to avert a two-front war. At length on August 23 the latter won; that day a treaty of non-aggression was signed in Moscow between Germany and the U.S.S.R., and in accordance with a secret protocol, Poland was to be divided between Germany and Russia. On the 24th the treaty was published, and on the following day the Anglo-Polish Agreement of March 27 was formally signed.

On September 1 – the anniversary of Sedan – without a declaration of war, German troops crossed into Poland, and President Roosevelt issued an appeal to Britain, France, Germany, and Poland to refrain from bombing unfortified cities and civil populations. Hitler immediately endorsed the President's plea, and on the 2nd the British and French governments issued a declaration in which they stated that they were in sympathy with the humanitarian sentiments expressed by the President.

At 9 a.m. on September 3 the British Ambassador in Berlin delivered an ultimatum to the German Foreign Office that unless before 11 a.m. assurances were given of a suspension of hostilities, Britain would declare war on Germany. At noon the French

[1] The writer met von Weigand in Berlin on April 19, and was told by him that he had learnt from a high authority that Germany expected to overrun Poland in a minimum of three weeks or a maximum of six: that there would be no attack on the Western Front, and that Italy would probably remain neutral. Of the British guarantee to Poland he said: "Well, I guess your Mr. Prime Minister has made the biggest blunder in your history since you passed the Stamp Act."

Ambassador handed in a similar ultimatum to expire at 5 p.m. Both were unanswered..

When Hitler received the British challenge he sat in silence unmoved, and when Paul Schmidt, his interpreter, left the room, Göring turned to him and said: "If we lose this war, then God have mercy on us."

CHAPTER 10

The Second Battle of Sedan and the fall of France, 1940

Hitler's war aim was Socratic and biological:[1] this is made crystal clear in *Mein Kampf*. "The foreign policy of a People's State," he wrote, "must first of all bear in mind the duty of securing the existence of the race which is incorporated in this State. And this must be done by establishing a healthy and natural proportion between the number and growth of the population on the one hand and the extent and resources of the territory they inhabit on the other. . . . What I call a *healthy* proportion is that in which the support of the people is guaranteed by the resources of its own soil and subsoil."[2] He pointed out that in 1914–1918 Germany was not a world power because she could not feed her people, and that she would never become a world power until she did. Her *Lebensraum* (living space) was to be sought not in the south or west of Europe, but in the east, in "Russia and the Border States subject to her."[3] His aim was to create a Carlovingian empire in eastern instead of western Europe, which would be so self-sufficient that no future combination of European Powers could threaten it.

As this meant that, were Hitler to succeed, he would establish a hegemony over Europe, naturally the British Government, following traditional British policy of keeping Europe divided, refused to tolerate it. But because neither Britain nor France was prepared to go to war, their policy should have been to let Hitler entangle Germany in eastern Europe where he would almost certainly become involved in a war with Russia, and meanwhile to rearm at full speed. Had they done so, whichever of the two dictators had won, Britain and France would have been well placed to have tilted the balance of power in their own favour. Instead, compromised as they were by their Polish alliance, they declared an ideological crusade against Hitlerism,[4] and on

[1] See vol. I, p. 3.
[2] *Mein Kampf*, trans. James Murphy (English edit., 1939), p. 523.　　[3] *Ibid.*, p. 533.
[4] This declaration was unanimous. Mr. Churchill said: "This is not a question of fighting for Danzig or fighting for Poland. We are fighting to save a whole world from the pestilence of Nazi tyranny and in defence of all that is most sacred to man."

September 4, 1939, in a broadcast to the German people, Mr. Chamberlain said: "In this war we are not fighting against you, the German people, for whom we have no bitter feeling, but against a tyrannous and foresworn régime."[1]

To effect this, the allies should have divided the Germans into two political groups, the pro- and anti-Hitlerites, and have offered the former the worst of terms and the latter the best. They should have gone into alliance with all Germans opposed to Hitler, and by helping them with every means in their power have attacked Hitlerism internally and overthrown it by revolution. That this was possible has been pointed out by Captain S. Payne Best, a British intelligence agent employed in Holland. "At the outbreak of the war," he writes, "our Intelligence Service had reliable information that Hitler was faced with the opposition of many men holding the highest appointments in the armed forces and civil service. . . . According to our information this opposition movement had assumed such proportions that it might even have led to revolt and the downfall of the Nazis."[2] This is corroborated by Walter Görlitz, who informs us that before Hitler invaded Denmark and Norway, Admiral Wilhelm Canaris, Chief of the *Abwehr* (the Counter-Intelligence Service of O.K.W.)[3] warned the Danish and Norwegian attachés in Berlin what was on foot; that General Franz Halder, Chief of the General Staff, arranged that King Leopold was warned of the impending invasion of Belgium; and that on May 9, 1940, Canaris "sent a last warning

---

[1] *Documents concerning German-Polish Relations*, Cmd. 6106 (1939), No. 144, p. 195.
[2] *The Venlo Incident* (1950), p. 7.
[3] The German Supreme Command was organized as follows:

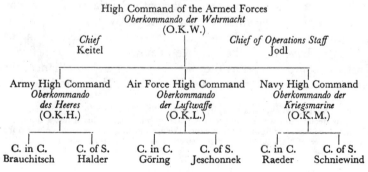

Supreme Commander
Hitler

High Command of the Armed Forces
Oberkommando der Wehrmacht
(O.K.W.)

Chief   Chief of Operations Staff
Keitel   Jodl

Army High Command *Oberkommando des Heeres* (O.K.H.)	Air Force High Command *Oberkommando der Luftwaffe* (O.K.L.)	Navy High Command *Oberkommando der Kriegsmarine* (O.K.M.)
C. in C. Brauchitsch C. of S. Halder	C. in C. Göring C. of S. Jeschonnek	C. in C. Raeder C. of S. Schniewind

through Oster, his Chief of Staff, to the Dutch military attaché in Berlin" to inform him of Hitler's intention to invade Holland.[1] Throughout the war, Hitler was surrounded by traitors.[2]

In spite of Mr. Chamberlain's pronouncement of September 4, once a psychological war aim had been fixed upon, the two allied powers set out to attain it solely by military means. This was their greatest political blunder of the war. Almost equally monstrous was their military blunder, which was to build their military forces on the experiences of the first half of the First World War – the period of stalemate – instead of on the second half – the period of mobility – whereas Hitler, in opposition to the majority of his generals, did exactly the reverse. To understand what this meant demands a brief outline of the new tactical theories to which the First World War gave birth.

As is usual in war, it was the losing side which learnt most. Whereas the victors looked upon the war as an incident which had been liquidated, the vanquished saw in it the consequence of faulty action. To Russia and Germany the supreme lessons of the war were: the increasing necessity for (*1*) political authority in war; (*2*) national discipline in war; (*3*) economic self-sufficiency in war; and (*4*) technology in war. And the same factors affected peace also, in order to be prepared for war.

Of the last requirement, three radically new weapons had been experimented with – the aeroplane, tank, and lethal gas – and in each case the experiments had pointed to an extension of gun power – the gun was the dominant weapon. The tank had been used as a self-propelled armoured gun; the aeroplane as a long range gun or machine-gun; and lethal gas as molecular shrapnel. Had the war lasted another year, it would have become apparent that in themselves tanks and aircraft were not weapons, but instead vehicles in which anything could be carried up to their maximum loads. Further, it would have been seen that as their dominant characteristic was a new means of movement, made practical by the common prime-mover, petroleum, entirely new fighting organizations could be built around them – namely, self-

---

[1] *The German General Staff*, Walter Görlitz (1953), pp. 364 and 372–373. See also *The Critical Years*, Genl. Baron Geyr von Schweppenburg (1952), p. 195. Fabian von Schlabrendorff (*Revolt against Hitler*, p. 39) calls Oster "the managing director of the resistance movement."

[2] The following books make this clear: *The von Hassell Diaries*, Ulrich von Hassell (English edit., 1948); *Revolt against Hitler*, Fabian von Schlabrendorff (English edit., 1948), *The German Opposition to Hitler*, Hans Rothfels (U.S. edit., 1948), and *Germany's Underground*, Allen Welsh Dulles (U.S. edit., 1947).

propelled armoured armies and airborne armies, and not merely self-propelled armoured guns and airborne artillery.

Two master theories emerged out of this experimental period, the one concerned mainly with tanks, and the other solely with aircraft. The former was worked out in considerable detail by the author in May, 1918, in a study entitled "The Attack by Paralyzation," which soon after was submitted to Marshal Foch, and when he accepted it as the basis of his projected spring campaign in 1919, was renamed "Plan 1919". The operative part of this project reads:

"Now, the potential fighting strength of a body of men lies in its organization; therefore, if we can destroy its organization, we shall destroy its fighting strength and so have gained our object.

"There are two ways of destroying an organization:

"(i) By wearing it down (dissipating it).

"(ii) By rendering it inoperative (unhinging it).

"In war the first comprises the killing, wounding, capturing and disarming of the enemy's soldiers – body warfare. The second, the rendering inoperative of his power of command – brain warfare. To take a single man as an example: the first method may be compared to a succession of slight wounds which will eventually cause him to bleed to death; the second – a shot through the brain.

"The brains of an army are its Staff – Army, Corps and Divisional Headquarters. Could we suddenly remove these from an extensive sector of the German front, the collapse of the personnel they control would be a mere matter of hours, even if only slight opposition were put up against it. . . .

"As our present theory is to destroy 'personnel', so should our new theory be to destroy 'Command', not after the enemy's personnel has been disorganized, but before it has been attacked, so that it may be found in a state of complete disorganization when attacked. . . ."

The means suggested were to use fast-moving tanks, supported by aircraft, and later followed by the traditional arms. The tanks, under air cover, were to break through selected points in the German front and make straight for divisional, corps and army headquarters and supply centres, and create pandemonium. Then the normal attack was to follow.[1]

---

[1] See *Memoirs of an Unconventional Soldier*, J. F. C. Fuller (1936), chap. XIII, and *On Future Warfare*, J. F. C. Fuller (1928), chap. IV.

The leading exponent of the aircraft theory was the Italian general Guilio Douhet, who in 1921 set down his doctrine on future air warfare in his book *The Command of the Air*. "The war of the future," he wrote, "will once more involve all nations and all their resources . . . the war on land . . . will take on a static character very similar to the World War . . . continuous fronts will be set up. . . . All theories and concepts of a war of movement will fail against these continuous fronts. . . ." What then is the answer? It is to transfer war into the air and attack the civil population, because once its will is broken by terror the whole machinery of government and with it of military direction will collapse. "This disintegration of nations in the last war," Douhet affirmed, "was indirectly brought about by the action of the armies in the field. In the future it will be accomplished directly by the actions of aerial forces," before armies and navies "have time to mobilize at all!"[1]

These two very different theories had two points in common. Their ultimate aims were moral instead of physical; the one to break the will of the enemy army command, and the other the will of the civil population. Both were intended to overcome the stalemate which had figured so largely in the last war by making continuous fronts indefensible, or by circumventing them.

The tactical policies derived from these two theories, as well as from lack of their appreciation, determined the character of the war on land. That of France was purely defensive, to shelter under cover of the Maginot Line, built to make the stalemate unbreakable. That of Great Britain was almost entirely economic, to blockade Germany, bomb her industrial cities and civil population, which was called "strategic bombing", and send a token army to France.[2] These twin policies were based on the assumption that Germany could be forced to accept a repetition of the stalemate period of the previous war, and that she was economically as dependent on others as she had been 20 years earlier. Except in the air, mobile warfare was not considered.[3]

The tactical policy of Germany was based on the offensive and designed to overcome the linear defensive of her opponents by

[1] *The Command of the Air* (English edit., 1943), pp. 142, 116, 51, 52.
[2] In the spring of 1939 the introduction of conscription modified this, but because of lack of armour the British army in France remained no more than a token force.
[3] In September, 1939, the British air force could muster 1,982 operative aircraft, of which 480 were bombers; the French 1,112, including 186 bombers, mostly of obsolete types; and the German 4,162, including 308 transport aircraft. The French were opposed to "strategic bombing."

means of the attack by paralysation, which was adopted as the basis of her *Blitzkrieg*. Her army was fashioned into an armour-headed battering ram which, under cover of fighter aircraft and dive-bombers – operating as flying field artillery – could break through its enemy's continuous front at selected points. The soul of German policy was mobility – a sharp, rapid and short war on one front only. This was to be the outstanding difference between the Second World War and its predecessor. Nevertheless, this policy was founded on a strategical oversight; it took no account of the possibility that, were England to support France, the next continental war would be a two-front war – a front on the land and a front on the sea. To break the second of these fronts was Germany's key problem, for should England throw in her lot with France, she would, as in the past, become the strategical centre of gravity of the alliance. Yet so ill-prepared was Hitler to break the sea front that, on the outbreak of the war, he had no more than an insignificant surface fleet; only 57 submarines, of which 26 were suitable for Atlantic operations; not a single landing-craft; an air force neither designed nor trained for an oversea invasion of the first magnitude; and above all – he had no plan.

On September 1, 1939 – the anniversary of Sedan – Hitler invaded Poland. Twenty-three divisions with no armour and few *Luftwaffe* aircraft were left on guard in the west, while 44 divisions, including six armoured and six motorized, in two Army groups, crossed the Polish frontier early that day, and within seven days the attack by paralysation had proved so effective that, except in Warsaw, Polish resistance collapsed. On the 17th the Russians crossed the eastern Polish frontier and the next day the Polish Government fled into Rumania. Although General Warlimont has said "that no German Army had gone to war so ill-prepared,"[1] it was not the German army, but as General Guderian has pointed out, the newly created German armoured and motorized divisions which were responsible for "the speed with which the campaign was won."[2] Supported by the *Luftwaffe*, they had achieved what appeared to be a miracle, but which in fact was a foreordained conclusion. In the west the French and British stood in their trenches, spectators of their ally's defeat.

---

[1] *The German General Staff*, Walter Görlitz, p. 348. Warlimont was Deputy Chief of Operations Staff O.K.W.
[2] *Panzer Leader*. General Heinz Guderian (1952), p. 84. Cited as Guderian.

Once Hitler had reduced the war on land to one front, his intention was to settle with France and Britain before he turned on Russia. Delays followed, partly because of the obstruction of his generals, qualms of treason within the army, and Russia's invasion of Finland on November 11. At length Z-day was fixed for January 20, 1940, but no sooner had it been chosen than Grand Admiral Erich Raeder, commander-in-chief of the Navy, urged Hitler to seize Norway first, in order to gain bases for the submarine war against England and to secure the sources of Norwegian and Swedish iron ore, which were vital to Germany. This operation was still under discussion when, on February 17, the British seized the German prison ship *Altmark* in Norwegian waters, an action which so infuriated Hitler that it put an end to his hesitation. On April 9 Denmark was suddenly occupied and, in face of the British fleet, Norway was invaded by sea and air. On April 15 a small British force landed near Narvik, to be followed on the 16th and 18th by two others which landed at Namsos and Aandalsnes. On May 2–3 the last two forces were withdrawn, and six days later this fiasco led to a vote of censure in the House of Commons. On May 10 Mr. Chamberlain resigned, and Mr. Churchill became Prime Minister.

The French plan was based on these considerations: (*1*) that the Maginot Line, which ran from the Swiss frontier to Longwy, was impregnable;[1] (*2*) that the Ardennes to the north, between Longwy and Namur, prohibited movement of large forces, particularly armoured ones; (*3*) that, because of the neutrality of Belgium (proclaimed in 1936), French forces could not cross the Belgian frontier until Belgium was violated by the Germans, and (*4*) that the Germans would repeat the Schlieffen manœuvre of 1914. This last was held certain, because the central Belgian plain favoured the movement of armoured forces. Because of this the aim of the French plan was how best to deny the central Belgian plain to the enemy.

There were three river lines on which this could be done: The Albert Canal–Meuse, Antwerp to Liége; the line of the Dyle, Antwerp to Namur; and the line of the Scheldt (Escaut),

---

[1] The frontier fortifications, known as the Maginot Line, were not continued from Longwy to the Channel because they could not be run north of the French industrial area south of Belgium without crossing the Belgian frontier; they could only be run through, or south of it. In the former case the industrial area would be largely destroyed in war, and in the latter lost altogether. Therefore it was decided not to extend them, and instead to advance into Belgium.

Antwerp–Tournai. But in 1939, because the Belgians decided to make the second river line their main line of defence, the defence lines were reduced to two, and their projected occupation by the French respectively became known as Plan D (Dyle) and Plan E (Escaut). On November 17, 1939, the former was adopted by the French Council of National Defence and approved by

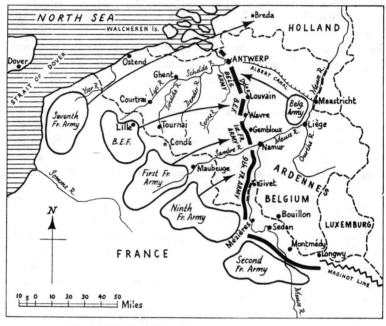

23.　ALLIED DEPLOYMENT, MAY 10, 1940

General M. Gamelin, the French commander-in-chief. While the Belgian Army (18 divisions) fell back from the Albert Canal–Meuse line to the Dyle between Antwerp and Louvain, the British Expeditionary Force (six divisions, eventually nine) under General Lord Gort, and the French First Army (six divisions) and Ninth Army (nine divisions), respectively commanded by General Blanchard and General Corap, which were in position between the English Channel and Mézières, were to pivot on the left flank of the French Second Army (seven divisions), under General Huntziger – which held the front between Mézières and Longwy – and advance to the Dyle. The B.E.F. was to advance between Louvain and Wavre; the First Army between Wavre and Namur; and the Ninth was to establish itself on the Meuse between Namur and Mézières. Besides this, the French Seventh Army (seven divisions) under General Giraud, was to be brought up behind the left of the B.E.F., not to reinforce the front or act as a reserve to it, but to push into Holland should Dutch neutrality be violated.

General Georges was appointed commander of the north-east theatre of operations, which extended from Switzerland to the English Channel. It was held by two Army Groups: Group I comprised the French Second, Ninth, and First Armies, and was commanded by General Billotte; and Group II, which lay on its right, garrisoned the Maginot Line. The British Expeditionary Force and the French Seventh Army were under the direct command of General Georges, who also had a general reserve of 13 divisions; but they were much spread out and their centre of gravity was not in Army Group I but in Army Group II.[1]

Although 48 divisions were numerically a formidable force with which to hold the Dyle front, because of its heterogeneous composition it was fragile. Further, the personnel of the four French armies differed widely; the best divisions were allotted to the First and Seventh, because they would have to operate in open country, and the remainder to the Ninth and Second, because they would be protected by the Ardennes. Their composition was as follows: First Army, two light mechanized divisions (Cavalry Corps), three active divisions and one Series A division;[2] Seventh Army, one light mechanized, two motorized, one active, one Series A and two Series B; Ninth Army, one motorized, one active, two Series A, two Series B, one fortress and two cavalry divisions; and Second Army, two active, one Series A, two Series B, and two cavalry divisions.

From this it will be seen that the link between the Maginot Line and Namur was weak in the quality of its men; but on the assumption that the Ardennes was bad offensive country, which it certainly was, there is little to criticize in this – the fatal error in the French plan lay elsewhere. Because the French General Staff expected that the bulk of the German armoured forces would

---

[1] See *La bataille de France Mai–Juin, 1940*, Commandant Pierre Lyet (1947), p. 42, cited as Lyet.

[2] Active divisions were those maintained in peace time; Series A, first line reserve; Series B, second line reserve; fortress, purely defensive; cavalry consisted of one horse brigade and one light motorized brigade; light mechanized equipped with light tanks, artillery and motorized machine guns; motorized, lorry-born infantry; and armoured, which were held in reserve, were each built round a core of about 150 tanks.

move over central Belgium, clearly then the three French armoured divisions should have been assembled behind the Dyle front to counter-attack the German armour directly it crossed the Albert Canal–Meuse line; or, should it not do so, but instead break through the Ardennes, then the French armour could have moved by way of Mons and have fallen on its right flank. The reason why this course was not adopted will be mentioned later.

Before we turn to the German plan, a few words must be said on the question of French morale, for the collapse of France in June, 1940, was not solely because of tactics.

To foreigners in general and to Englishmen in particular the French army was accepted as the most formidable in Europe. It was nothing of the kind; it was indifferently armed and tactically out-of-date, and its morale, which had never recovered from the shocks of the First World War, had been rotted by the corruption and communistic ideas of the *Front Populaire* government, created in 1936 by M. Léon Blum. The people were so apathetic and defeatist that many openly stated that occupation by Hitler was preferable to war.[1] Though all this was easily discoverable, no efforts were made to publicize it, mainly because the English did not want France to be thought weak and Germany strong. This is why it was a shock to Sir Edward Spears when, on May 25, 1940, he was told by Georges Mandel, French Minister of the Colonies, that in France "There is no will to fight", and that "There has been a general *défaillance*, a collapse of the whole nation."[2] These statements are corroborated by General Gamelin, who a week earlier had written in a report: ". . . the men mobilized to-day have not received, during the period between the two wars, the patriotic and moral education which would have prepared them for the drama which was to resolve the fate of the nation. . . . The break-through of our front was too often the result of flight (*sauve-qui-peut*), local at first, then almost general at key points, in the face of a bold adversary decided to take all risks and convinced of his superiority"[3] – words reminiscent of those of Colonel Stoffel before the war of 1870.

The German plan, known as "Plan Yellow," in which Major

---

[1] "Many French officials seemed to prefer Nazism to the danger of Communist domination" (*I Was There*, Fleet Admiral William D. Leahy, 1950, p. 40. Leahy was U.S. Ambassador to France).

[2] *Assignment to Catastrophe*, Major-General Sir Edward Spears (1954), vol. I, pp. 205–206.

[3] Quoted from *ibid.*, p. 159.

Ellis says "there is no contemporary evidence to suggest that Hitler was concerned,"[1] was based on three Army Groups, A, B, and C, respectively commanded by General Karl von Rundstedt, General Fedor von Bock, and General Wilhelm von Leeb. It was issued by O.K.H. on October 19, and it laid down that Army Group B with the bulk of the armoured divisions was to make the main thrust to the north of Brussels with a detachment to move through southern Holland, while Army Group A protected its left flank, and Army Group C faced the Maginot Line. Hitler did not like this distribution, and, according to General Jodl, he said that he had " 'originally wanted to use all forces south of Liége' with the idea of a break-through in the direction of Reims and Amiens."[2] The plan was then modified by Brauchitsch and Halder, who added to Bock's main thrust north of Brussels a subsidiary thrust south of Liége, and cut out the Holland detachment – this was the plan the French expected. Again Hitler did not like it, not only because it entailed a frontal attack on either side of Liége, but because he considered that the main blow should be struck to the south of Liége with an armoured and a motorized division directed on Sedan *via* Arlon.[3]

The next day – October 31 – Rundstedt and his chief of staff, General Fritz von Manstein, independently put forward a new idea. It was to cut off the enemy north of the Somme, not by pushing him back frontally, but by smashing through him with Army Group A. This plan was rejected by Brauchitsch. General Guderian informs us that in November Manstein called him to his headquarters and asked him whether he thought a tank thrust through southern Belgium and Luxemburg was a practical proposition. He agreed that it was, if made in strength.[4] Manstein then wrote a memorandum on this manœuvre, which Rundstedt approved on December 4, and signed and submitted to Brauchitsch, who refused to send it on to Hitler.

On December 28, a directive was issued that the western offensive would open in the middle of January, 1940, and that when the Führer had seen where the initial success was greatest, he would decide where the weight of the attack was to be concentrated. This was followed by an unexpected event. On January

[1] *The War in France and Flanders, 1939–1940* (British Official History), Major L. F. Ellis (1953), p. 335. Cited as Ellis.
[2] Ellis, p. 336, quoting Jodl's Diary of October 25, 1939.
[3] *Ibid.*, p. 337, quoting Jodl's Diary of October 30, 1939.
[4] Guderian, p. 89.

10 a German aeroplane, carrying a *Luftwaffe* officer-courier, made a forced landing in Belgium, and documents were found on him which revealed much of the German plan.[1] This and a bout of bad weather caused the projected offensive for January 17 to be postponed.

The next step was taken by Hitler. On February 13 he reopened the question of where the main attack should be made and proposed that the armoured divisions "should be concentrated in the direction of Sedan, where the enemy does not expect our main thrust", more especially because the documents captured on January 10 would have led the enemy to assume "that our concern is to occupy the Channel coastline of Holland and Belgium."[2] Manstein had pushed his idea so persistently that Brauchitsch, to get rid of him, promoted him to the command of an infantry corps, and, as was customary, before he took it over, Manstein paid his respects to Hitler. After he had dined with him he took the opportunity to press on him his plan, which so far Brauchitsch had refused to divulge to Hitler. As it tallied with the Führer's ideas, after two war games had been played, on February 22 Manstein's plan was adopted and the whole weight of the attack was transferred to Army Group A. Of this change Guderian writes that Rundstedt had no "clear idea about the potentialities of tanks," and that nobody, except Hitler, Manstein, and himself had any faith in the final edition of Plan Yellow.[3]

In detail the final plan was:

Army Group B, Eighteenth and Sixth Armies (28 divisions, including three armoured and one motorized) was to advance on the front Winterswijk–Aachen, overrun southern Holland and northern Belgium, seize airfields and cover the right flank of Army Group A.

Army Group A, Second, Fourth, Twelfth and Sixteenth Armies (44 divisions, including seven armoured and three motorized) was to advance on the front Aachen (exclusive)–Luxemburg, break through into France between Namur and Sedan, move on Amiens–Abbeville, and cut off the enemy north of the Somme.

Army Group C, First and Seventh Armies (17 divisions) was to watch, and feint at, the Maginot Line.

---

[1] *Belgium: The Official Account of What Happened, 1939–1940* (1941), p. 14.
[2] Ellis, p. 340, quoting Jodl's Diary of February 13, 1940.
[3] Guderian, p. 91.

O.K.H. Reserve was to consist of 45 divisions, including one motorized.

Such were the opposing plans, the one based on the fixed idea of the French General Staff, who could see nothing beyond a repetition of the Schlieffen manœuvre, and the other, thanks to

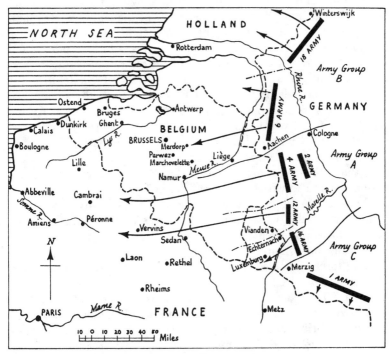

24. GERMAN DEPLOYMENT, MAY 10, 1940

a series of accidents, wrenched out of the fixed idea of the German General Staff, who were equally obsessed by Schlieffen, and based by Hitler and Manstein on audacity and novelty. Nor was this obtuseness of the two General Staffs their sole similarity; the German staff, as recorded, included some traitors and was not trusted by Hitler, who instinctively sensed it,[1] the French staff

[1] With reference to the November plot, hatched by Beck, Brauchitsch, Halder, Dr. Goerdeler and others – namely, to march the army on Berlin instead of on Paris – Görlitz writes that, on November 5, in a conversation between Hitler and Brauchitsch the former "screamed that he knew very well that the generals were planning something else than the offensive he had ordered" for November 12. Though Görlitz adds, "he knew nothing of the kind," with so mediumistic a man as Hitler this is to be doubted (*The German General Staff*, p. 365).

under General Gamelin, was profoundly mistrusted by M. Paul Reynaud who, on March 30, 1940, became Prime Minister and president of the War Council. Once in office he determined to get rid of Gamelin, who was supported by Daladier, the Minister of National Defence – called by his supporters "the bull of Vaucluse" and by his detractors "the cow with rubber horns." According to Paul Baudouin, Secretary of the Cabinet, Reynaud declared that Gamelin "might be all right as a prefect or a bishop," but that as a leader he was hopeless.[1] On May 9 Reynaud seized upon the Norwegian fiasco to rid himself of Gamelin, and that day at a War Cabinet council he skinned Gamelin to the bone, and ended the fracas which resulted with the shout: "In view of such serious opposition, I consider the Cabinet as having resigned, and I will announce its resignation to the President of the Republic."[2] The scene is altogether reminiscent of 1870, and its timing not very opportune, for barely had the meeting broken up than the Germans crossed the Belgian and Luxemburg frontiers, and unwittingly spared Gamelin a trip to Limoges.

Thus, at the moment when the great offensive in the west was launched, Hitler went to war with a commander-in-chief who would have preferred to march on Berlin, and Reynaud with a Generalissimo whom he had morally assassinated.

The forces involved in the invasion of Holland, Belgium, and France were:

Germans: 134 infantry divisions, 10 armoured[3] and four motorized. Dutch: eight infantry divisions.[4] Belgians: 18 infantry divisions. British: 10 infantry divisions, one army tank brigade (heavy tanks) and five mechanized cavalry regiments (light tanks).[5] French: 90 infantry divisions, three armoured divisions, three light armoured,[6] five light mechanized and 27 non-divisionalized tank battalions.[7] Of tanks, the Germans had 2,439 available for operations;[8] the French 2,460 modern machines;[9] and the British 229, of which 171 were light tanks. Many of the French tanks were superior in armour and gun-calibre to the German, but German tank theory was based on intact armoured

---

[1] *The Private Diaries of Paul Baudouin* (English edit., 1948), p. 10.
[2] *Ibid.*, p. 26. See also *Ci-devant*, Anatole de Monzie (1941), pp. 218–219.
[3] The first three were raised in 1935.
[4] Holland was overrun so rapidly that these divisions barely opened their eyes.
[5] On May 10 the total British forces in France numbered 394,165, of which 237,319 were combatants (Ellis, p. 19).
[6] Raised after the fall of Poland.　　　　[7] Lyet, p. 33.
[8] Guderian, p. 473.　　　　[9] Lyet, p. 33; also 600 old ones.

divisions – battering-ram tactics – and the French on the distribution of tanks to support the infantry – penny packet tactics.
This was the secret of German superiority. In the air the Germans
were unquestionably superior. They entered the campaign with
3,700 effective aircraft,[1] and some 600 transport aircraft, while
the French had only 1,500 effective aircraft.[2] The Dutch and
Belgian air forces were of little account, and of the British, 474
machines were based on France, the remainder were retained
in England.

On Wednesday, May 8, Hitler ordered the attack to be
launched at 5.35 a.m. on the 10th. Since October, on 10 previous
occasions he had massed his armies on the Belgian, Dutch, and
Luxemburg frontiers, but never before had his plan been more
likely to succeed. To carry out his part of the plan, von Rundstedt
had deployed three armies between Aachen and Merzig; the
Fourth (General von Kluge) on the right; the Twelfth (General
von List) in the centre; and the Sixteenth (General Busch) on the
left. The Panzer Group, under General von Kleist – the force of
decision – was also in the centre; it consisted of two Panzer corps,
the XIXth (1st, 2nd, and 10th Panzer Divisions) under General
Guderian, and the XLIst (6th and 8th Panzer Divisions) under
General Reinhardt. The former was deployed between Vianden
and Echternach, and faced the Luxemburg frontier; the latter lay
to its north. Guderian's goal was Sedan, and Reinhardt's Monthermé; both were to establish bridgeheads over the Meuse at
these places for the infantry, and close cooperation between the
Panzer divisions and the *Luftwaffe* was arranged; but no instructions were issued on what should be done were a complete surprise
gained.[3] Besides these armoured forces, the 5th and 7th Panzer
Divisions, under General Hoth, were allotted to the Fourth Army,
and the 7th, commanded by General Rommel, was given Houx on
the Meuse as its objective.

On May 7 rumours reached the Hague of an impending attack,
but because there had been so many false alarms they were largely
discounted. At 9.30 p.m. on May 9, the Belgian Foreign Minister
received a telephone call to inform him that the frontier posts
reported a continuous drone of moving vehicles. At 3 a.m. on
May 10, reports arrived that aircraft were flying over Holland,
and an hour later that the Dutch and Belgian airfields were being
bombed. Soon afterward the Arras airfields were bombed. At

---

[1] Ellis, p. 44.   [2] Lyet, p. 35.   [3] Guderian, p. 97.

5 a.m. the Dutch and Belgian Foreign Ministers appealed to London and Paris for aid, and at 6.30 a.m. Gamelin telephoned General Georges to put Plan D into effect. At 7.30 a.m. the van of the French cavalry crossed into Belgium and the left wing of the allied army, pivoted on Mézières, began to change front and advance on the Dyle.

The operations in Holland and Belgium developed at lightning speed. By the 11th the Dutch airfields at Waalhaven, Rotterdam, Wassennaar, Volkenburg, Dordrecht and other places were occupied by German paratroops, and the bridges over the Maas at Moerdijk were in their hands, while from Gennap a motorized column had smashed through the Raam–Peel position and advanced on Moerdijk. In Belgium, Brussels, Antwerp, and Namur had been bombed, and the bridges over the Maas at Maestricht (Dutch) had been seized and parachutists had captured those over the Albert Canal at Briedgen, Weldwezelt, and Vroenhoven, and had dropped on the fortress of Eben-Emael and captured it by vertical attack.

On this day – May 11 – the French cavalry in the Ardennes were hounded westward by waves of dive-bombers (*Stukas*) – the advanced guard of the XIXth and XLIst Panzer Corps. By 5.30 p.m., after they had blown the bridges, the French cavalry were driven over the Semois, and at 7.15 p.m. Guderian's leading tanks reached the outskirts of Bouillon. With his whole front now uncovered, and the German tanks advancing on him, General Corap appealed for reinforcements. The French High Command rightly gauged that the main German blow was coming south and not north of Namur – as they had planned for – and ordered one armoured and three infantry divisions to move on the 12th to support Corap, and another armoured and five infantry divisions to do so on the 13th. The former were to arrive on the Ninth Army front on the 17th and the latter on the 21st, in both cases, as we shall see, hopelessly too late.

On the morning of May 12, against strong resistance, Guderian made an all-out attack on Bouillon and carried it. Although the bridge over the Semois was found demolished, a ford was discovered close by, through which infantry crossed, and the motor cyclists used rubber boats. All resistance in the Ardennes collapsed; Rommel neared Houx; Reinhardt closed in on Monthermé; and before nightfall Guderian's 1st and 10th Panzer Divisions had occupied the eastern bank of the Meuse at Sedan and had captured the old fortress. Belgium had been left behind and the myth of the Ardennes exploded.

At 8.15 a.m. on May 13, Guderian issued orders for his three divisions to attack at 4 p.m. that day: The 2nd was to move on either side of Donchéry, force a crossing, seize ground south of Donchéry, swing westward, cross the Ardennes Canal and roll up the enemy's defences along the Meuse; the 1st was to force a crossing between Glaire and Torcy, mop-up inside the Meuse bend, and then move on the wood of Marfée; and the 10th was to do likewise in the Sedan–Bazeilles sector and capture the high ground about Pont Maugis.[1]

From noon until 4 p.m. the dive-bombers went to work on the French defences on the west bank of the Meuse.[2] They swooped on the French gun emplacements, pill-boxes and machine-gun nests and paralysed their defenders. At 4 p.m. artillery, anti-tank and anti-aircraft guns joined in, and tanks moved down to the eastern bank to add to the pandemonium. Hundreds of rubber boats were brought up and the crossing was begun. Although casualties were heavy, by 5.30 p.m. the Germans had gained a lodgment on the western bank, and immediately engineers started to bridge the river at Glaire, a work which took them until midnight. By 8 p.m. the wood of Marfée–south of Sedan–was occupied; at 10 p.m. Donchéry was captured, and by midnight the village of Chémery–eight miles south of Sedan–was in German hands. The break-through on Guderian's front was complete; it had taken eight hours of strenuous fighting.

While Guderian battered his way over the Meuse, Reinhardt set out to cross that river at Nouzonville and Monthermé. At the former village he was repulsed, and only after two attempts and a bitter fight did he succeed at the latter by the use of rubber boats, but this time unsupported by dive-bombers. Further north, at Houx–two and a half miles below Dinant–Rommel found the railway bridge intact, but no sooner did his men try to cross it than it blew up. Covered by tank fire from the eastern bank, a passage was eventually forced, a pontoon bridge built and a bridgehead established. When it is remembered that the French

---

[1] Guderian, p. 479.

[2] Lyet (p. 48) notes their psychological effect, and the French General Mittlehauser said: "The technical surprise in this sphere of aviation was decisive" (quoted from *The Six Weeks War*, Theodore Draper (English edit., 1946), p. 71). Also the anonymous author of *The Diary of a Staff Officer* (1941), p. 11, writes: "When the dive-bombers came down on them they stood the noise – there were hardly any casualties – for only 2 hours, and then they bolted out with their hands over their ears. . . ."

troops who opposed Rommel were of category B and most
indifferently armed, they put up a gallant fight as long as they
could hold on to their trenches; but once driven into the open
they rapidly lost heart. None of the German crossings was a
review performance, as many at the time assumed, three failed

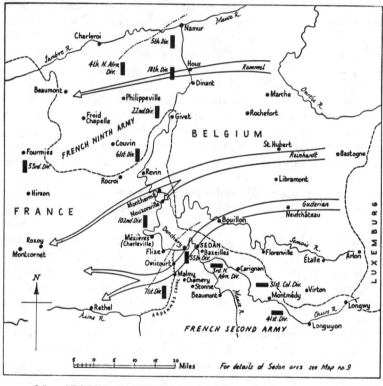

25. SECOND BATTLE OF SEDAN, MAY 13–15, 1940

and four succeeded, and had the French been better equipped
and trained and adequately supported by tanks and aircraft, a
very different picture would have been painted.

In accordance with Plan D, it was assumed that the Belgians
would be able to hold the Albert Canal–Meuse line until the
allied change of front to the Dyle had been completed; but, as
we have seen, in spite of its powerful fortifications, on May 10
and 11 it collapsed. On the 12th the Belgians were in full retreat
and General Blanchard sent forward his mechanized Cavalry
Corps to cover their withdrawal. This led to the first tank battle

of the campaign, fought around the small village of Merdorp, in which the superiority of the French 20-ton Somua and 31 ton/B tanks over the German 10-ton Pz. Kw. II and 22-ton Pz. Kw. IV was discounted by faulty French tactics. The result was that, after it had sustained heavy losses, the Cavalry Corps was forced to withdraw behind a strong anti-tank entrenchment between Perwez and Marchovelette. On the 14th a narrow gap was punched through it by the German guns, but to no purpose, for directly the German tanks tried to pass through it they were repulsed by the French artillery.

While this battle was fought, Dutch resistance collapsed, and at 11 a.m. on May 15 an armistice was signed and Holland ceased to be a belligerent. At the same time the French Seventh Army, which was moving on Breda, was flung back into Belgium, and on the 15th General Giraud was ordered to replace Corap in command of the Ninth Army. It was a useless change, because by the evening of the 14th, though the left and right of the Ninth Army were still in position, the whole of its centre had caved in. The hinge of the allied left wing was smashed Lyet writes, there were no reserves at hand to re-establish "a strong line of resistance which could check the enemy's armour."[1] This remark, made seven years after the event, is illuminating, for it shows how little, even in 1947, was understood of tank warfare. Throughout the campaign, the crucial tactical error was the persistence of the allies to maintain a continuous front, and the result was that they were never able to find sufficient forces to deliver a powerful counter-attack.

For the German XIXth Corps, as Guderian informs us, the night of May 14–15 was one of confusion because of difficulties with von Kleist, who forbade further advance. Guderian violently objected to this and there was a prolonged wrangle which ended when Kleist rescinded his order. On the 16th the bulk of the XIXth Corps advanced to a little west of Montcornet, and for the following day Guderian ordered the 2nd and 1st Panzer Divisions to move on St. Quentin–Péronne – while the 10th followed behind his left flank. But soon after the advance on the 17th had begun, again an order to halt was received. This time it came from O.K.H.[2]

[1] Lyet, p. 49.
[2] On May 17, *The Halder Diaries* carry the following entry: "Führer terribly nervous. Frightened by his own success. . . . Puts forward the excuse that it is all because of his southern flank." (See also Guderian, pp. 109–110.)

The halt did not last long, for it soon became evident that the French divisions which had been reported moving up on the southern flank of the gap intended to form a defensive flank and had no intention of counter-attacking. Rundstedt considered it was safe for Kleist to resume the advance, and the latter was ordered to push on to Cambrai–St. Quentin. There was nothing to impede him. Lyet writes: "On May 18 the enemy's armoured divisions were to find a void in front of them."[1] Guderian's advance was rapid; by 9 a.m. the 2nd Panzer Division had reached St. Quentin, and on its left the 1st approached Péronne. During this day, while on reconnaissance, General Giraud ran into a German post and was captured. This was the formal end of the French Ninth Army.

On May 19 the German advance reached the Canal du Nord at the following places: 7th Panzer Division at Marquion; on its left the 6th and 8th at Inchy-en-Artois and east of Beaumetz-les-Cambrai; the 2nd east of Combles; and the 1st at Péronne. The 5th protected the outer flank of the 7th and the 10th that of the 1st.

On Monday, May 20, while Rommel's 7th Panzer Division attacked Arras, a race for the Channel was made by the other German armoured divisions in front line. The 8th reached Hesdin and pushed on an advanced detachment to Montreuil; the 6th took Doullens and advanced to Le Boisle; the 2nd occupied Abbeville; and the 1st Amiens, where it at once established a bridgehead south of the Somme. The whole stretch of country between the Scarpe and the Somme was in German hands; the British lines of communication were cut, and the way to the Channel ports opened. In 11 days the Germans had covered 220 miles, and on the 20th the 2nd Panzer Division advanced well over 50 miles.[2]

In order to hold the Aisne and the Somme, between May 16–18 the French improvised three new armies: the Sixth (General Touchon) between Attigny and Soissons on the Aisne; the Seventh (General Frère) – incorporating a number of Giraud's old units – astride the Oise between Soissons and Péronne; and the Tenth (General Altmayer) along the Somme from Péronne to the sea.

While this front was formed, another new front was in process of formation in the north. On May 15 the allies in Belgium were ordered to fall back from the Dyle to the Scheldt (Plan E) in

---

[1] Lyet, p. 66.
[2] One reason for this rapid advance was that the armoured divisions were regularly supplied with fuel by air.

three stages: first to the Senne, next to the Dender, and lastly to the Scheldt, which was occupied on the 18th. The Belgians held the left, the British the centre, and the French First Army the right of this 75-mile line, which stretched southward to Arras, beyond which lay the 25-mile wide gap to Péronne.

Because of the rapidity of the German advance on May 20, the problem of the B.E.F. and French First Army were faced with was how to secure their right flank and rear – that is, how best to cover the northern flank of the gap. To improve his position, on May 21 Lord Gort made a tank attack southward from Arras. Although it was quite a small affair, it came as an unpleasant surprise to the Germans and showed how jumpy they were. It created, writes Guderian, "a considerable impression on the staff of the Panzer Group von Kleist, which suddenly became nervous."[1]

So much was this so that the 8th and 6th Panzer Divisions were pulled back to Anvin, St. Pol, Savy, and Saulty to form a flank guard to face the northern flank of the gap. This small and unsuccessful action clearly shows that had the French armoured divisions been trained for the counter-attack and assembled behind the allied left flank, which tactically was their correct position, Hitler's and Rundstedt's nervousness since May 15 would have been justified. The latter, we are told by General Blumentritt, his chief of staff, had a high opinion of General Gamelin and the French General Staff, and was wont to say: "My little Gamelin certainly knows what he is doing"![2]

Had Hitler and Rundstedt been able to glimpse events on the other side of the hill they would have found little cause for nervousness. They could have guessed correctly had they remembered the paralysing effect of the tank break-through at Cambrai and Amiens in the previous war. And had they coupled with this knowledge of the volatile temperament of the French, and then multiplied it ten-fold, they would have obtained a realistic picture of the pandemonium that raged in their enemy's camp.

On May 15 the news of the Ninth Army collapse fell on Paris like a thunderbolt. Reynaud seized his telephone, rang up Daladier, and asked him what counter-measures Gamelin proposed? The answer was, "he had none".[3] On the following day

[1] Guderian, p. 114.
[2] *Von Rundstedt the Soldier and the Man*, Guenther Blumentritt (English edit., 1952), pp. 64, 69.
[3] *The Private Diaries of Paul Baudouin*, p. 30.

the Cabinet met in a scene of indescribable confusion; archives were hurled out of the windows and burnt in the courtyard below; and deputies rushed about spreading the wildest of rumours. At 4 p.m. Mr. Churchill arrived[1] and, according to Baudouin, "kept saying that the further the Germans advanced the more vulnerable they would become to counter-attack." Counter-attack with what? Reynaud demanded fighter squadrons and Mr. Churchill agreed to send 10 squadrons and to divert the British strategic bombing force from the Ruhr[2] to the battlefield. "Crowned like a volcano by the smoke of his cigars," writes Baudouin, Churchill "told his French colleague [Reynaud] that even if France was invaded and vanquished England would go on fighting. . . . Until one in the morning he conjured up an apocalyptic vision of the war. He saw himself in the heart of Canada directing, over an England razed to the ground . . . and over a France whose ruins were already cold, the air war of the New World against the Old dominated by Germany."[3]

In England the wind blew less violently. Although the masses of the people, secure behind their sea wall, were not greatly perturbed by the German advance, the Government lost its head, and at the very moment when, in order to maintain internal calm, contempt of danger was imperative, the country was thrown into confusion by a host of ill-considered panic measures. Crazy obstructions were erected across the roads; signposts were up-rooted overnight; the names of railway stations, inns, villages and towns were suddenly obliterated; and hundreds of loyal people whose only crime was that they considered the war a blunder were arrested and held in custody, some for years on end, without charge or trial. It was anything but the finest hour in British history.

Panic in France was not restricted to the Government, and was possibly at its worst in the army. In the north it rushed through the headquarters like wildfire. On May 19 Lord Gort began to consider a withdrawal to the coast, and not without cause. On this day an anonymous diarist records: "The French General Staff have been paralysed by this unorthodox war of

---

[1] Mr. Churchill says 5.30 p.m. For his account of this meeting see *The Second World War* (1949), vol. II, pp. 42–46.

[2] The Ruhr was first bombed on May 15, and for what purpose it is hard to say, for the damage done was equivalent to dropping peas on the great pyramid (see *Berlin Diary*, William L. Shirer (English edit., n.d.), pp. 293–295 and 318).

[3] *The Private Diaries of Paul Baudouin*, p. 33.

movement. The fluid conditions prevailing are not dealt with in the textbooks and the 1914 brains of the French generals responsible for formulating the plans of the allied armies are incapable of functioning in this new and astonishing lay-out."[1] On May 20, General Weygand, who had been recalled from Syria on the 17th, visited the northern front, and "above everything else," writes Baudouin, "he had been struck by the panic that the Germans had succeeded in creating in our ranks by their armoured divisions and their aeroplanes. 'Their attempt to cause panic', said the General, 'has been crowned with complete success.' " And what was the answer? "In view of the paucity, one might almost say the non-existence, of our anti-tank equipment," writes Baudouin, "it was necessary 'to combine the 75's with the infantry and to use them like revolvers'."[2] Speed, novelty of tactics, the impossibility to readjust faulty initial dispositions, almost total lack of reliable information, and above all time to act, had paralysed the allied command.[3]

After the meeting on May 16 the traditional French panacea was applied to the crisis – the Government was reshuffled. On the 17th, Reynaud recalled Weygand from Syria and Marshal Pétain from Spain. On the 18th Daladier was made Foreign Minister, and Reynaud took over the Ministry of National Defence and made Weygand commander-in-chief in place of Gamelin, and Pétain deputy Prime Minister.

When General Weygand visited the northern front on May 20, he arranged for King Leopold, General Billotte, and Lord Gort to meet him at Ypres in order to consider a plan of action, but unfortunately Gort was unable to be present. The plan agreed was one which had already been considered by Gamelin, Georges, and Billotte, namely to carry out a dual counter-attack against the waist of the gap between Arras and the Somme. Part of the 1st Army Group was to strike south, and the Seventh Army north. Once this was settled Weygand returned to Paris by way of Cherbourg. Then fate stepped in, for soon after his departure, Billotte met with a fatal car accident, and his successor, General Blanchard, was unacquainted with the general situation.

[1] *The Diary of a Staff Officer*, p. 27.
[2] *The Diaries of Paul Baudouin*, p. 36. Weygand says: "The conditions prevailing in the higher ranks of the Army were chaotic, while in the lower ranks that staunchness of spirit that had in 1914 enabled them to stand up against the disasters of the first few weeks seemed no longer to be there" (*The Role of General Weygand*, Commandant J. Weygand, English edit., 1948, pp. 40–41).
[3] See Lyet, pp. 71–74.

On May 22 the Allied Supreme War Council met in Paris and it was decided that while the Belgian army withdrew to the Yser, eight divisions of the British Army and the French First Army would on the 24th attack south-west toward Bapaume and Cambrai, while the French Seventh Army, then south of the Somme, struck north.[1] Though sound enough on paper, this plan was unrealistic, for it failed to take into account the tense and confused situation which then prevailed in the north. On the 23rd the Seventh Army began to move as planned, but was immediately checked and only reached the Somme at one place; Gort reported that he could make no more than a sortie; and the French First Army was not ready to move. The next day it was realized by the British that the counter-attack was no more than a dream, and Gort was given permission to withdraw toward the coast. A war of words followed in which the French blamed the British and the British blamed the French.

The rapid German armoured advance on May 20 made Rundstedt grow nervous about his long, exposed southern flank, for naturally he expected that the cornered enemy would attempt to break back toward the Somme, also he was aware that French forces were on the move to the Somme from the south. Further, he and the German Supreme Command had begun to consider Plan Red – the southward move across the Somme – once the allied left wing had been rounded-up. "This growing preoccupation with plans for Operation 'Red' . . . is," writes Major Ellis, "the key to much that would otherwise be unexplainable in the German conduct of their campaign in the north from now onwards."[2]

To be in a position to meet the problematical allied counter-offensive, at about 6 o'clock on the evening of May 23, Rundstedt, through the German Fourth Army, ordered Hoth's and Kleist's Panzer Groups to halt until the situation became clearer, and at 11 a.m. on the 24th Hitler visited Rundstedt's headquarters and agreed that the mobile forces could be halted on the line Lens–Béthune–Aire–St. Omer–Gravelines, while Army Group B pressed on against the enemy Rundstedt's troops were to provide the anvil for Bock's hammer. Further, Hitler insisted that it was necessary to conserve the armoured forces for future operations. Lastly, when Hitler left, Rundstedt issued a directive which read:

[1] For the complete plan, see Ellis, p. 111, and Churchill, vol. ii, p. 50.
[2] Ellis, p. 120.

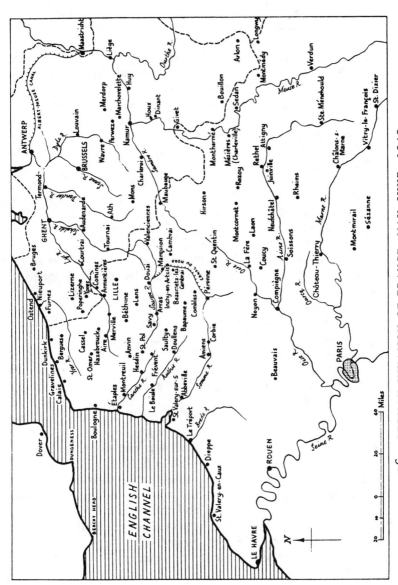

26. GERMAN INVASION OF FRANCE, MAY–JUNE, 1940

"By the Führer's orders . . . the general line Lens–Béthune–Aire–St. Omer–Gravelines (Canal Line) will *not* be passed."[1]

In the circumstances this was a sound decision. The German armoured divisions needed rest and overhaul–half Kleist's tanks and 30 per cent. of those of Hoth were out of action[2] – and because the bulk of the French armies south of the Aisne and Somme were still undefeated, it was imperative to halt. Also, as Major Ellis points out, the German leaders no more thought that a large-scale evacuation could be effected from the Channel beaches than did the British Admiralty and War Office.

Next, very early on May 25[3] O.K.H. authorized Rundstedt to cross the Canal line, but he did not do so until on the 26th Hitler intervened with an order to resume the attack in the direction of Tournai–Cassel–Dunkirk. After reading Major Ellis's careful analysis of the orders and diary entries issued and made between the 23rd and 27th, we can only agree with his final summing up: "Hitler's responsibility in connection with the halt has been completely misrepresented. He did not initiate it on the 24th, for Rundstedt had ordered it on the 23rd: Hitler merely endorsed it. He did not maintain it on the 25th and 26th for he had specifically left Rundstedt to decide on the next move. But he *was* personally responsible for terminating the halt and for the order to resume the attack on the 27th."[4] Even should this be rejected and Blumentritt's evidence[5] be accepted that the halt order was first issued to Rundstedt on Hitler's instructions by telephone, as we shall soon see, it was not this much disputed halt which was the main cause of the escape of the B.E.F. from Dunkirk.

When Rundstedt's Army Group halted, Bock's pushed on, and on May 25 it broke through the Belgian front on the Lys. At once Gort realized that were Bock allowed to exploit this success he would cut off the B.E.F. from the sea, so he abandoned all further thought of the southern counter-attack and ordered the 5th and 50th Divisions he had kept in hand for it to fill the gap. This he did on his own initiative, and had he not done so the B.E.F. would have been lost. On this day Boulogne was captured by the Germans and Calais fell to them on the morrow.

Fortunately for the allied left wing, when on May 19 the British

---

[1] *Ibid.*, pp. 138, 139.   [2] *Ibid.*, p. 151.   [3] *Ibid.*, p. 150.
[4] *Ibid.*, pp. 350–351. The opposite view is recorded by Captain Liddell Hart in his *The Other Side of the Hill* (1951), chap. XII.
[5] *Von Rundstedt*, p. 75. This is a sketchy book and would seem to have been written almost entirely from memory.

Admiralty was informed that Gort was considering a withdrawal to the coast, they at once began to plan for an evacuation, called "Operation Dynamo", and on the 26th, by when this plan was well advanced, the signal went out to put it into operation. It was only just in time, because at midnight the following day Leopold ordered his army to cease fire,[1] an action which stunned Paris, and caused Reynaud to accuse the King of treason and Pétain to exclaim, "We are finished. We must capitulate!" At the same time Weygand continued to inundate Gort with appeals to counter-attack!

On May 29 the allied left wing held a quadrilateral that extended from Nieuport to Comines, from Comines to Merville, and thence by way of Hazebrouck and Cassel to west of Dunkirk; it was about 30 miles deep and under 20 miles in breadth. On the 29th its southern face was withdrawn northward to Poperinghe–Lizerne, and on the 30th to the Bergues–Furnes Canal, six miles south of the coast. This left the allies in their final bridgehead, which fortunately for them was defensively exceedingly strong. South of the sand dunes that fringed the seafront the country was covered by a network of drainage dikes which, except by the roads flanked by ditches, made the whole area almost impassable by tanks.

By May 27 the Germans were fully aware that British troops were being evacuated from the Dunkirk beaches, and the question arose, how could a stop be put to this? Göring and Hitler, says Guderian, "believed German air supremacy to be strong enough to prevent the evacuation."[2] There was nothing exceptional in this point of view; if the British from May 15 on thought that bombing the Ruhr would slacken the German advance, Göring's and Hitler's error was certainly less flagrant.

Halder says that Hitler "prevented the complete destruction of the British army by withdrawing the German tanks which were already in their rear,"[3] and Rundstedt – in an interview he gave Milton Schulman after the war – says that he wanted to throw in five Panzer divisions but was forbidden to do so by Hitler – an "incredible blunder" he calls it.[4] Yet, on May 28, Guderian – his

---

[1] That this was done without prior consultation or warning, as Mr. Churchill (*The Second World War*, 1949, vol. II, p. 84) and M. Reynaud (*La France a sauvé l'Europe*, 1941, vol. II, pp. 234–237) have asserted, is incorrect: see *The Surrender of King Leopold*, Joseph P. Kennedy and James P. Landis (New York, 1950).
[2] Guderian, p. 120.   [3] *Hitler as War Lord*, p. 30.
[4] *Defeat in the West* (1947), p. 43.

leading tank general – after he had toured the forward positions, advised the chief of staff of Kleist's Group that "A tank attack is pointless in the marshy country which has been completely soaked by the rain [it had rained heavily in the past twenty-four hours]," and that the infantry of the Eighteenth Army of Army Group B, then approaching the XIXth Corps from the east, "are more suitable than tanks for fighting in this kind of country."[1] Von Kleist agreed, and all three of Guderian's armoured divisions were withdrawn, presumably by Rundstedt, for Kleist is unlikely to have ordered this on his own authority.

The truth is, that the whole area was one vast tank obstacle, and that Hitler, who had a better understanding of the capability of tanks than most of his generals, considered that their use in the Dunkirk area *would be* an "incredible blunder." As long ago as October 9, 1939, he had laid down that "The tank arm must be used for operations for which it is best suited. Under no circumstances must the tanks be permitted to become entangled in the endless confusion of the rows of houses in the Belgian towns."[2] This is far more true of the Belgian bogs.

The evacuation was a phenomenal success, as so many British retreats have been, and in spite of violent air attacks it was carried out methodically and without panic. Between May 26 and June 3, 366,162 men, of whom 224,320 were British, were brought back to England in 765 British ships of all sorts and sizes.[3] That Hitler wished them to escape, as some of his generals have asserted, is a myth, as also are the assertions that their salvation was due to Rundstedt's halt on May 23 and because Hitler held back the German armoured divisions.

The causes of the success were outside German control. They were the preparatory measures taken by the British Admiralty; the magnificent fighting of the French First Army rear guards; the stubborn resistance of Gort's men; the gallant work of the Royal Navy; the superb courage of the R.A.F. in face of the superior *Luftwaffe*; the initiative of hundreds of small craft owners; and not least, to the fact that the Dunkirk bridgehead was a natural fortress.

That, in face of the most powerful army and air force in the world, a third of a million men was safely brought back to Britain in nine days, thrilled the peoples of the British Empire. It was an

---

[1] Ellis, p. 208, quoting the XIXth Corps diary.
[2] *Ibid.*, p. 351.   [3] For types, see Ellis, pp. 219–321.

unique achievement, and its completion on June 3 marks the day when spiritually the British people full-heartedly entered the war. To France it was a catastrophe.

When the evacuation from Dunkirk was under way, the crossings over the Somme – seized by the Germans on May 20 – were developed into strong bridgeheads. The French improvised what was to be known as the Weygand Line, which extended from Abbeville to Longuyon. It was held by two Army Groups, the Third and Fourth, respectively commanded by General Besson and General Huntziger. The former consisted of the Tenth Army between the sea and Corbie, the Seventh Army from Corbie to Coucy, and the Sixth Army from Coucy to Neufchâtel; the latter of the Fourth Army from Neufchâtel to Attigny, and the Second Army from Attigny to Longuyon, where it linked up with the Maginot Line.

As will be seen, the basic idea was still one of a continuous front, and this although the French had no longer sufficient forces to hold it. Since Dunkirk they had been reduced to 43 infantry divisions, three armoured, three cavalry, and 13 fortress divisions in the Maginot Line which were immobile. Besides these, although there were 140,000 British troops in France, they included only one organized division – the 51st – and the British 1st Armoured Division, which had arrived at Havre on May 15.

On May 26 Weygand issued a new defensive plan. There was to be no retreat, and full use was to be made of woods, farms and villages to hold the front. They were to be organized into a network of "hedgehogs" (*herissons*) which, even if surrounded, were to be held to the last man, and the German tanks were to be allowed to by-pass them. Tactically the idea would have been sound had the French possessed a sufficiency of well-trained armoured forces to counter-attack between the hedgehogs, but as they did not, this strong-point system was suicidal.

There were now 137 German divisions facing the French, and with astonishing rapidity Army Groups A and B were reorganized for what Weygand called the "Battle of France". Army Group B was given six Panzer divisions, under von Kleist and Hoth, and was brought into line between Abbeville and La Fère, while Army Group A with four such divisions, under Guderian, took over the front La Fère–Montmédy.

Operation Red was issued by O.K.H. on May 31. Its general idea was that Army Group B (von Bock) should break through the French Somme front between Abbeville and Péronne, and when it had done so Army Group A (von Rundstedt) should do the same on the Aisne front. Both were to be based on the armoured divisions, and those under Bock were grouped in pairs, the 5th and 7th west of Amiens, the 9th and 10th at Amiens, and the 3rd and 4th at Péronne. The 5th and 7th were allotted to the German Fourth Army, which held the Somme front from the sea to west of Amiens. Their task was to break through the centre of the French Tenth Army, to drive its left wing – the IXth Corps and British 51st Division – against the coast, and penetrate to the Seine at Rouen, while the 9th and 10th Panzer divisions and the 3rd and 4th, under the German Sixth Army, on the left of the Fourth, broke through the right of the French Tenth Army and the left of the Seventh.

On May 28-29 and again on June 4 the French made two abortive attacks to wrest the Somme bridgeheads from the Germans. Then on June 5, while Reynaud again reshuffled his Cabinet, at four o'clock in the morning the German Fourth Army struck. As at Sedan, the break-through of the 5th and 7th Panzer Divisions was immediate, and when the Tenth French Army fell back to the river Bresle the two Panzer divisions cut in on the right flank of the French IXth Corps and forced it back toward Dieppe. On June 8, the two Panzer divisions reached the outskirts of Rouen, an advance of some 70 miles in three days. When Rouen was occupied on the 9th, the 5th and 7th Divisions swung north, and on the 10th they cut in on the rear of the French IXth Corps while its front was engaged by three German infantry divisions and one motorized division. The outcome was the surrender of the IXth Corps and the 51st Division on June 12. It was a superb manoeuvre – a Dunkirk in miniature, but without an evacuation. Meanwhile the 9th and 10th Panzer Divisions broke through the right of the French Tenth Army, and the 3rd and 4th escorted the infantry of the Sixth German Army through the initial stage of their advance, and when this had been done, all four Panzer divisions were withdrawn into reserve between Noyon and St. Quentin.

No sooner was Rouen in German hands than, at 4.30 a.m. on June 9, the battle of the Aisne was opened by a violent artillery bombardment on the fronts of the French Sixth and Fourth Armies, and at 5 a.m. the infantry of the German Twelfth Army, between Neufchâtel and Attigny, went over to the attack. They were followed by Guderian's 1st and 2nd Panzer Divisions, and on the 10th they fought a sharp and successful action with French armoured forces at Juinville, after which the 6th and 8th Panzer Divisions joined them, and together the four broke through the right of the French Sixth Army and the front of the Fourth, and pressed on toward Châlons and St. Dizier. On the 11th the four Panzer divisions in reserve were thrown in; the 3rd and 4th advanced on Château-Thierry, and the 9th and 10th on a course parallel with them. On the 12th and 13th, the eight Panzer divisions pushed into a wide gap between the French Sixth and Second Armies caused by the dissolution of the Fourth Army. When on the 12th General Réquin, commander of the Fourth, telephoned General Touchon, who commanded the Sixth, for aid, the latter replied: "I ought to assist you, but it is absolutely impossible. My right-hand corps is shattered. Between Montmirail and Sézanne there is a roundabout of tanks (*carrousel de chars*). I have nothing to ward it off."[1]

The rapidity of the German advance, which brought their leading troops to St. Dizier on June 14 and to Pontarlier on the Swiss frontier on the 17th – as the crow flies, 200 miles from Rethel – was due in part to the Weygand system of defence. Guderian tells us that because the French went into "hedgehogs" his tanks had a free run of the open spaces between them, and all they had to do was to push on and leave it to the following infantry to reduce the strong-points.[2] Also it was partly because Italy had declared war on France on June 10, which added to French despondency.

From the launching of the battle of the Aisne to June 25 we enter a dreamland of political fantasy, in which the tilting at windmills passed from fiction into history. On June 10 the French Government abandoned Paris, and followed by several millions of refugees[3] first sought refuge in Tours, and then in Bordeaux. On the 14th Paris was occupied by the Germans and the heart of France ceased to throb; nevertheless, utopian panaceas were proposed. For the most part they emanated from the fertile brain of Mr. Churchill: Brittany should be held as a redoubt; the French Government and 500,000 French soldiers should seek refuge in Algeria;[4] *a levée en masse* should be proclaimed; and more imaginative still, the French should take to guerrilla war and wear down

[1] Lyet, p. 133.   [2] Guderian, p. 124.
[3] Weygand (*op. cit.*, p. 108) says "some six million."
[4] *Ibid.*, p. 108, French N. Africa possessed "one very small cartridge manufactory!"

the Germans until they succumbed to famine. Of these fantastic schemes, it was fortunate for Mr. Churchill that the only feasible one, the transference of the French Government to Algeria was not adopted, for had it been, as Weygand points out, the almost inevitable outcome would have been a German invasion of North Africa, which was the one thing Mr. Churchill should most have dreaded.

On June 16, when the British Prime Minister's imagination hit the bottom of 1,000 years of cantankerous Franco-British history by a proposal of an "indissoluble union" of Britain and France, it so startled Monsieur Reynaud that at 8 p.m. he resigned the premiership and President Lebrun empowered Marshal Pétain to form a new Ministry. Pétain was 84 years old. In the First World War he had been proclaimed "the saviour of France", now he was called upon to become her undertaker. Although a slow and cautious soldier, he acted with a promptness which belied his years. At 12.30 a.m. on June 17 he asked the Spanish Ambassador to transmit to Hitler a request for an armistice. On the 22nd it was signed at Rethondes in the same railway coach in which the armistice of November 11, 1918, had been concluded.[1] Three days later hostilities in France ended, and Britain stood alone.

In six weeks France had been overwhelmed. What did it cost the Germans? According to Hitler, it cost 146,492 casualties, and according to the British official historian, 156,556; in either case less than one-third of the casualties suffered by the British in the battle of the Somme of 1916.[2]

The entire campaign was a dramatic vindication of the attack by paralysation. "The French High Command," writes Major Ellis, "was beaten not only by superiority of numbers and equipment, but by the pace of enemy operations, by inability to think ahead. . . ."[3] Lord Gort, who should know better than any man, wrote in his "Despatches": "The speed with which the enemy exploited his penetration of the French front, his willingness to accept risks to further his aim, and his exploitation of every success to the uttermost limits emphasized, even more fully than in the campaigns of the past, the advantage which accrues to the

---

[1] The armistice terms were lenient: The constitution of the Third Republic remained in full force; 40 departments were not occupied; an army of 100,000 men in France and 180,000 in Africa was allowed; the fleet was left intact, and so was the French Empire.

[2] It is of interest to note that after Dunkirk 191,870 British and other troops were evacuated from France.

[3] Ellis, p. 321.

commander who knows how best to use time and to make time his servant and not his master."[1]

After the fall of France England was left single-handed, and until she could raise another coalition it was manifestly impossible for her to win the war. But she was far from defeat, for she still held the initiative at sea, and as her sea power had enabled her to rescue one army, it also enabled her to plant another on the Continent whenever an opportune moment arose. As long as England refused to accept defeat, France would not merely have to be policed, but also garrisoned. In consequence, she would be a strategical liability to Hitler, and would become increasingly so were he compelled to add to the coast lines of his conquests. Thus the negative second front of the war was established, which demanded for its defence a dispersion of German fighting man-power at the cost of its full concentration against the positive front which, according to Hitler's war aim, was now Russia. It was of vital importance for Hitler to liquidate this negative front before he turned east.

When from the German point of view we consider the impor-tance of this problem, it is almost inexplicable that when in the autumn of 1939 the offensive against the west was determined, no invasion of England was envisaged, and the only possible reason why it was not is that Hitler cherished the belief that once France was defeated England would accept a negotiated peace.[2] It would appear that in spite of Clausewitz's irrefutable logic,[3] neither he nor his generals realized that because England was at war with Germany and because she could not be directly attacked, she automatically was the centre of gravity of all possible alliances against Germany, and that, as in the Napoleonic wars, the loss of a continental ally was of secondary importance to her as long as other potential allies were in the field. Were he to attack Russia before England had been subdued, he would automatically raise another coalition against Germany, which must inevitably lead to what he dreaded most – a conflict on two positive fronts.

[1] Supplement to the *London Gazette* of October 10, 1941, p. 5931.
[2] See *The Memoirs of Field-Marshal Kesselring* (English edit., 1953), p. 65. In 1935 Hitler told the writer that the one thing above all others which had struck him in the First World War was the tenacity of the English. This he would seem to have forgotten in 1939.
[3] "We may . . . establish it as a principle, that if we conquer all our enemies by conquering one of them, the defeat of that one must be the aim of the war, because in that one we hit the common centre of gravity of the whole war" (*On War*, English edit., 1908, vol. III, p. 108).

On June 18 – the day after Marshal Pétain's request for an armistice – Count Ciano, Mussolini's son-in-law, jotted down in his diary: "Hitler is now the gambler who has made a big scoop and would like to get up from the table risking nothing more."[1] But this he could not do as long as England was at war with Germany, and because, under Churchill's pugnacious leadership, she showed no willingness to abandon the war, he resorted to a gigantic bluff in order to bring her to heel: it was the threat of an invasion, called "Operation Sea Lion", and more appropriately might have been named "Sea Fox."

On July 2 the project was vaguely considered, and a fortnight later a directive was issued in which it was stated:

"As England, in spite of the hopelessness of her military position, has so far shown herself unwilling to come to any compromise, I have decided to begin to prepare for, and if necessary to carry out an invasion of England.

"This operation is dictated by the necessity of eliminating Great Britain as a base from which the war against Germany can be fought, and if necessary, the island will be occupied."[2]

The landing was to come as a surprise on a broad front from Ramsgate to the Isle of Wight, and all preparations were to be completed by the middle of August, a palpable absurdity, as 39 divisions were involved – 13 in first flight and 26 in support, and 1,722 barges, 471 tugs, 1,161 motor-boats and 155 transports had to be fitted and assembled in the Channel ports.[3]

On July 19, in a speech in the Reichstag, Hitler made an official offer of peace to England, but it had no effect whatever on the British Government. Operation Sea Lion was continued, and a few days later the date was put forward to September 15. On July 31, in a reply to Admiral Raeder, Hitler wrote: "The decision as to whether the operation is to take place in September or be delayed until May, 1941, will be made after the Air Force has made concentrated attacks on Southern England for one week."[4] This was another absurdity, for as Kesselring says: "It was clear to every discerning person, including Hitler, that England could not be brought to her knees by the Luftwaffe alone," if only

---

[1] *Ciano's Diary, 1939–1943* (English edit., 1947), p. 267.
[2] *Hitler and his Admirals*, Anthony Martienssen (1948), p. 69.
[3] When it is remembered that the preparations for the North Africa invasion in 1942 took well over nine months, the one month allotted by Hitler makes the operation ridiculous.
[4] Quoted from *Hitler's Strategy*, F. H. Hinsley (1951), p. 71. On this day for the first time Hitler mentions the invasion of Russia (see *Halder Diaries*, July 31, 1940).

because "The Luftwaffe by itself could not deal with the British Fleet."[1]

The truth is, with the possible exception of Göring, the *Luftwaffe* commander, nobody believed in Operation Sea Lion.[2] Certainly the German admirals did not, nor the generals, nor Hitler himself who, according to General Blumentritt, in July told Rundstedt privately that "he did not intend to carry out 'Sea Lion'."[3]

At the beginning of August the *Luftwaffe* had at its command 2,669 operational aircraft, of which 1,015 were bombers, 346 dive-bombers, 933 single-engine, and 375 twin-engine fighters; and opposed to it was the R.A.F. with 1,350 operational aircraft, of which 704 represented Fighter Command, under Air Chief Marshal Sir Hugh Dowding. In fighters, upon which the defence of the British Isles depended, German superiority was considerable. But set against this, the *Luftwaffe* would have to fight over the sea and hostile territory, and every aircraft shot down would mean a crew or pilot permanently lost; it would not be supported by anti-aircraft fire; the German Messerschmitt fighter was a slower climber than the British Spitfire; and above all, the R.A.F. could work on radar (radio-location) and the *Luftwaffe* could not.

The Battle of Britain, which at Hitler's bidding called the bluff, opened on August 12, and passed through two phases. In the first the radar stations were attacked, but as only one was put out of operation, Göring foolishly concentrated his offensive on the airfields in south-east England and on merchant shipping in the Channel. This phase reached its climax between August 24 and September 6, during which period the *Luftwaffe* put an average of almost 1,000 aircraft a day in the air.

On September 7, the second phase opened with the bombing of London. It was substituted for the invasion targets because Hitler looked "upon a large scale attack on London as possibly being decisive, and because a systematic and long drawn out bombardment of London might produce an attitude in the enemy which will make the 'Sea Lion' operation completely unnecessary."[4] Thus the Douhet theory was put into practice, and it was to prove a grotesque failure.

Whether Hitler really believed that the bombing of London would result in a British panic would appear doubtful; it seems more probable that his intention was to cover his initial failure,

---

[1] *Memoirs*, pp. 68 and 66.   [2] See *Guderian*, p. 138.
[3] *Von Rundstedt*, p. 87.   [4] See *ibid.*, p. 81.

as well as to retaliate for the R.A.F. bombing of Berlin on August 25–26, in order to stimulate his people and impress the Russians. That the latter were in his mind is supported by the fact that, on August 27, he decided to transfer 10 divisions from the west to the east, presumably because the failure of Phase I might have encouraged them. On September 3, the date of the invasion was postponed until September 29, and exactly a fortnight later the final decision was made. It was that, as the British air force was by no means defeated and showed increasing activity, and as the weather situation was doubtful, the Führer decided "to postpone 'Sea Lion' indefinitely."[1]

Rightly in England and throughout her Empire the Battle of Britain was turned into a great propaganda victory: yet never once were the British Isles in any real danger, nor was Fighter Command ever reduced to its last cartridge, as was put about in order to magnify the German peril. Because it came so soon on the heels of the fall of France, it not only showed that the Germans were not invincible, but it made Hitler look ridiculous, and in doing so it added vastly to British prestige. In consequence, the Battle of Britain was not the least of the factors which stimulated American support of England. Further, it persuaded Hitler to turn on Russia before Britain had been driven out of the war and this, as will be seen, was the road to his ruin.

[1] See *ibid.*, p. 89.

Operation Barbarossa and the Lend-Lease Act

As soon as the direct attack on England had been abandoned, Hitler turned to the indirect approach. Already on June 30, in a memorandum on the "Continuation of the war against England," General Jodl had suggested as an alternative to operation "Sea Lion" that the Mediterranean should be sealed off by the occupation of Gibraltar and Egypt; the former aim to be effected in cooperation with Spain, and the latter with Italy. Two months later – on August 21 – Ciano mentions in his diary that Mussolini was "entirely occupied" with his plan to attack Egypt on September 6, and that General Keitel had told the Duce that to take Cairo was more important than to take London. Significantly, on September 6 Admiral Raeder presented a report to Hitler to revive Jodl's suggestion. "Preparations for this operation," he wrote, "must be begun at once so that they are completed before the U.S.A. steps in. It should not be of secondary importance, but as one of the main blows against Britain." This was strategically sound, because Egypt was both the centre of Britain's imperial communications and her sole remaining oversea base within striking distance of Europe. Should Egypt and Gibraltar be wrested from her, the Mediterranean would become an Italian lake, Turkey could be pinched out, and the road to Russia by way of Armenia and Georgia opened; and finally Britain would be placed in so desperate a position that American ardour in her support might fall to zero. Could such a situation be brought about, England would be compelled to accept a negotiated peace, for without American economic support she could not continue the struggle.

Hitler did not set aside Raeder's suggestion, but seized on it and opened negotiations with Spain. First he decided that the submarine campaign should be intensified and the bombing of London continued, and then, on October 23, he met Franco at Hendaye in order to gain his consent to the free passage of German troops through Spain. He pressed for an immediate agreement which, to his annoyance, Franco refused to give. Five days later the whole situation was suddenly changed; without reference to Hitler, Mussolini invaded Greece. It was an act of strategic madness, because it involved Italy in a war on two fronts when she was having the utmost difficulty in supplying General Graziani's front in North Africa.

The immediate result of this piece of foolishness was the British occupation of Crete and Lemnos on November 3, and as this advance halved the bombing distance between Egypt and the Rumanian oilfields, Hitler decided, while preparations to seize Gibraltar continued, to impose his will on Bulgaria and Rumania and to invade Yugoslavia and Greece. On November 17 King Boris of Bulgaria was summoned to Germany and his good will won. Ten days later General Antonescu carried out a *coup d'état* in Rumania and joined the Axis.

Barely were these arrangements made than another unlooked for event upset Hitler's calculations. On December 9, Sir Archibald Wavell, British commander in the Middle East, routed Graziani in the Battle of Sidi Barrani, and the defeat was so complete that it became imperative for Hitler to succour the Italians. Without the loss of a minute, on December 10 he ordered formations of the *Luftwaffe* to the south of Italy in order to attack British sea communications, and ordered the despatch to North Africa of at least one armoured division under General Rommel. Further, and more important, the Italian defeat so alarmed Franco that the projected seizure of Gibraltar had to be dropped, and this, coupled with the British advance in the Aegean, led to Hitler's fateful decision – to strike at Russia before he had settled his accounts with England.

On December 16 he issued Directive No. 21, designated "Operation Barbarossa". In it we read:

"The German Armed Forces must be prepared to crush Soviet Russia in a quick campaign even before the end of the war against England. For this purpose the Army will have to employ all available units with the reservation that the occupied territories must be safeguarded against surprise attack. . . . Preparations are to be completed by May 15, 1941. . . . The ultimate objective of the operation is to establish a defensive line against Asiatic Russia from a line running approximately from the Volga river to Archangel."

Further, Hitler directed that the concentration of forces for "Barbarossa" was to be camouflaged as a feint for "Sea Lion" and his projected attack on Greece. It was to be made "the greatest deception in history."

This was not altogether a gesture of frustration; there was logic behind this decision: If England would not come to terms – so he argued – then her one and only hope must lie in the intervention of Russia and the United States. Were Russia, as a prospective British ally, to be eliminated, England would be left with the United States, and because neither would be able to recruit a continental partner, was it likely that America would continue to support Britain? If not, then Britain would be compelled to negotiate, and even were the United States to continue her support, the two allies would be faced with the whole might of Germany on one front, and probably by that of Japan on another.

In Martienssen's[1] opinion, Hitler's directive of December 18 was "perhaps the biggest military blunder of all time." Events proved that it was certainly the biggest blunder he made, although at the beginning there was one factor which had Hitler grasped it would in all probability have led to the complete overthrow of the Soviet colossus within a few months – that was, the composition of the Russian empire.

As discussed in Chronicle 9, Russia is a mosaic of subjugated peoples who in 1940 were as violently opposed to the autocracy of their Bolshevik masters as previously they had been opposed to the autocracy of their Tsars. Had Hitler only appreciated what this meant, he would have offered the Ukrainians, Bielorussians (White Russians), Turkomans, and the other subjected peoples liberation from Soviet rule and unfettered autonomy. He would have decided to have advanced into Russia as a liberator, not a conqueror, and had he done so he would have caused such an explosion that the U.S.S.R. would have disintegrated. It is true that this alone would not have given him the *Lebensraum* he sought; yet it is equally true that once the Soviet Imperium had been destroyed, he could have enforced his will on its shattered parts. As will be seen – setting morality aside – his barbarities toward the subjugated peoples as well as the Muscovites were not so much misplaced as mistimed; for they could only be profitable to him were they to follow the fall of the Soviet régime. Because of this they should have been rigorously excluded before the collapse. Although Hitler was as brutal as Lenin, he was less astute; while

---

[1] Editor of the *Fuehrer Conferences on Naval Affairs* and author of *Hitler and his Admirals* (1948).

Lenin understood how to make brutality his servant, Hitler through sheer grossness of mind became its victim, and ultimately it strangled him.

His most implacable enemy, President Roosevelt, had not been idle, and in spite of his manifold enunciations to keep the United States out of the war, he was bent on provoking some incident which would bring them into it. His aim, like Mr. Churchill's, was to destroy Hitlerism, root, trunk, and branch. He said, "There is absolutely nothing important in the world to-day but to beat Hitler," and as this would become impossible were Great Britain to accept a negotiated peace, in spite of international law, the laws of America and the neutral status of the United States, Roosevelt set out to do everything in his power to help her. His one great difficulty was to overcome isolationism at home, which meant that most Americans wanted to mind their own business. His policy to overcome this difficulty was double-faced. Like Mahomet II, "peace was on his lips, while war was in his heart." "We will not participate in foreign wars," he said, "and we will not send our Army, naval and air forces to fight in foreign lands. . . . I have said this before, but I shall say it again and again and again: Your boys are not going to be sent into any foreign wars. . . . Your President says this country is not going to war." But he left no stone unturned to provoke Hitler to declare war on the very people to whom he so ardently promised peace. He provided Great Britain with American destroyers, he landed American troops in Iceland, and he set out to patrol the Atlantic seaways in order to safeguard British convoys; all of which were acts of war.

The crucial danger which faced Great Britain was neither the German direct attack nor the German indirect approach. The battle of Britain had been won, and the battle of the Mediterranean was successfully waged; but the one battle in which Britain fought a desperate rear guard action remained – it was the battle of the dollar. Without dollars to pay for her food, munitions, and shipping, she was faced with strategical bankruptcy. Thus far she had paid for them on a "cash-and-carry" basis – that is, by selling her foreign assets; but by the end of 1940 she was scraping the bottom of her dollar barrel, and unless it could be replenished the ultimate issue before her was a negotiated peace. So desperate was her situation that, on December 8, Mr. Churchill, in a long letter to Roosevelt, informed him that the moment approached when further payment could not be made.[1] Rightly he says that this was one of the most important letters he ever wrote. It changed the axis of the entire war.

Roosevelt received this letter while on a cruise in the Caribbean, and for several days he pondered. On December 17, at a Press conference, he talked of how to "get rid of the silly, foolish old dollar sign", and on the 29th he delivered over the radio one of his educational fireside chats. It opened with the usual pronouncement that it was his purpose to keep the people, their children and their grand-children "out of a last-ditch war." In order to terrify them into one, he added, "Never before since Jamestown and Plymouth Rock has our American civilization been in such danger as now. . . . If Great Britain goes down, the Axis Powers will control the continents of Europe, Asia, Africa, Australasia (*sic*) and the high seas." Then "all of us would be living at the point of a gun loaded with explosive bullets." Then came the catch-line of his speech: "We must be the great arsenal of democracy. We have furnished the British great material support and we will furnish far more in the future." Typically, this chat ended with another wave of the olive branch – "We have every good reason for hope – hope of peace."

The great arsenal of democracy referred to the Lend-Lease Bill – "an Act to promote the defense of the United States" – introduced into Congress on January 10, 1941. On March 8 it passed the upper house by 60 votes to 31, and on the 11th was signed by the President, who on the same day proclaimed that the defence of Britain and Greece was "vital to the defense of the United States," and four days later China was included.

The powers granted to the President by this Act were unprecedented. It enabled him to designate as a beneficiary any country in the world; to manufacture and procure whatever munitions he wanted; to sell, transfer, exchange, lease and lend any articles of defence he liked; to repair and recondition the articles of defence of the designated governments; to communicate to these governments any defence information he considered necessary; and to determine the terms and conditions of receipt and payment. All

---

[1] "We had paid out over 4,500 million dollars in cash. We had only 1,000 millions left, the greater part in investments, many of which were not readily marketable. It was plain that we could not go on any longer in this way. Even if we divested ourselves of all our gold and foreign assets, we could not pay for half we had ordered, and the extension of the war made it necessary for us to have ten times as much" (Churchill, in *The Second World War*, 1949, vol. II, p. 493).

these things he could do at his pleasure "notwithstanding the provision of any other law."

The signing of the Lend-Lease Act on March 11, 1941, was as fateful an event in world history as the American declaration of war on April 6, 1917. By allying the United States with all countries fighting the Axis it enabled their President to make war, declared or undeclared, in any quarter of the globe. It meant that when America entered the war, again there would be no neutral arbiter left. In 1917, Woodrow Wilson had foreseen where he was going, but in 1941 Franklin D. Roosevelt stepped blindly on to the road of global war. In order to bracket the Lend-Lease Act with the Declaration of American Independence, he had numbered the Bill "1776". Yet instead of liberating Europe, under his leadership it was to become above all other instruments the one which was to bring half the world under the servitude of Moscow. Hitler's barbarities redounded to Stalin's profit and the blindness of the American President led to the triumph of the Muscovite dictator.

The first step in Hitler's projected invasion of Russia was to consolidate his position in the Balkans so that he might protect his right flank and rear and safeguard the vital Rumanian oilfields. By February 28 all was ready, and on that day, with the connivance of King Boris, Bulgaria was occupied and became party to the Three Power Pact, which had been signed by Germany, Italy, and Japan on September 27. Pressure was then brought on Yugoslavia and Greece and the latter called for British aid. On March 24, the Yugoslav Government capitulated, but three days later, when German troops were about to cross the Yugoslav frontier, General Simovitch carried out a *coup d'état* and repudiated the capitulation. With his accustomed celerity, on April 6 Hitler ordered his troops to cross the Yugoslav frontier, and 11 days later the Yugoslav army capitulated. Meanwhile, on March 7, British troops had begun to land at the Piraeus, but no sooner were they in line with the Greeks than, on April 8, they were attacked, and on the 21st Greece was out of the war. A month later a German airborne attack was launched on Crete, and on May 27 the island was in German hands.

Once Greece had been overrun, on April 30, at a conference of his generals, Hitler chose June 22 as the date to launch "Barbarossa". Actually, it must have been decided some days earlier, because on April 24 the German naval attaché in Moscow telegraphed O.K.M.: "Rumors current here of alleged danger of war between Germany and the Soviet Union. . . . According to the Counselor of the Italian Embassy, the British Ambassador predicts June 22 as the day of the outbreak of war."

While these campaigns were under way, Rommel opened his first offensive in Libya. By the middle of April he had won back nearly all that Graziani had lost. His success was so startling that on May 30 Admiral Raeder and the Naval Staff, in a memorandum they regarded as "one of the most important documents in all the war records," put forward the proposal of "a decisive Egypt–Suez offensive for the autumn of 1941"; a step which they considered would be "more deadly to the British Empire than the capture of London." Strategically they were right, for if Rommel had been reinforced with one or two armoured divisions, the probabilities are that he would have occupied Egypt long before the end of 1941. But Hitler would not listen to this until operation "Barbarossa" had been finished. What he failed to appreciate was that the conquest of Yugoslavia and Greece had added vastly to his negative front, and would increasingly do so as long as the British were left in occupation of Egypt and the Middle East. He had failed to occupy north-west Africa after the fall of France, now he set aside the opportunity to seize Egypt after the fall of Greece. Both were strategic blunders of the first order, and why he committed them would appear to be that he was incapable of appreciating the potentials of sea power, which became more and more formidable as his negative front was extended.

CHAPTER 11

The Battles for Moscow

With the occupation of Crete, Hitler had to his credit a series of conquests which no general in history had gathered in so brief a space of time. He had conquered Poland in 27 days, Denmark in one, Norway in 23, Holland in five, Belgium in 18, France in 39, Yugoslavia in 12, Greece in 21, and Crete in 11. Russia, in spite of her overwhelming might, had taken over 100 days to bring the Finns to heel. With this record behind him and with Russian inefficiency to mislead him, his assumption that he could overthrow Russia before winter set in was not only to his uncritical mind in no way astonishing, but it was accepted by the world in general as a high probability. He expected to destroy Russia's fighting power and to gain the line of the Volga–Archangel within three or four months; after which he could leave some 50 to 60 divisions to hold the conquered area and employ the remainder of his forces against England. This is why, before the campaign started, winter clothing for no more than a fifth of the invading armies was budgeted for.[1]

An essential of so rapid a campaign was the best of ground conditions at its start, and because the spring of 1941 had been exceptionally wet, and well into May the Bug and its tributaries were still at flood level,[2] it is improbable, as has so often been asserted, that the Yugoslav and Greek campaigns delayed the invasion by as much as six weeks, if at all, and in consequence that they were one of the main factors which led to its ultimate failure. The choice of objectives was more to blame. To destroy Russian fighting power demanded the selection of a goal which could not be abandoned by the Russian armies and which would compel them to accept battle within striking range of the Germans. The sole target which filled this bill was Moscow. It was the hub of Russian rail communications, and therefore strategically indispensable, and it was also the Mecca of world communism, the headquarters of a highly centralized government, and a great

[1] See *The German General Staff*, Walter Görlitz (1953), p. 389.
[2] See *Panzer Leader*, General Heinz Guderian (1952), p. 145.

industrial centre which employed over a million workers. This was the objective Field-Marshal Brauchitsch and General Halder wished to strike at, but Hitler would have none of it. " 'Only completely ossified brains, absorbed in the ideas of past centuries,' he said angrily, 'could see any worthwhile objective in taking the capital.' *His* interest lay in Leningrad and Stalingrad, the breeding grounds of Bolshevism. Destroy these two cities . . . and Bolshevism would be dead."[1]

This outlook is not as absurd as it may at first seem, because Hitler saw that his problem was very different from the one which had faced Napoleon. It was not wholly a strategical question – the defeat of the Russian armies; it was profoundly political – the defeat of the Bolshevik régime – not by the occupation of cities, but by the fomentation of revolution within Russia.[2] If he had from the start of the campaign assumed the role of liberator, he would have been right to consider his generals addle-pated. But to imagine that because of their names the occupation of Leningrad and Stalingrad would shatter the Soviet system was a piece of mystical bunkum, which he further confused when he coupled it with two primary economic objectives – the conquest of the Ukraine and of the Caucasus. The objective of the one was to deprive Russia of her main resources of food stuffs and 60 per cent. of her industries, and of the other to deprive her of the bulk of her oil. The result was a confused multiplicity of objectives which over-extended the German armies and meant the inevitable adoption of half-measures.

In spite of the "ossified brains" of the German generals, Directive 21 was a compromise between Hitler's views and theirs. Moscow was not to be abandoned, but given second place to Leningrad and the Ukraine, with the risk that unless the autumn were exceptionally dry it would not be occupied when winter set in.

The General Intention was:

"The mass of the army stationed in Western Russia is to be destroyed in bold operations involving deep penetrations by armoured spearheads, and the withdrawal of elements capable of combat into the extensive Russian land spaces is to be prevented.

"By means of a rapid pursuit a line is then to be reached, from beyond which the Russian air force will no longer be capable of

[1] *Hitler as War Lord*, Franz Halder (1950), p. 41.
[2] See Kleist's views in *The Other Side of the Hill*, B. H. Liddell Hart (1951), p. 259.

attacking the German home territories" – namely the line Volga–
Archangel, as already mentioned.

Next, after a paragraph on the tasks of the Finns and Rumanians, followed *The Conduct of Operations*, in which the more
important items were:

"The area of operations is divided into southern and northern
halves by the Pripet Marshes. The point of main effort will be
made in the *northern* half. Here two army groups are to be committed.

"The southern of these two army groups – in the centre of the
whole front – will have the task of breaking out of the area around
and to the north of Warsaw with exceptionally strong armoured
and motorized formations and of destroying the enemy forces in
White Russia. This will create a situation which will enable strong
formations of mobile troops to swing north; such formations will
then co-operate with the northern army group – advancing from
East Prussia in the general direction of Leningrad – in destroying
the enemy forces in the area of the Baltic states. Only after the
accomplishment of these offensive operations, which must be
followed by the capture of Leningrad and Kronstadt, are further
offensive operations to be initiated with the objective of occupying
the important centre of communications and armaments manufacture, Moscow.

．　　．　　．　　．　　．　　．

"The army group *south of the Pripet Marshes* will make its point
of main effort from the Lublin area in the general direction of
Kiev, with the object of driving into the deep flank and rear of
the Russian forces with strong armoured formations and of then
rolling up the enemy along the Dnieper.

．　　．　　．　　．　　．　　．

"Once the battle south or north of the Pripet Marshes has been
fought, the pursuit is to be undertaken with the following objectives:

"*In the south* the rapid occupation of the economically important Donetz Basin,

"*In the north* the speedy capture of Moscow.

"The capture of this city would be a decisive victory both from
the political and from the economic point of view; it would

27. THE MOSCOW CAMPAIGN, 1941–1942

involve, moreover, the neutralisation of the most vital Russian rail centre."[1]

The composition of the three army groups laid down in the directive was:

Army Group North, Field-Marshal von Leeb: Eighteenth Army, General von Küchler; Sixteenth Army, General Busch; and Fourth Armoured Group, General Hoeppner – a total of 20 infantry divisions, three armoured and three motorized, supported by the First Air Fleet, General Keller.

On its northern flank was the Finnish Army (Marshal Mannerheim), which comprised 16 Finnish divisions (150,000 men) and four German divisions – two infantry and two motorized.

Army Group Centre, Field-Marshal von Bock: Ninth Army, General Strauss, with the Third Armoured Group, General Hoth, and the Fourth Army, Field-Marshal von Kluge, with the Second Armoured Group, General Guderian – a total of 31 infantry divisions, nine armoured, seven motorized, and one cavalry, supported by the Second Air Fleet, Field-Marshal Kesselring.[2]

Army Group South, Field-Marshal von Rundstedt: Sixth Army, Field-Marshal von Reichenau; Seventeenth Army, General von Stuelpnagel, and the First Armoured Group, General von Kleist – a total of 30 infantry divisions, five armoured and four motorized. It also included the IIIrd Italian Corps (four divisions), General Messe; a Hungarian Corps, a Slovak division, and a Croatian regiment. The whole was supported by the Fourth Air Fleet, General Loehr.

To the south of this Army Group and attached to it were the Eleventh German-Rumanian and the Third and Fourth Rumanian Armies, nominally commanded by Field-Marshal Antonescu. Their task was to protect the right flank of Army Group South.

General Reserve: 24 infantry divisions, two armoured and two motorized.[3]

Two points should be noted about these forces; one refers to tanks, the other to transport.

When the campaign in the west was over, in order to multiply the Panzer divisions the number of their tanks was reduced by a

[1] Quoted from Guderian's *Panzer Leader*, Appendix XXII, in which Directive 21 appears in full.

[2] On July 3, 1941, both armoured groups were temporarily subordinated to the Fourth Army, and the infantry corps of the Fourth Army were formed into the Second Army under General von Weichs.

[3] The bulk of these figures are those given by General Wladyslaw Anders in his *Hitler's Defeat in Russia* (1953), pp. 32–34. Other authorities vary slightly.

half. The yearly output of tanks was then no more than 1,000, and when the invasion opened the total German tank strength was barely 3,200 machines. Later, the monthly output would appear to have risen from 80 to 210 machines, still a fantastically low figure to make good wastage, let alone to increase the number of Panzer divisions.

Even more important was the second point, which was governed by Germany's limited supply of motor fuel. There was only sufficient for a fraction of the transport to be motorized, and the lack limited the number of motorized divisions. Much of the divisional transport was horsed, and as enough lorries could not be produced in Germany, the new divisions were allotted lorries of French design, which were found not strong enough for the Russian roads. Without question it may be said that the lack of tracked supply vehicles was as vital a factor in the ultimate failure of the campaign as was Napoleon's lack of horse and ox shoes in 1812.

When we turn to the Russian plan, in fact to any Russian operation, the first and enduring difficulty is lack of documentation. It does not exist, because Soviet history is subordinated to Soviet politics, and as the latter is always changing, no general dare write his memoirs, nor can the Soviet Government produce an official history for fear that after publication it may contravene some future political change.[1] We are left with foreign sources, more particularly German, which are apt to be prejudiced.

What we do know is that instead of making use of the vast depths of Russia in order to wear down the German initial advance, and when its momentum was exhausted to counter-attack in strength, the Russian High Command deployed its forces close to the German frontier of 1941. According to General Alexei Mark ff, a former major-general in the Soviet army and air force, when the invasion began "There were no reserve echelons backing up the front-line troops, because defense in depth was waved aside as sheer nonsense. No defensive war plans were made or even contemplated. Giant supply depots were filled to bursting with arms, ammunition and fuel not in the safe rear, but so close to the frontier as to be within range of Nazi heavy artillery."[2]

[1] Colonel G. A. Tokaev, a Caucasian officer in the Russian army, who in 1948 sought refuge in the west, writes: ". . . it must be remembered that in the Soviet Union any attempt to reconstitute the true history of even the recent past is considered a capital offence" (*Betrayal of an Ideal*, 1954, p. 6).
[2] See his article in *The Saturday Evening Post* of 1950, vol. 222, No. 46; quoted by Raymond L. Gartoff in his *How Russia Makes War* (English edit., 1954), p. 437.

Further, we know that in June, 1941, the Red Army had not recovered from the purges of 1937–1938, in which three marshals, 13 army commanders, 57 corps commanders, 110 divisional and 220 brigade commanders were liquidated – that is, half its senior officers – and that it was still in a state of reorganization. Judged by western standards it was a primitive fighting force, and although it possessed, according to German estimates, about 15,000 tanks and 10,000 aircraft, most of these were of obsolete types. Its transport and supply systems were archaic,[1] and its attack tactics were heavy and clumsy; but, as in past campaigns, its soldiers were tough fighting peasants who, although they lacked initiative, were endowed with astonishing powers of endurance.

When the campaign opened, according to not very reliable German sources, the distribution of the Russian forces was:[2]

Finnish Group, Generals Meretzkov and Govorov; 20 infantry divisions, two cavalry divisions and five armoured brigades, east and west of Lake Ladoga, to operate against the Finns.

Baltic Group, Marshal Voroshilov: 19 infantry divisions, seven cavalry divisions and five armoured brigades, in Lithuania and Latvia, to cover Leningrad.

Bielorussian Group, Marshal Timoshenko: 50 infantry divisions and two armoured brigades, in east Poland and Bielorussia west of Minsk, to cover Moscow.

Ukrainian Group, Marshal Budienny: 69 infantry divisions, 11 cavalry divisions and 28 armoured brigades, in south-east Poland and Bessarabia, to cover the Ukraine.

According to General Halder, on June 21, 1941, the estimated strength of the Russian army in western Russia was: 154 infantry divisions, $25\frac{1}{2}$ cavalry divisions, and 37 armoured brigades, and that it was faced by 102 German infantry divisions, 19 armoured divisions, 14 motorized, five special, and one cavalry.[3]

The strength of Russia did not lie so much in her armed might, but as in the days of Charles XII and Napoleon, it lay in her immense spaces, her primitive roads, her vast forests, broad rivers and swamps, coupled with her short summer, long winter and spring thaws. Added to these were the scarcity and broad gauge of her railways, and she was a difficult country for tanks and

---

[1] See *An Outspoken Soldier*, Lieut.-General Sir Giffard Martel (1949), p. 226.
[2] Mainly quoted from *La défaite Allemande à l'est*, Colonel Léderrey (1951), p. 31.
[3] *The Halder Diaries* (copyright 1950, *Infantry Journal, Inc.*), June 21, 1941, vol. VI, p. 160.

motor vehicles. When it rained the roads became rivers of mud, and when it did not, either they were snow-bound, or the dust raised by traffic clogged the tank engines, and in winter the frost was frequently so intense that they could not be started until fires had been lit under them. It was imperative for the Germans to subdue Russia up to the Volga in the shortest possible time, and before her vast manpower could be called to arms, if not the campaign would tactically become an interminable struggle.

Hitler put his trust in the superiority of the German tactics to gain a rapid victory. His idea was to pinch out one Russian army after the other by a series of vast tank encircling manœuvres. The procedure was that two armoured groups were rapidly to advance against the flanks of the forces selected for destruction, to penetrate them, and then to wheel inwards well to their rear and cut them off from their communications and paralyse their command. Simultaneously the German infantry were to engage the Russian front, pushing in on the flanks of their enemy and so effect an inner encirclement, and then mop him up.

These tactics were set in motion on Sunday, June 22, 1941, when at 3.15 a.m. on the front of Army Group Centre – the one which most concerns us in this chapter – the artillery barrage opened, and 25 minutes later the first dive-bomber attack went in. At 4.15 a.m. from about Suvalki and Brest-Litovsk, the Third (Hoth's) and Second (Guderian's) Armoured Groups set out to encircle Timoshenko's group of armies west of Minsk. In this initial advance some of Guderian's tanks were waterproofed and equipped with the Schnorkel device – later adopted by the German submarines – which enabled them to cross the bed of the river Bug.[1]

In spite of the many warnings the Kremlin had received,[2] the attack surprised it. Halder says: "Tactical surprise of the enemy has apparently been achieved along the entire line. All bridges across the Bug river, as on the entire river frontier, were undefended. . . . That the enemy was taken by surprise is evident from the fact troops were caught in their quarters, that planes on the airfields were covered up, and that enemy groups faced with the unexpected development at the front inquired at their Hqs. in the rear what they should do. . . . A Gp. Center reports

[1] See *The Other Side of the Hill*, B. H. Liddell Hart, p. 268, and Guderian, p. 153. In 1918 a type of Schnorkel was suggested by the British Tank Corps in order to cross the Rhine in 1919.

[2] See *How Russia Makes War*, pp. 434–435.

wild flight on the Brest-Litovsk–Minsk road. Russian command organization in complete confusion."[1]

By June 24 over 2,000 Russian aircraft had been destroyed, either in the air or on the ground. "From the second day onwards," writes Kesselring, "I watched the battle with the Russian heavy bombers coming from the depth of Russia. It seemed to me almost a crime to allow these floundering aircraft to be attacked in tactically impossible formation. One flight after another came in innocently at regular intervals, an easy prey for our fighters. It was sheer 'infanticide'."[2]

On June 26 Hoth's Panzer divisions reached their objective, Minsk, and on the following day were joined by those of Guderian. While the German infantry were still far behind, the pincers closed on Timoshenko. On July 3, the first great battle of the campaign, that of Bialystok–Minsk, ended in pouring rain that turned the roads into bogs.[3] According to Admiral Assmann, it cost the Russians 290,000 men in prisoners alone, 2,585 tanks, and 1,449 guns.[4] In the meantime Army Group North captured Dvinsk and forced a crossing of the Dvina, while Army Group South crossed the Bug near Chelm, and advanced on Lutsk and Rovno.

Halder was so elated by the initial successes that, on July 3, he entered in his diary: "It is thus probably no overstatement to say that the Russian Campaign has been won in the space of two weeks."[5] By this he did not mean that the invasion was as good as over, but that its first phase had been won, and he was right. What of the second phase?

It opened with a tactical argument, which shows what little unanimity the German high command possessed. The original instructions were for the two armoured groups of Army Group Centre to drive straight to Smolensk–Roslavl, and O.K.H. still adhered to this idea. But because the infantry were now some 14 days in rear, Hitler, who wanted to gather prisoners, did not push on and disintegrate his enemy's command, but desired most of the armoured groups to fall back and help the infantry in their task of mopping up. In this he was supported by Kluge, though

[1] *Halder Diaries*, June 22, 1941, vol. vi, pp. 161–162.
[2] *The Memoirs of Field-Marshal Kesselring* (English edit., 1953), p. 90.
[3] *Halder Diaries*, July 3, 1941, vol. vi, p. 194.
[4] "The Battle for Moscow, Turning Point of the War," Vice-Admiral Kurt Assmann, *Foreign Affairs*, vol. 28, No. 2, p. 314. Throughout this campaign the enormous captures of tanks must have been because they ran out of petrol.
[5] *Halder Diaries*, July 3, 1941, vol. vi, p. 196.

Hoth and Guderian wanted to press on and Bock wanted both groups to be placed under Kluge so that he himself might be relieved of responsibility in their use. Hitler agreed to this on July 3.

A series of contradictory orders then followed, and Guderian – one of the few German generals who refused to be petrified by Hitler – cut the Gordian knot. He prepared to continue the advance, and by the time Kluge was able to intervene the preparations had gone so far that he was unable to stop them. The result was that, on July 7, the two groups pushed on, that of Hoth by way of Vitebsk and that of Guderian by Mogilev and Orsha. The semi-mythical Stalin Line, which ran from Narva to Polotsk, Vitebsk, Orsha, Mogilev, and thence by way of Vinnitza to the Black Sea, was broken through, and in spite of Kluge's intervention Guderian's leading tanks crossed the Dnieper on July 10, and undeterred by heavy Russian counter-attacks reached Smolensk on July 16. Four days later, Elnya – 50 miles south-east of Smolensk on the Dnieper – was captured, but here Guderian's forces were heavily counter-attacked. Hoth's group came in on the north of Smolensk.

Thus, by July 16, as the crow flies, two-thirds of the way to Moscow had been traversed – 440 miles had been covered at an average of 20 miles a day. The battle of Smolensk lasted until August 8 and ended in another encirclement, during which, between July 3 and July 25, Army Group Centre claimed as its booty 185,487 prisoners captured as well as 2,030 tanks and 1,918 guns.[1]

This bold and skilfully executed advance was one of the most remarkable tank operations of the war. According to General Blumentritt, the country was appallingly difficult for tank movements – "great virgin forests, widespread swamps, terrible roads, and bridges not strong enough to bear the weight of tanks." The great unfinished motor road leading from the frontier to Moscow, he tells us, was the only road a westerner would call a "road", all others were only sandy tracks. "Such country," he says, "was bad enough for the tanks, but worse still for the transport accompanying them. . . . Nearly all this transport consisted of wheeled vehicles, which could not move off the roads, nor move on them if the sand turned into mud. An hour or two of rain reduced the Panzer forces to stagnation. It was an extraordinary sight, with

[1] *Halder Diaries*, July 25, 1941, vol. VI, p. 270.

groups of them strung out over a hundred miles stretch, all stuck –until the sun came out and the ground dried."[1] An additional obstruction was that every time a difficulty arose in rear, Kluge stopped the advance until it had been overcome. Here it may be observed that, like a jockey, a bold tank general should have his eyes fixed on the winning post, and not, like a cautious transport leader, on the tail of his convoy.

When this remarkable operation was under way, on July 5 Army Group North burst through the Stalin Line in the region of Lake Peipus; captured Ostrov, Pskov, and Porkhov, and then advanced on Novgorod to cut off Leningrad from the east; and at the same time Army Group South broke through the Stalin Line between Zhitomir and Berdichev and thrust toward Kiev.

Hitler was a man who usually could no more break away from a preconceived idea than Joan of Arc could abandon her angelic voices. Once he had made up his mind, he stuck to his plan as if it were holy writ. This is why he would not abandon or modify Directive 21, and the deeper his armies penetrated into Russia the more pertinaciously he held to it.

When, on July 19, the battle of Smolensk was at its height, he did not wait for its outcome, but issued Directive 33. It comprised two operations to be carried out by the two armoured groups of Army Group Centre. The Second (Guderian) in cooperation with Army Group South, was to help to encircle the Russian forces about Kiev by moving on them in a southerly direction, while the Third (Hoth) was to advance northward, cut the Leningrad–Moscow line of communications, and help Army Group North in its assault on Leningrad. "Thus," writes Assmann, "began a turning point in the war, incomprehensible to the Russians – 'Marne miracle' as a Russian general called it – which was to save Moscow just as Paris was relieved in 1914."[2] Actually, there was no turning point, because the "Marne miracle" was implicit in Directive 21.

Timoshenko had succeeded in extricating nearly half a million men during the battle of Smolensk and he now withdrew them to a defensive line closer to Moscow. They had put up some very tough fighting, and to Halder's consternation he discovered that the Russians possessed more than the maximum of 200 divisions originally estimated by O.K.H.; 360 divisions had already been identified. In spite of this, O.K.H. wanted to press on to Moscow,

---

[1] *The Other Side of the Hill*, p. 271.   [2] *The Battle for Moscow*, p. 315.

but Hitler would not listen to Brauchitsch and Halder and, on July 26, in order to start off the southern operation, he instructed Guderian's armoured group, in collaboration with the German Second Army, to round up a strong enemy force at Gomel. Halder's comment on this is illuminating. "Such a plan," he writes, "implies a shift of our strategy from the operational to the tactical level. If striking at small local enemy concentrations becomes our sole objective, the campaign will resolve itself into a series of minor successes which will advance our front only by inches. Pursuing such a policy eliminates all tactical risks and enables us gradually to close the gaps between the fronts of the Army Groups, but the result will be that we feed all our strength into a front expanding in width at the sacrifice of depth and end up in position warfare!"[1]–this is almost exactly what happened.

While the Gomel operation was still under discussion, on August 4 a conference was held at headquarters Army Group Centre. Field-Marshal Bock, supported by Hoth and Guderian, pressed for a continuation of the offensive against Moscow. But Hitler brushed this suggestion aside and said that the industrial area about Leningrad was his primary objective, and after that the Ukraine, because its produce was vital to Germany for the further prosecution of the war. Further, to safeguard the Rumanian oilfields from Russian air attack, he considered it essential to occupy the Crimea. Six days later Army Group North's offensive on Leningrad was repulsed.

Between August 4 and 21, priceless time was wasted in arguments about objectives; but Hitler remained obdurate, and on the 21st issued Directive 34. Its opening paragraph reads: "The principal objects that must be achieved . . . before the onset of winter, is not the capture of Moscow but rather, in the South, the occupation of the Crimea and the industrial and coal region of the Donetz, together with isolation of the Russian oil region in the Causasus and, in the North, the encirclement of Leningrad and junction with the Finns."[2]

In accordance with Directive 33, the main operation was to ease the advance of Army Group South toward Rostov–Kharkov by means of a double envelopment carried out by the inner wings of Army Groups Centre and South to annihilate the Russian Fifth Army east of Kiev. "Not until we have tightly encircled Leningrad,

[1] *Halder Diaries*, July 26, 1941, vol. VI, p. 271. See also Guderian, pp. 182–183.
[2] *Halder Diaries*, August 22, 1941, vol. VII, p. 59.

linked up with the Finns and destroyed the Russian Fifth Army," we read, "shall we have set the stage and can we free the forces for attacking and beating the enemy Army Group Timoshenko with any prospect of success." Moscow, it was stated, "is of secondary importance."[1]

Brauchitsch sent Guderian to persuade Hitler to abandon this madness, which must lead to a winter campaign, but when Guderian met Hitler on August 23, all the latter told him was that the German generals knew nothing about the economic aspects of the war.[2] Guderian was ordered on August 25 to set out for east of Kiev.

Kesselring's opinion on this is worth quoting, because it shows the magnitude of Hitler's error. "If on the conclusion of the encirclement battle of Smolensk . . ." he writes, "the offensive had been continued against Moscow after a reasonable breather, it is my opinion that Moscow would have fallen into our hands before the winter and before the arrival of the Siberian divisions. The capture of Moscow would have been decisive in that the whole of Russia in Europe would have been cut off from its Asiatic potential and the seizure of the vital economic centres of Leningrad, the Donetz basin and the Maikop oilfields in 1942 would have been no insoluble task."[3]

On August 17, although Army Group North captured Narva, its second assault on Leningrad failed, and at the beginning of September Timoshenko, no longer confronted by German armour, launched a powerful counter-attack on the German Fourth Army and claimed the destruction of eight German divisions.

The battle of Kiev, which opened on August 25 and ended on September 26, was the greatest battle of encirclement of the war. Its aim was to annihilate the bulk of Marshal Budienny's Army Group in the vast salient which extended from Trubechevsk in the north to Kremenchug in the south, with Kiev as its apex. The German plan was to pinch it out by an inner and an outer encirclement. The former was to be carried out by the Second Army (von Weichs) moving southward from Gomel–Novosybkov, and by the Seventeenth (von Stuelpnagel) advancing northward from Kremenchug–Cherkasy, while the Sixth (von Reichenau) pinned the main Russian forces down on the Kiev front. The outer encirclement was the task of the Second and First Armoured Groups, commanded respectively by Guderian and von Kleist.

[1] *Ibid.*, vol. VII, pp. 60, 61.   [2] Guderian, pp. 199–200.   [3] *Memoirs*, p. 98.

The one was to advance southward from west of Trubechevsk on Lokhvitsa, and the other northward from Kremenchug on Lubny, both destinations were about 125 miles east of Kiev.

On September 9 Guderian captured Romny and on the 16th he established his headquarters there and made contact with

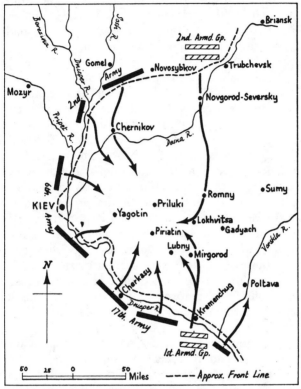

28. BATTLE OF KIEV, AUGUST–SEPTEMBER, 1941

von Kleist's group. The Second Army had crossed the Desna at, and on, the flanks of Chernikov, and the Seventeenth moved northward on a wide front between Kremenchug and Cherkasy, its right flank protected by a detachment directed on Poltava. On the 17th, the inner ring began to close in on Yagotin and Piriatin, 50 to 90 miles east of Kiev, and on the 19th, amid "wild chaos,"[1] Kiev was occupied by the German Sixth Army. On September 26, the day the battle ended, the Eleventh Army,

[1] *Halder Diaries*, September 19, 1941, vol. VII, p. 111.

under von Manstein, broke through the isthmus of Perekop and overran the Crimea.

The booty captured in the battle of Kiev was immense: besides 665,000 prisoners, it included 884 tanks, 3,718 guns and 3,500 motor vehicles. It is understandable that Hitler was elated. He called it "the greatest battle in the history of the world", but Halder termed it "the greatest strategic blunder of the eastern campaign."[1] Strategically the latter was right; yet had Hitler appreciated the political significance of the Ukraine, he could have turned the battle of Kiev into the most decisive operation of the war and could have exterminated Bolshevism.

Since the campaign began his armies had captured nearly 1,500,000 Russians, over 7,000 tanks, and approximately 9,000 guns. The first figure is significant, because the capture of such hordes of prisoners in the first phase of a war which was to last for nearly four years is unique in history. The reason is given by General Anders: "Even the first battles of 1941," he writes, "disclosed the widespread disinclination of the Soviet soldier to fight in the defense of the 'Fatherland of the proletariate', and his hatred of the régime, which was shared by the great majority of the population of the U.S.S.R. Many soldiers, seeing the war as an opportunity for a change of order in Russia, wished for German victory and therefore surrendered in great masses. . . . The surrender was not limited to enlisted men and lower ranks; many high Soviet officers went over to the enemy offering to fight against the Soviets."[2] One of them was Marshal Timoshenko's chief of staff.

What is astonishing is that Hitler, a man of exceptional political perspicacity, who had reckoned on the collapse of the Soviet régime as the first fruits of the invasion, made no effort to win over the subjugated peoples of western Russia, but deliberately set out to antagonize them. This colossal political blunder lost him his 1941 campaign and added insuperable difficulties to those that followed. With him it was *aut Caesar aut nullus*, and it would seem that the profusion of prisoners captured did not reveal to him the horror of the Russian masses for Soviet rule, but led him to assume that the surrenders were solely due to the brute force of his armies.

He would seem to have been oblivious of events: that when the invasion was in its initial stage, the Germans were everywhere

[1] *The Battle for Moscow*, p. 119.
[2] *Hitler's Defeat in Russia*, General Wladyslaw Anders, p. 168.

welcomed by the common people as liberators; that the Ukrainians looked upon him as the saviour of Europe;[1] that the Bielorussians (White Russians) were eager to fight on the German side; that whole regiments of Cossacks deserted to their enemy; and that Georgians, Armenians, Turkomans, Tartars, and Usbeks, as well as Ukrainians, Bielorussians and Cossacks surrendered in droves. Often the German soldiers were greeted with flowers and gifts by the peasantry, and Guderian tells us that "women came out of their villages on to the very battlefield bringing wooden platters of bread and butter and eggs and, in my case at least, refused to let me move on before I had eaten."[2] Even as late as December, 1941, Rundstedt, when he left Uman, was presented with flowers and an embroidered Ukrainian table cloth. At Rostov, writes Erich Kern, "all over the city there were people waiting on the streets ready to cheer and welcome us in," and on one occasion an old Russian woman thanked him for being kind to her and before he left, said, "I shall tell you a great truth; the Russian people will not be saved by the man with the bigger gun but by the man with the greater soul." "Never before," writes Kern, "had I seen such a sudden transformation. Of Bolshevism, there was no more. The enemy had gone. . . . Wherever we went now we met laughing and waving people. . . . The Soviet Empire was creaking at the joints."[3]

If Hitler had possessed the wisdom of the old Russian woman who told Erich Kern "the great truth", in spite of his strategic bunglings he might with ease have exploded the Soviet Imperium and have marched into Moscow garlanded with flowers. Many had foreseen this,[4] notably Alfred Rosenberg, a Balt who understood the conditions that prevailed within the U.S.S.R. Shortly after the invasion started he was made Minister of the Eastern Territories, and, on July 7, 1941, in an address he set forth his suggested policy:

"Russia," he said, "has never been a national State, but a State of nationalities", as Mommsen had appreciated when he wrote: "The Russian Empire is a dust-bin that is held together by the rusty hoop of Tsardom." The German task was not to reconstruct it, but to dissolve it; not to impose a new political

---

[1] *The Goebbels Diaries* (1948), p. 135.   [2] Guderian, p. 193.

[3] *Dance of Death* (English trans., 1948), pp. 102, 69, 94, 86. Kern was a n.c.o. in the *Leibstandarte Adolf Hitler*.

[4] Among them Halder, Count von der Schulenburg, former German ambassador at Moscow, Goebbels, and most of the generals.

system upon its subjugated peoples, but to recognize each nationality and foster each nation's independence. He proposed to do this by cutting out of western Russia three great blocks of peoples and forming them into buffer states between the rest of Russia and Europe. Besides Finland, which was already independent, Bielorussia and the Baltic States should form one block, the Ukraine a second, and Caucasia a third. Any attempt to hold down the Ukrainians, he said, "would mean to put a soldier behind every farmer." Of Russia proper – the area between Leningrad, Moscow, and the Urals – "We should declare," he proposed, "that we are not fighting the Russian people but the Bolshevik system," and that "our fight for re-organization will take place in the name of national self-determination of nations." He ended by stating that the two main German tasks in Russia were: "To safeguard the German food and war economies, and to free Germany for ever from the political pressure of the East: it is the political aim of our fight. . . ."[1]

Hitler would have none of this and on August 16, 1941, at a conference of his myrmidons he set forth his policy:

"Fundamentally," he said, "our policy is to cut the gigantic cake with skill, so that it can be first mastered, secondly administered, thirdly exploited. . . . The Russians have now given an order for guerrilla war behind our lines. This has its own advantage: it provides us with the opportunity to destroy whatever is against us . . . under no circumstances can anyone but Germans carry weapons. This is particularly important, for it is wrong to induce any subjected people into rendering us military assistance, even though it may appear more convenient at first sight . . . the whole Baltic area has to become Reich's territory. The Crimea, too, has to be incorporated in the Reich, with possibly a large area to the north . . . the German Volga colony has to become a territory of the Reich, and similarly the area around Baku. . . . The affiliation of Finland as a federal State has to be prepared," and Leningrad is to be razed to the ground and handed over to the Finns. . . . "Naturally, the vast territories have to be pacified as soon as possible; this can best be achieved by shooting everybody who shows a wry face."[2]

---

[1] Abstracted from *Russian World Ambitions and World Peace*, R. Ilnytzky (1953), pp. 4–12.
[2] *Ibid.*, pp. 12–15, citing Nuremberg Documents in evidence at the trial before the International Military Tribunal, Nuremberg, 1945–1946. See also *Hitler, a Study in Tyranny*, Alan Bullock (1952), pp. 633–644.

This policy was put into force, and although Rosenberg remained Minister of the Eastern Territories, their pacification – as it was called – was handed over to Himmler and his Security Service (*Sichereitsdienst*), a sister organization of the Gestapo and divorced from O.K.H., which was strongly opposed to it. It was this infamous Security Service, and not the army, which carried out the mass killings. Early in 1942 Dr. Berthold, a leading official of the German Administration in Poland, told von Hassell that the brutal treatment of the Russians and Ukrainians "exceed anything yet known."[1] For example, because a transmitter was found to be damaged 400 men were shot in Kiev.

Erich Kern points out that at the time when Bolshevism was politically bankrupt, it was saved by Himmler and his assassins. "By rousing the Russian people to a Napoleonic fervour," he writes, "we enabled the Bolsheviks to achieve a political consolidation beyond their wildest dreams and provided their cause with the halo of a 'patriotic war'."[2] And Görlitz writes: "The fact that the destruction of Bolshevism began soon to mean simply an effort to decimate and enslave the Slav people was the most fatal of all the flaws in the whole campaign."[3]

This madness went far to stimulate the guerrilla war proclaimed by Stalin within a fortnight of the invasion and first mentioned by the Germans on July 25, 1941. But it was not until December that the partisan menace grew formidable. This was firstly because of the atrocities perpetrated by the German Security Service, and secondly because of the scientific devilry of the N.K.V.D. (Russian Security Police) which controlled the partisan movement.

The first task of the N.K.V.D. was to end collaboration with the Germans, and only after this had been achieved did they turn to the allotment of military tasks to the partisans. As the simplest way to accomplish the former end was to terrorize the population, the N.K.V.D. at first left the Germans in peace and waged a war of terror against the population behind the German front. Men and women were trained for this purpose; they either passed through the German lines or were dropped from aircraft behind them, and then they organized bands of wandering soldiers and would-be partisans into terror squads. The Germans

---

[1] *The von Hassell Diaries, 1938–1944* (1948), p. 219. Even Goebbels wrote in his diary on April 25, 1942: "In the long run we cannot solicit additional workers from the East if we treat them like animals within the Reich" (p. 136).
[2] *Dance of Death*, p. 108.　　[3] *The German General Staff*, p. 397.

were little molested in this opening phase of the partisan campaign and they took no steps to protect the population; but as fear of the partisans grew the prestige of the Germans declined. When the population had been so terrorized that they would not collaborate, the partisans were instructed to kidnap German soldiers, torture them to death, and expose their mutilated bodies in places which would incriminate the local inhabitants. German reprisals followed; villages were burnt, hostages shot, cattle removed, and sometimes entire districts in which partisans operated were devastated. The results of reprisals were negligible, because all that the partisans had to do was to move into another district and repeat their devilry. But for the Germans they were disastrous. The peasants, deprived of means of living and filled with intense hatred for those whom they had welcomed as liberators, joined the partisans in tens of thousands. On March 6, 1942, Goebbels' entered in his diary: "The partisans are in command of large areas in occupied Russia, and are conducting a régime of terror there." Later in the war their numbers ran into hundreds of thousands, and they became so formidable a menace that Hitler was compelled to rescind his "wry face" policy; but it was too late.[1]

As soon as the battle of Kiev opened Hitler suddenly changed his strategy. Rebuffed before Leningrad, he decided to invest it, not to carry it by assault, and as soon as the battle of Kiev had been won – which he took for granted it would be in some 10 days – to annihilate Timoshenko's forces west of Orel-Rzhev, and then triumphantly to march into Moscow. This decision was embodied in Directive 35, issued on September 6. Army Groups North and South were to reinforce Army Group Centre with armoured troops, after which Army Group Centre was to carry out the offensive as follows:

The Fourth Army (Field-Marshal von Kluge) and Hoeppner's Fourth Armoured Group in the centre, between Smolensk and Roslavl, were to envelop Viazma from the south; the Ninth Army (General Strauss) and Hoth's Third Armoured Group on its left, between Smolensk and Olenino, were to envelop Viazma from

---

[1] Largely extracted from General Anders's *Hitler's Defeat in Russia*, chap. VII. What made the partisan war so formidable was that it could be controlled by radio and supplied by aircraft. The ruthlessness of the N.K.V.D., even toward their own partisans, is illustrated by the following order of May 11, 1943: "The repeated intercourse with women (partisans) resulted in several cases of pregnancy. These women are a nuisance to the regiment. Shoot them!" (Anders, p. 211).

the north; and the Second Army (General von Weichs) between Roslavl and Novogorod-Seversky, were to envelop Briansk. Unlike the previous battles, in which after two flanks had been created,

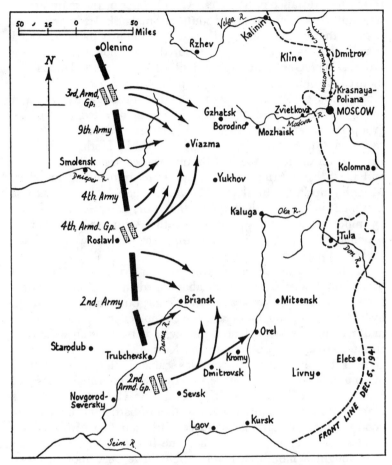

29. BATTLE OF VIASMA-BRIANSK, OCTOBER 1941

the enemy's centre was rolled up, two great mouthfuls were to be bitten out of his front on a frontage of over 300 miles – about the distance of London from Berwick-on-Tweed. Further, besides investing Leningrad, Army Group North was to cover the left flank of Army Group Centre, and Army Group South was to aid its attack by a simultaneous advance on Poltava–Kharkov–Izyum.

On September 30 the great battle of Viazma-Briansk was opened by Guderian, who set out from Novgorod-Seversky and completely surprised the Russians; by October 1 he had penetrated to a distance of 85 miles.[1] On October 2, the main attack was launched from north and south of Smolensk. Its impetus was so great that by the evening of the 3rd the infantry had penetrated to a depth of 25 miles and the armoured forces more than 30 miles. On this day Guderian captured Orel. On the 4th Hoth's Armoured Group began to wheel in on the north of Viazma; Hoeppner's group advanced to the north-east of Roslavl and swung in from the south, while Guderian directed part of his group northward on Briansk, and part on Mitsensk, which was captured. On the 7th Viazma was encircled by Hoth and Hoeppner, and on the following day Briansk was encircled by Guderian and the Second Army, which made some tremendous marches. Mopping up lasted until October 20, during which Gzhatsk was occupied on the 9th; Kaluga on the 16th; and Mozhaisk – only 65 miles from Moscow – on the 18th. Again the number of prisoners was astronomical: this time 663,000, as well as 1,242 tanks and 5,412 guns.

So great was the threat to Moscow that, with the exception of Stalin, the Soviet Government abandoned the capital and withdrew to Kuibishev (Samara) on the Volga; Budienny was replaced by Timoshenko, and Marshal Zhukov took over the latter's command to prepare to defend Moscow, not by resistance, but by counter-attack. It appeared to the Russians and to the world in general that the fate of Moscow was sealed. Hitler, in an outburst of excusable elation, announced that the Soviet armed forces had been annihilated, and even the pessimistic Halder jotted in his diary: "With reasonably good direction of battle and moderately good weather, we cannot but succeed in encircling Moscow."[2]

This was true enough, and had the battle of Viazma-Briansk been fought a month earlier it would have been more certain. But in October any large offensive could not be other than a gamble with weather, and when Mozhaisk was reached it rained. The roads became rivers of mud, and that of Orel-Tula so impassable that Guderian's Second Armoured Army – for so it became known on October 6 – was bogged down for days on end, and had to be supplied by air. On October 29 it splashed forward

---

[1] Guderian, p. 230.
[2] *Halder Diaries*, October 8, 1941, vol. VII, p. 147.

within two miles of Tula, but failed to take it; there it was compelled to halt until frost solidified the roads.

In the meantime Army Group North closed in on Tikhvin and Lake Ladoga, and gained contact with Army Group Centre at Ostashkov, south of the Valdai Hills. Army Group South approached Bielgorod and Kharkov, and in the battle of the Azov Sea 100,000 prisoners, 672 guns and 212 tanks were captured, and the First Armoured Army (von Kleist) in the south occupied Stalino, while in the Crimea the Eleventh Army advanced on Sebastopol and Kerch.

During the night of November 3–4 the first frost set in, and although it eased road movements, the German troops suffered severely because they had no winter clothing. On the 7th there were many cases of frostbite and on the 12th the temperature dropped to 5 degrees Fahrenheit. The question whether the offensive should be suspended or continued was brought to the fore. Rundstedt wanted to suspend it, but as Moscow was only 40 miles distant Hitler would not consider it, and for once he was supported by Brauchitsch, Halder, and Bock. On November 13 a conference of chiefs of staff was held, after which orders for what was called "the autumn offensive" were issued: Moscow was to be taken, and the Kremlin blown up, "to signalize the overthrow of Bolshevism."[1]

The plan of attack was that von Kluge's Fourth Army – 36 divisions in all – was to make a frontal advance on Moscow, while on its left Hoth's and Hoeppner's armoured groups were to encircle the capital from the north and west, and on its right Guderian's armoured army was to do the same from the south. The northern flank of this triple attack was to be protected by the Ninth Army and its southern by the Second.

The battle of Moscow was opened on November 16. Slowly Hoth advanced in a south-easterly direction; on the 23rd he captured Klin, and on the 28th reached the Moscow–Volga canal at Krasnaya-Poliana – 14 miles from the capital – and in the distance glimpsed the towers of the Kremlin. South of him Hoeppner advanced on Zvietkova, west of Moscow, and in the meantime Guderian by-passed Tula and advanced on Kolomna. For the first time during the campaign Siberian troops were captured.

The two armoured wings depended for their success on the

[1] *The Other Side of the Hill*, p. 285.

advance of the Fourth Army in the centre, for it if were held up they would be isolated north and south of Moscow. This is what happened, for no sooner had the battle opened than the right flank of the Fourth Army was so heavily attacked that Kluge had to commit his reserves in its support, and because of this he held back his left and centre until November 19, when his right again advanced. Although it made some progress, Field-Marshal von Bock was "so profoundly affected by the severity of the fighting" that, on the 22nd, he took over personal command of the battle and, as Halder writes, with "enormous energy" drove forward everything that could be brought to bear, because, as he said, the situation was similar to that on the Marne in 1914, "when the last battalion that could be thrown in turned the balance." But in spite of his energy the right wing of the Fourth Army was so exhausted that it could not move.

The Russians threw in more and more troops, but although von Bock feared that "the operation would become a second Verdun, *i.e.*, a brutish chest-to-chest struggle of attrition,"[1] the left wing of the Fourth Army pressed on, and on November 30 the centre was ordered to renew the offensive on December 1. At first it made good headway, but on the 2nd its advance was held up by strong defences in the forests round Moscow. Then, says General Blumentritt, von Kluge's chief of staff:

"A few parties of our troops, from the 258th Infantry Division, actually got into the suburbs of Moscow. But the Russian workers poured out of the factories and fought them with their hammers and other tools in defence of their city.

"During the night the Russians strongly counter-attacked the isolated elements that had penetrated their defences. Next day our corps commanders reported that they thought it was no longer possible to break through. Von Kluge and I had a long discussion that evening, and at the end he decided to withdraw these advanced troops. Fortunately the Russians did not discover that they were moving back, so that we succeeded in extricating them and bringing them back to their original position in fairly good order. But there had been very heavy casualties in those two days' fighting."[2]

Two days later, when the temperature fell to minus 32 degrees,

---

[1] The above is based on the *Halder Diaries* of November 16–29, 1941, vol. VII, pp. 164–192.

[2] *On the Other Side of the Hill*, p. 207.

because "the troops were no longer strong enough to capture Moscow", with a heavy heart Guderian decided to fall back.[1]

The final offensive on Moscow had petered out, not so much because of Russian resistance, but because of the frost. Snow had fallen for days on end, blizzards had covered the villages, and drifts had blocked the railways and roads. Lorries ceased to run, locomotives could no longer be fired, the troops could not be supplied, tanks would only start after hours of warming-up, aircraft dropped out of action because their lubricants froze, telescopic sights frosted over and became useless, machine-guns ceased to fire, and worst of all, thousands of men who lacked winter clothing were crippled by frostbite, and hundreds were frozen to death. That the German soldier, utterly unprepared for winter warfare, accomplished what he did is one of the greatest feats of endurance which the history of war records.

While this battle was fought, on November 21 von Kleist's First Armoured Army took Rostov, but on the 28th it was violently attacked by Timoshenko, driven out of the town and forced to fall back westward. This was the first successful big Russian counter-attack of the campaign, and when Field-Marshal von Rundstedt asked for authority for Kleist to withdraw to a defensive position on the Mius River, he was ordered by Hitler on no account to do so. Rundstedt felt unable to obey this order and asked to be relieved of his command. His resignation was accepted, and Field-Marshal von Reichenau, commander of the Sixth Army, was given command of Army Group South. Meanwhile von Kleist was forced back, and soon after this Hitler sanctioned his occupation of the Mius line.

The withdrawal of the Fourth Army on the night of December 3 was only just in time to avert a major disaster, because soon after it had fallen back Marshal Zhukov launched his long prepared counter-offensive, in which many fresh Siberian divisions took part. On December 6 he broke through the German positions east of Kalinin, and on the following day forced his enemy out of Klin. The blow was so formidable and the Germans so ill-prepared to meet it that Halder urged the withdrawal of the Fourth Army to the line Mozhaisk–Rzhev–Ostashkov. Hitler refused to countenance a retreat. On the 9th the Second Army front was breached at Livny, and on the following day Guderian's army was broken through west of Tula. Soon the counter-offensive

[1] Guderian, p. 260.

was taken up along the entire German front from the Gulf of Finland to the Black Sea. On December 18 Field-Marshal von Bock fell ill and was replaced by von Kluge, and on the following day Field-Marshal von Brauchitsch was relieved of his appointment and Hitler took over supreme command of the German army. On the next day his first order was issued: "Every man must fight back where he stands. No falling back where there are no prepared positions in rear."[1]

When reports of the Russian counter-offensive were received in Berlin, and with them the momentous news that the United States had become a belligerent, the capital was rocked to its foundations. "Unrest grew among the people," writes Arvid Fredborg. "The pessimists remembered Napoleon's war with Russia, and all the literature about La Grande Armée suddenly had a marked revival. The fortune-tellers busied themselves with Napoleon's fate and there was a boom in astrology. . . . Even the most devoted Nazi did not want a war with America. All Germans had a high respect for her strength. Nobody could help remembering how America's intervention had decided the first world war. The 1917 perspective was uncomfortable."[2]

Although the German generals repeatedly counselled retreat, both Guderian and Hoeppner were relieved of their commands because they fell back without authority; Hitler, the visionary, saw that a retreat could only end as did that of Napoleon. Although it was his obstinacy which had brought the campaign to the brink of disaster, it was his obstinacy which was to save it from plunging into the abyss. His refusal to draw out of Russia or to west of Smolensk undoubtedly saved his army from an even greater catastrophe than that of 1812.

Hitler's problem was to get his troops under shelter before they were frozen to death, and to hold on to communications so that the armies could be re-equipped and supplied.

The vital communications in the Moscow sector were the railways, Moscow–Rzhev–Velikye Luki, Moscow–Viazma–Smolensk, Moscow–Kaluga–Briansk, and Moscow–Tula–Orel, all of which were linked by the lateral line Velikye Luki–Vitebsk–Smolensk–Briansk–Orel. Also, from Orel a railway ran south to

---

[1] *Halder Diaries*, December 20, 1941, vol. VII, p. 235.
[2] *Behind the Steel Wall* (1944), pp. 60-61. Fredborg was a Swedish journalist in Berlin. It is interesting to be told that Caulaincourt's *Memoirs* were in great demand; they were diligently studied by von Kluge (*The Other Side of the Hill*, p. 284) and ultimately their circulation was prohibited (*How Russia Makes War*, p. 433).

Taganrog on the Sea of Azov. On all these railways there were one or more advanced depôts from which the front was fed. The more important were: Staraya Russa, Rzhev, Viazma, Kaluga, Briansk, Orel, Kursk and Kharkov. Between them there were minor depôts, and all were fully stocked and afforded shelter. It was essential to hold them and to get the troops back to them.

Hitler decided to turn these advanced depôts into entrenched camps, and to fall back on them. This would gain shelter for his troops, who could live on their dumps while the lines of supply were put into working order.[1] His plan was not a retreat, as had been that of Napoleon, but a manœuvre to the rear.

Each of the main fortified regions covered many square miles, and in some cases could shelter an entire army. The Germans called them *Igels* ("hedgehogs") after the squares of medieval Swiss pikemen formed to resist cavalry, because their defences bristled in all directions. Sometimes they were supplied by aircraft.

Generally speaking, the Russian advance was not so much a counter-offensive as a steady forward percolation which lapped round the points of German resistance and flowed between them. Because movements had to be made across country rather than by road, the Russians relied extensively on Cossack divisions reinforced with sledge-mounted artillery, sledge-borne infantry, and ski-troops; the landing-wheels of fighter aircraft were replaced by skis. Fighting became brutal in the extreme because of the guerrilla bands in rear of the German front.

The German withdrawal embraced the entire front and was deepest in the Moscow sector between Kalinin and Tula. Once these towns had been captured, extensive pincer operations were developed against Rzhev, Gzhatsk, and Viazma. At the close of December Kaluga was captured by the Russians. It was the most important single Russian success of the whole winter campaign, because Kaluga was a major "hedgehog."

From Kaluga the Russians advanced north-west on Yukhnov, a "hedgehog" south-east of Viazma, and pushed a deep salient into the German front. At the same time in the north they lapped round the west of Rzhev toward Vitebsk and to the north of the latter reached Velikye Luki. These two advances round Viazma brought the Russians within 50 miles of Smolensk. In the meantime, on January 20–22, Mozhaisk was occupied.

[1] Thousands of German lorries and hundreds of locomotives were frozen up. The damage took weeks to repair.

On the Leningrad front, Tikhvin was abandoned by the Germans on December 9, and when the Russians pressed on and crossed the Volkhov river the Germans linked up Schüsselburg with Novgorod, and position warfare set in. In the extreme south the Russians opened a counter-offensive in the Crimea, and north of the Sea of Azov the "hedgehogs" of Taganrog, Stalino and Artemovsk were by-passed in order to concentrate all available forces against the "super-hedgehog" of Kharkov. It stood firm, though Losovaya to the south of it was captured and the advance pushed to within 30 miles of Poltava.

With mid-winter and the increased depth of the snow, the Germans expected a respite. But the Russians continued their percolation although no decisive gains were won except on the Leningrad front, where they built a motor road over the ice of Lake Ladoga, regained contact with Leningrad, and on February 22 cut off a considerable portion of the German Sixteenth Army in the Staraya-Russa area.

On the central front, in February and March, the Russian gains were consolidated and the small "hedgehogs" of Sukhinichi and Yukhnov were captured. In April the thaw brought operations to a standstill except in the Crimea, where the Germans made some progress against Kerch, which earlier in the winter had been recaptured by the Russians, as also had Theodosia.

The German casualties in this campaign are given by Halder. Between June 22 and December 31, 1941, they were 830,403, including 173,722 dead,[1] and between June 22, 1941, and February 28, 1942, 1,005,636, of which the dead numbered 210,572.[2] Whether these figures include casualties from frost is not mentioned, but, according to Goebbels, up to February 20, 1942, they numbered 112,627, of which 14,357 required major amputations.[3] The Russian casualties cannot be ascertained and are probably unknown; but, according to Raymond Cartier, by January 1, 1942, the Red Army was reduced to 2,300,000 men which, he states, was the lowest strength up to the present day (1946).[4] Since in June, 1941, the total strength of the Red Army was over 5,000,000 men, the German claim to have captured well over 2,000,000 does not appear to be exaggerated.

[1] *Halder Diaries*, January 5, 1942, vol. VII, p. 248.
[2] *Ibid.*, March 5, 1942, vol. VII, p. 279.
[3] *The Goebbels Diaries*, p. 72.
[4] Quoted by Genl. Anders (p. 80) from *Les secrets de la guerre devoilés par Nuremberg* (1946), p. 297.

Although these enormous losses in Soviet manpower could in time be made good, the loss of war resources necessitated American and British aid, and then it could be made good only in part. According to Professor Prokopowicz, by December, 1941, the Germans had occupied 26·6 per cent. of Russia in Europe, which contained 40 per cent. of its population, and furnished 39·3 per cent. of its agricultural produce, 49 per cent. of its horses, 45 per cent. of its cattle, 66·6 per cent. of its iron, and 60 per cent. of its coal.[1] Set off against these staggering losses, the moral loss of the Germans was irreparable. In the "hedgehogs" of the winter months the cutting edge of the Grand Army of 1941 was blunted, and its temper could not be restored by the addition of the base metal of Italian, Rumanian and other satellite levies. Further, the economic gains in Russia were more than cancelled by the growing stranglehold of the British and American blockade.

Finally, what was the significance of Hitler's failure to take Moscow? Admiral Assmann's answer is that it was "the turning point of the war." But if this were so, would the turning point have been avoided had Hitler occupied Moscow? Beyond it extended 4,500 miles of unconquered territory, and since December 11 the United States had become involved in the war against Germany. Is it likely that, at this critical moment for Hitler, Stalin would have accepted a negotiated German peace, and even had he done so, would Hitler have trusted him to abide by its terms?

The turning point of the war was not Hitler's failure to occupy Moscow, but Roosevelt's astuteness in bringing the United States into the war, and this could only have been avoided, or its results mitigated, had Hitler grasped that, as Roosevelt's problem was how to unite the Americans in a war against Germany, his problem was how to detach the subjugated peoples of the U.S.S.R. from their masters in the Kremlin. Although this is a hypothetical question, it would seem probable that, had he come to them as a liberator, he would have dissolved most of the Soviet Army and have overthrown the Bolshevik régime months before Roosevelt had accomplished his self-appointed task, and had he succeeded in doing so, the one thing he dreaded most would have been avoided – namely, a war on two fronts. His error was political more than strategic; he struck at the iron head of his monstrous antagonist instead of at his feet of clay. Had he struck at the

[1] Quoted by Léderrey in *La défaite Allemande à l'est*, p. 58.

latter – that is, had he relied on counter-revolution and not on conquest – possibly there would have been no turning point at all. In any case, the whole outcome of the war would have been different; either Germany would have been defeated without Russian aid, or the war would have ended in a negotiated peace in which the Kremlin would have played no part.

The Russian problem and the extension of the war to the Pacific

At nine o'clock on the evening of the day Hitler invaded Russia, Mr. Churchill said in a broadcast to the British people: "I have to declare the decision of His Majesty's Government. . . . We have but one aim and one single irrevocable purpose. We are resolved to destroy Hitler and every vestige of the Nazi régime. . . . We will never parley, we will never negotiate with Hitler or any of his gang. . . . Any man or state who fights on against Nazidom will have our aid. Any man or state who marches with Hitler is our foe. . . . That is our policy and that is our declaration. It follows therefore that we shall give whatever help we can to Russia and the Russian people."

From this and similar utterances it is clear that Mr. Churchill had no conception of the task demanded of him in his capacity of Prime Minister and Minister of Defence. Firstly, it should have been to win a peace which would be profitable to his country, and there could be neither moral nor political advantage in substituting Stalin for Hitler. Secondly, because he had postulated the extirpation of Hitler and Hitlerism as his aim, he should have differentiated between the Nazi régime and the mass of the German people. Had he done so, he would have seen that his most profitable ally was the extensive anti-Hitler faction in Germany, and in accordance with his declaration he would have given it his aid. But, overmastered by his emotions, he committed the selfsame blunder that Hitler had made when he failed to distinguish between the pro- and anti-Stalinist peoples of the U.S.S.R. This blunder prolonged the war by years, and in spite of ultimate victory, it lost the peace and made the war an absurdity.

Thirdly, bound to Poland as the British Government was by the Anglo-Polish treaty, and faced with her partition – in which Stalin was as guilty as Hitler – Mr. Churchill should not have impulsively thrown his country into the arms of the Soviets, but should have paused until Stalin had sought his aid, and only then have proffered it on the understanding that the Ribbentrop-Molotov Pact of August 23, 1939, was first annulled, and that all Polish prisoners and deported Poles in Russian hands were released.

His partner in this negation of statesmanship was the American President who, obsessed by the collection of votes, sedulously cultivated the Communists and their fellow travellers, who held the balance of power in New York State. The outcome was, an American writer says: when Hitler invaded Russia the New Deal bureaux became the "roosting places for droves of Communist termites." Almost unbelievably, this infiltration was so successful that American Communists – agents of the Kremlin – obtained controlling positions in many of the government departments.[1] It was the work of these agents which deluded the President and thereby helped to shape his war policy toward Russia.

When Hitler invaded Russia, Roosevelt did not think to fix a price for American aid, such as specific guarantees against Soviet annexations of foreign territories, but, like Churchill, blindly espoused the Soviet cause and forthwith started the flow of lend-lease goods to Russia.

But the President's problem remained: how was he to bring the United States into the war? The answer was, since Hitler refused to be provoked into a declaration of war on the United States, Japan must be provoked into war.

Friction between Japan and the United States had been on the increase since 1931. That year, largely to find an outlet for her ever-increasing population and to gain raw materials for her factories, Japan annexed Manchuria, renamed it Manchukuo, and set over it a puppet government to protect her economic interests. This high-handed act roused the ire of Henry L. Stimson, President Hoover's Secretary of State, who announced that the United States would not recognize the puppet government. Further, he charged Japan with a violation of the Kellog-Briand Pact of 1928, which in 1929 had already been broken by Russia's attack on China. He exaggerated American economic interests in China, and was supported by a group of business men who

---

[1] For a score or more of these agents see *The Twenty-Year Revolution from Roosevelt to Eisenhower*, Chesly Manly (1954), pp. 99–103. Manly quotes the following evidence before the Senate sub-committee on August 14, 1951: "I would say that our best ones [Communist agents] were Henry Dexter White and Lauchlin Currie. . . ." The former became assistant secretary to the Treasury and the latter administrative assistant on eastern affairs to the President.

declared that American capitalism would collapse "if it failed to capture new markets", and that "China, with its more than four hundred million potential customers, was essential to the continuation of the American economic system". Further, he urged the application of sanctions and embargoes; but President Hoover would not listen to this.

It was different with his successor President Roosevelt who, as he said, had the deepest sympathy for China because his wife's ancestors had traded with her. Not only did he support Stimson's policy of non-recognition of Manchukuo, but as soon as he was in the saddle he set out to bring the American fleet up to the strength allotted by the 1921 Washington treaty – the Japanese fleet was already up to allotted strength – and late in 1934 Japan announced that she would no longer be bound by the Washington agreement, after the two years warning stipulated in that treaty had elapsed.

Next, in July, 1937, soon after Japan had renewed her war with China, Roosevelt began to plan to force the Japanese into submission by means of a joint British-American blockade to cut off Japanese trade, and in January, 1938, he sent a secret mission to London to arrange this. In March, 1939, it was followed by a plea from Lord Halifax, British Foreign Secretary, that, in order to bring the maximum psychological pressure to bear on Japan, the American fleet should be concentrated in the Pacific. A year later, in April, 1940, Roosevelt, against naval advice, ordered the Pacific fleet, then based on the Californian coast, to Hawaii.

In the meantime, Secretary Morgenthau, strongly supported by Stimson and some business men, had called for a boycott of Japanese goods and prohibition of the export to Japan of American oil. They were so successful that, in mid-June, 1941, all shipments of oil from the American east to west coast ports was prohibited, which led to a major cut in Japan's oil shipments. At the same time Morgenthau and Stimson urged that a stop should be put to Japanese trade by the freezing of Japanese assets.

When these suggestions were made, on July 23 Japan compelled the Vichy Government to agree to her temporary occupation of Indo-China, and as this was a direct threat to Burma and Malaya and an indirect threat to the Philippines, Roosevelt sought the opinion of Admiral Harold D. Stark, his Chief of Naval Operations, on the application of embargoes to Japan. The latter prepared a memorandum, in which it was pointed out that "an embargo would probably result in a fairly early attack by Japan on Malaya and the Netherlands East Indies," and that an embargo on exports "is almost certain to intensify the determination of those in power [in Japan] to continue their present course. Furthermore, it seems certain that, if Japan should then take military measures against the British and Dutch, she would also include military action against the Philippines, which would immediately involve us in a Pacific war." Reassured that embargoes would bring Japan into the war, on July 25 Roosevelt announced that Japanese funds in the United States would be frozen (Britain and the Netherlands followed suit), and on the 31st he forbade the export of aviation fuel and machine tools to Japan. Economic war was proclaimed against the Japanese.

As this meant that war in the Pacific was on the horizon, the next step was taken by Mr. Churchill, and it was to bring the United States into the war with the least possible delay. He arranged to meet the President in Placentia Bay, Newfoundland. There, between August 8 and 13, the Atlantic Conference was held, and shortly before it opened Roosevelt is reported by his son Elliott to have said that Churchill "knows that without America, England can't stay in the war." His difficulty was not how to enable her to do so, but that only Congress could declare war, and when the subject was broached,.his reply was: "I may never declare war; I may make war. If I were to ask Congress to declare war they might argue about it for three months." Already he was making war on Germany, now he would make war on Japan; therefore he promised Churchill that the United States, "even if not herself attacked, would come into the war in the Far East." Also he promised that on his return to Washington he would send a provocative note to Admiral Nomura, the Japanese Ambassador accredited to the White House. This was done on August 17, and among other things the Ambassador was told: ". . . this Government now finds it necessary to say to the Government of Japan that if the Japanese Government takes any further steps in pursuance of a policy or program of military domination by force or threat of force of neighboring countries, the Government of the United States will be compelled to take immediately any and all steps which it may deem necessary toward safeguarding the legitimate rights and interests of the United States and American nationals and toward insuring the safety and security of the United States."

As these commitments could not be made public, the notorious Atlantic Declaration, or Charter, was concocted. It was nothing more than a publicity hand-out, and was never intended to be a formal state paper, nor was it inscribed, signed and sealed; it was merely mimeographed and released. It was a highly idealistic document in which it was laid down that no territorial changes would be made which did not accord with the freely expressed wishes of the people concerned; that all peoples were to be given the right to choose the form of government under which they wished to live; that all States, victor or vanquished, were to have access on equal terms to the trade and raw materials of the world; and that after the final destruction of Nazi tyranny a peace was to be established which would permit all nations to dwell safely within their own boundaries, so that all men in all lands might live out their lives in freedom from fear and want.

Had it been adhered to, it would have been impossible to implement; as it happened, all it did was to delude the world. Nevertheless, until it was scrapped at the Teheran Conference, it was first-class propaganda, and probably the biggest hoax in history.

Because the embargoes imposed on Japan meant that, sooner or later, the Japanese would either have to withdraw from China or break the blockade, soon after the Atlantic Conference ended they opened conversations with Washington to get the embargoes rescinded. Further, in September, in preparation for war, coded messages began to be sent from Tokyo to the Japanese Consul General in Honolulu to seek detailed information on Pearl Harbour in the island of Oahu and on the American Pacific fleet stationed there. Little suspected by the Japanese, the Americans had pierced their cipher (called "Magic") and were able to read all their messages.

As the conversations led nowhere, on November 22 a message was sent to Admiral Nomura – now supported by an assistant ambassador, Saburo Kurusu – which insisted that unless negotiations were completed and signed by November 29 "things are automatically going to happen." Since this pointed to a surprise attack of some sort, and because the American fleet and army in the Pacific area were not yet ready to meet attack, between November 22 and 25 Mr. Cordell Hull, Secretary of State, worked out a *modus vivendi* proposal in which he suggested a 90-day truce during which the United States and Japan would resume economic relations on the understanding that the latter undertook to make no further conquests. This proposal was never handed to Nomura, because on November 25 Mr. Owen Lattimore, Chiang Kai-shek's American adviser, who was pro-Russian, sent a telegram to Mr. Lauchlin Currie, the President's assistant on eastern affairs, that "loosening of economic pressure and unfreezing would dangerously increase Japan's military advantage in China," and "would be disastrous to Chinese belief in America." Also, on the 25th, the President, after he had expressed a fear that the Japanese might attack as soon as "next Monday" (December 1), made the significant statement that "the question was how we should maneuver them [the Japanese] into the position of firing the first shot without allowing too much danger to ourselves."

Hull's *modus vivendi* would not do this and so a 10-point proposal was substituted for it. This, according to William L. Langer and S. Everett Gleason in their quasi-official history, *The Undeclared War*, was based on a memorandum submitted by Harry Dexter White to Henry Morgenthau, Secretary of the Treasury. It purported to set forth the American proposals to resolve the issue between the two countries; actually it was an ultimatum. In exchange for a new trade agreement and the unfreezing of each other's assets, Japan was required to conclude a mutual non-aggression treaty with Washington, Moscow, the Netherlands, Chungking, and Bangkok; to withdraw her forces from China and French Indo-China; to undertake to support no régime in China other than that of Chiang Kai-shek; to conclude a reciprocal trade treaty with the United States on the basis of the most favoured nation treatment; and to stabilize the yen with the dollar.

There could be no doubt whatsoever that these proposals were meant as an ultimatum. The Japanese Government decided to accept the challenge and to answer it by carrying out an operation they had for long prepared. Without a declaration of war, Japan intended to strike at British and American possessions in the Far East and at the American Pacific fleet in Pearl Harbour. As it was essential that this fleet should remain in harbour, Nomura and Kurusu were instructed to continue negotiations in order not to alarm the United States. According to Rear-Admiral Robert A. Theobald,[1] President Roosevelt, who· was fully informed of

---

[1] See his book, *The Final Secret of Pearl Harbor* (1954). Theobald was in command of destroyers at Pearl Harbour at the time of the attack, and a foreword to his book is written by Fleet-Admiral William F. Halsey, U.S. Navy, one of the most eminent of American sailors. See also *Admiral Kimmel's Story*, Rear-Admiral Husband E. Kimmel (1955).

what was in progress, decided, so as to make certain of carrying the United States into the war – and nothing was more likely to do so than a surprise attack on American territory – that nothing should be done to lead the Japanese to infer that the United States expected such an attack. Therefore, except for a war warning message sent out on November 27, which made no mention of Hawaii, he did not inform Admiral H. E. Kimmel, commanding the Pacific fleet, and General W. C. Short, commanding the Hawaiian garrison, what was afoot.

Between December 2–5, a series of messages was sent out from Tokyo ordering Japanese overseas consulates to destroy their codes, ciphers and secret papers, a sure indication of the imminence of war; none of this vital information was passed on to Kimmel and Short. Lastly, on December 6, the Japanese embassy in Washington received a 14-part message in relays; it was the reply to the American 10-point proposal of November 26, and it was preceded by an instruction that, when received in full, it was "to be put in nicely drafted form" and kept secret until the hour of its presentation to the United States Government was notified in a separate message.

By 5.30 p.m. that day the first 13 parts of this long message had been decoded and were in President Roosevelt's hands. After he had read them he said: "This means war." Yet, writes Admiral Theobald, ". . . that last critical day passed and no word was sent to the Hawaiian Commanders."

Early on December 7 part 14 came through. It was a thinly disguised declaration of war, and it was immediately followed by a message instructing the two Japanese ambassadors to present the whole 14 parts to the United States Government at 1.0 p.m. – "your time" – that day.

On December 7 Admiral Stark, Chief of Naval Operations, arrived at his office at 9.25 a.m., and although it was pointed out to him that 1 p.m. Washington time was 7.30 a.m. Hawaiian time, he did not consider it necessary to send Admiral Kimmel a warning order, although his aides urged him to do so. Two hours later, General George C. Marshall, Chief of Staff of the Army, arrived at the War Department. He also was handed the 14-point ultimatum, and as its time of delivery indicated a Japanese attack on the United States forces somewhere in the Pacific at or about 1 p.m., he drafted a message to the Commanding Generals, U.S. Forces in the Far East, Caribbean Defense Command, Hawaii

Department, and Fourth Army, to state: "Japanese are presenting at 1 p.m. eastern time today what amounts to an ultimatum . . . be on the alert accordingly. Inform naval authorities of this communication." But this most urgent message was not sent by trans-Pacific telephone, by which it would have reached General Short in 30 or 40 minutes, it was sent by commercial radio and was delivered at Short's headquarters six hours after the Japanese had attacked Pearl Harbour, and had sunk or damaged 18 of their enemy's ships – including eight battleships – and had killed and wounded 4,575 Americans and destroyed 177 American aircraft. Thus was America precipitated into the war, and not the least consequence of Pearl Harbour was that in effect it made her the ally of Moscow.

This astonishing story of how the Japanese were manœuvred into war by President Roosevelt is summed up by Admiral Theobald: "Thus, by holding a weak Pacific Fleet[1] in Hawaii as an invitation to a surprise attack, and by denying the Commander of that Fleet the information which might cause him to render that attack impossible, President Roosevelt brought war to the United States on December 7, 1941. He took a fully aroused nation into the fight because none of its people suspected how the Japanese surprise attack fitted into their President's plans. Disastrous as it was from a naval standpoint, the Pearl Harbour attack proved to be the diplomatic prelude to the complete defeat of the Axis Powers."

It would seem equally possible that the President and his leading advisers were so obsessed by the certainty that the Japanese blow would fall in the western Pacific that the possibility of an attack on Hawaii never entered their calculations, and this in spite of the fact that the grand manœuvres of 1932 had included a test of the joint army and navy defence of Pearl Harbour. Of this test Richard N. Current writes in his *Secretary Stimson: A Study in Statecraft* (1954): "At dawn on a Sunday morning 'enemy' carriers approaching Oahu from the northeast took the defenders completely by surprise. The attacking planes sank every battleship in the harbor, destroyed all the defending planes before they could get off the ground. So the umpires ruled." That so important a ruling should have been forgotten is in no way exceptional. As has been seen, in the Gallipoli campaign of the First World War,

---

[1] Weak, because the U.S. fleet was numerically inferior to the Japanese, and its three aircraft-carriers were not in Pearl Harbour at the time of the attack.

the 1906 and 1911 studies of the British General Staff, which pointed to the hazards of a landing on the Gallipoli peninsula, were overlooked or forgotten in 1915. So in 1941 was the decision, which arose out of British Staff College exercises of 1924–1925, that the main threat to Singapore would come on its landward side.

Whichever of these alternatives is accepted, the entrance of the United States into the war was the logical outcome of lend-lease, which kept Great Britain in the war, and of the embargoes which forced Japan into it. Both were economic instruments, the one positive and the other negative, and because the United States was the greatest industrial power in the world, from the moment she entered the war she became potentially the dominant belligerent. Unfortunately for the world, because her leaders lacked historic sense and looked upon war as a lethal game rather than an instrument of policy, battles began to lose their political value as soon as the United States entered the war. So much was this so that, during the latter half of the war, their results were as often as not neutralized by political events. Thus, it came about that conferences, such as those held at Casablanca, Teheran, and Yalta, were not only far more decisive than any battle fought, but they annulled the decisions the latter achieved. Further, whereas in the military sphere, because of the enormous strides made in technology, the generals-in-chief increasingly became the rubber-stamps of a host of technicians and industrialists, on the political plane power increasingly passed from cabinets and parliaments into the hands of single statesmen – heads of state – who at times, advised as they were by military simpletons and political crackpots and deluded by their own propaganda, committed the most egregious strategical and political blunders.

The first of these decisive conferences was assembled in Washington in late December, 1941, and it was code-named "Arcadia." Mr. Churchill left England on December 12, and arrived in Washington on the 22nd. Before his departure, Mr. Anthony Eden, the British Foreign Secretary, had left for Russia, and while still at sea Mr. Churchill received from him a report of his first conversations with Stalin, a statesman who never fell into the error of looking upon war as anything other than an instrument of policy. In some detail Stalin at once broached to Mr. Eden what he considered should be the shape of post-war Europe. He proposed the division of Germany into small states; the restoration of the positions of the Baltic States, Finland, and Bessarabia as they were immediately before the German attack; claimed the "Curzon Line" as the future Soviet-Polish frontier and pressed for its immediate recognition by Britain. With this bombshell in his portmanteau Mr. Churchill stepped into the White House.

The work of the conference may be divided under two headings: military and political.

The military planning was in every way excellent. To direct the strategy of the war, a controlling instrument known as "The Combined Chiefs of Staff" was created with its headquarters in Washington. It was a committee which included the British Chiefs of Staff, or their representatives, and the American Joint Chiefs of Staff; but significantly no Russian staff officers were members. Further, in spite of the Japanese attack, it was reaffirmed[1] that the offensive against Germany should take precedence over the war in the Pacific, and the following agreement was reached:

"In 1942, the methods of wearing down Germany's resistance will be . . . ever increasing air bombardment by British and American forces . . . assistance to Russia's offensive by all available means . . . [and operations] the main object [of which] will be gaining possession of the whole North African coast. . . . It does not seem likely that in 1942 any large scale land offensive against Germany, except on the Russian front, will be possible . . . [but] in 1943 the way may be clear for a return to the continent across the Mediterranean, from Turkey into the Balkans, or by landings in Western Europe. Such operations will be the prelude to the final assault on Germany itself."

The second was the fateful beginning of the end – the initiation of a policy which was to cost the two western allies the peace. It was the pet idea of President Roosevelt and was called by him the "Great Design." It was a reversion to the Wilsonian policy of 1917–1918 without the 14 points, and may be compared with a pot of political ale – all froth. His proposal was that, once the war was at an end, the nations of the world should be united into a great organization for peace. This association of sovereign Powers was to be modelled on the American inter-state system and be based on the principles of the Atlantic Charter. Since it was essential that this band of brothers should include Russia, nothing must be left undone to win Stalin's collaboration. In the President's opinion this presented no insuperable difficulty, because

[1] First affirmed at the Anglo-American staff conversations of March 27, 1941.

Harry Hopkins, his *eminence grise*,[1] who had visited Stalin soon after the German invasion, had told him that it was ridiculous to think of Stalin as a communist; he was nothing of the sort, he was a great Russian nationalist and patriot. Whatever his views might be about the future of Europe, he must be won over. Although the President did not then realize it, appeasement of Russia was to become the linch-pin in allied policy.

This sublime nonsense, christened by the President the "United Nations", was accepted by the conference as the peace programme of the allied Powers, and on January 1, 1942, a joint declaration was signed by the United States and United Kingdom, as well as 24 other nations, including the U.S.S.R. It endorsed the Atlantic Charter and proclaimed that the signatories were "convinced that complete victory over their enemies is essential to defend life, liberty, independence, and religious freedom, and to preserve human rights and justice in their own lands as well as in other lands, and that they are now engaged in a common struggle against savage and brutal forces seeking to subjugate the world."

Thus was created the policy which was to render abortive every victory won by the two great western allies; bring the Slav back to the Elbe; and replace Hitler by Stalin.

---

[1] Sherwood calls him "the *de facto* Deputy President" (*The White House Papers of Harry L. Hopkins*, 1946, vol. I, p. 267); Churchill – "high among the Paladins," and Representative Dewey Short of Missouri – "The White House Rasputin."

CHAPTER 12

The Battle of Midway Island, 1942

Japan was well placed to overrun Britain's and America's far eastern possessions, but was powerless to strike at their homelands; the most she could hope for was a limited victory. This was no new situation, for in her two previous major wars – with China in 1894 and Russia in 1904 – she had been faced with a similar problem. In both, her success had been due to her ability to use her sea power in such a way that she avoided an unlimited conflict. In both, because of her naval supremacy, she was able to seize limited territorial objectives and then to challenge her enemy to retake them, in the knowledge that he was incapable of doing so because the enemy naval power was inferior to her own. Japan thought that even were Germany defeated – which in 1941 seemed improbable – Britain would be too exhausted to put much punch into yet another gigantic campaign, and by then, though it would still be impossible to knock out America, Japan could have established herself in so strong a defensive position that the Americans would prefer to negotiate a peace rather than continue a war which might last for years.

To make as sure as she could of a long war, Japan would not only have to seize the Dutch East Indies, to make herself economically strong enough to sustain the war, but she would also have to push her conquests deep into the Pacific so as to deny sea and air bases to the Americans. Were she to do this, what, then, would her enemy's position be? A few figures will answer this question.

San Francisco to Honolulu is 2,400 miles, and London to Colombo is 5,600. Honolulu is 5,600 from Manila, and Colombo is 1,580 miles from Singapore. Singapore to Yokohama is 3,020 miles, and Manila, *via* Shanghai, to Yokohama, is 2,160 miles. Approximately 10,000 miles each way – that is, 20,000 miles of Anglo-American sea communications.

Because of this the Japanese decided to rely upon a strategy of exhaustion: to seize time by the forelock, and while the going was good first to eliminate the American Pacific fleet at Hawaii – the sole powerful naval force which threatened them – and secondly to deprive the British and Americans of Singapore and Manila, their main naval bases in the South China Sea. She would then push into the Pacific and establish a defensive zone of such depth that it would be possible to barter space for time and draw the war out to so unprofitable a length that her enemies might be brought to accept a negotiated peace.

This zone may be compared with an entrenched system, the front line of which ran southward from Paramushiro, the northernmost of the Kurile Islands, to Wake Island, and thence by way of the Marshalls and Gilberts to the Ellice Islands, from where it swung westward along the Solomons through New Guinea, and thence by way of Timor, Java, and Sumatra to northern Burma. In rear the reserve line ran from the Bonin Islands to the Mariana Islands, including Guam, and then to Yap, Palau, Morotai, Halmahera and Amboina to Timor, where it joined the front, or outer line. Like a communication trench, the Caroline Islands from Palau eastward to the Marshalls and Gilbert Islands connected these two lines, a "trench" which also flanked the American central Pacific line of approach, which ran from the Hawaiian Islands *via* Midway, Wake, and Guam to Manila in Luzon.

Although the strategy the Japanese adopted was in character defensive, their grand tactics, which were based on air power, were defensive-offensive. Already in possession of the Mariana, Caroline and Marshall archipelagoes, the Japanese had established on them a network of air bases within supporting distance of each other, and they planned to do the same on enemy islands they might capture. Then, should any one island be attacked, superiority of air support could be brought to bear against the attacker from neighbouring islands, and reinforcements sent from Japan. Within this network the Japanese fleet was to operate as a mobile striking force which, under air cover provided by the islands, could counter-attack in strength its enemy's naval forces: the system was that of "hedgehogs" and armoured columns transferred from land to sea.

Before the war, the naval air doctrine generally favoured was that, as in the past, battles at sea would be fought between gunships, therefore the primary task of the aircraft-carrier was to protect the battle fleet by opening over it an "air umbrella". This doctrine was questioned by the Japanese naval commander-in-chief, Admiral Isoroku Yamamoto, who was one of the first to appreciate that, because the aeroplane outranged the gun, the carrier should be given the leading offensive role.[1] It followed that its primary task was to strike at the enemy's fleet – particularly at its carriers – and that protection of its own fleet was secondary. Under his able direction, by December, 1941, the Japanese navy included 10 carriers, the newest of which were 30,000-ton vessels with a speed of 30 knots. At this date the Americans had seven, three of which were with their Pacific fleet.[2]

Once the American Pacific fleet had been crippled, and as three days later the British battleship *Prince of Wales* and battle cruiser *Repulse* had been sunk off Kuantan in Malaya, the road was clear to put the above strategy and tactics into effect. By the middle of April, 1942, they had proved so successful that not only had the Japanese wrested from their enemies the great naval bases of Singapore and Manila (except the island fortress of Corregidor) and had overrun Malaya, southern Burma, Borneo, the Dutch East Indies and the Philippines, but, with the exception of one small Australian post of Port Moresby on the northern shore of the Coral Sea in eastern New Guinea, they had established a chain of airfields down to Australia. On their defensive perimeter they had occupied the Gilbert Islands, and had established at Rabaul, in New Britain, and in the northern Solomons a chain of air bases with the intention of pushing farther south and south-eastward to the New Hebrides, New Caledonia, Fiji, and Samoa so that they might cut communications between the United States and Australia. In the four months since Pearl Harbour they had won an empire which, if they could hold it, would provide them with all the resources and manpower they needed to maintain the war indefinitely.

In spite of these initial successes, the Japanese plan was based on two miscalculations. It not only challenged the two greatest naval powers, but also the two greatest industrial powers in the world, and the United States could not be crippled permanently even were Germany to win the war in Europe. What the Japanese

---

[1] In 1937, when considering this problem, the author was of opinion that the aircraft-carrier would replace the battleship as the capital ship "because air carried bombs vastly outrange gun-fired shells," and that therefore "naval warfare will be very different from what it was in 1914–18" (*Towards Armageddon*, 1937, p. 196).

[2] The Japanese carriers were, (1) large: *Zuikaku, Shokaku, Soryu, Hiryu, Kaga* and *Akagi*; (2) light: *Ryujo, Hosho, Zuiho* and *Shoho*, the last two were converted submarine tenders. The American carriers were all large: *Lexington* and *Saratoga* (converted battle cruisers), *Ranger, Enterprise, Yorktown, Wasp*, and *Hornet*. The Japanese were building 5 large carriers and converting 2 large passenger ships to carriers, and the eventual American building programme included 17 large carriers, 9 light carriers and 78 escort carriers.

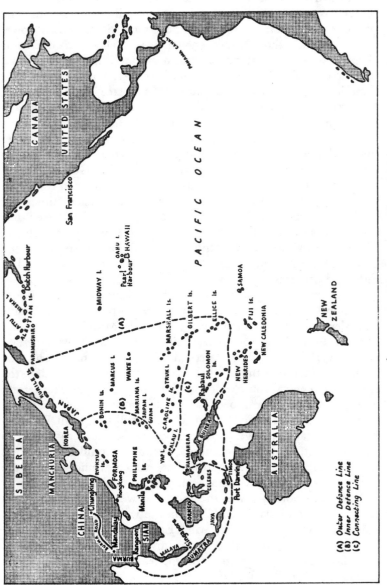

30. JAPAN'S STRATEGIC DEFENSIVE, 1941

overlooked was that the industrial potential of the United States was so vast that in time she could overcome all strategical obstacles of space and distance, and that the United States was a Power which, as they should have known, would choose to overcome them at whatever cost rather than negotiate a limited peace. Of all Japan's blunders this was the greatest: she believed that America would be willing to barter "losing face" for a short war, when she herself was willing to risk her existence in a long war rather than "lose face" by a withdrawal from China.

Once the Japanese had established their defensive perimeter and had securely installed themselves at Rabaul in New Britain and at Lae and Salamaua in north-eastern New Guinea, Yama-moto's problem became an equation of time, space and resources. He knew that were the Americans allowed sufficient time they could easily outbuild Japan's naval strength, and that, when they had done so, full command of the Pacific would pass to them. He decided, while the initiative was his, to exploit space in such a way that his enemy, weak though he was, would be forced to fight and progressively to weaken himself.

It was imperative to strike at objectives which his enemy could not afford to abandon. There were three: in the northern Pacific the Aleutian Islands, in the central Pacific Midway Island and Hawaii, and in the southern Pacific south-eastern Melanesia – the New Hebrides, New Caledonia, Fiji and Samoa. The first islands commanded the northern sea route across the Pacific, the second the central route, and the third the southern. The second was the most important, because Hawaii was the base of American naval power in the Pacific; but it was too distant from Japan to be a practical objective. Not so Midway Island, 1,135 miles to the west of it, for were it occupied, because it could be converted into an aircraft and submarine base which would restrict the use of Hawaii, the Americans would be compelled to fight for it.

Next in importance was the third, for were the United States to abandon south-eastern Melanesia she would lose contact with Australia, which was to her what Egypt was to Great Britain – an oversea base that flanked her enemy's homeland on the south.

Although the first objective was the least important of the three, in the northern Pacific the Aleutians were the link between the United States and north-eastern Russia and Japan, much as in the northern Atlantic Iceland was the link between America and Great Britain and north-western Russia.

To exploit this situation, which at present favoured Japanese strategy, Yamamoto decided first to draw his enemy's naval forces south, and then to draw them north and at the same time rapidly to concentrate his own forces in the centre, occupy Midway Island, and force his enemy to accept a major battle. For the southern operation it was decided to occupy Port Moresby, and Tulagi in the southern Solomons. Five separate forces were detailed for

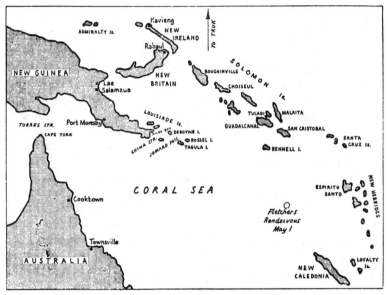

31. BATTLE OF THE CORAL SEA, MAY 4–8, 1942

these tasks: two Invasion Groups based on Rabaul, the headquarters of Admiral Inouyi, one bound for Port Moresby and the other for Tulagi, and three groups based on Truk in the Carolines. The latter comprised a Support Group with a seaplane carrier, which was to establish a seaplane base in the Louisiades, off the tail of New Guinea; a Covering Force with a light carrier – the *Shoho*; and, in order to secure the operation against enemy interference, a Striking Force, under Admiral Takagi, built around two large carriers, the *Shokaku* and the *Zuikaku*. Tulagi was to be occupied on May 3, after which the Support and Covering Groups and the Striking Force were to cooperate with the Port Moresby Invasion Group, which was to sail from Rabaul on May 4.

Through submarine scouts and broken code messages, it soon became known to Admiral Chester W. Nimitz, now in command of the Pacific fleet at Pearl Harbour, that something was afoot in the Coral Sea, and as he felt certain that a blow would be struck at Port Moresby, on April 29 he instructed Vice-Admiral Frank Fletcher, then in the Samoa area with a task force built around the carriers *Lexington* and *Yorktown*, to proceed to the Coral Sea and act as the situation developed.[1]

On the evening of May 6 Fletcher set out toward the Louisiades, 250 miles west-by-south of Espiritu Santo in the northern Hebrides, and started to refuel his ships. While so engaged he received a report from General MacArthur that Australian based aircraft had seen troops disembarking off Tulagi. Fletcher did not wait for the *Lexington* to complete her refuelling, but headed for Guadalcanal with the *Yorktown*, and at 7 a.m. on May 4, when 100 miles south-west of that island, the *Yorktown's* planes attacked the enemy's convoy at Tulagi, but did it little damage. After she had recovered her aircraft, the *Yorktown* steamed south, linked up with the *Lexington*, and spent the rest of the day refuelling.

On the evening of May 6 Fletcher set out toward the Louisiades, and next morning reached a point 115 miles south of Rossel Island, from where he sent out a search mission, which at 8.15 a.m. reported two carriers and four cruisers on the northern side of the Louisiades. Ninety-seven aircraft were launched, but no sooner had they taken off than it was discovered that the message should have read – "two cruisers and two destroyers." At about the same time Japanese aircraft located Fletcher, and when Admiral Inouye received this report at Rabaul, at 9 a.m. he ordered the Port Moresby Invasion Group, then heading for Jomard Pass, to turn back.

At 11 a.m. the *Lexington's* aircraft, which were ahead of those of the *Yorktown*, as they passed Tagula Island, sighted the light carrier *Shoho* of the Covering Group and attacked her. A few minutes later they were joined by the *Yorktown's* aircraft and by 11.30 the *Shoho* was so severely damaged that she sank.

Takagi's Striking Force had come down from the north, and at 6 a.m. on May 8, when about 100 miles east-south-east of Rossel Island, a search mission was sent out which had the good fortune to meet with some aircraft returning to the two American

---

[1] For the strength of the U.S. and Japanese forces see *History of United States Naval Operations in World War II*, Samuel Eliot Morison (1949), vol. III, pp. 17–20.

carriers. They followed the American aircraft and reported the carriers' position. At about the same time 18 search aircraft were launched from the *Lexington*, and at 8.15 a.m. they discovered the Striking Force some 175 miles to the north-east. At once Fletcher ordered both his carriers to launch air strikes, and at about the same time Takagi ordered his carriers to do the same. A criss-cross battle followed in which the *Zuikaku* disappeared in a rain squall; the *Shokaku* was badly damaged and set on fire; and both the *Lexington* and *Yorktown* were hit. By 11.40 a.m. the battle was over, and might have been claimed as a victory by Fletcher had not an explosion occurred in the *Lexington* which forced him to abandon her and have her sunk.

During the afternoon, Admiral Nimitz, who had been kept informed of the action, ordered Fletcher to withdraw from the Coral Sea, and Takagi, who was under the impression that both American carriers had been sunk, set out on his return to Truk.

"Thus," writes Admiral King, "ended the first major engagement in naval history in which surface ships did not exchange a shot."[1] It was the first battle of its kind.

Already on May 5 orders had been issued by the Japanese high command for the Midway Island and Aleutians operations. Five forces were to be employed:

Advance Expeditionary Force: Vice-Admiral Komatsu, 16 submarines.

Carrier Striking Force: Vice-Admiral Nagumo, four carriers (*Akagi*, *Kaga*, *Hiryu*, and *Soryu*), two battleships, two cruisers and 12 destroyers.

Midway Occupation Force: Vice-Admiral Kondo, Covering Group, two battleships, two cruisers, and seven destroyers; Close Support Group, four cruisers and four destroyers; Transport Group, 12 transports carrying 5,000 troops, and 11 destroyers; Seaplane Group, two seaplane carriers and 1 destroyer; Minesweeping Group, four minesweepers.

Main Body: Admiral Yamamoto (C.-in-C.), three battleships, one light carrier, two seaplane carriers and 13 destroyers. Detached from it the Aleutian Support Force, Vice-Admiral Takasu, four battleships and two cruisers.

Northern Area Force: Vice-Admiral Hosogaya, Second Mobile

---

[1] *A Report to the Secretary of the United States Navy*, by Admiral Ernest J. King, U.S.N., Commander-in-Chief U.S. Fleet and Chief of Naval Operations (1944), p. 37.

Force, two light carriers, one seaplane carrier and 12 destroyers; two Occupation Forces, six transports carrying 2,000 troops.[1]

The plan of operations was that on June 3, in order to confuse the enemy's command and cover landings on the islands of Attu and Kiska, in the western Aleutians, the Second Mobile Force was to deliver a paralysing air attack on Dutch Harbour, the United States naval base in the island of Unalaska. Immediately after this blow the Carrier Striking Force was first to soften-up Midway Island, and then, if challenged by the Pacific fleet, strike at it while the Main Body moved up to its support. In the meantime Midway was to be occupied and developed into an air base. The Aleutian Support Force was to take up a position half way between Midway and the Aleutians and be ready to intercept any enemy forces which came from, or went to, the north.

This plan was radically unsound and the distribution of forces was deplorable. Both were complex; the aim was confused and the principle of concentration ignored. Instead of deciding that the destruction of his enemy's carriers was his primary task, Yamamoto involved his own carriers in the occupation of Midway, which was his for the asking once the enemy carriers were destroyed. His best course would have been to have ignored Midway altogether until he had done so. Failing this, he should have held three of his carriers in hand until he had discovered the whereabouts of the American carriers, and meanwhile have handed over the softening-up of Midway to his battleships and cruisers – which were more suited for this task than aircraft – protected by one carrier. Instead, as will be seen, when his enemy discovered the whereabouts of his carriers, the latter had spent their shot and were neither able adequately to attack their enemy's carriers nor to defend themselves. It would seem that, either the recent activities of the Pacific Fleet and particularly an air raid on Tokyo on April 18 spurred him in his decision to attack Midway, or, what would seem as likely, he speculated on a complete surprise.

If the latter supposition is correct, unfortunately for him he was mistaken, for shortly before the battle of the Coral Sea Admiral Nimitz had got wind of a projected Japanese offensive in the central Pacific, and on May 14 from deciphered code messages[2] had learnt that the Japanese intended to attack both Midway and the Aleutians soon after June 1. Nimitz at once issued orders

[1] See Morison, vol. IV, pp. 77, 87–89 and 172–173 for full details.
[2] See *War for the World*, Fletcher Pratt (1951), p. 45.

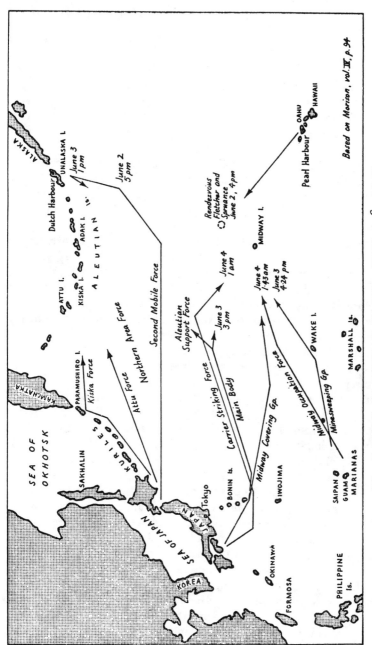

32. BATTLE OF MIDWAY ISLAND, JUNE 4–6, 1942

for the concentration of his forces at Pearl Harbour. Fletcher was recalled from the south Pacific, and Vice-Admiral Halsey, who with the carriers *Enterprise* and *Hornet* had, on April 18, carried out an air raid on Tokyo, and was on his way south to join Fletcher, was ordered back at top speed. When Fletcher arrived, the *Yorktown* was hastily repaired, and as Halsey was sick, Rear-Admiral Raymond A. Spruance took over command of his Task Force.

On May 27, Nimitz who, in supreme command, remained at Pearl Harbour throughout the battle, issued his final appreciation. He pointed out the vast superiority of the Japanese forces; that the high probability was that an attempt would be made to occupy Midway; and that the enemy's main target would be the American carriers.[1] He then instructed Fletcher and Spruance to take up their initial position north-eastward of Midway and out of range of enemy air attack, because he estimated that the Midway long-range aircraft would locate the Japanese carriers before the Japanese located the American carriers. The total forces under Fletcher's command were three carriers, seven heavy cruisers, one light cruiser, 14 destroyers and 19 submarines. These, except for the submarines, were divided into two Task Forces: No. 17, under Fletcher, comprised the carrier *Yorktown*, two cruisers and five destroyers; and No. 16, under Spruance – the carriers *Enterprise* and *Hornet*, six cruisers and nine destroyers. Midway was held by the 6th Marine Defense Battalion, under Colonel Harold D. Shannon; detachments from two Patrol Wings (32 Catalina patrol seaplanes); a Marine Aircraft Group (54 fighters and bombers); and an Army Air Force Detachment (23 heavy bombers – "Flying Fortresses").[2]

Air missions began to be sent out from Midway on May 30, to search the sea up to 700 miles from the island; but as the weather was thick, and the approaching enemy forces were covered by an area of low cloud, it was not until June 3 that anything was sighted. At 9 a.m. that day one of the Catalina pilots saw 30 miles ahead of him what he took to be the enemy's main fleet. At 11 a.m., 11 ships were sighted steaming eastward, and when this information was received at Midway, nine Flying Fortresses were sent out. At 6 p.m., when 570 miles from the island, they discovered the Japanese transport fleet. They bombed it, but made no hits; the battle was opened.

[1] See Morison, vol. IV, p. 84.   [2] For full details see *ibid.*, vol. IV, pp. 90–93.

When this attack was made the three American carriers were 300 miles east-north-east of Midway and 400 miles east of the planned launching point toward which the Japanese Carrier Striking Force sailed, and although the report received by Fletcher indicated that the ships attacked were the enemy's Main Body, he correctly judged that the Japanese carriers would approach Midway from the north-west, and that the force reported was more likely to be the transport group. To prevent the enemy's carriers from discovering his whereabouts he changed course southward and closed on Midway.

At 4.30 a.m. on June 4, when he was about 200 miles north of the island, 10 scout aircraft were launched from the *Yorktown*. At that hour Nagumo's carriers were 240 miles west of Midway, and were sending off their first strike. Although visibility was none too good, this strike was spotted by search aircraft from Midway, and at 5.45 a.m. the signal arrived: "Many enemy planes heading Midway distance 180 [miles from the island]". Then a signal was received that two carriers and battleships had been seen. Fletcher did not wait for further reports, but at 6.7 a.m. he ordered Spruance to "proceed southwesterly and attack enemy carriers when definitely located." He also informed him that he would follow with the *Yorktown* directly she had recovered her scouts.[1]

Fifteen minutes before this order was given, the first Japanese air strike – 36 torpedo aircraft, 36 dive-bombers, and 36 fighters, under Lieutenant Tomonaga, was picked up by Midway radar 43 miles north-west of the island. The alarm was sounded, every aircraft able to leave the ground took to the air, and at 6.16 a.m., when 30 miles out, the Marine Corps fighter squadron, 26 aircraft in all, encountered the Japanese van, but was outnumbered and almost annihilated.[2] "The entire island," wrote an American officer, "was deadly silent after the buzz of the planes taking off. It was a beautiful sunny morning. The men all strained for a first glimpse, and I had to sharply remind the lookouts to keep the other sectors covered against surprise. Then we saw the Japs, and the tension snapped. A moment later we were in action."[3] Although considerable damage was done to the installations on the island, few men were killed and none of the runways was rendered unusable. At 6.50 a.m. the attack was over.

[1] *Ibid.*, vol. IV, p. 130.
[2] See *Marines at Midway*, Lieut.-Col. Robert D. Heinl (1948), p. 27.
[3] Quoted from *ibid.*, p. 30.

A few minutes before the first Japanese bombs hit Midway Admiral Nimitz had ordered Captain Simard, in command of the Midway shore-based aircraft, to go all out for the enemy's carriers, and to leave the defence of the island to its guns. Ten torpedo aircraft took off just before the attack opened; at 7.10 a.m. they encountered the Japanese carriers, and without registering a hit, seven were shot down.

After his first strike had gone in, Nagumo sent out a search mission, and at 7 a.m. he received a message from Tomonaga, who had just finished bombing Midway, that a second strike would be needed; immediately afterward came the Midway counter-attack which proved that he was right. Nagumo then made a fatal decision, "he discontinued the stand-by condition of readiness of the 93 planes prepared for instant launching against surface forces, ordered them struck below to clear his flight decks for the recovery of the Midway strike, and ordered the torpedo planes' armament to be changed to bombs for a second attack on the atoll – a job that required a good hour's hard work."[1] Next, between 7.28 a.m. and 8.20 a.m., he received three signals. The first informed him that enemy ships had been sighted 240 miles from Midway; the second that they numbered five cruisers and five destroyers; and the third that they appeared to be accompanied by a carrier. Thus he learnt that in all probability he would have to deal with at least one enemy carrier; but for the time being he could do nothing, because he had to keep his flight decks clear for Tomo-naga's aircraft, which began to return at 8.35 a.m. Meanwhile his carriers had beaten off further attacks from Midway, all of which were ineffective.

Shortly before Nagumo made his fateful decision to carry out a second strike at Midway, Admiral Spruance had decided to make an all-out attack on his carriers, and at 7.2 a.m. aircraft from the *Hornet* and *Enterprise* began to take off. The strike comprised 20 fighters, 67 dive-bombers, and 29 torpedo aircraft, and as half of them had to be brought up from the hangar deck, over an hour was consumed in launching. Fletcher, who sailed on the same course as Spruance, was not certain whether there might be additional enemy carriers to those already reported and decided to hold back the *Yorktown* aircraft. But as by 8.38 a.m. no further carriers had been sighted he ordered half his dive-bombers and all his torpedo aircraft to take to the air with fighter escort. At

[1] Morison, vol. IV, p. 107.

9.6 a.m. 17 dive-bombers, 12 torpedo aircraft, and six fighters took off.

While these strikes were in preparation, Nagumo continued on his course toward Midway with his four carriers and their escort, and although his reconnaissance aircraft sent in signal after signal to notify him of the approach of enemy carrier-based aircraft, he could do nothing to meet their attack until 9.5 a.m., when Tomonaga's last aircraft had returned. Then he altered course by about 90° to port.

Because no American aircraft shadowed Nagumo, Spruance's striking squadrons assumed that the Japanese carriers were standing on toward Midway. The result was that when the *Hornet's* leading 35 dive-bombers reached the position at which they expected their enemy to be, they found nothing. They continued their course toward Midway, missed the carriers, and either landed on the island or ran out of fuel and splashed into the sea.

At the same time the *Hornet's* torpedo aircraft, under Lieutenant Waldron, who had lost their fighter escort in a cloud layer, were unable to find the enemy and turned northward. At about 9.25 a.m. Waldron sighted three Japanese carriers on the horizon. Although without fighter cover, he signalled the attack. His 15 aircraft went in; all were shot down, and of their 30 pilots and aircrewmen only one pilot survived.

The torpedo squadron of the *Enterprise*, under Lieutenant-Commander Lindsey, fared only slightly better. It had set out simultaneously with the *Hornet's* torpedo aircraft and had been allotted an escort of six fighters; but by mistake the latter linked up with the fighter escort of the *Hornet's* torpedo aircraft, which had lost touch with Waldron. The outcome was that when soon after 9.30 a.m. Lindsey sighted the Japanese carriers, he was without protection, and when he attacked 10 out of his 14 machines were shot down.

Barely had this action ended than, at 10 a.m., *Yorktown's* torpedo squadron, under Lieutenant-Commander Massey, came in. His escort of six fighters was soon overpowered, and of his 12 machines all but two were accounted for by the enemy.

Thus, of the 41 attacking American torpedo aircraft, only six returned, and not a single hit had been scored. "Yet," writes Rear-Admiral Morison, "it was the stark courage and relentless drive of these young pilots of the obsolete torpedo planes that made possible the victory that followed. The radical maneuvering that these imposed on the Japanese carriers prevented them from launching more planes. And the TBDs. [torpedo bombers] by acting as magnets for the enemy's combat air patrol and pulling 'Zekes' [Japanese fighter planes] down to near water level, enabled the dive-bombing squadrons that followed a few minutes later to attack virtually unopposed by fighter planes, and to drop bombs on full deckloads in the process of being refueled."[1]

It should be borne in mind concerning this that the Japanese ships had no radar for fighter direction, and because the Japanese held that torpedo attack was both the most dangerous and the most suited for attack at short notice, at this stage of the war their fighters were sent mainly against their enemy's torpedo-aircraft.[2]

As soon as the torpedo-aircraft attacks had ended, in came the dive-bombers from the *Enterprise* and *Yorktown*. Those of the former numbered 37 machines, and were in two squadrons under the command of Lieutenant-Commander McClusky. He had set out at 7.52 a.m. without a fighter escort, and half an hour later had reached the point at which he expected to find the enemy carriers, but he could see them nowhere. For a little over an hour he continued his search, and then turned northward. Twenty minutes later – at 9.55 a.m. – he sighted a Japanese destroyer steaming at high speed in a north-easterly direction; as he suspected that she was on her way to rejoin the enemy's Striking Force he took his course from her and about 10 minutes later in the distance saw two Japanese carriers manœuvring to escape torpedo aircraft attack. At once he ordered one of his squadrons to attack the *Kaga* and the other the *Akagi*. As they closed in to make their dives they met with little anti-aircraft fire, nor were they much interfered with by the Japanese fighters because the latter had come down low to tackle their enemy's torpedo aircraft and had not sufficient time to climb back.

The *Akagi* had 40 machines on her flight deck refuelling, and at 10.26 a.m., two minutes after she had evaded the last of the American torpedo-aircraft, she received two direct hits; the second penetrated to her hangar deck, and the explosion detonated the stored torpedoes. In a moment she was a mass of flames; it was found impossible to extinguish them and at 10.50 a.m. she was abandoned, and Admiral Nagumo transferred his flag to the

---

[1] Morison, vol. IV, p. 121.
[2] See *Sea Warfare, 1939–1945*, Captain John Creswell, R.N. (1950), p. 180.

light cruiser *Nagara*. Early on June 5 the *Akagi* was sunk by a Japanese destroyer.

Four bombs from McClusky's second squadron struck the *Kaga* whose aircraft had just finished refuelling; her flight and hangar decks were wrecked, and, like the *Akagi*, she became a raging inferno and also was abandoned before she blew up and sank.

A few minutes before the *Akagi* and *Kaga* met their doom, the 17 dive-bombers from the *Yorktown*, under command of Lieutenant Commander Leslie, who had taken a more direct route than the other squadrons, struck at the *Soryu*, whose flight deck was also crowded with refuelling aircraft. Three hits with 1,000 lb. bombs were scored on her and, like the *Akagi* and *Kaga*, she became a mass of flames and also had to be abandoned. At about 2 p.m. she was attacked ineffectively by the American submarine *Nautilus*, and five hours later blew up and sank. Of the dive-bombers engaged in these attacks, the *Enterprise* lost 14 and the *Yorktown* two.

There still remained the Japanese carrier *Hiryu*, which so far had escaped attack. She was well ahead of the other three, and when soon after 10.50 a.m., at which time Nagumo abandoned the *Akagi* and temporarily passed the command of the Striking Force over to Rear-Admiral Abe, who commanded his surface forces, Abe learnt from his reconnaissance aircraft that one American carrier with her escort had definitely been sighted 240 miles north of Midway. She was the *Yorktown*, and at once he ordered the *Hiryu* to attack her. At 11 a.m. 18 dive-bombers and six fighters took off, followed at 1.31 p.m. by a strike of 10 torpedo aircraft and six fighters. At about the same time, in preparation for a fleet action on June 5, Yamamoto ordered Vice-Admiral Kondo, in command of the Covering Group, to bring his battleships and cruisers forward; also he called in the Aleutian Support Force and the two light carriers of the Northern Area Force.

When the *Hiryu's* first strike was on its way, the *Yorktown*, under cover of 12 fighters, refuelled the aircraft which had returned to her, and while so engaged, a little before noon her radar located aircraft about 40 miles out approaching her from the west-south-west. A few minutes later, in came the *Hiryu's* dive-bomber strike; 12 were shot down or driven off minus their bombs, but six got through the *Yorktown's* fighter screen and scored three hits. One struck the *Yorktown's* flight deck, another exploded in her smoke-stack and disabled most of her boilers, and the third penetrated to her fourth deck and started a raging fire. Although it was extinguished, the carrier was unmanageable, and Admiral Fletcher transferred his flag to the cruiser *Astoria*. By 1.40 p.m. her boilers had been sufficiently repaired to permit her to make 19 knots, and she was about to refuel her fighters when a message was received from an escort cruiser that her radar had located a second strike. Four of the *Yorktown's* fighters were already in the air, and she had just sufficient time to launch eight others, partially refuelled. They were unable to cope with the enemy, and five of the *Hiryu's* torpedo aircraft flew in at masthead height or lower, broke through the splash barrage which had been put up to intercept them, and launched their torpedoes within 500 yards of the *Yorktown*. Two hit her, breached her port fuel tanks and jammed her rudder. Soon a heavy list developed, and as it was feared that the ship would capsize, at 3 p.m. she was abandoned.

Before the *Yorktown* was attacked, scout aircraft had been sent out from her, and at 2.45 p.m., at the time she was about to be abandoned, they sighted the *Hiryu* with battleships and cruisers a little over 100 miles west-by-north of the *Yorktown*. When he heard of this, Admiral Spruance ordered the *Enterprise* to launch an attack group of 24 dive-bombers, led by McClusky, and at 5 p.m. he came up with the *Hiryu*, attacked her and scored four hits at a loss of only three of his aircraft. Her fate was that of her sister carriers; she was immediately wrapped in a mass of flames, and as it was found impossible to extinguish the fires, at 3.15 a.m. on June 5 she was abandoned, and two hours later was sunk by Japanese destroyers.

When Yamamoto learnt of the fate of his four carriers, and that two American carriers were probably still fit for action, he abandoned all idea of a great fleet attack and at 2.55 a.m. on June 5 ordered a general retirement.

In the meantime, in order to avert a night fleet action with superior forces, Spruance withdrew the *Enterprise* and *Hornet* eastward. During Yamamoto's withdrawal, two of his cruisers, the *Mikuma* and *Mogami*, collided and were so severely damaged that they fell behind. On the morning of June 5 they were ineffectively attacked by shore-based aircraft from Midway, and at 9.30 a.m. Spruance altered course due west and set out to chase his enemy; but he was too late to catch up with Yamamoto.

Early on June 6 a reconnaissance flight was sent out from the *Enterprise*; it picked up the two crippled enemy cruisers, and between 8 a.m. and 1.30 p.m., 112 aircraft took off from the *Enterprise* and *Hornet* and attacked them. The *Mikuma* was sunk, but the *Mogami*, although hit by four bombs, which reduced her to a wreck, limped back to Truk.

At length, on the evening of the 6th, when 400 miles away from Midway, Spruance decided to abandon the chase. His pilots were exhausted and his ships were short of fuel; there was little prospect that he could catch up with the enemy. He altered course and steered eastward, back to where his tankers awaited him.

Thus ended the battle of Midway Island, but not without an unfortunate loss for the Americans, for during the evening of June 6, the *Yorktown* which, now in the hands of a control party, might have been saved, was torpedoed by a Japanese submarine, and with her went down one of her escorting destroyers, sent to the bottom by the same vessel.

"The Battle of Midway," writes Admiral King, "was the first decisive defeat suffered by the Japanese Navy in 350 years."[1] It was one of those rare battles in which a numerically inferior fleet suddenly snatched victory from a superior force, and thereby changed the course of war. The destruction of two-thirds of Japan's fleet carriers[2] knocked the bottom out of her grand tactical scheme to hold the Pacific by means of "hedgehogs" and mobile forces, and it threw her on the passive defensive. For the remainder of the war it secured the central Pacific for the United States; put into pawn the Japanese occupation of Attu and Kiska in the Aleutians, and restricted Japan's ambitious plan to conquer Fiji, Samoa and New Caledonia in order to sever Australia from North America. Finally, it struck a mortal blow at Japanese prestige.

As at the battle of the Coral Sea, except for anti-aircraft battery fire and submarine action, the battle of Midway Island was fought exclusively between carrier-borne aircraft – not a shot was fired between surface craft. The carrier had come into her own – she was the capital ship, and all other vessels of war were no more than her escort or her auxiliaries.

---

[1] *United States Navy, etc.*, p. 39. In 1592 the Japanese fleet was decisively defeated off the Korean coast by the Korean Admiral Yi-sun. In this battle the Koreans roofed in their ships with solid timber to protect their crews from missiles, and studded the roofs with *chevaux de frise* to prevent boarding. The Japanese were nonplussed.

[2] The only large carriers left were the *Zuikaku* and *Shokaku*, still under repair.

The War in North Africa

The United States' entry into the war made the conflict not only global in extent, but unlimited in character. The Pacific and Indian Oceans were added to the then main sub-theatres of the war – the Atlantic, Russia, and North Africa; and since no single great Power remained outside the circumference of the conflict as arbiter, the after-war problem – the shape of the peace to come – became of supreme importance.

Because the aim of the two western allies – the United States and the United Kingdom – was to exterminate Hitlerism, there could be no political advantage were Hitlerism to be replaced by Stalinism, and because Hitler's failure to occupy Moscow had shown that his expectations of driving Russia out of the war before the United States entered it, had been frustrated, the aim of the western allies clearly had become not only to extirpate Hitlerism, but simultaneously to prevent its replacement by Stalinism. Should they fail to do so, then, the more Germany was crushed, the more would the war politically be lost by the West.

This dual aim could only be attained if Germany were driven out of the war before Russia developed her full strength, and because the western allies could not hope to defeat the German armies and occupy Germany before this became probable, their sole rational course was to help Russia to withstand defeat while they entered into close cooperation with the extensive anti-Nazi faction in Germany to foment revolution within the Reich and at the same time to knock Italy out of the war. Could this latter aim be attained while they stimulated revolt in Germany, then except for the improbable event of a renewal of the Nazi-Soviet Pact of 1939–1941, whatever happened in Russia the western allies would strategically be well placed, not only to penetrate the centre of the German southern front, which extended from the Bay of Biscay to the Black Sea, but also to flank from the south a Russian advance into eastern and central Europe, and thereby bring Russia to heel. Vienna, and not Paris, was the goal of their military strategy. Could they but turn these two keys in their

478

respective locks; could they foment revolution within the Reich and simultaneously occupy, or even only threaten, Vienna, there would be every chance that they would be able to exterminate Hitlerism while Hitler was still engaged in Russia, and thereby become the arbiters of the peace which would follow the war. It was for this reason, and it should have been as obvious at the time as it was when the war ended, that Stalin so insistently pressed for the opening of a second front in northern France – that is, to get his allies as far away from Vienna as possible.

The importance of the political aim – revolution within the Reich – was ignored. Instead, on January 13, 1942, a conference of allied governments was assembled in London, not to consider cooperation with the anti-Nazis, but to pledge its members to punish Axis war criminals when the war ended: a piece of stupidity hard to equal, for obviously the most profitable way to punish them was to persuade and help the anti-Nazis to rid their country of Hitlerism *during the war*. Further, on May 26, the British Government committed the quite unnecessary blunder of signing with Russia a 20-year treaty of alliance without any territorial provisions attached to it: this implied a free hand for Soviet expansion in eastern Europe should Germany be defeated. Well may Mr. Churchill write: "Stalin was almost purring."

To drive Italy out of the war was in every way a feasible operation, and it was first discussed by the Chiefs of Staff at the Arcadia Conference, when a plan to invade north-west Africa was considered. It was considered because the British were already at grips with the Italians and Germans in Libya; because the French in Morocco and Algeria could not put up effective opposition; because the difficulties the Italians were faced with in supplying their forces in Libya were so great that it was impossible for them to maintain there more than an army of moderate size; and lastly, because the two western allies would soon have at their disposal sufficient men and means to warrant a successful invasion of North Africa.

When in April, 1941, General Rommel, the *de facto* commander of the Axis forces in Libya – the actual commander was General Ettore Bastico – opened his first campaign and drove his enemy back to the Egyptian frontier, Sir Archibald Wavell wisely held fast to Tobruk and so deprived his enemy of the only good sea port east of Benghazi – 340 miles west of Tobruk. Though its retention diminished Wavell's striking force in Egypt by two divisions, it put a stop to a further eastwardly advance of his adversary. It lengthened the enemy land communications and compelled him to invest Tobruk; not until he had reduced it would he have sufficient force to continue his advance on Alexandria.

Since it is not the intention here to consider in any detail the campaigns which immediately followed, it is as well to appreciate why Libya was for so long the racecourse of the war: each army in turn galloped forward until its momentum was exhausted, and then was compelled to gallop back to avoid annihilation. The reason centred almost entirely in supply and, like a piece of elastic, the line of supply of both armies could be stretched with comparative safety to between 300 and 400 miles from its base – Tripoli on the one hand and Alexandria on the other. But as these two main bases were over 1,400 miles apart, to try to stretch them farther before intermediate bases were established was to risk snapping the elastic. The supply problem of both sides was how to increase the elasticity of their respective supply systems. This could only be done by building up stockpiles at their respective main bases, and step by step pushing forward the advanced bases. As both sides were separated from their homelands by the sea, the tussle was governed by sea communications.

When Italy entered the war, the main British communications with Alexandria and Suez had to go by way of the Cape of Good Hope, a voyage of between 12,000 and 13,000 miles, some 37 times longer than the Italian communications between Messina and Tripoli. But as long as Malta remained a British submarine and air base the Mediterranean was incomparably more dangerous to cross than the Atlantic and Indian Oceans. The odds on spanning the 1,400-mile land communications overwhelmingly favoured the British, and had Hitler, after the fall of France, accepted Admiral Raeder's suggestion and occupied Gibraltar, which would have made Malta untenable, the reverse would have been the case.

On May 1, 1941, Rommel tried to storm Tobruk and failed. In August, 35 per cent. of his supplies and reinforcements were sunk on their way over the Mediterranean; yet not until October, when the sinkings approached 75 per cent., did the German Supreme Command try to alleviate the losses by the diversion of 25 submarines from the Atlantic to the Mediterranean. At once the situation improved, so much so that Rommel began to consider a renewal of his advance, but before he could set out, on October

18 General Sir Claude Auchinleck, who had replaced Wavell, attacked him in the vicinity of Sidi Rezegh, and after a stiff and wavering battle drove him back to Agheila, a naturally strong position at the southern extremity of the Gulf of Sidra.

Because by then the British elastic approached snapping point, Auchinleck should have ordered a retirement, especially as the German Supreme Command had realized the importance of Malta, which in December was violently attacked from the air. Simultaneously the British Mediterranean fleet was harassed by submarines, aircraft and mines. The aircraft-carrier *Ark Royal* was sunk, as also were the battleship *Barham*, two cruisers, two submarines and a destroyer, and on the night of December 18 the battleships *Queen Elizabeth* and *Valiant* were put out of action by "human" torpedoes in the harbour of Alexandria. So perilous was the British position that, by the end of 1941, British naval forces in the eastern Mediterranean were reduced to three cruisers and a handful of destroyers. Further, during January, 1942, not a single ton of Axis stores was lost on its way across the Mediterranean, and the outcome was that, on January 21 – five days after Auchinleck's campaign ended – Rommel struck for a second time and by February 7 had driven his enemy back to the line El Gazala–Bir Hacheim, some 20 miles west and south of Tobruk.

It was this offensive, so soon after the failure of his Russian campaign, that finally persuaded Hitler to listen to Admiral Raeder who, on February 13, 1942, pointed out that "an early Italo-German attack on the British key position of Suez would be of utmost strategical importance." Next, on March 12, Raeder raised the question of Malta and urged that its capture would greatly facilitate the Suez offensive. Hitler agreed, and during April the air attack on Malta was intensified, 5,715 sorties were made that month in preparation of a seaborne invasion of the island (Operation "Hercules") by Italian and German forces in May. Next, he changed his mind and decided to postpone the assault until mid-July and that before it was made Rommel was to take Tobruk, complete the conquest of Libya, and only when he was ready to advance on Alexandria was the Malta operation to follow.

Meanwhile, early in May, Auchinleck began to prepare for another offensive on June 7; but Rommel, now reinforced, got in ahead. On the evening of May 26 he struck at his enemy's left flank at Bir Hacheim, took that strong point, swung north, and after nearly four weeks of desperate fighting stormed Tobruk on June 21, and captured 33,000 prisoners and an immense booty. Two days later he crossed the Egyptian frontier, drove his enemy back to Mersa Matruh, and from there to a line running from Tel el Eisa on the coast, 10 miles west of El Alamein – 60 miles west of Alexandria – to the Qattara Depression, 35 to 40 miles to the south. This line was occupied by the British on June 30.

In the meantime, on June 15 – that is, when Rommel was still held before Tobruk – Hitler changed his mind again, and because he doubted the ability of the Italians to take Malta he decided not to assault the island until it had been bled by continuous air attacks and starved by blockade. Lastly, when Rommel was halted on the El Alamein line, and urgently called for reinforcements, those sent to him were taken from the forces earmarked for the capture of Malta. In the opinion of Field-Marshal Kesselring, who as C.-in-C. South was Rommel's nominal superior, this not only prohibited an invasion of Malta, but was "a mortal blow to the whole North African undertaking."

When Tobruk fell Mr. Churchill was in Washington discussing with President Roosevelt the possibilities of devising an atomic weapon; the submarine campaign; and the problem of opening a second front in France in 1943 and of the establishment of a subsidiary front in North Africa in 1942. He tells us that the fall of Tobruk was one of the heaviest blows he ever sustained, and that the President most chivalrously came to his aid. Although the American army was in urgent need of them, he gave him 300 Sherman tanks and 100 self-propelled guns which were at once shipped to Suez.

Immediately after this generous gift was made a conference was held to consider future strategy, and three problems were discussed. The first was the transference of American forces to the United Kingdom in preparation for an invasion of France in 1943 (code-named "Bolero"). But as it was considered essential, in order to help Russia, that something should be done in 1942, the second question was the invasion of French North Africa (code-named "Gymnast"), and the third a limited assault on France, the aim of which was to occupy either the Cherbourg or Brest peninsula (code-named "Sledgehammer").

The third had been accepted by the British War Cabinet on June 11 because it was a favourite project of General Marshall. But as the British Chiefs of Staff considered it totally impracticable, after his return home, Mr. Churchill wrote to the President on July 8, suggested that it should be dropped, and recommended "Gymnast" as the best means to help Russia. "Here," he said, "is the true Second Front for 1942," because, were the operation successful, it would threaten Italy and draw important German air forces away from Russia. But Marshall so strongly objected to this that the President replied that unless Churchill could convince Marshall that his project was unsound, America would have to reverse her strategy and concentrate her main effort in the Pacific. In order to solve the deadlock General Marshall and Admiral King came to London on July 18. Two meetings with the British Chiefs of Staff followed, and as the latter would not give way, the problem was referred back to the President, who replied that, as British opposition to "Sledgehammer" could not be overcome, his delegation should accept "Gymnast". Apparently, to placate Marshall, it was renamed "Torch", and on the following day – July 25 – the President sent a telegram that landings in North Africa should take place "not later than October 30." Eventually the date was changed to November 8.

When Auchinleck got back to the El Alamein line, for three days his situation was so critical that he prepared to withdraw to the Delta. But fortunately for him, Rommel's army was exhausted. Since it had stormed Bir Hakeim it had covered 400 miles and its momentum had petered out. It had only 50 German and 54 Italian tanks fit for action and was faced by superior tank forces. Although both sides tried to drive the other back, by the end of July the battle stabilized into position warfare.

On August 2 Mr. Churchill flew to Cairo, replaced Auchinleck by General Sir Harold Alexander as C.-in-C. Middle East, and gave him Lieutenant-General Bernard Montgomery to command his Eighth Army in Egypt.

CHAPTER 13

The Battles of El Alamein, 1942, and Tunis, 1943

The first three weeks of July, 1942, on the El Alamein line were devoted to attack and counter-attack. Rommel's one aim was that the front should not become static, and Auchinleck's aim was to make it so. The latter won the tussle and the outcome of the campaign became a question of reinforcements and supplies.

Faced with this situation, Rommel calculated that up to mid-September the advantage would be his; but in this he was badly deceived, because from the end of July on Auchinleck switched the main weight of his air offensive from the forward positions to the ports of Mersa Matruh, Bardia, and Tobruk, which left Rommel with Benghazi – 680 miles away – as his nearest secure base of supply. The results were that by the middle of August he was still short on establishments of 16,000 men, 210 tanks, 175 troop carriers and armoured cars and 1,500 vehicles; his army consumed double the amount of supplies that crossed the Mediterranean, and had it not been for the vast enemy dumps captured in Marmarica and western Egypt, "it would," as he says, "never have been able to exist at all."[1]

Rommel was severely criticized for not halting on the Egyptian frontier after he had taken Tobruk. True enough, had he done so he would have curtailed considerably his communications, but this in itself would not have solved his supply problem, because, as long as Malta remained in British hands in the long run it was impossible for him to out-stockpile his enemy. Further, once his attempt to rush the Alamein position failed, he could not fall back on a rear position because he had not sufficient transport simultaneously to supply his forward position and build up a position in rear. Since to remain where he was could not solve the problem of driving his enemy out of Egypt, he realized that he would have to attack, not when he was fully ready – that he could never hope for – but before his enemy's deficiencies had been made good.

[1] *The Rommel Papers*, edit. B. H. Liddell Hart (1953), p. 269.

It should be remembered that because Rommel was nominally subordinated to Marshal Bastico, Marshal Cavallero, the Italian Chief of Staff, whom Ciano calls "that crook" and "this charlatan,"[1] was responsible for the supply of Rommel's army. In order to clarify the supply situation, Rommel asked Cavallero and Field-Marshal Kesselring to meet him in Egypt. This they did on August 27, and when they guaranteed to supply him with 6,000 tons of petrol, one-sixth of which Kesselring promised to deliver by air, Rommel decided to attack. But to be doubly assured, he turned to Cavallero and said that the outcome of the battle would entirely depend on its receipt, to which the latter replied: "You can go on with the battle, it is on its way."[2] Unfortunately for Rommel, Kesselring failed to mention the recent arrival in Malta of Spitfire aircraft, which profoundly altered the situation.

When Rommel was thus engaged, General Alexander arrived at Cairo on August 8, and four days later he was joined by General Montgomery, who at once assumed command of the Eighth Army.

Montgomery was a man of dynamic personality and of supreme self-confidence. Known to his officers and men as "Monty", he was a past-master in showmanship and publicity; audacious in his utterances and cautious in his actions. Though at times smiled at by his officers, his neo-Napoleonic personal messages – "I am proud to be with you" . . . "YOU have made this Army what it is. YOU have made its name a household word" . . . "*YOU* and I together will see this thing through," etc., etc., interlarded with "The Lord Mighty in Battle" and "hitting the enemy for six," electrified his men. He was the right man in the right place at the right moment; for after its severe defeat the Eighth Army needed a new dynamo and Montgomery supplied it.

As soon as he arrived at his headquarters he summoned a meeting of his staff and said that his mandate was to destroy the Axis forces in North Africa, and if anyone doubted this he had better clear out. He added that he had ordered all withdrawal plans to be burnt; that the defence of the Delta meant nothing to him; and that in a fortnight he would welcome attack, but he did not intend to assume the offensive until he was ready to do so. In order to carry it out, it was essential to have a *corps d'élite*, like

---

[1] *Ciano's Diary* (1947), pp. 518–519.
[2] *Rommel*, Desmond Young (1950), p. 168. See also Kesselring's *Memoirs* (1953), p. 130.

the Afrika Korps; therefore he would at once create one out of two armoured and one motorized divisions. Further, it was also essential that Army and R.A.F. headquarters should live in close proximity, so that the planning of the great offensive he had in mind might be a joint effort from the start.[1]

Except for the Wadi Akarit position north of Gabes, the El Alamein Line was the only one in North Africa that offered no flank that could be turned from the south. Rommel's tactical problem was how to penetrate this position, and because of his enemy's minefields and the tactical features in rear of them, it was by no means easy to solve. The former ran from Tel el Eisa, close by the Mediterranean, to Hunter's Plateau, which fringed the Qattara Depression, the northern border of which was girt with precipitous cliffs; and the latter comprised two ridges, the Ruweisat, about 200 ft. above sea level, which ran from the centre of the front eastward, and the Alam el Halfa, to its south-east, which at its highest point was a little over twice the height of the former, and which extended in a north-easterly direction towards El Hamman on the Alexandria–Mersa Matruh railway.

Auchinleck's plan, which Alexander and Montgomery accepted as the basis of their own, was to hold as strongly as possible the area between the coast and the Ruweisat Ridge; lightly to hold but heavily to mine the area south of it to Hunter's Plateau; and to hold in strength the Alam el Halfa Ridge so that, should the enemy's mobile forces penetrate the front either north or south of the Ruweisat Ridge, they could be counter-attacked in flank, and should they break through along the ridge itself, then they could be met frontally.

When Montgomery assumed command of the Eighth Army he found the front held by the XXXth and XIIIth Corps, the former north of the Ruweisat Ridge and the latter south of it. The former consisted of the 9th Australian, 1st South African and 5th Indian Divisions and the 23rd Armoured Brigade; the latter of the 2nd New Zealand and 7th Armoured Divisions. Alexander had in reserve the 8th and 10th Armoured and the 44th and 51st Infantry Divisions, also the 1st Armoured and 50th Infantry Divisions, both refitting. At once Montgomery asked for the 44th and 10th Armoured Divisions, the one to hold the Alam el Halfa Ridge and the other to occupy its western extremity as a mobile striking force.

[1] See *Operation Victory*, Major-General Sir Francis de Guingand, Chief of Staff, Eighth Army (1947), pp. 136–138.

Rommel's army was disposed as follows: In the north the German 164th Infantry Division, then the Italian XXIst Corps, which consisted of the Trento and Bologna Divisions and Ramcke's German Parachute Brigade, and lastly the Brescia Division of the Italian Xth Corps; all these formations were in front line. As his striking force Rommel had the Afrika Korps, which consisted of the 15th and 21st Panzer Divisions; the German 90th Light Division (motorized infantry); and the Italian XXth Mobile Corps, which comprised the Ariete and Littorio Armoured Divisions and the Trieste Division. In rear, at Mersa Matruh and Bardia, were the Italian Pavia, Folgore, and Pistola Divisions in reserve.

Rommel's plan was to make a feint attack in the north, a holding attack in the centre, and the main attack in the south. On the night of August 30–31, lanes through the southernmost sector of his enemy's minefields – which he believed to be weak, but which were strong – were to be cleared by German and Italian infantry. Next, at dawn on the 31st, the Afrika Korps was to follow through, take the Alam el Halfa ridge and make for the area south-west of El Hamman. In the meantime the 90th Light Division and the Ariete and Littorio Armoured Divisions were to break through to the north of the Afrika Korps and cover the left flank of its advance. His idea was to cut off his enemy from his supply depôts, while the 90th Light Division and XXth Mobile Corps held the enemy, and then annihilate him. He sought a decisive battle, and for its success it was imperative that the Alam el Halfa Ridge should be overrun early on the 31st.

According to General Alexander, the opposing forces were evenly matched on the southern half of the front. Both had about 300 field and medium guns and 400 anti-tank guns; Rommel had 500 medium and light tanks, and the XIIIth Corps 300 medium and 80 light tanks and 230 armoured cars. Besides these, 100 tanks with the 23rd Armoured Brigade constituted a reserve.[1] Though numerically evenly matched, Rommel was badly out-classed, because half his tanks were Italian and they were very indifferent machines.

For Rommel, the battle of Alam el Halfa was a desperate gamble because the plan on which it was based was the only one feasible with the means at his disposal, and precisely because of this Montgomery expected Rommel to adopt it. For Montgomery, whose intention it was to maintain a firm defensive until he was

---

[1] *Despatches*, Supplement to *The London Gazette*, February 3, 1948, p. 845.

fully prepared to attack, it was a heaven-sent opportunity; not only did it enable him to rebuild the morale of his army, but at the same time it enabled him to weaken that of his opponent and thereby doubly assure the success of his eventual offensive. In order to impede an attack on the southern sector of his front Montgomery considerably added to its minefields so that on the night of August 30–31 when the Germans and Italians began to clear lanes through them, they were greatly delayed. To add to this difficulty, General von Bismarck, commander of the 21st Panzer Division, was killed by a mine, and the commander of the Afrika Korps, General Nehring, was severely wounded. Further, Rommel was so sick that he was unable to leave his truck. This, Desmond Young considers, was "perhaps the greatest handicap of all," because Rommel – like Charles XII – "relied much more on his personal observation and judgment during the progress of a battle than on a preconceived plan."[1]

The results of these misfortunes were that there was no surprise; the advance of the Afrika Korps was delayed; that of the 90th Light Division still more so; and the Ariete and Littorio Divisions could not penetrate the minefields. Rommel, bereft of half his striking force, was compelled to abandon his sweep to the north-east and restrict the attack of the Afrika Korps to the western end of the Alam el Halfa Ridge. But its advance was so impeded by soft sand and by air attacks that at 4 p.m. it had to be called off.

During the night of August 31–September 1 the Italo-German forces were so pounded by the R.A.F. that, on September 1, Rommel was compelled to abandon any attempt to carry out a major operation, and only desultory fighting on the Alam el Halfa Ridge followed. In the meantime Montgomery, when he saw that the battle was in his hands, switched the 10th Armoured Division from the south to the west of the ridge preparatory to carrying out a counter-attack southward with the 2nd New Zealand Division directly he had exhausted his enemy's offensive.

On September 2, still under constant air attack and desperately short of petrol, Rommel renewed his offensive, but with so little success that he ordered a withdrawal for the morning of the 3rd. Montgomery then launched his counter-attack, and at the same time ordered his 7th Armoured Division to harass the enemy's southern flank. After stiff fighting he drove him back to the minefields, and at 7 a.m. on September 7 called off the battle.

[1] *Rommel*, p. 169.

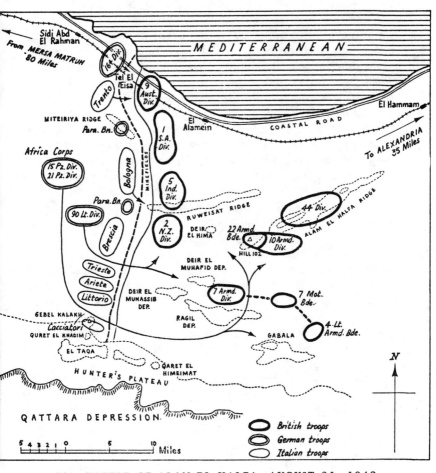

33. BATTLE OF ALAM EL HALFA, AUGUST 31, 1942

Rommel's losses were nearly 3,000 men killed, wounded and missing, 50 tanks, 15 guns, 35 anti-tank guns and 400 lorries lost,[1] and Montgomery's losses were 1,640 killed, wounded and missing, and 68 tanks and 18 anti-tank guns put out of action.[2]

Kesselring's opinion is that if Rommel had not been sick he would never have pulled out of the battle because he had "completely encircled his enemy."[3] This is a fantastic statement, and more especially as it is made by a highly experienced soldier. There was no encirclement, and once the battle had opened Rommel was under no illusion that his enemy's command of the air predoomed his defeat. He has much to say on this question, and among other things that, "Whoever enjoys command of the air is in a position to inflict such heavy damage on the opponent's supply columns that serious shortages must soon make themselves felt. By maintaining a constant watch on the roads leading to the front he can put a complete stop to daylight supply traffic and force his enemy to drive only by night, thus causing him to lose irreplaceable time. But an assured flow of supplies is essential; without it an army becomes immobilised and incapable of action."[4] This should be remembered when we come to the part played by Rommel in the Normandy campaign of 1944.

"With the failure of this offensive," writes Rommel, "our last chance of gaining the Suez Canal had gone."[5] He knew that the battle for supplies was irretrievably lost, if only because the large convoy of "well over 100,000 tons, laden with the very latest weapons and war material for the Eighth Army," which he expected "would arrive at Suez at the beginning of September,"[6] arrived there on September 3 with Roosevelt's gift of 300 Sherman tanks. He knew that his enemy would attack, and in all probability under a full moon.[7] Kesselring remarks: "Was it right under these circumstances to wait for the British offensive?" and adds that neither O.K.W. nor the Comando Supremo would have objected to a withdrawal.[8] Although this assumption is highly improbable, possibly the reason why Rommel stayed where he did was that either a voluntary withdrawal was repugnant to him, or that he had not the petrol and vehicles to carry it out. This latter reason is supported by Ciano, who, on September 2, entered in his diary:

[1] *The Rommel Papers*, p. 283.   [2] Alexander's *Despatches*, p. 846.   [3] *Memoirs*, p. 131.
[4] *The Rommel Papers*, p. 285.   [5] *Ibid.*, p. 283.   [6] *Ibid.*, p. 269.
[7] Before the battle of Alam el Halfa Rommel wrote: "The full moon, indispensable to our operations, was already on the wane. Any further delay would have meant giving up all idea of ever again resuming the offensive" (*ibid.*, p. 274).
[8] *Memoirs*, pp. 132–133.

"Three of our tankers have been sunk in two days," and on the 3rd, "Rommel's pause continues, and, what is worse, the sinking of our ships continues."[1] But had Rommel fallen back shortly before the next full moon, he would have disrupted his enemy's plans.

Whatever his reasons, he decided to stand and accept battle. His plan was to hold with outposts only his forward belt of mine-fields, in which some 500,000 mines and vast numbers of captured British bombs and shells had been sunk, and to fight his defensive battle in a mined zone one to two thousand yards behind. On his northern flank he posted the German 164th and 90th Light Divisions in depth; allotted to the Italians the defence of the front south of them; and divided his armoured divisions into two groups, the 15th Panzer and Littorio Divisions in the north, and the 21st Panzer and Ariete Divisions in the south. Tactically this was a faulty distribution and unlike any Rommel had hitherto adopted; possibly it was forced upon him through lack of petrol. In all he had 300 Italian tanks of little fighting value and barely fit for action, and 210 German tanks, of which 30 were Panzer IVs armed with 75 mm. guns, and the remainder Panzer IIIs with 50 mm. guns.

As he was then a very sick man he decided to return to Germany, and on September 22 he handed his command over to General Stumme, an experienced tank officer, and informed him that should the enemy attack he would at once return. This was not a very satisfactory arrangement. Back in Germany, on October 10 he was presented with his Field-Marshal's baton, which had been awarded to him immediately after the fall of Tobruk.

While Rommel was engaged on his unenviable task, his opponent, General Alexander, prepared for an all-out offensive. On August 10 Mr. Churchill had handed to him a directive to annihilate the German-Italian Army "at the earliest opportunity," but the date was governed by certain factors. Firstly, Operation "Torch" had been scheduled for November 8, and it was considered of vital political importance, in order to win over the French in Morocco and Algeria, that the Axis forces in Egypt should be decisively defeated before the invasion was launched. Secondly, because the 300 Sherman tanks would not arrive until early in September, and when they did several weeks' training with them was imperative, as well as a full moon under which to attack, the date fixed upon was the night of October 23–24.

[1] *Ciano's Diary*, p. 500

The next problem was one of grand tactics: where should the decisive blow be struck on the 40-mile front? Although in the front's southern sector the minefields were less extensive than in the northern, because a successful penetration in the south would drive the enemy northward towards his communications – the coastal road – it was decided to deliver the main blow in the north, to gain an outlet on to the coastal road, and to cut off the bulk of the enemy forces south of it. This settled, the next problem was one of minor tactics.

Because minefields can no more be rushed by tanks than wire entanglements can be rushed by infantry – and in the northern sector they were from 5,000 to 9,000 yards in depth – it was agreed that the initial advance would assume the form of an old-fashioned infantry attack accompanied by mine clearing parties and covered by artillery and bomber aircraft, with tanks in rear.

On October 6, Montgomery issued his plan. The main attack was allotted to the XXXth Corps (Lieutenant-General Sir Oliver Leese) on a four divisional front of six to seven miles in width. Its task was to cut two corridors through the minefields; the northern south of Tel El Eisa, and the southern across the northern end of the Miteiriya ridge. Once this had been done, the Xth Corps (Lieutenant-General Sir Herbert Lumsden) which comprised the 1st and 10th Armoured Divisions, was to pass through and engage the enemy's armour. In the meantime, to mislead the enemy and pin down the 21st Panzer Division in the extreme south, the XIIIth Corps (Lieutenant-General Sir B. C. Horrocks) and the 7th Armoured Division were to carry out two subsidiary attacks against the enemy's right flank. In all Montgomery had seven infantry divisions, a formation of Free French, a Greek brigade, three armoured divisions and seven armoured brigades; a total of 150,000 men and 1,114 tanks, of which 128 were Grants and 267 Shermans, both armed with 75 mm. guns, and 2,182 pieces of artillery, of which 1,274 were anti-tank guns of various types. The battle was to be opened by a short intense counter-battery bombardment, to be followed, once the infantry advanced, by a bombardment of the enemy's defences. From October 6 to the night of the 23rd the R.A.F. (500 fighters and 200 bombers) was to intensify its attack on the enemy's communications and transport, next, to support the artillery bombardments, and finally to concentrate on the areas in which the enemy's armour was located.

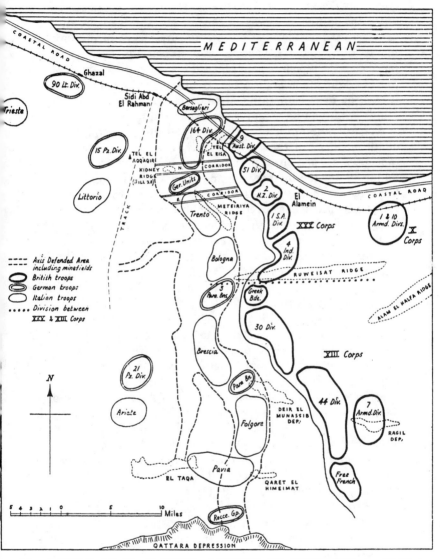

34. BATTLE OF EL ALAMEIN, OCTOBER 23–NOVEMBER 4, 1942

In addition, there was an elaborate cover plan, the aim of which was to make good lack of strategical surprise by deceiving the enemy. The first task was to conceal the various concentrations as much as possible, and the second, by means of dummy hutments, dumps, tanks, vehicles, gun emplacements, water installations and a pipeline, to mislead the enemy about the probable date, and direction, of the attack. Until the invasion of Normandy, it was the most elaborate fake undertaken, and its principle was –hide what you have and reveal what you haven't.[1]

At 9.40 p.m. on October 23, under a brilliant moon, the whole of the artillery of the Eighth Army, nearly 1,000 guns, simultaneously opened fire on the enemy battery positions. Twenty minutes later the infantry advanced,[2] and on the XXXth Corps front by 1 a.m. on the 24th the enemy forward defences were captured without serious loss. Half an hour's halt was then made in order to reorganize, after which the advance was resumed and met with stern opposition. Nevertheless, by 5.30 a.m. the Australians had secured most of their final objective, and the New Zealanders the whole of theirs; but in the centre the 51st Division was held up by strong points in the middle of the northern corridor some 1,500 yards from its final objective, and in the south the 1st South African Division was held up for several hours.

The Xth Corps crossed its starting line at 2 a.m., but the engineers, who worked behind the infantry, were so greatly delayed in lifting the mines that it was not until 6.30 a.m. that the southern corridor was sufficiently cleared to permit the 9th Armoured Brigade, followed by the 10th Armoured Division, to move forward. When the latter did go ahead it gained a footing on the eastern slope of the Miteiriya ridge, but came under such heavy fire that it could proceed no farther. In the meantime, the 2nd Armoured Brigade and the 1st Armoured Division had been seriously delayed by mines and artillery fire in the northern corridor, and it was not until 3 p.m., after an intense artillery bombardment and a combined attack by the 51st Division and the 1st Armoured Division, that the corridor was finally established. These delays put back the timetable and prohibited a break-out on the 24th.

In the south the operations of the XIIIth Corps met with so

---

[1] See *The Camouflage Story*, Geoffrey Barkas (1952), chap. 6.
[2] It is of interest to learn that, in order to help the troops to resect their positions and find out when they had reached their objectives, searchlight beams were directed on the sky (*Operation Victory*, p. 164).

limited a success that Montgomery instructed Horrocks to press
the attack no farther, but to resort to "crumbling" action – local
attacks of attrition – without the 7th Armoured Division being
involved.

On the Axis front the situation rapidly deteriorated, for
although the outposts had fought staunchly, the terrific enemy
bombardment so smashed the network of communications that
command was paralysed. General Stumme went forward at dawn
on the 24th to find out what was happening, and shortly after
had a heart attack and died. When this became known hours
later, General von Thoma, Commander of the Afrika Korps,
assumed the chief command.

When the battle opened, Rommel was in hospital at Semmer-
ing, and on the afternoon of the 24th he was telephoned by
Field-Marshal Keitel, who inquired whether he would be well
enough to return to Africa. He replied that he was, and at 7 a.m.
on the 25th took off for Rome. When he arrived there at 11 a.m.
he was met by General von Rintelen, the German military
attaché, who informed him that only "three issues of petrol
remained in the African theatre," which was equivalent to "300
kilometres worth of petrol per vehicle between Tripoli and the
front."[1] As experience had shown that one issue of petrol was
required for each day of battle, it was obvious to Rommel that
the battle was as good as lost, for without petrol the army could
no longer react to the enemy's movements.

That evening Rommel learnt from von Thoma that ammunition
was so short that Stumme had forbidden the bombardment of the
enemy's assembly positions on the night of October 23–24, and
that on the 24th and 25th the petrol situation had so deteriorated
that major movements were no longer possible, and that only
groups of the 15th Panzer Division had been able to attack;[2] that
they had suffered frightful casualties; and that the division was
now reduced to 31 effective tanks.

In spite of this crippling shortage of means, the Axis forces put
up so determined a defence that Montgomery realized that his
"crumbling" attacks were too costly. He decided to switch the
axis of the offensive more to the north, and instructed the XXXth
Corps to order the 9th Australian Division to direct its offensive

---

[1] *The Rommel Papers*, p. 304.
[2] This is corroborated by Alexander, who writes: "These efforts were not made in
great strength but by battle groups containing some twenty to forty tanks each"
(*Despatches*, p. 854).

toward the coast, to cut off the enemy in the salient which had been created north of the Tel el Eisa ridge. At the same time the 1st Armoured Division was ordered to fight its way westward toward what the British called Kidney ridge and the Germans Hill 28.[1] These attacks resulted in the most savage fighting of the battle. The Australian advance was successful, but the 1st Armoured Division made no appreciable progress until nightfall, because Rommel brought forward the 90th Light Division, elements of the 15th Panzer and Littorio Divisions, and a battalion of Bersaglieri. He writes: "Rivers of blood were poured out over miserable strips of land," and after it had grown dark: "Never before in Africa had we seen such a density of anti-aircraft fire. Hundreds of British tracer shells criss-crossed the sky and the air became an absolute inferno of fire."[2] At length, during the night, the 1st South African and 2nd New Zealand Divisions gained 1,000 yards more depth on the Miteiriya ridge, and the 7th Motor Brigade of the 1st Armoured Division established itself on Kidney ridge.

On October 26 it became apparent to Montgomery that the momentum of his attack was on the wane, and that his break-in area was still hedged in by a strong anti-tank screen. He decided to assume a temporary defensive, and to regroup his forces and build up fresh reserves for a renewal of the offensive in the north. He ordered the 2nd New Zealand Division to be relieved by the 1st South African Division and brought into reserve, and the front of the latter to be taken over by the 4th Indian Division, which was placed under the command of the XIIIth Corps. Further, he instructed the XIIIth Corps to send north the 7th Armoured Divisions and three brigades of infantry.

While these moves were under way, on the night of October 26–27 Rommel moved the 21st Panzer Division north, and on the 27th violently attacked Kidney ridge, but was repulsed at such heavy cost that Montgomery was able to withdraw the 1st Armoured Division and the 24th Armoured Brigade into reserve. At the same time he ordered the 9th Australian Division to attack the enemy in the coastal sector on the night of the 28th–29th. Apparently Rommel expected this attack, and in order to reinforce his left he was compelled to denude his southern front of practically all heavy weapons and German units and to replace

[1] Or "depression," see *Operation Victory*, p. 202.
[2] *The Rommel Papers*, pp. 306–307.

them by part of the Ariete Division which had been engaged in the north.

The Australian attack was launched under cover of an intense bombardment at 10 p.m. on the 29th in the direction of the coastal road between Sidi Abd el Rahman and Tel el Eisa. For six hours the battle raged furiously, and "again and again" writes Rommel, "British bomber formations flew up and tipped their death-dealing loads on my troops, or bathed the country in the brilliant light of parachute flares."[1] So intense was the fighting that, on the morning of the 30th, Rommel began to consider a withdrawal to the Fuka position, which ran from the coast 50 miles west of El Alamein southward to the Qattara Depression. This is the first intimation of a contemplated retreat which, irrespective of the severity of the fighting, was being pressed to the fore by petrol shortage. On October 27 only 70 tons had been delivered by the *Luftwaffe*, and on the 29th Ciano entered in his diary: "Another oil tanker was sunk this evening. . . . Bismarck has learned from Rintelen that Rommel is optimistic about the military quality of the troops, but that he is literally terrified by the supply situation. Just now not only is fuel lacking but also munitions and food."[2]

During the morning of October 29 Montgomery became aware that the 90th Light Division had been moved into the Sidi Abd el Rahman area, and as this indicated that Rommel had reacted to his intent to break out along the coastal road, he decided to shift the axis of his break-through attack southward so that it would fall mainly on the Italians. In order to cover this operation and pin down the 90th Light Division, he ordered the 9th Australian Division to resume its attack on the night of the 30th–31st. In the meantime the 2nd New Zealand Division was to be brought up in readiness to force a gap through the enemy's front a little to the north of the existing northern corridor, and once it had been made the Xth Corps with the 1st, 7th, and 10th Armoured Divisions was to pass through it into the open desert. This operation was code-named "Supercharge". Montgomery writes: The operation "was to get us out into the open country and to lead to the disintegration of Rommel's forces in Egypt. We had got to bring the enemy's armour to battle and get astride his lines of communication. Second New Zealand Division's tasks involved a penetration of some 6,000 yards on a 4,000 yards front. I made it

<hr>

[1] *Ibid.*, p. 312.   [2] *Ciano's Diary*, p. 515.

clear that should 30 Corps fail to reach its final objectives, *the armoured divisions of the 10th Corps were to fight their way through.*"[1]

On October 30, Rommel had the Fuka position reconnoitred, and although he realized that because the Italian infantry had practically no transport they would be no more than a dead weight in the open desert, he nevertheless planned to load as many of them as he could on his transport columns and withdraw them under cover of night, after which his remaining motorized forces were, on a wide front, to beat a fighting retreat to the west. "But first," he writes, "we had to wait for the British move, to ensure that they would be engaged in battle and could not suddenly throw their strength into a gap in our front and then force a break-through."[2]

It came that night, when the Australians resumed their attack toward the coast and, after they had reached it, they turned eastward and cut off the Panzer Grenadiers of the 164th Division in the northern salient. But most of the grenadiers, helped by counter-attacks delivered by elements of the 21st Panzer Division and the 90th Light Division effected their escape.

Montgomery's original intention had been to launch "Supercharge" on the night following this attack, but the situation compelled him to postpone it for 24 hours, and it was not made until 1 a.m. on November 2, after an intense artillery bombardment, reinforced by relays of bombers. Under cover of a creeping barrage two brigades of the 2nd New Zealand Division, supported by the 23rd Armoured Brigade, moved forward on a 4,000-yard front; their task was to drive a lane 4,000 yards in length through the enemy's position, clear it of mines and open a path for the 9th Armoured Brigade, which before dawn was to push forward another 2,000 yards to the track which ran south from Sidi Abd el Rahman, and establish a bridgehead from which the 1st, 7th, and 10th Armoured Divisions could debouch into the open desert and bring on a decisive armoured battle.

The lane was successfully cleared, but when a little before daylight the 9th Armoured Brigade reached the track, it ran into a formidable anti-tank gun screen and suffered a loss of 87 tanks —over 75 per cent. of its strength. In the meantime the 1st Armoured Division debouched and was at once engaged by the Afrika Korps. A fierce tank battle followed around Tel el Aqqaqir. Although Rommel's tanks were outclassed by his enemy's, and

[1] *El Alamein to the River Sangro* (n.d.), p. 22.   [2] *The Rommel Papers*, p. 314.

their 50 mm. and 49 mm. (Italian) guns could make little impression on the British Grant and Sherman machines, the attackers were brought to a halt and the penetration sealed off. Nevertheless, Rommel was under no illusions; he realized that the battle was lost. Not only were there signs of disintegration – units of the Littorio and Trieste Divisions streamed to the rear – but the supply situation, he writes, was "absolutely desperate." During the day his army had expended 450 tons of ammunition, and only 190 tons had been brought to Tobruk by three destroyers. He also states: "The Afrika Korps had only 35 serviceable tanks left."[1]

"This then," writes Rommel, "was the moment to get back to the Fuka line," and especially as "the British had so far been following up hesitantly and that their operations had always been marked by an extreme, often incomprehensible caution."[1] He then made what he acknowledges was a crucial blunder. Early on the morning of November 3 he sent his A.D.C., Lieutenant Berndt, to report direct to Hitler and to ask him for full freedom of action. He did not doubt that it would be given and ordered part of the Italian formations to retreat. At 1.30 p.m. he received Hitler's answer: stand fast and yield not a yard of ground. "As to your troops," it read, "you can show them no other road than that to victory or death."[2] Rommel then halted the withdrawal, and in the evening sent Berndt back to Hitler with a message to inform him that to stand fast meant annihilation.

Early on November 4 Kesselring arrived at Rommel's headquarters and, according to Rommel, said to him, "that the Führer had learnt from his experiences in the East that, in circumstances like these, the front must be held at all costs."[3] In his *Memoirs* Kesselring contradicts this, and writes that he told Rommel, "there could be no question of any such folly, that Hitler's order must be ignored," and that he would accept full responsibility for ignoring it.[4]

When on the morning of November 3 Montgomery learnt of his enemy's withdrawal westward, he asked the Desert Air Force to switch the whole of its weight to the retreating Axis columns. But it was not until nightfall that he ordered the 51st Division and a brigade of the 4th Indian Division to move forward on a

---

[1] *Ibid.*, p. 319.   [2] For the answer in full see *ibid.*, p. 321.   [3] *Ibid.*, p. 323.
[4] *Memoirs*, pp. 135, 136. It would appear that for some time Rommel and Kesselring had been on bad terms. This is supported by Ciano, who notes on September 9, 1942: "Now in Libya they are quarrelling, and Kesselring ran to Berlin to complain about Rommel. They are talking of a possible recall of Rommel" (*Diary*, p. 502).

four-mile front and to break through the southern sector of the enemy's anti-tank screen and win a gap through which he could pass his three armoured divisions. This was successfully done by the morning of the 4th.

Of this, the final action of the battle, Rommel supplies the following dramatic description:

"Enormous dust-clouds could be seen south and south-east of headquarters, where the desperate struggle of the small and in-efficient Italian tanks of XX Corps was being played out against the hundred or so British heavy tanks which had come round their open right flank. I was later told by Major von Luck, whose battalion I had sent to close the gap between the Italians and the Afrika Korps, that the Italians, who at that time represented our strongest motorized force, fought with exemplary courage. Von Luck gave what assistance he could with his guns, but was unable to avert the fate of the Italian Armoured Corps. Tank after tank split asunder or burned out, while all the time a tremendous British barrage lay over the Italian infantry and artillery positions. The last signal came from the Ariete at about 15.30 hours: 'Enemy tanks penetrated south of Ariete. Ariete now encircled. . . .' "[1]

By nightfall the XXth Italian Corps had been destroyed; the Afrika Korps on its left had been broken through and its com-mander, General von Thoma, captured;[2] a 12-mile gap had been driven through the Axis front; and Rommel had no reserves and no petrol. In spite of Hitler's insane order, retreat became com-pulsory, and Rommel tried to save what he could of his army. Next morning a message arrived from Hitler's headquarters to authorize the withdrawal.

That Rommel was ever able to withdraw even his motorized units was firstly because of Montgomery's instinctive cautiousness, and secondly to the reluctance of the R.A.F. to engage in low flying attack, as it had done so successfully after the battle of Vittorio-Veneto. According to General Alexander, the Eighth Army could still muster "very nearly six hundred tanks against eighty German;"[3] it needed only a modicum of audacity by Montgomery to turn his enemy's retreat into a rout. On the second point, de Guingand writes: "With the virtual air superi-ority we possessed, and the state of disorganisation of the enemy,

---

[1] The Rommel Papers, pp. 324–325.

[2] He was taken to Montgomery, who invited him to dine with him in his head-quarters mess (see Operation Victory, pp. 208–209).

[3] Despatches, p. 858. Actually the Germans had 20 serviceable machines.

it looked to us in the Army that here was the 'dream target' for the R.A.F. In the event, the results appeared very disappointing. When setting out along the road between Alamein battlefield and Daba, I had expected to see a trail of devastation, but the visible signs of destroyed vehicles were few and far between. After Daba much better results had been obtained but even here a lot of the vehicles we found had stopped through shortage of petrol."[1] This he rightly attributes to the R.A.F.'s trust in high level bombing instead of low level machine-gunning, with the consequence that training in low flying attack had been neglected. Had it not been for this, his opinion is that Rommel's withdrawal would have been paralysed.

The crux of Rommel's retreat was the pull-out on the night of November 4–5, when chaos reigned, but fortunately for him his methodical opponent, fearful of the difficulties of a night pursuit, halted his forces. "On 5 November," Montgomery informs us, "I regrouped for the pursuit."[2] Thus he lost some 18 invaluable hours. When he had regrouped he decided that the Xth Corps (1st, 7th Armoured and 2nd New Zealand Divisions) were to lead the chase; the XXXth Corps was to come into reserve between El Alamein and Mersa Matruh; and the XIIIth was to clear up the battlefield. In spite of this delay, by an outflanking movement through the desert he nearly cut off his enemy at Mersa Matruh. But on November 6 the van of the 1st Armoured Division was brought to a halt through lack of petrol[3] and Rommel succeeded, as he says, "in forming a fairly firm front and beat off all enemy attacks." He adds that his enemy "still continued to operate with great caution."[4]

It is also stated that "conditions on the road were indescribable. Columns in complete disorder – partly of German, partly of Italian vehicles – choked the road between the minefields [south of Mersa Matruh]. Rarely was there any movement forward and then everything soon jammed up again. Many vehicles were on tow and there was an acute shortage of petrol, for the retreat had considerably increased consumption."[5]

To add to the difficulties of both sides, and more particularly to the pursuers, on the 6th torrential rain made the desert tracks

[1] *Operation Victory*, pp. 209–210. Kesselring writes: "It was lucky for us that the enemy air forces had not yet been schooled to exterminate a retreating enemy albeit there were many opportunities, as, for example, at Halfaya Pass" (*Memoirs*, p. 136).

[2] *El Alamein to the River Sangro*, p. 25.

[3] For Captain Liddell Hart's comments on this see *The Rommel Papers*, p. 342.

[4] *Ibid.*, p. 341.   [5] *Ibid.*, p. 340.

impassable. For 24 hours the pursuit was bogged down. According to Montgomery the rain saved Rommel "from complete annihilation."[1]

At Sollum, in spite of air attacks, Rommel refuelled for another 60 to 100 miles. It was the last petrol in Cyrenaica, and from then on he had to rely on what could be delivered by transport aircraft. He abandoned Tobruk on November 12 and Benghazi on the 19th, and from there he pushed on to his old lair at Mersa el Brega, east of Agheila. On November 25 the van of Montgomery's pursuit came up with him.

Throughout this long and rapid pursuit of some 800 miles in 20 days, Montgomery's principal aim was not to annihilate his enemy, but to capture the ports of Tobruk and Benghazi as eventual supply bases. "This," writes Alexander, "was the task of the pursuit force, which had to be reduced in strength as the advance went on, owing to the increasing difficulties of supply."[2]

This was nothing new, because all previous campaigns in North Africa had shown, as Alan Moorehead observes, that "Nine-tenths of desert warfare is the battle of supply."[3] It is almost incomprehensible why, long before the battle of El Alamein was fought, an efficient air transport service had not been established in Egypt, but the answer is simple enough. It is that R.A.F. Command in England was so obsessed by strategic bombing that it almost entirely overlooked the importance of supply by air. Had it been truly air-minded, it would have appreciated that the revolution effected by the aeroplane was not that it enabled vertical bombardment to supplement or replace horizontal bombardment, but that it turned space into a road and thereby opened an entirely new sphere in logistics.

Montgomery's major supply difficulties would have been solved if there had been an adequate air transport service at his disposal. This, above all other lessons, was the most important of the campaign.

As usual, the casualties of the campaign vary with the recorder. According to Rommel, between October 23 and November 19, under the headings of killed, wounded, and prisoners, the German losses were 1,100, 3,900, and 7,900, respectively, and the Italian

---

[1] *El Alamein to the River Sangro*, p. 25.   [2] *Despatches*, p. 859.

[3] *The End of Africa* (1943), p. 104. On this problem in August 1942, Moorehead writes: "The enemy could get all his replacements and reinforcements three times quicker than we could. Often he used aircraft to carry many of his supplies and reinforcements to the front. They arrived ten times quicker than by land and sea. We don't use troop-carrying aircraft to any extent yet" (*A Year of Battle*, 1943, p. 237).

1,200, 1,600, and 20,000; a total of 35,700.[1] According to Alexander, between October 23 and November 7, the estimated figures for the Axis were 10,000 killed, 15,000 wounded, and over 30,000 prisoners; in all 55,000. The British losses given by him are 13,500 killed, wounded, and missing, and more than 500 tanks disabled.[2]

When, on November 8, Rommel was in full retreat, Operation "Torch" came into being, and an Anglo-American army, commanded by General Dwight D. Eisenhower, landed in North Africa at Casablanca, Oran and Algiers. These landings were respectively made by Major-General George S. Patton, Major-General Lloyd P. Fredenhall, and Lieutenant-General K. A. N. Anderson. The first two comprised American forces and the third British, and the second and third were formed into the First Army under Anderson.

Although the final decision to carry out "Torch" had been made on July 25, no plans to implement it were approved until six weeks later. The reasons for this delay, which prevented an invasion in early October, in time to reach a decision before the winter rains set in, were due to differences between Mr. Churchill and the American Chiefs of Staff on where the second front, so vehemently demanded by Stalin, should be opened. The former favoured the Balkans, in order to check Russian expansion toward the eastern Mediterranean as well as to defeat Germany; the latter pressed for northern France because they accepted Stalin in terms of their own propaganda and the political shape of Europe after the war lay outside their vision. This delay could only have been made good by a surprise occupation of Bizerta and Tunis – the keys of Tunisia – and it was because of this that from the first Admiral Sir Andrew Cunningham, the Naval C.-in-C. of "Torch," had urged a direct blow at the former, or at least at the port of Bone, regardless of the risks of air attacks from Sicily and Sardinia. Strange to say, although the American Chiefs of Staff had urged the opening of a second front in France in September, an incomparably more risky operation, the heavy casualties suffered by a strongly escorted convoy for Malta in August so perturbed them that they were unwilling to sanction a landing east of Oran. Further, because they feared that General Franco might seize Gibraltar and close the Mediterranean, they insisted that part of the invading forces should land at Casablanca.

[1] *The Rommel Papers*, p. 358.   [2] *Despatches*, p. 858.

In his subsequent report to the Combined Chiefs of Staff, as quoted by Chester Wilmot, Cunningham declared: "It is a matter of lasting regret to me that the bolder conception for initial assault in that area [Bone] or even further eastward was not implemented. Had we been prepared to throw even a small force into the eastward ports, the Axis would have been forestalled in their first token occupation and success would have been complete." Wilmot comments: "The consequent prolongation of the African campaign into the late spring of 1943 ruled out the possibility of any cross-Channel invasion that year. Allied strategy was never able to make good the months which were lost through the trans-Atlantic argument about TORCH."[1]

Nevertheless, it would appear that the invasion completely surprised Hitler,[2] although it is difficult to understand why, because as early as October 9 Ciano records in his diary: "All the information and the conversations lead one to conclude that the Anglo-Saxons are preparing to land in force in North Africa, whence, later on, they intend to launch their blows against the Axis. Italy is geographically and logically the first objective."[3]

The landings were only slightly opposed by the French, and on November 11, Admiral Jean Darlan, who was on a visit to Africa, opposed the Vichy Government, ordered the cease fire, and joined the allies.[4] Hitler, although quite unprepared to meet the invasion, reacted with astonishing promptness. He ordered the occupation of Vichy France, which caused the scuttling of most of the French fleet at Toulon, and rushed troops to Tunis and Bizerta by troop carriers. On November 10 two regiments arrived and were followed by a steady stream of troops, which included the 10th Panzer Regiment, the 334th Division, the 501st Tank Battalion, armed with the new Tiger tank,[5] the Hermann Göring Panzer Division, and various Italian formations, the whole under General Juergen von Arnim. If Rommel had received a half of these forces three months earlier a very different picture might have been painted at El Alamein.

After he had secured his bases, Eisenhower's task was to launch

---

[1] *The Struggle for Europe* (1952), p. 114.
[2] See *Behind the Steel Wall*, Arvid Fredborg (1944), p. 149.
[3] *Ciano's Diary*, p. 508. See also p. 520 for November 7.
[4] It may be noted here that the invasion was as flagrant an act of aggression against a neutral country as any perpetrated by Hitler, and Marshal Pétain considered it as such.
[5] It was one of the most formidable tanks of the war; it had frontal armour of 102 mm., an 88 mm. gun and a speed of 18 m.p.h.

35. THE TUNISIAN CAMPAIGN, NOVEMBER 8, 1942–MAY 12, 1943

the First Army eastward to seize the ports of Tunis and Bizerta, and immediately after the landings an advance was made. On November 12 the port of Bone was occupied by a seaborne commando and three days later American and British parachutists were dropped near Tebessa and Souk el Arba. Next, two brigades were rushed forward by all available transport, and after a brush with the Germans they occupied Medjez el Bab on the Medjerda river 25 miles south-west of Tunis on November 25.

The problem of allied supply became acute, and was made worse by torrential rain and air attacks on shipping. By November 29 air supply had beaten road supply. From Algiers to Medjez el Bab was over 300 miles and the best airfields were in Axis hands. While the roads became rivers of mud, the German transport aircraft continued to pour troops into Tunisia. By Christmas the stalemate was complete. Medjez el Bab was held by the First Army although the high ground to the north of it, in particular Jebel el Ahmera (Longstop Hill), was lost. The line extended to the south in a series of posts to Fondouk. Thus the situation remained until mid-February, 1943.

When this stalemate was at its height, on January 14, 1943, Mr. Churchill and President Roosevelt met at Casablanca to discuss the future direction of the war. The staff talks which followed, in which neither personally took part, ranged round the world and, so far as the North African campaign was concerned, the most important decisions were that once it had been brought to a successful conclusion Sicily would be invaded, and when the Eighth Army entered Tunisia General Alexander would become deputy C.-in-C. to Eisenhower, as well as commander of the Eighteenth Army Group, which would comprise all land forces in Tunisia. But these and all other decisions were completely overshadowed by the resolution of the President and the Prime Minister that the surrender of Germany, Italy, and Japan was to be unconditional.

How this fateful decision was arrived at is still obscured. According to Elliott Roosevelt, the President's son, his father first used the phrase "unconditional surrender" at a luncheon on January 23, attended only by the President, Churchill, Hopkins, and himself, and Churchill said: "Perfect! and I can just see how Goebbels and the rest of 'em'll squeal!" Further, Elliott writes that his father commented: "Of course it's just the thing for the Russians. They couldn't want anything better.

Unconditional surrender! Uncle Joe might have made it up himself."[1]

Goebbels – a past-master in propaganda – must have been over-joyed. On March 27, 1942, he had entered in his diary: "If I were on the enemy side, I should from the very first day have adopted the slogan of fighting against Nazism, but not against the German people. That is how Chamberlain began on the first day of the war, but, thank God, the English didn't pursue this line."[2] And, on April 12, 1943: "But, after all, the English are making the same mistake, no doubt at Churchill's instigation. They refrain in every way from saying anything tangible about their war aims. I can only add, thank God; for if they were to put up a peace programme on the lines of Wilson's Fourteen Points they would undoubtedly create great difficulties for us."[3] As to Uncle Joe, though he never had any intention other than the unconditional surrender of Germany, he was not such a simpleton as to inform his enemy of it. A true disciple of Lenin, on February 23, 1943, he publicly said: "It would be ridiculous to identify Hitler's clique with the German people and the German State" and that it was "a stupid lie and senseless slander" to proclaim, as the foreign Press did, that the aim of the Red Army was "to exterminate the German people and destroy the German state."[4]

The President's version differs widely. He says that the state-ment was unpremeditated, and that at a Press conference on January 23 "the thought popped into my mind . . . and the next thing I knew I had said it."[5] Though in Volume IV of his *The Second World War* Churchill is hazy on the whole affair, and acknowledges that later on he made "several erroneous statements about the unconditional surrender incident,"[6] at the time it was crystal clear to him, for on February 11, 1943, he told the House of Commons that: "It was only after full, cold, sober and mature consideration of these facts, on which our lives and liberties cer-tainly depend, that the President, with my full concurrence as agent of the War Cabinet, decided that the note of the Casablanca Conference should be the unconditional surrender of all our foes."[7] This is corroborated by Sherwood, a close associate and friend of Roosevelt, who informs us that the President's "announcement of

[1] *As He Saw It*, Elliott Roosevelt (1946), p. 117.
[2] *The Goebbels Diaries*, p. 102.   [3] *Ibid.*, p. 251.
[4] Quoted from *America's 2nd Crusade*, William Henry Chamberlin (1950), p. 289.
[5] *The White House Papers*, etc., vol. II, p. 693.   [6] P. 616.
[7] *Parliamentary Debates*, Fifth Series, vol. 386, col. 1473.

unconditional surrender was very deeply deliberated," and that it was a true statement of Roosevelt's considered policy and "what Roosevelt was saying was that there would be no negotiated peace . . . no 'escape clauses' provided by another Fourteen Points which could lead to another Hitler."[1] Later, on May 24, 1944, Churchill said much the same in the House of Commons: "But the principle of unconditional surrender . . . will be adhered to so far as Nazi Germany and Japan are concerned, and that principle itself wipes away the danger of anything like Mr. Wilson's Fourteen Points being brought up by the Germans after their defeat claiming that they surrendered in consideration of them."[2] "It apparently did not occur to Churchill," comments Mr. Chamberlin, "that the real cause for criticism was not the Fourteen Points, but the failure to embody these points honestly in the peace settlements."[3]

The implication of this slipshod slogan were even more fatal to the future of the western world than Woodrow Wilson's "self-determination". Here it may be remarked that a statesman should never publicly bind himself to an irreversible decision, and that of all men Mr. Churchill should, from constant practice, have been aware that the essence of successful politics is ability to turn somersaults without loss of face.

Firstly, what unconditional surrender implied was that war was no longer to be accepted as an instrument of creative policy – the establishment of a profitable and stable peace – but that it was to be an instrument of pure destruction. From Casablanca a vulture was unleashed to batten on the entrails of Europe.

Like the Bourbons, Roosevelt and Churchill had learnt nothing and forgotten nothing. Both had before them the example of the abortive peace-making of 1919, from which Hitler had sprung, and although both the American and British psychological warfare experts pressed for a definition of what "unconditional surrender" meant, all their efforts foundered on the rock of Roosevelt's opposition. When, on March 16, 1944, a committee set up by the United States Joint Chiefs of Staff to study the implications of the slogan recommended that the allies should declare that, although war criminals would be punished, there would be no indiscriminate penalization of the German people

[1] The White House Papers, etc., vol. II, pp. 693–694.
[2] Parliamentary Debates, Fifth Series, vol. 400, cols. 783–784.
[3] America's 2nd Crusade, p. 290.

because Germany's cooperation would be needed in the future peace, Roosevelt's reply on April 1 was an "uncompromising negative."[1]

Of all the judgments which have since been passed on this monstrous and momentous slogan, the most powerful is the one made by a statesman the best qualified to make it. In his book *Politics Trials and Errors*, Lord Hankey writes: "It embittered the war, rendered inevitable a fight to a finish, banged the door on any possibility of either side offering terms or opening up negotiations, gave the Germans and Japanese the courage of despair, strengthened Hitler's position as Germany's 'only hope', aided Goebbel's propaganda, and made inevitable the Normandy landing and the subsequent terribly exhausting and destructive advance through North France, Belgium, Luxemburg, Holland, and Germany. The lengthening of the war enabled Stalin to occupy the whole of eastern Europe, to ring down the iron curtain and so to realize at one swoop a large instalment of his avowed aims against so-called capitalism, in which he includes social democracy. By disposing of all the more competent administrators in Germany and Japan this policy rendered treaty-making impossible after the war and retarded recovery and reconstruction, not only in Germany and Japan, but everywhere else. It may also prove to have poisoned our future relations with ex-enemy countries. Not only the enemy countries, but nearly all countries were bled white by this policy, which has left us all, except the United States of America, impoverished and in dire straits. Unfortunately also, these policies, so contrary to the spirit of the Sermon on the Mount, did nothing to strengthen the moral position of the Allies."[2]

On the day this fatuous decision was made, Rommel, who had begun to withdraw from the Mersa Brega position on December 12, abandoned Tripoli to Montgomery and pressed on to Mareth, a naturally strong position on the Gulf of Gabes. There, while Montgomery was occupied in reopening the port of Tripoli, he decided to strike at the American IInd Corps west of Faid in order to clear his rear. On February 14 he smashed through the Americans and on the 20th occupied the Kasserine pass and advanced on Thala and Tebessa to disrupt the communications

[1] See *Persuade or Perish*, Carroll Wallace (1948), p. 320.
[2] Published in 1950, pp. 125–126. Since 1906 Lord Hankey was successively Clerk of the Privy Council, Secretary of the Cabinet and Committee of Imperial Defence, and member of the War Cabinet.

of his enemy's First Army. On the 23rd he was halted by British and American reinforcements and forced to fall back. On this day he was placed in supreme command of all Axis forces in Tunisia, which were formed into two groups, the Fifth Panzer Army in the north, under General von Arnim, and the Italian First Army in the south, which comprised the Afrika Korps and the XXth and XXIst Italian Corps under the Italian General Messe.

When Rommel returned to the Mareth position he decided to attack Montgomery's Eighth Army at Medenine before it could be built up to full strength, and on March 6 he fell upon it, but was severely repulsed. Three days later he temporarily handed over his command to von Arnim and flew by way of Rome to O.K.W. headquarters in Russia to place before Hitler certain plans he had in mind to bring his army back to Europe. It was a fruitless journey, and as he was a very sick man Hitler ordered him to take sick leave before he returned to Africa "for operations against Casablanca"![1]

On March 30 Montgomery attacked Messe at Mareth, and by a superb manœuvre – reminiscent of that of Lee at Chancellorsville – he turned his right flank and forced his withdrawal to the Wadi Akarit position. There, on April 6, he attacked him again and compelled him to fall back on Enfidaville. Next day, near Gafsa, an American patrol joined hands with a patrol of the 4th Indian Division; on the 10th the Eighth Army entered Sfax; Sousse fell on the 12th; and on the 13th contact was again made with Messe at Enfidaville. There the Eighth Army pursuit of 1,800 miles ended.

When, on February 19, General Alexander assumed command of the Eighteenth Army Group, his two most important tasks were to win sufficient of the coastal plain to enable him to establish airfields from which he could throttle his enemy's air communications with Sicily and to destroy the Axis forces as rapidly as possible and gain Tunis and Bizerta as bases for the invasion of Sicily.

By the middle of April he had accomplished the first of these tasks, and as a striking demonstration of what it meant, on April 18, of a large flight of German troop aircraft, over 50 were shot down.[2] The second task remained, and it was a formidable problem, not only because the whole of the enemy forces in Africa were concentrated in Tunisia, but because the mountainous nature of

---

[1] See *The Rommel Papers*, p. 419.   [2] Alexander's *Despatches*, p. 878.

the country made their rapid defeat most difficult. These forces numbered over 200,000 men, the equivalent of 14 divisions, of which three were armoured. In mid-April the position they held ran westward from Enfidaville to south of the defile of Pont du Fahs, thence northward to east of Medjez el Bab, and from there in a north-westerly direction through the rugged mountains of the Kroumirie to the coast some 12 miles east of Tabarka. To destroy these forces Alexander had at his disposal six corps: the Xth and XXXth of the Eighth Army; the Vth and IXth of the First Army; the U.S. IInd Corps; and the French XIXth Corps: in all 300,000 men.[1]

Alexander's plan was to hold by attack the enemy's left flank in the south with the Eighth Army; to strike at his right flank in the north with the United States IInd Corps with the aim of gaining Bizerta; to break through his centre about Medjez el Bab with the First Army and to open up the Medjerda valley and win the road to Tunis. Combined with this operation was a subsidiary northwardly thrust by the French XIXth Corps on Pont du Fahs. When the enemy had been split into two by the central attack, he then planned to wheel the greater part of the First Army southward and "drive the larger body of the enemy on the right flank of the penetration against the line firmly held by the Eighth Army" so as to prevent von Arnim and Messe from withdrawing powerful forces into the Cape Bon peninsula, where they might hold out for a considerable time.[2]

On April 11 Alexander ordered Montgomery to reinforce the First Army with the 1st Armoured Division, and on the following day he chose April 22 to open the general offensive. It was to be carried out as follows: As a preparatory move, the Eighth Army was to attack and carry the Enfidaville position on the night of April 19–20. On April 22 the First Army was to open the way into the Medjerda valley; and on an unfixed date the French XIXth Corps was to advance on Pont du Fahs. Lastly, on April 23, the United States IInd Corps was to attack on the Sidi Nsir road with the pass of Chouigui its final objective.

The Eighth Army attack was launched at 9.30 p.m. on April 19 and Enfidaville was carried, but to its north opposition was so fierce that, on the 21st, Montgomery decided to abandon his

---

[1] General Martel (*Our Armoured Forces*, 1945, p. 237) says that Alexander had 1,400 tanks, and his enemy 120.
[2] Alexander's *Despatches*, p. 878.

main thrust and concentrate on forcing the coastal defile. When he gained wind of what was in progress, on the following night von Arnim forestalled the First Army advance by a violent attack between Medjez el Bab and Goubellat, but it failed in its aim and on the morning of April 22 the First Army opened its offensive. Again fierce fighting followed, during which von Arnim concentrated the bulk of his armoured forces against his enemy, and it was not until April 26 that the 78th Division of the Vth Corps stormed and occupied Jebel el Ahmera (Longstop Hill), the key to the Medjerda valley. In the meantime, on the 25th, a German withdrawal from south of Pont du Fahs enabled the French XIXth Corps to advance to within striking distance of that defile. While the main battle in the centre was in progress, the United States IInd Corps made important advances on the whole front from the Medjerda to the coast, and on April 30, the United States 34th Division, after most bitter fighting, captured the formidable Jebel Tahent (Hill 609), north-east of Sidi Nsir, which opened the road to Mateur.[1]

Since the holding operation of the Eighth Army had proved a failure, Alexander sought to increase the striking power of the First Army and on April 30 he ordered Montgomery to transfer to it the 7th Armoured Division, the 4th Indian Division, and the 201 Guards Brigade, the original units of the Western Desert Force which had won the battle of Sidi Barrani. These were allotted to the IXth Corps, with which Alexander intended to deliver his decisive attack up the Medjez-Massicault road straight on Tunis. On its right it was to be supported by the 1st Armoured Division operating in the Goubellat area, and before its advance the Vth Corps, on its left, was to capture Jebel Bou Aoukaz in order to free its left flank. After this, the 46th Division on the north side of the Medjerda, and the 1st and 78th Divisions on the south side – all three of the Vth Corps – were to keep open the corridor through the enemy's position once it had been opened by the IXth Corps. Farther to the east, to pin down the enemy forces, the French XIXth Corps was to attack Jebel Zaghouan, and the Eighth Army was to carry out local attacks north of Enfidaville. Throughout these operations, the United States IInd Corps was to continue its advance on Bizerta.

The attack of the IXth Corps was fixed for May 6. It was to be

---

[1] In *A Soldier's Story* (1951), p. 87, General Omar N. Bradley gives an interesting account of the part played by tanks in the mountain warfare operation.

made on a frontage of 3,000 yards by the 4th British Division on the right and the 4th Indian Division on the left, followed respectively by the 6th and 7th Armoured Divisions. The first two were to advance under cover of an intense artillery bombardment, supplemented by bomber aircraft, to a depth of 6,000 yards, and to establish a mine-free corridor. Immediately afterward, the two armoured divisions were to forge straight ahead to within 12 miles of Tunis. No mopping up was to be done by them, nor were they to attempt to roll up the enemy to the right and left of them. Alexander hoped to seize Tunis before his enemy could organize its defence. "If these instructions," he writes, "could be strictly followed, I felt confident of turning the German 'blitzkrieg' technique on its inventors and preventing an African 'Dunkirk'."[1]

On the afternoon of May 5, after a stiff fight, the 1st Division of the Vth Corps stormed Jebel Bou Aoukaz, and at 3.30 a.m., the 4th British and 4th Indian Divisions advanced, supported by 400 guns and the Tactical Air Force.[2] The weight of the attack was too much for the defenders and at 11.30 a.m. the two divisions reached their objective. Immediately afterward, the 6th and 7th Armoured Divisions moved forward, brushed aside a few tanks of the 15th Panzer Division, burst through the enemy anti-tank screen, and by nightfall had occupied Massicault. In the meantime, under the constant pressure of the United States IInd Corps, the enemy front in the north had caved in and on May 2 the 1st United States Armoured Division captured Mateur. On May 7 the 34th Division of the IInd Corps broke through the Chouigui pass and made contact with the left of the First Army.

At first light on May 7, the 6th and 7th Armoured Divisions moved forward from Massicault; at 8.30 a.m. the village of St. Cyprien was taken; and at 2.45 p.m. the 11th Hussars and the 1st Derbyshire Yeomanry entered Tunis. Bizerta was immediately after occupied by tanks of the U.S. IInd Corps.

As soon as the situation was under control, the 7th Armoured Division was directed northward on Protville according to plan, and the 1st United States Armoured Division was directed from Mateur eastward on the same town; between them they entrapped the remnants of three German divisions, which surrendered on May 9. At the same time, in order to cut off the Axis forces

---

[1] *Despatches*, p. 881.
[2] 2,146 sorties were flown. See *Report of the Commanding General of the* [*U.S.*] *Army Air Forces*, 4th January, 1944, pp. 43–44.

between the First and Eighth Armies and prevent them from seeking refuge within the Cape Bon peninsula, the 6th Armoured Division, followed by the 4th Division, swung down the road from Tunis leading to the peninsula while the 1st Armoured Division came up on its right flank from Goubellat.

The first obstacle encountered was the Hamman Lif defile at the bottom of the Gulf of Tunis; an exceedingly strong position held by the Hermann Göring Division and some 88 mm. guns. Here the 6th Armoured Division was held up until the morning of May 10, when they by-passed a body of tanks through the edge of the surf and the position was turned. What followed next is graphically described by Alan Moorehead. "They broke clean through to Hammamet inside the next ten hours," he writes. "They roared past German airfields, workshops, petrol and ammunition dumps and gun positions. They did not stop to take prisoners – things had gone far beyond that. If a comet had rushed down the road it could hardly have made a greater impression. The Germans were now entirely dazed. Wherever they looked British tanks seemed to be hurtling past. . . . The German generals gave up giving orders since they were completely out of touch with the people to whom they could give orders, who were diminishing every hour. . . . In a contagion of doubt and fear the German army turned tail and made up the Cap Bon roads looking for boats. When on the beaches it became apparent to them at last that there were no boats – nor any aircraft either – the army became a rabble."[1]

Alexander Clifford writes: "The brain and nerve-centre of the army was paralysed, and nothing could function coherently any more"[2]—it was a repetition of the collapse of France.

On May 12 and 13 General von Arnim and Field-Marshal Messe surrendered; 250,000 Germans and Italians laid down their arms and only 663 escaped by sea. At 2.15 p.m. on the 13th, Alexander sent the following message to Mr. Churchill:

"Sir, it is my duty to report that the Tunisian campaign is over. All enemy resistance has ceased. We are masters of the North African shores."[3]

After two and a half years of tilting up and down North Africa, the decisive battles of El Alamein and Tunis ended the first victorious allied campaign of the war. A base had been established

---

[1] *The End of Africa* (1943), p. 201.
[2] *Three Against Rommel* (1943), p. 411.   [3] *Despatches*, p. 884.

from which Italy could directly be attacked and a road to central Europe opened. All that remained for America and Britain to do was with the utmost speed to exploit their success and drive Italy out of the war.

The first step taken to effect this was the invasion of Sicily on July 10, which on July 24 led to a *coup d'état* in Rome of the Fascist Grand Council, the fall of Mussolini, and the appointment by King Victor Emmanuel of Marshal Pietro Badoglio as head of State. As this portended proposals of peace, the western allies should have done their utmost to foster them, but their policy of unconditional surrender gripped them like a vice. In a speech on July 26 President Roosevelt proclaimed: "Our terms to Italy are still the same as our terms to Germany and Japan – 'Unconditional Surrender'. We will have no truck with Fascism in any way, shape, or manner. We will permit no vestige of Fascism to remain."[1] Because in the United States it was held that the Badoglio government was Fascist, its recognition was violently opposed.

In spite of the President's irrevocable dictum, on the same day he telegraphed Mr. Churchill: "It is my thought that we should come as close as possible to unconditional surrender, followed by good treatment of the Italian populace."[2] This soft pedalling of principle would appear to have been because General Eisenhower and the Combined Chiefs of Staff "recognized the enormous possible advantage of having any Italian Government, regardless of its political colouration, which would have the authority to deliver an immediate surrender."[3] But three days later Mr. Churchill telephoned the President that it was not for the allies "to broadcast armistice terms to the enemy." It was for their Government "to ask formally for an armistice on the basis of our principle of unconditional surrender."[4] This latter remark was a piece of nonsense, for according to Article 36 of the Hague Peace Convention of 1907, an armistice is a suspension of military operations by mutual agreement, which can be terminated according to its terms – it is not a capitulation.

A wrangle followed on what was meant by "unconditional surrender." On August 3, the Marquis d'Ayeta, an envoy of Badoglio, arrived in Lisbon to inform the British Ambassador

---

[1] *The White House Papers*, etc., vol. II, p. 738.
[2] *The Second World War*, Churchill (1952), vol. v, p. 51.
[3] *The White House Papers*, etc., vol. II, p. 739.
[4] *The Second World War*, vol. v, p. 56.

there that the whole of Italy longed for peace and was willing to cooperate with the allies. Three days later another envoy, Signor Berio, approached the British representative in Tangier with authority to open negotiations on terms. Mr. Eden, British Foreign Minister, sent a message to Mr. Churchill – then at sea on his way to Quebec – to ask: "Should we not reply that . . . the Badoglio Government must as a first step notify us that Italy surrenders unconditionally?" And should it comply, "we should then inform them of the terms on which we should be prepared to cease hostilities against Italy." On the margin of this message Churchill wrote in red ink, "Don't miss the bus," and replied: "Merely harping on 'unconditional surrender' with no prospect of mercy held out even as an act of grace may well lead to no surrender at all."[1] It is a pity he had not thought of this at Casablanca.

Thus the wrangle continued, envoys flitted forward and backward between Rome and Lisbon and Madrid, until at length, on September 2, in an olive grove near Syracuse, what were known as "short armistice terms," in other words "military terms of surrender," were signed by General Castellano on behalf of Italy, and by General Bedell Smith, Eisenhower's Chief of Staff, for the allies. Lastly, on September 5, Mr. Churchill informed Stalin of this political triumph, that the toe of Italy had been invaded on September 3, and that the dominant aim was "to kill Germans and make Italians kill Germans on the largest scale possible."[2] Unfortunately for the western allies the wrangling gave Hitler over four weeks to pour reinforcements into Italy. The first fruits of unconditional surrender were that the gilt was rubbed off the El Alamein and Tunis gingerbread, and that the offspring of these decisive battles was the most unprofitable allied campaign of the war.

But their immediate results were highly profitable to the two western allies because the conquest of North Africa had reopened the Mediterranean and so released millions of tons of allied shipping; it had doubled the area of occupied Europe which could be threatened and thereby had added vastly to the liabilities of Hitler's negative front; it tested the requirements of big amphibious operations; and it smoothed the rough edges off American and British cooperation and welded together their respective fighting forces.

[1] *Ibid.*, vol. v, p. 91.　　[2] *Ibid.*, vol. v, p. 99.

The foundations of the Stalingrad campaign

The situation which faced Hitler in the spring of 1942 was very different from that of nine months before. Then his prestige was at its height; his armies swept victoriously into Russia, England was isolated, and America, although truculent, was still nominally neutral. Now he was faced by a war on two fronts, the one thing he had dreaded most, and to disentangle himself from this disastrous situation it should have been apparent to him that, since his fatal policy had antagonized the subjugated peoples under Muscovite rule and had bereft him of all hope of the subjugation of Russia by internal revolution, he was left with two alternatives: either to destroy Russia's military power or to render it impotent before the Americans and British could develop their full fighting strength. The first he had already attempted and had failed, and as the Russians had unlimited space in which to fall back, which carried with it a progressive weakening of the German armies by lengthening their communications through hostile country, there was no reason to suppose that in 1942 it would prove more successful than it had in 1941. Hitler was left with the second alternative. What did it demand?

Firstly, the occupation of Moscow to cripple Russian communications; secondly, the occupation of Vologda to block the ingress of lend-lease supplies from Archangel; and thirdly, the occupation of Kirov, Kazan, Ulanovsk, Kuibishev, and Saratov to sever the Russian armies west of the Urals from the resources and manpower of Asiatic Russia. In brief, he had to establish a defensive line along the upper and middle Volga, approximately as laid down in Directive No. 21 of December 18, 1940. Could this be done in 1942, then a situation would be created in the east in which Russia's fighting power would progressively so weaken that, by the time America and Britain could take the field in strength, it would be possible to leave a minimum of forces in Russia and concentrate a maximum in the west. But Hitler did not implement this policy. The primary idea of the plan he adopted was to strengthen his military potential by the seizure of Russian oil, and the secondary consideration was that the enemy would be weakened because of its loss.

The plan decided on was his own, for since his failure to take Moscow Hitler seldom consulted his General Staff. He exaggerated the capacity of his own armies as grossly as he underrated that of his enemy, and when a statement was read to him in which it was pointed out that Stalin was still able to muster 1,500,000 men in the region north of Stalingrad, besides 500,000 in the Caucasus, according to Halder, "he flew at the man who was reading with clenched fists and foam in the corners of his mouth, and forbade him to read such idiotic twaddle." Halder remarks: ". . . his decisions had ceased to have anything in common with the principles of strategy . . . as they had been recognized for generations past. They were the product of a violent nature following its momentary impulses, a nature which acknowledged no bounds to possibility, and which made the wish the father of the deed."

He was profoundly influenced in this by his leading industrialists and economic advisers, who constantly impressed upon him that, unless the Caucasian oilfields were won, the Reich would collapse. Without further ado he accepted this at face value and decided that the occupation of these oilfields should be the goal of his 1942 campaign.

He was easily persuaded, for since the war began oil had been his nightmare. In 1941 his total supply had amounted to 8,929,000 tons, and he had only been able to carry on the war by withdrawing 1,140,000 tons from his reserves, which, excluding the needs of the navy, had by the end of 1941 fallen to 797,000 tons – barely one month's supply. In 1941 the yield of the Rumanian oilfields provided him with some 5,500,000 tons, half of which was earmarked for Rumania and her army, and synthetic production was about the same. Together they were insufficient to wage an extensive campaign on two fronts; sufficiency of oil was indeed a vital problem. Nevertheless the fact remained that wars are based on strategy, and although the foundations of strategy are in part economic – food, coal, oil, iron – economic security cannot compensate for the lack of military sanity. Hitler should have thought of this before he went to war, but once he had crossed the Rubicon, there was little chance of winning it were strategy subordinated to economics.

According to Goebbels who, on March 20, 1942, discussed the situation with Hitler, the latter had "a perfectly clear plan for the coming spring and summer. He does not want," he writes, "to overextend the war. His aims are the Caucasus, Leningrad, and Moscow. If these aims are attained, he is determined, whatever the circumstances, to end the campaign at the beginning of next October and to go into winter quarters early. He intends possibly to construct a gigantic line of defence and to let the eastern campaign rest there." On this Goebbels comments: "Possibly this may mean a hundred years' war in the East, but that need not worry us."

Save for local pressure on Leningrad, Hitler decided to assume the defensive on the whole front, except in the south, and whatever he may have said to Dr. Goebbels he had no intention to take Moscow. His aim was to occupy the Caucasus up to the line Batum–Baku and, in order to cover this operation, to establish a defensive front along the Don from Voronezh to Stalingrad. To accomplish this, he decided to break through the Russian front between Taganrog and Kursk.

This plan was radically unsound. Not only were the troops at his disposal – more especially German – insufficient simultaneously to carry out both operations, but to stretch the covering forces over a distance of 360 miles was to offer an enormous flank to Russian attack. If the Russians broke through this vulnerable flank and occupied Rostov the whole of the German forces in Caucasia would be cut off from their base.

It would appear that, when he came to these decisions, Hitler took no notice whatsoever of the Russian railway communications leading to the Voronezh–Stalingrad front, of which Saratov was their strategic centre. Saratov was linked to Moscow by rail; to the Ural industrial region by rail and river; to Astrakhan by rail east of the Volga; and to Chkalov on the river Ural by rail, near which a pipe-line ran to the north Caspian oilfields. Troops, munitions, fuel, and supplies could therefore be poured into the Saratov area from Moscow, Archangel, Siberia, Kazakh, Caucasia and Persia. Further, the lateral railways Tula–Penza–Syzran, Michurinsk–Tambov–Saratov, Tambov–Balashov–Kamishin, Voronezh–Rojestvenskoe–Stalingrad, when coupled with the longitudinal railways Moscow–Voronezh and Gorki–Penza–Bala-shov, made the area north of the Don well suited for the concentratior. of troops and supplies.

South of Stalingrad, Astrakhan played a similar though subordinate part. By way of Saratov it was linked by rail to the whole of unoccupied Russia, and by way of the Caspian to Persia and thence to the outer world; for in the south the Caspian Sea played the same strategic role as that of the White Sea in the north. Stalingrad was of little strategic importance; it was too distant to cover the forces operating in Caucasia, and it did not block the Volga any more efficiently than did Saratov. In any case, the Volga was ice-bound for five to six months in the year.

By the spring of 1942 Hitler had under his command 232 divisions, of which 171 were German and 61 satellite. The former consisted of 134 infantry, 24 armoured, and 13 motorized divisions, and the latter of 22 Rumanian, 10 Italian, 10 Hungarian, 17 Finnish, one Spanish and one Slovak, of which four were armoured. Though numerically a much larger army than that of 1941, it was weaker. The satellite divisions were indifferently armed and equipped – according to Antonescu, the Rumanians were next to worthless – and the strength of the German infantry divisions had been reduced from nine to six battalions, and only 10 of the original 20 armoured divisions had been brought up to full strength, because priority had been given to submarine construction.

Because of the enormous losses suffered in 1941, the Soviet Army of 1942 was largely composed of Asiatics, the tough Hunnish peoples of central Asia who centuries before had followed Attila and Genghis Khan. Although of low intelligence and almost wholly illiterate, they possessed immense natural tenacity and endurance. They not only replenished their supplies from the regions through which they advanced, but also their numbers; all able-bodied men found *en route* were conscripted straight into the front line units. Field-Marshal von Manstein says that "the dynamic of the Red Army was the same as that of the revolutionary armies of France, a combination of fanaticism and terror," and General Dittmar considered that the Russians' chief asset was "the soulless indifference of the troops" which was "something more than fatalism."

According to Field-Marshal von Rundstedt, none of the Russian generals of 1941 was any good; but by the spring of 1942, the war had winnowed away much of the chaff and not a few of the higher commanders were as efficient as the German, particularly Marshal Zhukov, who in 1921–1923 had studied strategy under General von Seeckt in Germany. Nevertheless, in order to fit the low intelligence of the bulk of the troops, tactical plans and operations had to be kept simple and rigid, and in consequence were easy to dislocate. According to Manstein, the Soviet Army was more effective in advance than in retreat. The vast numbers it could bring into the field enabled it simultaneously to attack at a large number of places; wave after wave of infantry advanced until a weak spot was found, when the armoured units would break through and the infantry follow.

In 1942 the Russian armoured formations were manned by picked troops, and the Russian T.34 tank, in design simple to the point of crudity, was superior to any German tank before the introduction of the Panther and Tiger in 1943. Cavalry were still employed in large numbers and were particularly useful during the spring thaws. The transport and supply services remained indifferent, and in General Geyr von Schweppenburg's opinion, had it not been for the thousands of lend-lease trucks which, in 1942, began to pour in from America, the Russian armies would never have survived the 1942 campaign. Against this must be set the statements of a considerable number of German generals made to Captain Liddell Hart after the war. They held that "the Russians' greatest asset was the way they could do without normal supplies," and General von Manteuffel told Liddell Hart that "The advance of a Russian Army is something that Westerners can't imagine. Behind the tank spearheads rolls on a vast horde, largely mounted on horses. The soldier carries a sack on his back, with dry crusts of bread and raw vegetables collected on the march from the fields and villages. The horses eat the straw from the house roofs – they get very little else. The Russians are accustomed to carry on for as long as three weeks in this primitive way, when advancing. You can't stop them, like an ordinary army, by cutting their communications, for you rarely find any supply columns to strike."[1]

Although Halder was still Chief of Staff, the 1942 plan of campaign was entirely Hitler's, and in April he reshuffled his forces. Army Group South was disbanded and replaced by Army Groups A and B. The former was commanded by Field-Marshal List; it consisted of the First Panzer Army (General von Kleist), the Seventeenth Army (General Ruoff), supported by the Fourth Air Fleet, and its task was to conquer the Caucasus. The latter, whose task was to cover the northern flank of Army Group A by

---

[1] This cannot have applied to the Russian armoured and motorized forces.

the occupation of the Stalingrad area, was commanded by Field-Marshal von Bock, and it comprised the Second Army (General von Weichs), the Fourth Panzer Army (General Hoth), and the Sixth Army (General von Paulus), supported by Luftwaffe Don Command. Behind these two groups in second *échelon* were the Second Hungarian, Eighth Italian, and Third Rumanian Armies, and apart from them in the Crimea General von Manstein's Eleventh Army, which included the Fourth Rumanian Army. In all, 60 German divisions, of which 10 were armoured and six motorized, and 43 satellite divisions were allotted to the southern front.

The combined operation of the two army groups was code-named "*Blau*" (Blue), and the campaign was to be carried out on the following lines:

From the south of Kursk, the Fourth Panzer Army of Army Group B was to advance on Voronezh, but not to occupy it. Followed by the Sixth Army, it was then to wheel south-eastward and move down the right bank of the Don toward Stalingrad, and as these two armies did so, the Second German, Second Hungarian, Eighth Italian, and Third Rumanian Armies were to take over the defence of the river to its bend west of Stalingrad; later the Fourth Rumanian Army was to hold the front south of Stalingrad. Under cover of this manœuvre, Army Group A was to advance from between Taganrog and Iyzum toward the lower Don about Rostov. The First Panzer Army was to pave the way for the Seventeenth Army, which was to join in the offensive once the former had crossed the Don, and by the Eleventh Army after it had reconquered the Crimea.

It is opportune here briefly to describe Hitler's system of issuing orders, because it led to endless confusion. Each evening the approximate positions of the forward troops were sent by wireless to Army Headquarters, and thence transmitted to Supreme Headquarters and placed before Hitler during the following morning, when orders for the day were issued. As they seldom reached the front line troops until late in the afternoon, by when their positions had frequently completely changed, as often as not they were inapplicable, and when they were not obeyed violent altercations followed. Compared with Napoleon's system that of Hitler was amateurish in the extreme.[1]

On May 8, 1942, the campaign in the Crimea was reopened by

[1] See vol. II, p. 414.

Manstein's Eleventh Army, which consisted of seven German and six Rumanian divisions; the defences around Kerch were broken through, and on May 15 the town of Kerch was occupied. In spite of the numerical superiority of the Russians, again their losses were phenomenal, for Manstein captured 150,000 prisoners, 1,133 guns, and 255 tanks. On June 2, he laid siege to Sebastopol, and after a month's severe fighting the fortress and 100,000 Russians surrendered to him.

In the meantime, Marshal Timoshenko opened a violent offensive north-east and south-east of Kharkov on May 12. He broke through the German defences and next struck at Krasnograd; then his momentum petered out. On May 17 he was counter-attacked by Kleist's First Panzer Army, supported by the Seventeenth and Sixth Armies, and was forced back. He was unable to withdraw his troops around Izyum and on May 26 they were surrounded. On the following day they were forced to capitulate. This abortive spoiling attack, which had little influence on the German preparations, cost Timoshenko 240,000 men captured, 2,026 guns, and 1,249 tanks. In subsequent operations in June around Volchansk, Izyum, and Kupyansk the Germans captured another 38,000 Russians.[1]

Understandably Hitler was elated by these captures, but unfortunately for him they would seem to have convinced him that he was right and his generals were wrong; that he had nothing further to fear from the Russians, and that by October Operation *"Blau"* would bring the war in the east to a victorious end.

[1] All these figures are from German sources, and therefore may be exaggerated.

CHAPTER 14

The Battle of Stalingrad, 1942-1943

On June 28, 1942, the Stalingrad campaign was opened by a sudden advance of the Second Army and the Fourth Panzer Army of Army Group B from about Kursk eastward on Voronezh. It came as a complete surprise to the Russians who, because of the lack of roads eastward of the line Kurzk–Izyum, did not expect a major German advance in that area, and in consequence the line of the Oskol river was held by little more than outposts. On June 30, the Sixth Army struck eastward from between Bielgorod and Volchansk and the advance of all three armies was so rapid that it appeared to Hitler that Russian resistance was at an end. On July 3 the advanced guards of the Second Army and Fourth Panzer Army neared Voronezh, and those of the Sixth, which by then had crossed the Oskol, pressed toward Korotoyak on the Don. Voronezh was reached on July 5, where the first severe fighting was experienced; but as Hitler did not intend to occupy the town, he ordered the Fourth Panzer Army, when relieved by the Second Army, to wheel southward down the Don, while the Sixth Army wheeled to the south-east on Rossosh.

No sooner were these movements under way than, on July 9, from between Izyum and Kupyansk the First Panzer Army set out down the northern bank of the Donetz, took Lisiachiansk, and on the 10th, when it approached Millerovo, the Fourth Panzer Army occupied Kantemirovka. The aim of these movements was to come down in rear[1] on the Russian communications in the Rostov area, and simultaneously to cover the advance of the First Panzer Army from the north and east. Because an attempt to enter Voronezh caused a delay which annoyed Hitler, on July 13 Field-Marshal von Bock was relieved of his command and replaced by General von Weichs, and the command of the Second Army was given to General von Salmuth.

General Halder describes the situation on July 16: "North of Kamiensk all the way to the Millerovo area a zone of confused

---

[1] *The Halder Diaries*, July 11, 1942, vol. VII, p. 347.

36. THE STALINGRAD CAMPAIGN, 1942-1943

battles, in which the enemy elements, squeezed between First Panzer Army from the west and Fourth Panzer Army from the north, are trying to break out in several groups in all directions. Meanwhile, east of this seething mass, the Grossdeutschland and 24th Armoured Divisions are racing to the Don without serious check by the enemy."[1]

The Russians abandoned Voroshilovgrad on July 17 and fell back to the south-east hotly pursued by the Seventeenth Army, which had advanced from north of Taganrog. On the same day the First Panzer Army crossed the Donetz at Kamiensk, and west of the Donetz in the north the Fourth Panzer Army moved down the Don with the Sixth Army on its western flank; neither met opposition. It was also on the 17th that Hitler took a step which went far to ruin the campaign. Fearful that von Kleist's First Panzer Army would not prove sufficiently powerful to force crossings over the lower Don he ordered Hoth to move the bulk of his Fourth Panzer Army to his support and thereby left the Sixth Army single-handed to continue its advance on Stalingrad. Halder strongly opposed this change.[2] But Hitler would not listen, although it should have been apparent to him that if the pace of the advance could be maintained Stalingrad was likely to fall before it could be put into a state of defence; and that the momentum of the Sixth Army depended on the Fourth Panzer Army's cooperation. Thus, again by a major diversion of his forces, Hitler ruined his campaign. As has been seen, in 1941 he failed to take Moscow because he diverted Guderian's armour toward Kiev, and his failure to take Stalingrad was primarily because of the diversion of Hoth's Panzer Army from the middle to the lower Don.

The battle for the crossings of the Don was vigorously pushed and on July 19 the advanced guard of Hoth's Fourth Panzer Army won a bridgehead over the river at Tsymlanskaya. Two days later Kleist's First Panzer Army came down on Rostov from the north and, according to Halder, broke through "a totally demoralized enemy."[3] On July 22, the Russian inner defences of Rostov collapsed and the Seventeenth Army crossed the Don in four places. The Sixth Army had continued its advance on Stalingrad and on July 24 approached the bank of the Don to the west of the city.

[1] *Ibid.*, July 16, 1942, vol. vii, p. 352.   [2] *Ibid.*, July 23, 1942, vol. vii, p. 358.
[3] *Ibid.*, July 21, 1942, vol. vii, p. 356.

By July 23 the confusion caused by the concentration of the two Panzer armies in and to the east of the Rostov area caused Hitler to assemble a conference at which in a violent scene he threw the entire blame for the muddle on his General Staff. Halder wrote in his diary: "The situation is getting more and more intolerable. There is no room for any serious work. This 'leadership', so-called, is characterized by a pathological reacting to the impressions of the moment and a total lack of any understanding of the command machinery and its possibilities (*i.e.*, Hitler is incapable of grasping that his constant interference is throwing everything in disorder)."[1] In spite of Hitler's interference the Russians had shown such incapacity to stay the German advance that the campaign had been an unqualified success. Their situation was so critical that the Kremlin, through its agents in America and Britain, launched a frenzied propaganda campaign in which the immediate opening of a second front in the west was demanded.[2] In August this led to the abortive British landing at Dieppe, which nevertheless so startled Hitler that he ordered two of his best divisions to be transferred to the west.[3]

When driven back from the lower Don the Russians withdrew to the river Manich, but were rapidly ejected by Kleist's First Panzer Army, which on July 27 began to fan out on a wide front in three columns toward the Black Sea; one on Voroshilovsk, one on Maikop, and, in between, one on Armavir.

By the end of July the situation was as follows: In the north the Sixth Army, because of lack of fuel and ammunition,[4] and shortage of armour due to the diversion of the Fourth Panzer Army, was, after violent fighting, halted on the Don immediately west of Kalach; the Fourth Panzer Army had reached Proletarskaya on the Novorossisk–Stalingrad railway; and in the south the First Panzer Army advanced on the line Maikop–Voroshilovsk, while the Seventeenth Army, and the Fourth Rumanian Army from the Crimea, after they had thrown the enemy into "wild rout,"[5] moved on Novorossisk and Tuapse.

On July 30, Hitler again made a fateful decision, through Jodl

---

[1] *Ibid.*, July 23, 1942, vol. VII, p. 358.
[2] See *Hitler's Defeat in Russia*, General W. Anders (1953), p. 105.
[3] See *The Other Side of the Hill*, edit. by B. H. Liddell Hart (1951), p. 313.
[4] Halder records, on July 25 (vol. VII, p. 360) "Lack of fuel and ammunition"; and on July 29 (vol. VII, p. 362) ". . . fuel supply to Sixth Army is not functioning. Insufferable tirades about other people's mistakes, which are nothing but duly executed orders of his [Hitler's] own congestion of armoured forces in Rostov area."
[5] *Ibid.*, July 30, 1942, vol. VII, p. 363.

he announced at a conference of his generals: ". . . that the fate of the Caucasus will be decided at Stalingrad, and that in view of the importance of the battle it would be necessary to divert forces from Army Group A to Army Group B . . . that the first Panzer Army must at once wheel south and southwest to cut off the enemy now being pushed back step by step from the Don by Seventeenth Army, before he reaches the Caucasus." Halder writes: "This is rankest nonsense. This enemy is running for dear life and will be in the northern foot hills of the Caucasus a good piece ahead of our armour and then we are going to have another unhealthy congestion of forces before the enemy front."[1]

To comply with the first item of these instructions, on August 1 Hoth's Panzer Army was returned to Army Group B[2] and ordered to move north-eastward along the Novorossisk–Stalingrad railway. It was little opposed at first and its advance was rapid. On August 3 it occupied Kotelnikovo, but from then on it was so fiercely opposed that on August 9 it was forced on the defensive and in consequence had to abandon all idea that it could seize Stalingrad single-handed.

While Hoth was thus engaged the Sixth Army resumed its offensive and, in spite of strong opposition, it gained a crossing over the Don; drove the Russians out of Kalach; and set out on its final lap towards Stalingrad. On August 23 it reached the Volga north of Stalingrad and occupied the northern outskirts of the city. Immediately afterward it closed the gap between the Don and the Volga – that is, from Kachalinskaya to Dubovka – and on September 2 established contact with Hoth at Kotelnikovo. On September 12 its commander, General von Paulus, received an order from Hitler to carry Stalingrad by storm on the 15th.

In the south, Army Group A advanced against little resistance at high speed; the Seventeenth Army on Krasnodar and Novorossisk; and the First Panzer Army on Voroshilovsk and Maikop. On August 3 Armavir and Voroshilovsk were captured, and on the 9th, when the Seventeenth Army seized Krasnodar, the First Panzer Army reached the Maikop oilfields, and on the following day its eastern column captured Piatigorsk. According to Colonel Léderrey – quoting Krylov's *Journal* – Kleist's rapid advance was partly because of the mutiny of the Kuban Cossack divisions under

[1] *Ibid.*, July 30, 1942, vol. VII, p. 363.
[2] *Ibid.*, August 1, 1942, vol. VII, p. 365.

General Lvov. Later, 15,000 of their officers and men were sent to Astrakhan and of every three, one was shot.[1] On August 22 men of von Kleist's army hoisted the swastika flag on the summit of Mount Elbrus (18,526 ft.),[2] and on the 25th Mosdok on the Terek river was captured. On September 6, Novorossisk, the last Soviet naval base on the Black Sea, fell to the Seventeenth Army.

In spite of these achievements, since the middle of August the momentum of Army Group A had rapidly declined, and on September 9 Keitel informed Halder that Hitler had decided to remove Field-Marshal List from his command.[3] He was succeeded by General von Kleist, and the command of the First Panzer Army was given to General Eberhard von Mackensen.

This change in command in no way solved the problem, because the primary cause of the loss of momentum was lack of petrol. "The bulk of our supplies," says von Kleist, "had to come by rail from the Rostov bottleneck, as the Black Sea route was considered unsafe. A certain amount of oil was delivered by air, but the total which came through was insufficient to maintain the momentum of the advance, which came to a halt just when our chances looked best." He adds: "But that was not the ultimate cause of the failure. We could still have reached our goal if my forces had not been drawn away bit by bit to help the attack on Stalingrad. Besides part of my motorized troops, I had to give up the whole of my flak [anti-aircraft] corps and all my air force except the reconnaissance squadrons."[4] Other generals, writes Captain Liddell Hart, "confirmed Kleist's evidence on the causes of the failure, especially the shortage of petrol – the armoured divisions were sometimes at a standstill for weeks on end, waiting for fresh supplies. Owing to this shortage the petrol lorries themselves were immobilized and petrol was brought forward on camels. . . ."[5]

By September 12, when Stalingrad was about to be stormed, the advance in the Caucasus had stopped on the line Tuapse–Elbrus–Ordzhonikidze–Mosdok–Elista;[6] the German front in the south, which ran from Kursk and Voronezh through Stalingrad, Elista, Elbrus to Tuapse, was stretched over more than 1,250 miles. When these miles are added to the 800 miles between Kursk and Leningrad, the total German frontage in Russia was

---

[1] *La défaite Allemand à l'est* (1951), p. 94.
[2] *The Halder Diaries*, August 22, 1942, vol. VII, p. 380.
[3] *Ibid.*, September 9, 1942, vol. VII, p. 391.
[4] *The Other Side of the Hill*, p. 303.   [5] *Ibid.*, p. 305.
[6] Elista, halfway between Mozdok and Stalingrad, was occupied on August 16.

well over 2,000 miles in length. This, when set against the forces and resources at Hitler's disposal, the vastness of the communications required to maintain this front, and the formidable proportions of guerrilla warfare in rear, shows the ineptitude of Hitler as a strategist more than anything else.

In 1942 Stalingrad was a long, narrow industrial city of about 500,000 inhabitants. It straggled for some 18 miles along the right bank of the Volga immediately north of its elbow, from where the river flows south-eastward into the Caspian Sea at Astrakhan. It was also an extensive inland port, ice-free for half the year, and in its northern sector were three large groups of factories which produced over a quarter of the tractors and mechanical vehicles of the U.S.S.R., as well as tanks, guns, and other armaments. West of the two southern groups rose the Mamaiev hill, also called the "Iron Heights", from which an extensive view could be obtained over the Volga. By September, thanks largely to Hitler's interference and the consequent slowing of the Sixth Army's advance, time had been gained by the Russians strongly to garrison the city. Its commander was General Chuykov.

East of the northern and southern quarters of Stalingrad the Volga, like the Piave, flows through several channels created by a number of islands and its main channel varies from two to two and a half miles in breadth. The river presented the Germans with a formidable bridging problem, and until it was solved it was not possible to invest the city on its eastern side. Could the Germans establish themselves on the left bank of the Volga, then a comparatively small, well-entrenched force would stop all river traffic, complete the investment, and reduce the city through starvation.

It is of some interest to examine this problem, because in nearly all opposed river crossings the determining factor is not width of river – though this is important – but the length of river frontage held by the attacker. Should the frontage be extensive, by feinting here and there the would-be crosser can so distract his opponent that, sooner or later, he will be able to throw a bridge over the river at some unprotected or lightly held point and establish a bridgehead on its far side. Because it takes longer to bridge a wide river like the Volga, the longer should be the operative stretch on which to feint. The initial German problem was to establish this operative front. But instead they resorted to direct attack – that is, an attempt was made to carry the city by batter and storm.

Once General von Paulus had sealed off the gap between the Volga and Don he established his airfields and supply dumps in the area between the two rivers. This was no easy task because he was dependent upon two indifferent railways – the Novorossisk–Stalingrad and the Rostov–Stalingrad. The latter ran by way of Tchirskaya, with a short branch line to Kalach; it was in a shocking state of repair and was constantly cut by partisans.

Hitler was not unaware that the troops which held the Don north-west of Stalingrad were inadequate for the task set them, but he trusted that a quick capture of Stalingrad would set free sufficient forces to reinforce them. Halder disagreed with this, and once it became obvious that Stalingrad could not be rushed, he urged the abandonment of the operation and a withdrawal westward. Instead Hitler took more and more German troops from the defensive wing and sent them to von Paulus.[1]

This piece of folly, coupled with a strong Russian counter-offensive in the Rzhev area, led to the final clash between Hitler and Halder, and the outcome was that the latter was relieved of his appointment and General Kurt Zeitzler, then in France, was ordered to replace him as Chief of Staff, O.K.H.[2]

The battle proper for Stalingrad opened on September 15, and after a week's desperate fighting the Germans penetrated to the centre of the city. On the 26th and 27th they broke into the factory district and seized the "Iron Heights", but on the 29th they were ejected. Reinforcements were then brought up and on October 4, supported by large numbers of tanks and bomber aircraft, the attack was renewed. For 10 days the attack was pressed with the utmost ferocity, street by street, house by house, both day and night, until the attackers were physically and morally exhausted. Stalingrad had become a second Verdun.

Hitler ordered a change of tactics; storming was to cease and the city systematically to be devastated by artillery fire and bombing. This was a senseless operation because it substituted rubble heaps for houses, and the former are the more easily defensible. The battle became one of prestige; Stalin was determined to hold the city which bore his name, and because of its name Hitler was equally determined to wrest it from his adversary. Yard by yard, over ground and under ground, the attackers

---

[1] See Warlimont's account in *The Other Side of the Hill*, p. 315.
[2] *The Halder Diaries*, September 24, 1942, vol. VII, p. 397. This entry concludes the *Diaries*, and the invaluable Halder deserts us.

fought their way through the ruins in what became known as the *Rattenkrieg* ("rat war"). On November 9 Hitler announced that "not one square yard of ground will be given up."[1] The battle continued until November 12, when in the last German general assault the Volga was reached in the south of the city.

By mid-November the German situation was as follows:

The Fourth Panzer Army, considerably reduced in strength and which on November 10 had been withdrawn to refit, was in the Kotelnikovo area.

The Sixth Army was in and around Stalingrad, and also held the gap between the Volga and Don as well as the Don between Kachalinskaya and Kletskaya, with the exception of a small bridgehead the Russians had established at Kremenskaya.

West of Kletskaya to Veshenskaya stood the Third Rumanian Army, and since November 2 the Fourth Rumanian Army – part of Manstein's Eleventh Army – had been brought up to hold the Ergeni Hills south of the Volga elbow in order to cover the right flank and the Novorossisk–Stalingrad railway. The rest of Manstein's army was ordered to the Leningrad front.

In the Caucasus the head of Army Group A was still about Mozdok, and a weak Rumanian force held Elista.

North of the Third Rumanian Army lay the Eighth Italian Army on the Don between Veshenskaya to west of Pavlovsk, and to its north stood the Second Hungarian Army as far as Korotoyak, where it contacted the right of the Second German Army in the Voronezh area.

It was early November and Hitler's attention was suddenly attracted to events in North Africa. The battle of El Alamein had been fought and won by Montgomery on November 5, and Morocco and Algeria invaded by Eisenhower on November 8. To counter this extension of the war in the south, German reinforcements were not sent east, but were sent west into France and to Tunisia. The moment was propitious for a Russian counteroffensive.

It was no sudden inspiration on the part of the Russians, for since early July they had prepared a counter-offensive, and by November, when winter would favour them, they had concentrated powerful forces in the forests north of the Don. Further, in preparation of their counterstroke, while their enemy pressed into the Caucasus and closed in on Stalingrad, they had carried out

[1] *Hitler's Defeat in Russia*, p. 119.

a series of violent attacks in the Voronezh area in order to pin down the German Second Army, and had also made many local attacks along the Don. They had seized a number of fords along the Don and had established several bridgeheads, including one at Serafimovitch. On October 25 a report was received at headquarters O.K.W. that the Russians had started bridging, and on November 2 this was confirmed by air reconnaissance. Two days later German agents reported that in the near future the Kremlin had decided to launch a powerful offensive, either over the Don or against Army Group Centre. They intended to do both.

These counter-offensives were planned and organized by Marshal Zhukov and his Chief of Staff, General Vassilevski. The attack over the Don was to be carried out in three phases by three armies north of the river in cooperation with an attack south of Stalingrad. The three northern armies were commanded by General Rokossovski, General Vatutin, and General Gorlikov, and respectively were deployed on the fronts Volga–Serafimovitch, Serafimovitch–Veshenskaya, and Veshenskaya to south of Voronezh. Approximately they faced the left wing of the German Sixth Army and the Third Rumanian Army, the Italian Eighth Army, and the Second Hungarian Army. The southern attack was to be made by General Yeremenko's army against the Fourth Rumanian Army on the Ergeni Hills. The second counter-offensive was to be launched against the German central sector between Vielikye-Luki and Rzhev, so as to impede reinforcements to the Don front; the attack began on November 25, and does not concern us.

The aim of the Don counter-offensive was to pinch out the German Sixth Army by a concentric attack on Kalach by the armies of Rokossovski and Yeremenko, and in which Vatutin's left wing was to protect Rokossovski's right flank. Once it was under way Vatutin was to break through the Eighth Italian Army and advance on Likhaya on the Stalino–Stalingrad railway, and thence on Rostov, the bottleneck of German communications. Gorlikov was to follow Vatutin and break through the Second Hungarian Army, force the German Second Army westward of Voronezh, and then advance south-westward on Bielgorod and Kharkov.

On November 19 the offensive was opened by Rokossovski. With three armoured corps and four cavalry corps in first line and 21 infantry divisions in second line, he debouched from bridgeheads between Serafimovitch and Kletskaya; broke through the right of the Third Rumanian Army, and while his right wing, in cooperation with Vatutin's left, pressed the enemy in rout toward the Chir river, with his centre he advanced on Kalach. Immediately after this attack his left wing moved against the Don–Volga gap, but was repulsed by the Sixth Army.

On the following day, Yeremenko, with two armoured corps and nine infantry divisions, broke through the Fourth Rumanian Army on the Ergeni Hills; then, while his left wing advanced on Kotelnikovo, his right wing swung northward toward Kalach where he linked up with Rokossovski on November 22. This meant that the Sixth Army, of about 200,000 combatants and 70,000 non-combatants, was surrounded; but the Russians were not sufficiently organized to prevent von Paulus from breaking out, which in all probability he could have done at any time during the following week.

When the news of the Russian offensive was received at Hitler's headquarters, General Zeitzler urged Hitler to order Paulus to cut his way out, and he nearly persuaded him to do so, but Göring – an incorrigible boaster – guaranteed that he would supply him by air with 500 tons a day of munitions, fuel, and rations. On November 24, because of this vain boast, Hitler ordered Paulus to "hedgehog" himself in, and commanded that his army should become known as "Fortress Stalingrad." The next problem was how to relieve it.

For once Hitler did the right thing. He called to his aid the ablest of his subordinates, Field-Marshal von Manstein, then at Vitebsk; renamed his Eleventh Army—largely dispersed—"Army Group Don", and subordinated to it the Sixth Army, Fourth Panzer Army, and the Third and Fourth Rumanian Armies. Manstein's task was not to open a way for the Sixth Army's retreat, because Hitler had no intention to withdraw it, but instead it was to defeat the Russians who encircled it and to re-establish the Stalingrad front.

Because of his indifferent railroad communications, Paulus's supply situation had throughout been precarious; now it grew critical. His army needed 700 tons of supplies daily and, according to General Anders,[1] O.K.W. were aware that once his reserves were exhausted he would require over double this amount.

[1] *Hitler's Defeat in Russia*, pp. 126–127, citing *Die Oberste Wehrmachtfürung*, Helmuth Greiner (1951), p. 425.

Göring had guaranteed to deliver 500 tons although there was only sufficient transport aircraft to lift 300 tons, and this amount did not allow for losses or the weather. The tonnage delivered between November 26 – when the operation was initiated – and January 3 is not specified by Greiner, but he records that on January 4 250 tons were delivered, on the 5th 150 tons, on the 6th 45, and from then to January 21, when it would appear that air supply ceased, the average was well under 100 tons daily.[1] During December alone this futile operation cost the *Luftwaffe* 246 transport aircraft.

When, on November 27, Manstein took over command of Army Group Don the situation with which he was faced was as follows: The remnants of the Third Rumanian Army, reinforced by improvised bodies of Germans, under command of General Karl Hollidt, precariously held the northern front from Veshen-skaya on the Don southward along the river Chir. On the southern front about Kotelnikovo stood Hoth's Fourth Panzer Army and remnants of the Fourth Rumanian Army, and to this group reinforcements were rushed from the north and the Caucasus. The Sixth Army was sandwiched between these two fronts in and around Stalingrad. Disturbing reports came in that the Russians north of the Don were concentrating large forces opposite the Eighth Italian and Second Hungarian Armies.

Manstein's plan, largely dictated by Hitler, was to advance Hoth's Fourth Panzer Army up the Kotelnikovo–Stalingrad railway against Yeremenko; to throw him back, and then to wheel against Rokossovski's right flank while Paulus struck at it from Stalingrad. Then he intended to launch the Hollidt group eastward over the Chir against Rokossovski's right – in brief, to defeat Yeremenko and then to encircle Rokossovski. The latter operation was an impossible task, and it would seem that Hitler had little information about the strength of Vatutin's army.

On December 12 Manstein's counter-offensive opened, and it made good progress for two days before it slowed. Nevertheless, by December 21 it was pushed forward to within 30 miles of the Stalingrad "hedgehog". Manstein's situation then became so critical that he decided to defy Hitler, and sent to von Paulus an order to be prepared to break out and join him within 24 hours. Paulus replied that he was unable to do so because his tanks had fuel only for 20 miles, and although he was urged by his generals to

---

[1] *Ibid.*, pp. 127–128 and pp. 425–435.

abandon his impedimenta and cut his way out with his infantry, he refused to do so. The truth would appear to be that he had no intention to withdraw from Stalingrad without a direct order from Hitler.

Why Manstein's request was so urgent was that on December 14 Hollidt had been violently attacked by Vatutin. On the 17th his front on the Chir collapsed, and on the following day Vatutin's right and centre crossed the frozen Don and struck at the Italian Eighth Army; on the 19th it was thrown back in rout toward the Donetz. Threatened as he was by encirclement, on December 24 Manstein ordered Hoth to send reinforcements to Hollidt, and then rapidly withdrew westward. On Christmas Day Hoth was in full retreat.

On December 29 von Paulus sent General Hube, commander of his XIVth Corps, by air to place the situation of the Sixth Army before Hitler. It was a futile journey, for the order Hitler sent back was to hold fast to Stalingrad until the spring. Nevertheless, on the same day, after he had repeatedly been pressed by Zeitzler to withdraw Army Group A from the Caucasus, he consented.

The next weeks were spent by Manstein in a desperate struggle to keep a corridor open for the retreat of Army Group A. He succeeded, and on January 18 Kleist reached the Don, and crossed it by the 22nd. While this retreat was in progress Gorlikov struck at the Second Hungarian Army and sent it back in rout. By the end of January, 1943, the whole of the German Don front had collapsed and a gap over 200 miles wide separated Manstein's left flank at Voroshilovgrad from Voronezh in the north.

The situation within Fortress Stalingrad rapidly deteriorated during Manstein's desperate struggle and Kleist's brilliant retreat. Soon rations had to be reduced to below subsistence level; artillery ammunition began to fail; medical stores and fuel, even for cooking, became exhausted; typhus and dysentery claimed thousands of victims, and frost as many more – the thermometer fell to 28 degrees below zero.

On January 8 Rokossovski called upon von Paulus to capitulate, and when he refused to do so, on the 10th Rokossovski ordered a general assault to be made on the doomed army. On the 14th the Pitomnik airfield, 14 miles west of the centre of the city, was captured by the Russians, and by then Paulus's situation had become so bad that he reported to Hitler that his troops could no longer bear their sufferings. The answer he received was:

"Capitulation is impossible. The Sixth Army will do its historic duty at Stalingrad until the last man, in order to make possible the reconstruction of the Eastern Front."[1]

On January 25 the Russians captured the last remaining German airfield, the loss of which deprived Paulus of all further physical contact with the outer world. On January 31 Hitler promoted him a field-marshal, and on the same day the radio of Sixth Army headquarters sent its final message: "The Russians are before our bunker. We are destroying the station."[2] Immediately after this, except for the XIth Corps, commanded by General Strecker, the Sixth Army laid down its arms, and on February 2 the XIth Corps surrendered.

When Hitler received the news of the surrender, first he compared the Sixth Army with the Three Hundred at Thermopylae, and declared that it had shown the world "the true spirit of National Socialist Germany and its loyalty to its Fuehrer," then he raved against Paulus and shouted that, like Varus, he should have thrown himself upon his sword rather than accept captivity.[3]

With Paulus, 23 generals, 2,000 field and junior officers, 90,000 other ranks, and about 40,000 non-combatant soldiers and civilians surrendered. About 34,000 wounded and sick had been evacuated by air during the siege, and over 100,000 were killed, died of sickness, hunger and frost, and left sick and wounded in Stalingrad. If Erich Kern is to be believed, these last-mentioned unfortunates were massacred by the Russians, who threw explosive charges into the hospital shelters, and on February 3 thousands were buried alive in the enormous Timoshenko bunker when its entrances were dynamited. Kern also informs us that "of the 90,000 prisoners, between 40,000 and 50,000 died of starvation within the first six weeks [of captivity] in the prison camp Bektoffka on the Volga, some forty miles south of Stalingrad."[4] As regards losses of material, Chester Wilmot states that "the records of the Army High Command show that at Stalingrad the Wehrmacht lost the equivalent of six months production of armour and vehicles, three to four months production of artillery, and two months production of small arms and mortars."[5] To these losses,

---

[1] *Hitler, a Study in Tyranny*, Alan Bullock (1952), p. 631, citing von Paulus's evidence at the Nuremberg Trials.
[2] Quoted by Anders, *Hitler's Defeat in Russia*, p. 142.
[3] *Hitler, a Study in Tyranny*, pp. 631-632.
[4] *Dance of Death* (1948), p. 246.
[5] *The Struggle for Europe*, p. 149.

according to General Pickert, who was in charge of the air supply of the Sixth Army, must be added over 500 transport aircraft.[1]

Stalingrad was a second Poltava in which Hitler was as much the architect of his own ruin as was Charles XII in 1709. Into the minds of a hundred million Muscovites flashed the myth of Soviet invincibility, and it forged them into the Turks of the North. If they could overcome the legions of Hitler, what had they to fear from the nations he had trampled in the dust? The German victories had thrown Europe into chaos and so had blazed a trail for the Third Rome. This decisive victory, which came on the heels of El Alamein, and at the moment when in Tunisia the Fascist cause had reached its nadir, inspired propaganda intoxicated peoples of the west. Stalingrad exalted Stalin into the champion of all for which they so ardently yearned. Tragically they were to be disillusioned.

In spite of the vastness of the German defeat, Stalingrad was only the signal of Hitler's ruin – it was not its cause. This, as described in Chapter 11, was because in his blind arrogance he had failed to differentiate between potential friends among the subjugated peoples of the U.S.S.R. and his active enemies. Also, Great Britain and the United States committed the same blunder when they did not distinguish between the Nazi and anti-Nazi factions in Germany, and did not establish the second front they were seeking within instead of outside the frontiers of the Third Reich. Had they done so, while still supporting Russia, the German *débâcle* at Stalingrad would have opened to them the road which almost certainly would have led to the end of the war in the spring or summer of 1943.

Because of the pointless sacrifice of the Sixth Army, never at any time during the war was revolt against Hitler nearer to success than in January, 1943. Generals Beck and Zeitzler and most of the field-marshals were involved, but without some assurance of British and American support they had nothing to offer the large middle group of officers who wavered. After the war one of the conspirators said to Mr. Francis Russell: "Our conspiracy was a great tragedy. We might have ended the war a year and a half earlier if your government had given us some encouragement. . . . We had our intermediaries in Sweden; we wanted to know what the Anglo-American conditions would be, what terms they would give a new government if we succeeded in doing away with Hitler.

[1] *Defeat in the West*, Milton Shulman (1947), p. 72.

They took our memorandum, it was given to Eden – but there was never any reply."[1]

On January 22 the two main rebel factions – those who wanted forcibly to remove Hitler, which could only mean assassination, and those who wanted to subject him to the General Staff – met in the house of Count Peter von Wartenburg in Berlin-Lichter-felde to square their differences. Then, on the following day, before they had arrived at a decision, Roosevelt's and Churchill's proclamation of unconditional surrender came from Casablanca; "a formula which," Görlitz declares, "gave the death blow to any hope that may have been entertained either by the 'shadow government' or by the oppositional elements in the General Staff, that their enemies would negotiate with a 'respectable' government."[2]

In spite of this setback, on March 13 the first definite plan to assassinate Hitler was put into force by a group of officers at von Kluge's headquarters. Unfortunately for them the bomb smuggled into Hitler's aeroplane failed to explode;[3] nevertheless, six other attempts on Hitler's life were planned in 1943. "Death," Görlitz says, "was already stalking Hitler unseen – which only shows how weak was the real basis of his authority."[4]

At this climax in the war, what staggers one is the political blindness of British and American statesmen. They completely failed to realize the politico-strategical situation with which they were faced, and this is so clearly unfolded in an exchange of notes between Sir Samuel Hoare (later Viscount Templewood), British Ambassador in Spain, and Count Jordana, the Spanish Foreign Minister, immediately after the German defeat at Stalingrad, that it is worth while to quote them at some length.

General Franco's views were "that there were two separate wars in progress, the war in the east against communism in which Spain was directly involved, and the war in the west between the Anglo-Saxon powers and Germany, in which Spain took no part."[5] To convince him that there was only one war, Sir Samuel

---

[1] "Pictures from Germany," *The New English Review*, June, 1948, p. 551.
[2] *The German General Staff* (1953), p. 430. Chester Wilmot writes that ". . . when the Allies proclaimed their demand for 'Unconditional Surrender' even commanders like von Kluge and von Manstein, who foresaw where Hitler's policy was leading Germany, refused to act against him. Since it seemed that the Allies were determined to destroy the German military caste. . . ." (*The Struggle for Europe*, p. 166).
[3] See *Revolt Against Hitler*, Fabian von Schlabrendorff (1948), chap. VI.
[4] *The German General Staff*, p. 434.
[5] *Ambassador on Special Mission*, Rt. Hon. Sir Samuel Hoare (1946), pp. 184-185.

Hoare entered into correspondence with Count Jordana, and on February 19, 1943, he stated in a memorandum to the latter: "The victory at the end of this war will be an Allied, not a Russian victory, namely a victory in which the British Empire and the United States of America will exercise the greatest possible influence. Moreover, M. Stalin declared on November 6th, 1942, that it was not the future policy of Russia to interfere in the international affairs of other countries."

On February 21 Jordana replied to this note, and among other things wrote:

"If events develop in the future as they have done up to now, it would be Russia which will penetrate deeply into German territory. And we ask the question: if this should occur, which is the greater danger not only for the continent but for England herself, a Germany not totally defeated and with sufficient strength to serve as a rampart against Communism, a Germany hated by all her neighbours, which would deprive her of authority though she remained intact, or a Sovietized Germany which would certainly furnish Russia with the added strength of her war preparations, her engineers, her specialized workmen and technicians, which would enable Russia to extend herself with an empire without precedent from the Atlantic to the Pacific? . . .

"And we ask a second question: is there anybody in the centre of Europe, in that mosaic of countries without consistency or unity, bled moreover by war and foreign domination, who could contain the ambitions of Stalin? There is certainly no one. . . . We may be sure that after the German domination, the only domination which could live in these countries is Communism. For this reason we consider the situation as extremely grave and think that people in England should reflect calmly on the matter, since should Russia succeed in conquering Germany, there will be no one who can contain her. . . . If Germany did not exist, Europeans would have to invent her and it would be ridiculous to think that her place could be taken by a confederation of Lithuanians, Poles, Czechs, and Roumanians which would rapidly be converted into so many more states of the Soviet confederation. . . ."

On February 25, Sir Samuel Hoare replied:

"The Minister says that the great danger to Europe is Communism and that a Russian victory will make all Europe Communist. . . . The British view is very different. . . . Will any single country be able to dominate Europe at the end of this war? Russia, at least, will need a long period of reconstruction and recovery in which she will depend greatly upon the British Empire and the United States of America for economic help. . . . Whilst, however, giving full credit and admiration to the Russian army, we are convinced that the final victory will not be the victory of any single Ally but of all the Allies. . . . There will then un-doubtedly be great British and American armies on the Conti-nent. . . . They will be composed of fresh, first line troops, whose ranks have not been previously devastated by years of exhausting war on the Russian front.

"As for ourselves, I make the confident prophecy that at that moment Great Britain will be the strongest European military Power. . . . British influence, it seems to me, will be then stronger in Europe than at any time since the fall of Napoleon. . . . We shall not, however, shirk our responsibilities to European civilisa-tion or throw away our great strength by premature or unilaterial disarmament. . . . There is no reason to think that the alliance formed under the stress of war will not continue in the peace and provide a peaceful and stabilising force in European politics."[1]

This correspondence reveals, against the sombre background of Spanish realism, the idealistic war policy which the American and British governments followed, and how misjudged this policy was became fully apparent to Mr. Churchill four days after his war aim of June 22, 1941 – "to destroy Hitler and every vestige of the Nazi régime" – had been attained. On May 12, 1945, in a telegram addressed to President Truman – which he calls "the 'Iron Curtain' telegram" – he said:

"I am profoundly concerned about the European situation. . . Anyone can see that in a very short space of time our armed power on the Continent will have vanished, except for moderate forces to hold down Germany. . . . What will be the position in a year or two, when the British and American Armies have melted and the French has not yet been formed on any major scale, when we may have a handful of Divisions, mostly French, and when Russia may choose to keep two or three hundred on active service? An iron curtain is drawn down upon their front. We do not know what is going on behind. There seems little doubt that the whole of the regions east of a line Lübeck–Trieste–Corfu will soon be completely in their hands. . . . Thus a broad band of many

[1] *Ibid.*, pp. 190–195.

hundreds of miles of Russian-occupied territory will isolate us from Poland. . . . Meanwhile the attention of our peoples will be occupied in inflicting severities upon Germany, which is ruined and prostrate, and it would be open to the Russians in a very short time to advance if they chose to the waters of the North Sea and the Atlantic."[1]

In this apocalyptic appeal to the new President is revealed the political importance of the battle of Stalingrad. Because of the allied policy of unconditional surrender, which crystallized all that President Roosevelt and Mr. Churchill stood for, it was, with the exception of the battle of Normandy – its copestone – the most decisive of all the battles of the war. It was, Lieutenant-Colonel F. O. Miksche declares, "a defeat for Europe as a whole."[2]

[1] *The Second World War*, vol. VI, pp. 498–499.
[2] *Unconditional Surrender* (1952), p. 254.

The political and second fronts

The year 1943 was one of decisive political changes that shaped the outcome of the war and radically influenced the course of history. It opened with the proclamation of unconditional surrender at Casablanca and by its emphasis on a war of annihilation bereft the western allies' cause of a sane aim, a decision which Stalin was not slow to capitalize.

Stalin sought to exploit the West's enthusiasm over the Soviet victory at Stalingrad, and resorted to Lenin's maxim: "one step back to gain two steps forward." On May 22 he announced the dissolution of the Comintern and so deluded the British and American peoples and governments into a belief that the Kremlin had abandoned for ever its policy of interference in the internal affairs of other countries; Russia could be accepted by them as a friendly, near-democratic partner. Because of this chameleon-like change and their own policy of unconditional surrender, the western allies left the political initiative to Russia at the very moment when Italy was on the point of collapse and the road was about to open to them to seize their opportunity in southern Europe and establish a profitable second front.

In the meantime Hitler inverted everything he had so far held to be essential. He abandoned his plan to impose his will on Europe and establish a German *Lebensraum* in western Russia and instead set out to champion European freedom in order to prevent the establishment of a Soviet *Lebensraum* in eastern and central Europe. He knew that all continental nations were terrified at the prospect of a Russian victory, and that the age-old policy of England was antagonistic to the dominance of Europe by any one Power. He substituted *Festung Europa* for *Lebensraum*, made propaganda capital of the unconditional surrender policy and so turned it into a blood transfusion for the Germans, and proclaimed a crusade of Europe against Asia. Such were the main political transformations of 1943.

Although their policy was dismal, the strategic prospects of America and Britain were bright. By the summer of 1943 the submarine had been mastered and the so-called Battle of the

Atlantic won;[1] supremacy in the air had been gained; the output of American industry reached its peak; an enormous American army was in training; and Great Britain had recovered from her disaster at Dunkirk, and was in the process of raising a powerful army at home. The allied problem was how best to employ these enormous and ever-increasing assets; in other words, how to establish the long awaited Second Front which had been accepted as their strategic goal as early as the Arcadia Conference, and at which three possible directions were foreshadowed – across the Mediterranean, from Turkey into the Balkans, and in western Europe.

Because the Second Front could not be opened in 1942, when Stalin vociferously demanded it, and because something had to be done to satisfy him, the invasion of North Africa had been undertaken as a stopgap, but only on the understanding that the preparations for the invasion of France ("Bolero") would in no way be impeded. It was decided at the Casablanca Conference to set up an inter-service staff, under Lieutenant-General F. E. Morgan as Chief of Staff to the Supreme Allied Commander designate (COSSAC), to prepare a definite plan for the invasion of France in the spring of 1944. It superseded "Bolero" and was code-named "Overlord". Lastly, the successes which sprang from "Torch", especially the invasion of Italy, introduced a strategical complication that was to become a bone of contention between Mr. Churchill and the Joint Chiefs of Staff – more particularly General Marshall – and bedevil allied strategy up to and beyond the establishment of the Second Front in Normandy.

The crux of this question would appear to have been that Mr. Churchill's ideas on where he wanted the second front to be opened were mixed. Although he agreed with "Overlord", once a front had been established in Italy he did not want "Overlord" to cripple it. Nor – and he is most emphatic about this – did he want to open a second front in the Balkans. Nevertheless, from the earliest days of the war his thoughts were directed on the possibilities of a south-eastern front, and in September, 1941, he had considered that the only means to help Russia was to establish with Turkish aid "a second front somewhere in the Balkans".

---

[1] In the opinion of the author, the struggle for the mastery of the Atlantic is erroneously called a "battle". It was a series of co-ordinated and *ad hoc* operations in which their sum, and no single engagement, was decisive. It may be compared with the struggle for air or industrial supremacy. It was a continuous operation which only ended with the termination of the war.

When Sicily was invaded he expressed the opinion that "the Balkans represented a greater danger to Germany than the loss of Italy," and he hoped to bring in Turkey when allied troops "had reached the Balkan area" – presumably Venezia Giulia. In spite of this, on October 20, in a note to Mr. Eden – then in Moscow – he wrote: "I would not debouch from the narrow leg of Italy into the valley of the Po. . . . Would they [the Russians] be attracted by the idea of our acting through the Aegean, involving Turkey in the war, and opening the Dardanelles . . . so that we could ultimately give them our right hand along the Danube?"

Because of this persistent reference to the Balkans the Joint Chiefs of Staff assumed that Mr. Churchill's heart was in the south-eastern front and not in "Overlord" – the north-western front. Although we do not wish to ascribe to Mr. Churchill an opinion he never held, it would seem that his outlook at this time, when compared with that of the Joint Chiefs of Staff, was not far removed from that of Constantin Fotitch, the Yugoslav Minister in Washington. On October 16, Fotitch broached to President Roosevelt the question of an invasion of Europe by way of the Balkans, and pointed out that this strategy, "already suggested by Churchill, would prevent the installation of Soviet puppet régimes in the Balkans and in Central Europe." The President replied that the problem would be decided "purely upon its military aspects." Fotitch observed, ". . . that it was a costly absurdity to fight a war for purely military reasons, with no moral and political objectives." The bone of contention would appear to be that while the President and his Chiefs of Staff aimed at a purely military victory, Churchill had his eye on the political outcome of the war, and this involved Russia as fully as it did Germany. Should this be correct, then undoubtedly he was right, for a war without a political aim is military nonsense. But was it correct? It is difficult to determine, because on July 25, the day Mussolini resigned, Churchill decided to send Mr. Fitzroy Maclean, M.P., on a mission to Marshal Tito, and when Maclean pointed out to him that if the Yugoslav partisans were victorious Tito would in all probability establish a Communist régime in Yugoslavia closely linked to Moscow, and asked for His Majesty's Government's views on such an eventuality, Churchill replied: "So long as the whole of western civilization was threatened by the Nazi menace, *we could not afford to let our attention be diverted from the immediate issue by considerations of long-term policy. . . ."* "My task," writes Maclean, "was simply to find out who was killing the most Germans and suggest means by which we could help them to kill more. *Politics must be a secondary consideration.*"[1] Even as late as February 27, 1945, 10 weeks before the war ended, Churchill told Parliament that the two principles which guided his approach to continental problems were: "While the war is on, we give help to anyone who can kill a Hun; when the war is over we look to the solution of a free, unfettered democratic election." Apparently it never occurred to him that as Russia would by then have done most of the killing, she would seek a solution of her own.

On August 17, when the Germans had just suffered in the great battle of Orel–Kursk as catastrophic a defeat as that at Stalingrad, Churchill and Roosevelt, attended by the Combined Chiefs of Staff, met in Quebec to discuss "Overlord". Their main decisions were that as a prerequisite of "Overlord" highest priority was to be given to the strategic bombing of Germany; that resources for the prosecution of "Overlord" were to have priority over operations in the Mediterranean; that a landing in the south of France, code-named "Anvil" (later changed to "Dragoon"), was to supplement "Overlord"; and that the "target date" for "Overlord" was to be May 1, 1944.

These important decisions were overshadowed by a forecast made in a document which Harry Hopkins brought with him to the conference. It was entitled *Russia's Position*, and was attributed to "a very high level United States military strategic estimate." It stated that: "Russia's post-war position in Europe will be a dominant one. With Germany crushed, there is no power in Europe to oppose her tremendous military forces. It is true that Great Britain is building up a position in the Mediterranean *vis-à-vis* Russia that she may find useful in balancing power in Europe. However, even here she may not be able to oppose Russia unless she is otherwise supported.

"The conclusions from the foregoing are obvious. Since Russia is the decisive factor in the war, she must be given every assistance and every effort must be made to obtain her friendship. Likewise, since without question she will dominate Europe on the defeat of the Axis, it is even more essential to develop and maintain the most friendly relations with Russia.

[1] *Eastern Approaches* (1949), p. 281, italics added.

"Finally, the most important factor the United States has to consider in relation to Russia is the prosecution of the war in the Pacific. With Russia as an ally in the war against Japan, the war can be terminated in less time and at less expense in life and resources than if the reverse were the case. Should the war in the Pacific have to be carried on with an unfriendly or a negative attitude on the part of Russia, the difficulties will be immeasurably increased and operations might become abortive."

This estimate is reflected in a telegram sent by Mr. Churchill to Field-Marshal Smuts a few days after the conference ended. "I think," he said, "that Russia will be the greatest land Power in the world after this war, which will have rid her of the two military Powers, Japan and Germany."

These predictions meant that once Germany was crushed, the totalitarian rule of Stalin over Europe would replace that of Hitler; as far as the western allies were concerned, the war would lose its political aim, and in consequence it would be absurd to continue it.

It would appear that this vitally important inference was not discussed for a moment. Had it been discussed it would have become apparent that in order to attain their political aim, it was essential for the western allies not only to destroy Hitlerism, but simultaneously to prevent its replacement by Stalinism. And if psychological attack is omitted, this could only be accomplished if they adapted their military operations to this political end.

In the time at their disposal there was only one course they could have taken, and that was to accept the front, then about to be established by General Eisenhower and General Alexander in Italy, as the Second Front, and to have put "Overlord" into cold storage. Had they done so, then, when Alexander had been reinforced with the resources earmarked for "Overlord" – more particularly landing craft – by a series of amphibious operations up the leg of Italy he rapidly could have compelled Field-Marshal Kesselring to withdraw beyond the river Po, and by a landing in the Trieste area he could have forced him either to abandon Italy or risk the loss of his communications. Such an eventuality, which was by no means impracticable, would win for the western allies the road to Vienna, Budapest, and Prague. In any case the Chiefs of the Combined Staff should have seen that, instead of striking at the apex of the German salient Leningrad–Brest–Athens, strategy dictated that, were the means available, its reduction should be sought by striking at its waist – Lübeck–Trieste. Because it was more difficult to strike at the former target than the latter, a second front in the Trieste area was the only practical operation in the time available to eliminate the rival totalitarian systems.

The next conference, that of the allied Foreign Ministers, which had been agreed at Quebec, assembled at Moscow on October 18. Mr. Eden there broached two main subjects. The first was a meeting of the three heads of the allied governments, which Roosevelt had long requested. Stalin agreed, but insisted that the conference should be held at Teheran. The second subject was the problem of the Second Front, and Mr. Eden reported to Mr. Churchill "that the Russians were completely and blindly set on our invasion of Northern France." The latter replied that Eden should tell Stalin: "I will not allow . . . the great and fruitful campaign in Italy . . . to be cast away and end in a frightful disaster, for the sake of crossing the Channel in May. The battle must be nourished and fought out until it is won. We will do our very best for 'Overlord', but it is no use planning for defeat in the field in order to give temporary political satisfaction. . . . Eisenhower and Alexander must have what they need to win the battle, no matter what effect is produced on subsequent operations." This was a brief glimpse of strategical daylight.

That the daylight lasted so short a time was largely because of Roosevelt's obsession that he was Beauty and Stalin a Beast who could be charmed into a fairy prince with whom Europe could live happily ever after. When William C. Bullitt, former United States Ambassador in Moscow, protested that his Russian policy would fail because Stalin could not be trusted, the President replied: "Bill . . . I don't dispute the logic of your reasoning. I just have a hunch that Stalin is not that kind of man. Harry says he's not, and that he doesn't want anything but security for his country. And I think that if I give him anything I can and ask nothing from him in return, noblesse oblige, he won't try to annex anything and will work with me for a world of peace and democracy." In this frame of mind the President set out on November 13 for Cairo, where he conferred with Churchill and Chiang Kai-shek, and on November 27 he flew with Churchill to Teheran to meet Stalin.

Before they left Cairo he and Churchill had agreed to suspend a final decision on Anglo-American strategy for 1944 until after the conference. Nevertheless, the American Chiefs of Staff had long made up their minds, and, according to Sherwood, were prepared "for battles at Teheran in which the Americans and Russians would form a united front." This was facilitated by the arrangements made to house the President and Prime Minister. Churchill was lodged in the British Legation, and to make sure that he had the President in his pocket, on a pretext of security Stalin invited him to take up residence in the Soviet Embassy and not in the American Legation.

The first plenary meeting was held on November 29, and as there was no agenda discussions were *ad hoc* and confused. It would appear that, as usual, Churchill did most of the talking, and this suited Stalin admirably, because he alone of the "Big Three" knew exactly what he wanted. Above all his wish was for a Second Front in France in May, and bluntly he asked Churchill whether he really believed in "Overlord", or was "only thinking about it to please the Soviet Union?" Churchill replied that there was no question of shelving "Overlord", and that it would be launched in May, June, or July; but that the immediate problem was what to do in the Mediterranean during the next five months. He emphasized the importance of the Balkans and suggested that support should be given to Tito's partisans in Yugoslavia and withdrawn from those of Milhailovich. After the capture of Rome, he said, there would be "no advance in Italy beyond the Pisa–Rimini line." Nevertheless, when the subject of an invasion of southern France cropped up – which Stalin favoured – he said that although he was not opposed to it, he "preferred a right-handed movement from the north of Italy, using the Istrian peninsula and the Ljubjana Gap towards Vienna." Stalin was adamant against this and any Balkan or Turkish venture.

The subject of Poland was raised by Churchill. "Nothing was more important," he said, "than the security of the Russian western frontier." Poland should relinquish all her territory east of the Curzon Line (approximately the Ribbentrop–Molotov line) to Russia, and move westward into Germany. "If Poland trod on some German toes," he remarked, "that could not be helped, but there must be a strong Poland." He added that he "would always support the movement of Poland's frontier westward."

Stalin suggested that the Poles should be allowed to move west as far as the Oder. He said that he did not want anything belonging to other people, but would like Königsberg – which did so belong. Churchill replied that the Poles would be foolish if they did not accept the Curzon and Oder frontiers, and that he would remind them "that but for the Red Army they would have been utterly destroyed." Anyhow, he was not going to break his heart about the cession of part of Germany, although it meant shifting 9,000,000 people. This was the end of the Atlantic Charter and the Anglo-Polish Guarantee of 1939. Apparently Mr. Churchill had forgotten that, on December 27, 1941, he had said to Mr. Jan Ciechanowski, Polish Ambassador to the United States: "We shall never forget what glorious Poland has done and is doing. . . . Great Britain has set for herself the aim of restoring full freedom and independence to your nation overrun by Hitler. That is, and will remain our foremost concern. I can assure you that Great Britain will never tarry in the fight until that aim is achieved."

After Poland came Finland. Churchill urged that "Russia must have security for Leningrad and its approaches," and that the Soviet Union must be assured "as a permanent naval and air Power in the Baltic." As with Poland, no mention would appear to have been made of Russia's unprovoked attack on Finland in 1939, but because the Finns had retaliated in 1941 Stalin demanded the restoration of the 1940 treaty, the cession of Hangö or Petsamo, and compensation in kind for 50 per cent. of the war damage suffered.

The problem of Germany was examined at considerable length. Stalin said he wanted Germany to be split; the President warmly agreed and suggested that it should be divided into five parts: (*1*) Prussia; (*2*) Hanover and north-west Germany; (*3*) Saxony; (*4*) Hesse-Darmstadt and Hesse Cassel; and (*5*) Bavaria, Baden, and Württemberg. Each part should be self-governing; but Kiel, the Kiel Canal, Hamburg, the Ruhr, and the Saar should be governed by the United Nations.

Churchill put forward another scheme. He considered that the root evil lay in Prussia, the Prussian Army, and the General Staff[1] and proposed that Prussia should be isolated; Bavaria, Württemberg, the Palatinate, Saxony, and Baden detached, and that Bavaria with Austria and Hungary should be formed into a non-aggressive confederation. "We all deeply feared," he comments, "the might of a united Germany. . . . It would be possible, I thought, to make a stern but honourable peace with her,

---

[1] An astonishing statement, which shows how ignorant Mr. Churchill was of the antagonism of the General Staff to the Nazi régime.

and at the same time to create in modern forms what had been in general outline the Austro-Hungarian Empire. . . ." Stalin thought not. He saw no fundamental difference between north and south Germany – "all Germans fought like beasts," he said – Austria and Hungary should exist independently, and after the break up of Germany it would be most unwise to create a new Danubian combination. The President fully agreed.

Stalin assured the President that the United States need have no fear about the Pacific, since the Soviet Union would declare war on Japan once Hitler had been defeated. "Then," he said, "by our common effort we shall win." This Delphic utterance vastly pleased the President and his Chiefs of Staff, and, so it would appear, out of gratitude and behind Churchill's back, Roosevelt, in one of his several private conversations with Stalin, discussed the question of a common front against the British and proposed that he and Stalin would back Chiang Kai-Shek against Churchill on the question of Hongkong and Shanghai. Elliott Roosevelt's explanation of this is that "the biggest thing was" to make "clear to Stalin that the United States and Great Britain were not in one common block against the Soviet Union." Further, Roosevelt mentioned to Stalin "the possibility that Russia might have access to the port of Darien in Manchuria" (incidentally, this was Chinese territory).

In the end little was formally agreed: the partisans in Yugoslavia were to be supported; Turkey was to be encouraged to enter the war; "Overlord" was to be launched in May, 1944; and the Staffs of the three Powers were to keep in close touch with each other. Actually, Stalin scooped the pool; Churchill got nothing, except the arch-Communist Tito as a collaborator; and the President received Stalin's grateful thanks. "Pushed by the Russians and pulled by the Americans," writes Wilmot, "the overall strategy of the Western Powers had been diverted away from the area of Soviet aspirations. Even before Teheran it was inevitable that the enforcement of 'Unconditional Surrender' upon Germany would leave the U.S.S.R. the dominant power in Eastern Europe, but it was by no means inevitable that Russian influence would extend deep into Central Europe and the Balkans. After Teheran it became almost a certainty that this would happen. Thus the Teheran Conference not only determined the military strategy for 1944, but adjusted the political balance of post-war Europe in favour of the Soviet Union."

On December 1 the conference ended and on the following day Roosevelt and Churchill were back in Cairo. Eisenhower was selected as Supreme Commander for "Overlord" on December 6, and the Combined Chiefs of Staff decided that "Overlord" and "Anvil" would be "the supreme operations for 1944. . . . They must be carried out during May. Nothing must be undertaken in any part of the world which hazards the success of these two operations."

CHAPTER 15

The Battle of Normandy, 1944

The invasion of Normandy was the supreme effort of the western allies in Europe, but although it was tactically decisive, it utterly failed to win the peace of President Roosevelt's dreams. The reason was, as the American official historian points out, that the Joint Chiefs of Staff developed "a purely military perspective that considered political implications chiefly with an eye to avoiding them."[1] This is fully corroborated by the President who, in a conversation with his son at Teheran, said:

"Elliott: our chiefs of staff are convinced of one thing. The way to kill the most Germans with the least loss of American soldiers, is to mount one great big invasion and then slam 'em with everything we've got. It makes sense to me. It makes sense to Uncle Joe. It makes sense to all our generals, and always has, ever since the beginning of the war. . . . It makes sense to the Red Army people. That's that. It's the quickest way to win the war. That's all.

"Trouble is, the P.M. is thinking too much of the *post*-war, and where England will be. . . . He's scared of letting the Russians get too strong.

"Maybe the Russians will get strong in Europe. Whether that's bad depends on a whole lot of factors.

"The one thing I'm sure of is this: if the way to save American lives, the way to win as short a war as possible is from the west and from the west alone, without wasting landing craft and men and materials in the Balkan mountains, and our chiefs are convinced it is, then that's that!"[2]

Throughout this chapter the reader should bear these words in mind, because they explain why and how the invasion of Normandy and the events which followed it led to the establishment over half of Europe of a Soviet dictatorship equally vile to the one Russia had helped to destroy.

[1] *United States Army in World War II* (American Official History), "Cross-Channel Attack", Gordon A. Harrison (1951), p. 92.
[2] *As He Saw It*, Elliott Roosevelt (1946), p. 185.

Soon after General Eisenhower's nomination to command "Overlord" the following appointments were made: General Sir Henry Maitland Wilson to become British Supreme Commander in the Mediterranean; Air Chief Marshal Sir Arthur Tedder to be Eisenhower's deputy Commander; and General Sir Bernard Montgomery to command the cross-Channel invasion forces, known as the Twenty-First Army Group, until such time as Eisenhower could transfer his headquarters to France. Besides these appointments, Admiral Sir Bertram Ramsay was given command of the Allied Naval Expeditionary Force, and Air Chief Marshal Sir Trafford Leigh-Mallory was given command of the Allied Expeditionary Air Force.

On January 1, 1944, Montgomery left Italy for England; broke his journey at Marrakesh, where Mr. Churchill was convalescing, and was shown by him the draft COSSAC plan prepared by General Morgan. It was proposed to launch the invasion in the Bay of the Seine between Grandcamp and Caen with one corps of three divisions, with a build-up to nine divisions by the fifth day. After his arrival in England on January 2, Montgomery considered this plan in detail and came to the conclusion that the frontage was too narrow and the assault force too weak. At a conference with Ramsay and Leigh-Mallory it was decided that the assault should be made on a frontage of two armies, the First United States Army on the right with two divisions in first wave, and the Second British Army on the left with three divisions. To meet this increase of force, the front of assault was extended westward to les Dunes de Varreville, on the eastern coast of the Cotentin peninsula, and eastward to Cabourg, east of the river Orne. The dividing line between the two armies was to be Port en Bessin–Bayeux, both inclusively allotted to the Second British Army. Because this increase of force demanded additional landing craft it was proposed to postpone the date of the invasion (D-day) from May 1 to May 31, in order to obtain an additional month's production of craft, and to take over the landing craft earmarked for "Anvil" – the invasion of southern France.

The shortage of landing craft was not the fault of production, but of allocation, for by May 1 Fleet-Admiral King, C.-in-C. U.S. Fleet, had at his disposal the bulk of the landing craft, but as his heart was in the Pacific and not in Europe he allotted only a small fraction of the number as the American quota to "Overlord". The crux of the difficulty, as Mr. Henry L. Stimson, United

States Secretary for War, points out, was that the Joint Chiefs of Staff were "incapable of forcing a decision against the will of any one of its members. . . . Only the President was in a position to settle disagreements" between them, which he was reluctant to do.[1] The results of King's close-fistedness were that the date of "Anvil", which was to coincide with "Overlord", had to be postponed, and that General Alexander was deprived of the means to carry out amphibious operations up the leg of Italy, in consequence of which his campaign was ruined.

On January 21 Eisenhower accepted the revised plan, the general idea of which was: (*1*) to secure a footing on the Normandy coast from north of the Carentan estuary to the river Orne; (*2*) to occupy Cherbourg and the Brittany ports; (*3*) when once firmly established, to threaten to break out with the Second British Army in the Caen area, in order to draw the enemy reserves toward that sector; (*4*) once this had been done, to break out with the First and Third U.S. Armies[2] on the western flank and advance southward to the Loire; and (*5*) to pivot the whole front on Caen and swing the right wing eastward to the Seine.[3]

Across the Channel Eisenhower was faced by Field-Marshal von Rundstedt who, in March, 1942, had been appointed C.-in-C. West, a command which included France, Belgium, and Holland. In the spring of 1944 he had at his disposal two Army Groups and the Panzer Group West. They included these formations:

Army Group B (Field-Marshal Rommel) consisted of the LXXXVIIIth Corps (General Christiansen) of three divisions in Holland; the Fifteenth Army (General von Salmuth) of four corps of 17 divisions, between Antwerp and the river Orne; and the Seventh Army (General Dollmann) of three corps of 15 divisions (one in the Channel Islands) between the Orne and the Loire.

Army Group G (General Blaskowitz) comprised the First and Nineteenth Armies, the one of five and the other of eight divisions. The former garrisoned the area between the Loire and the central Pyrenees, and the latter the Mediterranean coast from Perpignan to Mentone.

In all there were 48 divisions, of which 38 were located along, and 10 behind the coast. Of the latter, five were between the

---

[1] *On Active Service in Peace and War* (English edit., n.d.), p. 287.
[2] The Third Army was to follow the First Army at a date subsequent to D-day.
[3] *Normandy to the Baltic*, Field-Marshal Montgomery (n.d.), pp. 15–16.

Scheldt and the Somme, two between the Somme and the Seine, and three in Normandy.

Panzer Group West (General Baron Geyr von Schweppenburg) was responsible for the administration and training of 10 Panzer and Panzer grenadier divisions, located as follows: North of the Loire, 1st S.S. Panzer Division (*Leibstandarte Adolf Hitler*) at Beverloo (Belgium); 2nd Panzer Division in the Amiens area; 116th Panzer Division east of Rouen; 12th S.S. Panzer Division (*Hitler Jugend*) in the Lisieux area; 21st Panzer Division in the Caen area; and the Panzer-Lehr Division in the Orléans area south of the Loire; the 17th S.S. Panzer Grenadier Division was in the Poitiers area; 11th Panzer Division in the Bordeaux area; 2nd S.S. Panzer Division (*Das Reich*) in the Toulouse area; and 9th Panzer Division in the Avignon area. Of these divisions the 2nd, 116th, 21st and 12th S.S. were under Rommel's command, and the rest in O.K.W. reserve.[1]

The Third Air Fleet (Field-Marshal Sperrle), which was reduced to 90 bombers and 70 fighters fit for action, came under Göring's orders, although it was centred in France.

Taken as a whole the troops were of poor quality, reinforced with invalids and foreigners, and most of their divisional transport was horse drawn.

The so-called Atlantic Wall, which skirted the coasts of Holland, Belgium, and France, had been laid out by the Todt Organization, and in 1943, with the exception of port defences and the Pas de Calais section, consisted of little more than coastal earthworks. In November, 1943, when Rommel was appointed to command Army Group B, he was instructed to inspect the coastal defences, independently of Rundstedt, and in his report to Hitler, dated December 31, he expressed the opinion that "the focus of the enemy landing operation" would "probably be directed against the Fifteenth Army's sector . . . between Boulogne and the Somme estuary. . . ."[2] Nevertheless, he turned his attention to the Normandy stretch, possibly because Hitler was one of the few who believed that the landing would be attempted there.[3] The result was that the coastal defences in the Seine Bay were extensively added to: concrete works were built, minefields and entanglements extended, anti-tank obstacles constructed on the

[1] *Panzer Leader*, General Heinz Guderian (1952), pp. 331–332.
[2] *The Rommel Papers*, edit. B. H. Liddell Hart (1953), p. 453.
[3] See *Von Rundstedt*, Guenther Blumentritt (1952), p. 218, and *The Struggle for Europe*, Chester Wilmot (1952), p. 205.

beaches, and under-water obstacles added. Extensive areas were flooded in the marshy ground bordering the Carentan estuary.

The question of the location of the strategic reserve led to a somewhat academic argument between Rundstedt and Rommel, because ever since 1941 Hitler had decided that were a landing attempted it was to be fought *à outrance* on the beaches. Rommel was of the same opinion, and because of the enemy's air superiority, which he rightly maintained would prohibit daylight movements, besides holding the beaches in strength he wanted the reserves, particularly the armoured divisions, to be located near the coast.[1] Rundstedt, supported by Geyer and General Guderian, Inspector-General of the Panzer Troops,[2] with equal right maintained that until it was known where the enemy intended to land such a course might mean that the reserves would be wrongly positioned when the enemy did land. The outcome was a compromise: the 21st Panzer Division was left at Rommel's disposal, but the 116th, 12th S.S., and Panzer-Lehr Divisions were on no account to be used without Hitler's authority. The greatest defect in the whole defence scheme was that Hitler arrogated to himself the right to issue orders direct to those who should have been Rundstedt's subordinates – Rommel, Sperrle, and others – but who actually were no more than his collaborators. There was no unity of command during the campaign.

The forces in England ready for use at the time of the invasion were: 17 British divisions, including three Canadian; 20 American divisions, one French and one Polish; 5,049 fighter aircraft, 3,467 heavy bombers, 2,343 other combat aircraft, 2,316 transport aircraft, and 2,591 gliders. The total landing craft, merchant vessels and warships exceeded 6,000 vessels.[3] There were also assault engineer tanks; tank-carried bridges for crossing anti-tank ditches; mat-laying tanks for crossing soft patches on the beaches; ramp-tanks over which vehicles could scale sea walls; flail tanks for exploding land mines; amphibious tanks, known as D.D. tanks because of their duplex drive – twin propellers as well as tracks[4] – and C.D.L. tanks, which were fitted with projectors for night operations.[5] Seventy old merchant vessels and four old warships were prepared for the planting of breakwaters (code-named "Gooseberries") in each divisional sector; two artificial harbours

---

[1] *The Rommel Papers*, pp. 468–469.   [2] *Von Rundstedt*, p. 213.
[3] *Crusade in Europe*, Dwight D. Eisenhower (U.S. edit., 1948), p. 53.
[4] *Normandy to the Baltic*, p. 24.
[5] *The Second World War*, J. F. C. Fuller (1948), Appendix, pp. 413–415.

(code-named "Mulberries") built of concrete caissons, which could be towed over the Channel, were in readiness, and a cross-Channel pipe line (code-named "Pluto") was available through which sea-going tankers could discharge petrol direct on the Normandy shore.

The order of battle of the initial assault forces was:

Airborne: the 6th British and the 82nd and 101st American Airborne Divisions.

First U.S. Army (Lieutenant-General Omar N. Bradley): VIIth Corps (Major-General J. L. Collins) four divisions – the 4th, followed by 90th, 9th, and 79th. Vth Corps (Major-General L. T. Gerow) three divisions – 1st and 29th, followed by the 2nd.

Second British Army (Lieutenant-General M. C. Dempsey): XXXth Corps (Lieutenant-General G. C. Bucknall) three divisions – 50th Division and 8th Armoured Brigade, followed by the 7th Armoured Division and 49th Division. Ist Corps (Lieutenant-General J. T. Croker) three divisions – 3rd Canadian Division and 2nd Canadian Armoured Brigade, followed by Commandos and 4th Special Service Brigade; and the 3rd British Division and 27th Armoured Brigade, followed by the 1st Special Service Brigade, 51st Highland Division and 4th Armoured Brigade.

On land, sea, and in the air there were in all 2,876,439 allied officers and men.

The objectives of the forces are shown on the assault plan. It will be seen that the two airborne groups were to form flank guards, the U.S. 82nd and 101st Airborne Divisions around Ste. Mère-Eglise on the right of the assault area, and the British 6th Airborne Division between Cabourg and the river Orne on its left. Five landing areas were allotted to the four assault corps: "Utah" for the U.S. VIIth Corps; "Omaha" for the U.S. Vth Corps, and "Gold", "Juno" and "Sword" for the British XXXth and Ist Corps. The final objectives for D-day are shown on the plan.

Probably the most important step in readiness for invasion was the adoption of a rational strategic bombing policy. Since May 11, 1940, when Mr. Churchill inaugurated the bombing of German cities,[1] the policy of obliterating the enemy's industrial and residential areas had proved a failure; it had not reduced production, which had advanced by leaps and bounds, and it had fortified, not lowered, German civil morale.[2] It was too scattered

---

[1] See *Bombing Vindicated*, J. M. Spaight (1944), pp. 68 and 74.
[2] See *United States Strategic Bombing Survey, Over-all Report (European War)*, 1945.

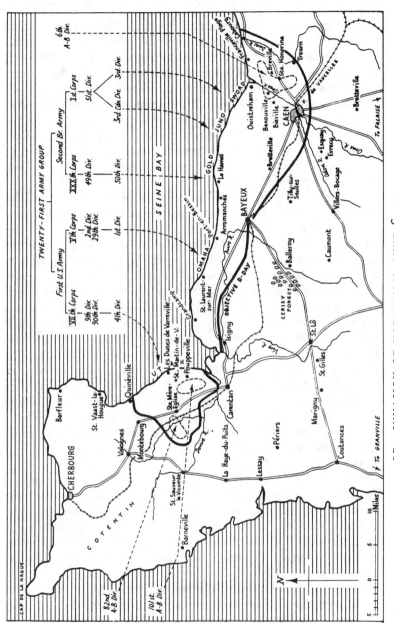

37. INVASION OF NORMANDY, JUNE 6, 1944

to be decisive and it was decided to concentrate on two vitally important targets – transport and synthetic oil plants. General Carl C. Spaatz, Chief of the U.S. Strategic Air Force, favoured the latter, and Air Chief Marshal Sir Arthur Tedder the former. Of the two, Tedder's was the better choice, and it was given priority because the bombing of transport offered the only prospect of disorganizing the enemy in the time available, while the effect of bombing oil plants might not be felt for several months. On March 30, 1944, Tedder's proposal was put into force and at long last "strategic" bombing, for the time being at least, was to become truly strategic.

The plan adopted was to restrict the enemy's mobility by crippling the French and Belgian railways. The underlying idea was, not merely to isolate the allied landing area, but also the whole forward zone of operations between the Seine and the Loire by demolishing the rail and road bridges over these rivers. Should this be effected, it would be difficult for the enemy to move the Fifteenth Army westward of the Seine, and his troops in the south of France northward of the Loire. Except for the gap between Orléans and Fontainebleau, these demolitions would turn the whole forward zone into a strategic island. Beyond these two rivers, a second line of "interdiction" was selected along the Meuse and Albert Canal, the crossings over which were vital to the supply of the German Fifteenth Army. It was decided to demolish these crossings so that the supply lines of the Fifteenth Army would be crippled and its westward lines of advance restricted. This would mean that the German Seventh Army could not be rapidly reinforced from the east.

In the attack on the railways the primary objective was the destruction of motive power by bombing the locomotive depôts. Eighty of these "nerve centres" were selected and by D-day more than 50 had been heavily damaged. Early in May, Colonel Höffner, who was in charge of rail transport for von Rundstedt, reported to O.K.W. that 100 trains a day were required to maintain the *Wehrmacht* in France, and that the average for April had been 60, and had fallen to 32, because the French railways could no longer be supplied with Belgian coal.[1] By D-day, in the Région Nord, of 2,000 locomotives 1,500 were immobilized by air action, or lack of maintenance and fuel, and traffic had fallen to 13 per cent. of its January level. By June 5, "of the 24 road and rail

[1] Cited by Wilmot in *The Struggle for Europe*, p. 211.

bridges over the Seine between Paris and the sea, 18 had been destroyed, three were closed for repair, and the remaining three were under such threat of air attack that they could not be used for any large-scale movement in daylight."[1]

During the three months before D-day 66,000 tons of bombs were dropped, "thus creating," Mr. Churchill writes, "a 'railway desert' around the German troops in Normandy."[2] Besides these operations, preparatory attacks were made by the allied air forces on the enemy coastal defences, radar stations and airfields, which for several weeks before D-day were systematically bombed, and on the eve of D-day 10 super-heavy radar-sighted batteries on the Normandy coast were obliterated. In all, more than 14,000 tons of bombs were dropped on these targets. On the same night the remaining enemy radar stations were jammed, so that when the airborne attacks were launched they were not intercepted, nor were the invasion forces discovered until they neared their objectives.

The more important naval tasks were to escort the invasion fleet, to sweep channels through the enemy's mine barrier, and to cover the landings by bombardment. Admiral Ramsay had two task forces at his disposal; the eastern force, under Rear-Admiral Vian, R.N., to assist the landings on the British sector, and the western force, under Admiral Kirk, U.S.N., to help the American landings. In all, 29 flotillas of minesweepers were allotted to these forces.

An elaborate deception plan was put into force to cover the tactical operations. Its aim was to mislead the enemy about the date of the attack by persuading him that the attempt to cross the Channel would not be made until about six weeks after the actual day selected, and to indicate that it would be delivered in the Pas de Calais area. For every air mission flown over Normandy, two were flown over the Pas de Calais, and for every ton of bombs dropped west of le Havre, two tons were dropped north of it. In addition, many dummy landing craft were assembled in the ports of south-east England; an elaborate dummy headquarters was erected at Dover; and dummy roads, railways and sidings were laid in Sussex and Kent.

Of the many perplexing problems Eisenhower was called upon to solve, one of the most intricate was the choice of D-day. "It was decided," Montgomery states, "that the best conditions would

---

[1] *Ibid.*, p. 212.   [2] *The Second World War*, vol. v, p. 465.

obtain if H-hour [the old zero-hour] were fixed at forty minutes after nautical twilight on a day when at this time the tide was three hours before high water mark,"[1] but because the flow of the tide up the Channel did not permit these conditions to be obtained on all beaches simultaneously, a separate H-hour had to be fixed for each beach; they varied from 6.30 a.m. to 7.45 a.m. Also, as it was desirable that the invasion should be made under a full moon, D-day was restricted to one of three days in each lunar month, and the first three after May 31 were June 5, 6, and 7. The first date was selected; full moon was on the 6th.

June opened with high winds and rough seas, and on June 3 and 4 meteorological predictions were so unfavourable that Eisenhower decided to postpone the invasion for 24 hours. Although conditions had only slightly improved on the 5th, at 4 a.m. that day he took the bold decision to launch the cross-Channel assault on the 6th.

The timetable was that airborne troops, carried in 2,395 aircraft and 867 gliders, were to land at 2 a.m.; the air bombardment, in which 2,219 aircraft were to participate, was to open at 3.14 a.m., to be augmented by a naval bombardment at 5.50 a.m.; and the first wave of the invading forces, carried in 4,266 landing ships and landing craft, were to land between 6.30 a.m. and 7.45 a.m.

At the appointed hour the bombardment was opened by an intense bombing of the enemy's coastal defences and beach obstacles; 7,616 tons of bombs were dropped on them. Then, while the 2nd British and 9th U.S. Tactical Air Forces covered the invasion flotillas, the heavy guns of the combined fleets bombarded the enemy's fixed batteries and concrete defences.[2] At closer range, the lighter defences were bombarded by the lighter ordnance. Finally, as the first wave of the assault neared the shore, a standing barrage was placed on the beaches, which was timed to lift immediately the troops landed. For this, Commander Edwards states, destroyers and L.C.G.'s (landing craft gun) – the modern equivalent of the old floating batteries – literally "drenched" every yard of the beaches with high explosives. Further to increase the density of the fire, rockets were fired from landing craft – L.C.R.'s. "For purposes of short-range 'drenching fire'," Commander Edwards writes, "one such craft

---

[1] *Normandy to the Baltic*, p. 26.
[2] Both bombardments did little damage to the concrete casemates (see *Supreme Commander's Report*, p. 27).

has a fire-power equivalent to over 80 light cruisers or nearly 200 destroyers."[1] These operations were covered by a standing patrol of 10 fighter squadrons, and as far as the high seas permitted the troops were led to the beaches by D.D. (amphibious) tanks. Eisenhower writes: "The use of large numbers of amphibious tanks to afford fire support . . . had been an essential feature of our plans, and, despite the losses they suffered on account of the heavy seas . . . it is doubtful if the assault forces could have firmly established themselves without the assistance of these weapons."[2]

The airborne invasions were eminently successful in spite of the stormy weather. The 6th British Airborne Division was dropped around Breville; the 101st American Division south of Ste. Mère-Eglise, and the 82nd to its west. The first division captured the bridges over the Orne and blew those over the Dives; the second occupied the villages of Pouppeville and St. Martin-de-Varreville, west of "Utah" beach; and the third, in spite of wide dispersion, seized Ste. Mère-Eglise and thereby blocked the Caen–Carentan–Cherbourg road.

These operations came as a rude shock to the enemy who, because of the bad weather, had been taken off-guard. But he was not completely surprised, because between 9.15 and 9.30 p.m. on June 5, a wireless signal had been intercepted and decoded which called all the French Resistance Movement to battle at midnight June 5–6. By 10.30 p.m. both Army Groups B and G and the Third Air Fleet were put on the alert, but unfortunately for the Germans Rommel was on a visit to his wife at Heerlingen, near Ulm; Sepp Dietrich, commander of the 1st S.S. Panzer Corps, was in Brussels; and Dollmann, C.-in-C. Seventh Army, was at Rennes directing a war game.[3] About 1 a.m. on June 6 O.K.W. was informed of the intercepted message, and between 2 a.m. and 3 a.m. it was informed of the airborne landings. When the seaborne landing was announced Rundstedt asked O.K.W. to release the Panzer divisions in reserve. But permission to use them was not given until between 3 and 4 p.m., when it was too late to bring them into action that day. This, according to Blumentritt, was because it was Hitler's habit to work into the

---

[1] *Operation Neptune* (1946), p. 89.
[2] *Supreme Commander's Report*, p. 30. The author first proposed the use of amphibious tanks in a lecture given at the Royal United Service Institution on February 11, 1920, entitled "The Development of Sea Warfare on Land and its Influence on Future Naval Operations."
[3] See *Von Rundstedt*, p. 221.

early hours of the morning and then to sleep until a little before noon, and as no one at O.K.W. had the courage to wake him, "he received detailed information only when the invasion had been in full swing for several hours."[1]

None of the seaborne landings was repulsed; all were successful, though in varying degrees. On Utah beach the 4th U.S. Division, preceded by amphibian tanks that had been launched 5,000 yards off shore, penetrated to a depth of over six miles and made contact with the 101st Airborne Division. On Omaha beach, the two regimental combat teams of the 29th and 1st U.S. Divisions, deprived by the rough sea of full amphibious tank support, were vigorously opposed by the 352nd German Division and were pinned down on the shore line until late in the day, when they fought their way forward to the coastal road. The Second British Army, which also used amphibious tanks, was more fortunate, for although the right of the 50th Division on Gold beach was strongly opposed at le Hamel (two miles east of Arromanches), its left rapidly advanced inland almost to the Bayeux–Caen road. The 3rd Canadian Division on Juno beach met with stiff resistance on the beach, but it pushed forward steadily to a depth of nearly seven miles. On the left of the Second Army the 3rd British Division's assault on Sword beach went according to plan, and by the late afternoon Bieville and most of Ouistreham had been secured, and a counter-attack by German infantry supported by some 20 tanks of the 21st Panzer Division had been repulsed by the 3rd British and 3rd Canadian Divisions.

This counter-offensive was a muddled affair. In the absence of Rommel, General Speidel ordered forward the 21st Panzer Division. But, meanwhile, its commander, General Edgar Feuchtinger, had advanced part of it against the enemy airborne troops east of the Orne, and before it could accomplish its task he was ordered to withdraw it to deal with a critical situation west of the Orne. He was unable to intervene until 3 p.m., and for lack of sufficient infantry support his counter-attack, after it had penetrated to the coast, was beaten back by self-propelled anti-tank artillery.

---

[1] *Ibid.*, p. 225. According to Fabian von Schlabrendorff, when General Hans Speidel, Rommel's chief of staff, telephoned General Jodl at O.K.W., the officer on duty did not dare wake him until 9 a.m., and in his turn Jodl waited for another hour before he informed Keitel. "Both men then considered themselves bound by the strict order never to disturb Hitler's sleep. So it was not until his usual midday meeting that Hitler heard the news" (*Revolt against Hitler*, pp. 129–130).

Throughout the day the allied command of the air was absolute. The *Luftwaffe* did not shoot down a single aircraft of the 14,600 sorties that were flown. By nightfall, between the Vire and Orne the allies had broken through the Atlantic Wall on a front of some 30 miles; but gaps between the landing stages still remained to be filled in, and not one of the final objectives had been gained.

Hitler, Rundstedt, and Rommel – who had returned on the afternoon of the 6th – for once agreed in the belief that the assault west of the Seine was a feint intended to cover the main invasion in the Pas-de-Calais. They decided not to call in the Fifteenth Army, and to deal with the immediate situation. Rommel's plan was to seal off the American penetrations with infantry, and to counter-attack the British in the Caen sector with the 1st Panzer Corps. So that this might be done without delay, Dietrich was instructed not to wait for the Panzer Lehr Division, but to attack all out with the 21st and 12th S.S. Panzer Division as early as he could on June 7.

Soon after midnight on June 6–7, General Kurt Meyer, Commander of the 12th S.S. Panzer Division, arrived at Feuchtinger's headquarters in Caen. Between them they had some 160 tanks, a formidable force, but because of delay in refuelling, aggravated by a fighter-bomber attack at dawn and the involvement of the 21st Panzer Division in a British attack north of Caen, Meyer went forward with only part of his division. He struck at the Canadians who then threatened Caen from the west, and early on June 8 Rommel ordered Dietrich to strike again, this time with all three of his divisions, between Caen and Bayeux. But this was not possible, because the Panzer Lehr Division had not yet come up and the 21st was unable to disengage. All Dietrich could do was to reinforce Meyer, and again Meyer struck at the Canadians, who had advanced to the Caen–Bayeux road at Bretteville. But his infantry was cut off from his tanks and before dawn on the 9th a Canadian counter-attack took back the ground he had gained. After this abortive operation Rommel decided to postpone further counter-attack until he could concentrate his armour.

"From 9th June onwards," writes Speidel, "the initiative lay with the Allies, who fought the battle entirely as it suited them."[1] This is corroborated by Rommel who, on the 10th, in a long report to Hitler, wrote: "During the day, practically our entire

[1] *We Defended Normandy*, p. 99.

traffic – on roads, tracks, and open country – is pinned down by powerful fighter-bomber and bomber formations, with the result that the movements of our troops on the battlefield is almost entirely paralysed, while the enemy can manœuvre freely. Every traffic defile in the rear areas is under continual attack and it is very difficult to get essential supplies and ammunition and petrol to the troops."[1]

Montgomery had firmly established his bridgehead by June 12, and 326,000 men, 54,000 vehicles, and 104,000 tons of stores had been landed.[2] By then the VIIth U.S. Corps had pushed out to Montebourg, north-east of Ste. Mère-Eglise, and also had occupied Carentan, east of which it had linked up with the Vth U.S. Corps. The latter had advanced its front to the Vire, eight miles north of St. Lô; had occupied the Forest of Cerisy, and had pushed its left well beyond Balleroy. On the British front the XXXth Corps had captured Bayeux and had fought forward to the Balleroy–Caen road. On its left the Ist Corps had established itself on a front that ran from Bretteville round Caen and thence to Ste. Honorine, from where its left was swung northward to Franceville-Plage on the Channel, west of Cabourg.

In spite of Rommel's failure to drive his enemy into the sea, on the night of June 12–13 renewed hope was awakened in Germany. The first flying-bomb had fallen on London. It was a pilotless jet-propelled aircraft with a warhead of 1,000 kg., but although it did considerable damage the expectations placed in it were soon found to have been grossly exaggerated.[3]

Once the German counter-attack had been repulsed, Montgomery set out to take Cherbourg and Caen; the former in order to gain a port which would supplement his precarious prefabricated harbours and beach supply, and the latter to establish a fulcrum for his strategic lever – the break-through on his western flank. Rommel, after his failure at Caen, set out to frustrate an advance on Cherbourg, and on June 13–15 he made a violent attempt, in which the 17th S.S. Panzer Division was committed, to break through the junction of the VIIth and Vth U.S. Corps in the Carentan area; but again he was repulsed. Simultaneously

---

[1] *The Rommel Papers*, pp. 476–477.   [2] *Normandy to the Baltic*, p. 57.
[3] In all some 8,000 flying-bombs were launched against London, of which 2,400 got through; 23,000 houses were destroyed, over 700,000 damaged, 6,000 people killed and 18,000 injured. On September 8 the first long-range rocket-bomb (V2) fell in London. It was a novel and revolutionary weapon, its maximum range was 200 miles and its speed remarkable, but it was too inaccurate to be anything more than a terror weapon.

the Americans captured Montebourg, and on the 14th the 9th
U.S. Division and the 82nd Airborne Division advanced westward
on St. Sauveur-le-Vicomte. They captured it on the 16th and two
days later reached the west coast of the Cotentin Peninsula at
Barneville. The VIIIth U.S. Corps then became operative and
took over command of the two airborne and 90th divisions and
faced south so as to cover the advance of the VIIth Corps on
Cherbourg.

On June 19 the allied calculations were upset by a furious and
unforecasted gale. It blew hard for three days, wrecked the
American "Mulberry" at St. Laurent-sur-Mer, and damaged the
British "Mulberry" at Arromanches. When the storm subsided
it was found that 800 craft were stranded on the beaches and that
allied shipping had sustained five times the damage caused by
the enemy on D-day.

On June 21, the 4th, 79th, and 9th Divisions of the VIIth U.S.
Corps closed on Cherbourg, and on the following day, supported
by naval gunfire, they opened an assault on the fortress, which
was commanded by General Karl von Schlieben. On the 25th
they broke through its defences, captured von Schlieben on the
26th, and on the 27th Cherbourg surrendered with 39,000 men.
The port was found so thoroughly wrecked that it did not become
operative until late in August.

While Cherbourg was stormed, on June 25 the XXXth, VIIIth,
and Ist Corps of the Second British Army made a determined
attack on Caen. The country was exceedingly difficult and strewn
with land mines, and although in the centre the VIIIth Corps
reached the river Odon west of Caen, the other two corps made
little progress. On the 29th the 1st and 2nd S.S. Panzer Divisions
were encountered, and were soon followed by the 9th S.S. Panzer
Division with elements of the 10th S.S. Panzer Division, both
from the eastern front. This stiffening of the enemy armour
decided Montgomery to hold the ground he had won and to
re-group.

When the Second Front, so long called for by Stalin, was opened
in Normandy, the Russians made ready their summer offensive.
On June 23 it was opened between Vitebsk and Gomel, and by
the end of July the Niemen was reached. South of the Pripet a
second great offensive followed on July 13, and 17 days later the
Vistula was crossed south of Sandomir. By mid-August the
German situation was catastrophic – the Russians were at the

Carpathians and the borders of east Prussia. On August 22 after a *coup d'état* in Bucharest the Rumanian Government capitulated, and three days later the Finns sued for an armistice. From July 1 the doom of the Third Reich was no longer in doubt; the hour for the break-through in Normandy was about to strike and at long last the end of the war was in sight.

On the day after the fall of Cherbourg, Rundstedt and Rommel were summoned to Berchtesgaden and, on June 29, in conference with Hitler, Rundstedt demanded a free hand, and Rommel urged that the Seventh Army should be withdrawn to the Seine. Hitler would not listen to these proposals and the outcome was that on July 3 Rundstedt tendered his resignation and was succeeded by Field-Marshal von Kluge.

Meanwhile Montgomery decided to take Caen, and at the same time to advance the First U.S. Army toward the line Coutances–St. Lô, preparatory to a break-out on the western flank. This dual offensive was opened by Bradley on July 3, but because of the difficult *bocage* country and the stubborn resistance of the enemy it made slow progress. On July 7–8 came the attack on Caen, a typical Montgomery battle of *matériel*. Bomber Command R.A.F. was called in to support Dempsey's advance, and although Montgomery asserts that "it played an important part in the success of the operation,"[1] eyewitness reports do not corroborate this.[2] Two thousand five hundred tons of bombs were dropped on Caen, the streets of which were so blocked by rubble that it was impossible for tanks to move along them until passages had been cleared by bulldozers.[3] The delay caused by the bombing enabled the Germans to withdraw from Caen, on the northern side of the Orne, to the Faubourg de Vaucelles, on the river's southern side, and so to frustrate a complete break-through.

By July 10, a crisis was reached: the American offensive was bogged down; the Germans in Vaucelles still blocked the way to the Falaise plain; and four German divisions from southern France had been brought up to reinforce the right of the Seventh Army. Because these reinforcements enabled Rommel to relieve his Panzer divisions, which he began to move toward the American

---

[1] *Normandy to the Baltic*, p. 74.
[2] See *Eclipse*, Alan Moorehead (1945), p. 112, and *European Victory*, John D'Arcy-Dawson (n.d.), pp. 87–88.
[3] General de Guingand, Montgomery's Chief of Staff, records: "The trouble then was that *too much disruption* was caused, and our advance was impeded by the effects of the bombing" (*Operation Victory*, 1947, p. 396).

front, it became imperative for Montgomery to attack again in order to put a stop to this.

His plan was that while Bradley restocked his ammunition dumps and made ready to capture St. Lô and drive the enemy back to the Périers–St. Lô road, in preparation for a break-out (Operation "Cobra") on July 20, on the night of July 15–16 Dempsey was to make a feint attack to the west of Caen, which on the 18th was to be followed by a decisive attack (Operation "Goodwood") by his VIIIth Corps and three armoured divisions from the Orne bridgehead southward and to the east of Caen. In a note to Lieutenant-General Sir Richard O'Connor, G.O.C. VIIIth Corps, Montgomery explained his project as follows: "A victory on the eastern flank will help us gain what we want on the western flank. But the eastern flank is a bastion on which the whole future of the campaign in North-West Europe depends."[1] In brief, his plan was to draw in the maximum German forces on Caen so that the minimum would be left to operate against Bradley's First Army in the St. Lô area.

The feint attack at first succeeded in deceiving the Germans, and was notable for its use of an expedient called "artificial moonlight." Beams of massed searchlights were focussed on the clouds, from which their light was reflected back to the ground.[2] But on the following night a *Luftwaffe* reconnaissance, using flare-lights, reported traffic across the Orne bridges. As this pointed to a break-through, early on July 17 Rommel went forward to make sure of the defensive dispositions. On his return in the afternoon, when on the road from Livarot to Vimoutiers, near the village of Ste. Foy-Montgomery, his car was attacked by a British fighter aircraft and he was so severely wounded that at first it was thought he was dead. When von Kluge heard of this, he did not appoint a successor to Rommel, but took over command of Army Group B.

The attack on July 18 (operation "Goodwood") was a super-Montgomery operation. The plan was to bridge the Orne canal; to send over three armoured divisions (the Guards, 7th, and 11th) with supporting tanks and infantry, and then, under cover of a "super-colossal crack", to swing southward toward Falaise and cut off and destroy three German divisions. To clear a way for the tanks, heavy bombers were to bomb on each side of an area

---

[1] Cited by Wilmot in *The Struggle for Europe*, p. 354.

[2] Montgomery's assumption that this expedient "was used for the first time in battle" (*Normandy to the Baltic*, p. 78) is incorrect. As we have seen (Chapter 8, p. 314) it was first employed in Italy by the British 7th Division in August, 1918.

4,000 yards in width and silence the enemy anti-tank guns on the flanks of the attacking armour. Between these two walls of bursting bombs lighter aircraft were to drop fragmentation (non-cratering) anti-personnel bombs, so as not to make the ground impassable. The tanks were then to advance through the bomb-swept lane under cover of a creeping artillery barrage. Eisenhower informs us that the attack was preceded "by what was the heaviest and most concentrated air assault hitherto employed in support of ground operations." Twelve thousand tons of bombs were dropped, 5,000 "in less than forty-five minutes. . . . At the same time, a strong naval bombardment was made to supplement the air effort."[1]

Unfortunately for Montgomery, the Germans withdrew their troops and prepared a zone of anti-tank defences on a line a few miles behind the prospective lane. Their gunners remained under cover until the bombing was over and then they emerged and opened fire on the hundreds of vehicles deployed across the plain. They knocked out between 150 and 200 of the attacking tanks – the 11th Armoured Division lost over 100 – after which some 50 German aircraft heavily bombed the British position during the night. On the following day the weather broke and the plains of Caen became a sea of mud; the battle ended.[2]

The break in the weather persuaded General Eisenhower to postpone Bradley's attack (Operation "Cobra") until July 25, when the plan was to advance on a three-divisional front west of St. Lô, with the line Marigny–St. Gilles as the primary objective. Then it was planned that three fresh divisions would leap-frog through the leading three divisions, and lastly a turn westward was to be made in order to strike at Coutances and Granville.

The air tactics were that fighter-bomber attacks were made on all enemy bridges over the river Vire south of St. Lô, so as to isolate the area of advance. Then, "at 1.40 hours," writes General H. H. Arnold, Commanding General U.S. Army Air Forces, "P.47 Thunderbolts with bombs and incendiaries crossed east to west in seven waves, 2 or 3 minutes apart. Then for an hour more than 1,500 Fortresses and Liberators dropped 3,431 tons of explosives. P.38 Lightnings followed in eight waves lasting 20

---

[1] *Supreme Commander's Report*, pp. 45–46.
[2] According to General Wisch, commander of the 1st Panzer Division, on the evening of July 18 his Panther tanks surprised approximately 100 British tanks in leaguer and knocked out 40 during the night and another 40 next morning (*Defeat in the West*, Milton Schulman, 1947, p. 141).

minutes, laying more incendiaries. Then 400 medium bombers attacked the southern end of the area with 500-pound bombs, concentrating on crossroads and German concentrations of tanks and troops in the village of St. Gilles. Incendiaries started flames that swept unchecked over German bivouac areas and dugouts."[1]

As in the Caen attacks, this mighty air blow "did not cause a large numbers of casualties to the enemy, but it produced great confusion." And "Again, as at Caen, this stunning effect was only temporary. . . . The advance was met with intense artillery fire, from positions not neutralized by the air bombing."[2]

The infantry attack was made on a four-mile front, with tanks in support, and the most interesting thing about it was the air cooperation. "As our troops went forward," writes General Arnold, "fighters and fighter-bombers in closest communication and under common direction ranged ahead of them destroying military targets. . . . Fighters in direct communication with tanks by radio flew constant alert over our armored columns. Ground officers called on the fighters to bomb or strafe artillery or armor in their path. Pilots warned tank commanders of traps at crossroads or woods. German armored units, without aerial eyes, fought at a disadvantage."[3] This was *blitzkrieg* on the grand scale.

During July 27 the towns of Périers and Lessay were occupied, and on the 28th the escape route through Coutances was closed and 4,500 Germans captured. In the meantime, to the east, the Canadian IInd Corps' advance toward Falaise had been halted by a strong defensive belt of anti-tank guns, dug-in tanks, and mortars.

Five days later, the Third U.S. Army, which consisted of the VIIIth, XIIth, XVth, and XXth Corps, under General Patton, officially came into being; Lieutenant-General C. H. Hodges was given the command of the First U.S. Army (Vth, VIIth, and XIXth Corps), and the two armies were formed into the Twelfth Army Group under General Bradley. This left Montgomery in command of the Twenty-First Army Group, namely the Second British Army and the First Canadian Army, under Lieutenant-General H. D. G. Crearer, which had become operational on July 23. Nevertheless, until September, Montgomery continued in control of all of Eisenhower's land forces.

---

[1] *Second Report*, 27th February, 1945, pp. 11 and 14.
[2] *Supreme Commander's Report*, pp. 47–48.
[3] *Second Report*, 27th February, 1945, p. 14.

When Coutances was taken, the plan for the Third U.S. Army was to drive south, break through Avranches into Brittany, and seize the area Rennes–Fougères. Then it was to turn westward and secure the ports of St. Malo and Brest while the First U.S. Army advanced south to seize the Mortain–Vire area. At the same time the Second British Army was to thrust forward in the Caumont area. This time, whatever the weather, Eisenhower decided "to indulge in an all-out offensive and, if necessary, throw caution to the winds."[1] It was high time to do so, because he had absolute command in the air, at least two men to his enemy's one, and a tank and gun superiority of about three to one in his favour.

On July 29 Patton's leading tanks crossed the river Sienne (south of Coutances), and two days later Avranches was captured. "No effective barrier," writes Eisenhower, "now lay between us and Brittany, and my expectations of creating an open flank had been realized. The enemy was in a state of complete disorganization. . . ."[2] At the same time Montgomery launched his thrust south of Caumont, preceded by a smashing air bombardment delivered by 1,200 aircraft. Évrecy and Esquay, south-west of Caen, were stormed on August 4, and Villers-Bocage occupied on the 5th.

After the capture of Granville and Avranches, Patton met negligible resistance. On August 2 Rennes was entered and St. Malo by-passed. By August 6, the line of the Vilaine river was held from Rennes to the sea and the Brittany peninsula cut off. On August 7 the 6th U.S. Armoured Division stood before Brest, and on the 10th Nantes was in American hands.

The day after the occupation of Rennes, Bradley ordered Patton to leave a minimum of force in Brittany, and with the bulk of his army to drive all out for Paris. Patton set out to do this on August 4.

It was clear to von Kluge, threatened as he was by Patton's break-out from Avranches, that the only sane thing to do was to withdraw to the Seine. But Hitler would not listen to this, and on the day Patton set out for Paris Hitler ordered Kluge to assemble eight of his nine Panzer divisions and, on the night of August 6–7, to launch them from Mortain against the bottleneck of Patton's communications at Avranches. This would have been a sound enough proposition had Kluge held command of the air,

---

[1] *Supreme Commander's Report*, p. 50.
[2] *Ibid.*, p. 50.

but as he did not, it was suicidal.[1] Kluge was fully aware of this, but as he had been involved in the plot of July 20 to assassinate Hitler[2] he feared that were he to press his disagreement Hitler might suspect him of treason. In spite of this fear he found it impossible to disengage from the battle more than four Panzer divisions – 250 tanks in all – and two infantry divisions.

Unfortunately for Kluge, his preparations could not be hidden from his enemy's air reconnaissances, and directly Bradley learnt of them he deployed five divisions between Vire and Mortain to meet the threatened thrust. He also ordered Patton to hold back three divisions at St. Hilaire on the southern flank of the German advance. On August 6 Bradley struck against Vire, which compelled General Paul Hausser, in command of the Seventh German Army, to throw in part of the counter-attacking force in order to secure its right flank. Lastly, on the night of August 6–7, Hausser struck westward, advanced seven miles toward Avranches, and then was halted by American armour.

On August 7 the German columns that crowded the roads around Mortain were mercilessly bombed by American Thunderbolt and R.A.F. Typhoon aircraft and Montgomery ordered the First Canadian Army to thrust southward down the Caen–Falaise road against the rear of Hausser's right flank. "The plan," writes Montgomery, "was to attack under cover of darkness after a preliminary action by heavy bombers; the infantry was to be transported through the enemy's zone of defensive fire and forward defended localities in heavy armoured carriers. These vehicles, which became known as 'Kangaroos', were self-propelled gun carriages converted for transporting infantry."[3] On August 8 Montgomery asked Bradley to order Patton to swing his XVth Corps, which the day before had occupied Le Mans, northward on Alençon, so as to meet the Canadian thrust on Falaise and thereby close in from south and north on the enemy's communications.

[1] According to General Bayerlein: "Without the U.S.A.A.F. and the R.A.F. this attack . . . would almost certainly have resulted in a resounding victory. Hence, like the invasion battle itself – and this was the opinion of Rommel and most of the leading commanders – the battle was lost only because of the total supremacy which the Allies enjoyed in the air" (*The Rommel Papers*, pp. 490–491).

[2] For this plot see *Revolt Against Hitler*, Fabian von Schlabrendorff, chap. x. So little did the Allies appreciate the value to themselves of the anti-Nazi revolt that after July 20 they indicated "that Hitler's removal from power would not mean any modification in the demand for 'Unconditional Surrender' " (*The Struggle for Europe*, p. 318). Actually the attempted assassination strengthened more than weakened Hitler's position.

[3] *Normandy to the Baltic*, p. 97. It is strange that these vehicles were not used earlier because armoured infantry transporters were built in 1918.

This thrust became apparent to Kluge on the morning of the 10th, and as he could not meet it, a withdrawal from the Mortain area was imperative. Nevertheless he hesitated to suggest it to O.K.W. until midday on the 11th, and then only in a vague way. The reply he received was that, once he had driven back the XVth American Corps, he was to adhere to the counter-attack. But before he could act on this order the XVth Corps captured Alençon on August 12, and by the evening of the following day had advanced to Argentan. This placed most of the Seventh German Army in an impossible position. It occupied a sausage-shaped salient, 40 miles in length and 15 miles in breadth at its base – Falaise–Argentan – and whatever Hitler might dictate its withdrawal had become compulsory.

So that Patton might resume his advance on Paris, on August 12 Bradley relieved his XVth Corps at Argentan by the Vth Corps of the First U.S. Army, and on the 14th the Canadians resumed their advance on Falaise, but failed to occupy it until the 16th. On that day Patton's XIIth Corps captured Orléans and his XXth entered Chartres, and 24 hours later his XVth was in Dreux, from where it was ordered to advance to the Seine at Mantes – north-west of Paris. There it established a bridgehead over the Seine on the 19th. In the meantime Hitler, who suspected that Kluge had betrayed him, replaced him by Field-Marshal Walter Model.[1]

On August 17 the Vth American Corps from Argentan, and the 4th Canadian and 1st Polish Armoured Divisions from Falaise set out to close the exit of the shrinking pocket in which the remnants of 15 German divisions and elements of others were now squeezed into a space 20 miles long and 10 wide at its eastern end. Their only escape routes were through Chambois and St. Lambert, which were under fire from both flanks and unceasingly bombed. "P.47 Thunderbolts," writes General Arnold, "caught German tanks and trucks in column moving three abreast, bumper to bumper, on three highways of Argentan. The planes bombed the leaders of the columns, blocking the roads, and then roamed over them strafing and bombing. . . . A.A.F. Fighters kept up the attack all day despite intense flak and foul weather. The smoke was so thick along some roads that pilots could not tally the destruction exactly, but they estimated 1,000

---

[1] Kluge handed his command over to Model on August 16, and a few days later committed suicide. Rommel was compelled to do the same on October 14.

vehicles destroyed. Next day in the Royal Air Force area, Spitfires, Mustangs, and Typhoons destroyed another thousand."[1]

In spite of this terrific pounding, on August 20 the 2nd Panzer Division broke through the Canadians at St. Lambert and for six hours kept open an escape road for the fleeing remnants of the Seventh Army. That any of its men escaped, and over a third did, would appear to be because the thrust from Falaise had been made in insufficient strength and because of the relief of the American XVth Corps by the Vth, which must have delayed the advance northward of Argentan. The destruction of the Seventh German Army and not the occupation of Paris should have been the strategical objective at that time. But later, in April, 1945, as we shall see, when Berlin was within Eisenhower's grasp, it was the reverse.

On August 15, when the battle of Falaise was at its height, Operation "Dragoon" – previously code-named "Anvil", was put into force. Had this happened immediately before or simultaneously with "Overlord", strategically there might have been some slight profit, but after D-day "Anvil" had lost its *raison d'être*. This diversion of forces from Italy wrecked Alexander's campaign, which after the fall of Rome, on June 4, had progressed rapidly northward, and prevented Alexander from advancing into central Europe and so went far to deprive the victory in Normandy of its political significance. After the successful landing on June 6, in any set of circumstances the defeat of Germany was assured in the immediate future; the time had come to suit strategy to policy. Although in the circumstances that prevailed, Normandy and Poland were strategically the decisive theatres of the war, the backbone of the decisive political theatre remained the line Vienna–Prague–Berlin. Were the western allies the first to gain that line, in spite of their purblind commitments at Teheran they would still be able largely to shape the eventual peace; but were the Russians to do so, then, faced by Russia's military might, they would be compelled to toe the line.

This was foreseen by Mr. Churchill, by the British Chiefs of Staff, and by General Wilson, General Alexander, and General Montgomery. On June 19 Wilson had pointed out to Eisenhower that should the strategical aim be to defeat Germany in 1944, "the strategy best calculated to aid the assault on Northern France," was "to strike a blow which would force the enemy to

[1] General Arnold's *Second Report*, pp. 14 and 28.

divert divisions from France and, at the same time, confront him with the prospect of defeat in 1944." Instead of "Anvil" he urged "a continuation of General Alexander's campaign into the Po Valley and to the Ljubjana gap – thereby threatening an area vital to the enemy,"[1] and, incidentally, vital to the Russians also.

But Eisenhower would have none of this and he was strongly supported by the American Chiefs of Staff, more particularly by General Marshall. Mr. Churchill points out that they held "rigidly to the maxim of concentrating at the decisive point, which in their eyes meant only North-West Europe."[2] What they failed to understand was that a decisive point of the first importance must be politically profitable as well as strategically attainable, and that to land an army in southern France in order eventually to storm the winter sports resorts of the Black Forest was about the most indecisive thing they could do. On the contrary, Wilson's suggestion, which led toward Vienna, would endow a victory in France with the utmost political profit, because it would bring the Americans and British into central Europe, and only in central Europe could the war be won politically. Eisenhower's contention that "there was no development of that period which added more decisively to . . . the final and complete defeat of the German forces than did this secondary attack coming up the Rhone Valley,"[3] shows that, even as late as 1948, he still failed to realize that war is a political instrument.

Eisenhower was supported by the President, who had political reasons for doing so. In a long cable dispatched to Churchill on June 29, Roosevelt said: "Since the agreement was made at Teheran to mount an 'Anvil', I cannot accept, without consultation with Stalin, any course of action which abandons this operation. . . . Finally, for purely political considerations over here, I should never survive even a slight set back in 'Overlord' if it were known that fairly large forces had been diverted to the Balkans."[4] For the President, the decisive point was neither in north-west France nor central Europe, it was the November presidential elections, and in part, at least, "Anvil" was launched to secure for him his fourth term in office.

That was why early in July Alexander was ordered to withdraw the VIth U.S. Corps (three divisions); the French Expeditionary

---

[1] *Report by the Supreme Allied Commander Mediterranean, etc.* (1948), part II, p. 35.
[2] *The Second World War*, vol. VI, p. 52.   [3] *Crusade in Europe*, p. 294.
[4] *The Second World War*, Winston S. Churchill, vol. VI, p. 664.

Force (three divisions in Italy and four in North Africa); and a considerable part of his air force in order to build up the Seventh U.S. Army, under Lieutenant-General Alexander M. Patch, for the invasion of southern France on August 15. Mr. Churchill points out that thereby General Mark C. Clark's Fifth U.S. Army in Italy alone was reduced from some 250,000 to 153,000 men,[1] and Alexander's campaign wrecked.

Ten days after the Seventh U.S. Army had landed – virtually unopposed – between Cavalaire and Agny on the French Riviera,[2] Paris was liberated by the 2nd French Armoured Division, under General P. E. Leclerc. The battle of Normandy was at an end; the Seventh German Army was in rout. "From the point of view of equipment abandoned," says General Dietrich, who conducted the withdrawal, "the Seine crossing was almost as great a disaster as the Falaise Pocket."[3] The battle had cost the Germans little short of half a million men, of whom 210,000 were captured; 3,000 guns; 1,500 tanks; 2,000 aircraft; 20,000 vehicles; and masses of equipment and supplies.

On September 1, Eisenhower took over personal command of all his land forces, and Montgomery, promoted field-marshal, was left with the Twenty-First Army Group. A second Jena had been won and the western road to Berlin opened; all that remained was to exploit the victory, as Napoleon had done in 1806. But unfortunately for the allies, through force of circumstances, and even more because of difference of character, Eisenhower was neither a Montgomery nor a Napoleon.

When the war began Eisenhower was a junior lieutenant-colonel in the Philippines on General Douglas MacArthur's staff. Since then, and until July, 1942, when he was selected over the heads of 366 senior officers to command "Torch", he had held no command other than that of an infantry battalion. His outlook on the war was typical of most Americans. He says that the war was a crusade in which "the utter destruction of the Axis" was demanded, in order to create "a decent world."[4] "Throughout my life," he said during his 1952 electoral campaign for the presidency, "the major events have always had that extra spiritual factor to make them a crusade. . . . How else can you explain

---

[1] *Ibid.*, vol. VI, p. 76.

[2] On September 15 the French divisions were grouped into the First French Army (General de Lattre de Tassigny) and with the Seventh U.S. Army were formed into the Sixth Army Group, under General J. L. Devers.

[3] Cited in *The Struggle for Europe*, p. 434.   [4] *Crusade in Europe*, p. 157.

the successful landings in North Africa and the campaigns that followed through Sicily and Italy except in terms of a crusade? . . . How could Hitler's Fortress Europe have been breached, and how could the Nazi armies have been rolled back to ultimate destruction unless the spirit of every man involved was a spirit of crusade?"[1] In 1944, Henry Morgenthau quotes him as characterizing "the whole German population" as "synthetic paranoid;"[2] he held that "membership in the Gestapo and the S.S. should be taken as *prima facie* evidence of guilt," and that the war-making power of Germany should be eliminated.[3] Whether this was to be the task of the western allies or Russia does not seem to have concerned him, because in his opinion, "The ordinary Russian seemed to" him "to bear a marked similarity to what we call an 'average American',"[4] and that, "In the past relations of America and Russia there was no cause to regard the future with pessimism. . . . Both were free from the stigma of colonial empire building by force."[5]

When his generalship is criticized, it should be borne in mind that his upbringing placed him in an exceptionally difficult position as an allied commander. It would appear that he was not a highly educated or deeply read soldier, and he had little comprehension of the relationship between strategy and policy. "Political estimates," he writes, "are functions of governments, not of soldiers,"[6] which though true in the abstract, is often fatal in the concrete, more especially when the soldier is a general-in-chief. Because in service he was a comparatively junior officer, and a man of amiable rather than forceful character, he was dominated by General Marshall and over apt to yield to his subordinates. It was made more difficult for him not to give way to the latter because he commanded an allied army, and in such a body envy and jealousy, if not active, are always latent. It was imperative for him to establish harmony between his leading generals, and this he did admirably. But it was equally imperative in order to win the war in the shortest time and at the least cost, that strategy should not be subordinated to concord. Because he failed to understand this, as a general-in-chief he was more of a coordinator than a commander. In order to keep his turbulent

---

[1] *The Times*, London, October 22, 1952.
[2] *America's 2nd Crusade*, William Henry Chamberlin (1950), p. 303.
[3] *Crusade in Europe*, p. 287.   [4] *Ibid.*, p. 474.
[5] *Ibid.*, p. 457. This would be an extraordinary statement even for a schoolboy.
[6] *Ibid.*, p. 80.

barons occupied and tranquil he cut the strategic cake into slices and gave each a slice to eat; in so doing he violated the principle of concentration and prolonged the war.

On August 31 the rosters of Allied Supreme Headquarters showed that by then a total of 2,052,297 men and 436,471 vehicles had been landed, and that in northern France Eisenhower had at his disposal 23 infantry divisions and the equivalent of 15 armoured divisions. "The ratio of combat effectives," states Mr. Cole, "was approximately 2 to 1 in favor of the Allies. . . . Allied superiority in guns was at least 2½ to 1, that in tanks approximately 20 to 1;" and allied air strength numbered 13,891 combat aircraft, as well as hundreds of reconnaissance, liaison, and transport aircraft, against 573 serviceable aircraft of all types in the German Third Air Fleet.[1]

Although Eisenhower was unaware of these ratios, at least he knew as much as Bradley, which was that "By the first of September the enemy's June strength on the Western front had been cut down to a disorganized corporal's guard. The total of all German remnants north of the Ardennes equaled only 11 divisions, of which but two were panzers."[2] The problem Eisenhower had to solve was clearly one of pursuit. His four armies in northern France were in line: the First Canadian on the left, the Second British and First American in the centre, and the Third American on the right; and together they had pushed out a great salient from Abbeville in the north and Orléans in the south, with its apex at Verdun. To launch a pursuit with all four armies was out of the question because, Eisenhower points out, truck supply of petrol had become "utterly inadequate" and, in order to maintain the momentum of the Third Army, he had already been compelled to supply it by air-lift.[3] His problem was to decide which of his armies to halt so as to accumulate sufficient petrol to sustain those which were to pursue.

Montgomery had considered this problem; already on August 17 he had suggested to Bradley that, once the Seine was crossed, a powerful thrust should be made, not along the whole front, but north of the Ardennes. On August 23, he proposed to Eisenhower, "one powerful full-blooded thrust across the Rhine into the heart

[1] *The United States Army in World War II*, "The Lorraine Campaign," H. M. Cole (1950), pp. 2–4.
[2] *A Soldier's Story*, p. 411.
[3] *Supreme Commander's Report*, p. 60. See also General Arnold's *Second Report*, p. 30, and Sir Trafford Leigh-Mallory's "Despatch", *London Gazette*, December 31, 1946.

of Germany" by way of Belgium so as to gain the plains of northern Germany, where superiority of armour could be exploited. "If we could maintain," he writes, "the strength and impetus of our operations beyond the Seine sufficiently to keep the enemy on the run straight through to the Rhine, and 'bounce' our way across that river before the enemy succeeded in reforming a front to oppose us, then we should achieve a prodigious advantage."[1] But to supply this thrust demanded that Patton's Third Army should be halted temporarily. Eisenhower would not agree to this: he considered it politically impossible, because "the American public would never stand for it."[2] And from a military point of view he held that the proposal was "completely fantastic"; he called it a "pencillike thrust."[3]

Eisenhower's plan was to "push forward on a broad front, with priority on the left," and at the same time to advance the Third Army eastward toward the Saar Basin, to make contact with the Sixth Army Group, then advancing up the Rhône Valley. "This linking up of the whole front," he writes, "was mandatory," it "would allow us to use all our troops in facing and fighting the enemy and would prevent the costliness of establishing long defensive flanks along which our troops could have nothing but negative, static missions. . . . We wanted to bring all our strength against him, all of it mobile and all of it contributing directly to the complete annihilation of his field forces."[4]

It would appear that it was because of Bradley's and Patton's protests that Eisenhower did not allot the leading rôle to Montgomery, and also that he entirely misread the situation. He did not exploit his victory, but began preparations for another major battle and so missed the opportunity to make his victory strategically decisive.

Whether Montgomery's "full-blooded thrust" would have succeeded, we cannot say, but what we do know is that it was what the Germans expected. "Since the war," writes Wilmot, "Rundstedt and other German generals . . . have declared that a concentrated thrust from Belgium in September must have succeeded. . . . Blumentritt says: 'Such a break-through *en masse* with air domination, would have torn the weak German front to pieces and ended the war in the winter of 1944'."[5]

---

[1] *Normandy to the Baltic*, p. 119.
[2] Cited by Wilmot, *The Struggle for Europe*, p. 468.
[3] *Crusade in Europe*, pp. 252 and 306.
[4] *Ibid.*, p. 226.   [5] *The Struggle for Europe*, p. 539.

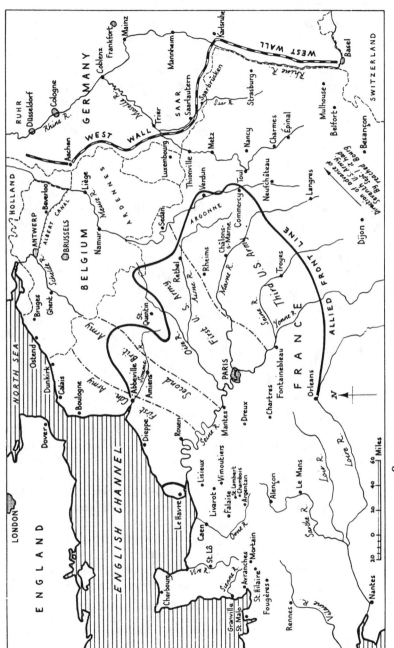

38. ALLIED FRONT LINE, SEPTEMBER 1, 1944

Liddell Hart corroborates this: "All the German generals to whom I talked," he records, "were of the opinion that the Allied Supreme Command had missed a great opportunity of ending the war in the autumn of 1944. They agreed with Montgomery's view, that this could best have been achieved by concentrating all possible resources on a threat in the north, towards Berlin."[1] Finally, General Speidel says: "The events of the last weeks of August were like a foaming torrent that nothing could stem. . . . Then something unexpected occurred, a German variation of the 'miracle of the Marne' for the French in 1914: the furious advance of the Allies suddenly faded away. . . . The method of Allied Supreme Command was the main reason. . . . Had the Allies held on grimly to the retreating Germans they could have harried the breath out of every man and beast and ended the war half a year earlier. There were no German ground forces of any importance that could be thrown in, and next to nothing in the air."[2]

Still further to cripple allied strategy, during the Second Quebec Conference, which assembled on September 10, Mr. Henry Morgenthau, Secretary of the United States Treasury, who in 1944 began to play a decisive part in shaping American foreign policy,[3] brought forward a plan on how to deal with Germany. It was largely the work of Harry Dexter White, Morgenthau's assistant secretary, who, in August 14, 1951, was cited before the Senate security sub-committee, and was found to be a Soviet agent.[4] The main features of the plan[5] were that Germany was to be deprived of east Prussia, most of Silesia, the Saar, and an extensive area on the left bank of the Rhine. The rest of Germany was to be partitioned into North and South and an International Zone, the latter to extend from Frankfort to the Baltic and Bremen, and to include the Ruhr. In this zone it was laid down that "all industrial plants and equipment not destroyed by military action shall be completely dismantled or removed from the area, or completely destroyed, all equipment shall be removed from the mines and the mines shall be thoroughly wrecked." Forms of restitution were to include, besides transfer of plant and equipment, "forced German labor outside Germany." The last proviso is of particular interest, for had it been put into effect it would have led to the

---

[1] *The Other Side of the Hill*, p. 429.   [2] *We Defended Normandy*, pp. 151–153.
[3] See *Memoirs of Cordell Hull* (English edit., 1948), vol. I, p. 207.
[4] See *The Twenty-Year Revolution from Roosevelt to Eisenhower*, Chesly Manly (1954), pp. 102, 103.
[5] See *Germany Is Our Problem*, Henry Morgenthau, Jr. (1945), pp. 1–4.

domination of Germany by Russia. It reads: "The primary responsibility for the policing of Germany and for civil administration in Germany should be assumed by the military forces of Germany's continental neighbors. Specifically these should include Russian, French, Czech, Polish, Greek, Dutch, and Belgian soldiers. Under this program United States troops could be withdrawn within a relatively short time."

The Morgenthau plan was accepted by the President and Mr. Churchill, and on September 15 they initialled an agreement providing that the industries in the Ruhr and the Saar would be "put out of action and closed down." The two areas were to be placed under some international organization, "which would supervise the dismantling of these industries, and make sure that they are not started up again by some subterfuge. This programme for eliminating the war making industries in the Ruhr and the Saar is looking forward to converting Germany into a country primarily agricultural and pastoral in its character. The Prime Minister and the President were in agreement upon this programme."[1]

On September 24 the plan was made public,[2] and as it appeared to define in detail what unconditional surrender meant, it convinced the millions of Germans who were opposed to the Nazi régime that it was better to go down fighting under Hitler than to accept a Carthaginian peace. It awakened in them the spirit of 1813. In the words of Macbeth, the cry of every German was:

> "Ring the alarum-bell! Blow wind! come wrack!
> At least we'll die with harness on our back."

After this insane spiritual blood transfusion, coupled with Eisenhower's broad-front strategy, throughout the autumn there was a series of desperate offensives, desperately resisted, along the 350 miles from Nijmegen to Colmar, until in mid-December Hitler's counter-offensive in the Ardennes clearly demonstrated the folly of Eisenhower's linear strategy. Though it failed, it cost the allies 77,000 men, and it was almost as great a blow to American prestige as the Japanese surprise attack on Pearl

---

[1] In full see *On Active Service in Peace and War* (English edit., n.d.), Henry L. Stimson and McGeorge Bundy, p. 33.

[2] It was heavily criticized, and when Stimson, U.S. Secretary of War, read to the President the words about converting Germany into a pastoral country, Stimson records that: "He was frankly staggered by this and said he had no idea he could have initialled this; that he had evidently done it without much thought" (*ibid.*, p. 336).

Harbour. It so impressed Stalin that he seized the opportunity, while his western allies were embarrassed, to agree to another Big Three meeting toward the end of January, for which the President had pressed since his re-election. Also, since Hitler had committed his entire strategic reserve in the Ardennes offensive, Stalin decided to open the Russian winter campaign in mid-January; he hoped that by the time the "Big Three" met his armies would have overrun the whole of Poland and be in a position to present his allies with a *fait accompli*.

The Russian offensive, led by Zhukov and Koniev, opened on January 12. It burst like an avalanche through the German front and swept forward at such speed that by February 4 the two marshals had carried their armies to the Oder at Küstrin and Breslau. That same day the Big Three met at Yalta in the Crimea. On Mr. Churchill's suggestion, it was prophetically code-named "Argonaut", for Stalin played the part of Jason and in triumph carried back with him to the Kremlin the fleeces of Poland and several other countries.

Roosevelt left America for the Crimea with high hopes and little preparation;[1] the war in Europe neared its end and peace glimmered on the horizon. The moment had come to assure himself of Stalin's full-hearted collaboration. This appeared an easy task, for he could see no fundamental clash of interests between the Soviet Union and the United States. Also, although Churchill was a full-blooded imperialist, Stalin, so he fondly held, was nothing of the kind, and, in order to liquidate the British, French, and Dutch Asiatic empires, he needed his support. He also needed Stalin's aid to finish off the Japanese, because his Chiefs of Staff had warned him that without Russia it might cost the United States "a million casualties" to conquer Japan.[2] Before the conference assembled, he had made up his mind to give Stalin a free hand in Europe as a *quid pro quo*.

Because of Stalin's realism and the President's idealism – he was advised by Harry Hopkins, and among others by Algar Hiss of the State Department – the results of the Yalta Conference were a super-Munich.

It was unanimously agreed that Germany was to be partitioned into zones and each zone occupied by an allied army; that unconditional surrender was to be enforced; that forced labour was to

---

[1] See *Speaking Frankly*, James F. Byrnes (English edit., n.d.), p. 23.
[2] *On Active Service in Peace and War*, Henry L. Stimson, p. 365.

be imposed; and that 20 billion dollars in reparations, of which Russia was to receive half, should be considered.

Once Stalin had agreed to take part in the United Nations Conference in April, Poland, for whose integrity Great Britain had entered the war, was thrown to the Russian wolves. Her eastern frontier was approximately fixed on the Curzon Line; her western frontier provisionally pushed out to the Oder and western Neisse; and the Lublin Committee of Soviet stooges, which at the instigation of the Kremlin had, on December 31, 1944, proclaimed itself the "Provisional Government of Liberated Democratic Poland", was, when diluted with a few members of the émigré government, to be accepted, on condition that free elections were held, but these were not to be supervised by neutral observers, as this would insult the Poles!

Lastly, once Poland had been pledged to the Soviets, at a secret meeting, from which Churchill was excluded, Roosevelt secured Stalin's aid against Japan. In exchange he agreed to acknowledge the *status quo* in Outer Mongolia; the restoration to Russia of all territories lost in 1904–1905, southern Sakhalin and the Kurile Islands; and also he agreed to Russian joint control with China of the eastern and southern Manchurian railways. As much of these territories was Chinese, it would appear that the President had either forgotten about imperialism and the Atlantic Charter, or was *non compos mentis*.

The conference ended on February 10, and at the dinner which followed, when he proposed Stalin's health, Mr. Churchill, with true prophetic vision, said: ". . . he knew that in peace no less than in war Marshal Stalin would continue to lead his people from success to success."[1] The following day a statement was signed and issued by the Big Three. It contained, among other things, many of the economic proposals of the Morgenthau Plan, and ended with a declaration that "in the words of the Atlantic Charter" the agreements offered assurances which would permit all men in all lands to "live out their lives in freedom from fear and want."[2]

Three days before these hopeful words were published, the final stage of Eisenhower's phalangial advance on the Rhine opened in appalling weather. On the left the Rhine was reached by the

---

[1] *The White House Papers, etc.*, vol. II, p. 857. "Stalin replied in the best of tempers" (Churchill, vol. VI, p. 343).
[2] In full see *Roosevelt and the Russians, etc.*, Edward R. Stettinius, pp. 295–302.

First Canadian Army opposite Emmerich on February 14, but not until March 3 was the Ninth U.S. Army, on the right of the Canadians, able to make contact with it at Geldern, for besides the evil weather the enemy put up fanatical opposition. Next, on March 5, advanced elements of the IIIrd Corps of the First U.S. Army captured the bridge over the Rhine at Remagen. Lastly, on March 22, Patton crossed the Rhine near Oppenheim, south of Mainz, and on the following day the Twenty-First Army Group and the Ninth U.S. Army, both under Montgomery, crossed at Wesel.

From the Rhine the Germans fell back on the Ruhr. There they put up a desperate resistance, but were surrounded, and on April 13 Field-Marshal Model with 325,000 officers and men capitulated. The road to Berlin was now unbarred and the Russians, under Zhukov and Koniev, were still on the Oder and Neisse. On this same day in the south Marshal Malinovsky occupied Vienna, the southernmost of the three great political and strategical centres in central Europe.

There still remained Berlin and Prague. There was little between Eisenhower and the former, neither prepared defences nor field army, and although Berlin was in the centre of the agreed Russian zone of occupation it had never been suggested that it was the perquisite of any one allied army. It was imperative that Eisenhower should advance on it because the Russians had broken or disregarded every important item of the Yalta Agreement which by then had been put to the test, and Berlin in Anglo-American hands would place Great Britain and the United States in a strong position from which they could insist that the Russians honoured their agreements. "If we did not get things right," says Mr. Churchill, "the world would soon see that Mr. Roosevelt and I had underwritten a fraudulent prospectus when we put our signatures to the Crimea settlements."[1]

Although this should have been obvious, political values were of secondary importance to Eisenhower, and coupled with this outlook was his belief that Hitler intended to abandon Berlin and fall back on what was called the "National Redoubt" – western Austria and southern Bavaria.[2] "Military factors, when the enemy

[1] *The Second World War*, vol. vi, p. 370.
[2] Bradley writes: "Months before, G.-2 had tipped us off to a fantastic enemy plot, for the withdrawal of troops into the Austrian Alps . . . for a last-ditch holdout. . . . I am astonished we could have believed it as innocently as we did" (*A Soldier's Story*, p. 536).

was on the brink of final defeat," he writes, "were more important in my eyes than the political considerations involved in an Allied capture of the capital. The function of our forces must be to crush the German armies rather than dissipate our strength in the occupation of empty ruined cities."[1] That was why his plan was to leave Berlin to the Russians, and, under Bradley, to move the axis of his advance through central Germany toward Marshal Koniev in the Leipzig–Dresden area and so cut off Hitler from the National Redoubt, while his right wing, under Patton, occupied that mythical lair, and his left wing, under Montgomery, moved on Hamburg and the Baltic. Already, on March 28, he had cabled the gist of his plan to Washington, London, and Moscow; Stalin was delighted and Churchill furious, but the latter was hamstrung because the American Chiefs of Staff supported Eisenhower. On March 31 Marshall cabled the British Chiefs of Staff: "The battle of Germany is now at a point where it is up to the Field Commander to judge the measures which should be taken. To deliberately turn away from the exploitation of the enemy's weakness does not appear sound. The single objective should be quick and complete victory."[2] On April 6 he stated: "Such psychological and political advantages as would result from the possible capture of Berlin ahead of the Russians should not override the imperative military consideration which, in our opinion, is the destruction and dismemberment of the German armed forces."[3]

The van of the Ninth U.S. Army entered Magdeburg on April 11, and on the following day it crossed the Elbe. "At that time," writes Bradley, "we could probably have pushed on to Berlin had we been willing to take the casualties Berlin would have cost us. Zhukov had not yet crossed the Oder and Berlin now lay midway between our forces."[4] On the 14th, two days after President Roosevelt died and Mr. Harry S. Truman had succeeded him, Eisenhower halted his troops on the Elbe, and on the 21st he informed the Soviet High Command that, except for an advance on Lübeck, he did not intend to advance east of the Elbe, nor beyond the western frontier of Czechoslovakia; instead his Third and Seventh Armies would occupy the National Redoubt! Prague also was abandoned to the Russians.

The doom which, since the allied landings in Normandy, had

---

[1] *Supreme Commander's Report*, p. 131.   [2] *Crusade in Europe*, p. 402.
[3] Cited by Wilmot in *The Struggle for Europe*, p. 693.   [4] *A Soldier's Story*, p. 537.

threatened Hitler like the open jaws of some monster, closed with a snap. On April 29 General Heinrich von Veitinghoff, in command of the German forces in Italy, with nearly one million men,

39. ALLIED ZONES OF OCCUPATION AND RUSSIA'S
WESTERN FRONTIER IN 1945 COMPARED WITH
CHARLEMAGNE'S EASTERN FRONTIER IN 814

surrendered unconditionally to Field-Marshal Alexander. At 3.30 p.m. on the following day Hitler shot himself, and on May 2 the Russians established themselves in Berlin. Two days later,

Admiral Friedeburg and other representatives of the German High Command, at Montgomery's tactical headquarters on the Lüneburger Heide, where in 1935 Hitler had held his first manœuvres, signed an armistice providing for the surrender of all German forces in north-west Germany, Denmark, and Holland. Three days later the instrument of the *Wehrmacht's* unconditional surrender was signed by Jodl and Friedeburg at Eisenhower's headquarters in Rheims; at midnight May 8–9 hostilities ceased, and on May 9 the Russians marched into Prague.

For the United States and Great Britain, the fruits of the battle of Normandy were apples of Sodom, which turned to ashes as soon as they were plucked. Hitler and his legions were destroyed, and in their stead stood Stalin and his Asiatic hordes. Because "Victory – victory at all costs"[1] had been the western allies' aim, and because of their insistence that "it was to be the defeat, ruin, and slaughter of Hitler, to the exclusion of all other purposes, loyalties and aims,"[2] Stalin, the supreme realist, whose strategy had throughout kept in step with his policy, had been able to impose his messianic cult upon Estonia, Latvia, Lithuania, part of Finland, Poland, eastern and central Germany, a third of Austria, Czechoslovakia, Yugoslavia, Hungary, Rumania, and Bulgaria. Vienna, Prague, and Berlin, the vertebrae of Europe, were his, and except for Athens, so was every capital city in eastern Europe. The western frontier of Russia had been advanced from the Pripet Marshes to the Thuringerwald, a distance of 750 miles, and as in the days of Charlemagne, the Slavs stood on the Elbe and the Böhmerwald. A thousand years of European history had been rolled back. Such were the fruits of the battle of Normandy, fructified by inept strategy and a policy of pure destruction.

[1] *The Second World War*, Winston S. Churchill, vol. II, p. 24.
[2] *Ibid.*, vol. III, p. 21.

Progress of the war in the Pacific, 1942-1944

After the battle of Midway Island, the problem that faced the United States was how to sap forward through the outer and inner defences of the Japanese ocean fortress and ultimately to storm its citadel – the home islands of Japan. This problem was solved, as sieges so frequently have succeeded, by taking advantage of the contour of the fortress, which was, as noted earlier, that of a huge salient. Its base extended from Burma to Paramushiro in the Kuriles, and its apex rested on the Ellice Islands, pointing toward Fiji and Samoa.

Strategically, the salient commanded the western Pacific, and to a lesser extent the Indian Ocean; but fortunately for the United States and the British Empire Japan had not strength enough to occupy the strategic centres in the latter ocean and simultaneously wage a life or death struggle in the Pacific. Had she been able to do so, she could have strangled her enemy's sea routes to the Middle East and India, which in all probability would have led to the occupation of Egypt by Rommel, and possibly also to the collapse of Timoshenko in Caucasia, who could not have been supplied by way of Persia. It might also have caused the collapse of Chiang Kai-Shek in China. It was the Indian Ocean, as much as the U.S.S.R., which separated Japan from her western allies.

It was because Japan could not simultaneously hold the two flanks of the salient in sufficient force that she lost the war, and from the start it must have been apparent to her that her danger lay in the likelihood of a simultaneous attack on both. Her enemies saw this with equal clarity, and that their grand tactical problem was to fight a stupendous Cannae operation at sea. They also saw that directly they had accumulated sufficient means, they were well placed to carry out such an operation, because they could approach the salient from four separate bases: from India and Alaska to strike at its haunches, and from the Hawaiian Islands and Australia to strike at its flanks.

Although the salient enabled Japan to operate on interior lines,

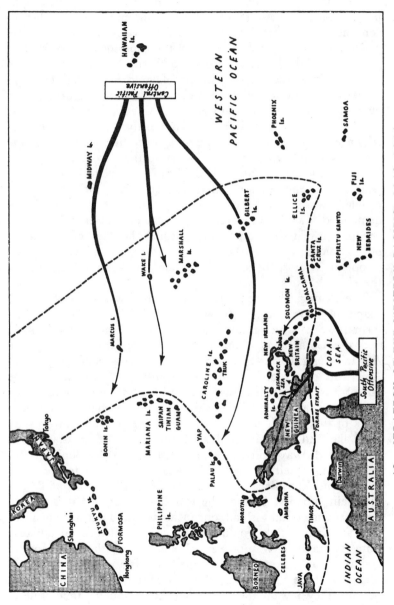

40. STRATEGY OF THE WESTERN PACIFIC, 1942–1944

a decided advantage as long as her enemies were weak, directly they became strong enough to threaten it from several directions her shipping and air power were insufficient to enable her to concentrate her forces against more than one point at a time and simultaneously hold the rest of the enormous circumference. In fact, from the battle of Midway onward, the limited nature of her strategy worked in her enemies' favour, for it enabled them to gain the time to build up their strength and to force her to over-extend her own and so wrest the initiative from her.

It was clear to the Americans and British that their lines of advance from Burma and Alaska against the haunches of the salient were in importance secondary to those from Hawaii and Australia against its flanks. Also, because the victory of Midway Island had definitely secured the Hawaii base, their immediate problem was to make certain the security of Australia. This demanded that the Japanese be prevented from extending their occupation of New Guinea and pushing the apex of the salient out to Samoa; for were they to do this they would be well placed to operate against the south Pacific line of communications from the United States to Australia.

The strategic centre of this sub-theatre was Rabaul, in the island of New Britain. It was centrally placed between the Bismarck Sea, which flanked the northern coast of New Guinea, and the Coral Sea, which flanked the north-eastern coast of Australia and Torres Strait; once Rabaul was neutralized or in American possession, no further extension of the apex of the salient was to be feared. Also, Rabaul lay on the left flank of the line of approach from the Hawaiian Islands through the northern flank of the salient. It was a threefold line. Its axis ran by way of Wake and the Marshalls to Guam and Saipan islands; its right *via* Midway and the Marcus Islands to the Bonin Archipelago, and its left *via* the Gilbert Islands and Truk to the Palau Islands and Yap. Because Rabaul was 800 miles south of Truk – the main Japanese base in the Caroline Islands – that is, within aircraft range of that island, once Rabaul and Truk were neutralized an air-free link would be established between an advance from Australia by way of New Guinea to the island of Morotai and an advance from Hawaii to the Palau Islands. These terminal islands, and the Marianas, were vitally important strategic points, because they lay on the circumference of Japan's inner line of defence.

In brief, the allied solution of the problem was as follows: To neutralize Rabaul and thereby to breach the southern flank of the salient; to breach the northern flank between Wake and the Gilberts; then, once these two operations were successfully accomplished, to assault the inner line between Morotai and Saipan and storm the Philippines and so cut off Japan from her recently gained southern empire. Lastly, to advance from the Philippines to the home islands of Japan.

This vast strategical plan was to be carried out by two forces, one under General MacArthur based on Australia, and the other under Admiral Nimitz based on the Hawaiian Islands. Its execution was powerfully aided by the events already recorded. The battle of the Coral Sea had frustrated the Japanese occupation of Port Moresby in Papua and so for the time being had secured for the Australians and Americans the vitally important Torres Strait – the northern moat of Australia – and the battle of Midway Island had inflicted such aircraft-carrier losses on the Japanese that they were forced to abandon their plan to advance on New Caledonia and the Fijis, and instead look to the security of their base at Rabaul. To effect this they decided on two closely related and simultaneous operations. The first was to establish a chain of strong outposts in the Solomons, and the second to take Port Moresby: were this done, the northern approach on Rabaul could be blocked by air power. The latter operation was to be initiated by an advance from Gona and Buna, on the northern coast of Papua, across the Owen Stanley range in order to draw the Australians at Port Moresby northward into the jungle. Next, Milne Bay, at the eastern end of Papua, was to be occupied and the airfield in its vicinity seized. From this airfield, aircraft, in cooperation with those on Guadalcanal, were to gain command of the northern entrance to the Coral Sea. Lastly, once this command had been won, and while the Australians were entangled with the Gona–Buna column, a seaborne force from Rabaul was to seize Port Moresby. Thus the Japanese hoped to cut the Australian line of communications between Port Moresby and Darwin, which was the northern terminus of the Adelaide–Alice Springs trans-Australian railway. It was a bold project, but complex, and the Japanese had not force sufficient to carry it out.

To frustrate the first half of this threat, on August 7, 1942, an American expedition, based on New Zealand, landed on the islands of Florida and Guadalcanal; at first it met with slight opposition, and it occupied the partly finished Japanese airfield on the latter island. This provoked a series of naval engagements, which opened with the battle of Savo Island on August 9 and ended with the battle of Tassafaronga on November 30, by when the position of the Japanese on Guadalcanal became untenable. In the meantime the Japanese situation in Papua had gone from bad to worse, and by January, 1943, had become so critical that in February the reinforcements assembled in the Rabaul area for Guadalcanal were diverted to Papua and the remnants of the Japanese forces on Guadalcanal withdrawn.

The second half was set into motion on July 21–22 by the Japanese occupation of Gona and Buna, which was followed by an advance inland on the Australian post of Kokoda, about half-way to Port Moresby. Next, on August 26, a force of some 2,000 Japanese was landed at Milne Bay, but it met with such stubborn opposition that it was compelled to withdraw, and because all reinforcements were required for Guadalcanal, no repetition of the landing was attempted. Freed from this threat, on November 3 the Australians, supplied by aircraft, drove the Gona-Buna column out of Kokoda and pushed it back to the northern coast of Papua, where it was largely exterminated. It was this disaster which compelled the Japanese to abandon Guadalcanal and throw all reinforcements into Lae and Salamaua in north-eastern New Guinea in order to block the way to New Britain and thence to Rabaul. Lastly, on March 3–4, 1943, came the battle of the Bismarck Sea, in which a Japanese convoy carrying reinforcements and supplies from Rabaul to Lae was largely destroyed by allied air attack. The second half of the Japanese plan ended as disastrously as the first, and together they clearly showed that the strategic initiative was slipping from their hands.

When the Papua campaign ended MacArthur moved his forces toward Salamaua, while the Japanese reinforced their defensive line from Rabaul to Hollandia in Dutch New Guinea to strengthen their right flank. But it was not until August that MacArthur was ready to advance in force to gain command of the Vitiaz and Dampier Straits, which separate New Guinea from New Britain. By means of amphibious forces staged from Milne Bay and Buna he landed on the Huon Peninsula, and on September 16 seized Lae. Next, on October 2, he occupied Finschafen, at the apex of the Huon Peninsula, and there developed a great supply base

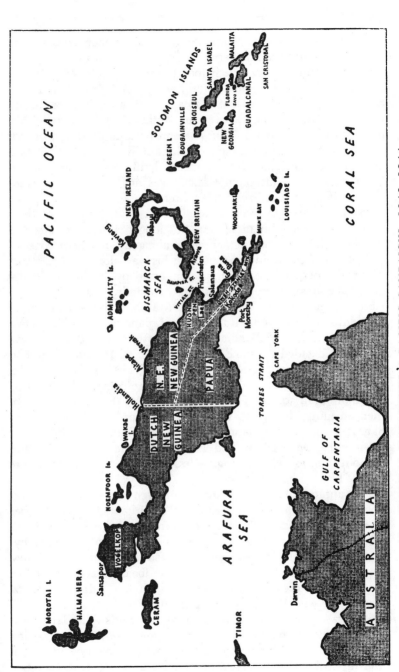

41. GENERAL MACARTHUR'S PACIFIC CAMPAIGNS, 1942-1944

capable of use as a staging area for amphibious operations against New Britain and the northern coast of New Guinea.

The first of these operations took place on December 15, when a landing at Arawe in New Britain was made. Meanwhile in the Solomons, on November 1 American marines had landed on the island of Bougainville, where they established airfields within fighter range of Rabaul. Thus, it soon became possible to carry out round-the-clock air attacks on Rabaul from both New Britain and Bougainville, and from Green Island to the north of the latter island, and although Rabaul was not occupied by Mac-Arthur, it was neutralized by his aircraft.

As it became apparent to MacArthur that, because of their losses at sea, the Japanese were no longer able adequately to supply their numerous detachments along the northern coast of New Guinea, he decided not to inch his way along, but to resort to a series of amphibious jumps supported by carrier-borne aircraft. The first of these was made to the Admiralty Islands, which were occupied during February and March, and as it constituted an additional threat to Rabaul the Japanese decided to move their main base to Hollandia. But MacArthur divined their intention, and decided to make his next jump to Hollandia, and so by-pass all enemy detachments *en route*. This leap of 600 miles was made on April 22. The Japanese were completely surprised and more than 50,000 of them were cut off to the eastward. From then on jump after jump was made westward until, on July 30, Sansapor on the Vogelkop was occupied. Thus, in a little over 12 months, MacArthur had advanced some 1,300 miles and without much severe fighting no less than 135,000 Japanese were cut off beyond hope of rescue.

At Sansapor the New Guinea campaign ended, and the next bound opened the campaign for the Philippines. On September 15 a leap was made to the island of Morotai, on the Japanese inner line of defence, and 30,000 Japanese in Halmahera were by-passed. It brought MacArthur within 300 miles of the Philippines. Equally important, Morotai lay in the focal area in which the second of the great Pacific campaigns, that of Admiral Nimitz, was to fuse with the first in a single offensive.

Nimitz's problem differed from MacArthur's. The latter was land-based, but Nimitz had to move his base along with him, which meant that his fleet had to be both his base of operations and his striking force. It was, therefore, a four-fold organization

– a floating base, a fleet, an air force, and an army, combined in one. That it was designed, built and assembled within 18 months of the battle of Midway Island is without question the greatest organizational feat of naval history.

This great instrument of destruction enabled Nimitz and his subordinate admirals to operate on so broad a front that the Japanese were compelled to deploy their inferior strength – particularly their air force – over such wide spaces that they could seldom, if ever, concentrate it at any critical point. The consequence was that because most of the Pacific islands are too small to be converted into really formidable positions and are incapable of housing garrisons of sufficient strength to put up a prolonged resistance, they could be knocked out before aid could be brought to them. Further, once one or more air bases in a group of islands had been seized and put into use the remaining islands could be so completely cut off from succour that they could safely be by-passed and left to starvation. Because the instrument was not only most powerful, but also because it was self-sufficient and carried out all operations, including its own supply, maintenance and repair, and therefore possessed indefinite range of action, it rapidly knocked the bottom out of the Japanese defensive strategy and transformed the vastness of the Pacific from an ally into a deadly enemy of the Japanese.

In the summer of 1943, the attack on the northern flank of the salient was heralded by a series of preparatory operations. They consisted of air attacks from carriers on Wake Island on July 24 and 27; on Marcus Island – an important Japanese air base which served as a relay point on the Japan-mandated islands supply line – on August 30; and of attacks on key islands in the Marshalls. Baker Island in the Phoenix group, and Nuku Fetau and Nanumea in the Ellice Islands, were occupied in early September.

The initial phase of the campaign comprised the invasion of Makin Island, Abemama Atoll in the Gilbert Islands, and Tarawa Atoll. Landings were successfully made on the first on November 1, on the second on the following day, and on the third on November 21. Makin was taken on the 23rd, and Tarawa on the 24th; the landing on Abemama was unopposed. The object of these operations was to relieve the Ellice Islands from further risk before the main central advance was made. It misled the Japanese into a belief that their enemy's intention was to make his main thrust toward the Solomons in support of the Rabaul campaign. It was not until Nimitz struck his next blow that they discovered their error.

The blow fell upon the Marshall Islands – 500 miles north-west of the Gilberts. Again the aim was not to occupy all the islands, but only those selected because they had good airfields. On January 1, 1944, Majuro, with its fine harbour, was occupied without fighting, and on February 2 Kwajalein Atoll was attacked, it resisted stubbornly for four days. On February 2 American marines invaded Namur and Roi, and between the 19th and 22nd Eniwetok Atoll was taken.

Because Nimitz's intention was to by-pass the Caroline Islands and open the third phase of his campaign against the Marianas, and because the island of Truk in the Caroline group was the main Japanese naval base in the central Pacific, Nimitz ordered Admiral Spruance to reduce it to impotence. This the latter did by carrier attack on February 17–18, and the Japanese withdrew from the island.

The operations in the Marianas were directed against the islands of Saipan, Tinian, and Guam. Between June 10 and 12 they were heavily bombarded, and a landing on the first was made on the 15th. It was the most important operation yet staged in the central Pacific; for not only would the possession of the Marianas breach the enemy's inner line of defence, but it would enable the Americans to cut their enemy's direct line of communications with the Carolines and also provide a base for operations against the Bonin Islands, from where the Japanese home islands could be bombed.

At the time of the landing on Saipan, a powerful Japanese fleet, including nine aircraft carriers, entered the Pacific to the west of that island. It was commanded by Admiral Ozawa, and his intention was to destroy the U.S. carrier task force, under Admiral Spruance, which was covering the landing. He planned to shuttle the planes from his carriers to air bases in Guam and then back to his carriers, attack the U.S. fleet on both trips, while his own carriers remained out of range of his enemy's carrier aircraft. On June 19 he opened his air attack; it was the most powerful yet made against surface forces, and it involved an unprecedented number of aircraft. But it was so badly coordinated that over 350 of its planes were shot down, and two of Ozawa's carriers were sunk by American submarines. On the 20th Spruance's task force headed west, and when the Japanese fleet had been located, between 6.20 p.m. and sunset 216 aircraft were launched against it. One aircraft carrier and two naval oilers were sunk, and four carriers, one battleship, one heavy cruiser and one oiler damaged. Though this battle, known as the battle of the Philippine Sea – the most important since that of Midway Island – did not result in the hoped-for destruction of the Japanese surface fleet, the loss of three of its carriers and the almost complete destruction of the trained air groups of the three carrier divisions engaged meant that Japanese carrier air power was virtually finished as an operative force.

The fighting on Saipan lasted for 25 days, and it was not until July 9 that organized resistance ceased. The immediate result of its capture was the fall of General Togo and his Government and the formation of a new Japanese Cabinet under General Koiso.

The next island to be invaded was Guam. A landing was made on July 21, and by August 10 its garrison was annihilated. Lastly, the island of Tinian was invaded on July 24, and after nine days' fighting it was occupied.

After the conquest of Tinian a pause in operations followed until September 8. On that day the U.S. Third Amphibious Force, commanded by Vice-Admiral Wilkinson, appeared off the Palau Islands, and on the 15th American marines and infantry landed on the island of Peleliu. On the same day that MacArthur invaded Morotai, the Central Pacific Fleet came up on his right flank. The stage was set for the reconquest of the Philippines.

CHAPTER 16

The Battle for Leyte Gulf, 1944

By the late summer of 1944 the advance of the forces of General MacArthur and Admiral Nimitz had put Japan in the gravest peril. Although her Combined Fleet, under Admiral Soemu Toyoda, was still intact, the losses her mercantile shipping had sustained afflicted her economy with a creeping paralysis, and an enemy advance farther westward would stop entirely the trickle of commerce which still flowed behind the Philippines–Formosa–Ryukyu islands screen. Already lack of oil had become her crucial naval problem, so much so that she was no longer able to fuel the whole of her fleet in home waters and had been compelled to base part of it on the Lingga Islands in the vicinity of Singapore. When, after the war, Toyoda was questioned on the situation which faced him in September, 1944, he explained that, were the Philippines lost, even though the fleet should be left, the shipping lane to the south would be so completely cut off that even if the fleet should come back to Japanese waters it would not be able to obtain its fuel supply. If it should remain in southern waters it could not receive supplies of ammunition and arms. "There would be," he added, "no sense in saving the fleet at the expense of the loss of the Philippines."[1] How, then, were they to be held?

In spite of lack of fuel, and although Japan's carrier-borne air power had been shattered in the battle of the Philippine Sea, the position of the Japanese was not altogether hopeless. Their enemy operated thousands of miles from his home base, with his nearest airfield some 500 miles away, but they could fight in range of the scores of airfields they had built. As he had to fight, Toyoda decided that wherever his enemy struck he would rely on surface fleet action covered by land-based aircraft. The project built on these decisions was called the *Sho* plan (*Sho* meaning "to conquer") and it was to be Japan's supreme effort of the war. It was also one of the most daring naval operations ever undertaken. But

[1] Cited in *The Battle for Leyte Gulf*, C. Vann Woodward (1947), p. 21. Woodward was Intelligence Officer in the Office of the Chief of Naval Operations.

600

before we discuss it, it is necessary to outline the events that immediately followed MacArthur's and Nimitz's advance, because they drew the teeth from the plan.

Since it was obvious to both MacArthur and Nimitz that the Japanese fleet would choose to fight under cover of land-based aircraft, shortly before they established themselves on Morotai and Peleliu they decided to extend their conquests before they leapt on to Mindanao in the middle of November, and at the same time, Admiral Halsey, in command of the Third U.S. Fleet, began a series of strikes on the Japanese airfields in Mindanao. The opposition he encountered was so weak that, on September 13, he recommended that all intermediary landings should be dispensed with, and an assault made on Leyte Island as soon as it could be mounted. With this MacArthur, Nimitz, and the Joint Chiefs of Staff agreed; October 20 was chosen for the landing and the main base of the Pacific Fleet was moved from Eniwetok in the Marshalls 1,000 miles westward to Ulithi Island, which was occupied on September 23. Meanwhile, since their withdrawal from Truk, the Japanese had established their base at Brunei Bay in western Borneo. Between October 10 and 16, Halsey struck at Okinawa, Luzon, and Formosa with such effect that Toyoda denuded his carriers, under Admiral Jisaburo Ozawa, of most of their aircraft and aircrews and sent them to Formosa. In the battle which ensued, the greatest up to then between ship- and shore-based aircraft, 650 Japanese aircraft were destroyed. As this meant the loss of most of Ozawa's half-trained aircrews, more than anything else it wrecked the *Sho* plan.

The *Sho* plan was devised to meet one of four alternatives: an American thrust against either the Philippines, or Formosa and the Ryukyu Islands, or Kyushu, Shikoku and Honshu, or Hokkaido. Each was to be based on the full exploitation of the gunnery strength of the fleet, and land-based air power was to be substituted for carrier-borne aircraft.

The Combined Fleet was organized into two divisions to effect this, one composed of the bulk of the battleships and cruisers, under Admiral Takeo Kurita, based on the Lingga Islands, and the other of the remaining carriers, denuded of most of their aircrews, under Admiral Ozawa, based on the Inland Sea. If the *Sho* plan was adopted, Ozawa was to proceed toward the point of invasion, and then act as a decoy, to lure the enemy carrier forces toward him. Next, freed as he would then be from carrier threat,

Kurita, under cover of land-based aircraft, was to fight his way to the enemy beachhead and destroy the invasion shipping. "The whole plan," we read, "revolved about the strong surface gunnery force, and was designed to get it in to where it could do the greatest damage. Little thought was given to getting it out,"[1] nor was it expected that Ozawa's carrier force would survive. In brief, the operation was to be a forlorn hope, and a point worth noting is that even were it to succeed, the suicidal loss of ships it entailed prohibited a repetition – it was to be neck or nothing. After the war this was corroborated by Ozawa who, when questioned, answered: "A decoy, that was our first primary mission, to act as a decoy. My fleet could not very well give direct protection to Kurita's force because we were very weak, so I tried to attack as many American carriers as possible, and be the decoy or target of your attack. . . . The main mission was all sacrifice."[2] How desperate was the gamble at once becomes apparent when we compare the strengths of the opposing forces.

The two American fleets concerned were the Third and Seventh, the one commanded by Admiral William F. Halsey and the other by Vice-Admiral Thomas C. Kinkaid, respectively under Admiral Nimitz and General MacArthur. There was no supreme commander. The Third Fleet consisted of eight aircraft-carriers, eight light carriers, six new and fast battleships, six heavy cruisers, nine light cruisers, and 58 destroyers. It was organized as Task Force 38, under command of Vice-Admiral Marc A. Mitscher, and was divided into four Task Groups: No. 1, Vice-Admiral John S. McCain; No. 2, Rear-Admiral Gerald F. Bogan; No. 3, Rear-Admiral Frederick C. Sherman; and No. 4, Rear-Admiral Ralph E. Davison. The Seventh Fleet comprised in all 738 vessels, and was organized into three Task Forces – the Covering and Support Force and two amphibious forces. In the first there were six old battleships, five heavy cruisers, six light cruisers, 18 escort carriers, 86 destroyers, 25 destroyer escorts, 11 frigates, and 44 motor-torpedo-boats. Among these vessels were ships of the Royal Australian Navy.

Opposed to this vast assemblage of warships were the fleets of Admiral Ozawa and Admiral Kurita. The first comprised one large aircraft-carrier – the *Zuikaku* – three light carriers, two battleship

---

[1] *The Campaigns of the Pacific War*, United States Strategic Bomb Survey (Pacific), 1946, p. 281.
[2] Cited by Woodward in *The Battle for Leyte Gulf*, p. 129.

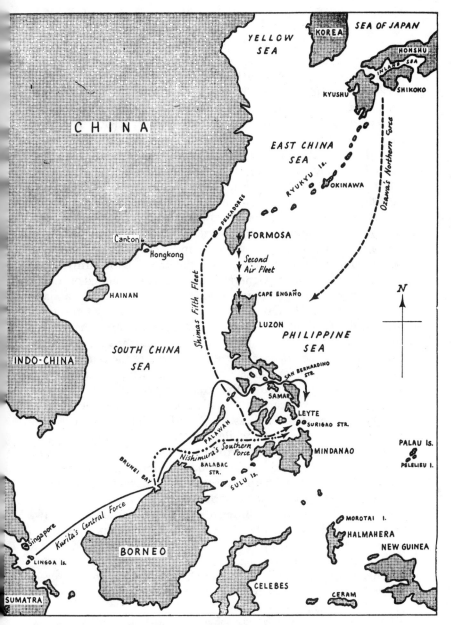

42. REVISED SHO NO. I OPERATION, OCTOBER, 1944

carriers – the *Ise* and *Hyuga*[1] – two heavy cruisers, four light cruisers, and 17 destroyers; and the second fleet comprised seven battleships, including the *Yamato* and *Musashi*,[2] 11 heavy cruisers, three light cruisers and 19 destroyers. Ozawa's air component had been whittled down to 52 fighters, 28 fighter-bombers, and 29 torpedo-aircraft, the crews of which were so indifferently trained that once their machines were launched they were instructed not to return to the carriers, but to land on the airfields. Before the battle, the navy transferred to the Philippines the First and Second Air Fleets, approximately 400 aircraft, and in the islands the army had some 200 aircraft fit for action.

On October 16, MacArthur's attack and support forces arrived off Leyte Gulf in a heavy storm, and although carrier air support was impossible, the islands of Suluan, Dinagat, and Homonhan were occupied, and by the 19th mine-free lanes to the beach on Leyte had been swept. On the 20th, under cover of a terrific naval bombardment and carrier strikes, the Sixth U.S. Army, commanded by Lieutenant-General Walter Krueger, landed on Leyte.

Immediately the landing became known in Tokyo, a hasty readjustment of *Sho* Operation No. 1 was made to fit the topographical situation. Leyte Gulf is situated between the eastern shore of Leyte and the southern shore of Samar islands, and from the west it can be approached either by way of the Surigao Strait on its southern side, or by the San Bernardino Strait on its northern side. To take advantage of this dual approach, Toyoda decided that, while Ozawa carried out his mission to lure the enemy's carrier forces toward him east of Cape Engaño in Luzon, Kurita should split his fleet, and while with the larger number he proceeded by way of San Bernardino Strait to strike at Leyte Gulf, the smaller force, under Vice-Admiral Shoji Nishimura, which consisted of two battleships – the *Fuso* and *Yamashiro* – one heavy cruiser – the *Mogami* – and four destroyers, struck at the gulf by way of Surigao Strait. In order to strengthen Nishimura, Ozawa was instructed to detach two heavy cruisers, one light cruiser, and seven destroyers (the Fifth Fleet) under Vice-Admiral Kiyohide Shima, to move west of Luzon and cooperate with Nishimura.

This readjusted *Sho* plan, although complicated, looks exceedingly astute on paper, but for success it depended upon most

[1] Battleships converted to carriers.
[2] They were of 64,000 tons instead of the agreed 35,000 tonnage, and were the most powerful battleships in the world. Their speed was over 26 knots, and each mounted nine 18·1 inch guns,

careful coordination, and this was not provided for. No supreme commander was appointed, and Shima knew nothing of Kurita's plan, nor was Nishimura subordinated to him. While Ozawa and Kurita came directly under Toyoda, Shima came under the South-West Area Command, as also did all naval land-based aircraft. The result was confusion.

At 8 a.m. on October 17, in accordance with the revised plan, all Japanese naval forces were put on the alert and Kurita set out from Lingga for Brunei Bay, where he was to refuel. He arrived there on the 20th, and on the 22nd stood out northward west of Palawan Island for the Sibuyan Sea. He was followed by Nishimura, who steered for Balabac Strait and the Sulu Sea, Shima set out from the Pescadores and on the afternoon of the 23rd arrived at Coron Bay, and Ozawa, who left the Inland Sea on the 20th, arrived on the 23rd off the northern tip of Luzon.

These movements led to four separate, closely related and very different actions, which together became known as the battle for Leyte Gulf – one of the most extraordinary in naval history.

The first of these actions – the battle of the Sibuyan Sea – fought between Kurita's ships and Halsey's carrier-borne aircraft, was heralded by a stroke of unpredictable ill luck for Kurita. A few hours after his fleet, which we will call the Central Force to distinguish it from Ozawa's northern, and Nishimura's southern force, set out from Brunei Bay, it was located by two American submarines – the *Darter* and *Dace* – who at once reported to Admiral Halsey that they had contacted an enemy force, estimated at 11 vessels, standing up the Palawan Passage. Kurita was unaware of their presence and he was rudely awakened when, early on October 24, his flagship, the heavy cruiser *Atago*, was suddenly torpedoed by the *Darter*. Later she sank. Next, the *Maya*, another of his heavy cruisers, was torpedoed by the *Dace* – she sank in four minutes – and a third, the *Takao*, was so seriously damaged that she was left dead in the water. Within 24 hours of its start, the Central Force was deprived of nearly one-third of its heavy cruisers.

When Halsey received the contact report from the *Darter* and *Dace* he was sailing some 300 miles east of Luzon. A few hours earlier he had ordered McCain's task group to proceed to Ulithi to reprovision. He did not recall it, and as his task was to destroy the Japanese fleet, while Kinkaid covered the landing, he turned westward to within 60 miles of the Polillo Islands, from where his

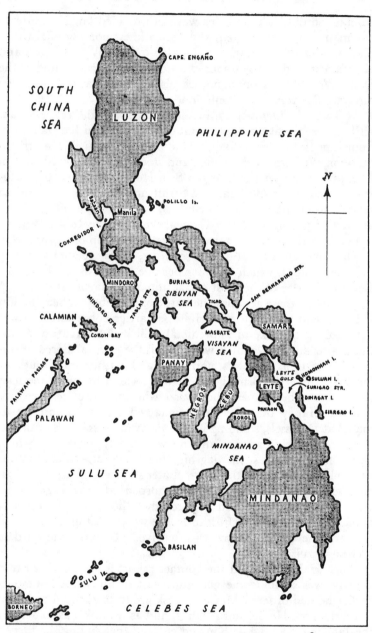

43. BATTLE FOR LEYTE GULF, OCTOBER 23–26, 1944

search aircraft could cover the Sibuyan Sea, but he did not think it worthwhile to search to the north and north-east of Luzon.

At 8.20 a.m. on October 24 Halsey received a report from a search aircraft that, a little over half an hour earlier, two large groups of enemy ships had been seen to the south of Mindoro Island on an easterly course, but no aircraft-carriers were reported. This was Kurita's Central Force, and as it was clear that by way of San Bernardino Strait it could reach Leyte Gulf by dawn the 25th, Halsey concentrated on his centre, which was then off the strait, and prepared to launch strikes westward. At the same time he ordered McCain's group, then about 600 miles to the east, to put about.

Soon after, another contact report came in from a search group over the Sulu Sea, which stated that a fleet was steaming south-west of Negros Island. This was Nishimura's Southern Force, and soon afterward it was attacked by 26 aircraft, which, as usual, claimed numerous hits. Actually, only the battleship *Fuso*, and a destroyer, the *Shigure*, were slightly damaged.

Although both the Central and Southern Forces could reach Leyte Gulf by daylight on the 25th, Halsey decided to throw the whole of his carrier aircraft against the former, the more powerful of the two forces. Then a search aircraft reported a third force to the north-east of Nishimura's force. This was Shima's Fifth Fleet, which was assumed to be part of the Southern Force, which actually it was meant to be. Because the Southern Force was heading for the Mindanao Sea, Kinkaid prepared to meet it.

At 9.10 a.m. Halsey's first strike was sent off from Bogan's group, and was about to be followed by a strike from Sherman's group when a raid of some 40 enemy aircraft was discovered on its way toward Sherman. It was followed by a second raid, and then by a third, estimated at 60 aircraft. Sherman's strike had to be postponed and a furious *mêlée* followed in which Sherman claimed to have shot down 120 Japanese aircraft at a loss of 10 of his own. During the action the American light carrier *Princeton* was hit by a 550 lb. bomb and later blew up and sank. What was peculiar about this attack was that the Japanese aircraft appeared to be of carrier type, and no carriers had been reported in either the Central or Southern Forces. The explanation was that they came from Ozawa's Northern Force, of which, because he had omitted to send out a search to the north-east of Luzon, Halsey was unaware.

At 10.20 a.m. Bogan's strike sighted the Central Force steering through Tablas Strait, eastward of Mindoro Island. It was met by a terrific anti-aircraft fire, and although it claimed many hits Kurita continued on his course. But his position gave cause for anxiety. Although he had heard from Nishimura that the latter had been engaged, he had received no word from Ozawa, nor of the progress made by land-based aircraft on the enemy's task forces. Worst of all, he was totally without air cover, because the aircraft which should have cooperated with him had been sent to Leyte Gulf. At 1.15 p.m., he reported his position to Ozawa, and 15 minutes later another enemy strike came in, then another and yet another. Four of his battleships, including the giants *Yamato* and *Musashi*, had been hit, and the latter was in a sinking condition. Also, one heavy cruiser and two destroyers were so seriously damaged that they had to put back. With these mounting casualties it seemed to him that his mission was breaking down, and as he feared further attacks in the narrowing seas, at 3.30 p.m. he turned his ships westward to regain broader waters. At 4 p.m. he reported this move to Toyoda, and repeated the message to Ozawa and the commanders of the First and Second Air Fleets. Then, as no further attacks were made on him, at 5.14 p.m. he turned about and headed for San Bernardino Strait. Sometime after he received Toyoda's reply to his dispatch, which read: "Advance counting on Divine Assistance." After the war this cryptic message was explained by Toyoda to convey: "That damage could not be limited or reduced by turning back, so advance even though the fleet should be completely lost."[1]

When, at 8 p.m., Ozawa received Kurita's message to Toyoda to announce his retirement, as it seemed to him that he would be left single-handed to face the entire enemy fleet, he called in his advanced guard and withdrew northward; but when further messages had clarified the situation, at midnight he turned again south-east, determined to commit his fleet to destruction.

When the third Japanese air strike was made on Sherman's group, Halsey, by then thoroughly puzzled that no enemy carriers had been reported, sent out a search group to the north-east of Luzon, but it was not until 4.40 p.m. that he received a report from the group which stated that an enemy force of four battle-ships, five or six cruisers, and six destroyers had been located

---

[1] Cited in the *Japanese at Leyte Gulf: The Sho Operation*, James A. Field, Jr. (1947), p. 72.

130 miles east of the northern coast of Luzon. But still no carriers were mentioned. A few minutes later another report arrived to inform him that, through a cloud gap, two large and one light carrier, and four cruisers, accompanied by destroyers, had been spotted some 15 miles to the north of the former group. Thus, at length, was the mystery of the carrier aircraft solved – the two groups of ships comprised Ozawa's Northern Force.

Two hours before he received this vitally important information Halsey had instructed Admiral Mitscher to be prepared to form a subsidiary task force, numbered 34, to engage the Central Force if it should attempt to force San Bernardino Strait. It was to consist of four battleships, two heavy cruisers, and two light cruisers, and two squadrons of destroyers drawn from Bogan's and Davison's groups. Then, when the Northern Force was located, Halsey, who meanwhile had received from his air strikes reports of enormous losses inflicted on the Central Force, instead of discounting much of them, as he should have done, for he was an experienced carrier admiral, accepted them at face value, and on their faulty estimate he made the most momentous decision of the battle.

He knew that he was faced by three separate enemy forces, and as he had been informed by Kinkaid that he (Kinkaid) was preparing to repel the southern force, he could leave it out of his calculations. But of the remaining two he assumed that the Central Force was virtually *hors de combat*, and from reports received he considerably overestimated the strength of the Northern Force. On these faulty premises, as he says, he decided to "strike the Northern Force with all of our own striking strength concentrated, and leave San Bernardino Strait unguarded."[1] Further, he calculated that he would be able to destroy the Northern Force and return to the strait in time to meet the Central Force should any of its undamaged ships attempt to pass through it. It would appear that he was so carried away by the idea of destroying the Northern Force that the security of Kinkaid's northern flank was entirely overlooked. Well may it be asked, would so immense an oversight have been possible, had there been present a supreme commander who could have viewed the battle as a whole? The lack of such a commander would seem to have been the crucial American error.

At 8.20 p.m. Halsey put his new plan into operation. Bogan's and Davison's groups were ordered to join Sherman's group, to

[1] Cited by Woodward, p. 80.

the north of them, and after the three had united, to be ready to form Task Force 34, when Mitscher with over 90 ships was to proceed northward and attack the Northern Force at dawn. "Everything," writes Woodward, "was pulled out from San Bernardino Strait. Not so much as a picket destroyer was left."[1] Besides this, Halsey ordered McCain's group not to steer for Leyte Gulf, but instead to set course northward and to join in the attack on the Northern Force on the following morning. Lastly, he informed Kinkaid of his plan, and added that he was going north *"with three groups* to strike the enemy carrier force at daybreak."[1]

Sixteen minutes later Halsey received a radio signal from the light carrier *Independence* to inform him that one of her night "snoopers" had sighted the Central Force between Burias and Masbate Islands. If correct, this meant that the Central Force must have moved at a speed of 24 knots from the position it held when last attacked, which was impossible for a badly crippled fleet. It was assumed therefore that, were the report correct, the ships seen could be only a few undamaged vessels, and the message was repeated to Kinkaid to inform him that *part* of the Central Force had been seen at the position indicated. In spite of this report, Halsey raced northward with Bogan's and Davison's groups.

Other reports – one garbled – came in from the *Independence*, and in the last, received at 12.11 a.m. on October 25, another "snooper" reported that a column of battleships had been sighted 40 miles west of San Bernardino Strait; nevertheless, Halsey continued north at 25 knots, and through an oversight Kinkaid was not informed of the sighting.

After he had received Toyoda's "Divine Assistance" message Kurita, now without the battleship *Musashi* and the heavy cruiser *Myoko*, pushed ahead for San Bernardino Strait, and at 10.24 p.m. he transmitted the following order from the *Yamato*: "The First Division Attack Force [battleships] will proceed south along the east coast of Samar and penetrate Tacloban [the northernmost American landing beach in Leyte Gulf]. It is strongly desired that the whole force throw its entire power into the fray so as to attain its aims."[2] At midnight the Central Force passed through San Bernardino Strait unopposed and unseen and nothing lay between it and Kinkaid's Fleet, then engaged with the Southern Force in the battle of Surigao Strait.

[1] *Ibid.*, p. 81.   [2] *Ibid.*, p. 87.

When the presence of the Southern Force in the Sulu Sea was reported to Admiral Kinkaid, as he knew that Halsey was guarding the San Bernardino Strait, he confidently set about to meet it. Later he learnt that Halsey was about to form Task Force 34; so when he received Halsey's message announcing that he was proceeding north "with three groups," he naturally assumed that Task Force 34 would be left off San Bernardino Strait.

His plan was to block the Surigao Strait with three groups of ships: a line of battleships and cruisers above the northern end of the strait; south of it three destroyer squadrons between Leyte and Dinagat Islands; and beyond these, pushed out into the Mindanao Sea, all of his motor-torpedo-boats. In all, the forces detailed for this operation comprised six battleships, four heavy and four light cruisers, 26 destroyers, and 39 motor-torpedo-boats, under the command of Rear-Admiral Jesse R. Oldendorf.

When the M.T.B.s took up their position about 100 miles from the battle line, the night was dark and the sea calm. At 10 p.m. their radar screens picked up the leading enemy ships off Bohol Island. Soon after they opened fire and star shells illuminated the sea and searchlights criss-crossed over it. But because of radio damage, it was not until after midnight that the first reports of the engagement were received by Oldendorf. The action continued until 2 a.m., and a little later Oldendorf's flagship, the heavy cruiser *Louisville*, at a range of over 25 miles, located the advanced Japanese ships on her radar screen. The leading ships of Destroyer Squadron 54 were then ordered to form into two groups and attack the flanks of the approaching enemy column, and at about 3 a.m. the left group opened fire at 11,500 yards. Next, the right group did the same at 9,000 yards, and at 3.19 a.m. its attack was followed by a series of explosions. Destroyer Squadron 24 was then thrown in and opened fire at 7,000 yards range, and at about 3.45 a.m. Nishimura's flagship, the *Yamashiro*, received a salvo of torpedoes which exploded her magazine and blew her in half; but before she went down Nishimura ordered the captain of the *Fuso* to continue the attack with all ships.

While this signal went out the American battleships still held fire, awaiting the range to close. Next, Oldendorf threw in Destroyer Squadron 56 in two groups, one to port and the other to starboard of his enemy's column. "The important and almost incredible thing," writes Woodward, "was that the Japanese continued to plod up the strait into the jaws of the trap prepared for them. The nearer they approached the nearer was the realization of the gunnery admiral's dream – 'T-ing' the enemy's column and enfilading it with broadsides from all ships. 'We were in the ideal position,' exclaimed the flag captain, 'a position dreamed of, studied and plotted in War College maneuvres and never hoped to be obtained.' It was old-line, text book tactics, perfect in conception, but very nearly impossible of realization."[1]

At 3.50 a.m. all ships of the American battle line opened fire at ranges of 15,000 to 21,000 yards and steered down the centre of the strait with Destroyer Squadron 56. "It was the most beautiful sight I have ever witnessed," wrote the captain of the destroyers. "The arched line of tracers in the darkness looked like a continual stream of lighted railroad cars going over a hill. No target could be observed at first, then shortly there would be fires and explosions, and another enemy ship would be accounted for."[2] Ten large explosions were counted, six after the battleships opened fire. The *Fuso* and *Mogami*, which had turned to the south, flamed brilliantly; but soon the destroyer *mêlée* became so confused that at 4.10 a.m. Oldendorf ordered all ships to cease fire so that they would not hit his own destroyers[3]. A few minutes later a big Japanese ship disappeared from the American radar screen – she was the battleship *Fuso*.

When this action was at its height, American destroyers and M.T.B.s reported contact with a new group of five or more enemy ships – it was Admiral Shima's Fifth Fleet. Shima had observed radio silence so as not to reveal his position and had not informed Nishimura of his approach. At midnight he picked up a radio voice message, which announced that Nishimura was under M.T.B. attack, and three hours later he overheard a reverse course signal to avoid torpedoes. He was then entering the strait, and at 3.21 a.m. the *Abukuma*, flagship of his destroyer screen, was hit by a torpedo and dropped out of line. Twenty minutes later, as he advanced at 28 knots, from his flagship, the *Nachi*, between two dense smoke screens, a ship on fire was sighted. She was the *Mogami*, and although she appeared to be stationary, actually she was moving at some eight knots. In the smoke she was lost to sight and the *Nachi* collided with her and was badly holed in her port side. This collision, writes Field, "effectively ended the tragicomic

---

[1] *Ibid.*, pp. 110–111.   [2] *Ibid.*, pp. 113–114.
[3] The *Grant*, of Destroyer Squadron 56, was hit by some 20 shot, 11 from American cruisers.

efforts in Surigao Strait. The Second Diversion Attack Force [Shima's Fifth Fleet] milled round for a few minutes, laid a protective screen, and retired."[1]

At 4.31 a.m. Oldendorf ordered the pursuit; but an hour later he abandoned it, and–as prearranged with Kinkaid–an air attack by escort carriers off Samar was made on the enemy cripples; it sank the battered *Mogami* and the *Abukuma*. Of Nishimura's ships, only one survived the battle–the damaged destroyer *Shigure*. Except for one M.T.B. no American ship was lost.

At 7.28 a.m. on October 25, Oldendorf received a signal from Kinkaid to congratulate him in his victory. Ten minutes later came a second and very different signal. It was that Japanese battleships were approaching the eastern entrance of Leyte Gulf, and were firing on the Seventh Fleet's escort carriers. The lure had worked–it was Kurita's Central Force. With his fuel and torpedoes almost exhausted and his ammunition dangerously low, Admiral Oldendorf set course for Leyte Gulf.

While the battle of Surigao Strait was fought, Halsey steamed north-eastward to strike the Northern Force off Cape Engaño at dawn. At 2 a.m. on the 25th one of his search aircraft reported contact with six enemy ships some 80 miles ahead of him, and half an hour later another reported contact with a larger group astern of them. He at once instructed Mitscher to form Task Force 34 by withdrawing six battleships, two heavy and three light cruisers, and 18 destroyers from the three task groups and to place them under command of Vice-Admiral Willis A. Lee and instruct him to proceed ahead of the carrier groups. At 3 a.m. Halsey informed Nimitz and Kinkaid of the position of the Northern Force, and that his own force of "three groups" was concentrated. This message would seem to have perplexed Kinkaid, because at 4.10 a.m. he urgently inquired whether Halsey's battleships were still guarding San Bernardino Strait. Unfortunately Halsey did not receive this message until 6.4 a.m., and when he did, he replied that the battleships were with the carrier groups.

In the meantime, at about 5 a.m. Mitscher's first strike took off, but it was not until 7.35 a.m. that the Northern Force, then concentrated, was discovered 140 miles to the north-east steering on a southerly course. Very few aircraft were seen over it, and what was more remarkable, none was observed on its carriers' flight decks. Mitscher's strike went in, and although it met with

[1] *The Japanese at Leyte Gulf*, p. 92.

intense anti-aircraft fire, it severely damaged the *Zuikaku*, sank one light carrier, and left another dead in the water.

Shortly before this action opened Halsey had ordered Lee to stand toward the enemy, and at 8 a.m. he instructed McCain's group, then some 260 miles to the south-east, to join in the attack as soon as possible. No sooner had he sent this order than he received an urgent dispatch from Kinkaid, which informed him that Japanese battleships and cruisers were firing on his escort carriers north-east of Leyte Gulf. A few minutes later a second message came in to say that the Third Fleet battleships were urgently needed off Samar Island.

Halsey was 350 miles to the north of Leyte Gulf, and because to put about appeared to him to be useless, he ordered Lee to close the enemy at 25 knots, and at the same time instructed McCain, who was even more distant from the Gulf, to go to Kinkaid's aid.

Next, in rapid succession, a third and fourth appeal came in from Kinkaid, in which he informed Halsey that he was faced with four battleships and eight cruisers, and that his battleship ammunition was nearly exhausted. This seemed incredible to Halsey because, if true, it meant that Kurita's Central Force was virtually intact, and the day before, from the air strike reports he had received, it had been almost blasted out of existence. He replied to Kinkaid that McCain was on his way to assist him – not very helpful – and continued to steam north at full speed.

At 10 a.m. Halsey received a message from Nimitz to ask what had become of his battleships, and immediately after yet another urgent appeal arrived from Kinkaid. No notice was taken of it; Task Force 34 continued to race north, and Mitscher's second strike went in. Then, at 11.15 a.m., when the battleships were within 45 miles of their enemy, Lee received from Halsey an order to reverse course southward – the pursuit was abandoned.

After this order was given, four of the cruisers and 10 destroyers were detached from Task Force 34 and instructed to rejoin their original task groups, and Bogan, whose task group included one large and two light carriers, was ordered to steer south with the battleships. Mitscher was left with Sherman's and Davison's task groups to continue the attack on the Northern Force, which was known to include two battleships. As Halsey had six, and with his best endeavours could not reach Leyte Gulf until 8 a.m. on the 26th, it is strange that he did not leave two with Mitscher.

This became stranger still when at noon he dissolved Task Force 34, and at 4 p.m., when fuelling was completed, he formed a new task force of two of his fastest battleships, three light cruisers and eight destroyers, and half an hour later at high speed sped southward. Thus Bogan was left with four battleships to follow him. If two of them had been left with Mitscher, in all probability the Northern Force would have been annihilated and Halsey's aim attained.

In the meantime Mitscher continued to launch strikes against the Northern Force, which had turned north. These led to the sinking of the *Zuikaku* and the light carrier *Zuiho*, and the crippling of the light carrier *Chiyoda*. Mitscher next sent out a force of cruisers and destroyers, under Rear-Admiral Du Bose, to sink the *Chiyoda* and any other stragglers he might find.

When Ozawa turned north, he still had with him his two battleships, the *Ise* and *Hyuga*, three light cruisers and some eight destroyers. This force was attacked by Mitscher's fifth and final air strike, and although 22 hits were claimed on one of the battleships and 15 on the other, neither received more than slight damage. At 7.30 p.m. Ozawa received word from a destroyer that Du Bose's force consisted of two battleships – incorrect – accompanied by cruisers and destroyers, and as he felt strong enough to cope with it, he ordered all his surviving ships to reverse course and close on Du Bose. Woodward points out the battle took "an ironic turn in its closing phase. The pursuer had now become the pursued, the decoy the aggressor, and though they did not make the assumption, it was the Japanese and not the Americans who had the superior gun power in the end."[1]

For two hours Ozawa steamed south, but Du Bose eluded him. Then Ozawa reversed course and the battle off Cape Engaño ended, much as the battle of Quatre Bras had done, when D'Erlon's corps wandered to and fro between two battlefields. In both battles faulty information and over-impulsive generalship were the causes of the respective fiascos.

When Kurita cleared the San Bernardino Strait after midnight on October 24 he ran eastward until 3 a.m. and then he turned south-east and swept down the coast of Samar. Two and a half hours later he received a dispatch from Shima that Nishimura's battleship division had been destroyed and that the *Mogami* was seriously damaged. This placed Kurita in a critical position,

[1] Woodward, p. 161.

because it meant that he was now left single-handed to cope with the enemy. At 6.14 a.m. the sun rose, and 10 minutes later his flagship, the *Yamato*, made radar contact with aircraft.

Kinkaid's 16 escort carriers and their destroyer escorts, under command of Rear-Admiral Thomas L. Sprague, were distributed in three groups, Southern (Rear-Admiral Thomas L. Sprague), Middle (Rear-Admiral Felix B. Stump), and Northern (Rear-Admiral C. A. F. Sprague), which respectively lay 90 miles south-east, 50 miles north-east, and 60 miles north-north-east of Suluan Island. The third, which bore the brunt of the oncoming attack, consisted of the escort carriers *Fanshaw Bay*, *Saint Lo*, *White Plains*, *Kalinin Bay*, *Kitkun Bay*, and *Gambier Bay*, and of a screening force of seven destroyers and escort destroyers. At 5.30 a.m. routine air patrols had been sent out, and at 6.47 a.m. an aircraft from the *Saint Lo* reported that it had sighted an enemy force of battleships, cruisers, and destroyers 20 miles to the north of the Northern Group. A few minutes later, to his dismay, a signalman aboard the *Kitkun Bay* saw through his telescope the pagoda masts of Kurita's battleships and cruisers loom above the horizon. Immediately a salvo of heavy shells fell among the carriers; it was from the main battery of the *Yamato*, and the range was about 35,000 yards. The battle off Samar had begun.

At once C. A. F. Sprague appealed to Kinkaid for aid, and it was his appeal which caused the latter to send his first urgent message to Halsey. From the position reported by Sprague the Japanese were within three hours sail of Leyte Gulf and the entire Seventh Fleet, the transports, and the beachhead were in dire jeopardy. The situation appeared catastrophic to Kinkaid because he was in no way prepared to meet it. His battleships and cruisers were still deep in Surigao Strait and he knew that their fuel and ammunition must be largely exhausted. His first action was to order Oldendorf to organize a force of three battleships, five cruisers, and two destroyer squadrons, to proceed to the eastern entrance of Leyte Gulf and refuel. His second move was to order the middle and southern escort carrier groups to launch all available aircraft against the approaching enemy. When these orders went out, fortunately for Sprague's carriers, a rain squall swept over them and reduced visibility to half a mile. Had it not been for the squall they might have been annihilated.

In the meantime Kurita advanced in three columns, his four battleships in the centre and his cruisers and destroyers on their flanks. Though he over-estimated his enemy's strength, he was nevertheless determined to take advantage of "the heaven-sent opportunity" presented to him, and "we planned," he said, "first to cripple the carriers' ability to have planes take off and land, and then mow down the entire task force."[1] His immediate aims were to reduce range and get to windward of the escort carriers to hamper them from heading into the north-easterly wind and launching their aircraft. This done he intended to enter Leyte Gulf, to fight a battle, to destroy his enemy's transports, and then to retire through Surigao Strait.

When the rain squall ended, the Japanese had closed to 25,000 yards, and as Sprague's carriers were in imminent danger of encirclement, at 7.40 a.m. he ordered a destroyer torpedo attack. While under cover of a smoke screen the carriers sped southward, the destroyers attacked and a *mêlée* followed in which they steamed in and out between the enemy's columns. They acted with supreme daring, scored several hits, and three of them were sunk. Kinkaid called this attack "one of the most gallant and heroic acts of the war."[2] Woodward writes: "The tall columns of water caused by shell splashes were becoming familiar features of the seascape to the CVE's [escort carriers]. They soared up suddenly, those of the major-caliber 18-, 16-, and 14-inch shells, to a height of 150 feet or more, easily distinguishable from the shorter 8-inch and 5-inch shell splashes. The carriers twisted in and out among them as through a forest of water spouts."[3] The *Fanshaw Bay* received six 8-inch shells; the *Kalinin Bay* 15, and the *Gambier Bay* one, which left her dead in the water; later she was hit again and again and sank.

In spite of this tremendous pounding, within 30 minutes of the action opening, the carriers of the Northern Group managed to launch 65 fighters and 44 torpedo-bombers; but many of them carried only 100 lb. bombs, which could produce little effect. Nevertheless four from the *Kitkun Bay*, loaded with 500 lb. bombs, severely crippled one of the Japanese cruisers, which later blew up and sank. From 8.50 a.m. strikes arrived from the Middle Group. They were much heavier, and, according to Woodward, "probably had much to do with turning the tide of battle."[4]

At about 9.25 a.m., when the fate of the Northern Group

---

[1] *The Japanese at Leyte Gulf*, James A. Field, p. 100.
[2] *The Battle for Leyte Gulf*, C. Vann Woodward, p. 182.
[3] *Ibid.*, p. 183.   [4] *Ibid.*, p. 190.

seemed sealed, suddenly Kurita broke off the engagement and turned north. The reason for this most unexpected movement would appear to be that he utterly lacked information beyond his immediate field of vision. He had previously sent out two observation aircraft, and neither had returned; he was ignorant that over the horizon his cruisers were within five miles of his enemy's carriers, and he thought that they had escaped. "Still intent on penetrating the Gulf," writes Field, "mindful of the need for fuel conservation, especially in his destroyers . . . and anticipating that he would soon be subjected to increasingly heavy air attack, he decided to break off and reform his widely scattered force."[1] So at 9.11 a.m. he sent out the signal for all ships to cease fire and assemble on a northerly course. At 9.30 a.m. the chase was broken off and the surface phase of the battle ended.

No sooner had the American escort carriers got clear of the *mêlée* than they were subjected to *Kamikaze*,[2] or suicide-aircraft attack; earlier in the day similar attacks had been launched on the Southern Group. On an organized scale, these attacks were the first of their kind, and during the remainder of October 25 and on the 26th they sank one escort carrier and severely damaged four others. The Japanese resorted to this form of attack because of the insufficient training of most of the Japanese pilots, and they were first suggested to Ozawa in the previous June. They became the main attack tactics of the Japanese air forces.

After he had broken off action Kurita's fleet milled around for two hours, during which, according to Rear-Admiral Koyanagi, Kurita's chief-of-staff, it assembled, and assessed information. Also, four badly damaged cruisers, under constant air attack, had to be attended to.

Kurita's effective force had been reduced to four battleships, two heavy and two light cruisers, and some seven to 10 destroyers, and until noon, it would appear, the question he discussed with his staff was whether it was of sufficient strength to battle against an enemy fully on the alert. Until noon, so he says in his report, he was determined to carry out his mission to the full. Then he changed his mind, and after the war explained why he did so. "There was no question of fuel," he said. "There was no consideration of how to get home. We had enough ammunition . . .

[1] *The Japanese at Leyte Gulf*, p. 109.
[2] The *Kamikaze* Corps took its name from *Kami* (gods) in the shape of the Divine Wind of Ise, which legend affirmed destroyed Kublai Khan's invading Mongol fleet in August, 1281.

it was not a question of destruction. That was neither here nor there. It was a question of what good I could do in the Gulf."[1] At 12.36 p.m. he decided to abandon his mission and set out northward, so as to clear San Bernardino Strait and get as far west of it as he could during the night.

Since 4.30 p.m. on October 25 Halsey had steamed southward at 28 knots, and soon after midnight he arrived off the eastern entrance of San Bernardino Strait, but by then Kurita's Central Force had passed through it. On his way he had ordered Bogan's and McCain's groups to rendezvous north-east of the strait at 6 a.m. on the 26th, and to launch search missions westward. This was done, and two hours later the Central Force was located in Tablas Strait, north-west of Panay Island. Strikes were then sent out from four of McCain's carriers and two of Bogan's carriers; many hits were claimed on the *Yamato* and Kurita's remaining two heavy cruisers, but again the damage done was overestimated and they continued to steam westward at high speed. Other strikes followed in which one light cruiser and one destroyer were sunk. Except for *Kamikaze* attacks on Kinkaid's escort carriers, the battle for Leyte Gulf was at an end, and on the night of October 28 Kurita was back at his starting point – Brunei Bay.

For the Americans, the battle for Leyte Gulf was a cheap victory; for the Japanese it was a catastrophic defeat. In the four days' fighting the former lost a light carrier, two escort carriers, two destroyers, a destroyer escort and a motor-torpedo-boat, and the latter lost three battleships, one large and three light carriers, 6 heavy cruisers, four light cruisers, and nine destroyers. The Japanese Navy had ceased to exist, and, except by land-based aircraft, their opponent had won undisputed command of the sea. When Admiral Ozawa was questioned on the battle after the war he replied: "After this battle the surface forces became strictly auxiliary, so that we relied on land forces, special [*Kamikaze*] attack, and air power. . . . There was no further use assigned to surface vessels, with exception of some special ships." And "Admiral Mitsumasa Yoni, Navy Minister of the Koiso Cabinet, said he realized that the defeat at Leyte 'was tantamount to loss of the Philippines.' As for the larger significance of the battle, he said, 'I felt that that was the end.' "[2]

[1] Cited by Field, p. 125. Another reason may be that throughout the action he believed he was attacking big carriers and not escort carriers, and as he had given his enemy a respite he felt that were he to close on him all his ships would be sunk.
[2] *Ibid.*, pp. 230–231.

This "larger significance" was missed by President Roosevelt and his advisers, who failed to appreciate the political implications of their overwhelming victory. They looked upon the war as a contest between Christian and Appollyon, instead of regarding it as a surgical operation. They failed to understand that, what the scalpel is to the surgeon, war should be to the statesman, and whatever the causes of war may be, should the aim of the states-man be purely destructive, then the activities of the soldier will become those of the slaughterhouse. But if, instead, the aim is constructive and curative, then these activities become those of the surgery. Because of mischance or misunderstanding, or lack of knowledge or skill, a surgical operation may fail; but when the aim of the slaughterer becomes the aim of the surgeon, it must fail, there can be no possible alternative. To be a sane political instrument, war demands a sane political end, and to be attainable that end must be strategically possible.

After the battle for Leyte Gulf, this strategical possibility had been fully established: there could be no question that Japan could win the war. As she was doomed to lose it, the American problem was predominantly political – how could her defeat be brought about at the highest profit to the United States?

It was a far simpler problem than the one that faced the President in Europe. There he had to consider his allies, but the war with Japan was 95 per cent. an American war, and to win it at the highest profit it was essential, in order to avert complications, that the United States should win it single-handed. Had this been understood, it would have been appreciated that as Russia was the only Power who could complicate the issue it was highly desirable for the United States to bring the war with Japan to an end before or immediately after Germany collapsed – that is, while Russia was still at grips with her. Was this possible? The answer is an unqualified "yes", provided that the strategical and political centres of gravity of the problem were firmly kept in mind.

The economic position of Japan, because of industrialization, had become more fragile since we referred to it in Chronicle 4. In 1941, when Japan struck at Pearl Harbour, her economic potential was approximately 10 per cent of that of the United States, and the acreage of her arable land no more than three per cent., yet it had to support a population over half as large. Because Japan depended on Manchuria and Korea for most of her raw materials and large supplies of grain, which had to cross the Sea of Japan and the Yellow Sea, Japan's merchant navy was the centre of gravity of her entire strategy. The attack on Japanese shipping became the main task of the American submarines. According to Admiral Spruance, the part they played in bringing about the defeat of Japan would be difficult to overestimate, and the correctness of this may be judged from the following figures: At the opening of the war Japan had 6,000,000 tons of merchant shipping of over 500 tons gross weight, and during the war an additional 4,100,000 tons were built or captured. Of the total, 8,900,000 tons were sunk, and of this loss 54·7 per cent. was attributed to submarines.[1]

Instead of concentrating against Japan's shipping and forcing her surrender through economic collapse, the strategy adopted by the Joint Chiefs of Staff was based on an invasion of the Japanese home islands, and in preparation, long-range bombing offensives from the Mariana Islands were initiated shortly after the battle of Leyte Gulf. In the aggregate 104,000 tons of bombs were dropped on 66 urban areas, and 29,400 tons on industrial areas.[2] Although this bombing reduced production, loss of shipping remained the dominant factor in Japan's economic decline, because it was the interdiction of coal, oil, other raw materials and food, and not the destruction of factories and urban areas that struck the deadliest blow at her economy. Loss of shipping limited the import of iron ore, and want of steel limited the building of ships; labour efficiency declined for want of food, and food for want of ships. In the *Survey* we read:

"Even though the urban area attacks and attacks on specific industrial plants contributed a substantial percentage to the overall decline in Japan's economy, in many segments of that economy their effects were duplicative. Most of the oil refineries were out of oil, the alumina plants out of bauxite, the steel mills lacking in ore and coke, and the munition plants low in steel and aluminum. Japan's economy was in large measure being destroyed twice over, once by cutting off of imports, and secondly by air attack. A further tightening of Japan's shipping situation, so as to eliminate remaining imports from Korea and coastwise and inter-island shipping, coupled with an attack on Japan's extremely vulnerable railroad network, would have extended and cumulated the effects of the shipping attack already made.

[1] *United States Strategic Bombing Survey*, Summary Report (Pacific War), 1946, p. 11.
[2] *Ibid.*, p. 17.

"Much of Japan's coastal and inter-island traffic had already been forced onto her inadequate railroads. The principal coal mines of Japan are located on Kyushu and Hokkaido. This coal traffic, formerly water borne, was moving by railroads employing the Kanmon tunnels and the Hakkodate–Aomori rail ferry. The railroads of Honshu include few main lines and these lines traverse bridges of considerable vulnerability. . . . A successful attack on the Hakkodate rail ferry, the Kanmon tunnels and 19 bridges and vulnerable sections of line so selected as to set up five separate zones of complete interdiction would have virtually eliminated further coal movements . . . and would have completed the strangulation of Japan's economy. . . .

"The Survey believes that such an attack, had it been well-planned in advance might have been initiated . . . in August, 1944. . . . The Survey has estimated that the force requirements to effect complete interdiction of the railroad system would have been 650 B–29 visual sorties carrying 5,200 tons of high explosive bombs."[1]

When these figures are deducted from the 15,000 sorties flown and the 104,000 tons of bombs dropped during them on the 66 Japanese cities, the residue is a fair measure of the strategic error committed by the Joint Chiefs of Staff.

Unfortunately for the aftermath of the war, Japan's political centre of gravity eluded the vision of the President and his advisers. It lay in the person of the Emperor, or Tenno ("Heavenly King"),[2] and because he was the godhead of the armed forces, and in the eyes of his people a divinity, he was the supreme symbol of Japanese life and thought. Yet there was one thing he could not do, and that was to order his people to surrender unconditionally and thereby acquiesce in his becoming a war criminal, to be placed on trial or shot at sight.[3]

Early in 1944, Rear-Admiral Takagi, of the Japanese Naval General Staff, after he had analysed the events of the war, came to the conclusion that Japan could not win it, and therefore should seek a compromise peace. But it was not until the loss of Saipan,

[1] *Ibid.*, p. 19.

[2] According to the *Kojiki*, the Shinto bible, the first sovereign of Japan was the grandson of the sun goddess Amaterasu, whose shrine was at Ise. From him in unbroken succession all the emperors of Japan descended; therefore each was looked upon as a Tenshi (Son of Heaven).

[3] In accordance with the Morgenthau Plan, when captured, all listed as war criminals were to be shot, and "the President had expressed himself in favour of execution without trial" (*On Active Service in Peace and War*, Henry L. Stimson and McGeorge Bundy (English edit., 1949), pp. 338–339).

in July, that his views were so far accepted as to force the retirement of General Hideki Tojo, prime minister and head of the military faction. He was succeeded by General Kuniaki Koiso, who created a Supreme War Direction Council of six members to consider the war problem, and as things drifted from bad to worse, on April 5, 1945, four days after the American landing on Okinawa, he resigned and Admiral Kantaro Suzuki took his place. On the same day the Soviet Government announced that it would not renew its neutrality pact with Japan, which was due to expire in 12 months. Although Suzuki's task was to bring the war to an end[1], he was unwilling to do so as long as the only alternative to its continuation was unconditional surrender. Because of the status of the Emperor, he decided to prosecute the war.

In June, the Emperor, who since January had become increasingly convinced that the war must be ended, agreed that Hirota, a former prime minister, should approach Jacob Malik, the Soviet Ambassador in Tokyo. On June 24 conversations between them were opened, but as they led nowhere, it was next decided to send Prince Konoye on a mission to Moscow to seek Soviet mediation. At the same time Sato, the Japanese Ambassador in Moscow, was instructed to inform the Soviet Government that under no circumstances could Japan accept unconditional surrender; he was to persuade the Kremlin to bring about peace on other terms.

In the meantime Washington also considered ways and means to end the war, and although the War Department urged invasion and the Air Force mass bombing, others were of opinion that were "a rationalised version" of unconditional surrender adopted, the Japanese might give in, and that "the only doubt which still forestalled a decision was the future status of the Emperor."[2] One opinion, based on interrogations of prisoners of high rank, was "that the Japanese were on the point of giving up but were held

[1] At the time of the San Francisco Conference, which opened on April 25, 1945, it would appear that rumours of Japan's desire to end the war were current. On April 29, in a dispatch to the *Washington Daily News*, Mr. John O'Donnell reported:

"Another hot yarn is that the Japs have sent to Washington their specific conditions for unconditional surrender. Behind this is the argument that the Japs want to come to terms with us before Russia, now at peace with Tokyo, moves into the war picture in the Pacific and demands by way of spoils a lot of real estate that the Japs would rather see under American than Soviet control.

"Because the Kremlin has been getting very hard-boiled with Great Britain and the United States since the Yalta love session, the story is that the new Jap cabinet, convinced that utter defeat is only a matter of time, would like to make peace now while Russia doesn't figure in the settlement." – (Reprinted in the *Daily News*, April 25, 1955).

[2] See *United States Army in World War II*, the War Department, Washington Command Post: The Operations Division, Ray S. Cline (1951), pp. 333–347.

back by a fear that the imperial institution would be abolished and the emperor himself punished as a war criminal."[1]

While these proposals were under review, progress on the atomic bomb had advanced to a point at which its success was almost certain.[2] In April, 1944, Mr. Stimson appointed a committee to advise him on its use. On June 1 the committee recommended that, should its final trial be successful, the bomb should be used against Japan and without an advanced warning.

Stimson, who had been President Roosevelt's adviser on atomic policy and was also Truman's adviser, considered the report, and on July 2 set forth his views in a memorandum to the President. He proposed as an alternative to an invasion of Japan the use of the atomic bomb, if its final trial, then in preparation, succeeded. He suggested that its use be preceded by a warning, which should point out "the varied and overwhelming character of the force we are about to bring to bear on the islands," and "the inevitability and completeness of the destruction which the full application of this force will entail." Further, he personally thought, "we should add that we do not exclude a constitutional monarchy under her present dynasty, it would substantially add to the chance of acceptance."[3]

On July 17 the Potsdam Conference assembled in the Cecilienhof, the residence of the former Crown Prince of Germany, and on that day Stimson, who was in attendance on the President, received the momentous news that, on July 16, at Alamogordo, New Mexico, the final test of the bomb had proved an unqualified success.

When President Truman and Mr. Churchill were informed of this, they decided that because it had been calculated that an invasion of Japan would cost 1,000,000 American lives and half that number of British, the use of the bomb would obviate these losses. "Now all this nightmare picture had vanished," writes the latter. "In its place was the vision – fair and bright indeed it seemed – of the end of the whole war in one or two violent shocks. . . . Moreover, we should not need the Russians."[4]

His great ally thought otherwise, for Mr. Stettinius informs us: "Even as late as the Potsdam Conference, after the first atomic

[1] *Secretary Stimson: A Study in Statecraft*, Richard N. Current (1954), p. 224.
[2] Mr. Churchill first mentions this weapon on August 30, 1941 (*The Second World War*, vol. III, p. 730) and Dr. Goebbels on March 21, 1942 (*The Goebbels Diaries*, p. 96).
[3] *On Active Service in Peace and War*, p. 368.
[4] *The Second World War*, vol. VI, pp. 552–553.

bomb had been exploded . . . the military insisted that the Soviet Union had to be brought into the Far Eastern War. At both Yalta and Potsdam the military staffs were particularly concerned with the Japanese troops in Manchuria. Described as the cream of the Japanese Army, this self-contained force . . . was believed capable of prolonging the war even after the islands of Japan had been surrendered, unless Russia should enter the war and engage this army. . . . Actually Russian entry into northern Korea was agreed to after Yalta by American military authorities as part of the taking of the surrender of Japanese troops."[1]

Before the conference assembled, all the messages that passed between Tokyo and Sato in Moscow were deciphered in Washington by means of the same "Magic" as had been done before to the Japanese attack on Pearl Harbour, and on July 13 the following dispatch from the Japanese Foreign Minister to Sato was deciphered: "See Molotov before his departure for Potsdam. . . . Convey His Majesty's strong desire to secure a termination of the war. . . . Unconditional surrender is the only obstacle to peace. . . ."[2] Although this made Japan's desperate position crystal clear and opened the road to the immediate end of the war, on July 26 the following ultimatum was presented to Japan: "We call upon the Government of Japan to proclaim now the unconditional surrender of all the Japanese armed forces and to provide proper and adequate assurance of good faith in such action. The alternative for Japan is complete and utter destruction."[3] Not a word was said about the Emperor, because it would be unacceptable to the propaganda-fed American masses.

Two days later Suzuki rejected the ultimatum; he announced that it was "unworthy of public notice."[4] As Russia's entrance into the war had been fixed for August 8, it was decided to drop two bombs, one on Hiroshima on August 6, and the other on Nagasaki on August 9.[5]

[1] *Roosevelt and the Russians: The Yalta Conference*, p. 96. At this time the "cream" of the Japanese army in Manchuria consisted of skimmed milk. Its trained men had long been removed and replaced by raw recruits and convalescents; besides, it had no petrol.

[2] *Japan's Decision to Surrender*, Robert J. C. Butow (1954), p. 130.

[3] For reply in full see *Ibid.*, Appendix C, pp. 243–244.

[4] *On Active Service in Peace and War*, p. 369.

[5] Professor P. M. S. Blackett, in chap. x of his *Military and Political Consequences of Atomic Energy* (1948), suggests that the bomb was dropped in order to force the Japanese to surrender to America instead of to Russia. This is a fantastic suggestion, because peace with Japan, short of complete humiliation, could have been arranged by negotiation any time since the previous May.

Early on August 6, a B-29 aircraft, carrying one of the two atomic bombs then in existence, approached Hiroshima. At 8.15 a.m. the projectile, attached to a parachute, was released, and the aircraft raced away to escape the blast. A minute or two later a ball of fire appeared over the north-west centre of the city. Its explosive force was equivalent to 20,000 tons of T.N.T.; at its core its temperature was about 150,000,000° C. – "more than seven times greater than the temperature at the solar centre,"[1] and the pressure exerted was estimated at hundreds of thousands of tons to the square inch. A "fire storm" resulted in which hundreds of fires were simultaneously started, the most distant was 4,600 yards from the centre of the explosion. Four and a half square miles of the city were completely burnt and from 70,000 to 80,000 people killed and some 50,000 injured.

At 1.00 a.m. (Toyko time) on August 9 the Russians crossed the Manchurian border and met with little opposition. The same day Nagasaki was atom bombed, and the Supreme War Direction Council agreed to refer the issue of unconditional surrender to the Emperor. He decided for peace, and on the 10th a broadcast from Tokyo announced that the Japanese Government was ready to accept the terms of the Allied Potsdam declaration of July 26, "with the understanding that the said declaration does not compromise any demand which prejudices the prerogatives of His Majesty as a Sovereign Ruler."[2]

When, by way of Switzerland, official notifications of this reached Washington, Truman sought Stimson's advice, and the latter told him he considered that "even if the question hadn't been raised by the Japanese we would have to continue the Emperor ourselves under our command and supervision in order to get into surrender the many scattered armies of the Japanese who would own no other authority and that something like this use of the Emperor must be made in order to save us from a score of bloody Iwo Jimas and Okinawas all over China and the New Netherlands. He was the only source of authority in Japan under the Japanese theory of the state."[3]

This was common sense, and the allied reply on August 11 contained this paragraph: "From the moment of surrender the authority of the Emperor and the Japanese Government to rule

---

[1] *The Nature of the Universe*, Fred Hoyle (1950), p. 42.
[2] For reply in full see Butow, Appendix D, p. 244.
[3] *On Active Service in Peace and War*, p. 371.

the State shall be subject to the Supreme Commander of the Allied Powers."[1]

Finally, on August 14, the Emperor accepted the provisions of the Potsdam agreement; the "cease fire" was sounded, and on September 2, exactly six years since Britain and France had declared war on Germany, Japanese envoys signed the instrument of surrender on board the U.S. battleship *Missouri* in Tokyo Bay and the Second World War had ended.

Stimson's comments on this are illuminating. "This question in Stimson's view," we read, "was based on a double misunderstanding – first of the meaning of war, and second, of the basic purpose of the American Government during this period.

"The true question, as he saw it, was not whether surrender could have been achieved without the use of the bomb, but whether a different diplomatic and military course would have led to an earlier surrender. Here the question of intelligence became significant. Interviews after the war indicated clearly that a large element of the Japanese Cabinet was ready in the spring to accept substantially the same terms as those finally agreed on. Information of this general attitude was available to the American Government. . . . It is possible, in the light of the final surrender, that a clearer and earlier exposition of American willingness to retain the Emperor would have produced an earlier ending of the war; this course was earnestly advocated by Grew and his immediate associates during May, 1945."[2]

If the war had ended in May, 1945, and but for the political and strategical lunacy induced by the policy of unconditional surrender it might well have done so, Russia – whatever she might eventually have done – would not have been given a free and cordial hand to expand her influence over the Far East. Equally important, the atomic bomb would not have been dropped by Americans. "My own feeling was," writes Fleet Admiral William D. Leahy, Chief of Staff to Presidents Roosevelt and Truman, "that in being the first to use it, we had adopted an ethical standard common to the barbarians of the Dark Ages. . . . There is a practical certainty that potential enemies will have it in the future and that the atomic bomb will sometime be used against us. . . . Employment of the atomic bomb in war will take us back

---

[1] For reply in full see Butow, Appendix E, p. 245. In effect the Supreme Commander became the Shogun.

[2] *On Active Service in Peace and War*, pp. 371–372. Joseph C. Grew was Acting Secretary of State.

in cruelty towards noncombatants to the days of Genghis Khan.
. . . These new and terrible instruments of uncivilized warfare
represent a modern type of barbarism not worthy of Christian
man."[1]

[1] *I Was There* (1950), pp. 441–442. Words very similar were voiced by the Vatican in the *Osservatore Romano* of August 7, 1945. "This war," we read, "provides a catastrophic conclusion. Incredibly this destructive weapon remains a temptation for posterity, which, we know by bitter experience, learns so little from history."

The Second World War in retrospect and prospect

The second American crusade ended even more disastrously than the first, and this time the *agent provocateur* was not the German Kaiser but the American President, whose abhorrence of National Socialism and craving for power precipitated his people into the European conflict and so again made it worldwide. From the captured German archives there is no evidence to support the President's claims that Hitler contemplated an offensive against the western hemisphere, and until America entered the war there is abundant evidence that this was the one thing he wished to avert.

One of the first to warn his fellow countrymen against involvement in the European quarrel was Roosevelt's predecessor, the former President, Mr. Herbert Hoover. "I opposed and protested every step in the policies which led us into the Second World War," he said in a broadcast on August 10, 1954. "Especially in June, 1941, when Britain was safe from German invasion due to Hitler's diversion to attack on Stalin, I urged that the gargantuan jest of all history would be our giving aid to the Soviet government. I urged we should allow those two dictators to exhaust each other. I stated that the result of our assistance would be to spread Communism over the whole world. I urged that if we stood aside the time would come when we could bring lasting peace to the world. I have no regrets. The consequences have proved that I was right."

Soon after the United States entered the war, there appeared a book by a Yale professor[1] in which he pointed out that, "If the foreign policy of a state is to be practical, it should be designed not in terms of some dream world but in terms of the realities of international relations in terms of power politics." He urged that the two objectives of United States policy should be predominance in the New World, and a balance of power in the Old, and because

[1] *America's Strategy in World Politics: The United States and the Balance of Power*, Nicholas J. Spykman (1942), pp. 446, 460.

this balance had been upset on the opposite shores of the Atlantic and Pacific, the war aim of the United States should be to restore it. This, he wrote, did not demand the annihilation of Germany and Japan, lest Europe and the Far East be opened to domination by Russia. "A Russian state from the Urals to the North Sea," he said, "can be no great improvement over a German state from the North Sea to the Urals." The same reasoning applied to the Far East and he wrote: "The danger of another Japanese conquest of Asia must be removed, but does not inevitably mean the elimination of the military strength of Japan and the surrender of the Western Pacific to China or Russia."

This policy, which was to be adopted after the war,[1] applied equally to Great Britain, for her position was analogous to that of the United States. Her objectives should have been the security of her empire and the maintenance of the balance of power in Europe and Asia, and for the identical reason given by Spykman, neither objective demanded the annihilation of her enemies. When the two great western powers were united in arms, Russia became the crux of their war problem. That they had to support Russia in her fight against the common enemy was obvious, but it should have been equally obvious that support should not lead to her dominance; for were it to do so, then their problem would remain unsolved.

As we have seen, Roosevelt's policy was diametrically opposed to Spykman's; "Unconditional Surrender" had nothing to do with the balance of power, and everything to do with its negation. Nor had Churchill's policy which, three days after his advent to power in 1940, he proclaimed to be: "Victory – victory at all costs."[2] These policies were the obverse and reverse of the same idea – annihilation; and that Churchill, a man of incomparably greater military insight than the President, should have fixed on such an aim is bewildering when it is compared with his epitaph on the First World War:

"Governments and individuals," he wrote, "conformed to this

[1] Some years after the war, a French historian pointed out: "The goal that Western strategy has [now] set itself in Japan as well as in Germany is not very different from the situation that would have arisen of its own accord if peace had been concluded before the entry of Soviet troops into the Reich and Manchuria, and before complete destruction of both armies and countries. We are trying to efface the consequences of a too complete victory, and get back to a victory compatible with the resurrection of the vanquished" (*The Century of Total War*, Raymond Aron, English edit., 1954, p. 194).
[2] *The Second World War*, vol. II, p. 24.

rhythm of the tragedy and swayed and staggered forward in helpless violence, slaughtering and squandering on ever-increasing scales, till injuries were wrought to the structure of human society which a century will not efface, and which may conceivably prove fatal to the present civilization. . . . Victory was to be bought so dear as to be almost indistinguishable from defeat. It was not to give even security to the victors. . . . The most complete victory ever gained in arms has failed to solve the European problem or to remove the dangers which produced the war."[1]

His choice of "Victory at all costs" becomes even stranger when we read his epitaph on the Second World War:

"The human tragedy," he writes, "reaches its climax in the fact that after all the exertions and sacrifices of hundreds of millions of people and the victories of the Righteous Cause, we have still not found Peace and Security, and that we lie in the grip of even worse perils than those we have surmounted."[2]

What a confession of failure.

When we remember that both Roosevelt and Churchill are to be reckoned among the most prominent of the presidents and prime ministers of the United States and Great Britain, it is perplexing to have to record this. What persuaded them to adopt so fatal a policy? We hazard to reply – blind hatred! Their hearts ran away with their heads and their emotions befogged their reason. For them the war was not a political conflict in the normal meaning of the words, it was a Manichean contest between Good and Evil, and to carry their people along with them they unleashed a vitriolic propaganda against the devil they had invoked. As this was the identical process adopted by Hitler, it is in no way strange to read in *The Economist* of August 11, 1945: "At the end of a mighty war fought to defeat Hitlerism, the Allies are making a Hitlerian peace. This is the real measure of their failure."

After Stalingrad, when it was obvious that Hitler's star was sinking and Stalin's rising, it is astonishing to look back on the views then held on Russia by allied statesmen, such as those of Sir Samuel Hoare;[3] and it is even more astonishing to believe that it was possible at the First Quebec Conference for the policy toward Russia, as set forth in the Hopkins document,[4] to have been discussed and adopted.

---

[1] *The World Crisis, 1915* (1923), pp. 17–18.
[2] *The Second World War*, vol. I, p. viii.
[3] See *supra*, pp. 539–541. [4] See *supra*, pp. 546–547.

This blind trust in Russia's motives can only be explained by Roosevelt's and Churchill's ignorance of her history, or by the trance into which they had been induced by their pro-Soviet propaganda. For 200 years Russia had knocked at the eastern door of Europe, and for well over a century European statesmen and historians of note had warned the peoples of Europe against her designs. It is more than a matter of interest to refer to what they said, not only because the results of the war reveal how profoundly right they were, but because the future is rooted in the present.

What these men recognized was that Russia has never belonged to Europe; her civilization owes nothing to Latin culture; she never took part in the Crusades, the Renaissance, the Reformation and the Thirty Years War, and was unaffected by the discovery of the New World and the French Revolution. Since the battle of Poltava the Muscovites have been to Europeans "the Turks of the North" – the spearhead of the Asiatic threat to Europe.

Châteaubriand realized this and he longed to visit Russia because he believed that she threatened to overwhelm the world.[1] Custine visited Russia in 1839 and he wrote: "They wished to rule the world by conquest; they mean to seize by armed force the countries accessible to them, and thence to oppress the rest of the world by terror";[2] and De Tocqueville pictured a disunited Europe conquered by a Russian Philip.[3] In 1823 the Abbé de Pradt, at one time Napoleon I's ambassador at Warsaw, wrote: "On the other side of the Vistula falls a curtain behind which it is most difficult to see clearly what is happening within the Russian empire. In the manner of the Orient, from which it has derived its character, the Russian government is concentrated in the court of the prince: he alone speaks, writes little and publishes nothing. In a country constituted to hide everything from public knowledge, one is more or less limited to guesswork, and this limitation also applies to the Russian army. . . . Since the days of Peter the Great, the policy of Russia has never ceased to be one of conquest; one might say that for a whole century her government has consisted in one and the same man, with one and the same idea – methodical aggrandizement."[4] And in 1850 Donoso

---

[1] See *Liberty or Equality: The Challenge of our Time*, Erik von Kuehnelt-Leddihn (1952), p. 75.
[2] *Journey for our Time: The Journals of the Marquis de Custine*, trans. Phyllis Penn Kohler (1953), p. 164.
[3] See *Liberty or Equality*, p. 77.
[4] *Parallèle de la puissance anglaise et russe relativement à l'Europe* (1823), pp. 154, 156.

Cortés was as prophetic: ". . . when nothing is left in the West," he said, "but two camps, that of the despoilers and that of the despoiled – then, gentlemen, the hour of Russia in the clock of time will have struck. Then Russia will be able to march peacefully, arms shouldered, into our lands; then, also, gentlemen, the world will witness the greatest chastisement in all history; this tremendous chastisement, gentlemen, will be the chastisement of England. Her ships will be useless against the colossal empire which grips Europe with one hand and India with the other. . . . Russia will fight in order to inflict defeats . . . in order to protect the defeated country. And in the moment the defeated nation considers itself an ally it becomes Russia's victim and prey. The victories of Russia lead to 'protection' – her protection to death."[1]

Later historians have been no less prophetic. In 1878, Constantin Frantz, writes Keuhnelt-Leddihn, ". . . was convinced that Russia would invade Western Europe and that in the coming war between Britain and Russia the United States would play a decisive role," and that "the future belonged to the United States and Russia."[2] And shortly before the First World War, Richard von Kralik, an Austrian historian, in connexion with the invasions of Asiatic hordes on the European continent, wrote: "Europe has even now to fear the Russian Empire and Eastern Asia which represents elements half or fully Mongol. This issue marks the most decisive struggle in world history which is the antagonism between East and West. . . . Here the future will by no means spare us disagreeable surprises. It is possible that Asiatics penetrate France and Spain, as it happened in the 8th century, or that they get to Germany, as in the 13th century the Mongols, or that they appear before Vienna, as the Turks in the 16th and 17th centuries. . . . Nor is it unthinkable that it will, perhaps, be America which pushes back the Asiatic East on European soil."[3]

Surely, before the Second World War engulfed Europe, western statesmen should have been aware of these predictions, and although no one would suggest that presidents and prime ministers can find the time to delve into dusty history, at least one would expect that their foreign offices and intelligence staffs would do so, for "to know your enemy" – potential as well as actual – is every bit as important as knowledge of his country, resources, and

---

[1] Quoted in *Liberty or Equality*, pp. 78, 79.
[2] *Ibid.*, p. 76.   [3] *Ibid.*, p. 302.

armed forces. At least they might have borne in mind Lenin's prediction of the inevitable clash between the bourgeois states and the Soviet Union. Instead they bandied witticisms between each other on Uncle Joe!

The Asiatic hordes are back in Germany, and this time they penetrated within the walls of Vienna. The wheel of history has turned full circle, and the threat which faces Europe to-day is not far removed from the threat which faced her in the days of Xerxes and Darius. Added to this, Japan, the counterpoise to Russia in the Far East, was eliminated, and thereby the sluice-gate opened for Communism to inundate China. Such were the political consequences of the war.

The military consequences were no less remarkable. At Hiroshima the nuclear theory of the atom and the ability of man artificially to transmute one element into another, which had revolutionized physics, became a demonstrable fact to the most ignorant and illiterate of human beings. It inspired a universal terror, not because 70,000 to 80,000 people had perished, but because one bomb, manipulated by a single man, had slaughtered this multitude.

The repercussions of August 6, 1945, shook the accepted theory of war to its foundations. If one bomb could wreck a great city, what would hundreds effect in another war? It bereft organized international warfare of its political significance; for it reduced this type of war to an absurdity. It knocked the bottom out of the theory that armed conflicts are the instruments of policy, by transforming their threat into a deterrent of war between armed men.

Does this mean that war is approaching its end? Assuredly no, because in an ideological age the fundamental causes of war are profoundly psychological; they cannot be eliminated either by a negation, or a surplus, of physical force. All it means is that one form of war has become obsolete, and that another will replace it. For lack of a better name, the new form in this age of man in the mass is called "cold war." It is a combination of psychological war, the weapons of which are the emotions; of economic war aimed at destroying financial stability; of guerrilla war, the most primitive form of war; and civil war, its most brutal form. M. Aron points out that cold war is a limited war, limited "not as to the stakes, but as to the means employed";[1] it may be compared

[1] *The Century of Total War*, p. 171.

with the limited methodical wars which for a century and a half
followed the Thirty Years War. But there is this profound difference: it is the readiness to wage nuclear war which, by deterring
an opponent from resorting to physical war, makes cold war
so deadly.

Russia is the leading exponent of this form of conflict, and by
waging it on methodical lines, immediately after the shooting war
ended she established her dominion over a third of Europe without
firing a shot, since when she has waged it by propaganda, sabotage
and subversion in every non-Communist country in the world;
for all countries which have not accepted Soviet Communism are
held to be active enemies of Russia. Further, as Aron observes:
Western military experts are not sufficiently freed from traditional
conceptions to realize that the cold war is the real war which is
raging all the time and that the battle against propaganda and
subversion must be waged indefatigably; "the elimination by
trade unions of Stalinist ringleaders," he writes, "often signalizes
a victory comparable with the formation of an additional army
division."[1]

Another limitation of the means to wage physical war is the
enormous cost of nuclear and supersonic weapons. No longer is
it possible for even medium sized nations to equip themselves with
the full panoply of war, and even were they wealthy enough to do
so, most could neither obtain the requisite raw materials with
which to fashion nuclear weapons nor find the necessary unin-
habited territory in which to test them.

These limitations have led to the strategical division of the
world between two super-States, the United States of America
and the Soviet Union, each possessed of an ideology which neither
will abandon. As in the days of Abraham Lincoln, "a house
divided against itself cannot stand." It "cannot endure half slave
and half free . . . it will become all one thing or the other."
Coexistence of incompatibles is the father of war.

In 1823, faced with the outcome of the Napoleonic wars, on
the opening page of his essay on a comparison between the power
of England and Russia, the Abbé de Pradt wrote these words:
"Two flags are now raised at the two extremities of Europe; one
over the land and the other over the sea"; and in his concluding
pages he observed: "England and Russia are the two prepon-
derant powers in Europe. . . . The political aim of England is to

[1] *Ibid.*, p. 233.

oppose whosoever would dominate the continent; she watches over the political liberties of Europe. Russia is this dominant power and through necessity the born enemy of the liberties of Europe."[1]

The Union Jack, the banner of the *Pax Britannica*, has now been furled, and to-day in its stead floats the Stars and Stripes to face the Hammer and Sickle. The supreme question set by the Second World War is: Which will be hauled down? Is the future to see a *Pax Americana* or a *Pax Tartarica*? We hazard to suggest that the answer will be found, not in the contending military strengths of the United States and the Soviet Union, but in their antagonistic political, social, economic and cultural systems. Which of the two is the more fitted to solve the crucial problem set to mankind by the Industrial Revolution – the status of man, his government and way of life in a fully mechanized world?

[1] *Parallèle de la puissance anglaise et russe, etc.*, pp. 1 and 168–9.

Index

Index

Other DA CAPO titles of interest